D1327714

Sybil Thorndike

Sybil Thorndike

A Star of Life

JONATHAN CROALL

HAUS BOOKS
London

For Lesley, with much love, as always

Copyright © Jonathan Croall 2008

First published in Great Britain in 2008 by Haus Publishing,
26 Cadogan Court, Draycott Avenue, London SW3 3BX
www.hauspublishing.co.uk

The moral rights of the author have been asserted

A CIP catalogue record for this book is available from the British Library

ISBN 978-1-905791-92-7

Typeset in Caslon by MacGuru Ltd
info@macguru.org.uk
Printed in Slovenia by DZS – Grafik

Contents

List of Illustrations

Acknowledgements

Mander and Mitchenson Theatre Collection 5, 11, 14, 21, 25, 27, 29, 30, 36, 38, 39, 40, 41, 47, 51
Harvard Theatre Collection 45, 50
John Vickers 42, 44
John Topham Library 48
Alexander Murray 15
Thorndike family archive 1–4, 6–8, 12, 13, 16, 22–24, 26, 31–35, 49, 52

Introduction

Sybil Thorndike was on the stage for 65 years, and played well over three hundred parts. She appeared in virtually every theatrical genre: Greek tragedy, drawing-room comedy, Grand Guignol, revue, Shakespeare, poetic drama, farce, and much else besides. It is an astonishing record, an indication of her remarkable versatility and her desire to tackle every kind of role, whether it was Medea or a Welsh schoolteacher, Lady Macbeth or a prostitute, a New Woman or an old bag lady, or even Lear's Fool.

John Gielgud described her as 'one of the rarest women of our time'. She became a national institution, loved, admired and respected. Her dedication to her work and her profession was legendary, as was her unstinting support for good causes, and her steadfast socialist and pacifist beliefs. She was a profoundly spiritual woman, an ardent Christian but never a dogmatic one. She cared little about money, always believing that it would be found when needed. Strong-willed, courageous and outspoken, generous and magnanimous, she invariably looked for the best in people. 'No one likes anyone as much as Sybil loves everyone,' Noël Coward was said to have remarked.

She worked with and knew intimately the greatest actors of her day. She was, by his admission, a surrogate mother to Laurence Olivier, whom she gave his first break in the theatre. She stood by John Gielgud when a scandal threatened to end his career. She acted opposite Ralph Richardson when he played what many considered to be his finest role. Her years on stage ran parallel to that of Edith Evans, who was seen as her great rival, but the reality was rather different.

She faced certain handicaps in getting to the top of her profession: her looks were not the conventional ones then expected of a star actress, nor did she have the sexual allure that made others popular and marketable. With her fierce blue eyes, broad forehead and strong cheekbones, she was striking rather than beautiful. It was her crusading spirit, moral force and vibrant personality which made her so compelling to watch.

A West End star for much of her career, she preferred working in simpler theatrical conditions, as she did in the First World War, as leading lady at the Old Vic during its first four Shakespeare seasons. Unlike many actors she loved touring, especially when she could play to audiences unused to theatre. She relished especially the months she spent in the towns and villages of Wales, staging fit-up productions of Euripides and Shakespeare in miners' institutes and parish halls during the Second World War. Simplicity was also the hallmark of her hugely popular poetry recitals, which in her later years she performed all over the world, so indulging her great passion for travel.

She was a doughty campaigner for a National Theatre, a persistent seeker after new and experimental work, and a lifelong opponent of theatre censorship. She believed theatre could be a force for good, that it should not merely entertain, but help people understand themselves better, stimulate their imaginations, and encourage them to think about the world around them. Personally ambitious, she loved acting for its own sake, and was always looking to improve her art. 'If you've got no audience,' she once said, 'then act to the kitchen poker.' But she was also driven by a desire for the theatre itself to succeed, and for the lives of those working in it to be improved. It was this that led her, along with other leaders of her profession, to help found Equity, the actors' trade union, and over the years to fight within it for her ideas.

She spoke on many platforms, holding forth passionately on countless topics, from Votes for Women in the suffragette years to nuclear disarmament in her eighties. She marched through the streets in the peace movement, and sought to help refugee children during the Spanish Civil War. She fought and spoke up for groups struggling against their government, whether they were conscientious objectors, striking miners, or the native blacks in apartheid South Africa. She was on Hitler's hit-list of individuals to be eliminated once Germany had invaded Britain. She visited leper colonies in Essex and Hong Kong, and held the hands of dying children in Belsen concentration camp. She was, in the writer A P Herbert's words, 'a star of life'.

The role which made her name in the theatre, and with which she was forever associated, was Saint Joan. Shaw wrote it especially for her, and she played it with all the warrior-like fervour and heartfelt conviction of her deeply held religious faith. Afterwards he gave her a copy of the play, inscribing it 'To Saint Sybil Thorndike from Saint Bernard Shaw'. There were many people, then and later, who believed the label an appropriate one for her. So did 'Saint Sybil' really exist? Who was the private person behind the ebullient, famously worthy public personality? While researching her long and extraordinarily rich life, I talked to nearly two hundred people who had known or worked with her. They included family and friends, and many of the actors, directors and playwrights whose careers intertwined with hers over the decades. Their vivid personal memories reveal an infinitely more complex and human woman than the word 'saint' would suggest.

There was, I discovered, a tough, astringent side to her personality – Ralph Richardson called it her 'stiletto' – and she could be acerbic about people. She had a violent temper, though she rarely showed it outside the home. Rarely ill herself, she was none too tolerant of illness in others. She had a hunger for drama offstage as well as on, which sometimes made her presence overwhelming to those around her. Although her family loved and admired her, they found her energy and enthusiasm at times exhausting, even intimidating. As her son John put it: 'To be with Sybil is to see everything through an enormous emotional magnifying glass.' Her four children went into the theatre for some or all of their lives, but three of them moved abroad at certain times of their careers, in part to escape from her shadow.

Her marriage of sixty years to the actor and director Lewis Casson seemed from the outside to be the perfect partnership. He directed her in some of her greatest successes; they shared many aims and values, both about the theatre and society at large; and they had an intensely loving relationship. But it was one in which two very forceful people often clashed temperamentally. Their arguments, sometimes violent, were usually about plays or politics rather than personal matters. But on one or two occasions there was more serious turbulence.

As a public speaker she could move an audience by the force of her personality and the obvious sincerity of her feelings, but she was sometimes wildly inconsistent. Her political views could be naïve and simplistic, stemming from a very human response to people and events. It was Lewis who, though a passionate man himself, provided the more rational, sophisticated and informed analysis of the world around them.

Her real personality is seen vividly in her many surviving letters. Written to and from all corners of the world in her large, flowing hand, addressed equally to the famous and the obscure, they reveal many aspects of her personality beyond the familiar enthusiasm, optimism and love of life. They show the gay, fun-loving woman, delighting in theatrical gossip; the doting but anxious mother and grandmother; the avid reader exchanging views on the latest novel or book about philosophy. Perhaps the most poignant are those in which she writes of her struggle to care for Lewis during his bouts of depression and later infirmity.

One of the questions raised during my research was whether the enormous quantity of work she and Lewis did together in the theatre hampered their individual careers. One view was that his development as a director was held back because he committed himself too often – more than a hundred times – to directing her. Another was that she would have achieved even more if she had not been subject to his often dogmatic and pedantic method of direction and, in later years, to the need to find plays in which he could be cast alongside her. A more common view was that their partnership was mutually beneficial, and that on stage she needed him, a fearless and often ferocious critic of her acting, to rein in her more violent tendencies.

Was she a great actress? In the opinion of the director Tyrone Guthrie, she and Laurence Olivier were the two actors 'who best combined protean skill with star quality'. Theatre critics such as W A Darlington, J C Trewin and Ivor Brown had no doubt of her greatness. James Agate, probably the most influential in her heyday, felt she achieved greatness, but only in great roles. Many felt that, unless restrained, she could descend into caricature, or revert to the grand manner, with all the appropriate gestures: 'She was magnificent, if you could keep her arms below her shoulders,' one theatre manager observed.

Comparisons were inevitably made with other leading actresses of the time, most notably Edith Evans. She and Sybil could hardly have been more different in style, temperament and personality, and in the parts in which they excelled. Gielgud, who knew and admired both of them, thought Edith Evans the greater actress, but Sybil Thorndike the greater woman. Opinion on the first question was divided in their lifetime, and continues to be so today. On the second, there has been only one opinion.

Prologue

By noon it was a full house in Westminster Abbey. Two thousand people had come to give thanks for her life and work. In the congregation were stars of the stage and screen, family and friends, diplomats and academics, and numerous people from theatres and charities throughout the country. Sybil Thorndike was being laid to rest. As her ashes were lowered into a grave in the choir aisle, her children stood near with bowed heads. Trumpets sounded, muffled bells pealed, the standard was at half mast.

She was the first of her profession to be so memorialised since Henry Irving 71 years previously, and the first actress to be given the honour. During the service, held on 2 July 1976 three weeks after her death, three great actors saluted their friend: Ralph Richardson with the 91st Psalm, Paul Scofield with 'Fear no more the heat o' the sun' from Shakespeare's *Cymbeline*, and John Gielgud with an affectionate address about 'the best-loved English actress since Ellen Terry'.

A life that ended in an ancient abbey had its roots in an ancient cathedral....

Sybil Thorndike grew up in Rochester by the river Medway in Kent. The cathedral, which dominated the city and her childhood, was her first playground and theatre. Here she acted out her fantasies with her brother Russell, gaining her feeling for drama by watching the traditional church rituals. Here she absorbed the stories and beliefs of her parents' religion, and developed her intense love of music.

The services, the daily round of sung matins and evensong, delighted the lively young girl – musically, visually and spiritually. She knew all the hymns and anthems by heart, and sang them lustily in her piping treble voice. She loved too the colourful hangings on the altar, the 'costumes' worn by the different ranks of churchmen, and the dramatic moment when the cathedral door opened and the clergy arrived.

Music was a central element in her young life. From an early age she showed a precocious talent as a pianist. Encouraged at home by a ferociously ambitious mother, she applied herself with extraordinary application to developing her talent, practising at all hours of the day. She became a pupil of a distinguished musician, gave a recital in London, and seemed destined to become a concert pianist.

Acting, religion and music were the three great passions of her childhood. Along with her love of family, they were to remain as such for the rest of her life.

1

When Arthur Met Agnes

'I could marry that handsome man'
Sybil's mother, on seeing Arthur Thorndike in church

Acting, religion and music all featured prominently in the lives of Sybil's parents and grandparents, though in many different ways and circumstances.

Her paternal grandfather Daniel Thorndike, born in 1794, was a general in the Royal Artillery, though he never saw active service. Living in Bath, he was a successful amateur actor, who compelled his children to learn the flute, cello and harp. His first wife, the beautiful Miss Faunce, ran away to Australia with her lover, a namesake of the Irish playwright and actor Dion Boucicault. He divorced her, and her name was never mentioned again in his lifetime.

Of the two children, Charles entered the army, and later became ordained. He had a beautiful voice, which he passed on to his children, two of whom, Herbert Thorndike and Emily Hart Dyke, became well-known professional singers. Julia, the daughter, is remembered for her fine, deep contralto voice, and the trembling emotion she displayed during family prayers. This quality of voice was a family characteristic: they all sang very dramatically and with tremendous emotion.

The general married again, and restored the home to one of God-fearing Victorian respectability. His second wife Isabella Russell, Sybil's paternal grandmother, was a vivacious younger woman, but obedient and properly religious. She played the piano at family theatricals and musical entertainments. The couple had four sons and a daughter. The first two children, Godfrey and Russell, died in infancy, the fourth and fifth, Francis and another Isabella, survived. The middle child, Sybil's father, was born in Quebec on 26 November 1853, and named Arthur John Webster Thorndike.

Amiable and good-looking, fair-haired, with a strong profile and fine cheekbones, he entered St John's College, Cambridge in 1872. He studied the Latin and Greek classics, and theology, for which he had to study the Old Testament in English, one of the four gospels in Greek, and English church history. A talented but not outstanding scholar, he showed a passion for tennis and mountaineering, but particularly rowing, where he rowed bow in the college first boat, only missing selection for the annual university boat race through being slightly under weight. Although he hoped for a career in the army, General Thorndike insisted he go into the church, a command which, having been religious from boyhood, he found easy to obey. He too was very musical, with a good singing voice. He had tremendous vitality and zest, a mystic religious sense, a social conscience, and a delight in overcoming difficulties – all characteristics he would pass on to his eldest daughter.

John Bowers, Sybil's Scottish maternal grandfather, could be seen as a role model for her life-long passion for self-improvement. The son of the local postman in Elgin in northern Scotland, he assisted his father in the post office, and tended the sheep in the surrounding meadows. He made good use of these hours, reading voraciously and teaching himself the elements of mathematics. A determined, ambitious young man with a flair for ships and engineering, he joined a boat going to England as an apprentice, and ended up in Southampton, where he eventually became a consulting engineer for the Union Castle shipping line. Hospitable and generous, he too embraced religion fervently: every Sunday after church, in a round-house he had erected in his garden, he would discuss the local vicar's sermon with those of the shipping line's captains then ashore.

His three sons all went into the church. The eldest, Jack, had a distinguished career, becoming first a canon, then Archdeacon of Gloucester, and finally Bishop of Thetford. Renowned for telling funny stories even in the pulpit, his memorial in Norwich Cathedral shows him with a broad grin on his face. The youngest son, Ted, did brilliantly at Oxford, but got into financial difficulties through his reckless behaviour. His father paid off his debts, and gave him money to go to North America, where he married a Canadian woman, and ended up a dignitary of the Episcopal Church in Texas. The youngest son, William, known as Willie, was also wild, and should, according to some, have been an actor. His theatrical and emotional sermons in his church at Gillingham in Kent often reduced his congregations to tears. In the vestry afterwards he'd declare, 'I got 'em, didn't I – not a dry eye in the place!'

John Bowers' wife, Sybil's maternal grandmother, was Betsy Allcot, who came from Portchester on the Hampshire coast. In addition to their three boys, the couple also had three daughters, Adela Fanny (Amy) the eldest, Belle the youngest, and their middle child Agnes Macdonald, Sybil's mother, known as 'Donnie'. Agnes too was strongly religious: in Southampton she played the organ for church services and temperance meetings, and taught in the local Sunday School. Attractive and strong-featured, with blue eyes, a gay, smiling face, and a plump figure, she was much courted by young officers on the shipping line, one of whom proposed to her, but without success. Like her brothers Ted and William, Agnes too had a wild streak, coupled with an innate gaiety, and a strong sense of the ridiculous.

Sybil's parents first met while Arthur Thorndike was at Cambridge. Agnes would visit her brother Jack Bowers, a fellow-student and friend of Arthur. A good pianist, she accompanied Arthur when he sang at informal musical sessions. She made a great impression on him, but she thought him conceited. They met again a few years later at St Mary Redcliffe Church in Bristol, where Arthur was taking his first steps up the ecclesiastical ladder. After Cambridge he had been ordained a deacon, then taken two curate posts in Dorset, at Canford Magna and Bere Regis. A concern for people's welfare, which would influence his daughter, was already apparent: Thomas Hardy remembered him at Bere Regis as a 'beautiful fair-haired lay reader, who used to be in and out of the cottages with great diligence and persistence, his Bible under his arm'.

He had then become a curate at St Mary Redcliffe, as had his friend Jack Bowers. In May 1881 Jack was to preach his first important sermon, and had invited his sister Agnes, now twenty-two, to attend. She noticed a young curate walking beside her brother as they processed down the aisle and, according to legend, said: 'I could marry that handsome man walking with Jack.' She had apparently failed to recognise him from their encounters in Cambridge. They met again that night at supper, and this time the attraction was mutual. Within two weeks they were engaged, and Arthur was given the curacy at Barley, a pretty Hertfordshire village near Royston. The wedding took place at Holy Trinity Church in Southampton on 15 September. After a honeymoon in Folkestone, the pair moved to a small house in Barley in October.

Living on Arthur's stipend of £250 a year they struggled to make ends meet, and must have been grateful for the generosity of Agnes' mother Bessie.

Her letters to her daughter show her plying them with postal orders 'to help to fill some little corners', with substantial supplements to their 'little stock of wines and spirits', and with the occasional food hamper. Then, in February 1882, Agnes confided to her mother that she might be pregnant. 'Fancy Arthur a father!' her mother wrote to her gleefully. 'It will be sure to be pretty, having Papa and Mama's beauty combined.' She continued to support Agnes with maternal advice – 'If you suffer with a pain in your back, take a warm bath' – and the couple with plenty of drink: 'I shall send you 2 bottles of brandy, 2 whiskey, 2 Gin, 2 Port, 2 Sherry and 2 of Champagne.'

In the summer the couple moved yet again, this time to Gainsborough in Lincolnshire. Whether for financial reasons, or because of pressure from Agnes, who was more ambitious for her husband than he was for himself, Arthur had secured the post of senior curate at All Saints' Church. He thought the move appropriate, as his mother-in-law noted: 'I am so pleased you are going to Gainsborough,' she wrote to Agnes. 'Arthur is perfectly right, he is far too good for Barley.'

The baby was born on 24 October. Her parents first thought of calling her Isabella Marian, but then christened her Agnes Sybil. Later her brother Russell fantasised about their mother's memory of the birth. 'As the doctor bent over the natal bed, this newcomer extended one hand to him in true leading-lady manner, as much as to say, "Thank you for working up my entrance," and then gave him a push to convey that she was quite ready to play her part on the great stage of the world, without any further support from him.'

2

A Kentish Lass

1882–1895

'Would be a good pupil if she would cultivate repose'
Sybil's school report

Sybil was born in The Olde Vicarage, her parents' new home, which stood across the road from All Saints. A large parish church with an impressive square steeple, it reflected the importance of Gainsborough as a wool town in the Middle Ages. In the 1880s it was a generally dreary place of some 12,000 inhabitants; George Eliot had reputedly used it as the model for St Ogg's in *The Mill on the Floss*.

As senior curate Arthur Thorndike was kept busy, both in Gainsborough and other parishes, where he was sent as a 'locum'. Agnes soon became involved in church and other social activities. In February 1884 they moved from the vicarage to another house in the town, Cleveland House. On the same day Arthur was interviewed for the post of minor canon at Rochester Cathedral. Agnes wrote to him: 'I have been thinking of you so much this morning and wondering how those old guns are treating you. I do hope for the best, but never mind darling, if you don't get it, we shall still love each other all the same, so don't think I shall grieve, will you?' Arthur wired her to say he had been offered the post. 'You cannot tell how delighted I was to receive the telegram,' she replied. 'You did so well, you old pet.'

Two weeks before the move, Arthur took temporary lodgings on Boley Hill in Rochester, and started to prepare their new house. 'What a delight it will be to have you with me to arrange the house,' he wrote. 'Tomorrow I make my debut in the cathedral by taking the litany in the morning service and helping in the celebration at mid-day. In the afternoon I take the service in the nave.' Agnes wrote fervently from his mother's house in Bath: 'I am longing, my darling, to see you, it seems years to me since we met: how thankful I shall be, my dear one, to get to my own home. I am very happy here, but there is such a dreadful want which only my Artie can supply. I never spent such a long fortnight in my life.'

Agnes and Sybil arrived in Rochester in May. As an adult Sybil retained few memories of Gainsborough. Her first at around eighteen months was of taking her wax doll to bed, and finding it melting under her. She remembered the pleasure of being allowed to toddle from somebody's garden into a field of new-mown hay, the smell of which in later life always prompted the cry 'Oh, Gainsborough!' The rest of her childhood memories related to Rochester, where she would spend the next 16 years.

An ancient city in Kent, it stands on the river Medway, above which towers the great square keep of its Norman castle. It contains many ancient buildings, including a seventeenth-century Guildhall, and Restoration House, so called because Charles II stayed there in 1660 on his way to reclaim the throne. It has many associations with Charles Dickens, who lived in nearby Gad's Hill and knew Rochester from his childhood: 'I peeped about its old corners with interest and wonder when I was a very little child,' he wrote. Some things had not changed by the time the Thorndikes moved there: cattle were still being driven down the high street.

Their new home was at 2 Minor Canon Row, set within the precincts of the ancient cathedral in a row of seven redbrick houses built in 1723, and close to the chapter offices, the cloister house and the handsome Georgian deanery. Dickens used Rochester as the setting for much of his last, unfinished novel *The Mystery of Edwin Drood*, in which Rochester is thinly disguised as 'Cloisterham'. His description of the row of houses evokes the 'blessed air of tranquillity' a few years before Sybil and family moved there. 'Minor Canon Corner was a quiet place in the shadow of the cathedral, which the cawing of the rooks, the echoing footsteps of rare passers, the sound of the cathedral bell, or the roll of the cathedral organ, seemed to render more quiet than absolute silence.'

A solid and spacious three-storey house with a long, narrow garden at the back, the family's new home had in addition to the usual rooms a separate dining-room, a nursery and a dressing-room. The servants, then the norm for the middle classes, included Sybil's nurse, a cook, and a between-maid; they also employed a cleaning woman and a gardener. Agnes took a great interest in the house, enjoying choosing the décor for the various rooms. As she had in

Gainsborough, she helped Arthur with his church work, and became heavily involved in parish activities. Nine months after the move she gave birth to a second child, Arthur Russell.

He and Sybil quickly became close companions, revelling in the myriad opportunities for games and mischief provided by their proximity to the country's second-oldest cathedral. They loved to race down the long wide nave, hide under the choir stalls and play games in the crypt, from where they were often chased by the verger. From their nursery window they would observe the comings and goings of the clergy, lay-clerks and choirboys, then gleefully imitate their ways of walking; later they would imitate the sermons they heard in the cathedral.

Both children were blessed with vivid imaginations. One of their chief amusements was to see who could tell the most frightening story, after which they would enjoy the feeling of fear as they went upstairs in the dark. They also liked to play at detectives, tracking in sleuth-style the various inhabitants of the precincts whom they suspected of intent to murder or rob. Sybil was, according to Russell, 'a stormy petrel in the nursery': her vitality was already there in abundance. So too was her concern for others. One day, finding Russell inconsolable because the snow he loved had stopped falling and was melting, she created a fake snowstorm out of torn-up paper.

A lively and outgoing girl with a great sense of fun, Sybil made friends easily. She and Russell got to know children of other church families in the precincts, most notably the Jelfs, whose father was a canon, and whose house looked out on to the cathedral. It was there when she was four that her acting career began. The two families performed a play, with Sybil and Kitty Jelf cast as fairies, and Russell as a gnome. The experience whetted their appetite for performance, and they set up their own stage at home on the nursery table. Here they acted out gruesome home-made dramas, bloodthirsty shows in which murder was a prominent feature. 'Acting came to my children as naturally as did eating their breakfast,' their mother observed later.

At five, after a spell at kindergarten, Sybil joined a local school run by a Miss Rivett. The children, ranging in age from 5 to 10, were taught in a single group, and did their sums on slates. Sybil had already learned to read, and made good progress. She enjoyed being called up to read aloud. But her precocious musical ability brought her into disgrace, when it was discovered she was playing piano exercises by ear rather than by sight. This was considered deceit, and she was kept in for an hour after school. When her mother collected her she sobbed all the way home. Another day she was thoroughly shaken when a big backward boy was caned because he couldn't do his sums. His crying, and the sound of the cane on his hands and back, frightened her horribly, but also revolted her, because it was done in cold blood, and seemed wrong. The incident, she argued later, marked the beginning of her pacifist feelings.

The beating particularly shocked her because, unusually for the time, her parents refrained from using physical punishment. Her upbringing was a liberal one. A humble and patient man, who took a cold bath every morning, Arthur Thorndike was dedicated to his work, and took his faith very seriously: after returning home from early service at the cathedral he would go to his dressing-room and pray until breakfast time. He was tolerant and easy-going, and from an early age encouraged his children to argue over religion and other subjects. When they quarrelled, he would make each of them act being the other, so they would better understand the other's point of view. He was prepared to flout convention, allowing Sybil to play with her toys on Sunday, an activity frowned on in church circles. She worshipped and adored him: he seemed the perfect father. When he preached in his fine voice she swelled with pride; when she got into trouble at school it was him she felt she was letting down. He never became angry or raised his voice, but just became sad if she did wrong, causing her to feel devastated she had upset him. 'My dear Daddy,' she wrote aged six, as a postscript to a letter her mother wrote to him. 'Come back soon as we miss you so much. We are always talking about you. Mother guided my hand. We are taking care of her. Write soon. Ever your own loving Sybil Thorndike.'

Agnes Thorndike was a more exuberant, high-spirited character than her husband, with an original sense of humour. Her ribald remarks at the expense of the clergy and the cathedral services sometimes got her into hot water in the precincts, where she was considered 'racy' and a bit of a 'card'. 'I think she provided my father with a gaiety and a sense of the ridiculous which saved him from being the complete religious,' Sybil suggested later. 'She was wildly dramatic.' She influenced her husband's sermons: if they went on too long, she used to cough and he would stop. She was known for her modern ideas, especially about interior decoration. She was keen on the new Liberty furniture, and would accompany friends to London by train to advise them what to buy. She was full of ambition for her children – 'Neither Caesar nor Napoleon had more,' Russell recalled – but also for her husband, whom she hoped would become an archbishop. This proved a bone of contention in what was otherwise a close, loving marriage between two very different characters. They provided their children with the perfect background against which their fantasies could be played out, and their artistic talents allowed to flourish. 'Mother gave me my zest for living and Father made me love people,' Sybil said later.

After the nursery table, she and Russell created a theatre in the spare room. Their productions, including *The Blood on the Bedpost*, *The Murder of the White Mice* and *The Nun's Revenge*, came with stern health warnings, such as 'A play that is very frightening' or 'A play for much crying'. A particular favourite was a lurid melodrama written by Sybil, *The Dentist's Cure, or, Saw Their Silly Heads Off*, the plot of which was not dissimilar to that of *Sweeney Todd*. Their audience consisted of the family servants who, to Sybil's annoyance, were not always able to keep a straight face during her tragic speeches. Their mother also broke the spell at critical moments: when Sybil spattered stage blood at the end of *The Dentist's Cure*, she would call out 'Mind the best bed', or 'Mind the lamps'. She disapproved of the Grand Guignol element in the plays, and tried to persuade her children to exercise more restraint.

Russell spent a year with Sybil at Miss Rivett's before they went their separate ways, Russell to the preparatory school of the sixteenth-century King's School situated behind Minor Canon Row, Sybil to the newly built Grammar School for Girls, where just before her eighth birthday she became a pupil in the first intake. The school, a large house situated on a corner in the Maidstone Road, was established as a sister school to Sir Joseph Williamson's Mathematical School for Boys, where the actor David Garrick had once been a pupil. It was a fee-paying school for 200 girls, with those under ten such as Sybil charged £2 13s 4d per term, and girls over ten £3 6s 8d. At a time when the education of young women was by no means universally approved of, it was one of the country's first girls' grammar schools. Yet even the enlightened citizens of Rochester who founded it had limited ambitions for its pupils, expressing the hope that it would turn out girls 'fit to adorn the homes of England'.

Sybil started each term full of good resolutions, determined to achieve top marks. Yet she had limited success as a scholar, finding other areas of life much more interesting. One of her teachers, a Miss Eastgate, later wrote of a wistful-eyed young girl of twelve with 'a questing expression', for whom lessons seemed dull, and who showed a longing for self-expression, 'a longing that could not be satisfied by reading, writing or arithmetic'. Quiet study was clearly not her forte: 'Inclined to be noisy', 'Good, but apt to be boisterous', and 'Would be a good pupil if she would cultivate repose' were typical comments in her reports. Russell remembered: 'If she didn't want to learn a thing, she didn't. She was never quite bad enough to be bad, and never quite good enough to be brilliant.'

She felt a strong urge to learn history, but was frightened by the history mistress. She only liked geography when it dealt with exploration. She enjoyed the scripture lessons, taught by a Miss Bartolemy who, she recalled, 'made Samuel, Kings and Chronicles and even the prophets sound like a Robert Louis Stevenson adventure', and for whom she experienced her first girlhood passion. But she often fared badly, and had to give excuses for failing to do her work. Eventually the headmistress came to see her father, while a petrified Sybil hid in the garden.

Her great thrill was the Shakespeare class. Her teacher, Miss Ashworth, read passages from *Julius Caesar* with such great emotion that Sybil, captivated, went home and recited them to Russell, imitating her teacher's voice. Sybil's talent was soon recognised, and she was cast as Brutus in *Julius Caesar* in the school play. For weeks the house rang with the noblest Roman's speeches, with Sybil, who loathed needlework, spending hours sewing red braid on her mother's old sheets to make a toga. Her performance was greatly applauded. 'She was awfully bucked for weeks afterwards,' Russell remembered. Whenever a dignitary visited the school, Sybil was brought out of class and asked to recite 'Romans, countrymen and lovers!' No illustrated record of the production survives, but in photographs Sybil seems a solid young girl, attractive rather than beautiful, with wavy, shoulder-length hair and a fringe surrounding regular features. Dressed variously as a sailor, a shepherdess and herself, she seems at ease in front of the camera.

Meanwhile the dramatic performances continued at home, sometimes in the cellar, at other times in the kitchen, with the servants dutifully applauding. When the spare bedroom started to be used for visitors, Sybil persuaded their mother to let them use the box-room instead. Their new theatre had the luxury of proper curtains, and a bath hung up for use as a thunder sheet. Plays about missionaries now became the order of the day. In one of them, *The Great Thunderstorm of Central Africa*, Sybil, playing a missionary, was struck by a poisoned thunderbolt, but was saved from death by a passing doctor, played by Russell on a wooden horse. All this 'playing' was a useful channel for the young Sybil's powerful emotions, though they didn't prevent a recurring dream: in it she was walking down an alleyway between bales of cotton, her feet getting tangled in cobwebs, and hearing a noise growing louder and louder. The dream would continue throughout her life, especially when she was ill or troubled.

Her and Russell's games included playing at 'services' or 'church' or 'processions'. Imitating sermons heard in the cathedral, they preached to a congregation of boots, tennis rackets and watering-cans, using an edition of *Don Quixote* as the Bible, and bobbing and genuflecting with great zest. One day they conducted a High Mass communion service, using their father's bicycle bell, and reverently drinking cough mixture from his college rowing cup. Discovering them, Arthur Thorndike imposed a ban on such blasphemous games, to Sybil's indignation. Their melodramas were influenced by a visit to the Corn Exchange to see Poole's Myriorama, a horror show involving shipwrecks, volcanoes and army hospitals under fire, these being interspersed with a prima donna singing 'Abide with Me' and 'Rock of Ages'. This was the first professional actress Sybil had seen, and she was greatly impressed. 'Everyone sobbed, except us,' Russell remembered. 'We were too excited.'

A familiar figure in Rochester until his death in 1870, Dickens loomed large in their childhood. He had used the town as the fictitious setting in several novels, including *The Pickwick Papers*, *Great Expectations* and, most notably, *The Mystery of Edwin Drood*. Plenty of people in the town remembered him, and liked to repeat stories of him looking at Restoration House (the model for Miss Havisham's house in *Great Expectations*), or standing in front of Eastgate (the Nun's House and Miss Twinkleton's Seminary for Young Ladies in *Edwin Drood*). There were also more personal associations. Their neighbour Dean Hole had been a friend of Dickens, and would pass on his memories of him to them. They went to tea with the verger, Mr Hoadley, on whom the disreputable stonemason Durdles in *Edwin Drood* was supposedly based. There they would listen to his stories, and be shown pictures of characters from the novels.

The children liked to fantasise that Mr Crisparkle in *Edwin Drood* was based on their father; Dickens described him as: 'Minor Canon, early riser, musical, classical, cheerful, kind, good-natured, social, contented, and boy-like.' Arthur Thorndike himself was a Dickens enthusiast: he took the children to Gad's Hill, impressing on them how lucky they were to be living in the same place as one of the world's great men. He read to them from *The*

Pickwick Papers and *The Old Curiosity Shop*, and, Sybil remembered, 'being an amateur actor of the old school who liked exaggerating all the parts, he gave the characters a colourful quality of something larger than life'.

But Dickens was also a source of fear. On the dining-room mantelpiece there stood a large plaster-cast of the novelist. For a while, because they were forbidden to say 'What the Dickens' since it meant 'What the Devil', the children got the two confused, and became terrified of the bust, thinking it was Dickens' ghost. One night Russell woke screaming from a nightmare, in which he imagined the bust had come into their nursery. This prompted Sybil, now seven, to organise its destruction: while their father was safely at prayer in his room, she and Russell pulled it from the mantelpiece to the floor, where it smashed into pieces. Since, as they explained, they had broken it in order to destroy the Devil, the only punishment their father gave them was the task of burying the remains in the garden.

They were often involved in the parish entertainments, in mission rooms and at ecclesiastical garden parties. Sybil first performed in public at the age of four, standing on a table in the archdeacon's garden and, held by her father, singing 'The Maid of the Mill'. Later she and Russell sang duets, performing them with large gestures and intense emotion, in a melodramatic style. Once, when they were re-enacting a circus on the cathedral lawn, Sybil was supposed to jump through a paper hoop, but it failed to break. When Russell burst out laughing, Sybil picked up the hoop and smashed it over his head, reducing him to tears, and the audience of local servants to hysterics. Like other members of the family she had a strong temper, though she and Russell rarely quarrelled, and then not usually violently.

Music had been important from her early days, and in Minor Canon Row she was surrounded by it. In addition to his fine voice, which he used to good effect in the cathedral, Arthur Thorndike played the cello. Agnes, a good musician with a beautiful voice, was also a natural pianist and organist, and regularly played for the Rochester Choral Society. Once a student at the Guildhall School of Music in London, she harboured ambitions for Sybil, and taught her the rudiments of the piano when she was just five. Sybil showed obvious musical talent, and studied the piano and violin at school. She made little progress with the violin, which she disliked, but became good enough on the piano to accompany the drill classes and play in school concerts.

One of her favourite pastimes was dancing. Her debut in public, at the age of five, was in a charity musical show. Later, at the grammar school, she attended a class at the Mission Hall formed by her mother and the headteacher of the King's prep school, Mrs Langhorne. The dance teacher Miss Turner taught them fan dances, hornpipes, minuets and gavottes, Irish jigs and Scottish reels, waltzes and barn dances, with Sybil's mother providing a spirited piano accompaniment. Sybil revelled in the chance to show off: 'We were quite a company of exhibitionists,' she remembered. 'And no band has played dance music like Mother. She had such go, such dash.'

Her mother gave birth to another girl, Eileen, in January 1891, and the following year Arthur Thorndike was appointed vicar of St Margaret's-next-Rochester, the largest parish in Rochester. The family moved up the hill to the vicarage next to the church in St Margaret Street, a handsome, rambling three-storey house set behind high walls, with the children's nursery looking out over the Medway. To Sybil's delight she and Russell were given an attic room each, and permission to move the furniture around for theatrical purposes. She placed a backless wardrobe against her bed, so that at bedtime she could make an 'entrance' through its double doors.

The children now staged their plays in the parish room attached to the vicarage. A parental ban prevented Eileen joining the company until she was three. To Sybil's chagrin, they were not allowed to perform publicly the plays they considered the most interesting. One day their father, feeling they should use their talents for the benefit of the parish, suggested that if they could find a suitable play, they could perform it with scenery and footlights at an entertainment in the Mission Hall. Excited at the prospect, Sybil and Russell performed a selection of their dramatic works for him. But their mother intervened, suggesting that 'some nice play with a pretty plot' would set a much better example to the local children.

'Sybil went off the deep end into one of her awful rages,' Russell remembered. 'She always had a vile temper, which was liable to go off quite unexpectedly. Things that most children go into tempers about didn't affect her, but a chance word about something that she thought vastly important, like plays, would suddenly fire the mine.' There would be tears and angry words, with Sybil being sent to her room in disgrace for her 'unladylike' behaviour. Quick to argue, she was also furious when their father forbade her to read novels such as Rider Haggard's *She*, but allowed Russell to do so. She got round the ban by having her brother tell her the stories, after which they secretly acted them out in the cellar.

She had no desire to be a lady. One of her first ambitions was to be a nun in winter and a gleaner in summer, although this soon gave way to being an explorer. Strong and vigorous, she envied boys their capacity for adventure, and loved to join in their activities. She took part in trips to the Vines, a new public park, and to the grounds of the ruined castle, where she and Russell climbed into every nook and cranny. A local woman who made dresses for the Thorndike girls remembered Sybil as 'happy and talkative and full of energy'. Later she became one of the first girls in the town to ride a bicycle, an increasingly popular activity, but one considered unladylike by some. Having taught Russell, she joined him and other boys on exhilarating rides through the lanes and fields of Kent, imagining they were army officers on horseback exploring the Himalayas or conquering and subduing their enemies. She was a fast runner who loved running for its own sake, but hated competitive races, or being forced to play cricket. She was terrified of the sea, and spent several seaside holidays refusing to go in. Yet once she learnt to swim she became wildly keen.

Her early love of theatre came directly from her home. The Victorian drama exemplified by Henry Irving and Herbert Beerbohm Tree and other star actor-managers was still firmly entrenched. The great partnership of Irving and Ellen Terry at the Lyceum had made Shakespeare fashionable again. Sybil's parents went there regularly, Agnes sometimes paying for tickets by selling a fender or a poker to the local antique shop. 'They always came back from seeing them with starry eyes, and thrilled us with the tales, so that I felt Ellen Terry was some kind of magic person,' Sybil remembered. Her first contact with Shakespeare came when her father read *Hamlet* to them after seeing it at the Lyceum. A keen amateur actor, Arthur Thorndike loved poetry, and would learn a new work every morning while shaving. He read poems to the children, while Agnes, who had harboured ambitions to be an actress, read them stories in a theatrical style that made them seem like plays.

It seems surprising in the light of her parents' enthusiasm that, apart from a visit to see *Aladdin* at the Victoria Hall in Rochester, Sybil was not taken to the theatre until she was ten. It was treated as a very special occasion. Dressed in their best clothes, the family took a taxi to the Chatham Opera House, where they sat in the front row of the dress circle to watch Charles Hawtrey's farce *The Private Secretary*. Despite being warned to be on her best behaviour, Sybil laughed raucously, got violent hiccups, and was threatened with being taken out.

After this they were taken every year to the pantomime in Drury Lane. Yet despite Sybil's love of acting and growing fascination with the theatre, it was music that gradually took over her life. Her passion was the piano. Encouraged by her mother and her schoolteacher Mary Symons, she worked hard at her playing, waking early in order to practise. She was soon good enough to graduate from accompanying drilling to playing solos in school concerts and the occasional Mission Room entertainment. Yet she soon began to suffer from the nerves that as a performer she was to battle with all her life. Significantly, she found the only way she could overcome them was to pretend she was a great pianist – in other words, to act the part.

At eleven she took part in a local concert, playing a Mendelssohn Scherzo and a Beethoven Contretanz: the local paper reported that 'this little girl's very clever execution of the pieces secured for her a persistent encore, which she complied with'. Her teacher then arranged for her to play the Beethoven piece at a concert in London's Steinway Hall (now the Wigmore Hall). Overcome with fear shortly before it began, she announced she couldn't go on. Fortunately the baritone and musical-comedy star Charles Hayden Coffin was also on the bill. When he saw this podgy figure trembling backstage, he led her to a chink in the curtain, and said: 'Just play to that nice old man in the front row, and don't think of anyone else.'

His advice calmed Sybil down, and she played well enough to gain two encores. Afterwards the singer kissed her and said: 'Little Miss Paderewski – splendid.' She never forgot his kindness, as it gave her back some self-confidence, a quality she would need in abundance as she embarked on her planned musical career.

3

The Young Musician

1895–1902

'I wish there was nothing but Shakespeare and the piano, I do loathe
lessons so unless they are to do with plays'
Sybil in a letter to her brother Russell

Sybil's ambition to be a pianist continued to grow. At the local choral
society concerts she was inspired by the playing of first-class musicians,
including the eminent Brahms and Schumann specialist Leonard Borwick,
then touring the provinces. She now put pressure on her parents to let her
leave school and study the piano in London. Her mother would have been
happy for her to concentrate solely on music, but her father insisted she
continue with her education, an unusual attitude at this time towards the
education of girls. Meanwhile Russell, whose musical talent lay in his voice,
became a chorister and a boarder at St George's School in Windsor, and for
the first time Sybil and he were separated.

At thirteen an audition was arranged for Sybil at the Guildhall School of
Music in London. She was to play for Professor Francesco Berger, in the hope
that he would take her on as a pupil. Then in his early sixties, a distinguished
composer and pianist, Berger was famous for producing virtuoso performers.
He was a friend of Dvorak, and as a director of the Philharmonic Society had
dealings with Saint-Saëns and Arthur Sullivan. He too had a connection with
Dickens, being a close personal friend. He had composed the music for two
plays by Wilkie Collins, *The Frozen Deep* and *The Lighthouse*, which had been
written for and were performed by Dickens' amateur troupe, with Berger at
the piano.

Sybil's mother took her to the audition, insisting she wear her new velvet
frock and a large hat with a feather in it. Her long, breathless letter to Russell
suggests a keen-eyed, warm-hearted, enthusiastic girl.

'Darling Russell, – It's over, and I'm a pupil at the Guildhall School of Music. Mother took me up by the 9.20 yesterday. All the cathedral people were going up by the same train, as it's the cheap one, and I felt terribly important. Well, we got to the school at ten minutes to eleven, and there was a most glorious noise going on, millions of pianos and violins and singing all going on at once, I felt awful quirks. The porter at the door was an awfully nice man, very like a verger and just as interested in everything. I was taken, and Mother too, into Professor Francesco Berger's room – he's the most fascinating person, I simply adore him. Lots of pupils, about five of them, were sitting on chairs against a wall under a picture of Bach, and one of Wagner opposite, and a girl called Gertrude Meller, older than me, awfully pretty, and a tiny waist, well she was playing some Chopin thing. Oh! Russell, I'll never be able to play like her, she's glorious, she can lift her hand higher than her head and it always comes down on the right note and all the time she looks as if it's awfully easy. I sat and shivered on my chair. Mother made me feel worse by saying, "Now don't be shy," and then Prof. Berger said, "Now, let's see what this little girl can do." So I played a lot then, all without my music – the Beethoven thing you like, more Beethoven things, then a bit of Bach, and lots of pieces I'd learnt with Miss Symons. I felt after the beginning I was getting on finely, then he stopped me and laughed and said, "Very nice little girl, you've got some feeling." Then he turned to Mother and said, "She has no technique at all; she must give up everything and work at technique." Mother said, "Yes, she shall", and I said, "Oh yes" too; then he said I must give up the violin – oh! I was glad, Russ – and that I must give up games, everything I do with my hands except the piano. I was gladder still then, I do hate tennis and cricket and all the things you want me to play, and now I needn't ever again – and that I was to practise three hours a day and then I might possibly be able to play the piano in a few years – I'm so happy I don't know what to do. Oh! and I'm to go to hear a man called Emil Sauer play next week, and I'm to go every week and hear a pianist if I can. Good-bye angel….You'll be frightfully proud of me when I'm as good as Leonard Borwick, won't you? – Your loving Sybil.'

In the same letter she told Russell: 'I wish there was nothing but Shakespeare and the piano, I do loathe lessons so unless they are to do with plays.' Her parents agreed to let her leave school, continuing her general education with a governess, whom she shared with five children living nearby, the Smiths. Her regime was excessively demanding. Once a week she went up to London for a piano lesson at the Guildhall. On other days she rose at five, took a cold bath, and at 5.30 practised her scales for an hour. After breakfast with the cook she practised for another two hours, then had lessons in the Smiths' house from 9 until 1. After lunch there was a walk with the governess and the Smith children, during which they had to speak French. Then followed another hour's practice, more lessons, the evening meal, and yet more practice.

In her new role as student she moved from the attic to a large downstairs sitting-room. Her mother had the room specially furnished and decorated, with Liberty wallpaper and a frieze of tulips, and pictures of Bach, Beethoven and Wagner for inspiration. She installed a grand piano given to Sybil by her aunt Isabella, keeping her upright piano there so that she and Sybil could play duets. 'I adored Mother, but she was terribly critical, which helped but also irritated me,' Sybil remembered. 'She was awful over the piano, because she was such a clean, lovely player herself, and every time I messed up anything she'd jump right down bang on me. She was wildly ambitious for me, much more than I was myself. She'd not been able to fulfil any of her own ambitions, so she worked it all off on me.' Later her mother claimed that 'the real secret of my children's happy youth lay in the fact that my husband and I let them alone…our part was to merely act as their guides'. But the pressure she put on Sybil was clearly more than mere guidance.

Sybil's determination and capacity for hard work were already remarkable. Russell remembered that 'she practised nearly all day long, and no one was allowed to disturb her'. Occasionally she flagged, as she confessed to Kitty Jelf, her closest friend: 'I have been such a wretch last week, and was alto-gether low, but on Monday I made a fresh start and practised my five hours quite well….Last Saturday I went out for a bike ride with Margie she has just learnt she rides very well wobbles occasionally, but that's nothing. I had to be home at six o'clock because I was so slack about practising and Mother was rather annoyed about it.' Her friendship with Ketty Jelf was intense: they kept a secret diary together, and wrote each other Private Letters. Sybil signed hers with expressions such as 'Goodbye darling from your own loving Sybil', and clearly enjoyed passing on her family and other news. Another letter of the time, with its wayward punctuation, catches her chatty nature.

'The cat is a wretch, she keeps scratching, and is altogether unsociable. Eileen has rather a toothache this evening, poor girl….Do you remember Hares and Hounds, how I lost my coat and Phil and Gordon got waxy wasn't it a lark….How are the Liberty curtains, do tell me what they're like. Oh

Mother's room is being papered and painted so pretty. The Nursery has been done with a pretty poppy kind of paper, you know yellow with bunches of poppies wheat and oats on....I'm making myself a petticoat with warm weather pink print 6¾ a yard. I had my 5/- allowance yesterday don't you think it's dreadfully difficult to save I do.'

There was also no doubting her religious fervour. 'Last Friday I went with Father and Mother to hear Canon Rhodes Briscoe preach at the Cathedral, it was lovely. I *do* like the Cathedral. Oh we've got the most beautiful new choir stalls in our church you ever saw, they're simply magnificent.' This intensified when, after her confirmation, her father had to do temporary duty at a church in Brighton, and she and Russell attended a High Mass. 'From that moment we were the most extreme Anglo-Catholics you could possibly have,' she recalled. 'We bowed and crossed ourselves to practically every word.' Her mother bought her a large oak crucifix with a silver Christ figure to hang over her piano, and 'I dedicated myself to the Lord and the piano'.

Her brother Frank was born in May 1895. With Russell at Windsor during term time, Sybil became involved in amateur dramatics. If music was her work, acting was her relaxation. She played the lead in the annual Christmas operetta *The Goose Girl*, and appeared in numerous farces, one-act comedies and charity shows for the parish. Hoping to extend her talent further, her energetic mother started a company to stage musical comedies. Sybil appeared in several of these, including *Rumpelstiltskin* (in which she played an elf), *Beauty and the Beast* and *Jedediah the Scarecrow*. They were directed by Claude Aveling from the Royal College of Music, who lived nearby in Restoration House. Later to write lyrics for shows in the West End and on Broadway, he took a great interest in Sybil's development. According to Russell he was tough with her in rehearsal, but she responded well, being very willing to learn.

Under his tutelage she progressed from small parts to leading ones, including the title-role in *Princess Zara*, which Aveling wrote for her; it had a score by Arthur Somervell, whose recent song cycle *Maud* ('Come into the garden...') had proved immensely popular. Aveling remarked: 'Never mind if the voice isn't much – she can act.' It was a meaty part, full of chances to play mock tragedy, and it proved Sybil's biggest success so far. She was now roped in to other shows, staged by officers of the Royal Engineers and their wives in the theatre at Chatham. Her performance in one production apparently prompted a local woman to remark: 'If the Thorndikes aren't careful, that girl Sybil will get ideas into her head about the *real* stage.'

This view that the profession was a dangerous one was common. It was associated with late hours, drinking, and general loose living: as a writer put it in the *Theatre*, 'the actor is regarded as an outcast, the actress as something worse'. Many actresses of the day faced opposition from their parents. When Marie Tempest told hers of her stage aspirations, they brought in William Gladstone to steer her away from such depravity. Lilian Braithwaite's similar ambition was met with a storm of family protest; Lena Ashwell was locked in an office strong-room and advised to re-consider such a step; and when Eva Moore's father discovered she was secretly acting, he threw her out of the house.

During Russell's holidays, he and Sybil were taken by their parents to the West End theatre, including the pantomime in Drury Lane. Sybil's interest in musical comedy was fired by *The Geisha*, a hugely popular musical at Daly's about a Japanese girl falling in love with a British naval officer. Afterwards her acting came under the influence of its star, Marie Tempest. This embarrassed Russell and his friends: 'We used to look the other way when Sybil let out a high note, very tremolo and actressy,' he remembered. They saw many of the great actors of the time, including Johnston Forbes-Robertson as Hamlet, Henry Irving, Lewis Waller, John Martin Harvey, and Ellen and Marion Terry. Although the plays of Ibsen and Shaw were starting to stir up the London stage – Shaw had announced that the production of *A Doll's House* 'gave Victorian domestic morality its death-blow' – there is no evidence that Sybil's parents had any interest in the New Drama.

One of their most memorable trips was in 1896 with their Aunt Isabella to the recently built His Majesty's, where the actor-manager Herbert Beerbohm Tree was staging his spectacular Shakespearean productions. *Julius Caesar* starred the matinee idol Lewis Waller as Brutus and Tree as Mark Antony, with costumes by Lawrence Alma Tadema. Sybil and Russell sat in the dress circle, holding hands, enthralled, and by the end emotionally drained. Sybil was often in tears, and completely transported – an early sign of her capacity to react extremely emotionally to the drama. She became obsessed by the play, and started to read Roman history. She was fascinated by Waller, and persuaded her father to take her to the play again.

Sometimes her mother took her to a matinee after her Guildhall lesson. After one performance she wrote to Russell of her burgeoning delight in Shakespeare: 'There are two kinds of plays in the real theatre, plays that you enjoy because things happen that surprise you and the story is interesting

– and plays like *Julius Caesar* where you are part of it and want to join in because you know it belongs to you.' Shakespeare now became a new element in their repertoire: they learnt many speeches, and performed them in their room to an imaginary audience.

Sybil occasionally spent holidays in Southampton with her Aunt Fanny and Uncle James. She took part in amateur dramatics, though not always happily: told once she should play a part as others had done before, she replied: 'What about me? Haven't I got anything to put into it?' She was rebuked for being presumptuous. Yet she was still bent on a musical career. After her success in *Princess Zara*, a well-known music critic who had seen the production, and also heard Sybil play the piano, observed: 'She's not a pianist, she's an actress.' On hearing this she cried, and vowed to work harder than ever at the piano.

Ebenezer Prout, an elderly professor at the Guildhall, told Sybil she would be a happier person if she played one Bach Prelude and Fugue every day, and she took his advice. Professor Berger would sometimes storm at her in his lessons, but this only spurred her on to improve. It transpired that she had perfect pitch, and she became interested in music theory. At fifteen she started to learn harmony and counterpoint with a Dr Greenish, who encouraged her in composition, telling her she had great technical aptitude, but no idea how to harness her imagination. 'This work seized her mind with terrific enthusiasm,' Russell remembered. 'She used to be glued to her manuscript-books, writing, scoring and launching out into composition.'

She was happy in her musical life, exchanging ideas with her fellow-students and teachers, going to concerts, including her first promenade concert, and hearing many of the top performers. Bach's St Matthew Passion gave her a special thrill. Yet she was rarely satisfied with her own performance, and always nervous about playing publicly. Soon she was invited to take part in one of Professor Berger's celebrated *après-midis instrumentals* at his home. At these afternoons of chamber music his more talented pupils were given the opportunity to play with professional instrumentalists, and occasionally to perform solo pieces.

'I'm to play in an afternoon recital at Madame Berger's drawing-room next week,' Sybil told Russell. 'It's the first time Mr Berger has let me play to people. I feel awfully frightened. He won't even allow me to play without the music – it's a Raff suite and awfully long – I don't feel I shall do it very well somehow.' As usual, she and her mother disagreed about what she should wear. 'Mother is buying me a green velvet frock from Liberty's. I don't think I shall play nearly as well as if I could wear my everyday dress.' But afterwards she wrote more cheerfully: 'I got on all right after the first few bars, but I did feel so awful before. Madame Berger was very kind to me – she said I was a clever child, and a Monsieur Jacoby, who was the violin player, he was a darling and said I must learn to play a trio with him and the cellist, who was awfully handsome but looked more like an actor. So I'm going to, I'm going to learn a trio by Weber and shall play it in 3 or 4 weeks' time, isn't it splendid?'

Madame Berger, once a celebrated singer, became fond of Sybil, and she and the professor would take her to concerts. Although she was usually inspired hearing professionals play, she could be cast down by a talented contemporary. One day the professor gave her a ticket to hear the child prodigy Jenny Hyman play. 'She played Beethoven gloriously,' Sybil told Russell. 'I felt very despondent, Russ, I can't ever be like that, and I'm years older, so even with work I can't catch up – but still you never know. I *might* be able to.' Jenny Hyman became a student at the Guildhall (and later a professor), and the two girls, who became close friends, played music together for hours on end. When they performed with other students in a public show at the school, Sybil was greatly envious when her friend walked away with the honours.

Determined to succeed, at sixteen she persuaded her parents to let her give up her education completely, go to the Guildhall twice a week, and concentrate solely on her music. She had enjoyed some lessons with her governess, but felt she wasn't really suited to this kind of learning. She also believed it was time to start earning her living. Soon she was performing in concerts in private houses, earning a guinea a time accompanying a singer or playing a solo. At her professor's suggestion she decided to do some teaching, and put an advertisement in the *Chatham News* offering 'lessons on the pianoforte at St Margaret's Vicarage'. She began to attract young pupils from local families, but proved a temperamental teacher. 'She had no patience with other people,' Russell remembered. 'She used to see red if a pupil couldn't do a thing at once.' Her pupils included their sister Eileen, whom Sybil often reduced to tears.

Professor Berger now decided she was ready for her first solo piano recital. This took place in May 1899, in the long, high-ceilinged Corn Exchange, before a capacity audience. Wearing a floor-length white dress, Sybil played a duet with Monsieur Jacoby the violinist, then performed a lengthy programme of solo pieces by Chopin, Schumann and Bach. The applause was warm, and a career as a pianist seemed a real possibility. But afterwards she confessed to Russell that an agony of nerves had nearly prevented her from playing at all, and that she had only got through the ordeal by pretending she was 'a new Paderewski and that it was all in a play'. It depressed her, she said, that she made people believe she was better than she really was, and that she could never perform as well in public as she heard herself do in her head.

Despite her demanding musical studies, she found time for activities linked to St Margaret's, including school treats and choir outings. She had been teaching in the local Sunday School since she was ten, initially in charge of infants, now with boys aged 9–13. The secret of their good behaviour, she confided to Russell, lay in her habit of racing through the Lesson for the Day, then reading *Dracula* or *The Werewolf* to them. At the vicarage she was encouraged to discuss religious matters with the young assistant priests and organists who came to supper. She was enthralled by the missionaries from Central Africa, some of them black, who came to stay with them.

She began to attend services daily at St Margaret's, and make frequent visits to the cathedral for evensong. 'I went to early service this morning,' she wrote to Kitty. 'There is a daily Communion now, there has been since the beginning of advent in our church. It was rather in a muddle this morning new choir stalls being put up.' She had never questioned her parents' faith: church-going and church affairs had always been part of her daily life, although she and Russell disliked 'holy-bobs', their name for people who were over-reverent and solemn about God and the Church. Their father was evidently not one of them: when Sybil, noticing his distraction one day during a blessing, asked him afterwards what he was thinking about, he said: 'I was thinking how wonderful it would be if I had been on a trapeze swinging across the aisle.'

She continued to indulge her love of dancing, both as a regular member of the dancing class, and now at parties and balls in Chatham, where she danced with great gusto with the young Royal Engineers officers. She loved especially the wilder, more dashing dances: the polka, the gallop, the fast waltz, the Sir Roger de Couverly. Despite having to wear stays, she and the other girls danced as vigorously as the young men. 'The end of a ball was always a gallop, and at the finish we were all dropping with exhaustion,' she recalled.

With the onset of puberty came a sudden concern with her appearance. She had a strong jaw and a straight, prominent nose, but was jealous of Kitty Jelf, whose features were more delicate. As she became interested in the opposite sex there were the usual adolescent jealousies and heartaches. In the dance class one boy, who was the idol of all the girls, chose her several weeks in a row as his partner. This was, she remembered, 'complete bliss', but was followed by total despair when the boy callously 'hopped off with Freda Jelf and left me stranded'. She also, according to Russell, fell for Kitty Jelf's brother Arthur, who generally played the prince in the theatricals in which she and Russell took part in the Jelfs' home.

She kept her hand in as a playwright. After returning one spring day from 'a glorious music lesson' in London, she wrote to Kitty Jelf: 'I'm going to tell you that secret today so don't tell, it's in the Private Letter.' In this letter, sent in a separate envelope marked 'Quite Private/Miss Kitty', she sought her friend's advice about casting her latest work. 'Don't tell Russell, I am composing a play Little Red Riding Hood. I'm doing the music and doing both words and dances. Now give advice. We wanted Cicely to be RRH but she can't sing or act so we think we'll have a bigger one, will you be it.' After listing her ideal cast, with Russell marked down as a Woodcutter and Eileen as an Attendant Fairy, she ended: 'Do you think that would do, it would be a lark wouldn't it. Only tell Freda, not even the boys yet. Goodbye sweet, write Private Letter – Sybil.'

Her main problem as a pianist had been nerves. But now she began to feel a twinge in her left wrist. She tried to ignore it, but it became very painful, and finally a lump appeared there. The professor sent her to a doctor, who diagnosed cramp, and advised her to wear a wrist strap. With her usual enthusiasm she had been practising too much, and was advised to stop playing for a few days. Her distress was acute. 'Oh, I feel utterly and entirely wretched,' she told Russell. 'Everything I've been working for has stopped. I shall never be a pianist. When I do octave passages, Russ, it's torture, and I never was good at octave passages.' But she retained some hope. 'De Pachmann worked fourteen hours a day for two years, so I read last week – once this wrist gets well, I'll do that.' Four days later the rest appeared to have worked: 'I'm quite all right again,' she wrote. 'My wrist seems well, and I'm preparing for another recital which Mr Berger thinks I ought to give.' Her confidence was boosted when she won an exhibition and a small scholarship to the Guildhall. Since her mother sometimes had to sell shares to pay for her extra tuition, this came as a relief.

Russell was now nearly sixteen, and a soloist in the Chapel Royal choir at Windsor. To his chagrin, he had to leave Windsor at the end of 1900, since his voice was breaking; though he returned a month later to sing a solo at Queen Victoria's funeral. For many years his father had hoped he would follow him into the Church. Sybil was convinced he could become an archbishop and, before he became a chorister, had tried to help him achieve this goal by suggesting he write plays based on the Bible. 'If you want to do a thing, you can do it if you work frightfully hard at it,' she told him.

Now, home again and back at King's School, ostensibly in order to study for Oxford and the Church, he told her that his real ambition was to be a writer. This confession prompted him and Sybil to form The Vigilist Club, a solemn, elite organisation with a membership of two, which laid down rigorous rules designed to help its members achieve their primary callings of writer and musician. Sybil was required to learn by heart three lines a day of a Bach fugue, and twenty lines of Shakespeare, while both of them had to study one of his plays a week. Russell wrote a Bible play, *Saul, a Tragedy in Five Acts*, which Sybil told him was quite as good as the worst of Shakespeare.

In 1902 the family moved again. Arthur Thorndike was offered the living of vicar at Aylesford, a village seven miles from Rochester, and made an honorary canon of Rochester. He was delighted to accept what was considered the most desirable living in the Rochester diocese, not least because of its respectable income. The beautiful church of St Peter and St Paul stood on a hill among a cluster of old red-roofed houses, looking down on the winding Medway below, and on the medieval bridge that spanned it. Once again there was a Dickens connection: the writer's family had reserved a burial plot for him in the large churchyard, but in the event he had been buried in Westminster Abbey.

The handsome, substantial nineteenth-century vicarage (now part of St Peter's School) stood across the road from the church. Here Sybil was to spend many happy years. The tithe barn next to the kitchen garden became their new theatre. Eileen, aged ten, was now a full member of their troupe, while five-year-old Frank was also showing acting talent. Productions of *Richard II*, *Sherlock Holmes*, parts of *Saul* and other works by Russell were staged in the barn, with boys from the village playing minor parts, and the sexton acting as the company's low comedian – he was the First Grave-Digger when Russell cast himself as Hamlet, with Sybil as Ophelia.

Sybil found new musical contacts in Aylesford, including the cobbler, a keen violinist, who was happy to play Mozart and Beethoven sonatas with her. 'Anyone she could get to play strings to her piano she seized on,' Russell recalled. 'Her whole day was music, from five in the morning till ten o'clock at night, only giving the afternoons to the village and villagers.' Eileen and Frank were having their ordinary lessons with a governess, but it was Sybil who took on their musical education. Frank was enthusiastic about music, and with Sybil's help he started to learn the cello. These separate artistic enthusiasms were formalised within the house, with Sybil's room becoming the Beethoven Club, exclusively for her and Frank, and Russell's the Garrick Club, with Eileen and himself the sole members.

It was Arthur Thorndike's duty as vicar to visit the poor of the parish. Not long before, Charles Booth's celebrated survey of working-class life, *Inquiry into the Life and Labour of People in London*, had found a third of the capital's population living in abject poverty. But Rochester and Chatham also had their share of poor families: Sybil had accompanied her father on his visits to the worst slum areas around St Margaret's, where men were known to beat their wives, and 'slops' were thrown out of windows. 'We used to go out to places not fit to live in,' she remembered. 'Father used to say: "This has got to be altered. You have got to see to it when you are older."' Such sights perturbed her greatly, making her aware of poverty, misfortune and injustice, and planting the seeds of her socialism.

Later she described the contrast between herself and Russell, he giving himself airs and graces about processions and royalty at Windsor, while she squatted on the floor shouting 'What about the starving poor?' Her parents, she felt, were less concerned than she was about such conditions, her father seeming to be mainly interested in the souls of the families, her mother in the drama of their very different lives to hers. Both were staunch Conservatives, much in favour of Lord Salisbury, who in these years, as governments rose and fell, regularly alternated as prime minister with the Liberal leader William Gladstone. 'We knew Mr Gladstone to be little better than Satan,' Russell recalled.

In Aylesford Sybil again joined her father on his parish visits. She was under strict instructions to accept tea in every cottage whenever it was offered, however bad it made her feel. She remembered him telling her that in life she should treat everyone alike, 'whether you are talking to Lady Sniddle or the poorest of the poor'. The conditions of the poorest families again excited her sympathy, and she became notorious for her careless generosity, often distributing a month's worth of grocery tickets in a week, and giving away clothes belonging to her parents without their permission. She also assisted her father in other duties, walking on Sundays to Pratling Street, a hamlet in his parish, to play the organ when he preached at evensong. As a welcome respite from her hours of piano practice and teaching, and her anxieties about her wrist, these times were her happiest of the week.

During these walks she had long talks with her father about religion and philosophy, which had begun to interest her greatly. A Roman Catholic friend, noting Sybil's interest in argument, had lent her books on church history, and introduced her to the works of Carlyle and Emerson. Meanwhile, on the train to London, she had met a young science student by the name of Bulbrooke, whom she later described as 'my first boy-friend'. It seems though to have been an intellectual friendship: just sixteen, Bulbrooke had advanced ideas, and got her interested in the theory of evolution, lending her books by Darwin, Huxley and Spencer. Her father wondered whether she should be reading such 'atheist literature', but fell short of forbidding her to do so.

She carried on with the piano, with further engagements in London at the St James's, Bechstein and Steinway Halls. She even played two piano concertos with an orchestra, the Schumann and the Mendelssohn in G minor. Just before her eighteenth birthday in October 1900 her teacher suggested she give another recital in Rochester. This time she played a trio with the celebrated violinist Henry Such and his cellist brother, then performed an extended programme of solo pieces. Both press and public were enthusiastic about her developing talent, but the agonising pains in her wrist were becoming more frequent, and her nerves were as bad as ever. Once more she was advised to refrain from playing for a while.

During one of these enforced rests her mother suggested she consider singing as an alternative. With the help of her two well-established singer-cousins Herbert Thorndike and Emily Hart Dyke, she gained an audition with Madame Anna Williams, an expert in oratorio. But she was discouraging, telling Sybil after she had sung a soprano aria from *The Messiah* that she had a true ear, a sense of rhythm and feeling, but no voice. Upset and angry, Sybil sought advice from Professor Berger. He in turn sent her to Madame Bessie Cox, a teacher famous for her tone production. She worked on the principle that everyone has a voice, but that some are large and some are small, and it depends on the individual whether they can make it beautiful and express what they want. She agreed to give Sybil lessons, but warned her not to go at it full tilt. Her singing improved, but she was still conscious of her lack of power.

Meanwhile the pains in her wrist were becoming more frequent; after one recital she couldn't move her arm for two days. The tension brought on by nerves was exacerbating the problem. Finally the doctor insisted she should stop playing for a year. It was a devastating moment: all her dedication and hard work over the years seemed to have been wasted, her hopes of becoming a professional pianist shattered. 'The bottom dropped out of my world, and I thought I'd die,' she remembered. 'I really could have committed suicide if I had been brave, I was so miserable.'

It was at this moment that her brother came to her rescue, with a plan that was to determine the course of the rest of her life.

4

Drama School and Ben Greet

1903–1904

'Of course I can act, I've acted since I was four'
Sybil at her audition for the Ben Greet Academy

S eeing Sybil's despair, Russell came up with a bold plan: he suggested the two of them go into the theatre together. At first she resisted the idea and, despite the constant pain in her wrist, continued to practise the piano and have lessons at the Guildhall. But one day she came home from London in great distress, and told Russell she was giving up the idea of being a professional musician.

However hard she worked, she felt she would never be as good as she wanted to be. She also thought it unreasonable to expect their parents to go on paying the Guildhall fees, and that she should be earning more money herself. The idea of stopping made her miserable, but at least it would enable her to give up piano teaching. So, hoping she might still be able to play the piano for herself, she agreed reluctantly to Russell's plan. In theory Russell was still headed for Oxford and the Church, but in addition to his real ambition to be a writer, he now also wanted to be an actor.

Sybil's uncertainty about a theatrical career was influenced by an incident the previous year. Her mother had written to the actor-manager Charles Wyndham, enclosing photographs and notices of her performances in Rochester, and asking if he would see her. On the morning of the interview the normally healthy Sybil had a bilious attack, and was unable to move. The interview was re-arranged, but again she felt ill in the morning. To her father, this was a clear sign the theatre was not for her.

Agnes Thorndike was understandably disappointed that Sybil was giving up the piano. But she clearly had no qualms about putting her daughter on the stage. 'Mother wouldn't have minded how I made my name, as long as I was to the fore,' Sybil suggested later. This was an unusually liberal attitude for the time, though the theatre, helped by Irving's knighthood in 1895, was gradually becoming more respectable. Sybil and Russell persuaded their mother to keep their plan secret from their father, and set about finding a suitable training course.

At this time there were no major established drama schools, although the Academy of Dramatic Art (later the Royal Academy of Dramatic Art – RADA) was to be established in 1904, to be followed soon after by Elsie Fogerty's Central School of Speech Training and Dramatic Art. Many aspiring actors took private lessons from star actors and actresses, or joined a company with a training school attached. The actor-manager Frank Benson had formed one in 1883. His main rival was Ben Greet, who began as an actor, then made his mark as a producer of open-air Shakespeare. He had toured extensively in rural Britain, having at one stage 25 companies on the road. He would play anywhere: stately homes, castles, zoos, botanical gardens, pavilions, recreation grounds, aquariums and piers.

Heavily influenced by the scholarly producer William Poel, he favoured a return to the simpler staging of the Elizabethan theatre, though for economic and practical reasons as much as historical ones. In 1896 he founded an Academy of Acting in London, in the middle of the West End theatre district at 3 Bedford Street, a five-storey redbrick Victorian building (now offices) just a few yards from the Strand. A room at the top of the building had a small stage, known as the Bijou Theatre. Here Greet had trained scores of young actors, many of whom – notably Mrs Patrick Campbell, H B Irving, Lillah McCarthy and Harley Granville Barker – had made names for themselves.

When Sybil, dressed inappropriately in a veil, arrived with her mother at the academy for an audition, they were met by an old monocled actor, Frederic Topham, in charge while Greet was touring America. The entry requirements were not rigorous: he took one look at Sybil and said: 'I don't think I'll bother her to do anything – she looks as if she can act.' To which the cocksure Sybil replied: 'Of course I can act, I've acted since I was four. Anybody can act, it's the easiest thing in the world.' Obviously desperate to recruit students, Topham said he couldn't judge whether she had talent until she enrolled, but would tell her at half-term if she would make an actress. He also accepted Russell as a student – sight unseen.

As Sybil had feared, her father initially proved less amenable to their scheme than their mother. He had set his heart on Russell going to Oxford and following him into the Church. The children pleaded with him: Russell confessed he hated the idea of being a parson, while Sybil argued that she would go mad if she taught piano without becoming a great pianist. Arguing that Oxford would be expensive, they pointed out that they could earn money more quickly in the theatre. Russell told him that if they were both in the theatre he'd 'always be able to look after Sybil'. Arthur Thorndike was not a man to force a career on his children, so he agreed.

Sybil and Russell were in a frenzy of excitement. Before starting at the academy, they revived many of their plays in the barn, with Eileen, Frank and local boys in the smaller parts. Meanwhile they were mapping out their immediate future, hatching a utopian plan which underlined their closeness: 'We rearranged our lives and made plans never to marry, but to take a travelling company round the world and show people what really terrifying acting could be,' Russell recalled. In autumn 1903, with Sybil nearing twenty-one, they started their training with two dozen other students.

The course was basic in the extreme. There was no voice, movement or technical work; after being given some rules and told when and how to make the appropriate gestures, the students simply rehearsed plays, then performed them. Sybil and Russell were thrown in at the deep end, being drawn in on the first day to a rehearsal of *Twelfth Night*. Sybil was cast as Fabian, but when the girl playing Viola proved shaky on her lines, she took over the part, which she already knew from having played scenes at home. After she and her Orsino had done one scene twice, Topham said: 'That was as well played by these two young people as I've ever seen it played.'

Despite this encouraging accolade, Sybil was at first miserable at the academy. She missed the piano intensely, and for the first term carried on with her singing lessons and her studies at the Guildhall. But then she decided that, if she was going to earn her living as an actress, she must buckle down to it. Her dancing classes in Rochester helped compensate for the lack of movement teaching. There was also that invaluable Shakespearean acting experience at home, especially with *Julius Caesar*: 'Russell and I had practised with the sheets and the blankets – we knew exactly what to do with togas and things,' she remembered. But she had to work by herself on her voice. Topham was delighted with her, and she quickly made progress, taking on parts with violent enthusiasm, enjoying especially playing Puck in *A Midsummer Night's Dream*. However she struggled with *The Merchant of Venice*, telling Topham she didn't want to play Portia because she didn't like her. He told her not to be foolish, that she had to learn to understand all kinds of characters.

At half-term Topham told their mother that Sybil and Russell both had 'the stage instinct'. Russell, he said, was an odd, unexpected actor, with potential as a clown. He thought Sybil had great gifts, but they were in character and comedy parts; having seen her play Portia he felt she had no potential as a tragedienne. This greatly upset Sybil, who had decided she could play tragedy better than anyone else. She had a violent quarrel with Russell, insisting that tragedy was her forte, on the dubious grounds that 'I feel so perfectly awful myself sometimes that I must be able to act it'.

During those first two terms, Russell recalled, 'Sybil and I were in heaven'. They had classes two days a week, and spent the rest of the time rehearsing and performing in the barn at Aylesford, inviting fellow-students to take parts in their productions. They had now created a proper auditorium and stage in the oak-beamed and panelled barn, and had been given a magnificent pair of eighteenth-century brocade curtains, which had once hung in their grandfather's home in Bath. Their repertoire had become more ambitious: as well as *Sherlock Holmes* it included *Macbeth*, *Richard II* and *Hamlet*.

They also went often to the theatre, queuing for the cheapest seats in the pit and the gallery, and afterwards waiting for their favourites to emerge from the stage door. In a West End marked out by gas lamps and hansom cabs, several of the great names were in action. Eleanora Duse was in town with a repertoire that included *Hedda Gabler*, Sarah Bernhardt was playing in *Pelléas et Mélisande* opposite Mrs Patrick Campbell, while Harley Granville Barker was appearing in Shaw's *Candida* at the Court.

As their student year drew to a close they worked hard on two productions. On the eve of rehearsals Sybil had another dispute with her mother, who wanted her to wear a silk frock and matching hat with feathers. According to Russell, Sybil said firmly: 'If you put a feather near me, I shan't be able to act at all. So I shall wear my old clothes that no one notices.' It was a sign of her growing independence, but also her disregard for fashionable or glamorous clothes, an attitude that was to remain with her always. 'I do hate clothes, I wish we could live in combinations,' she told Russell.

For the first production Ben Greet, now back from America, directed a mixed company of professionals and students in *As You Like It*, with Sybil as Phoebe and Russell as William. They were agog to meet professional actors for the first time, see them at work, and listen to the gossip. Greet, as many other directors would do, tried to restrain the ebullient Sybil: 'You'll be all right if you don't bounce too much,' he said. 'You come on stage now as if you were going to do a song and dance.' He advised her to walk round with a book on her head to improve her balance, and this she did religiously.

The other production was the academy's public performance. *The Cabinet Minister* is one of Pinero's lesser farces, a silly story of debts, disasters and dancing, with a cast of thinly drawn characters and some heavy-handed satire on Scottish stereotypes. Russell had the title-role, with Sybil clearly well cast as the forty-year-old Lady Twombley, described by Pinero as 'a handsome, bright, good-humoured woman', and by members of her family as an 'inexhaustible spirit', who was 'too good-hearted and impressionable'. The character – impulsive, scatterbrained, extravagant – gave her some lively scenes to play. Pinero came to the performance and was, according to Russell, 'sweet and kind to us'.

Greet liked what he saw, and offered her a place as an understudy and walk-on in a company due to tour America. She accepted instantly, but Greet told her she must discuss it with her parents. He also engaged Russell, but as he was too young for any part in the American tour, he was given a place in a home-based company, with the promise that if he did well he could join his sister the following year. Sybil's parents were not sure they should let her go abroad: she was a very young twenty-one, blazing with enthusiasm but startlingly naïve. But Sybil showed her determination: after much intense argument she won the day, and was then engaged at $25 a week.

Before they set sail she and Russell gained valuable experience. In May Sybil had her first taste of Shaw, playing Dolly Clandon in *You Never Can Tell* at the King's Hall, Covent Garden, for the Romany Amateur Dramatic Club. She learnt a lot from the experience, and began to make some useful contacts. The following month she and Russell joined Greet's annual Pastoral Tour, then in its twentieth year. It was a strong company, led by the star actor Matheson Lang, his wife Hutin Britton, and Helen Haye; it also included Nigel Playfair and his future wife May Martin, Sydney Greenstreet, and two young actors, Eric Blind and Frank Darch.

Sybil made her professional debut in a small part in *The Palace of Truth*, a 'Fairy Comedy' written by W S Gilbert in his pre-Sullivan days. The first performance was on 14 June 1904, in the gardens of Downing College, Cambridge. During one performance Sybil was ticked off by the stage manager for speaking through the audience's laughter. Greet gave her a decent part in

H M Paull's *My Lord from Town*, in which she had scenes opposite Matheson Lang: according to the *Era* critic, 'Miss Sybil Thorndike scored a big success as Phyllis'. In *The Merry Wives of Windsor* she walked on as a Green Fairy, and Russell made his own debut as John Rugby. At the end of their first day as professionals they each received a guinea.

It was hard but absorbing work: for six weeks they played in college grounds, private gardens, castle grounds and other outdoor venues, ending in the Botanical Gardens in London's Regent's Park. Once they performed in a private garden of a grand house in Surrey, and afterwards were sent to the servants' hall to have tea. 'We felt we were real strolling players,' Russell recalled. Like the other actors, they had to supply their own wigs, shirts, tights, daggers, broaches, boots and shoes for Greet's ramshackle productions. They survived on meagre pay, gaining useful experience of theatrical digs and landladies.

As the tour ended, Sybil prepared to make her first journey abroad, one that would dazzle her with new experiences.

5

An Innocent Abroad

1904–1907

'I'm having my eyes opened to the wickedness of the world,
and I simply loathe it'
Sybil in a letter home from California

On 23 August 1904 Ben Greet's company assembled at Euston station. Sybil was seen off by her parents and brother. According to Russell, 'she looked bright-eyed and thrilled, as if she was off on a sort of adventure that no one had ever been on before'. He told her later that their parents had debated whether to tell her the facts of life – about which, though now twenty-one, she knew nothing – but decided she would be all right. Though attitudes were changing, it was still a common belief that young people should only learn about them when they were married.

Although she cried on parting from her family, by the time they reached the *Numidian*, berthed at Greenock in Scotland, her high spirits had returned. 'I've never felt so excited in my life – it's glorious,' she told her parents before she sailed. 'I'm awfully happy and terribly excited, and we are to swot fearfully hard, and I'm sorry if I've ever been in beastly tempers, I never mean it, and I'll write a bit every day.' She was to be as good as her word. As the company travelled all over America and Canada, she wrote home almost every day, spilling out her thoughts and emotions about life, men, religion and the theatre.

The company, led by Constance Crawley and her husband John Sayer Crawley, also included Frank Darch, Eric Blind and Sydney Greenstreet from the summer season, and Ben Greet's niece Daisy Robinson, with whom Sybil struck up a friendship. She began 'swotting' as soon as the ship left port. Greet, knowing she was 'a quick study', suggested she learn everyone's parts, as there were bound to be illnesses, and she might have to go on at any time.

Sybil agreed, boasting that she never got ill. She already knew all *Twelfth Night* and much of *As You Like It*, so she started in on *Hamlet*.

This was Greet's third successive North American tour, in a series that would continue until 1914. Although visits by companies such as those of Max Reinhardt, Jacques Copeau's Vieux-Colombier, and the Irish Players from the Abbey in Dublin were still to come, native audiences were already familiar with leading European actors. The great Sarah Bernhardt had played in 50 cities while touring in 1880; Ellen Terry and Henry Irving had brought their Lyceum company over six times, the last in 1901; Mrs Patrick Campbell had spent most of 1902 in the States; and Eleonora Duse had toured the country the following year. But while these major stars played mostly in New York and the big cities, Greet's 'Woodland Players' performed at a lower level, where there was a greater demand for Shakespeare.

Ben Greet was a benevolent despot, 'a dear tyrant', as the actress Nora Nicholson later labelled him. Aged 47, a tall, burly man with deep-blue eyes and a great shock of hair, he combined a kindly, cheerful disposition with great vitality and a violent temper, when his cherubic face would turn scarlet. 'Any sign of being pleased with oneself, either in parts, or physical health, and he'd knock one flat off one's perch,' Sybil recalled. He was a genuine Shakespeare enthusiast, who knew the plays inside out, but also a practical man of the theatre. 'Shakespeare to him was bread, breathing and a cup of tea,' observed Margaret Webster, a member of one of his later companies. 'He had no time for fancy theories, far-fetched analogies, scholarly discussions or gimmickry.' His productions were broad, lusty, often crude, but clear; costumes were simple, sets minimal. He had little interest in innovation: the plays were to be done with all the traditional 'business', and without any pauses.

Sybil was thrilled by her first sight of New York: 'My dear, the skyscrapers are marvellous, I think they look very beautiful, and the Statue of Liberty is splendid,' she told Russell. 'I can't help feeling it's all a dream.' One of the first plays they tackled was *Everyman*, which they performed for a week at the Lyric Hall in Brooklyn. 'It's a morality play and simply gorgeous,' Sybil explained. 'I'm going to learn all the parts because I'd like to play them all. Mrs Crawley plays Everyman – she's absolutely beautiful, with a lovely voice, and her tears pour down – well, so did mine when she did the big prayer – I'd give anything to be able to play that part. I'm playing Beauty – don't laugh – she's an abstraction, if you know what that is. I shall look ghastly, as I saw the clothes and wig.' The company also performed a Shakespeare double-bill 'in the Elizabethan manner'. Sybil's description suggests her work was yet to satisfy Greet (known to all as BG). Of her lady-in-waiting to Olivia in *Twelfth Night* she wrote: 'I don't think I looked very nice, though I managed my skirts all right – my hair isn't tidy enough for Elizabethan. Ben Greet said I looked like a ragbag – he said it under his breath on the stage – it wasn't very encouraging.'

There were fifteen plays in the company's repertoire, mainly cut versions of Shakespeare, but also Goldsmith's *She Stoops to Conquer*, *Everyman*, and the old shepherd plays. Travelling in a special train that also carried their scenery and costumes, the company played in colleges and universities, private houses, holiday camps, and several one-horse towns – sometimes two in one day. They staged up to twelve plays a week, rehearsing most mornings and travelling through the night. In these pre-cinema days even the smallest town had a theatre, and for several weeks they played a succession of one-night stands only. Most productions were in the open air: there would rarely be a proscenium arch in sight, and if they were in a theatre they would never have the curtain down. For Sybil it was the start of a lifelong preference for an open stage, where actors and audience could be in close contact.

After their fortnight in New York they called in on Syracuse, sent postcards from Rochester NY to Rochester Kent, shuffled off to Buffalo, and blew in to the Windy City. In Chicago Sybil had her first taste of American theatre: Greet took her and Daisy to see *Romeo and Juliet*, with the great husband and wife team E H Sothern and Julia Marlowe. Sybil thought the English-born actress, at thirty-eight 'rather square and not very thin', would be wrong for the part, 'but she'd not been going long before I'd forgotten all this and I only saw the young lovely Italian girl. I can't tell you what I felt during the balcony scene. You know how love bores me – well, it wouldn't if it was like *Romeo and Juliet*....I thought I would never stop crying.' Seeing the play for the first time stirred sudden longings: 'Oh! I would love to play Juliet...but I don't suppose anyone would want me to, I don't look tragic, romantic, do I? How I wish I did.' Later, in Los Angeles, she was terrified by the great Polish actress Modjeska's playing of Lady Macbeth. Meeting her at a tea party soon afterwards, she could hardly believe 'that this kind, gracious lady was the creature I had seen so horribly and tragically working with evil'.

Despite enjoying her new life, she felt guilty about having given up music. 'Acting is absolute pleasure all the time,' she wrote to Russell. 'You never have that awful agonising feeling that you won't be able to do things that you get when you are working at music – the enormous amount you have to know is so tremendous before you begin to be an artist yourself, and it appals you. With the stage it's *being* something that counts.' Ironically, she was worried about being so happy. 'I seem to be living a life of pleasure, and no drudgery or effort at all, and tho' of course we work hard – some of the company think it's next-door to slavery – yet when one compares it with the way one swots at music, it's not to be called work at all.'

She unburdened herself to a Mrs Love, a friend of Greet who dropped in on the company *en route*. A keen musician herself, she told Sybil that acting was different from the piano, but just as hard, 'that the medium I use is myself, and I must make myself as perfect as I want to make notes or strings, and, Russ, not only walking and dancing, moving and speaking beautifully, but mind too.' Mrs Love seems to have been an acute judge of Sybil's potential, telling her she had talent, and that 'if I swot just as hard as I did at music, I shall be able to be in the front rank of actors'.

This conversation increased her desire to perfect her new art, and she spent many hours learning the repertoire by heart. On the long train journeys she was always the first to wake and start on her lines. She had now got to *Much Ado about Nothing*, and 'that Beatrice woman'. Soon she knew all the leading parts, so that 'it only needs for someone to fall ill for me to say, "Ere, I know that part," and go on and make my name and fortune.' She kept up her piano playing by hiring rooms in music shops in the towns where they played, and working on bits of harmony and counterpoint in her manuscript book. Prompted by Mrs Love, and ashamed at the little she had learnt in school, she bought a French and German grammar, and started studying both languages. Already her capacity for hard work seems to have been exceptional.

They continued up into the snows of the Sierra Nevada, then down again through the orange and lemon groves around Sacramento. At the University of California at Berkeley they were to play *Hamlet* uncut. The venue was the Greek-style theatre set on the hillside, with a view of San Francisco's Golden Gate, and a stage three times the width of that in New York's Metropolitan Opera House. During rehearsals Sybil disgraced herself. According to Russell: 'Anybody could make her giggle on stage. You only had to whisper something silly to her or do something unusual and she would collapse.' This now happened when she laughed out loud at a funny story Eric Blind was telling Frank Darch, causing Greet, playing Hamlet, to 'dry' during a soliloquy. He was furious: 'He called me a giggling schoolgirl – wasn't it too appalling?' she reported. 'I felt utterly and entirely dejected….I feel I've put myself back quite a lot by being such a little fool….I feel all disgraced and most miserable.'

Performing the play was a magical experience. 'I was simply in a dream,' she wrote. 'Everything seems to be much bigger than it really is and every little thing seems to matter more than anything can matter really. The end of the play was almost unbearable, it was so beautiful – it was at sunset – and it was setting over the Golden Gate, and we had real guns in the hills when Fortinbras says, "Go, bid the soldiers shoot." It's the best ending that's ever been written to any play.' It was, she later recalled, 'the occasion of the most wonderful emotion I have ever experienced'.

In San Francisco, where they staged *Everyman* again, Greet took her and Daisy to a theatre in Chinatown. The artificial style of the staging of the play reinforced her view that it was foolish to try to convince an audience they were seeing real life. 'I don't believe the theatre is meant for that at all, any more than sculpture or painting is actual. The Greeks realised this marvellously, didn't they, and Shakespeare? You don't want actual life, you want a more concentrated thing, a life that you don't see really because eyes are not clear and hearing not acute – in the theatre your sense must be sharpened, and with that you've got to have a child's mind that will believe dreadfully seriously in it, and yet at the same time know it's playing.' Here is a glimpse of the other side to the jolly, giggling, impulsive girl: the serious, thoughtful young woman trying to articulate an artistic philosophy.

Greet told her that she'd have to 'keep the fat away' if she wanted to play leading roles, and she tried desperately to reduce it. Unfortunately her appetite was usually stronger than her resolve, or the effect of Greet's reproachful looks. 'I swear I won't eat another meal today, because I must get to look more poetical,' she said after a solid lunch on the train. That evening she wrote home: 'Had an enormous meal. Thoroughly enjoyed it. Two helps of everything and hoped BG wouldn't notice. As he walked out of the dining-car he said, "Old fat Syb." It made me feel rather depressed.' She also was aware of how stylish her friend Daisy looked when they went dancing one night in Chicago. 'She's very good at clothes,' she admitted. ' I'm beginning to wish I were keen on them, but it's no good I'll never alter that way.'

She had another anxiety. 'Mine is really a vicar's wife face,' she complained to Russell. 'It's tragic for me the way I want to do all things my face doesn't fit.' But it was not her face that attracted criticism in *The Merchant of Venice*, in which she played several parts. When someone told Greet that as Balthazar her legs looked like the legs of a piano, she was upset. 'I had foul-looking pale blue tights – well, I must get thin – it's no good, I'd give anything to be elegant – only I do get so hungry, dash it.' She felt more comfortable in a dress, and as one of Portia's attendants she tried each night to be a different person: 'It's exceedingly difficult as I have to have the same make-up and dress, but I feel differently inside, and that's the main thing.' But she was in trouble again as a crowd member during Antonio's trial: 'Ben Greet told me I made too much noise, that I was to fill in and not be conspicuous, as the audience wanted to watch the principal action. I felt this was quite right. I got carried away, I suppose.' Greet was not to be the last director to have to curb her enthusiasm.

In Stockton she had her first real break when Constance Crawley, playing Viola in *Twelfth Night*, became ill. Sybil had no rehearsal: she went through the part on her own, and then with Eric Blind ran through her scenes with Orsino. Daisy told her to keep her knees straight, and not 'waggle your head at every word when you get emotional'. Her first performance in a leading Shakespearean role was a success. A local reviewer, not knowing she was an understudy, praised 'Mrs Crawley' for 'a most charming performance, naïve and touching'. Greet complimented her: 'Good girl, Syb, you never missed a word.' On stage she had felt immediately inside the part: 'I've never enjoyed myself so much in all my life. In fact, I felt I *was* Viola, she didn't seem different to anything I felt deep down.' Her reunion with her lost twin brother Sebastian struck a particular chord: 'I felt exactly like seeing you, Russ, after years and ages of separation, and I cried like anything, but it didn't matter really, did it?' Her joy was unconfined: 'Ha! ha! Now my foot is on the ladder truly and really.'

At she travelled around California, gorging herself on the abundant fruit, her energy and dedication to work seemed boundless. Having learnt all the leading parts in the company's repertoire, in Fresno she took her volume of Shakespeare on a visit to a vineyard, where she started to learn Katharine in *Henry VIII*. When Daisy became ill in Redlands, she played her part of Kindred in *Everyman*, as well as her own roles, Beauty and the White Angel. In Los Angeles she played Valentine in *Twelfth Night*: 'I simply love it because I'm on such a lot. I'd like to be on the stage the whole time – if only one could play heaps of big parts all at once.' She also took over from Daisy as Nerissa in *The Merchant of Venice*, but once again went over the top: 'Oh! I did enjoy myself and got heaps of laughs – two of them Ben Greet said I oughtn't to have got at all, as they were what he calls clowning laughs, and that I must be careful not to let my spirits run away with me....I don't really agree with him, altho' I do what he says because he's the producer and he knows more about it.' Going back to behind the scenes was difficult. From Stanford she wrote: 'We're playing *Hamlet* here – and woe is me, I'm having to be prompter.' Even here she had a minor spat with Greet: 'BG furious with me – he said after the matinee he couldn't hear my prompt – so I said it very loud at night, and he called me a little devil.'

Her quick and eager mind was absorbing the new ideas buzzing all around her. In their hotel rooms the company would discuss the newest developments in the London theatre. Here she learnt about the pioneering repertory work of Granville Barker at the Court; of the championing of Ibsen by his translator William Archer; of J T Grein, the ardent advocate of avant-garde European drama, who had started the Independent Theatre to stage non-commercial plays. One person who seemed 'like a dynamo under all these activities' was Bernard Shaw, whose plays were just becoming known in America.

She became interested in the New Thought and the works of Annie Besant, and promised to send her father copies of her books *Karma* and *Reincarnation*. 'I was so enchanted with *Reincarnation* that I could hardly go to sleep,' she wrote. She began to show signs of an intense interest in religion combined with a tolerance of its different forms: 'I'm in a whirl with religion – it's all around me,' she wrote from Santa Barbara, 'people believing so hard and knowing that no one else has ever believed anything fit for believing, and really they're all only different bits of the Church.' At Leland Stanford University she met a Theosophist, and decided that 'it's the most sensible way of thinking I've yet discovered....Now I'm a Theosophist, I'm also a Christian Scientist, and I'm still Church – how's that for broadmindedness!!'

At this time she knew nothing about sex: 'Why I didn't get into the most awful fandangles I don't know,' she later observed. 'Nobody could be innocenter than I was.' Given her naïvete, her desire to think the best of everyone, and her outgoing, warm personality, this was indeed a miracle. In San Francisco there was one potential fandangle. 'What misery it is being a girl – how I loathe men who get keen on me,' she wrote home. She and Daisy had been to a fair with a man connected with the theatre they were playing in. Although 'he looked harmless and kind and middle-aged', he soon started 'saying things to make you believe he was in love with you'. The outing took a turn for the worse when they rode in a boat on a switchback: 'There were tunnels, and he would hold my hand, and I gave myself up for lost.' Afterwards she couldn't imagine why they had agreed to go with the man: 'You never know with men how abominable the kind ones can be,' she complained wearily to Russell

The man had told her that she hadn't got the 'instincts of a girl' and ought to have been a boy, sentiments with which Sybil agreed. There was a strong masculine element in her make-up, which she acknowledged while learning the part of Beatrice in *Much Ado*. 'She's great fun, but I'm afraid I prefer all the men's parts. I hope I'll be a man in my next incarnation.' She also perhaps had a fear of sex. 'Oh dear me, I feel so relieved to think that I won't ever marry,' she told Russell. 'I couldn't stand anyone saying "in love" things all the time. I shall adopt lots of children, and you and I will live together, Russ, won't we? Much more fun than lots of hateful people married to you.'

There was another incident, possibly of a sexual nature, although Sybil never said what caused her distress. It occurred in San Diego, 'the most horrible place I've ever been in – miserable I was the whole time,' she wrote. 'I'm having my eyes opened to the wickedness of the world and I simply loathe it; some things I didn't know could be so awful – I wish you were here, Mother – you and Daddy would make it all seem so different.' The next day in Santa Barbara, feeling depressed and having a rare night off, she wrote a lengthy letter to her father about this 'wickedness', then tore it up and got into bed, saying, 'Oh! Father, Father, I hope you'll understand.' Curiously, at the same hour in England, Arthur Thorndike was woken by hearing her voice call out these exact words. Fearing Sybil was in trouble he woke his wife, then immediately sat down and wrote her a sympathetic letter, as if he knew the cause of her distress.

In one letter from San Francisco she reflected on how the theatre can help you to achieve a philosophy of life. 'A play makes you see suddenly what life can show you if you keep your eyes open. The stage – perhaps all art – does that – it kind of focuses everything for you; you get it into shape, and real life is such a messy business – ends hanging out and bits lopped off and not tidied – well, art never does that. Sometimes I feel if I could just get hold of something that is always escaping me I could see life all shaped.' Certainly life on tour could be a 'messy business', for she could, she admitted later, 'fall in love so easily with anybody who looked actory and exciting'.

At first she affected an indifference to men: 'You know how love bores me,' she reminded Russell. But this indifference soon melted: 'I've not decided which I like best of all the men,' she wrote from the Mid West. 'It's very difficult as they are all great fun.' Soon she started to fall for Eric Blind, whom she thought a 'glorious' Orsino. The son of an artist, and of German lineage, his obvious good looks – thick dark hair, noble nose, full lips – fascinated her: 'He's got the most lovely face I've ever seen in my life, don't you think so too? – not counting Father,' she asked Russell. 'He has got a glorious voice too, and when you get a glorious voice and a glorious face – well, what is there else? Oh, and he's a lovely character, I'm sure, because everyone likes him.' Not a churchgoer himself, the young actor sometimes joked with her about Christian Science, while she talked to him about Annie Besant. 'Eric Blind encourages me in everything', she wrote; when she talked to him 'there's something sound and solid and laughable in the world, and all the awful feelings I get, like nightmares about life and things, aren't real at all.'

Eric Blind enjoyed teasing the hearty, healthy young woman 'fresh from the vicarage', and trying to make her laugh during rehearsal. When she argued that Beatrice in *Much Ado about Nothing* 'was a bit too bright, I mean always making jokes and tripping people up,' he replied that 'there was more to her than that, and that as yet I was only half awake'. She respected his judgement: 'Eric Blind says I'm improving a lot,' she reported from Los Angeles. Wider read than she was, he inspired in her a greater interest in poetry. 'He's told me to read Browning – do you know Browning, Russ? Well, it's terrific. I can't imagine why I've never read him before. And I'm reading a lot of Shelley too. I've always liked poetry vaguely, but I've suddenly got it all new – like music, only with something that is very close to one's real self – something awfully intimate.' Blind introduced her to Walt Whitman, whose *Leaves of Grass* filled her with excitement. When she shared rooms with another actress, Gilda Veresi, they stayed up half the night 'spouting Browning to each other'. Poetry was suddenly a passion.

Sybil later admitted that if Blind had proposed to her she would have accepted. 'He was just adorable and had a good and very innocent lark with me, and when he left I thought I'd die.' The other young actor, Frank Darch, seemed to make less impact. Six years older than Sybil, according to his grand-daughter Julia Jarrett he was a good-natured, gentle, humorous man; photographs show his fair hair, and an open, cherubic face; he had hoped to go into the Church, and was later often cast as a vicar. He had been with

Benson's company, and had a resonant tenor voice. Later, when he played Hamlet for Greet, the critic J C Trewin noted 'Darch's gentle tenor which left no line unclarified', and 'singularly beautiful hands and a gentle courteous manner'; he praised him for being 'direct, untrammelled', and having a delivery untainted by the 'sonorous and echoing' manner of the rest of the company.

He, Sybil and Eric Blind often made a threesome: there were walks on board ship at the start of the tour, and meals shared on long train journeys. Frank Darch also liked to lark around in rehearsal: during one solemn moment in *Everyman*, when he was kneeling behind Sybil – he was playing Strength, she Beauty – he tickled her foot with his sword, causing her to burst out laughing ('I managed to turn it into a cough, but imagine an abstraction with a cough'). She described him affectionately as 'that pig Frank Darch', but there were no admiring comments of the kind she made about Eric Blind. So it comes as a surprise – as it must have done to her family – when she describes a night boat journey the company took up the Puget Sound to Victoria on Vancouver Island. Early in the morning Frank Darch woke her and persuaded her to come and see the glorious view along the coast.

'Frank then proposed to me, sitting up in the bows. Laugh! We both laughed till I thought we'd wake the whole shipload. I expect it was the air so fresh. Anyway, we're engaged, I thought we might as well be – and it won't last for more than two days, we both said that. Very amusing.' The news also apparently amused the company, who 'shrieked with mirth over breakfast'. Greet told her she was a foolish girl for letting her spirits carry her away so often, but Sybil was unrepentant. 'I rather like spirits carrying one away – spirits are great fun, and I'm sure have very nice faces.' As she predicted, this light-hearted engagement didn't last, though it may have continued for longer than two days. According to the Darch family, it was Sybil who ended it.

After Christmas the company headed south, to play *As You Like It* and *Hamlet* again at Berkeley: 'I suppose I shall have to do all my million walk-ons,' Sybil wrote in frustration. 'I wish I could play a part and speak.' Once more fortune was kind to her: half an hour before the play began it was discovered that the students, who were playing the Players, had omitted to cast anyone as Lucianus, the murderer in the play within the play which catches the conscience of the king. Greet summoned Sybil, who was taking on a different small part every two or three days. To her dismay he told her to put on a beard. 'Couldn't I just make a face?' she asked, and cried a little when he insisted on the beard. For her one six-line speech she pulled out all the melodramatic stops – 'I did all the *Dentist's Cure* quirks' – and enjoyed the experience. She seems to have been convincing enough: John Sayer Crawley, unaware of the late change, asked afterwards if 'the funny little fat man' was joining the company, as he was 'rather odd, but if suited might be clever'.

Later Sybil played both Rosencrantz and Guildenstern, but though she wanted to play Ophelia, the part she most coveted was Hamlet. 'Really he's not more male than female, he's everybody who's got something to do and keeps failing,' she told her brother. 'I know a good bit of it – but I suppose you'll play it before me, Russ, and I don't think I really look it, though I feel it.' In rehearsals she watched Greet closely, observing how he was interpreting the Prince, and 'planning what I'd do when I play it'. It would not have been unusual for her to do so: in England there was already an established tradition of women taking on the role, and she would have known of Sarah Bernhardt's performance at Stratford only five years earlier.

The company travelled through the Midwest for several weeks, performing one-night stands in places such as Reno, Salt Lake City, Denver and Kansas City, until they reached Chicago. The conditions were often unusual. On one occasion the actors had to change in a hencoop. On another, they arrived in a horse-drawn bus at a private estate in Deephaven on the shores of Lake Minnetonka, where on the grass tennis courts overlooking Carson's Bay they performed *As You Like It* in the afternoon, and *A Midsummer Night's Dream* in the evening.

They moved on to Canada, where they concentrated on pastoral productions of scenes from the plays – on university campuses and private estates, in forests, beside lakes near 'Red Indian' settlements. Sybil still lacked discipline. Playing Juno in *The Tempest* at McGill University in Montreal, she tripped in a rabbit-hole, tried to restrain her laughter, but finally gave way while singing the marriage song, inciting both actors and audience to collapse in hysteria. The local paper noted: 'A most charming performance of *The Tempest* was given by the Ben Greet Players, marred only by the unseemly levity of one of the goddesses, Miss Sybil Thorndike.' She was fined $2 for spoiling the show. But there were also high spots. In Kansas City, Constance Crawley had a fall an hour before a matinee of *Everyman*. Called on to play the lengthy title-role with no rehearsal, Sybil acquitted herself admirably. The accident also gave her chance to play Beatrice, and a couple of performances as Rosalind in *As You Like It*.

By the end of the tour she had played 35 roles. *Everyman* was her first shot at a tragic one, prompting Greet to tell her he thought she might be able to cope with tragedy after all – though he warned her she would have to 'keep thin and not let her face look too healthy' if she was to succeed. Her mother took a similar line when she met an exceedingly plump Sybil on her return in August. 'You look like a little German girl,' she remarked in horror. 'You can't play leading parts if you're fat.' Since she was engaged to return to America with Greet in a month's time, she went on a strict regime, cutting out bread, pastry and potatoes. By the time she re-joined the company her figure, according to her brother, had altered considerably. So had her salary: she was now on $35 a week.

Russell joined her on this second American tour, for which Greet had added *Henry V* and *The Comedy of Errors* to their repertoire, and Milton Rosmer and St Clair Bayfield to the company. While crossing the Atlantic Sybil talked with an American professor, then president of Princeton, whose face she liked. They discussed their respective careers, and Sybil in her girlish way told him he looked exactly as she had imagined Rudolf Rassendyll of Ruritania, in *The Prisoner of Zenda*. At the end of the voyage the professor gave a short speech, in which he thanked Sybil for accompanying everyone on the piano. He invited her and Russell to stay with him when the company came to Princeton. Seven years later, after giving up his academic career, Woodrow Wilson became president of the United States.

Once again there were adventures as they toured around the country. In Florida during a performance of *A Midsummer Night's Dream*, when Sybil as Helena lay asleep on the ground, with Ben Greet as Bottom asleep nearby, a snake suddenly crept over her legs. Though terrified, she was obviously even more fearful of her producer. 'I couldn't move, I didn't dare,' she explained to Russell. 'Ever since Mr Greet rowed me for spoiling *The Tempest*, I've been scared of doing the wrong thing.' She did it again though, during a perform-ance in a college of *The Comedy of Errors*, in which she was the Lady Abbess. Normally she kept away from alcohol, which tended to go to her head. On this hot day, weighed down by her heavy costume and the long wait before her entrance, she drank two mint juleps, wandered off, and fell asleep in a nearby field. When her cue came it took ten minutes to find her. Eventually she was gleefully chaired back to the stage by a group of students. Greet's reaction is not recorded, but from that day on she never drank alcohol before a performance.

Playing in the open air had many hazards. Probably the worst was the presence of mosquitoes, which thrived on the actors' grease-paint. Often fires had to be lit on each side of the stage to keep them off, while the audience held burning joss-sticks, and the actors wore them in their hair. One actress got stung so badly she had to leave the company, thus providing Sybil with several more parts to play. But there were light-hearted moments too. While they were performing *The Comedy of Errors* in a ravine in a holiday camp in Michigan, Greet came off stage in a fury: he had spotted two members of the audience creeping into the back row, apparently without paying, and asked Sybil and Russell to confront them. But when they reached the spot they discovered two bears 'with their arms round one another's neck like a pair of lovers'. Greet laughed when told of the interlopers – 'You see, even animals like Shakespeare' – then talked about staging a performance of *The Winter's Tale* specially for them.

The company played in some unexpected venues. Briefly stranded in the small town of Cordele, Georgia, which had only come into existence fifteen years before, they performed in the courthouse, which was also used as a prison. As the one cell was occupied and couldn't be used as a dressing-room, the actors were offered the execution shed as an alternative. Sybil and Russell volunteered to use it, learning later that a man due to be hanged there had escaped the night before. While rehearsing *The Tempest* in their hotel in Spartanburg, South Carolina they witnessed the aftermath of a murder. With the corpse lying outside their window, their talk took a ghoulish turn: 'We piled horror on horror's head,' Russell remembered. That night the seed was sown for the character of Dr Syn that was to bring him success as a writer.

It was at Princeton, while they were staying with Woodrow Wilson, that an accident occurred that threatened to end Sybil's career. While playing Good Deeds in a matinee of *Everyman*, a piece of fluff became stuck in her throat, and temporarily prevented her from speaking. Refusing to give up, she found next day a deeper voice, and with Greet's encouragement continued to play a variety of parts, including Beatrice and Rosalind, in a low growl, often twice a day, for a further two months. She insisted her voice was getting better, but Russell saw things differently, and said she had to stop. Eventually in Philadelphia he persuaded Greet to let her see a specialist. Though he recommended she stop acting immediately, she refused to do so for another month. Russell told her she was a fool for endangering her career, and threatened to send for their father. 'She burst out crying and didn't stop for hours, but agreed, if BG would allow her, to go home,' he recalled.

She and Russell had already been engaged for the following year's American tour, and had intended to remain in America during the break, staying on the coast of Maine. But when they arrived back in England Sybil was hardly able to speak. Her parents were angry with Russell for letting her carry on. He in turn blamed Sybil's stubbornness, which was certainly a factor, though her desire not to let Greet down also played its part. It was arranged for her to see St Clair Thomson, one of the king's medical advisors, who found her vocal chords covered in growths. He doubted she would ever act again. Devastated to think she might have to give up a second career, she asked if there was any possible chance of a cure. The doctor said that, if she could remain totally silent for six weeks, he could give her a answer.

She rose to the challenge with characteristic determination. She went for long walks with their dog in the countryside around Aylesford, using a notebook to communicate with anyone she met. At home she played the piano for hours, and read lots of poetry. She remained completely silent – a great trial for someone so naturally sociable – and to her surprise enjoyed the experience. The doctor was astonished to find the growths had disappeared, telling her she must have a will of iron and the constitution of an ox. Noticing that she had got into bad vocal habits, he sent her to a voice specialist, who worked with her for a month and gave her a set of daily exercises. Before long she had her voice back, and was able to return to America.

There are few records of her third season with Greet. A surviving programme shows she played Ophelia at Michigan University in January 1907; and in March the company, which included Sydney Greenstreet and Milton Rosmer, had a short season at the Garden Theatre in New York, where they staged five Shakespeare productions, plus *Everyman* and *Masks and Faces*. It had become a tradition for the tour to end at the resort of Bar Harbour in Maine. Here, while playing Rosalind and Touchstone in *As You Like It*, Sybil and Russell were introduced by Greet to a distinguished-looking man in a white suit they had noticed in the audience. He told them his name was Clemens, but they might know him better as Mark Twain. 'We nearly fell through the greensward, we were so thrilled,' Sybil remembered.

When the company sailed for home, Russell stayed behind in the hope of finding further work in New York. In three years Sybil had performed in all but four of the American states, and by her own reckoning had played 112 parts. In *Macbeth*, typically, she had played both Duncan's sons, all three witches, Lady Macduff, the Bleeding Child, and the offstage Cries of Women.

The tours had given her a comprehensive grounding in Shakespeare, and shown that she could play a wide range of parts, including tragic ones. They had also opened her eyes to the realities of the world beyond her sheltered, comfortable family life.

Her experience was now put to the test, as within a year she would meet three men of the theatre who would have a profound effect on her professional and personal life.

6

Fallen Among Highbrows

1907–1908

'I belong now to the Women's Social and Political Union,
and I hobnob with the spirits of the age'
Sybil in a letter to Russell

Back in England in the summer of 1907, Sybil was determined to establish herself as an actress. It was not a promising moment to start her career. Aside from Shakespeare at His Majesty's, Irving's productions at the Lyceum, and Shaw's plays at the Savoy – *Caesar and Cleopatra* and *The Devil's Disciple* were staged this year – the theatre was dominated in the West End and the major provincial cities by the conventional well-made plays, notably the 'cup and saucer' dramas set in an elegant, upper-class world. The critic William Archer complained: 'The English playwright concerns himself exclusively with the manners and the emotions of the idle rich.'

Returning first briefly to Aylesford, Sybil was hit by a familiar problem. 'I am worried sick about my voice,' she told Kitty Jelf. 'I must talk in a whisper.' Greatly frustrated, she was forced to stick to this regime for several weeks. Then, her voice restored, she took a room in a flat in a workman's dwelling opposite Lambeth Palace. It belonged to a family friend, Ethel Cunliffe, a prison visitor. She worked with women discharged from Holloway and Maidstone prisons, some of whom came to her flat. Sybil listened to their stories, glimpsing lives startlingly different from hers. She visited Holloway, where the 'dingy walls' and 'austere dreariness' made a strong impression on her, and sparked her later interest in prison reform.

With Russell still in America, she was on her own for the first time in her life: apart from Nigel Playfair and Frederic Topham, she knew no one in London. Like hundreds of other hopefuls she did the rounds of the theatrical managers, but no offers came. Russell believed her wrist and voice problems had dented her confidence. 'She didn't, I'm sure, go in as if the world belonged to her, as she used to in the old barn days.' There was a moment of hope, when Playfair secured her an audition with Beerbohm Tree. But the role was an unlikely one, the lead in the musical play *The Beloved Vagabond*, and she was not successful.

She did a little work with amateur societies, who would pay a professional to play the lead in their productions. In the autumn Playfair introduced her to the Play Actors' Society, formed that year by members of the Actors' Association, with J M Barrie as its president. The second of such societies to be established – the Stage Society was the first – it put on Sunday night productions, enabling young actors to display their talents, and offbeat plays to be staged in the hope of attracting the attention of West End managers. Sybil was cast as O Chicka San in *His Japanese Wife*, a one-act play by the American writer and actress Grace Griswold, which was staged at the Bijou. She was then cast as a naïve American girl in *The Marquis*, a sentimental farce by Cecil Raleigh and Sidney Dark, staged for a single performance at the Scala.

In the latter she caught the attention of the *Era* critic. 'Miss Thorndike is pretty, and singularly well endowed. She has sensibility, charm, and plays with conviction, being always delightfully fresh and natural.' More importantly, she impressed another member of the audience. The next day she received a note from Playfair, who was rehearsing for a tour of Shaw's *Candida*. 'Shaw saw your ridiculous play last night – liked you very much – says you might do as an understudy for Ellen O'Malley as Candida. Come along quick and read the part.' The next day, feeling 'completely confident and in ecstatic mood', she went to read for Shaw. She knew nothing of *Candida*, Shaw's 'modern pre-Raphaelite play', his counterblast to Ibsen's *A Doll's House*, written in 1895 but not publicly performed until 1904. Candida herself, caught between her socialist clergyman husband Morell and the idealistic poet Marchbanks, was, in Shaw's words, a 'clean, dry, strong and straight heroine'.

When Shaw asked Sybil to read for him, she went at it with all guns blazing. 'I thought, this is jam, this is as easy as pie after Shakespeare,' she recalled. 'I put everything into it – Lady Macbeth, Rosalind, Beatrice, everything.' She finished breathless with excitement. Shaw burst out laughing, and said with a twinkle: 'Splendid, my dear young lady. Only you must go away quietly, learn housekeeping and have four children, or six if you'd rather, and then perhaps you'll be able to play Candida.' Clearly she needed more experience of life to play a part which, in Shaw's stage direction, required 'largeness of mind and dignity of character'. But he gave her the understudy job – while confiding to Playfair that he hoped she'd never go on – and the title-role and only female part in *The Subjection of Kezia*, a popular curtain-raiser, based on a short story by Edith Lees, the wife of Havelock Ellis.

Shaw had seen certain qualities in the green but enthusiastic young actress. He believed she would learn from watching and understudying the beautiful Ellen O'Malley, to his mind the best Candida yet. He invited her to sit next to him in rehearsal, during which he talked to her about acting, about Ellen Terry and Mrs Patrick Campbell. He told her she reminded him of Janet Achurch – a voluptuous, Amazonian fair-haired actress with whom he had been in love, and for whom he had written *Candida* – and that if she worked hard she might one day match her achievement. 'You'll make a big return later,' he told her. Little wonder that, as Russell recalled, she was 'in a state of adoration towards Mr Shaw'.

Candida opened in Belfast in the spring of 1908, where it alternated with Shaw's first play, *Widowers' Houses*. Both productions, performed by separate companies, were staged by the Gaiety in Manchester. Sybil had now, she reported, fallen among 'highbrows', and was struggling to be one herself. 'The highbrows are led by – or rather they follow – Shaw and Granville Barker, and people like John Galsworthy and Arnold Bennett are all highbrows, and people talk of them in an odd and very familiar voice, and you feel when you listen to them that you are very cheap and that if you aren't careful you'll drop your aitches or giggle; but I keep a tight hold on myself….I feel very ignorant. I don't know anything about the new movement in the theatre, but I shall find out I expect if I go wary and mind my ps and qs.'

One night she went to see *Widowers' Houses*, Shaw's fierce attack on slum landlords. Playing the hero Harry Trench was a young actor with a beautiful, deep voice and a formidable air, who immediately caught her eye. That night she wrote: 'Darling Russ, I've seen a man I could marry – it's most absurd. His name is Casson, Lewis Casson.' She had seen his picture outside the theatre that morning, and been attracted by his strong features and 'nice face'. May Playfair told her that he was a good actor, but 'rather difficult to get on with'; he was also a socialist. Sybil was intrigued and, when she saw him act, impressed, telling Russell: 'I liked him better than any young man I've ever seen on the stage because he spoke so fast that it woke you up and made you puzzle a bit, instead of going to sleep as a lot of actors who are highbrow make you. He sort of barks out things.' She failed to find him backstage, but hoped to meet him soon – 'though he'll probably hate me and find me a country Jane'. All the actors, she noticed, were interested in politics, 'but the prince of the lot is this man Casson'.

Two days later, out walking with the Playfairs, she met this prince in the street, wearing 'a very shabby overcoat and a hat all down over his eyes like a tramp – he looks as if he would fight you if you gave him a chance'. At first he merely 'barked a sort of huffy how-do-ye-do', but later when he laughed she noticed 'his face looked quite different, and he's got a really lovely voice, very direct'. She concluded: 'He's the sort of man I like, but you needn't worry, he'll never be interested even – he hasn't even *looked* at me.' He didn't look at her again the following week in Dublin, when she and May met him at the zoo, where 'he was standing in front of a tigress trying to hypnotize it'. As they walked round he talked theatre to May. 'He never spoke a word to me and I don't think he remembered I existed,' Sybil complained to Russell. He looked, she thought, 'as if he ought to be an engineer or a sailor or something to do with real life – not a bit like an actor, but fearfully highbrow'. But when she was left alone with him she decided 'he's the sort of man I'd like for a pal – really love is such an awful effort – being pals is much better and far more amusing.'

Like Sybil, Lewis Casson had been exposed to the theatre at an early age. Born in Birkenhead in 1875, one of seven children, he was brought up in Denbigh in north Wales in a deeply religious family. His father, a bank manager who later designed organs, had been in his youth a well-known amateur actor in Liverpool, and had played with Lewis' mother in Gilbert and Sullivan. He read *Macbeth* to his children when they were small, and at six Lewis played Orlando in a shortened home-version of *As You Like It*. The family were poor, so he and his brother Will built their own elaborate toy theatre, and wrote their own plays. But his family were opposed to him going on the stage, so after leaving school at sixteen and going to London, he tried other occupations: organ-building, chemical engineering, and teaching. When his father's organ business collapsed the family endured a period of severe poverty.

Thinking of entering the Church, he was briefly a pupil teacher in a church elementary school, then first a student and later a tutor at St Mark's Teacher Training College in Chelsea. Here he discovered socialism, the ideas of Robert Blatchford and his book *Merrie England*, and politics, where he became a supporter of the Labour leader Keir Hardie, and his efforts to spread socialist ideas by gaining representation in Parliament. Acting had initially been a spare-time amusement, in which he played more than a hundred Shakespeare parts, from Second Murderer to Hotspur and Romeo, and including Troilus in the first public production of *Troilus and Cressida* since Shakespeare's time. These semi-professional productions were staged in halls, swimming-baths and other venues, often in the East End; some matinees were for girls' schools whose students were forbidden to go to the theatre. This pioneering work was staged by Charles Fry, a leading actor of the old 'rhetorical' school.

Lewis was 25 before he decided on a career in the theatre. His break came when Fry recommended him to William Poel, whose determination to get back to an Elizabethan way of staging plays led him to favour continuity, a full text and a platform stage. Poel cast him as Don Pedro in *Much Ado About Nothing* in a production touring London's town halls in an evening-class programme. It was his first professional engagement, and he quickly came under Poel's influence, attracted by his call for 'a rapid, highly coloured musical speech of great range and flexibility'. Then Granville Barker recruited him in 1903 to appear in *The Two Gentlemen of Verona*, and the following year to understudy and play small parts at the Court.

The three repertory seasons that followed there under Barker and J E Vedrenne set new standards of acting and production, and were later recognised as the beginning of the modern British theatre. The plays included works by Galsworthy, Masefield, St John Hankin, Yeats, and Barker himself, and translations of European dramatists such as Ibsen, Maeterlinck, Hauptmann and Euripides. Also staged were eleven works by Shaw, who was then virtually unknown: they included *Candida*, during which Lewis as an understudy watched Shaw directing; *Man and Superman*, in which he created the part of Octavius Robinson; and *Major Barbara*, where he took over the role of Adolphus Cusins from Barker. The experience provided him with a rich theatrical apprenticeship, which would strongly influence his ideas about acting and directing.

So how and why was Sybil drawn to this socialist actor, seven years her senior? Was she really looking for a 'pal', or something more? Was she trying to hold back the first stirrings of love? Why was she certain before she met him that he was a man she could marry? The attraction was partly due to his resemblance to her cousin Basil Bowers, with whom she later claimed she was 'very much in love and very unhappy'. Lewis was good-looking in a stern way, with a strong chin, a determined mouth and an intent and penetrating gaze. While his manner was often reserved or gruff, his intimidating exterior concealed a man of passion, kindness and humour. Though frightened by his sharpness, Sybil admired his intelligence, his air of quiet authority, and his lack of interest in clothes. Best of all, she realised, he was 'raving mad about the theatre'.

Sybil was now 25, of medium height, slimmer than she had been in America, with wavy brown hair, strong blue eyes and an expressive face. Her vitality and animated spirit had instantly drawn Lewis to her. During their first meeting in Belfast she had hung back and not spoken, but he had noticed her eyes. Now having met her again, he went that evening to see her in *The Subjection of Kezia*. 'It was a simple part, but I was very much struck by her playing,' he recalled. In Dublin Zoo they had had what he called 'a real talk', when he 'got to know her as a person rather than as an actress'.

Sybil quickly took to her life among the theatrical highbrows. 'I'm getting to be one very fast,' she told Russell. 'There's a boy called Basil Dean with a very special highbrow face, and one called Clarence Derwent who is a wit and makes jokes that I'm beginning to see; but they're too clever.' Dean had joined the previous year, and remembered being impressed with her boundless enthusiasm, her devotion to the theatre, and her sense of mission. Meanwhile she was coming under the influence of a style of acting very different from Greet's: 'It's a new way of looking at acting these people have,' she explained to Russell. 'I mean, they're not in the least exciting like you and me, you can't imagine them making such terrible faces that they'd frighten people like you and I can, but they're being very real and very restrained and there's nothing actory in their acting. It's rather attractive. I'm starting to try it; you probably won't recognise me when you come home.'

After playing in Dublin the two Gaiety companies split up, Lewis returning to Manchester, Sybil to London. She spent the early summer acting in pastoral plays for Playfair and Topham, among others. She was also reunited with Greet, for a production of *The Comedy of Errors*. The difficulty of acting in the open air was highlighted by a critic who saw the production in a garden in Downton in Wiltshire. Sybil played Adriana 'with a sympathetic sense of its strong dramatic qualities; it suited her admirably and her characterisation was full of spirit', although at times 'it was difficult to hear the speeches of the actors' because of 'the sighing of the wind in the trees'. Safer indoors, she played in a charity matinee at the Lyceum, appearing as a Lady-in-Waiting in the concluding item, W S Gilbert's *Rosencrantz and Guildenstern*, a burlesque version of *Hamlet*, with Gilbert himself playing Claudius.

Soon afterwards she returned to the Gaiety, now being run by Ben Iden Payne, an actor and director who had also been inspired by the Court seasons. She was to understudy Candida, and a lead actress in George Paston's comedy *Clothes and the Woman*. She took digs at 32 Ackers Street in the suburb of Chorlton-cum-Hardy, in a row of soot-blackened houses where noisy backyard squabbles were the norm. She told Russell: 'I pay 12s 6d a week and that includes breakfast and a fire – jolly good, and then I go out with Hilda Bruce-Potter a lot – she's ripping and awfully clever. Margaret Halston is the leading lady – she has a most lovely face and the people adore her, crowds wait at the stage door to see her come out. She is extremely nice and kind to us all….I shall learn a great deal about acting from these people here.'

Lewis was also in the Paston play, and offered to help her learn her understudy part. They worked on the theatre roof in the smutty Manchester air. Sybil told Russell: 'I've got such yards to tell you about this new acting – very different to Shakespeare, but I think Shakespeare would be all the better for a dose of it.' She was impressed and fascinated by Lewis' more intellectual style of acting: 'You're frightfully conscious of a brain, not so much that he's *become* the person, but as if he was making *you* see the person and he was giving you suggestions – it's not the way I could work, but it's very interesting, and his speed is most exhilarating.'

But when she saw him in St John Hankin's *The Return of the Prodigal*, in which he played 'a very prim precise sort of Conservative prig', she had 'an awful feeling that he did it so well because he was like it'. She was soon disabused of this idea, and began to notice other qualities in him: 'We got on rather well,' she reported, 'at least better than I ever imagined we could, because he has that vile quality of seeing through me. I should imagine he'd never tell a lie – not for any moral reason but simply because he doesn't care what anyone thinks about him.' She also liked his apparent lack of conceit, and his ability to listen attentively to her: 'He never talks about himself at all, which is very attractive.'

One day Lewis invited her, Clarence Derwent and Hilda Bruce-Potter to take a trip in the country beyond Didsbury. They walked together, and this time Sybil made him talk about himself. 'He's had rather the same bringing up as us,' she explained to Russell, 'you know, all holy and church and being able to laugh at it because you know it too well to be solemn, which is gladdening to my heart.' Lewis for his part was beguiled when they dropped into a café, found it empty except for a piano, and Sybil played a Rachmaninov prelude.

On other country walks they discovered a shared interest in poetry. Since discovering Browning, Shelley and Keats, Sybil had spent many hours reading their works. Lewis, too, loved poetry, and already had a fascination bordering on an obsession with matters of phrasing, intonation and pitch. Sybil's response to the poems was a predominantly emotional one, his more analytical. On these walks they began to learn poems by heart, and Sybil enjoyed his vigorous delivery and his deep, melodious voice with its Welsh lilt. They began to give poetry readings, including one in a working-men's club in the slum area of Ancoats.

Nervous of her feelings, Sybil tried to conceal the nature of their relationship from Russell, and also herself: 'I'm not falling in love, so don't worry – he's much too nice; and he told me that he wasn't going to marry till he could afford a valet and a secretary, because he couldn't be bothered, and I said, "I'm just like you, I never have intended to marry, Russell and I are always going to live with each other," so that's all right.' In fact she was already smitten, both with the man and his politics. Lewis was a thoroughgoing socialist and advocate of women's rights. He had made a pact with the actor Johnston Forbes-Robertson that they would talk at a meeting on women's suffrage in whatever town they were playing in. A regular reader of the *Clarion*, a newspaper reflecting the socialist ideas of William Morris, Robert Owen, H G Wells and Shaw, he and other 'Clarionettes'– including Basil Dean – had recently cycled to Shrewsbury, where they sang uplifting songs and listened to speeches from socialists such as Robert Blatchford and H M Hyndman. He had also recently become involved with the Actors' Association, an early attempt at a union for the profession.

Sybil quickly came under the influence of his ideas. 'Manchester is full of politics,' she told Russell, after Lewis had taken her to a general-election meeting, at which Lloyd George spoke in support of the Liberal candidate Winston Churchill. 'Do you know anything about politics? I don't, except that you're supposed to vote Conservative if you're respectable, and be anything but a socialist. Well, most of these highbrows are socialist – full of "the people".' Her political allegiance shifted with startling rapidity: 'I don't think I'm going to be a Conservative any more – it's so boring – Well, and there's women's suffrage too. You know Russ, I'm terribly ignorant. I said to Lewis Casson, "Whatever do you want to go fussing like this – there's only just time enough to learn about acting without wanting votes and such-like." He said, "Your acting won't be much good if you don't think about the world in which you live and the conditions of the people."'

This excellent advice, a variation on Shaw's remark about her lack of life experience, affected her deeply. Overnight she began to take more interest in the wider world. Lewis took her round some of the Manchester slums, talked to her about women's suffrage, and outlined the political situation. He took her to a meeting at the Free Trade Hall, where two leaders of the movement, the charismatic Emmeline Pankhurst and her daughter Christabel, were speaking. Sybil was entranced by Emmeline, though thinking first what a lovely part she would be to play on stage. 'She got me right from the start, quietly dramatic, dignified, and such well-chosen phrases,' she recalled. 'I thought, Well, she can convert anyone, she had a voice of most remarkable sweetness'. She was less sure about Christabel, who was 'more violent, with wild arguments – too much, I thought, but exciting'. Afterwards she signed up for the cause, though not without misgivings: 'I belong now to the Women's Social and Political Union and I hobnob with the spirits of the age,' she boasted to Russell. 'What Father will say to me when I return I do not know.'

Founded in Manchester by the Pankhursts five years before, the Women's Social and Political Union (WSPU) was the more militant wing of the suffrage movement: its slogan was 'Deeds, not Words'. Women were still legally bracketed with 'children, criminals and lunatics' as being incapable of casting a vote. The WSPU held public meetings, lobbied and demonstrated, and were labelled suffragettes by the press after disrupting a House of Commons debate. Having failed to convince the Independent Labour Party and the Liberal government of the justice of Votes for Women, the WSPU was using more violent tactics, leading to many women being arrested, going on hunger strike and being force-fed in prison. More than a thousand actresses became involved in the struggle during the Edwardian era, many joining the WSPU, and then the Actresses' Franchise League, the aim of which was 'to convince members of the theatrical profession of the necessity of extending the franchise to women', and to produce propaganda shows for suffrage societies.

Sybil signed up alongside stars such as Ellen Terry, Lillah McCarthy, Lena Ashwell, Lily Langtry, Nina Boucicault and Elizabeth Robins. Already imbued with pacifist feelings, she refused to take part in violent demonstrations – although there were rumours, never substantiated, that she had once done so and thrown a stone through a window. But she greatly admired and became friends with the WSPU leaders, especially Emmeline Pankhurst and her two other daughters, Adela and Sylvia. She went to meetings and, after just three weeks, was persuaded to take the chair at one of them. 'I never felt such a fool, but after a bit I got quite worked up about women's wrongs, and in a minute I shall feel I shall be an anarchist too and throw bombs,' she wrote merrily to Russell. But she also questioned her own sincerity. 'It's awful being an actor because you can make yourself feel anything at any time,' she confessed. After-wards Lewis, who had watched from the front row, asked her if she believed everything she was saying. 'No, I just got carried away,' she replied.

At the end of her spell in Manchester she travelled back to London with Lewis. Before she took the train to Aylesford he invited her to tea in his top-floor flat at 16 Clifford's Inn, which he shared with the actor Kenelm Foss. Here she sewed two buttons on his coat, which was very uncharacter-istic behaviour. 'I was really very smitten,' she confessed later. Soon Lewis invited her to play Rosalind opposite his Orlando in his production of *As You Like It*, at St Mark's in Chelsea. One night the audience included his three sisters – a social worker, a school-teacher, and the wife of a school-teacher. 'Very learned they were,' Sybil recalled. 'They put the wind up me.'

Then came another boost to her confidence. Payne offered her a place in the company for the 1908/09 season in Manchester, to play whatever parts were going, beginning with a summer tour. And so, four years after being sent away by Shaw to learn about life, she finally got to play Candida in Exeter. Initially she found it hard to create her own interpretation after having under-studied Ellen O'Malley. But Dean, also in the cast, thought her an unqualified success, remarking sixty years later: 'I still consider her the finest Candida I ever saw.'

She was now reunited with Lewis, and their friendship deepened: 'I'm very glad Lewis Casson is in the company again,' she told Russell. 'That man argues a dreadful amount but I find he likes heaps of the things I like.' These apparently included standing for hours watching performing dogs on Brighton pier, and every morning swimming and diving off the end of it. She had worried initially to see him with golf clubs, but now relief came. 'Oh, Russell, such a mercy he doesn't like games. Not that it really matters to me, but the love of games is such a barrier, I do so dislike them.'

Under Lewis' influence she was fast becoming an ardent Shavian: she read the prefaces, studied the plays, and began to question her 'vicarage values'. She found Lewis' comments on her acting valuable, if somewhat blunt. In Exeter he admired her performance, feeling she captured well Candida's serenity. Afterwards he offered to give her some notes. It proved a discouraging session: he made only criticisms, telling her she was 'too bouncy' and talked too fast. But Sybil already had the ability to listen to and act upon any advice she thought valid. 'That man fairly laid me low,' she told Russell. 'I came out of that coffee-shop feeling like a used 2-cent stamp, but all the same he said some jolly good things, and I shall do everything he says because he knows more about it than I do.'

When Lewis talked of his admiration for Barker as a director, Sybil was intrigued but sceptical: 'I'd like to see this man who everyone thinks is like God,' she told Russell. 'No, more like Napoleon, I imagine – if he says a thing, all these highbrow actors say it's right.' Barker, who was staying with Galsworthy in Devon, cycled over to Exeter that week, so Lewis was able to introduce him to Sybil. Dressed in knickerbockers and a Norfolk jacket, his dynamic manner impressed her immediately: 'He had this wonderful face, and alert speech, and a curious, very vibrant high voice,' she remembered. 'I don't think I've ever met anybody so fascinating in my life.'

Her relationship with Lewis now blossomed rapidly, even though he still addressed her as 'Miss Thorndike'. He invited her to tea in his digs, and showed off his athleticism by climbing up a steep balcony. The following week the company were in Birmingham, where the courting signals grew stronger. With two other actors they went for a midnight walk in Edgbaston, then countryside, and lay down in a cornfield under the harvest moon. On the way back Lewis held her hand, 'which I thought was very forward of him, but I was really rather far gone then,' she recalled. The next day, discovering she had lost a glove on their walk, he bought her a new pair. The following day Sybil reported to Russell: 'Lewis Casson has asked me to marry him. I'm so taken aback. He's never even called me by my Christian name. I didn't fall flat on my face when he proposed in the Kardomah restaurant over coffee and toast, but the whole room spun round and so did the houses outside.'

The proposal took her by surprise, and her first response was muted. 'I suppose it means I shall marry him though everything doesn't look quite as Mother says it ought when you're in love. I really don't feel as if he's on earth at all, so I expect it comes to the same thing.' She was too overwhelmed to give him an answer immediately. The next morning he came to her digs, bringing a baby, and explaining: 'It was crying, so I brought him in to see you.' This test of her maternal instincts touched her emotionally, and she agreed to marry him. To Russell she was more casual, writing: 'On the Sunday we went to early service together, and then somehow or other we found we were engaged.' Her emotions were clearly in a turmoil, her decision clearly impulsive, based perhaps on an intuitive feeling that Lewis would make a good husband, rather than a careful weighing-up of his merits. She had imagined herself in love several times before, but this seemed a more adult experience.

The news came as a shock to her parents, who felt her impetuosity had run away with her, that she had been rushed into the engagement. Her father travelled to Carlisle, where the company was playing, to try to persuade her to think further before taking such a step. He met Lewis, and discovered that his background was similar to Sybil's: the two men got on well. But when Sybil's mother came to Blackpool, the next touring date, she told Lewis she wanted Sybil to marry someone more distinguished. There was a row, and Sybil was in despair; but eventually her mother gave way. She was however adamant on one point: although Sybil and Lewis wanted to get married at once, and with as little fuss as possible, she insisted the clergy and people of Rochester and Aylesford would expect Sybil to have a full-blown wedding, and would think it extremely odd if she didn't. Lewis tactlessly asked: 'Would that matter very much?' She was only a little mollified after he and Sybil staged a dramatic performance that night in their hotel. 'He certainly has a beautiful voice,' she told Sybil, but added: 'I hope he won't make you hard, you've always been such a sweet girl in the village.'

The wedding was fixed to take place in Aylesford just before Christmas. Sybil's life was about to be transformed.

7

Annie Horniman and the Gaiety

1908–1909

'I admire her, and would like to do what she is doing'
Sybil on Annie Horniman, manager of the Gaiety

The daughter of a wealthy Quaker tea merchant, with a passion for the drama of Ibsen and Shaw, Annie Horniman was a pioneer in the development of the repertory movement in British theatre. It was Sybil's good fortune to be able to work in Manchester during these formative years in a theatre dedicated to challenging the existing system, the first provincial repertory theatre, and one that gave her a variety of roles in new plays, many of them critical of contemporary society.

A determined, energetic woman, Annie Horniman had been one of the founders, along with the poet W B Yeats and Lady Gregory, of the Abbey Theatre in Dublin, for which she provided a substantial annual subsidy. After a bitter quarrel with her co-founders she left for England. Now 47, and known affectionately to many as 'Hornibags', she cut a striking figure. She smoked Turkish cigarettes in a long holder, and dressed unconventionally in the evenings, in rich brocades of startling colours, and wore a long pendant containing three hundred opals. Despite her wealth she took the tram to the theatre, and lived modestly in her rooms in the Oxford Road, surrounded by her cats and books on astrology, feminism, travel and politics.

A firm believer in the equality of the sexes, she favoured plays about the position of women. Despite the developing battle for women's rights and the struggle for the vote, the images of women on the stage remained traditional ones. Christopher St John wrote in the newspaper *Votes for Women*: 'There is not one play on the London stage at the present time which takes any account of women, except on the level of housekeepers or bridge players – the actual or potential property of some man, valuable or worthless as the case may be. It is strange to go out of the world where women are fighting for freedom, into the theatre, where the dramatist appears unaffected by the new renaissance.'

Sybil was immediately impressed by her employer: 'I like her awfully on first acquaintance,' she told Russell. 'She looks as if she's stepped out of a mid-Victorian picture – tall and dignified and I think just a beautiful face, and she wears the most wonderful clothes, all made in the same mid-Victorian style of the loveliest materials – Beautiful stuff that you'd only think of for curtains, and are surprised to see how well it furnishes the human body. She makes a real picture.' She also saw her as a possible role model. 'She is a very enterprising woman. She spends most of her money on the theatre and lives very simply herself in a sort of bachelor way. I admire her, and would like to do what she is doing. I often wonder whether the people in this city appreciate what she's doing – one wonders if pioneer work is ever appreciated.'

Annie Horniman had made clear her intention to do for Manchester what the revolutionary Barker and Vedrenne seasons had done for London, 'to give in the provinces the same earnest care and attention to the selection of the pieces, the casting of the characters and the general ensemble that has made the name and fame of that celebrated management'. Her artistic director Ben Iden Payne was another refugee from the Abbey, and like her a devotee of the New Drama. Both wanted to break down the star system and the tradition of long runs. Their policy was 'to produce good new plays, to revive old master-pieces, and to present translations of the best works of foreign authors'. She was also determined to give opportunities to local writers. The Gaiety, her manifesto asserted, would be 'not wedded to any one school of dramatists, but quite catholic, embracing eventually the finest writings, both comedy and tragedy, by the best authors of all ages, with a specially wide-open door to present-day writers, who will not now need to sigh in vain for a hearing, provided they have something to say worth listening to, and say it in an interesting and original manner'.

It was a strikingly serious and ambitious aim for a provincial theatre, but Manchester was potentially a suitable place for the New Drama. Its eight theatres staged musical comedies, farces, melodramas and romances, but there was little to satisfy the playgoer looking for intellectual stimulation from plays that mirrored real life. An important industrial centre, Manchester was a city of perpetual grime, rain and mist, its dingy, narrow cobbled streets echoing to the clang of trams and the rumble of horse-drawn drays loaded with cotton. Yet it had a strong cultural heart, boasting the Hallé orchestra at the Free Trade Hall, a Literary and Philosophic Society, the Manchester Royal College of Music, and the *Manchester Guardian*, whose influential theatre critics included C E Montague and Allan Monkhouse – and the young James Agate, with whom Sybil was later to have many disagreements.

As the *Manchester Guardian* put it: 'The strength of the Manchester Repertoire Theatre will be in its power to feed and so strengthen a genuine theatrical appetite which now exists in abundance, but is almost paralysed by despair of its own satisfaction.' Annie Horniman had kept her promise to keep ticket prices 'popular'. But though she had hoped to present a varied repertoire each week, she quickly abandoned this radical idea in favour of running each production for a week, then reviving the successful ones, occasionally taking them for a week to another town.

The plays staged suited Sybil down to the ground, both politically and artistically. In her two seasons at the Gaiety she would play roles in new work by writers such as Barker, John Galsworthy, St John Hankin, Eden Phillpotts, St John Ervine, Arnold Bennett and Elizabeth Baker, and by others in what came to be known as the Manchester School: Stanley Houghton, Harold Brighouse and Allan Monkhouse. The conditions were basic: her salary was £5 a week (Lewis' was £7), with rehearsals unpaid, while her contract compelled her 'to provide all own modern costumes, wigs, tights, stockings and shoes if required, the same to be approved by the manager'.

The opening night in September 1908 drew a fashionable audience. The season began with *When the Devil Was Ill*, a satire on the 'back to nature' cult, written by one of the local writers, Charles McEvoy. It was preceded by a curtain-raiser by Basil Dean, *Marriages Are Made in Heaven*, an apt title to mark Sybil and Lewis' first time on stage together. Dean, who was making his debut both as playwright and director, recalled the first day of rehearsal: 'I arrived at the theatre to find the actors having a brisk argument among themselves in a corner. But when Sybil saw me she immediately turned to the others with an all-embracing gesture, and said: "Now come along, don't be silly. Let's all help the young man to have a success."' The eager, unworldly young member of Greet's company was starting to mature.

In October Euripides' enduring tragedy *Hippolytus* gave Sybil her first chance to work in Greek drama, and Lewis his second professional production as director. Since childhood she had been fascinated by the Greeks: she knew about Hecuba, and had read about the Argonauts, Perseus, Theseus and many others in Charles Kinglsey's *Heroes*. During a country walk with Lewis he had talked of his plans to direct *Hippolytus*, and the possibility of her playing in it. 'I felt from the tone of his voice that I was to learn and know something very wonderful,' she recalled. She was not disappointed. Studying the part of the goddess Artemis, she felt 'a new world was being opened for me, and that I was to learn of a beauty I had never even glimpsed'.

Her main guide in this new world was a man who, like Shaw and Lewis, would become a powerful mentor. Born in Australia, Gilbert Murray had just been made professor of Greek at Oxford. A scholar, poet and dramatist, his translations of the Greek tragedies were generally reckoned to be superior to previous ones. Barker had recently staged at the Court his versions of three of Euripides' plays – *Hippolytus*, *The Trojan Women* and *Electra* – and also directed *Medea* at the Savoy, where Lewis had played the Messenger. At this time the ancient tragedies were hardly ever staged, and certainly not in conventional theatres. But both Barker and Murray, who were close friends, believed the Greek playwrights could and should be treated like modern ones. In giving the plays new life Murray wanted them to have a 'sustained and rapid action on the stage'. His scripts were almost entirely devoid of stage directions, leaving the focus on the words. Although his lyrical English verse aroused academic controversy – critics such as William Archer believed the beauty of the text required rhyme – his romantic translations made the plays accessible both to actors and audiences.

It was Barker who had suggested to Payne that Lewis should direct a Greek tragedy. The cast included Penelope Wheeler as Phaedra, Jules Shaw as Hippolytus, and Lewis, who had been an understudy in the Court production, as the Henchman. He had been corresponding with Murray about staging his translation. They discussed the Choruses – Murray preferred them to be spoken rather than sung – and the music, to be provided by Granville Bantock. Then, while on tour in Carlisle with *Candida*, Lewis wrote casually to Murray: 'I had a long talk with Bantock in Birmingham and have been meaning to write to you ever since, but private affairs, which have resulted in my engagement to Artemis, have kept me a bit away from such mundane matters.'

Lewis brought Murray in to advise him, and Sybil met him for the first time. 'He was very gentle and quiet,' she remembered, 'but he knew exactly the sort of effect he wanted to get, and by a word could put one on the right track.' Murray was not opposed to actors speaking the words passionately, but he required above all sincerity. His aim was to get Sybil to change the way she characterised her performance, to cut out her distinctive personal traits. Yet his suggestions were not always crystal-clear. After watching her play one scene Murray said, 'Charming, my dear. Now what I want is opalescent dawn.' This brought Sybil up short – partly because she was not sure what he meant, but also because she realised the role was more complicated than she had thought. Murray advised her to listen to her director, observing: 'Casson will show you how to do it – he moves and speaks like a Greek.'

Hippolytus was the first of the many productions in which Sybil was directed by Lewis, and she confessed later that she was terrified of him. Yet she was exhilarated and excited by the rehearsals, during which so many new ideas and thoughts were given to her. In the evening she and Lewis would go back to their digs, where she would sit at the piano for hours with Bantock's score, while he fitted the words with the music. Her difficulties with Artemis seem to have been overcome. Afterwards Lewis wrote to Murray: 'It is really splendid that you think so highly of the performance.' The critics praised the production, seeing it as an admirable attempt to make a great play seem modern, while retaining its beauty. It established Lewis' reputation within the company, and with the Gaiety's audiences.

It also had a profound effect on Sybil. '*Hippolytus* is surely one of the most beautiful plays in the world,' she suggested later. 'It has every quality that makes a great tragedy. Rehearsing and studying it for the first time was like being in a magic country.' She now took to reading all the Murray translations as they appeared, becoming especially fired up by *The Trojan Women* and *Medea*, and longing for a chance to play in them. This was also the beginning of a lifelong friendship between the two families. Sybil and Lewis went to the Murrays' home in Oxford, where Mary Murray gave her some 'wise help and advice…as a young married woman…for which I have always been grateful'. Like Sybil's mother, she was musical and played the organ; and was, in her own description, 'a keen suffragist and a quasi-socialist radical', so she and Sybil had much in common. Murray espoused many liberal causes, and was to be a leading figure in the peace movement. Sybil said years later that Murray was 'one of the guiding lights of my life'.

She and Lewis were not in all the season's productions, but in the run-up to their wedding they played together in a one-act play by Charles McEvoy, *Gentlemen of the Road*, and in *The Charity That Began at Home*, a comedy by St John Hankin about the impracticability of practising Christian principles in

Edwardian society, which had been in Barker's Court repertoire. In the latter, according to the *Manchester Guardian*'s eminent critic C E Montague, Sybil as the well-bred and woolly-minded Lady Denison acted 'with faultless intelligence and humour'. The company then took *Candida* to Ireland, with Lewis playing Marchbanks opposite Sybil's Candida.

Shortly before this trip they had spent a day with Barker at Court Lodge, his small Elizabethan house in Stansted in Kent. Sybil had played on his pianola, a gift from Shaw, and then on his piano, Barker telling her: 'I don't want any expression, I only want notes.' This curious request may have caused what Sybil later described as 'a tremendous argument about music'. Now in Dublin they met him again. Barker had contracted typhoid fever from drinking infected milk, collapsed, and nearly died. On recovering he met Sybil and Lewis, and Sybil played Bach to him. The company then moved on to Cork where, because of a tight schedule, they had to speed up the last performance, reducing *Candida* to an hour so they could catch their train and boat connections to be home in time for their wedding.

Beneath the heading 'A Village Wedding', the invitation read: 'The Vicar of Aylesford and Mrs Thorndike wish to invite you to the marriage of their eldest daughter Sybil with Mr Lewis Casson, which will be solemnised in the quaint Old Parish Church at Aylesford, on December 22nd at a quarter before 2 o'clock, and will you come to the Vicarage directly after the service to meet the Bride and Bridegroom.' Lewis, having lost his battle for a quiet wedding, had refused at first to buy a new suit for the occasion. He had threatened to wear one of his stage suits for the ceremony, and another he had worn in Shaw's *Widowers' Houses* for going away. But in the end he relented, and wore more formal dress for the church.

The night before the wedding, at a ceremony in the barn, Sybil received many presents, and Lewis made a speech in which he tactfully described Sybil as 'the jewel of the village'. That night Kitty Jelf shared Sybil's bedroom with her. The next morning Sybil and Lewis went to the early service together. Sybil cried at the thought of leaving the village and the home she so loved. Later, dressed in an embroidered white satin dress and orange-blossoms, she drove to and from the packed church in an open carriage, so that she could see and be seen by those who couldn't get in. Her hopes that there would otherwise be 'no fuss' were not realised, as Russell remembered: 'The procession seemed to include all the clergy of the diocese, canons of Rochester, a dean, two bishops – Rochester and Thetford – two train-bearers in white swansdown and scarlet cloaks, and a huge choir in scarlet cassocks. Christmas music supplied by members of the Royal Engineer Band in full uniform.'

The imposing fifteenth-century church was decked with holly as Sybil walked down the wide aisle on the arm of her father, dressed in his white cassock. They were followed by her two bridesmaids – her sister Eileen and a young friend of hers – in white dresses and red cloaks, with her mother sitting at the magnificent organ at the side of the church. Jules Shaw, Lewis' friend, was best man. Afterwards the couple, with Sybil dressed in a squirrel coat and matching toque with a long blue feather, drove to the station at a funereal pace, preceded by the village brass band. Halfway there the carriage stopped for a presentation, and Sybil made a speech to the villagers lining the road. It was a bright but frosty day, and her nose was red, both from the cold and from her overflowing emotion at leaving Aylesford.

For their honeymoon she and Lewis spent two weeks in Miller's Dale near Buxton in the Derbyshire Peak District, where they drove around in a borrowed Rolls-Royce and, Lewis recalled, enjoyed 'tramping in the blizzards and the snowdrifts, talking our heads off, and thrashing everything out'. They went on to Portmadoc in North Wales, where they stayed for a further fortnight at Bron-y-garth ('Garden Ridge'), a spacious stone mansion owned by Lewis' Uncle Randal and Aunt Lucy, with a breathtaking view of the surrounding mountains. They had violent arguments, and Sybil was intensely homesick: 'I could have gone straight back home – Lewis then didn't quite make up for it – I cried and cried – little silly ass I was – Lewis was so sweet!' she recalled. Instead they returned together to their suburban theatrical digs in Didsbury. Shortly afterwards, while touring in Edinburgh, Sybil discovered she was pregnant.

During their engagement Lewis had argued endlessly with her about voice and phrasing matters. Finally he suggested she should see Elsie Fogerty (known as Fogie), the founder of the Central School, and a specialist in voice training, who would later help Edith Evans, Laurence Olivier and others when they had vocal problems. A woman of tempestuous enthusiasm, another follower of Poel, when she first met Sybil with Lewis she terrified her by saying: 'You're a lucky girl to have married Lewis Casson. It's the best voice on the stage, the purest production – and I hope you are worthy of it.' She then added: 'You must free those head resonances – you're not using the head notes at all.' Lewis said: 'Oh, Sybil's stage voice is all right.' Fogie replied briskly: 'Can't have one voice *on* the stage and another *off*. She must come and do some work with me.'

Sybil remembered feeling 'a complete worm', but agreed, and thereafter experienced 'many happy hours of study'. Her voice, Fogie noted, was inclined to escape her control, so she showed her how to save it. She gave her breathing and vocal exercises, which Sybil practised regularly first thing in the morning, a habit that would last a lifetime. Later, whenever she had vocal troubles, she would go immediately to Fogie for help. 'She always put it right,' she recalled. 'She never tried to impose a false manner of speech, but she was wonderful at teaching you how to make the most of your natural voice.' They became friends, disagreeing about many things, but enjoying hammering out their differences.

After their honeymoon, Sybil and Lewis' first production was John Galsworthy's first play, *The Silver Box*. This had been a success at the Court, where it was praised for its dispassionate realism. An attack on the class system, its story of the theft of a silver box was designed to show the different rules of justice for rich and poor, both in life and in the law courts. Galsworthy attended rehearsals to advise Payne, who hired some unemployed men as extras in an attempt to enhance the production's realism. Lewis was cast as the Magistrate, while Sybil played the haughty and hard-hearted Mrs Barthwick, the wife of a wealthy Liberal MP, 'a lady of nearly fifty, well dressed, with greyish hair, good features and a decided manner'.

It was a potentially tricky role for a burgeoning young socialist to tackle, and Galsworthy thought she would find it difficult. He wanted her to play it more impersonally, but in rehearsal she despaired of being able to do so. It was the same problem that had arisen with Murray and Artemis: too much Sybil Thorndike, not enough of the 'universal' quality of the character. But by the first night Galsworthy was satisfied. Although the characters now seem stereotypes and the plot laboured and predictable, the play made a profound impression on the audience. Allan Monkhouse wrote in the *Manchester Guardian*: 'To many of us it was a deep experience revealing, indeed, fresh possibilities in the art of the theatre.' The lord mayor thought differently, declining to attend on the grounds that you could see this kind of incident daily in the police courts.

During a short tour in February Sybil heard that Kitty Jelf needed an operation. From Glasgow she wrote anxiously to Kitty's fiancé Monier Bickersteth, in a letter that reveals her strong Christian faith: 'I'd no idea anything of the sort would have to be. Oh! I am thinking of you both, and the anxiety you will feel….I always think it's worse for those who are waiting – such huge strengthening given to the ones who have actually to go thru' the ordeal. Dear old Monier, you'll be in me prayers, you and darling Kitty, it's something I know to have those who love one praying for and with one. She writes such a cheery bright letter – so full of hope, her faith is so grand. I know God will bring her all right and we shall have her strong and well when this time of trial is over. God bless you both, Monier. Your affectionate Sybil.'

In the next three months she took on a range of parts. In *Cupid and the Styx*, a light-hearted comedy about love and death set in a hospital written by J Sackville Martin, a local doctor, she gave a charming performance as a nurse engaged to two house surgeons at once. She was also in *Tresspassers Will Be Prosecuted*, a first play by another local writer, M A Arabian, about a group of people who, Ibsen-style, challenge conventional morality; Montague noted that 'Miss Sybil Thorndike acted throughout with the greatest spirit and incisiveness'. It was followed by *The Feud* by Edward Garnett, a romantic drama set in Iceland in the twelfth century, a spectacular production, full of scenic splendours, of a crude and wordy play. The work was demanding, especially on tour. In Oxford the company presented six different plays on six successive nights, each preceded by a curtain-raiser, and ended with two performances of *Candida* on the Saturday.

Sybil later recalled: 'It was such a strange thing for me, who had been taught in a real old Shakespearean manner, to have to speak very much in the lingo of Manchester. It was so different from anything I had done before.' The audience covered every shade of opinion: according to Basil Dean, it included 'intellectuals from the university, vegetarians, nature lovers, weekend hikers in the Derbyshire hills, and general marchers in the advance guard of public opinion'. Dean also recalled the actors' work schedule: 'The routine of work was exacting: we rehearsed from 10.30 to 4, with only half an hour's interval for lunch, then a scamper through the rain to tram or train to one's lodgings, then back through the rain once more for the evening performance.'

During the season Sybil made one of her many enduring female friendships. Florence Bell wrote plays for adults and children, and adapted novels for the stage. Married to the industrialist Hugh Bell, and stepmother to Gertrude Bell, later famous as an explorer, she was fascinated by the theatre. She was an intimate friend of the actress Elizabeth Robins, with whom she had anonymously written *Alan's Wife*, a play about infanticide which caused a sensation in London, where it was thought to be by a man. Hoping the Gaiety might stage another of her works, *The Way the Morning Goes*, she had written to Lewis, saying: 'There's a girl in your company I'd like for the lead. She's called Sybil Thorndike.' Lewis replied: 'I'm glad you think she's good. I've just married her!' Sybil was unable to play the part, but sat with the author on the first night, and they became close friends.

In June the company staged a three-week season in London at the Coronet in Notting Hill, featuring seven of their best productions. They attracted widespread praise from both critics and audiences, especially for their fine ensemble playing. William Archer, a leading critic, stated that 'this Manchester movement is the most important fact in our theatrical history since the opening of the Vedrenne-Barker campaign at the Court Theatre... The flexibility, the adaptability of the company was altogether admirable and the sense of living artistic endeavour gave excellence a new charm.' However, Sybil's advancing pregnancy meant she could only be in one play, Hermann Sudermann's *The Vale of Content*.

They now decided that Lewis should strike out on his own, so he resigned from the Gaiety. Manchester had been a valuable experience for both of them. It had enabled Sybil to define more clearly the purpose of her work as an actress. 'We all thought the era of the New Theatre was being created,' she observed later. 'The theatre which was to be the reflection of the life of the people...a theatre which was to be Daily Bread, food and stimulant, as opposed to the escapist theatre of the time. I can't describe what that zest and inner fire of the movement meant to the individual actor.'

8

Granville Barker and America

1909–1911

'He had an electric personality: you came away from rehearsals
feeling you'd got a new vision'
Sybil on Barker as a director

Sybil went down to Aylesford to await the arrival of the baby. Lewis had recently bought a motorbike for a few pounds, so she travelled there in the side-car. But soon another family upheaval brought her back to London: her father had been offered the living of St James-the-Less in Westminster, a large, red-brick church just off Vauxhall Bridge Road in what is now Thorndike Street. She and Lewis moved into the vicarage in nearby St George's Square, close to the Thames. Here, after an appallingly difficult and painful labour, Sybil gave birth on 28 October 1909 to her first child, John.

She was delighted to be a mother, but with little money coming in she and Lewis had to live very modestly. Fortunately he had a talent for exploring markets and finding apparently useless or decrepit objects, then adapting or restoring them, and in this way he furnished their home. But work was thin on the ground: he had been in a play with Lewis Waller, and a short run at the Haymarket of *The Fires of Fate* by Arthur Conan Doyle, but otherwise had only acted in a few one-off matinee productions. One of these, *Love in a Tangle*, which he directed for The Playwrights' Association, featured 'Master Frank Thorndike' as the Duke of St Austell.

Like his sister, young Frank had at first been drawn to music. Sybil had taught him the piano, having terrible rows and pushing him off the piano stool; later he had become an accomplished cellist after taking lessons at the Guildhall. He went to boarding school in Oxford, but ran away, claiming he was learning nothing. Still only fourteen, he decided to join his siblings in the theatre. In a matinee performance of *Cousin Kate* at the Court he was spotted by Gerald du Maurier, and joined him in *Alias Jimmy Valentine*, in which he made a considerable impact. Gay and urbane, more sophisticated than his sisters and brother, he was thought to have great promise.

Eileen was also starting out in the theatre. Having spent some weeks with Sybil as part of the Gaiety company, she had recently walked on in *As You Like It* and *Romeo and Juliet* at the Court. Russell, having done a further American tour with Ben Greet, was also there, playing character roles such as Montague and the Apothecary in *Romeo and Juliet*, Turbal and Old Gobbo in *The Merchant of Venice*, and Corin in *As You Like It*, while doubling as assistant stage manager.

Sybil and Lewis had agreed from the start of their marriage that their children would have to fit round their careers. With all her siblings involved in the London theatre, Sybil was keen to return to it as soon as possible. She eased her way in at the beginning of 1910 with two single-matinee productions at the Court for the Play Actors, both directed by Lewis. In *Peg Woffington's Pearls*, a 'comedietta' by C Duncan Jones and Dennis Cleugh, the *Era* noted that 'Miss Sybil Thorndike made a typical Irish beauty of Sal Fortescue, acting and speaking prettily'. This was followed by the title-role in Harold Chapin's *The Marriage of Columbine*. But then came a much more significant opportunity.

London was still the only European capital of any importance without a repertory theatre. A company was being formed for a season of modern plays at the Duke of York's. The idea had come from J M Barrie, and quickly gained the support of Shaw and Galsworthy. Barrie had convinced Charles Frohman, the theatre's American manager and his close friend, of its desirability. Frohman, a small, shy, balding man, known as the Beaming Buddha of Broadway, was an impresario of great influence and discerning judgement, who produced over five hundred plays in his lifetime, including the first *Peter Pan*. An astute businessman, he was also a great gambler. If he had a failure, he preferred to forget it. 'Don't revive the past,' he said. 'Pulverise the future.' Tragically, he was to die in 1915 aboard the torpedoed *Lusitania*.

Mounting this kind of repertory season, the first in the West End, was a risk. While Frohman was the producer, Barker was its moving spirit. 'It is hard work to push push push at the blessed old English, and repertory is our salvation,' he wrote to Murray. The company he and fellow-director Dion Boucicault engaged was of a high quality: stars such as Gerald du Maurier, Lillah McCarthy, Hilda Trevelyan, Lena Ashwell and Irene Vanbrugh, and actors with solid repertory experience, notably Sybil and Lewis from Manchester and Mary Jerrold from Glasgow. The programme was to include plays by Barrie, Galsworthy, Masefield, Laurence Housman, Meredith, Maugham, Pinero, Shaw and Barker. It was another attempt by Barker to lay down a blueprint for a national theatre, to treat theatre as art rather than just entertainment, and provide an antidote to the farces and musical comedies dominating the West End.

Sybil was invited to play small parts and understudy others. The salary was £3 10s a week, thirty shillings less than Miss Horniman had paid her. On the strength of their engagement she and Lewis found a small flat at 75 St George's Square, two doors from her father's vicarage. Her first two roles gave her little chance of making an impact. George Meredith's 'unfinished comedy' *The Sentimentalists* was a fragment in prose and verse found in the novelist's papers after his death, and given to Barrie to arrange a performance. It featured May Whitty, Charles Maude, Dennis Eadie and Mary Jerrold, while Sybil, in the words of the *Era* critic, was among those who 'had little to say and less to do', but who did it 'without flaw or failing'. It formed part of a triple bill with two short Barrie plays, but ran for just six performances.

Barker's *The Madras House* was a more substantial piece, a play about the economic, social and sexual status of women which chimed in with the concerns of those struggling for equal rights for women. Barker described it as 'the best play I've written yet', and it later was seen as a brilliant, innovatory piece. But although the first-night audience received it with uproarious delight, its minimal plot and lengthy philosophical dialogue were too revolutionary for the West End, and it only managed ten performances. Sybil was one of the six virginal Huxtable sisters living in suburban Denmark Hill ('angular, ill-dressed, vulgar daughters who twaddle', observed *The Times*), and again received only a group review in the *Era*, its critic noting that the actresses, 'though without opportunities of individual distinction, supplied careful and satisfactory performances'. The following month she was Romp, a 'jolly girl' and one of the masqueraders, in a revival of the pierrot play and tragic fantasy *Prunella*, a collaboration between Barker and Laurence Housman.

All three plays were directed by Barker, who was keen to avoid the declamatory style of acting based on vocal histrionics and abundant gestures, favouring instead a new realism. Once an actor himself, he liked them to use their minds and be creative with ideas, and would give them a wealth of psychological background. Sybil was excited by his method. 'He would explain things so beautifully,' she recalled. 'His movements, his gestures – he had something of the dancer in him. He had wonderful style and a flexible body, that could move, and this astonishing alive face. He had an electric personality: you felt you were in the presence of something so vibrant. And you came away from rehearsals feeling you'd got a new vision.'

It was Barker who made directing into a system, who invented the professional director whose sole job was to bring together all the elements of a production. 'To suggest, to criticise, to coordinate – that should be the limit of his function,' he wrote. Its impact on the British theatre was profound. One of his revolutions was to institute a lengthy series of rehearsals, at which the emphasis would be not on a star performer but on the ensemble and the text, which he aimed to make coherent in a manner as faithful as possible to the author's intentions. He preferred rehearsals to be on the stage, and liked to get actors on their feet as soon as possible, rather than engage in lengthy discussions about the play. He worked to develop even the smallest part to maximum effect, seeing himself as essentially the author's representative.

Barker was often regarded as a god. Sybil reflected this in a letter to Russell during rehearsals for *Prunella*: 'There's one of his gestures, Russ, that no one but God would have thought of – and things he does with his voice when he's showing people what he wants – things that not a single one of us can do. I shall go on practising hard and try to do what he does.' Like others, she admired his ability to capture the emotional and intellectual spirit of a play through an accumulation of realistic and poetic details. He was determined but not autocratic, and reasonable and charming in his manner. Lewis recalled him in rehearsal as 'eager and tireless, blazing with an inner fire that yet remained always under the steely, flexible control of a keen calculating brain'.

Sybil's willingness to learn soon paid dividends. In May the company was to stage Elizabeth Baker's grimly realistic play *Chains*, directed by Boucicault. When Lillah McCarthy, Barker's wife, became unwell, Sybil was asked to take over her part. The story, set in suburbia, concerned a wife who tries to prevent her husband from leaving her for a new life in Australia by pretending she is pregnant. Sybil played the wife's sister Maggie, a strong, adventurous New Woman who wants to break away from the suburban life.

Boucicault was a more traditional director than Barker. Lewis was impressed with his methods, but May Whitty thought him a martinet: 'His chief weapon was irony, and he was never charming until he had impressed you with his power,' she remembered. 'He insisted on definite movements, never varying….One's coffee was drunk at a given second, and gloves were taken off by numbers.' Sybil disliked being treated like a child, being told: 'You must say it like that, don't you see the sense of that, or are you completely without brains?' She struggled as Boucicault tried, as other directors had, to tone down her acting. 'Not one single thing I do is right,' she complained to Russell. 'My face moves too much. My body moves too much. I do everything too much. Mr Boucicault says if I stop doing everything and do nothing at all, he thinks I shall be a great success in the part; and that's what all these West End managers and authors say to one, it seems – "Don't do anything." Well, Mr Galsworthy said it, and it proved right, so I'd better try it again.' Mr Boucicault also seems to have proved right: *The Times* thought her 'capital as a type of suburban *revoltée*', while P P Howe in his record of the season noted that she 'succeeded very well in making plausible the enthusiastic Maggie'. She and Lewis, he wrote, were among those 'who did persistently good work in nearly every play'.

The company had achieved a high standard of acting, and staged an impressive number of new plays and revivals. However, with so many stars involved it had not been a true repertory event. The season was cut short in June, mainly because the early productions brought in £100 a night instead of the required £300 minimum, losing Frohman a great deal of money. Sadly, he increasingly had to bring back Pinero's popular *Trelawny of the 'Wells'* (in which Sybil walked on) at the expense of the more ground-breaking work. The death of King Edward VII in May, which forced the theatres briefly to go dark, provided a respectable excuse for him to close the season after just 17 weeks and 128 performances. Barker concluded that 'a repertory theatre cannot be made to pay in the commercial sense of the word'.

Sybil had clearly made progress for, having watched a rehearsal of *Chains*, Frohman offered her and Lewis a season in America. With no money in the bank, and the chance of returning to a country that had captivated her, the offer was extremely tempting, and a great compliment. She would be acting on Broadway with a star of the American stage, John Drew, and earning a decent salary for the first time. But she now faced a mother's classic dilemma, whether to put career or family first. The thought of. leaving her eight-month-old John for several months caused Sybil much anguish. The matter was resolved when her mother offered to look after him, with the help of his nurse Alice Pearce. Sybil and Lewis borrowed £20 from an actors' charity to tide them over until their first salary cheque, and in July set off by train to Liverpool, Sybil crying all the way at being parted from her son.

These were early days on Broadway, with its 40 theatres, and where, as one critic put it, 'even the best of American plays contained a large profusion of claptrap'. Sybil and Lewis were to appear in an import, Somerset Maugham's *Smith*, which had just completed a successful West End run. 'Cynicism driven to its highest pitch,' was how one critic described it. A minor Maugham, it was a misogynistic attack on the upper reaches of society. The hero, returning from the colonies to seek a wife, is shocked by the behaviour of the upper-class women and their endless bridge parties, and marries Smith, a decent, hard-working parlour maid. The female lead was played by the charming comedienne Mary Boland. Sybil played the adventuress Emily Chapman, a showy part which gave her some good scenes with Drew.

Now fifty-seven, the debonair Drew, admired for his courtliness and gentility, was known in America as 'the first gentleman of the stage'. The uncle of Lionel, Ethel and John Barrymore, all later great actors, he made a striking figure, with his drooping moustache and large, heavy-lidded eyes. Earlier he had shared a fine stage partnership with the great comedienne Ada Rehan. Although he had done a great deal of Shakespeare, he was best known for his drawing-room comedy technique, which led to him being dubbed 'the American dress-suit actor par excellence'. One theatregoer, paying tribute to his finesse, remarked: 'John Drew doesn't act, he just behaves.'

Directed by William Seymour, *Smith* opened at the Empire on 5 September, and ran successfully for 112 performances over four and a half months. Sybil thought Drew 'angelic', and she and Lewis spent long hours talking theatre with him. Outside of work they fell among artists and writers in downtown Manhattan. Sybil enjoyed hours of music-making with Nikolai Sokoloff, later conductor of the Cleveland Symphony Orchestra, then a young violinist. She and Lewis spent many enjoyable days in the New Jersey home of Charles Battell Loomis, the writer of comic monologues and short stories. She talked poetry with a Mrs Lemoine, a well-known interpreter of Browning, whose dramatic poems she began to read again, believing them to be good for the study of acting. They also got to know Alice and Irene Lewisohn of the Neighborhood Playhouse, a centre for the performing arts in the heart of the Lower East Side ghetto, where plays were produced in English and Yiddish.

With more leisure hours than they were used to, they went for long walks along the Hudson river, and immersed themselves in books. 'We find our time pretty well occupied, as we do quite a lot of studying together and we have so many friends,' Sybil wrote to Monier Bickersteth. Faith healing had recently caught her interest. 'I've just been reading the most wonderful book on the subject, *The Law of Psychic Phenomena* by Dr Anderson. He knows the marvellous cures that have been affected by faith, and one can't help feeling it's a much sounder, saner thing than this abnormal use of drugs medicine.' She also noted a growing interest in one brand of religion: 'Nearly every other person one meets here is a Christian Scientist. It's growing tremendously.'

A long tour, through the eastern states and ending up in California, was to start early in 1911. But before they left New York Frohman made Sybil an astonishing offer. Promising to make her a star, he offered her and Lewis another play with Drew the following autumn, and a deal guaranteeing her three months a year in a Broadway production, with a tour to follow. Sybil told Monier Bickersteth. 'We shall in all probability be returning in the early autumn bringing John too, and I shall set up in a little home, as Mr Frohman has promised me that if I work I need not do anything. It's such good money and we must think of the future, tho' I wish England would give us the same opportunity. However, we can't arrange everything just as we want, and we've such a lot to be thankful for.'

The idea of being away from home for such an extended period made her wretched, but Lewis, always more practical, persuaded her of the advantages of Frohman's offer, including the warmth and encouragement of the American people. After much discussion Sybil gave way, they signed, and took to the road with Drew's company. It was a demanding tour, as Sybil admitted in a letter to Kitty Jelf from St Louis, Missouri: 'I meant to have written when we sent the books off from Detroit, but we were having a most harassing time on one-night stands, and everything goes blank in front and behind!' The books, a set of the works of Robert Louis Stevenson, were a wedding present for her old school friend, now recovered in health, whose imminent marriage provoked an outpouring of intensely felt nostalgia on Sybil's part.

'How gloriously happy you must be! I wish I were going to sleep with you the night before the wedding, as you did with me – do you remember? We always understand each other, don't we darling? It's wonderful to think what the years have brought for us both – such different sorts of lives we've had, and yet we haven't been less friends, but even closer. I was having lunch at a little restaurant today, and in the middle I went off into fits of laughter – Lewis, very perturbed, demanded in a stentorian aside, What on earth is the matter? – I felt so foolish because I was just thinking about drilling at school, when I used to make up waltzes for the bending exercises and fancy them hugely, until I saw you in convulsions because they were such silly tunes – do you remember? We *were* jokes at school. I just feel inclined now for a good talk and laugh over all the old days.'

Kitty's wedding also prompted her to brood on her own marriage. 'Men *won't* see to their own selves,' she complained. 'Really one has to be mother and everything when one marries, and it's queer the way a woman has all the maternal feelings for the man she loves just as if he were a little child, isn't it?' Her sentiments give an early glimpse into the nature of her relationship with Lewis, hinting at his lack of interest in his appearance, and her reluctance to mother him. Another difficulty was what Lewis called her 'father-fixation', which Sybil admitted made life hard for him.

As usual she filled every hour of the day. 'I am just in the middle of learning Pompilia for *The Ring and the Book* – a gigantic task I set myself for Lent – I am truly glad I'm doing it. She's the most beautiful character I've ever studied, because one makes all characters from within oneself, and she has taught me such a lot.' But she was unhappy to be cut off from friends and family, and sad that while Kitty could see John, she herself could not. 'I wish very much we were going to stay in England, there is nothing like one's own land after all, but other things have to be considered, don't they? I'm glad you saw my little darling and liked him so. He *must* be such a pet.'

Lewis wrote to Murray: 'We are both terribly bored with the play, as we have hitherto had the good fortune to escape long-run work, but the money is certainly some slight compensation.' Sybil finally suggested the way out was for them to have another baby. An afternoon in a room in Dubuque in Iowa saw the plan put into action. Once her pregnancy was confirmed Sybil wrote to Frohman, explaining she would have to break her contract. To her surprise he offered her a new one to start after the baby was born, assuring her he could find her continuous work in New York so that she could have her children with her. This prompted further agonising discussions with Lewis before she turned down Frohman's offer.

A week later, while playing in Salt Lake City, they received a letter from Manchester. Iden Payne was leaving the Gaiety, ironically to work for Frohman in America; Miss Horniman offered the job of director to Lewis, with the promise of parts for Sybil when she was available. Delighted at the vindication of their decision, they accepted immediately. 'Now we're out of it!'

Sybil exclaimed. They returned to England in July, having been away for just over a year. John was nearly two, and didn't recognise his parents, preferring the company of his nurse: after a few minutes with them he would say 'Want Alice.' Sybil was understandably distressed.

9

The Gaiety Revisited

1912–1914

'I do not think she will go very far'
Allan Monkhouse, critic and playwright, on Sybil

Within days of their return from America Sybil and Lewis were off again to Manchester. They found a small semi-detached house at 106 King's Road, Sedgley Park, in the suburb of Heaton Park, and settled in there with John, his nurse and a cook. Lewis took over the Gaiety company, and directed no less than nine productions before Christmas. It was hard work, but with his great appetite for it very much to his taste.

Sybil found time during her pregnancy to arrange some Beethoven sonatas as incidental music for his boisterous and successful production of *Twelfth Night*. Olivia was played by Eileen, who had recently joined the company, and was with Sybil when her second son Christopher – dubbed 'the broken contract baby' – was born on 20 January 1912. A fortnight later Lewis took a Gaiety company for a six-week season in Canada, where they staged 11 plays from the repertoire, plus *Man and Superman*. It was a formidable task and Lewis, away from Sybil for the first time since their marriage, had a brief, passionate affair with Edyth Goodall.

A lively, handsome 30-year-old Manchester actress, she was playing Candida, and was later to play the title-role in the first London performance of *Mrs Warren's Profession*. She too was a socialist, her London home later becoming the base for the Romney Street Group, a forum for non-Christian socialists. Whether the affair was driven by politics, sex, loneliness, or a combination of all three, is a matter of conjecture. Lewis' biographer Diana Devlin, his and Sybil's granddaughter, believes 'Sybil felt guilty about sex, about not having been responsive enough to Lewis. The impression one

got was that she liked sex for having babies, but was never particularly interested otherwise – which is why he strayed.' When Sybil found out about the
affair she was deeply upset, so that when he returned from Canada in April
'emotions were fairly high', but there was little time 'to begin straightening
things out' before Lewis plunged into the next production. Lewis in turn felt
exceedingly guilty, and continued to be so for a long time.

Annie Horniman was staging a seven-week London season of fifteen
plays at the Coronet in Notting Hill, on the strict repertory basis of a changed
programme each night. The critics were impressed: Herbert Farjeon called it
'the finest all-round little band of actors we have seen in London for many
a day', adding that 'while they do not possess the poetical imagination of
the Abbey Theatre Players they certainly exceed them in versatility'. Calling
for other repertory theatres to be established, he suggested that seeing these
plays was 'a liberal education in the art of acting and a complete exposition of
the inefficiency of our present system'. Shaw wrote to Miss Horniman: 'Your
shadow grows and grows across these islands.'

Although Sybil enjoyed being a mother, she was bored with domesticity,
and desperate to be working with the company. Her chance came in June
when she appeared in *Hindle Wakes* by Stanley Houghton, a Lancashire businessman, and one of the local writers Annie Horniman encouraged. Directed
by Lewis, the play caused an uproar. The plot centred on Fanny, a mill girl,
who goes off for a weekend with Alan, her employer's son, and then refuses
to marry him, considering their jaunt no more than 'a lark'. It ends with
her leaving home and declaring both her economic and social independence. With its echoes of Nora's defiant exit in Ibsen's *A Doll's House*, the
play was considered daring for the time, and became the most discussed in
London. In the press and the pulpit, and among the theatre-going public,
arguments about Fanny's behaviour and the issue of double standards for men
and women raged for weeks, and provoked some extreme opinions.

'The play produced in me the sensation as if someone had spat in my face,'
one disgusted playgoer wrote. 'Toleration of such a character in a London
play is one of the most sinister symptoms of social illness that have arisen in
my lifetime.' The critic of the *Referee*, criticising a scene where the possibility
of Fanny being pregnant is raised, wrote: 'To talk of such things familiarly
and without restraint, if persisted in on the stage, must inevitably tend to the
degradation of public manners.' Local-authority watch committees registered
their disapproval, while the vice-chancellor of Oxford University declared

the theatre where it was later staged on tour to be out of bounds to undergraduates. Posters appeared in the London Underground carrying the slogan 'Should Fanny marry Alan?' The furore was a reflection of the continuing debate about women's suffrage.

The play was first given two performances by the Stage Society at the Aldwych, then brought in to the Coronet season. Its success – the *Graphic* headlined it 'The Play with the Tightest Grip in London' – brought an immediate transfer to the Playhouse in the West End, after which it moved to the Court. While the public was fiercely divided on the moral issues it raised, the critics were almost unanimous in their praise, especially of the ensemble acting: the *Pall Mall Gazette* noted 'its repose, its truth to type, its mastery of art and its concealment of it…a rare joy in a London theatre these days'. Alan was played by J V Bryant, Fanny by Edyth Goodall, while Sybil was cast as Beatrice, Alan's wronged fiancée. The parallels between the stage story and Lewis' affair with his leading lady must have made this a difficult experience for Sybil. Whatever her feelings, she gained good notices: the *Evening News* observed that she 'played with an admirable reticence, sincerity and intensity of feeling'. In a company setting new standards of excellence, she was learning more about the arts of restraint and subtlety.

For the new Gaiety season Lewis was keen for her to have more opportunity to make her mark. She now shared the leading parts with Irene Rooke, whose husband Milton Rosmer became the new leading man. Eileen had moved across to the repertory company at the Liverpool Playhouse, now run by Dean, where she was to play over ninety parts in the next five years. Russell, having completed a world tour in *Mr Wu* with Matheson Lang, joined the Gaiety company. Although the emphasis was on the ensemble, the actors were not all paid the same; Sybil was probably getting something close to the top salary of £12 a week, as opposed to £3 for the lowest paid. Rehearsals were never more than two weeks for each production, which put a heavy onus on the actors, especially as dress rehearsals often went on into the night. Under Lewis' direction they were marked by squalls of Welsh fury. Often violently impatient, he would bark and roar at his actors, some of whom retaliated. Foremost among them was Sybil: their arguments were verbally violent, with neither wanting to give way. If he vented his anger on others, she would act as peace-maker or confront him with his behaviour, which would generally result in an apology to his victims.

Despite these outbursts, his method, unlike Iden Payne's more intuitive approach, was generally clear and workmanlike, if somewhat authoritarian. Like Poel, he would insist on first spending a lot of time round the table 'to get the general musical interpretation of the play right', an approach disliked by many actors, who felt their ideas only came once they were on their feet. His admiration for Poel was underlined by his and Sybil's presence at a dinner given in his honour that autumn in London, with Ellen Terry, Lillah MacCarthy and Nigel Playfair among the guests, and Shaw in a speech describing Poel as 'one of the greatest and finest influences on the English theatre'.

While in London they saw Barker's production at the Savoy of *The Winter's Tale*. Together with the *Twelfth Night* and *A Midsummer Night's Dream* which followed, this landmark production subverted the conventional notions of staging Shakespeare. Barker did away with the elaborate scenery, the shortened text and the ponderous verse-speaking that characterised Tree's productions. Instead he offered simple but beautiful sets, and uncut texts spoken with speed and vigour. Such ideas would influence generations of directors, including Lewis. Henry Ainley's Leontes in *The Winter's Tale* moved Sybil greatly. 'I was in sobs, it was out of this world,' she recalled. 'Ainley had a very classical face, a really lovely voice, and beautiful eyes. He was the perfect instrument for a mind like Barker's. It was an electrifying moment. I could have screamed, jumped in the air, grown ten feet tall. It was a feeling of exultation – a liberation.'

Back in Manchester she further extended her range. She repeated her roles in *The Charity That Began at Home* and *Prunella*, and appeared in the one-act play *The Question*, providing, according to Montague, 'good sincere acting'. He also praised her work in Harold Brighouse's *The Polygon*, in which she 'had shadows to grasp and grasped very respectable handfuls of them'. She increased her knowledge of Shaw by playing Judith Anderson in *The Devil's Disciple*, a difficult part which Allan Monkhouse felt she dealt with skilfully. She produced a fine piece of acting as the vigorous and idealistic young heroine Renie Dalrymple in George Calderón's *Revolt*, a prophetic play about a scientist who discovers how to split the atom. She also had roles in Galsworthy's *The Pigeon*, a fantasy about the futility of charity administered by the rich, and Harold Chapin's *Elaine*, a witty, gently satirical comedy about attitudes to love and money in marriage. At Christmas she was cast as the romantic but sensible Julia in Sheridan's *The Rivals*, in which, according to the *Courier*, the cast 'very nearly succeeded – but not quite – in being perfectly artificial'.

In May 1913 Annie Horniman and Lewis organised a London season at the Court of five plays from their repertoire. One of these was *The Whispering Well*, a morality play about avarice by the socialist journalist Frank H Rose. A kind of Lancashire version of the Faust legend mixed with *A Christmas Carol*, it was described by the *Morning Post* as 'a queer jumble of fairy-tale, folklore, symbolic morality and realistic irony'. With Russell cast as The Spirit of Desire, Sybil had a tricky, chameleon-like part as the wife. She was praised by the critics, but also warned: the *Observer* noted: 'Miss Sybil Thorndike showed a real power of acting (though a power that needs restraining and pruning)', while *The Times* observed that 'if she not infrequently overdid it, she showed a clear power of transforming herself by hearing and facial expression from good wife to shrew, from shrew to slut, from slut to pointed baggage, and back again to good wife'.

It was her playing of the title-role in St John Ervine's *Jane Clegg* that started the critics talking about her as a new tragic actress in the making. In some respects a middle-class version of *Hindle Wakes*, the play was a grim, realistic tale of a long-suffering wife, who makes a bid for independence from her lying, philandering husband after inheriting a small legacy. 'It doesn't seem right to have a mind and not use it,' Jane says, reflecting the voice of protest of the women's movement of which Sybil was a part. Both in rehearsals and at home Sybil and Lewis had frequent violent clashes, ostensibly about her acting style, but perhaps also in response to Lewis' infidelity. Through a mixture of guidance and bullying he tried to persuade her to do less, while she indignantly argued the case for identifying emotionally with her character. It was not to be the first such conflict.

Lewis seems to have won the day, for Sybil was widely praised for her restrained, harrowing performance, considered the finest of her career so far. When she had given it first in Manchester, Monkhouse had written: 'The stern logic of her character with its underlying and repressed emotion was given with perfect understanding and discretion by Miss Thorndike. She never stressed a note unduly, she maintained the type with unfailing fidelity: it would not be easy to recall a piece of acting at the Gaiety more austerely right in the expression.' In London the eminent critic Desmond MacCarthy observed: 'She hardly raises her eyes during the three acts, but when she does, it is with tremendous effect.' Ervine, taking a curtain call at the first night, said the credit for the play's success was mostly down to Sybil. But the *Observer* critic warned: 'In watching her through several parts, one seems to feel that her assumptions of character, though full of cleverness, lack to some extent conviction and depth.'

During the season, invited by Beerbohm Tree to a supper party at His Majesty's, she met Ellen Terry, who congratulated her on being 'married to that nice clever boy Lewis Casson'. He and Sybil had discussed his affair with Edyth Goodall and, according to Diana Devlin, 'established their marriage on a stronger footing than before'. But a small incident that occurred while they were at the first night of the Diaghilev Ballet's performance of Stravinsky's *The Rite of Spring* in London that summer suggests it was still in a volatile state. Excited by the passionate music and dancing, Sybil reflected: 'If Lewis doesn't go for this, it's the end for us. It's too important to disagree about.' But he was as exhilarated as she was.

Back in Manchester she wrote enthusiastically to a friend: 'We're having such an interesting season here. We've a new Eden Phillpotts next week, *The Shadow* – beautiful writing! – a new Elizabeth Baker – and then *Julius Caesar*, which we are all very excited about. Lots more too – it is jolly work here, one never gets bored with existence for a moment.' Yet she seemed weary of the tragic and realistic nature of so many of the plays: 'I'm tired of them rather, aren't you? One longs for Shakespeare.' She did however have another chance to play Candida, with Lewis as Marchbanks.

Milton Rosmer and Irene Rooke had now left the company, leaving the way clear for Sybil to take on more leading roles. Elizabeth Baker's family drama *The Price of Thomas Scott* was a disappointment, leading the *Manchester Guardian* to accuse the Gaiety of having fallen into 'rather a dreary realistic rut'. Agate later wrote: 'Time after time the curtain would go up on a Welsh dresser and a kitchen table, with Sybil weeping in frustration. Sometimes the dresser would be to the left, sometimes to the right. But the table and Sybil were constant.' He also recalled: 'What an indifferent actress she was, mournfully tending the flame of Repertory in Manchester....How she moaned and wailed, and waved her thin arms like some animated hat-stand.' Yet this was not his view at the time: after seeing her in *The Silver Box* he wrote: 'Miss Thorndike has lately made enormous strides in the scope and variety of her art.'

Before *The Shadow* was performed, its novelist author Eden Phillpotts wrote to Miss Horniman: 'I make bold to believe I have written a big part for a woman, but belike I am wrong.' He wasn't. A story of passion and crime among working people set on Phillpotts' native Dartmoor, which used dialect as the medium, the play had echoes of Hardy. It gave Sybil a powerful, emotional role: the *Manchester Guardian* found her performance 'moving in its intensity, and in the naturalness of its transition from gaiety to sorrow to terror'. According to Russell, offstage the part 'took a fearful hold on her', which suggests Lewis' restraining was crucial. Forty years later Phillpotts recalled her 'wondrous versatility' at this moment: 'I marked her rare sense of humour in a comic part she was just then playing at night, and watched her rehearsing by day a stricken heroine with every apt and poignant emotion, mien and gesture, even to the expression on her face and the woe in her voice.' Allan Monkhouse was less enthusiastic, writing to Agate: 'Thorndike is all right for Galsworthy's Mrs Barthwick, St John Ervine's Jane Clegg and the more depressing women in my own plays. But I do not think she will go very far.'

Lewis later described Miss Horniman as 'a difficult woman, full of high ideals in the theatre and much generosity, but subject to sudden and unpredictable prejudices and caprices'. His next production provoked a serious dispute between the two of them. Shakespeare was popular at the Gaiety, and there had been murmurings that no play of his had been done for a while. Lewis decided, with Miss Horniman's agreement, to stage two experimental productions: *Julius Caesar* for two weeks, with Sybil playing Portia and he taking on Brutus, followed by *The Tempest*. Influenced by Poel and Barker, he decided to do them uncut, to use an apron stage, and use lighting from the front, a revolutionary move. To enable the action to be continuous he commissioned a set for *Julius Caesar* which consisted of permanent arches, pillars and steps in the spirit of Edward Gordon Craig, whose iconoclastic *On the Art of the Theatre* had just been published.

Many critics applauded his innovations: Montague's review was 'a whoop of joy', while the *Courier* thought it 'one of the greatest things the Gaiety has done'. But there was an outcry from the more traditional critics and the conservative elements in the Manchester audience. More crucially, Miss Horniman disliked the concept, though she had made no criticisms during rehearsals. The morning after the first night she told Lewis the production was 'freakish', 'Gordon Craigish' and self-indulgent, an example of experiment for experiment's sake. Her pejorative use of Craig's name was no surprise: three years before, the famous designer had arrogantly attacked women in general and her in particular, advising her to 'learn that woman is nothing but a selfish accident drifting aimlessly or to the bad without the guiding influence of a man'.

The argument with Lewis reached boiling point: she cancelled his planned production of *The Tempest*, and he immediately resigned in protest, though he agreed to stay until Christmas. He and Sybil continued with the company, in revivals of *Jane Clegg*, *The Silver Box* and *The Shadow*, and in Arnold Bennett's *What the Public Wants*. At a large farewell dinner at the Midland Hotel, Lewis was asked to reply to the usual polite speeches. He let loose a tirade, attacking the people of Manchester for being smug, conservative and failing to support their theatre. 'Manchester hadn't founded it, didn't work for it, and didn't pay for it,' he thundered. In the silence that followed his speech Sybil burst out laughing, and others followed suit. According to Russell, who was present, this intervention 'healed the deadly stings which Lewis had caused' and 'made everybody agree that the attack was more than justified'.

In the *Manchester Guardian* Agate praised Miss Horniman and her directors for 'the noblest, the best-sustained and most consistent theatrical achievement that this city has ever known'. Lewis' work at the Gaiety had revealed him to be a dedicated, skilled and meticulous director. It was later said of him that 'he gave the company everything that could be given by intelligence, technique and sincerity not raised to the power of genius'. In a farewell address to the Manchester Playgoers' Club, in which he complained about the dearth of 'intellectual plays of a light character' available to a theatre outside London, he referred to two kinds of actors: those who used the author to exploit their own personality, and those who used their personality to serve the author. Sybil clearly fell into the second category: her second spell at the Gaiety had increased her versatility, and deepened her belief in the importance of a repertory theatre. She now appeared for the first time in *Who's Who in the Theatre*.

During those final weeks in Manchester she discovered she was pregnant again. The baby was conceived before Lewis' row with Miss Horniman, so it seems that there was no ulterior motive. Returning to London, they were found a place to live by Sybil's mother, a house she had bought at 40 Bessborough Street in Pimlico, near Vauxhall Bridge and close to the vicarage. She rented out the top floor to her widowed sister-in-law, and gave Sybil and her family the use of the rest of the house. Sybil's father had become good friends with Father Gerard Olivier, who was vicar of another Pimlico church, St Saviour's, in the neighbouring parish, and who had a son called Laurence. 'They were great friends, and thought alike in church matters,' Sybil recalled. The two families often mixed, and Eileen would take the baby Laurence out in his pram. Before long, his life would begin to intertwine with Sybil's.

The imminent arrival of a third child made it vital, in an increasingly crowded profession, for Lewis to find work. Early in 1914 he was offered a temporary job as artistic director of the Scottish Repertory Theatre at the Royalty, Glasgow, the first provincial theatre to follow the Gaiety down the repertory path. There he directed twenty-one plays, including Shaw's *Man and Superman*, in which he played the leading role of John Tanner. Apart from brief weekend visits, he and Sybil were apart. 'It's horrid without Lewis,' she wrote to Lillah McCarthy. 'He's having a most successful time, which is a comfort, tho' it's very popular stuff! I've a baby coming in May, so I'm having a fairly exciting time – it's quite a nice rest all the same.' Her 'rest' consisted of learning new parts, so she could return to work as soon as possible; playing Bach for hours a day; and in between looking after her boys.

The Glasgow season enhanced Lewis' reputation as a director. In April he came home and, when the midwife failed to arrive in time, was able to assist Sybil with the birth of their daughter Mary on 22 May. Lewis took the boys in his old Ford car down to Dymchurch in Kent, where they were looked after by Alice Pearce until Sybil and Mary were able to join them. They stayed in one of two tiny, primitive adjoining cottages bought by Sybil's mother, situated behind the sea-wall in the wide bay between Dungeness and Folkestone. Sybil spent the time playing with her children, and teaching the boys to swim. 'Day after day,' John remembered, 'she and I used to go out on to the wonderful sandy beach and build exciting castles and elaborate irrigation systems. Or, best of all, we would sit together on the shingle under the sea-wall, while we played a game, which she had invented, called Making Plans. It consisted of making plans for a ship, of which she and I were to be the owners. We would talk for hours about it.'

That summer Sybil was surrounded by her family. Nearby in the lifeboat house, Russell was writing *Dr Syn*, the first of his novels in the series about smuggling in Romney Marsh, which he and Sybil had first talked of in America ten years before. After her children were in bed he would come over to the cottage, and by the light of an oil lamp read his day's work to her. The other cottage was occupied by her parents, and occasionally by Eileen and Frank. Good-looking, popular, with an excellent voice, Frank was already proving a skilful actor of considerable spirit. He had spent a year training at the Central School, where Elsie Fogerty believed he would become 'one of our most brilliant young players', and had progressed from small parts for the Sunday societies to acting in farces, burlesques and straight plays.

Lewis undertook a few minor productions for the Stage Society in London to bring in some money, but was able to come down for long weekends. He and Sybil would explore the little churches dotted about the marsh, and tour Kent in their ramshackle Ford (named 'Hindle Wakes' after their Gaiety success). Sitting on the sea-wall, they also played their version of Making Plans. They talked of what they might do if Barker started a repertory theatre. Lewis wondered whether to revive an earlier plan, to visit Europe and see the theatrical experiments being carried out by Max Reinhardt in Germany and Stanislavsky in Russia. They also talked about the possibility of risking their savings and getting someone to back them in a management venture in London, in which Russell too would be involved.

But in August their dreams, like everyone else's, were rudely interrupted.

10

The Old Vic and Lilian Baylis

1914–1916

'There's a strange woman running a theatre in the Waterloo Road; you'd
find her exciting, Syb, because you're as mad as she is'
Letter from Ben Greet

Sybil and Lewis were in Dymchurch on 28 June 1914 when the Archduke
Franz Ferdinand was assassinated in Sarajevo. A few days later, standing
on the beach looking across to France just thirty miles away, Lewis announced:
'There's going to be war in Europe.' According to Russell, Sybil's instant reply
was: 'Thank God you're not a soldier then.' The war was to bring tragedy and
hardship to her and her family, but prove a rich and rewarding period in her
development as an actress.

She and her family moved back to Pimlico just as war was declared on
4 August. The days that followed were marked by widespread fervour, with
crowds cheering, waving flags, riding on taxi roofs and singing patriotic songs,
as thousands of soldiers said goodbye to their families. In the theatre new
productions were suspended and old ones closed, leaving Sybil, Lewis and
thousands of others unemployed. On 6 August Lord Kitchener issued the call
to arms, 'Your King and Country Need You'. Russell had joined the Westminster Dragoons the previous year, and Frank, now 20, enlisted in the same
regiment, but without telling the family.

Within three weeks the brothers had set sail in high spirits for the Middle
East. Sybil's father wanted to enlist, but at 60 was barred from doing so, even
as a chaplain. Lewis meanwhile was in a dilemma. As a socialist he opposed
the idea of war, and sympathised with the anti-war elements in the Labour
Party, led by Keir Hardie. He was also attracted to the idealistic pacifism
of the Neutrality Committee, which included Gilbert Murray and Ramsay
MacDonald. But he also felt it his duty to defend his country. On the day he

and Sybil saw Russell and Frank off, he told Sybil that he had to join up, in what he hoped would be 'a war to finish war for ever'.

Sybil was naturally unhappy: 'I hated, hated the thought of his fighting Germans, because I'd worked with German musicians, and had such lovely friendships with people of that country,' she later wrote. 'It seemed a most hideous and wretched betrayal of that friendship.' But having discussed the matter with her parents, who supported Lewis' view and promised to look after Sybil and the children, she reluctantly gave way. While she opposed the war, she was not yet a full-blooded pacifist, believing that 'this country is going to smash the beastly engine of war and make a new world, something bigger and better than has ever been known before'.

Although the age-limit for recruitment had been raised to thirty-five, Lewis still had to slice four years off his age in order to join the Army Service Corps in St Alban's, where he was soon fully occupied. 'He is driving a motor lorry and being a cook and doing stews, and washing up, and working from 4.15am all the livelong day,' Sybil told a Manchester friend in October. 'I believe he is quite enjoying himself – he certainly is developing unsuspected talents!' But the war was now impinging on her life too, as wounded soldiers and Belgian refugees poured into London. 'Isn't this war awful? One really cannot believe all the tragedy and frightfulness is true, but when one sees the wounded here in London it does suddenly come home.'

The house in Bessborough Street echoed to the sound of troops marching over Vauxhall Bridge on their way to Waterloo and France. John and Christopher dressed up as soldiers, Sybil playing 'Tipperary' and 'The British Grenadiers' on the piano as they marched about. 'We all felt thrilled with lumps in our throats, and firm resolution in our hearts,' she recalled. She told her children a little about the Germans, who were 'against us', but never suggested they should hate the enemy. She argued, according to Russell, that 'England ought to set an example to other nations, because that's what England's for'. Like many others, she believed England was somehow morally superior to other nations.

One day she received a letter from Ben Greet, who had been brought in to direct a few Shakespeare plays at the Royal Victoria Hall, popularly known as the 'Old Vic'. A former music-hall, once described by the writer Charles Kingsley as 'a licensed pit of darkness', it was located in a working-class district near Waterloo Station with a reputation for vice and violence. Opposite the theatre was a gin palace, a dangerous place on a Saturday night, when no actress was allowed to leave without a male escort. Robert Atkins, who was soon to join the company, recalled: 'Many a murderous quarrel started up when the naptha lamps were flaring and smoking above the market stalls in the New Cut and the Lower Marsh.'

The theatre aimed to provide entertainments 'suited for the recreation and instruction of the poorer classes', at prices 'as will make them available to artisans and labourers'. The person behind this attempt to bring Shakespeare and opera to the people was Lilian Baylis, an eccentric, motherly woman, driven by a belief that God had chosen her for this task. People who knew her later described her variously as looking and behaving like 'a seaside landlady', 'a charwoman', 'a schoolmarm' or 'a parish visitor'. Dumpy, dowdy and plain, with a slight squint and a drooping mouth – probably the result of Bell's palsy – her rasping voice mixed the tones of south London with those of her native South Africa. She could be bossy, brusque and tactless, and often crushing in her criticisms. Yet she was shrewd and practical, loyal to her directors, and protective of her actors, whom she called 'my boys and girls'. Though she was reputed never to have read a play right through, or watched a performance to the end, she had a working knowledge of Shakespeare, and a rough, commonsense feeling for his characters. Her method of selecting actors was idiosyncratic: if a name came to her while she was taking communion, he or she would be hired, since God had spoken. He also frequently spoke about salaries, many a frustrated actor being told that He had advised against granting them an increase.

Having staged a production of *The Tempest*, Greet wrote to Sybil: 'There's a strange woman running a theatre in the Waterloo Road; you'd find her exciting, Syb, because you're as mad as she is.' He then invited her at short notice to join the scratch company. '*Comedy of Errors* week after next – you play Adriana; I've told them you'd be wonderful, though I don't think you'll really be very good. You always bounce too much....Still you'll like Lilian Baylis, she's got ideals, and don't tell her you've not played the part before because she says she wants the best and she's going to get it.' Sybil had never been to the Old Vic, nor heard of Lilian Baylis. She was now thirty-two but, despite her seasons at the Gaiety and her occasional West End appearances, she was certainly not a star. She accepted immediately. She would be paid ten shillings a show, a small but useful sum to which, once Lewis was sent to France, she could add her 'soldier's separation allowance', and the 25 shillings he would send home.

The actress Nora Nicholson remembered her arrival, 'rather breathless, rather wind-blown, and bringing with her a sense of good health, good humour, and above all goodness'. Lilian Baylis greeted her in characteristically blunt fashion: 'Well, you won't get much pay, but you like the work, don't you,' she said. 'And if your husband's in the army you'd better be doing decent work too – good for you and the children. Your father's a priest, isn't he? Church and stage – same thing – should be!' Sybil was intrigued: this extraordinary woman didn't seem to care whether she could act or not. She wrote to Russell, now in Egypt: 'She is the most original woman I've ever met. Simply dying to play her. She'd be a gorgeous part. She's not a bit like a theatrical manager. Much too keen on the "People", and really the whole thing promises to be great fun. I shall love working for her as she's one of those people who just make you do things. It's rotten pay, but anything is a godsend in these times, and we all eat such a lot. At the Vic we live on coffee and buns. There's no time for anything else, and I find them very nourishing.'

Lilian Baylis believed that 'great music and great drama at cheap prices are very real necessities in the life of the people'. She kept prices low so even the poorest could afford seats. Conditions were primitive, as Robert Atkins recalled: 'After theatres such as His Majesty's and other lovely ones I had known, the ramshackle disinfectant-breathing fit-up at the Vic struck a chill.' The stage and auditorium were lit by gas; there was virtually no wardrobe, costumes had to be shared with the opera company; the sets were makeshift, and the same décor was used for each play. Nora Nicholson recalled: 'Sybil and I shared an apology for a dressing-room where we chatted and joked and jostled each other as we dressed elbow to elbow.' The acoustics were far from ideal: the actors' words were often drowned out by 'noises off', either from the canteen at the back of the pit, or the market in the New Cut. Greet observed: 'I defy everyone to hear everything in any place built in the middle of a populous and busy thoroughfare.'

During that first season of combined opera and Shakespeare, the Old Vic staged sixteen operas and sixteen plays: thirteen by Shakespeare, plus *The School for Scandal*, *She Stoops to Conquer* and *King René's Daughter*. There was a different play each week, with four or five performances weekly, the other nights being devoted to opera. It was a demanding regime for the actors: Henry Kendall, who was taken on with no Shakespearean experience, had to play thirty parts in nine months. Sybil shared the leading parts with Estelle Stead – 'a shocker of an actress, but she had the money,' she recalled – and otherwise played 'as cast'.

As the opera company needed the stage, rehearsals took place in odd corners of the theatre such as the saloon. During breaks Sybil and her fellow-actors frequented Pearce and Plenty, the small, sawdust-strewn eating-house at the front of the building, where they could enjoy a steak for fourpence, or a pint of tea with a slab of bread and butter for twopence. At other times they ventured out to the nearby Express Dairy, or to Wagner's Eating House, 'where for a bob you could get a meal to last three days,' Sybil remembered. But there were other sources of food. Lilian Baylis liked to cook her meals on a gas ring in the box by the prompt corner; often towards the end of a matinee the smell of sausages, bacon or kippers would reach the audience's nostrils. Some days she would catch the ever-hungry Sybil in the wings: 'I'm having steak and tomatoes afterwards,' she would say. 'You'd better have it too – must feed you up.'

Lilian Baylis believed that 'the theatre is our greatest power for good or evil', a philosophy that Sybil was soon to embrace herself. At first she thought her even odder than the eccentric Annie Horniman. 'She's an absolute scream,' she told Russell. 'She uses old-fashioned slang – words like "bounders" and "mucky". Poor old BG doesn't know what to make of her sometimes, especially when she used "mucky" in connection with Shakespeare…. She runs the place exactly like we've seen people organise parish rooms. She looks like a church worker, and is one. She's High Church, untidy, works like a nigger, and counts the "takings of the house" as a church worker as if it were an offertory. I'm longing for you to meet her.'

Because the Old Vic had yet to attract the critics, there is no record of how much bounce or other qualities Sybil showed in her debut. But she made a good enough impression to be asked to stay on. After playing Adriana she appeared in *The Taming of the Shrew, Twelfth Night*, as Nerissa in *The Merchant of Venice*, and as Hermia in *A Midsummer Night's Dream*. She had been Helena in the *Dream* in America, and not enjoyed the role. But seeing Lillah McCarthy play her in Barker's Savoy production had changed her view, and she was soon to revert to it: 'I've always hated Helena before, she's always been made such an old thing, and just dull and talky,' she wrote to the actress. 'Yours was young and made one feel fresh and springy and you looked so beautiful. The whole thing made me happy somehow.'

Early in 1915 Greet suggested she play Lady Macbeth opposite Fisher White. This was a significant moment: at last she was to play a big tragic role. Yet the idea of playing Lady Macbeth initially appalled her: she felt she had nothing of her 'foulness'. But Lilian Baylis, who was no Shakespearean scholar but often had shrewd insights into character, suggested Lady Macbeth's love for her husband was the key. 'If it wasn't that you go to communion, I daresay you'd do all sorts of wicked things to help Lewis!' she said. This idea, Sybil recalled, got her started: 'I thought of it through Lewis, and through doing things for the children, and being willing to do any awful thing as long as they were all right.'

Greet wanted her to play Lady Macbeth as totally evil, as if, Sybil said, she had 'horrible sparkles shooting out of her eyes'. She resisted this melodramatic interpretation, taking the unexpected line that Lady Macbeth was not a wicked woman, but just 'very like all women who are quiet and violent and want the best for the one they love, and despise anyone who gets in their way'. She had many arguments with Greet, including one about the sleep-walking scene: Greet wanted her to wake during it, but Sybil thought this wrong. 'Oh! how I argued, and how miserable I was,' she recalled. 'She couldn't have woken up, I knew she couldn't.' She did as Greet wanted, and was rewarded when, after three performances, he admitted he was wrong.

Nora Nicholson thought her performance a fine one: 'You are a great actress!' she told Sybil. But in her own eyes, and apparently those of certain critics, it was a failure. 'Played Lady Macbeth last night,' she told Russell. 'Don't laugh. I was too appalling. The critics that I read all said I was unsuited to tragedy as my voice is too light and my features too small. That's rather depressing, isn't it? Never mind, something's got to be done about it, and I mean to jolly well swot until they do think me suitable.' She admitted she found tragedy difficult 'because it's so much larger than real life. I suppose real comedy is too, but one can enjoy quite small performances of comedy, but tragedy is either tragic, with a big T, or it's nothing. If it's pathetic, it's awful. I simply loathe pathos, Russ, it's so soft and weak. Tragedy has fight.' Though she loved the part, she confessed that 'my performance so far is nothing like her'.

Sometimes with *Macbeth* the fight was offstage. During a matinee, Lilian Baylis and Greet were seen to be quarrelling violently in the wings, arguing so loudly that the audience could hear them. Robert Atkins remembers how Macbeth's line 'How is't with me, when every noise appals me?' got an unexpected laugh. 'At that moment we seemed to be living in an earthquake. Sybil's voice joined in, imploring them to keep quiet.' Afterwards she was so upset she actually swore at Greet.

On the day that she opened in *Macbeth* Lewis, now a sergeant, left for the Front. 'I'm thankful I'm doing tragedy, as it will relieve my feelings,' Sybil wrote to Russell. When the war began people had said it would be over by Christmas. But after the First Battle of Ypres in October 1914, the unremitting trench warfare began. Lewis wrote to her every day. At Christmas the opposing soldiers met in no-man's-land in a bizarre exchange of presents. A few weeks later, walking down the Waterloo Road with Nora Nicholson, Sybil said: 'Nick, I believe I'm going to have another baby.' It was, she noted cryptically, 'Lady Macbeth that did it.' Tackled later by her son John as to why, when they were so hard up, she and Lewis had conceived a fourth child, she replied: 'It was Lewis' last night before going to France.' Like millions of others during a war that was to bring tragedy to so many, she thought she might be seeing him for the last time. It was in fact eight months before he came home on leave.

She continued at the Old Vic until April, playing Rosalind in *As You Like It*, Perdita in *The Winter's Tale* and Emilia in *Othello*. Audiences at first were scanty: when *Hamlet* was first staged the takings amounted to a mere £2, and some nights *Macbeth* was performed to an audience of less than a dozen. Sybil remembered an evening 'when about five people were in the pit and three boys and an orange in the gallery'; it was a time when 'casualty lists were long and people had heavy hearts'. Some days Lilian Baylis would say, 'Only a handful in front, dears. Would you like me to give them their money back and all go home?' But, Sybil recalled, 'a look in her eyes made us realise that she'd kill us outright unless we said, "Let's ring up!"' Meanwhile word was spreading of a talented and powerful actress in the Waterloo Road. Audience numbers began to improve, and the 'Standing Room Only' notices went up.

The work was demanding: usually there were only five rehearsals for each play. Greet's productions were plain, simple and speedy. He used the traditional bowdlerised and censored versions of the plays, and cut the text heavily, feeling the full texts were beyond the capacity of the Vic's audiences. Simplicity was forced on him: he had no more than £2 for the production expenses of each play. His method of acting, and also directing, was broad and often crude, but without affectation. He had no time for new theories, scholarly discussions or gimmicks. When directing he would sit in the stalls with a bag of sweets, giving occasional instructions. According to Robert Atkins, his main exhortations were 'Get on with it!' and 'I want sincerity,' while his greatest term of praise was 'Not too bad'.

One of his favourite plays was *Everyman*, in which Sybil played the title-role. It moved her tremendously, and sometimes caused her to shed tears on stage. After one performance Lilian Baylis said: 'That's right, I like to see you have a good cry; you mustn't cry because Lewis and all the other dear boys are fighting, we none of us must – but you can let it out when you are Everyman, and let's hope some of the poor things in the audience are having a good cry too.' As she was to do increasingly, Sybil used acting as an outlet for her strong, often violent emotions.

Throughout the war the Old Vic was the only London theatre to stage a continuous programme of Shakespeare and the classics. Writing to Mrs Patrick Campbell after Sybil's first season, Shaw noted that the Old Vic 'seems to be at the centre of the dramatic movement nowadays'. Good plays had virtually disappeared: Barrie's *Dear Brutus* was one of the few serious ones to emerge. The West End was given over mainly to propaganda spy stories such as *The Female Hun*, and to musicals, revues and thrillers. The popular successes were *Peg O' My Heart* with Laurette Taylor, *Chu Chin Chow*, *A Little Bit of Fluff*, and *The Bing Boys*, in which George Robey famously sang 'If you were the only girl in the world'. This, the managers believed, was the kind of escapist fare audiences, especially the troops, needed. But Lilian Baylis believed many people, including the troops, might want more. So she allowed servicemen in at half price, and wounded soldiers and refugees from allied countries in free.

Sybil was fully in agreement with her ideals. Theatre, she believed, should not be mere entertainment or escapism; it should make people more aware, more alive to their surroundings and to others, sending them back into real life with a heightened consciousness. 'The Old Vic got more than its share of soldiers on leave,' she wrote later, 'and one feels perhaps they found comfort and solace in beautiful words and beautiful ideas, and full-blooded human comedy, something that may have sent them back to their horrors with a vision and a faith, instead of a lulling drug which is all that a great many ask of the Theatre.' Many of the troops wrote to her, saying how helpful it had been to see their fears dramatised on the stage.

At the end of the season, when the Old Vic organised its first Shakespeare Birthday Festival, she played eight roles in a fortnight. The festival – she described it as 'a kind of stew after the joint and cold meat of the season' – quickly became an annual event. It included a programme of scenes from the plays, featuring many leading lights of the West End theatre, who would dash across the river in taxis to fit in a scene or two while appearing in shows in the West End. Once Mary Anderson, the great American-born beauty, came out of retirement to play Lady Macbeth in the sleep-walking scene, with Sybil in support as the Gentlewoman. She was able to watch Ellen Terry as Portia in scenes from *The Merchant of Venice* –'a glorious lovely person, all sunshine and beauty', she remembered, 'a new wondrous light seemed to shine from her, and the absolute truth that came with every word, her enunciation perfect'. Another year she saw her play Queen Katharine in *Henry VIII*: 'I shall never forget the glorious indignation with which she rose up to the cardinals.'

But she positively disliked another institution, the school matinees. They were hugely popular: in one week 4,000 children saw the production of *As You Like It*. Two seasons later, as many as 90,000 would attend the matinees. The actors were not keen on them, but they were the saviour of the Old Vic financially. Sybil approved in principle of introducing Shakespeare to the young, but hated the reality. 'How intensely we actors disliked them – and their fidgets,' she recalled. 'Some kind friend would occasionally provide the little darlings with bags of buns and sweets at the beginning of the perform-ance – give me a raid any time before this experience.'

Her pregnancy meant she had to miss *Julius Caesar*, the final produc-tion of the season. She moved down to Dymchurch, where gunfire could be heard across the Channel. She wrote daily to Lewis, as she did whenever they were separated. His letters to her, later lost, described the horrors of trench warfare, as well as the courage and self-sacrifice he witnessed. He was briefly on leave in August, after which she returned to London. But in September the Zeppelin airships continued to drop bombs on the city. Curiosity about these strange but beautiful machines gave way to fear and panic: traffic came to a standstill, anti-aircraft guns mounted on trucks tore through the streets, lights were extinguished. One Zeppelin flew over the Houses of Parliament near the Thorndikes' vicarage, and emptied its bombs on theatre-land.

Often Sybil had to wake her children in the night to take them down to the basement. 'She saw to it that we were never frightened by the bangs and the booms,' John recalled. 'She made us think of it as some sort of grown-up skylark.' In October the raids became more dangerous and Sybil's mother, fearing for the children's safety, found another country cottage, to which they were dispatched with Alice, and their other nursemaid Nellie. Situated on a farm in Kent, Grey Cottage (now demolished) stood in the middle of West

Kingsdown village, some twenty miles from London. The rent was half a crown a week, which even the impoverished Sybil could afford.

'The baby comes in a day or two,' Sybil wrote to a friend. 'I've sent the children to the country to get away from raids and am trying to let my flat because I can't afford it on war money.' Her second daughter Ann was born on 6 November 1915. The next day Lilian Baylis arrived, and asked how soon she could return to the company, where rehearsals for Hamlet had been held up. Sybil's protestations that her baby was three weeks late were brushed aside: that, her manager made clear, was Ann's fault, not hers. 'I took it from her because it was for the Old Vic, and never for herself,' Sybil explained later. Within a month she was back for her second season.

Edward Gordon Craig once said of his mother: 'I don't see how you can rock the cradle, rule the world, and play Ophelia perfectly, all in the day's work.' Sybil did her best to prove him wrong, playing Ophelia opposite Will Stack's Hamlet, with Robert Atkins as Claudius and Beatrice Wilson as Gertrude. It was the first time the company had staged *Hamlet* in its entirety. Sybil was, the *Era* stated, 'a sweet and pathetic Ophelia'. But though she was excited to be playing the part again, it was, she remembered, a tiring and trying time, 'rushing back and forth and feeding the baby – doing mad scenes – trying to get into dresses much too tight for me – Ben Greet at me again because I wasn't a sylph, and I laying the blame on the baby this time.'

During 1915 the casualties in France had been mounting in their thousands, and soon conscription was introduced. Sybil and Lewis suffered a loss in September when Lewis' brother Will was killed by a sniper during the bungled Battle of Loos, becoming one of its 50,000 casualties. The actor and play-wright Harold Chapin, in whose *The Marriage of Columbine* and *Elaine* Sybil had appeared, was killed at the same time. Sybil wrote a warm and consoling letter to his wife Calypso Valetta: 'Oh! Calypso, it seems sometimes it's not possible that he's had to give up his life with all his genius and loveableness…. The trouble and pain must be almost too much. I feel it dreadfully, and so does Lewis. Harold was one of the men he cared for really – he's not one to care deeply for a lot of friends, he's too reserved, but he loved Harold.'

In her second season she played an astonishing range of leading Shake-spearean parts, including Portia, Viola, Rosalind, Hermia, Perdita, Emilia, Beatrice in *Much Ado about Nothing*, Katharina in *The Taming of the Shrew*, Lady Anne in *Richard III*, Portia in *Julius Caesar*, Katharine in *Henry V*; she was also Everyman, Lydia Languish in *The Rivals*, and Kate Hardcastle in

She Stoops to Conquer. Considering her family circumstances, it was a staggering achievement, both mentally and physically. She would rise at six, bath the children and give them breakfast before going to rehearsal. She would rush back from the Vic to give them meals at lunch and tea, and fit in a story before returning for the evening's performance. The problem of combining the two roles was neatly reflected in an incident in her kitchen. While learning her lines for *Macbeth* she managed to drop the small red Temple edition of the play into a stew she was making. She fished it out and carried on cooking, rightly banking on Lewis not noticing any difference in the flavour or the colour.

Since Lilian Baylis refused to invite the critics to what she now billed as 'The People's Opera, Play and Lecture House' – 'Let the bounders buy their own tickets!' she declared – few notices exist of these productions. At first only the trade papers such as the *Era* and the *Stage* came. The *Era* critic, not the sternest of his breed, was much taken with Sybil's looks and personality. 'Miss Sybil Thorndike (mighty pretty!) put a deal of spirit into the part of Lydia,' he concluded after seeing *The Rivals*. He enjoyed her 'very natural and girlish Perdita' in *The Winter's Tale*; thought her 'delightfully impetuous' as Viola in *Twelfth Night*, in which she 'spoke her lines as if she had been brought up on blank verse'; and liked her 'dignified and convincing performance' in The *Comedy of Errors*. He approved of her also in *Everyman*, where 'her sincerity and earnestness make her performance both moving and impressive'.

Sybil spent Christmas at Grey Cottage with the children. Early in 1916, to her huge relief, Russell and Frank returned to England. Both had been in the botched Gallipoli campaign, and had witnessed slaughter all around them; the playwright George Calderón was one of the casualties. Frank's return was due to fever and jaundice, from which he soon recovered, but Russell's condition was more serious: a machine-gun had fallen on him and dislocated his spine, he had suffered from shell shock, and was invalided out of the army. The experience left him with a slight stammer, which fortunately disappeared when he was on stage. Sybil reflected on the human cost of the war: 'We'd seen him and Frank ride away with the regiment looking so jolly and fit – both pretending I'm sure to be either Douglas Fairbanks or General Ian Hamilton…and us all in the crowd, cheering, none of us knowing what was ahead – and now Russell looked an old man – bent nearly double – high spirits nearly gone – not quite ever – and just crawling along.'

Russell's novel *Doctor Syn: A Tale of the Romney Marsh* – in which Rochester became Dullchester – had been published while he was still in the army, and had scored an immediate success. He had originally conceived it as a play, but it had proved too costly to produce. Now he wanted to return to the theatre. Sybil's anguish at his injury was balanced by her delight in having him back in her life; during a lengthy convalescence at his home in Westminster he listened to her lines. In the spring Lewis was briefly home on leave, before returning to a very different job in France. Because of his knowledge of chemistry he had been asked to work on the development of poison gas, a task he abhorred. As he rose to captain he was given his own company, and the job of preparing and placing cylinders and projectors of poison gas along the line. The memory of the work would haunt him for many years to come.

As spring shifted into summer Sybil was able to spend more Sundays with her children. John Casson remembered first seeing the English countryside through her eyes: 'She took us into the woods and fields and made us see it all with that intensity of focus that only the great artists seem to be able to manage....We skylarked our days in a sort of open-eyed delight, with Sybil's visits injecting us each time with new and lively enthusiasms.' She taught John to recite Brutus' forum speech from *Julius Caesar*, and made him repeat it in front of the bemused village schoolchildren. 'We were also persuaded by Sybil to dress up as elves and fairies, and she wound us up in all sorts of wispy veils and scarves,' he recalled. 'She explained the rudiments of classical dance to us so that we could float and glide among the woodland trees, casting magic spells on moles and rabbits.' This whimsical spell was brutally broken one day when, to the astonishment of all parties, they floated and glided into the middle of a Boy Scouts' camp.

In May the Old Vic played for a week at the Theatre Royal in Portsmouth, where they performed the remarkable feat of staging eight Shakespeare productions in six days. This visit was a precursor of later excursions outside London. Both Sybil and Lilian Baylis saw the importance of the Vic becoming more of a national theatre. 'A theatre is more than just the building,' Sybil argued. 'It's the plays and the players, and these should travel and bring the good fare to the country – to the other towns.' In August the company was invited to Stratford-upon-Avon where, despite the war, the annual Shakespeare Summer Festival was still being held.

The festival had a distinctly improving character: in addition to the plays at the Memorial Theatre there were recitals, courses in speech training and elocution, demonstrations and lectures organised by the English Folk Dance Society, sessions of Dalcroze Eurythmics, and 'peasant dances of the Allies' performed by children of the Guild of Play. The Old Vic company was replacing Frank Benson's, which was performing in Europe. The tercentenary of Shakespeare's death was being widely celebrated, and Greet had drawn up an ambitious programme, of nearly thirty performances in four weeks: nine Shakespeare plays, two Sheridans and *She Stoops to Conquer*. The company included Robert Atkins, Ion Swinley, Florence Saunders, Austin Trevor and Jerrold Robertshaw. To Sybil's delight Russell, still recuperating, was invited to play a few minor roles.

Sybil was in ten of the twelve plays, and during an intensive month of work received mixed notices. The opening performance was the rarely played *The Comedy of Errors*, in which, the *Birmingham Post* critic wrote enigmatically, 'Miss Sybil Thorndike gave a decided and unusual particularity to the wife Adriana'. The *Era* thought she gave the part 'distinction and charm', but another critic noticed 'the extreme of the theatrical manner' in her playing. She also played Perdita in *The Winter's Tale*, Lady Teazle in *The School for Scandal*, Lydia Languish in *The Rivals*, and Julia in *The Two Gentlemen of Verona* – in which, the *Birmingham Daily Post* noted, 'she touched high levels of feminine caprice and pathos'. In *Othello*, according to the *Stratford Herald*, her playing of Emilia was 'high-strung, a woman of the people, virile; and its over-accented technique suited its thrilling moments'. Though the same critic disliked her Ophelia ('far from the mark') and her Beatrice ('there was harshness throughout'), his enthusiasm for her Kate Hardcastle suggested her comic skill was improving: 'Her method in such prose comedy is delightful. She gave pace which is never too hot, kept cautiously and naturally on the surface of the girl, and made her interesting, picturesque, consistent and vivid.'

There was one moment of crisis. The Stratford manager Archibald Flower hired the star actress Nancy Price to play Lady Macbeth, but Lilian Baylis refused to allow one of her 'girls' to be pushed aside. 'Oh! dear no!' she announced. 'That's Sybil's part. She's very good in it, and I won't have her turned out.' It was Russell who came up with a solution, suggesting they should alternate in the role. But the local critic – who incurred Greet's wrath for being so consistently critical of his productions – was again unimpressed by Sybil: while he felt Nancy Price brought to the sleep-walking scene 'power, insight, realism, and marked originality', with Sybil he noted only 'the theatrical effect and not the horrifying pathos'.

A family friend who saw her perform was impressed: 'Sybil is really a beautiful actress, very pretty, and without affectation, and great vivacity. And to this she adds 4 babes under 6!' The festival was an enjoyable interlude away from the strains of the war in London. In September Sybil returned to the Old Vic for two more seasons, during which she would make further strides as an actress, but suffer great personal losses.

11

The Pity of War

1916–1918

'I seem to want Daddy every minute – he was so part of everything'
Sybil on the death of her father

As Sybil began her third season at the Old Vic, Lewis, now an officer in the Royal Engineers, remained in France, only rarely coming home on leave. He was still involved with the poison-gas work that he loathed. It was a job he continued to do right through the Battle of the Somme, which caused nearly half a million British casualties, and finally killed any remaining public enthusiasm for the war.

Sybil, desperately short of money, had moved from Bessborough Street to lodge temporarily at the Pimlico vicarage in St George's Square. Her three older children remained in Kent but, as Saturday night was opera night at the Old Vic, she saw them every other weekend. It was an exhausting life: lacking Lewis' support, as well as his ramshackle car, and unable to afford a taxi, she had to walk four miles from the station to the cottage. Eventually Lilian Baylis persuaded her that, despite the bombing raids, she and her children would be happier if she brought them back to London and the vicarage. 'She was right,' Sybil remembered. 'Though the raids went on, we became used to them, and took them as part of the tiresomeness of life.'

During the 1916/17 season she continued to play the main Shakespearean heroines, but also smaller roles, including Portia in *Julius Caesar*, the Duchess of York in *Richard II* and the Old Lady in *Henry VIII* – a part which the *Era* thought she played 'with livery malice'. One night she emerged from the tube at Waterloo station to find an air-raid in progress. With considerable bravery, she put the theatre before her personal safety. Later she gave a vivid account of the incident: 'I met crowds pouring down the stairs with the air-raid look on their faces, and in their talk too. Lilian was more to be reckoned with, however, than any raid, so I fought my way up to the street. I was stopped by a bobby, who said: "You can't go outside here, my dear, raid's on." "I can't help the raid," I cried, clinging to his brass buttons, "the curtain's up at the Old Vic, and I shan't be on for my entrance." "Old Vic is it?" he said. "Oh, I know Miss Baylis; yes, you're right," and a lull coming in the bomb sounds, he gave me a push into Waterloo Road with a: "Now run for your life, and if you're killed, don't blame me – blame her!" I got to the pit door – first door I reached – and found Lilian in a fume and fret. "Why on earth weren't you in before this?" "A raid," I said, "everybody underground at Waterloo – everything impossible." "Raid!" she snorted. "What's a raid when my curtain's up!"'

Though Lilian Baylis could be a hard taskmistress, Sybil admired her enormous energy, her lack of dignity or pretension, her down-to-earth directness, and her absolute dedication to her theatre. The two of them also had their religious faith in common, though Sybil never claimed to have 'her hot-line to God'. Her main charitable concern was a leper colony, the Home of St Giles at East Hanningfield in Essex. She insisted her actors should visit the place with her to meet and entertain the patients. While many went reluctantly, Sybil had no qualms, and was moved to observe how easily this loud, earthy woman related to the men and women living in the shadow of death: 'Into every little separate house she'd go, bringing breeziness and good comradeship, never letting them see that they were different to any of us,' she recalled.

She herself was liked and admired within the company. This year it included Ray Litvin, whose daughter Natasha Spender recalls: ' Mother always said it was a very friendly, close company. She and the other young actresses all adored Sybil, and regarded her as tremendously brave when she ran through the air raid, and got a wigging from Lilian Baylis.' Henry Kendall, another youngster in the company, wrote: 'I don't think it is an exaggeration to say that whatever I learned about acting, I learned from Sybil Thorndike. Apart from her tremendous sense of fun and her extraordinary vitality, her knowledge of Shakespeare was quite incredible.'

She was also proving adept at classical comedy. As the erring Lady Teazle in *The School for Scandal* the *Era* critic felt she showed 'a rare sincerity and true pathos' in the scene where she is discovered behind Joseph Surface's screen. Joseph was played by Russell, who was now the leading man, and often on stage with Sybil. His range was impressive: during this season he played

Richard II, Iago, Cassius, Claudius, Macbeth, Sir Andrew Aguecheek and Don Pedro, in addition to comic roles such as Touchstone, Launcelot Gobbo and Bardolph. An actor of wit, panache and versatility, he was a great favourite with Lilian Baylis, who confessed to a partiality for his legs. Like Sybil, he was blessed with ferocious energy and a mischievous sense of humour.

The uniquely informal atmosphere in the theatre was captured by a reviewer from the popular *Pall Mall Gazette*, who noted that the Vic was the only theatre in London staging the classics: 'Threepence will secure you an excellent seat in which, if you follow the prevailing fashion, you sip your coffee from a saucer, munch your bun, smoke your gasper, and watch the strutting and fretting of the players with one arm round your best girl's waist....There are serious students of the Bard among the threepenny public, and in the intervals they foregather round the coffee urn (filled from a bucket) and discuss nice points.'

For Christmas Sybil and Russell wrote a satirical revue. *The Sausage String's Romance; or, A New Cut Harlequinade* was a burlesque of the plays and operas staged at the Vic, and of the theatre's actors, staff and governors. Russell as Joey and Sybil as Columbine presented the evening, while Sybil arranged the music, turning tunes from *Hymns Ancient and Modern* and Handel's *The Messiah* into dances. *The Times* noticed 'Miss Sybil Thorndike, that very intellectual young actress, revelling in the wildest absurdities'. Russell saw how she took to her clowning role: 'For the first time since our box-room theatre days I felt she was really doing the thing she enjoyed most – burlesque – for exaggeration is a form of acting she is most partial to.'

She was also partial to the family atmosphere at the Vic, and the good rapport with its enthusiastic, loyal audience. 'It's an awfully interesting theatre and tremendously hard work, but I love the work and the audience,' she wrote to Allan Monkhouse. 'I'm sure it's a very good training ground because the theatre is so huge it is necessary to have clear good speaking, or not a word can be heard.' But combining childcare with playing major roles sometimes proved too much for her. During the final rehearsals for the revue she caught a cold and was in agony on the first night, having to be drugged to dull the pain, and then given brandy to bring her round from the drugs. A few weeks into 1917, clearly overworked, she was compelled to ask for a week off. Fearing a slump in the box-office, Lilian Baylis engaged the West End star Viola Tree to play Viola in the next production, *Twelfth Night*. Tall, beautiful, but extremely vague, on the night of the fourth performance she was nowhere to be found (she was in the Savoy Grill). There were no understudies, so in desperation Lilian Baylis sent Robert Atkins to fetch Sybil. Henry Kendall, playing Sebastian, recalled what followed: 'Robert found Sybil bathing the children, and dragged her into the waiting taxi, up to her wrists in soapsuds.... She was pushed into Viola Tree's costume (which was about five times too large) and on to the stage....She went through the entire performance word perfect, without a single prompt.'

The company was starting to make further forays beyond the Old Vic. They staged *The Tempest* in the Queen's Hall, with no curtain and no scenery. They gave performances at the Northern Polytechnic in the Holloway Road, at an East End settlement, and at the Excelsior Hall, a swimming bath in Bethnal Green converted on Saturdays into a theatre, where the audience was mainly Jewish – 'the most vivid and intelligent audience I've ever played to', Sybil remembered. In May the actors again visited the Theatre Royal in Portsmouth. The plays included *Twelfth Night* and *Hamlet*, with Sybil playing Gertrude. Afterwards she and others decided it would be fun to do a few weeks of Twice Nightly shows, which they did for three weeks at the Prince's, again in Portsmouth. One play they staged in Dickens' home town was *Oliver Twist*, with Sybil playing Nancy. Harcourt Williams, later the Vic's artistic director, noted of the Twice Nightly scheme: 'It was of course the high-spirited Thorndike enthusiasm that brought this about.'

One June weekend at the country cottage Sybil received a telegram. Her son John recalled: 'Never as long as I live will I forget the look of abject terror on her face as she tore it open.' The news was not as bad as she feared: Lewis was wounded, but not dangerously. While on a mission to lay gas cylinders in no-man's land he had received a shrapnel wound in his shoulder. After a spell in hospital he was sent home. Sybil wrote to Allan Monkhouse: 'In a way it's a relief to know he's out of things for a few weeks and really having to rest; he has been through a pretty awful time, and the responsibility was making him feel aged. He's just got the military cross too – he's been inventing things – horrible things – but they've been quite successful. He's working out plays all the time too, and in a way he says one gets an utterly new vision of the theatre, seeing it from the midst of horror – Lear – Hippolytus – all those tremendous things are more alive to one than anything else.'

During his convalescence Lewis worked with the Army Camp Theatres run by Basil Dean, and once fit he was offered a job at the War Office. But Sybil was still anxious about Frank, now in action in France. Earlier, while recovering from an appendicitis operation in an Egyptian hospital, he and Russell had discussed plans for writing and producing plays, and acting in them with Sybil, Eileen and Lewis. To their parents he had written: 'Russ and I are so determined to get on and make a lot of money and a great name that absolutely nothing short of an earthquake can stop us.' Then came the disastrous Gallipoli landings. The following year he applied to join the Royal Flying Corps, qualified as a pilot and, with only four hours solo flying in training, was posted to a squadron in France. The casualty rate for pilots was high – the average life expectancy was eleven days – but with typical bravado he told his family that 'flying is so exciting you don't care what happens to you'.

In February 1917, while home on leave, he had visited Sybil and Russell backstage at the Old Vic, where they were playing the Macbeths. They had suggested he play the small part of Young Siward for one night. Serving soldiers were forbidden to appear on the professional stage, but Lilian Baylis scorned such regulations, insisting a spot of acting gave them a welcome break. Frank duly appeared, disguised in the programme as 'Frank Burroughs'. A week before his return to France he walked with Sybil and Russell through the large graveyard of St Peter and St Paul's in Aylesford. Pausing at the war memorial, he said: 'I've been on every list in the parish – choirboy, choirman, bell-ringer, server – and sure as anything I'll be on that roll of honour.'

The end of July saw the launch on the Western Front of the calamitous Passchendaele offensive, which would claim 324,000 lives in the next four months. Three weeks later, while Frank was on patrol, his plane got lost in the clouds, stalled and crashed. A telegram delivered to the vicarage informed his family he had been wounded. Canon Thorndike wrote to him at once, his anxiety mingling with joy and relief: 'Well, God has been very good to us in keeping you from being either completely squashed up or a prisoner or missing. Now you are out of reach of the Hun.' Two days later an army chaplain arrived with the news that Frank had unexpectedly died of his wounds. He was twenty-three. His father's letter was returned marked 'Deceased'.

The family received the news just before evensong. Canon Thorndike was too upset to preach a sermon. His distraught wife broke down, and Sybil had to take her place at the organ. In the ensuing weeks her father tried to hide his grief, as Russell remembered: 'Father was terribly affected by Frank's death, but never would give it away – always saying what a splendid thing it was to die for England, and hiding the sorrow he felt.' At Frank's memorial service he spoke of the great cause for which his son had died. Frank was buried in France, at Douisson near Arras, and in the church graveyard at Aylesford his name was put on a family memorial cross next to the war memorial. On it, beneath the words 'Frank Thorndike, Actor and Airman', was inscribed the poignantly apt words spoken about Young Siward after his death in battle at the hands of Macbeth:

> He paid a soldier's debt.
> He only lived but till he was a man;
> The which no sooner had his prowess confirmed
> In the unshrinking station where he fought
> But, like a man, he died....
> Why then, God's soldier be he.

Sybil had adored Frank – 'he was twelve years younger than me, but he was my belonging, somehow,' she remembered. 'He was my great pal.' For Sybil's father, his suppression of his grief at the loss proved fatal. Two weeks before Christmas, accompanied by his wife and Sybil, he took evensong at the church. He sang the vestry prayer in his magnificent voice and, as the choir sang Amen, suffered a heart attack. By the time his wife and daughter reached his side, he was dead.

It was a devastating blow for Sybil's mother, who for 36 years had not been separated from her husband for a single day. For weeks afterwards the family feared for her sanity. For Sybil herself, coming so soon after the loss of her brother, her father's death was a terrible shock. He had been the lodestar of her young life, the one whose values had most shaped hers as she grew up. She wrote to Kitty Jelf: 'It's been a dreadful business getting dear old mother cleared out of the vicarage. You have been this way, so you know the heartache, and isn't the miss awful, Kitty! I seem to want Daddy every minute – he was so part of everything. Poor Mummy can't get reconciled to life at all – but I suppose it's a question of time – she is so brave and splendid, but it's too pathetic the way she clings on to the memories of when they first met – and they were lovers always.'

Arthur Thorndike was buried in Aylesford, in the graveyard of the church where he had been vicar for seven years, and where Sybil and Lewis had been married in 1908.

After Christmas Sybil, now in her fourth season, returned to the Old Vic.

She found an outlet for her great sorrow in Shakespeare, sublimating it especially in *King John*, in which Russell played the title-role. 'What a releasing Constance was for me,' she recalled. Lilian Baylis helped to keep her spirits up: 'Your Frank won't want long faces, he's happy now, his duty done, and you must do the same,' she reassured Sybil.

During these emotionally difficult weeks Sybil found solace in yet another demanding variety of roles within the company. 'I don't believe I've looked at a newspaper for ages,' she told Kitty Jelf. 'I've *never* worked so hard.' More often than not she was acting in partnership with Russell, playing Kate Hardcastle opposite his Young Marlow in *She Stoops to Conquer*; Imogen in *Cymbeline* while he took on Iachimo. They were also together in the *Dream* as Helena and Lysander; in *Twelfth Night* he was Sir Andrew Aguecheek to her Viola; they were Hermoine and Leontes in *The Winter's Tale*; she was Queen Margaret when he took on Richard III.

As the war dragged on, and more and more men were called up to become cannon-fodder in the trenches, the number of actors available fell drastically. Lilian Baylis realised she had to ask her 'girls' if they would be willing to play 'boys'. For Sybil the opportunity was a thrilling one. 'When you're an actor you cease to be male or female, you're a person,' she remarked. Ever since touring America with Greet she had been jealous of the men in Shakespeare, aggrieved that for every good female part there were ten male ones. 'I would so much rather have been a man,' she said, referring to life as well as the theatre. 'I never much liked being a woman.' This masculine streak was a crucial and valuable part of her personality. She had already donned male attire the previous season, to play the Chorus in *Henry V*. Over the next few months she played several others, including Puck, Touchstone, Prince Hal, Ferdinand, Launcelot Gobbo and Rugby in *The Merry Wives of Windsor*. Male impersonation was everywhere: when Sybil played Prince Hal, fourteen of the male parts were played by women.

She also played the Fool in *King Lear*, with Russell in the title-role. At Lilian Baylis' suggestion she exploited the family resemblance by playing 'Lear's shadow' as a blank of her brother. 'I made the Fool look like an egg – blank – no eyebrows, nothing but the shape of a face that could reflect Lear's moods,' she remembered. The scholar Gordon Crosse, who saw all the great Lears from Irving to Wolfit, later wrote that her Fool 'over-topped all the rest', that her 'halting gait, hanging lip and nervous demeanour suggested the half-witted youth perfectly, and the childish pleasure the Fool took in his little jokes and snatches of song completed a brilliant piece of acting'. She was delighted when Barker came and at first failed to recognise her. Afterwards he told her: 'You work too hard – don't do it from the outside – live inside – it's all there in the play if you just live and be.'

The season's final production was *Hamlet*, played in its entirety, a version then never done in the commercial theatre. With Russell cast as the Prince, the bizarre situation was created in which Sybil as Gertrude was playing his mother. They were joined by Lewis, who had been organising concert parties in France, in which he recited patriotic pieces such as Kipling's 'If' and Henry V's 'Once more unto the breach'. Home on leave, and disguised in the cast list as 'Christopher Holland', he was roped in to play Fortinbras. To complete the family presence, the production, all four and a half hours of it, was watched by eight-year-old John from the steps of the circle.

Bombing raids were now a regular occurrence in London, and continued until May, often causing widespread panic: by the end of the war some 1,400 people had been killed and 3,400 injured. Many performances at the Old Vic were interrupted, with audiences forced to stay on after the end, and being offered 'impromptu performances and songs'. Sybil recalled Lilian Baylis' response to the news that enemy aircraft were approaching London: 'I remember her seizing on those of us who had children and saying, "You better go home as fast as you can," but we said, "No, let's go on," realising that all her doubts and fears were for us, and that she hated to give in. We had to keep a stiff upper lip like true English men and women, and not show our feelings.'

After this the company played through all the raids. One night during *King John* a raid on Waterloo station left neighbouring houses destroyed and the streets outside the theatre littered with glass. The observation that 'Some airy devil hovers in the sky/And pours down mischief' was suddenly topical. And while the Germans were unable to bring the house down, the actor playing Faulconbridge certainly did, with the lines, 'This England never did and never shall/Lie at the proud foot of a conqueror'. The audience roared their approval, and the defiant words were soon after inscribed above the proscenium arch, where they remained until the war ended.

In these dark times Lilian Baylis refused to be cowed. She would tell the audience they were safer in the theatre than trying to make their way home, then announce brusquely, without consulting the actors: 'Will all those who wish to leave please do so at once. We are carrying on.' Henry Kendall remembers a typical speech she made following the first act of *Romeo and*

Juliet, after the performance had been disrupted by a deafening raid: 'Now, boys and girls, we're not going to let Kaiser Bill interfere with the Vic, and so we shall carry on with this beautiful play, and if you up there on the top shelf would feel any safer you can come down and sit in the stalls – and I won't charge you any extra!' One afternoon she discovered members of the opera company sheltering in the wings after a raid had interrupted rehearsals. 'I'm ashamed of you all,' she exploded. 'If you have to be killed, at least die at your job!'

The second night of *King Lear* was played out against the sound of dropping bombs and heavy gunfire. In the middle of Lear's great speech in the storm, 'Blow, winds, and crack your cheeks!', a bomb landed on Waterloo station, and a loud explosion shook the theatre. In a moment of inspiration Russell strode downstage, with Sybil at his heels, shook his fist at the roof of the auditorium, and put a special emphasis into the next line, 'Crack Nature's moulds, all germens spill at once!' The audience applauded wildly, and did so again when Sybil responded with the Fool's comment: 'Here's a night that pities neither wise man nor fool!'

With the death of Canon Thorndike the Pimlico vicarage had passed to the next incumbent. While they looked for a home they could afford, Sybil and Lewis rented Holly Tree Cottage, one of two seventeenth-century brick and stone cottages in West Kingsdown. Their options in London were severely limited, and they had to settle for a tiny house at 35 Wood Street (now demolished) in Westminster behind Millbank Gardens. It was a slum area, with barefoot children a common sight in the street, even in winter. The house was a converted shop over an archway, which led into a court containing two rows of small, scruffy houses, 'a funny little rabbit warren of a place', Russell remembered. It had been damaged by a bomb, leaving a hole in the roof and through every floor, and the windows boarded or bricked up. Sybil still had her grand piano, but Lewis had to go to Caledonian Market to find some second-hand furniture. 'Perhaps I'll see more of you when I get fixed in my comic house,' Sybil wrote cheerfully to Kitty Jelf. 'It is looking so sweet.' It was to be their home for the next two years.

Her two families – her own and that at the Old Vic – sometimes overlapped. When they were seven and five respectively John and Christopher walked in a procession in *Julius Caesar*, playing Brutus and Portia's sons. When she appeared in *The Merchant of Venice*, all four children were allowed to sit in a box with their nurse. But when Portia made her first entrance Ann, aged two, yelled out, 'Mum, Mum, Mum!' The audience roared with laughter. 'Girls are so utterly adorable, and I'm revelling in Ann and Mary,' Sybil told Kitty Jelf. 'I think it's killing, you and me with such a lot of children, and we were such funny little things ourselves at school!'

In February 1918 a roll of honour was unveiled at the theatre, to commemorate the 142 actors, writers and musicians who had died on war service. Lewis, home on leave, read out the 142 names. In the autumn he was back again from France, now working as secretary to the Chemical Warfare Commission. With John and Christopher at school, he tried to persuade Sybil that, with the Old Vic paying just £4 a week, she should aim for the West End. But Sybil resisted: she was less anxious about money than Lewis, always believing something would turn up, and, according to Russell, at her happiest in the Waterloo Road: 'The Old Vic was unstylish…it had a feeling about it that nothing else outside its gloomy walls mattered, and Sybil liked that, as she thought she had nothing in common with West End people.'

But where Lewis had failed to budge her, Lilian Baylis succeeded. While retaining Russell as leading man for the following season, she told Sybil that she was becoming too settled, even stale, that it was time for her to 'learn something new somewhere else'. Reluctantly, she agreed to fly the nest – although she did return to it twice in the autumn. On the first occasion she played Portia opposite Ernest Milton's Shylock in *The Merchant of Venice*. Then in October she appeared in a centenary celebration of the theatre's history, in a programme compiled by Russell for a matinee in the presence of Queen Mary. The Thorndikes were well represented: while Sybil again played Columbine to Russell's Joey, Eileen took part in a scene from *Paganini*, and John and Christopher played the children of Athene Seyler in an excerpt from the melodrama *Simon Lee, or The Murder of Five Fields Copse*.

Looking back later at this sad and gruelling time, she reflected: 'We were all caught up in such big emotions that nothing mattered but getting on with the job in hand.' During her four years there the Old Vic had staged 25 plays of Shakespeare, eight classical comedies, two Christmas plays, and *Everyman*. Sybil had been the cornerstone of the company, helping to develop the theatre's artistic reputation, and justify its label of 'The Home of Shakespeare'. In Agate's view her work there had made her a great actress, while Gordon Crosse later reckoned that her playing of Shakespeare's heroines made her, after Ellen Terry, the greatest Shakespearean actress he had seen. She had played all the parts she had wanted to – except Hamlet. She had widened her range by playing Lady Macbeth, Gertrude, Constance and Queen Margaret, roles which tested her skills as a tragic actress. Her sustained work on the classics had laid the foundation for the next stage of her career.

On 11 November 1918 the armistice was declared. In London everyone took to the streets in celebration. In the evening the families in Wood Street made an enormous bonfire out of old furniture and junk. 'At the edge of the patch we all stood and watched,' John recalled. 'Lewis and Sybil had tears rolling down their cheeks, and we four children gazed in wonder as the fire blazed red and everybody sang lugubrious songs.' The nightmare of war, which among many millions of victims had claimed the lives of Lewis' brother, Sybil's brother and, indirectly, her father, was finally over.

12

The New Tragedienne

1919–1921

'It wasn't what I meant to do. It wasn't right'
Sybil to actress Colette O'Niel, after the first night of Medea

In the immediate post-war period there were few serious opportunities for Sybil to develop her art. Following 'the war to end all wars', the public taste was for shows that would make them forget the conflict, for glitter and frivolity or tough, sophisticated drama. Classical revivals were a rarity, while the more experimental work was confined to the outer fringes of London in theatres such as the Everyman, Hampstead and the Lyric, Hammersmith, or staged by the small Sunday societies. Barker, having divorced Lillah McCarthy, had married an American heiress and left the theatre, a move seen by many, including Sybil and Lewis, as a betrayal. The actor-managers were a dying breed, and most of the West End theatres were owned or run by businessmen, whose values were commercial rather than artistic. In addition there was substantial unemployment among actors. Yet within little more than a year Sybil would dazzle London with two electric performances.

Her start was not promising. The first person to offer her work was the impresario C B Cochran, who had earlier brought Sarah Bernhardt, Eleonora Duse, the Guitrys and Diaghilev's Russian Ballet to London, but was best known for staging revues and extravaganzas. In a recent Old Vic revue Sybil and Russell had performed a skit on Ibsen's *Ghosts*, called *Spooks*, playing it mock-tragically in an invented language. Cochran's manager saw the show, and immediately summoned Sybil to his office. Still in mourning for her father, dressed in black and, as she put it, 'looking like last week's governess', she was unrecognisable from the night before. A disappointed Cochran fell back on the familiar 'We'll let you know' formula.

The press agent Tom Kealy, dubbed by Lewis 'a little Irish firebrand', was a great admirer of Sybil's work, and had tried to publicise her work at the Old Vic. He now persuaded Cochran and the actor-manager Seymour Hicks to see her play Lady Teazle in *The School for Scandal* at the Old Vic. Impressed, Cochran offered her a contract at £7 a week. And so on 27 June 1918, at the relatively late age of thirty-five, Sybil made her West End debut on a variety bill at the London Pavilion. In *The Profiteers*, a one-act play translated from the French, she played opposite the comedian Léon Morton, whose stage tricks both horrified and delighted her. 'Vulgarity wasn't the word for it,' she recalled. 'Every night he came on with a piece of fruit in a different part of his anatomy, to break me up. You can imagine what fruits he would use. It was absolutely awful, but I liked him tremendously.'

Six weeks later Cochran cast her in the short play *The Kiddies in the Ruins*, which he inserted as an episode in *The Better 'Ole*, playing at the New Oxford. This popular show, set in no-man's-land, was sub-titled 'The Romance of Old Bill, A Fragment of France in Two Explosions, Seven Splinters and a Gas Attack'. It had been running for a year, its cockney humour and dogged patriotism catching the national mood. Sybil played in it until the armistice, when the show was taken off. She shared a dressing-room with half a dozen actresses from a very different background from her own. 'I didn't know about their kind of lives before,' she admitted later. 'I think Cochran did it on purpose, to break me down from the Old Vic and the vicarage.'

Cochran however was not impressed with Sybil's acting. Her performance in *The Profiteers* made him think wistfully of the actress who played the part in the original French version, and he was critical of her work in *The Kiddies in the Ruins*. 'Her performance was a little too restless,' he wrote in his memoirs. 'She had a number of mannerisms and lacked repose. Her voice also lacked flexibility. But she was a conscientious artist, and a charming woman to be associated with.' He now gave her the chance to understudy the star Madge Titheradge in the naval drama *In the Night Watch*. Out of work and hard up, Sybil accepted this apparent demotion: with four children to support, and Lewis experiencing depression brought on by the war, she needed the £7 a week badly.

Life was hard in their Westminster slum, although they were still able to escape occasionally to the Dymchurch cottage. It was here that they got to know Noël Coward, who lived nearby in Goldenhurst. 'He and my mother were tremendous pals, and he was wonderful with the children,' Sybil recalled.

'One day he brought us down a play to read, called *I'll Leave it to You*. I thought it was an excellent play, and we all knew that he was going to do things.' She also met Edith Evans for the first time. She had seen her on stage before the war, playing in a duologue with Gwen John, both of them then amateurs. Afterwards she had told Lewis: 'I've just seen the most wonderful actress: she's almost plain, almost ugly, but she's absolutely marvellous.' Now she came to the stage door of the London Pavilion, asking Sybil if she would help her get in to the Old Vic. Sybil persuaded Lilian Baylis to see her, then received an irate phone call from her: 'How dare you send me such an ugly woman?' she said.

The outlook for Sybil remained bleak in the early weeks of 1919, and she only found work sporadically. She returned briefly to the Old Vic to play Everyman again for eight matinee performances. She earned a couple of guineas for a single performance of an abridged version of Farquhar's *The Beaux' Stratagem*. The production, staged at the Haymarket with a cast that featured Russell and sister Eileen, was directed by Russell, and mounted on behalf of the newly founded 'Art Theatre'. But the art seemed in short supply: the actors, according to the *Era* critic, seemed uncertain whether they were in the eighteenth or twentieth century. Sybil also played the title-role in a single performance of *Savitri*, part of a double-bill of Indian plays staged at the Comedy by the Indian Art and Dramatic Society, under the hopeful banner of 'Union of East and West'. Based on a legend from the *Mahabharata*, it was, according to the *Observer*, 'beautifully played' by Sybil, Russell and the cast.

Like many actors, both established and rising, Sybil often worked for just a guinea or two in productions mounted by the small stage societies. An early version of fringe theatre, groups such as the Stage Society, the Phoenix Society and the Play Actors staged single performances on Sunday nights, sometimes adding a second on Monday afternoons. Some societies existed to mount foreign or forgotten plays, others to provide opportunities for new young actors, or interesting new writers unable to get their plays staged commercially.

The oldest and best-known was the Stage Society. Founded in 1899 by a group of amateurs, its aim was to produce plays of distinction and social significance which were otherwise unlikely to be staged, either because of censorship or the conservatism of the commercial managers. It had a distinguished record, having put on the first productions of works by Shaw, Maugham, Barker and, against fierce opposition, Ibsen and Chekhov. Murray was a supporter, and a member of its reading committee. It was under its auspices that Sybil appeared for two performances at the Queen's in Herbert Trench's poetic drama *Napoleon*, the cast including Leslie Banks, Basil Rathbone, Harcourt Williams and the talented young Meggie Albanesi. *The Times* thought she 'acted with tragic beauty, charm of voice, and nobility of manner and feeling' in the part of Leon Quartermaine's mother.

But it was a production by the Pioneer Players that gave her the chance to show her potential in tragedy. Founded in 1911, the society specialised in exploring the work of foreign dramatists, experimenting with new theatrical forms, and staging plays that gave expression to political, social and feminist ideas, a policy very much to Sybil's taste. According to Shaw, who was on its advisory committee, the Pioneer Players, 'by singleness of artistic direction, and unflagging activity, did more for the theatrical vanguard than any of the other coterie theatres'.

Its founder and moving spirit was Edith Craig, the illegitimate daughter of Ellen Terry, known to everyone as Edy. She had acted with her mother and Irving when young, and designed and made costumes for productions at the Lyceum and elsewhere. Now approaching fifty, tall, thin and dark, she had been producing plays in churches and pageants in parks and gardens. Virginia Woolf satirised her as Miss La Trobe, bossily organising the pageant, in her novel *Between the Acts*. She lived in a *ménage à trois* with the writer Christopher St John (real name Christabel Marshall) and the artist Clare (Tony) Atwood in the cottage next to Ellen Terry's at Smallhythe in Kent; the writer Vita Sackville-West labelled them 'The Trouts'.

Edy was an enthusiastic Ibsenite and a knowledgeable and talented director, but widely seen as a dragon – 'Boney' was one of her more polite nicknames. She once threatened to fine any actor who forget their lines. 'We don't want Edy here, she would upset the staff,' Lilian Baylis said, when it was suggested she come to the Old Vic. Always in her mother's shadow, she was handicapped by a slight lisp: both factors probably contributed to her brusque manner, and her dictatorial method of directing – as perhaps did the fact that she was a woman trying to make her way in a almost exclusively male field. Sybil had got to know her when she and her mother had taken part in the Shakespeare birthday shows at the Old Vic. Ellen Terry's memory was fading, and she never remembered Sybil's name, referring to her as 'that big girl'. Sybil was mildly hurt by this, knowing that, since she wasn't tall, 'it must have referred to my rather square bounciness'.

Edy asked her to play the only female part in a single performance at the Scala of Paul Claudel's poetic drama *The Hostage*, alongside Milton Rosmer, Brember Wills and Felix Aylmer. Sybil later described how her eagerness was checked by Edy's scathing manner: 'I remember arriving for the first rehearsal at her flat in Bedford Street, full of beans, loving the words of the play even when I didn't know what on earth they meant, but dashing at them in the forthright way one dashed at Shakespeare, hoping that verve and nerve would carry one through, then being completely laid low by Edy, who could "scathe" as few people knew how.' But though Edy criticised her acting ('Keep still – don't flounce and bounce!' was a frequent and no doubt necessary note), she helped Sybil to grasp the meaning of the play, and to get inside her character. Sybil considered her a genius, and they became friends. Later she wrote: 'I trusted Edy utterly. I would have done anything she told me, blindfolded; her instinct was so unerringly right....She broadened the significance of the acting art for me.'

Claudel's plays were noted for their religious fervour and moments of great dramatic intensity. In *The Hostage*, adapted by Christopher St John, Sybil played Sygne de Coufontaine, an emotional and idealistic woman who is forced to marry a man she hates. She later intercepts a bullet meant for him, and suffers a slow, agonising death. The critics were enraptured by Sybil's performance, *The Times* in particular: 'We knew that Miss Sybil Thorndike was a very clever actress, but we had never before seen her act with so much passion, so much sensitiveness, such a flow of agonising beauty.' Sybil later described it as 'one of my biggest spiritual experiences in the theatre'. But she was frustrated at playing it only once: 'In a play like that one feels one has only just begun to realise the part at a first performance,' she told Edy.

One producer who helped keep her spirits up was the actor-manager Leon M Lion. On a previous visit to his office, when London's theatre managers were turning her down or simply refusing to see her, she had been encouraged by his telling her she would eventually make the grade. 'I went out all cock-a-hoop and two inches taller, and felt success around the corner,' she told him. Now he was searching for an actress to replace Ethel Irving, the leading lady in his own melodrama at the New, *The Chinese Puzzle*. His later account of his meeting with Sybil provides a revealing picture of her attitude: 'When I asked if she would read the part on approval, her instant reply was, "Of course, as often as you like, and sack me if I'm bad." When I tentatively ventured into that awkward domain of salaries, she cut me short with Sybillian forthrightness. "Cochran is paying me eight pounds at present. What do you think I'd be worth to you?" A little taken aback, I believe I smiled before replying, "Well, if I think you're going to be as good as you should be, would forty pounds a week for a start make you happy?"'

This was beyond her dreams, and Sybil accepted immediately. Lion called a rehearsal for the next morning, and was astonished when she turned up word-perfect. After her first night she wrote to a fellow-actor: 'It's over thank goodness – now I've got to try and play the part!' She stayed in the show for four months, and made a success of it. 'She's damned fine,' Gerald du Maurier was heard to remark. At moments, according to *The Times*, 'she really rose to the heights', its critic concluding: 'Much as the Old Vic will regret it, it is hardly conceivable that Miss Thorndike will be allowed to cross over to the south side of the river again.'

Meanwhile the claims of motherhood remained strong, as Henzie Raeburn, an assistant stage manager on the production, remembered: 'After a matinee Sybil would rush out in full war-paint, to get home for tea with the children. "That girl will never get on," was Lilian Braithwaite's verdict.' Sybil later thanked Lion for what his directing had taught her, 'your watchfulness at every performance, never letting pass any opportunity for improving a line here, a movement there – every time some new, better way opened, whereby one's technical knowledge might be increased, one's rendering of the part strengthened and deepened.'

This role prompted two further offers of West End leads, in Arnold Bennett's *Sacred and Profane Love*, directed by her Gaiety colleague Basil Dean, and in Louis Parker and George Sims' melodrama *The Great Day*, directed by Arthur Collins. She opted for the latter, relishing the challenge of tackling a melodrama for the first time. But she was also apprehensive, writing after the first night to her friend and fellow-actress Colette O'Niel: 'I'm glad last night's over – always when one tries something entirely new in style and everything, one is anxious and horribly nervous.' With her hair dyed a garish gold, that nervousness made her, the *Era* critic observed, 'a little jerky in the first act', but her subsequent playing of the noble heroine 'won our entire sympathy, both for her clever acting and her charming personality'.

Sybil enjoyed telling her children the play's story. 'We listened open-mouthed as she strode round the tiny sitting-room at Wood Street telling us all the details,' John remembered. Sybil played a young girl working in the Paris embassy, who is kidnapped by the villains and threatened with torture unless she reveals the secrets of an international treaty. At the last minute she is rescued by the hero, played by Stanley Logan, described in *The Times* review as 'dashing'. The play ended with Sybil falling into the hero's arms. It seems this came near to being repeated offstage, as she fell heavily for Stanley Logan, who was ten years younger than Lewis. Although it was probably not a sexual relationship, Lewis got wind of her feelings; John Casson remembers 'odd moments of mysterious tension, which we thought were part of some play'. Whether Sybil brought up his affair is unknown, but like him she felt guilty, and her vicarage upbringing soon reasserted itself.

Colette O'Niel, who admired Sybil as 'une grande artiste', provides a clear picture of her. One day, soon after *The Hostage*, she called at her house. 'She came to the door in the alley where they lived, in a shabby blue serge skirt with a cotton dressing jacket round her shoulders. Her skin was rough and there wasn't a vestige of powder on it....Her hands were large and rather hard – and she wore a heavy gold wedding ring. Her eyes were very wide open and very blue....Her voice and her eyes express a peculiar quality of spiritual vision. The quality is rare; and the ability – the technical equipment – to transmit to your audience that sense of the terror and beauty of great, impersonal things – that, also, is rare. It is little short of genius.'

The carnage of the war had turned Sybil into a pacifist – a position to which, unlike many of her contemporaries, she would adhere for the rest of her life. Her decision was influenced by the feminist and pacifist Maude Royden, a remarkable woman preacher, and later a peace activist on the international stage. Sybil's parents had taken her to hear her speak in a Pimlico church, and later they would become friends, and share platforms. 'Her method of putting a message across to an audience was almost an actor's method,' she recalled. 'Her words were charged with a sort of electricity.'

Lewis was still brooding about the war and struggling with depression, but as his thoughts turned back to the theatre his state of mind began to improve. He became active in union affairs, and was involved in setting up the British Drama League, the first national organisation for drama. He also directed three of Sybil's performances in the second half of 1919. It was the first time they had worked together since the Gaiety days. During the next decade he would direct the majority of the plays in which she appeared, including her greatest successes. Even when he was not directing her, she would discuss the play with him. It was already proving an immensely fruitful professional relationship, but often a stormy one.

The first play was *Sakuntala*, a sixth-century Hindu classic drama by Kalidasa, translated by the poet and playwright Laurence Binyon, and staged at the Winter Garden by the Indian Art and Dramatic Society. Dressed in a sari, Sybil, in the eyes of the ever-admiring *Era* critic, provided 'a very tender and beautiful study of the shy young nymph-maiden'. Lewis also directed her in *Dr James Barry* by Olga Racster and Jessica Grove. Staged as a charity matinee at the St James', it was about a famous woman doctor who lived most of her life in South Africa as a man. Sybil, dressed part of the time in a red wig, cocked hat, black cloak, tight white breeches, top boots and spurs, was able to express her masculine side and, according to Russell, revelled in the part. The *Daily Express* critic wrote: 'Manner, voice, gait – all were convincing.'

The third play directed by Lewis was Euripides' *The Trojan Women*. Ever since the war Sybil had been enthralled with the Greek tragedies, in part because she felt they had 'a lot of masculinity in them'. She thought Murray's translations worked in the theatre because of 'the beauty and clarity of the verse and its dramatic speakableness'. Euripides' passionately anti-war play, set at the end of the Trojan War as the city goes up in flames, suited her politically as well as artistically. Its depiction of the ravages of war is brutal and stark, and its story chimed in with the mood of a nation exhausted by the recent conflict. It also fitted in with Sybil's desire to play her part in working for a stable and peaceful Europe. 'It spoke to a war-ridden world, and made us one with those who had suffered thousands of years ago,' she wrote later.

It was staged under the banner of the newly formed League of Nations Union (LNU), established to further the League's ideals through lectures, study sessions and other events. In the 1920s it became the largest and most influential peace organisation in Britain. Murray was its vice-chairman, and it was he who suggested Lewis direct a production to publicise the LNU. To write the music Lewis recruited John Foulds, a pacifist with a particular interest in the music of the ancient Greeks and Celts. For the simple sets and costumes he hired Bruce Winston, a large, well-read and talented designer and actor, who agreed to co-finance the production. Lewis wrote: 'His generous, adventurous spirit, his love of colour in life and in the theatre, broke down much of my caution and Puritanism.'

The Trojan Women was first performed in September at a peace conference in Oxford, presided over by Murray. It took place in a tiny cinema in Cowley Road, with Evelyn Hall playing Hecuba, and Murray helping Lewis with rehearsals. Lilian Baylis then agreed to host four matinees at the Old Vic, with the proceeds to go to the LNU. Sybil took over as Hecuba, while Beatrice Wilson played Andromache. After a couple of her performances Lewis, playing Poseidon, confided coolly to Murray: 'Sybil is a much more passionate Hecuba than Evelyn, although perhaps lacking in some of the latter's royalty.' That passion was sometimes directed at him, for during rehearsals they often drove each other to despair. She was angered by his staging of some scenes in the half-dark. Colette O'Niel, playing Helen, recalled one performance: 'I had to steady her in my arms when she came off the stage, shaking in every limb, sobbing bitterly, cursing between her sobs: "If only Lewis would give me more light! I can't work without light!"'

The production was a sensation, and Sybil's Hecuba the talk of the town. It sent the critics into paroxysms of delight: Archibald Haddon of the *Daily Express* said she seemed born for the role, adding that her 'transition from it to that of the girl-heroine at Drury Lane on the evening of the same day constituted almost a freakish exhibition of versatility'. The *Daily Telegraph*'s new critic W A Darlington thought it 'a great part, greatly played'; forty-five years later he wrote that it 'still glows in my mind as the greatest tragic performance I have seen a woman give'. The *Observer* vividly described her bold performance: 'She was afraid of nothing. She rolled in her gait; she mopped and mowed; she clawed and clutched; she howled; she grimaced.' The result, he felt, was not a grotesque, 'but a grief that attained grandeur'; Sybil was an actress 'who can do any big work she chooses'. T S Eliot, then critic of the *Athenaeum*, pinpointed her qualities: 'To have held the centre of the stage for two hours in a role which requires both extreme violence and restraint, a role which requires simple force and subtle variation; to have sustained so difficult a role almost without support; this was a legitimate success.' Allan Monkhouse, having at the Gaiety predicted Sybil would not go very far, had the nerve to state on a postcard to Agate: 'Thorndike is a very great actress – as I always said she would be.'

Her performance also attracted members of the peace movement: 'We pacifist sympathisers flocked to a superb performance of *The Trojan Women*,' Dora Russell recalled. 'Sybil Thorndike, as Hecuba, shook me to the core.' Colette O'Niel, also a pacifist, was overwhelmed: 'She wiped the stage with every one of us – towered above us – swept the play from end to end. Never for one moment did she let the audience out of her grip.' Yet according to Russell, who came round after the first performance, Sybil was deeply depressed by her playing. Lewis had tactlessly told her she had neither the voice nor the face for Hecuba, and she feared he was right. 'I loathe the way I play her more than he does, but I will play her properly one day,' she told her brother, hurling her costume at her face in the mirror. Russell reported: 'She carried on like this for days, and utterly refused to believe any of the lovely things the papers said about her. Then she said she wasn't going to read any more notices of her own acting as they only put her off the things she was trying to do.'

A gala performance in aid of the LNU, mounted at the Alhambra and attended by King George and Queen Mary and other eminent people, brought Sybil more good publicity. Lewis then looked round for another theatre where he and Winston could stage further matinees. There were 42 theatres in London, but their managers were concerned with providing light entertainment for war-weary audiences, and refused to consider staging this great classic. The surprising exception was Charles Gulliver, manager of the Holborn Empire, one of the few surviving pre-war music-halls, popularly known as the 'O'burn' (it was destroyed in the Second World War). In these very different surroundings, where performing elephants appeared on the bill, and comedians such as Harry Tate and George Robey plied their trade twice nightly, Sybil drew the crowds to four further matinees.

Much encouraged, Lewis and Winston decided to go into management properly, with the aim of giving Sybil a chance to play the great classical roles for which she was clearly now ready. It was a risky step, and one that was soon to land them in trouble. They had already financed the Old Vic matinees, with some success: 'We are rather pleased with ourselves, and have some hope of coming out nearly square after paying production costs,' Lewis wrote to Murray. They also had Gulliver's agreement for them to make further use of the 'O'burn'. But after the initial matinees there they only had £200 with which to float the venture. Then, at a British Drama League dinner which Sybil also attended, Lewis unleashed a tirade. After listening with growing anger to a series of complacent and self-congratulatory speeches, he attacked the growing commercialism of the theatre, accusing those present of not caring about serious plays or good acting, and suggesting that unless people woke up and took action, there would soon be no English drama left of any value.

The speech had an effect where it mattered: the British Drama League president, Lord Howard de Walden, congratulated Lewis on his candour and courage, then offered them backing of £1,000. Other backers, including the steel magnate Sir Hugh Bell, contributed smaller sums, giving them a capital of around £1,700. In January 1920 Lewis wrote optimistically to Murray: 'We are forming a small syndicate to run the Holborn matinees.' After asking for the rights for a year to four of his Euripides translations, he added: 'Can we stick to a seven and a half flat royalty rate? It seems mean to ask for it, but it really is going to be rather a gamble.'

Before it began, Sybil took a rare, if brief, break from work. 'We're having a rest,' she wrote to Colette O'Niel in January. 'The country is great – and the cold and the air make me new again.' The opening production, *The Trojan Women*, was followed by a successful week of *Candida* matinees. Having long ago satisfied Shaw's conditions for becoming a good actress, Sybil had written to ask his permission to stage the play, in which she would be playing Candida for the first time in London. Shaw not only agreed, but offered to direct the production himself. He conducted rehearsals in the afternoons, having spent the mornings doing battle with Mrs Patrick Campbell, playing Eliza Doolittle in a revival of *Pygmalion*. Sybil recalled: 'He took our rehearsals with extraordinary vigour, and was most exacting – always polite, he never made any of us feel uncomfortable. But if an actor or actress put on airs, he never failed to admonish them with a snub.' Shaw was still not quite satisfied with her, remarking afterwards – though not to her face – that she was 'too strong for the part'.

With the next production her strength was to prove a virtue. Even in Greek tragedy there are few more demanding roles than Medea, a tigress of a woman of 'uncontrollable, tempestuous spirit, blent with wrongs'. Medea has been abandoned by her husband Jason, who has married the daughter of Creon. In revenge she poisons Creon and his daughter, and kills her two young boys to prevent Jason from seeing them again. Nicholas Hannen was cast as Jason, while Lewis himself played the Messenger. Sybil was not sure if she was right for the part, but as with Lady Macbeth she tried to find positive qualities in her character to justify her evil deeds. 'I don't believe in complete evil,' she explained later. 'Medea had given up everything and done awful things to help Jason, and all she expected in return was his love. He rejected her and oppressed her, and she had the most terrible time.' The play made her reflect on wider matters. 'As I studied the part I thought a lot about the position of women in the world, the position of the under-dog – their endless struggle for freedom and fulfilment – and I came to see very clearly how oppression breeds hatred.'

Murray told her that *Medea* 'might have been written for the woman movement'. The role is a more passionate, full-throttled one than Hecuba, where the grief is more controlled and drawn-out. It demands huge energy and power and, not surprisingly, Sybil found it a formidable task in rehearsal. 'Hannen as Jason is promising well,' Lewis told Murray a fortnight before they opened. 'Sybil is just going through the despairing stage which always affects her halfway through rehearsals. It's going to be a very vivid piece of work.' Yet once again her first-night performance failed to match her ideal. Colette O'Niel was in the audience, and thought her magnificent, but when she went round afterwards she found Sybil in tears. 'She put her arms round me, and said, "It wasn't what I meant to do. It wasn't right."'

The critics disagreed. 'A great piece of acting was given on the stage of the Holborn Empire,' declared the *Daily Express*. 'Her Medea is a near approach to histrionic greatness.' Darlington 'praised an exhibition of sheer power which is in itself enough to refute the criticism that the actress of today has not the physique for a tragic part'. Louis J McQuilland topped them all with a fulsome tribute: 'England has at last discovered a great tragedienne,' he wrote. 'Miss Thorndike is comparable with the greatest of them. Henceforward she takes rank with Rachel, with Ristori, with Janauschek, with Genevieve Ward, with Bernhardt, with Duse – with all the sceptred race and the forms divine of the high enchantresses of the theatre.'

According to Russell, these glowing reviews made Sybil furious, and fuelled her growing contempt for the critics' judgement. 'They don't know anything about Greek plays, or they'd never say I can play tragedy,' she told her brother. 'You wait, I will do it one day, and they'll all say what a pity it is I've gone off.' Yet not all the critics were totally admiring. In a thoughtful piece that, paradoxically, might have met with her approval, Darlington suggested she was unable to keep up the high pitch of emotion with which she started, and that her reading of the part made Medea too inhuman to command sympathy: 'She is the barbarian sorceress, aching and thirsting for revenge, rather than the wronged wife seeking just retribution,' he wrote.

She herself later pinpointed why the Greek drama suited her. 'There's something in me which is male. I'm not attractive in a feminine way at all and I've known that all along. I've got an enormous number of men friends, but none of them fell in love with me. And a woman on the stage needs to make men fall in love with her. Otherwise she's terrifically hampered. The reason it didn't hold me back is that I recognised it and played very big, huge parts that required a lot of masculinity, as in the Greek plays.'

The matinees were a success. 'We had a wonderful wind-up on Saturday,'
Lewis told Murray at the end of the first week of *Medea*. 'A nearly full house
(£240), hundreds turned away from the cheaper seats, and much cheers at
the end.' Often the lunchtime traffic in Holborn was brought to a standstill
by the crowds around the theatre. A typical reaction was that of the explorer
Gertrude Bell, who wrote to her stepmother Florence: 'I was very grateful
for the *Medea* – tremendous wasn't it – but I think *The Trojan Women* is even
more magnificent.' Many of the leading actors of the day came to see Sybil's
high-octane performances. One night Ellen Terry was in the audience, sitting
in a box with Edy Craig. Now seventy-three and a little deaf, at one point she
fell asleep. Soon after, Sybil made one of her wailing entrances. The famous
actress woke suddenly, and announced for all to hear: 'There's someone in
the room!'

In the evenings the comedian George Robey would come on to the stage
and remark, 'I can sniff the air of Greece.' But he was unable to do so for
long. Lewis had earlier asked Murray for the rights of two further Euripides
plays, *Hippolytus* 'and (dare I say it!) *The Bacchae*! We are seriously thinking
of plumping for the last if we could get the money and a Dionysus.' Unfortunately they plumped instead for a new play, *Tom Trouble*, a north-country
comedy by John Burley. It got the thumbs-down from the critics, and lasted
only a week. According to Russell, the switch came because Sybil suddenly
said she was 'tired of grand parts'. But she quickly realised her mistake: 'I was
better today in the rotten play – make-up too – and I got more grip,' she wrote
to Colette O'Niel. 'I *loathed* myself yesterday.'

Their management was now in trouble. They next staged *The Showroom*,
a light comedy by Florence Bell which lasted just a dozen performances, in
which Sybil, according to the *Observer*, was 'rather triumphant in an exhibition of the pure science of acting'. She also had to exhibit the pure art of
improvisation when Lewis, who liked to play practical jokes, strolled on unexpectedly with Bruce Winston, and asked her the way to the dress department.
'Through the jumpers, gentlemen,' she answered with aplomb, but afterwards
was furious with Lewis for behaving so unprofessionally.

In April they took the Duke of York's to do a fortnight of evening performances of the two Greek tragedies, and there were discussions about touring
them to other music-halls. But the gamble was lost. 'We have to raise more
money before we can start again,' Lewis wrote disconsolately to Murray: 'It's
rather a disappointing end to another ambitious scheme!' The *Manchester*

Guardian summed up Sybil's qualities at the end of the venture. 'Her acting appears to be the product of two very different sources of inspiration. At times she seems the extraordinarily gifted and enthusiastic amateur doing things by the light of imagination and will-power only, and at others – chiefly in modern comedy – she shows herself the hard and accomplished technician, accomplished enough almost to hide the technique, doing things perfectly in the light of study and calculation and long experience.'

While Sybil was playing Hecuba at the Old Vic, Florence Bell brought to her dressing-room the woman who, with William Archer, had been largely responsible for bringing Ibsen and the new realism to the attention of English audiences. The beautiful American actress Elizabeth Robins was a powerful personality, who had toured with the great Edwin Booth, and once threatened to shoot Shaw when he interviewed her about *The Master Builder* and became over-familiar. She was the first to play Hedda Gabler in London, but left the stage in her prime in order to write. Sybil, at nineteen, had seen one of her last performances, in *Paolo and Francesca* with Henry Ainley. She had written suffrage plays, most notably *Votes for Women*, a powerful piece of suffrage propaganda staged by Barker in his first Court season. She had been a founding member of the Women's Social and Political Union and the Actress' Franchise League. Leonard Woolf observed that she possessed 'that indescribably female charm which made her invincible to all men and most women'.

She had sent Sybil an appreciative note about her performances in *Medea* and *The Trojan Women*, to which Sybil replied hastily: 'Dear Miss Robins (Forgive pencil – I'm waiting in the wings – it's Candida!) I must write to say thank you for your kind letter. I need not tell you how much I appreciated your thought, and I feel if you like Hecuba and Medea there is something I can be glad about. Please let us meet one day. I'd love to talk about them.' Sybil remembered their first meeting, the start of a thirty-year friendship. 'I will never forget the effect of her eyes. I think, except for Eleonora Duse, I have never seen such eyes. There did actually seem to be a light behind them that could pierce through outward and visible things and see the invisible.'

From then on they talked often of plays and parts and interpretations of Ibsen, Sybil feeling she was 'lifted into another plane of being'. She almost believed she had witnessed her new friend's trail-blazing performances. 'I can literally see her as Hedda Gabler burning the Lovborg manuscript, see her vivid hands thrusting it away in the fire, so keenly did she represent it to me; and the spurring on of Solness in *The Master Builder* to mount the tower he had built, I can see that too, sitting as we used to in Florence Bell's music room, and her with those eyes of fire, and voice haunting and vibrant, making me almost leap in the air with excitement.'

Sybil's growing fame prompted many people to write fan letters, or seek her advice. One of these was Robert Speaight, who had just played Mark Antony in *Julius Caesar* at Haileybury School. Sybil's response to his request for help in interpreting the part underlines her instinctive, non-academic approach to acting. '*Julius Caesar* is my favourite play (*Macbeth* runs it close) – but the parts are wonderful studies, aren't they? Don't bother about anybody's ideas about them – go straight to the play and get all its meaning for yourself – that's the advice I give to anyone who acts. Acting is one of the greatest studies in the world – whether it is your living or not, the study of it helps you in every walk of life. Write and tell me how you get on.'

She also received invitations to pass on her skills. Flora Robson, a student at RADA, recalled her directing rehearsals of *The Trojan Women* there. 'We worshipped Sybil, she was so kind and generous. When she left I cried into a towel in the dressing-room, and one girl rushed into the lavatory and kissed the seat where she had been!' Rehearsing another class in scenes from *Medea*, she told the students they were 'like a lot of governesses', with no fire or guts – except for one tall, pale, willowy youth, the only one with any spark. When she asked his name, he said: 'It's John Gielgud.' Later Gielgud recalled the moment. 'She had sandy hair, arranged in coils round her ears like radio-receivers, and wore a long straight dress in bright colours with strings of beads around her neck. She told me Jason was a self-righteous prig and I must play him so. She exuded vitality, enthusiasm and generosity, and we were all spellbound.'

In staging the Greek tragedies, she and Lewis were way ahead of their time. Most of the post-war theatre-going public wanted lighter fare. The cool restraint of the Gerald du Maurier naturalistic school of acting was more to their taste than Sybil's outpouring of emotion. But the Greek drama was therapeutic: throwing herself into the great tragic parts with unstinting energy and gusto enabled her to channel the violent streak in her personality, and the frustrations involved in juggling a career with marriage and mother-hood. 'I felt as though I'd been in a bath,' she recalled. 'All the foul tempers, wanting to knock Lewis' block off, wanting to spank the children, I got rid of them all. The family used to say I was angelic after playing Medea.'

Although the comparisons with Duse and Bernhardt were extravagant, Sybil was now seen by many as England's finest tragedienne, with a rapidly growing band of admirers. Agate felt Euripides was her spiritual home. 'In Greek tragedy she buried the nursery governess, the provincial grande dame, the lady mayoress,' he wrote. 'Now as Hecuba she can hold a candle to the greatest.' But she also had her critics, among them John Francis Hope, one of the first to write in detail about her abilities. In a lengthy piece in the *New Age* he described her as the most powerful actress on the London stage, but wondered whether that power wasn't sometimes a handicap.

'She yells at the audience, and the audience thunders back at her – but the lightning flash of which the thunder is only an effect is never visible.' He faulted her for her indiscriminate choice of parts and fellow-actors: 'She will play anything – which is practically a condemnation – and with anybody, which is a proof of bad taste.' He criticised her for the way she wore her costumes: 'An actress like Irene Vanbrugh can tell us what she means by the swing or hang of a skirt, and she really seems to alter with the fashions. But Miss Thorndike is Miss Thorndike whatever she wears – her sense of clothes is as elementary as that of a girl at boarding school.' He concluded that she had power, but not genius; she could convince in character parts, but not in the more psychologically complex ones. 'She knows and can do all the technical tricks, but is incapable of creation. She remains provincial, because she does what the public has already applauded, instead of compelling it to applaud a new personality. She is derivative, and not creative; and is of more interest to history than to drama.'

It was a harsh, sometimes unfair piece, but one that contained several valid criticisms. Ever keen to improve, in the next few years Sybil would battle to deal with them.

13

Grand Guignol

1920–1922

'Horrors have been my meat and drink day and night
since I was a tiny child'
Sybil in the Grand Guignol Review, *1921*

During her success in the Greek drama, Sybil and family were still living in the tiny house in Wood Street, Pimlico, where her mother had a flat. They had been there for nearly two years and, although their finances were improving slightly, they were not well off, and were living austerely. Unable to afford a car, Lewis rode around on a battered woman's bicycle. Their pleasures were simple ones: they would take the children for walks on Sunday afternoons, and in the evenings all sing hymns at the tops of their voices, with Sybil or her mother at the piano. 'My grandmother also used to play for us to dance round the sitting-room, and Ann and I loved that,' Mary Casson recalls. 'And she used to recite the Victorian poems she had learnt in her childhood.' Supper after the show invariably consisted of cocoa, bread and marmalade.

The families in Wood Street were mostly poor, a situation which, John remembered, prompted Sybil to play the Lady Bountiful on their first Christmas there. 'She had laid in a great pile of jolly little toys, and at eleven o'clock the mothers from the court at the back came one by one with their children into our sitting-room, to receive such Christmas cheer as Lewis and Sybil could afford to give them – a toy for each child and a shilling for the mothers. All four of us children had to be there to give our greetings, and to learn that if we were going to enjoy ourselves we had to see that others had something too.' They mixed with the locals, and widened their vocabulary: John came in one day and asked: 'What's a bugger, Mummy?'

The house had become too small for the growing family. Luckily friends offered them a house in Kensington rent-free for a year while they were abroad. New House, a vast building with 42 rooms, was on the corner of Airlie Gardens and Campden Hill. It could hardly be more of a contrast to Wood Street: the children had their own flat on the second floor, while Sybil for the first time was able to have members of her and Lewis' family to stay. They included Russell and Eileen, who was expecting her first child. Agnes Thorndike, who had always harboured social ambitions for her daughter, was delighted with Sybil's grand new home.

One frequent visitor was Tom Kealy, who became Sybil and Lewis' press agent. A huge enthusiast for Sybil's work, he had a false hand covered by a glove, and spent his time hobnobbing with the journalists in Fleet Street, persuading them to write about her. Sybil began to feature in papers such as the *Daily Mirror* and *Daily Sketch*, which emphasised her role of mother. She was pictured supervising her children at the piano, playing toy trains and 'puff billiards' with them, overseeing her daughters' bath-time during the maid's night off ('A great actress who scrubs and tubs'), or frolicking with all four children in the sea at Dymchurch ('a great tragic actress in merry mood'). There was even a picture of her scrubbing the floor at home, with a caption containing the surprising information that 'She can play most Shakespearean parts and a number of others at an hour's notice'.

The family stayed at New House for nine months while looking for a permanent home. At one stage it seemed they might have to return to Wood Street, as they couldn't find a house they could afford. Then, with the help of a loan of £700 from Lewis' wealthy aunt, they obtained an eleven-year lease on a Victorian house at 6 Carlyle Square in Chelsea, just off the King's Road, to which they moved in October. Chelsea, once the home of George Eliot, Mrs Gaskell, Swinburne, Carlyle, Dante Gabriel Rossetti and other literati, was becoming more bohemian as actors and artists moved in. The three-storey house had no garden, just a small paved space at the back, but they had access to the communal garden in the square. Sybil and Lewis, to the initial amazement of other residents, used it as a place for hearing each other's lines. Their voices, her contralto and his bass, could also be heard at St Mary's Church near Sloane Square, where they became regular attenders.

Russell was a frequent visitor. 'He was very much the favourite uncle,' Mary recalls. 'He'd join in our games as if they were absolutely serious.' The house had a long, spacious central room well suited to the children's plays, which they devised themselves. Their audience comprised Sybil, Lewis and their governess, with Sybil occasionally called upon to accompany a song on the piano. John remembers his parents 'sitting there with rapt attention', Sybil no doubt delighted to see her children carrying on the family tradition of home-made drama.

Sybil began to learn to drive, but decided it wasn't for her; and Lewis thought her 'too jumpy'. He invested in a battered 1916 Maxwell bought at an army disposal dump, enjoying taking the engine to bits and strewing it all over the road. Life now began to open up again for the family. Approaching forty, Sybil was exchanging her previously makeshift life for a relatively more stable existence. In her new home there was room for her mother, who came to live with them, and often played the piano to the children. There was also a nursery-governess, a parlourmaid and a cook, who would have been especially welcome, since Sybil showed no enthusiasm for cooking.

She tried to see as much of her children as she could: 'I should like to come and see you very much indeed, but am terribly busy just now,' she explained to Dora Russell. 'I seem to spend all my days in the theatre except when I rush home to see my four babies!' She loved being with them, and relished reading stories to them, just as they loved listening to them. John remembered her reading Frances Hodgson Burnett's *The Secret Garden* to them in St James' Park. 'We were completely transported into another world. I can still quite vividly see every character as though we had spent large parts of our summer in that strange household on the Yorkshire moors.'

Norman Edwards, a young journalist, was equally captivated when he visited Carlyle Square: 'Perhaps you wonder what our greatest actress is like offstage? A woman with abundant golden hair (bobbed in a way that ennobles the art of bobbing) sits in front of a cheery fire in a cheery house in Chelsea. Quiet as mice are grouped about her four children – two girls and two boys. Their eager faces are turned toward their mother: their ears, as well as their eyes, are intent upon her….The story-teller grips those children as the fascinating adventures of *Alice in Wonderland* are unfolded. And such a story-teller! Such a thrill where a thrill should be emphasised; such a marvellous story – when told by Sybil Thorndike.'

The children were gradually drawn into their parents' world. Mary, aged six, made her debut this summer on the steps of St Paul's Church in Covent Garden, in *The Mystery of the Rose*, a religious play by Elsie Fogerty; according to *The Times* 'she played the silent part of Innocence with perfect composure'. Christopher, aged eight, played Astyanax in *The Trojan Women*, a part which Mary was to play the following year, and Ann a little later. Christopher alternated with John as one of Medea's two children, while Mary and Ann sometimes played the parts together.

'My two little daughters are for ever acting,' Sybil commented. 'They act in the nursery and in the garden. They never stop. I shall certainly allow them to go on the stage if they want to, but I also want them to see it while they are young.' The assumption that they would follow her into the theatre seemed to be there when she observed that the children 'must have no illusions about the stage when they take it up seriously as a profession'. But Mary says their parents put no overt pressure on them to follow in their footsteps. 'They didn't push us into anything, although it was rather assumed that we would go into the theatre, and we didn't demur from that.' But she found acting with her mother difficult. 'I couldn't bear it, it made me terribly self-conscious,' she recalls. 'When she and Lewis put on matinees of the Greek plays, we all got roped in. But I absolutely loathed it. I used to find it particularly difficult with *Medea*, just standing there without a line while this torrent of passion came out. Mummy didn't go out of her way to make me feel at ease, she just played her part. I couldn't deal with it at all, and I fought it on one or two occasions.' Meanwhile Christopher showed an early grasp of technique. During one performance of *The Trojan Women*, when he was about to be thrown from the city walls, Sybil noticed tears in his eyes. Complimenting him afterwards on the way he had felt himself into the part, she was disappointed when he replied: 'Yes, I have learnt how to produce tears: you just puff your cheeks out, hold your breath, and they come.'

Much of their early education was at home. Mary didn't go to school until she was seven: John taught her to read, while Sybil taught her the piano from an early age. 'Although she didn't like teaching it, she thought we should all make a start,' Mary remembers. 'She was pretty good, she taught us what keys to use when improvising, she went beyond just teaching you the five fingers.' All four children went to Albert Bridge School, a small private school in Battersea run by the mother of the dancer Penelope Spencer. Many of the pupils were from theatrical families, and were allowed time off to perform. But when John and Christopher moved to the fee-paying King's School in Wimbledon, the situation changed. 'They can't be children in the show, I'm afraid,' Sybil wrote to Ellen Terry: 'They are at school and are never allowed off by the authorities! Ann and Mary will love to and will come to the rehearsal on Monday.'

The show was a charity performance of Saint-Georges de Bouhélier's

Carnaval des Enfants, a play based on nursery rhymes, which Edy Craig was directing at the Kingsway for the Pioneer Players. During rehearsals Sybil, who played Celine, stood in for Ellen Terry as The Old Woman who Lived in a Shoe. Mary played Little Bo-Peep, and the other children included Daphne du Maurier, and the daughters of Athene Seyler and Gladys Cooper. The author met Sybil, and was struck by 'une jeune femme au visage modelé à ravir et aux yeux profonds' and 'sa voix tendre et grave'. Sybil remembered Edy's fiercely critical approach to her actors: 'She gave us such a lashing, we'd come away from rehearsals bruised beyond words – but with a feeling that there was something we *might* be able to achieve if we went down to the nethermost hell and then struggled back and up.' After the performances she wrote to Edy: 'I should always jump quite selfishly at the chance to being produced by you because you teach me such a lot. I wish I had more work with you.'

This was the first of three occasions when she appeared in a full-length play with Edith Evans. The two actresses were, Mary Casson says, 'enormous friends who admired each other's work'. She and Ann once went to stay for the weekend at Washendon Manor, Edith's period farmhouse in Biddenden, Kent. Although her and Sybil's very different lives and temperaments meant they were never close, Edith was a frequent visitor to Carlyle Square, as John Casson recalled: 'It was best when she was the only guest. Lewis' thrusting logic and disciplined thought underpinned by immense artistic sensitivity and insight, Sybil riding her bounding imagination like a battle-charger galloping over everybody, but making them get up and gallop too, and Edith's gorgeously orchestral voice commanding attention by its more smoothly flowing magic, was all like watching and hearing not a play, but a kind of Olympian circus.'

The demanding roles in the Greek drama had aggravated Sybil's trouble with her voice. 'I'm going away on Sunday for a week's silence – away from Lewis and the babes,' she wrote to Colette O'Niel. 'I hate that – but the silence will be good. My voice is awful.' Happily the rest did the trick, for they now had no money and no management, and were compelled to accept parts in a feeble thriller, *The Mystery of the Yellow Room* by Gaston Leroux, directed at the St James' by the American J Harry Benrimo. *The Times* critic recommended it to all who wished to know 'how human and at times really pathetic Miss Sybil Thorndike can be as the heroine of a theatrical "shocker",' but confessed to be in the dark about what the mystery was. 'The new play is great fun,' she told Colette O'Niel. 'I do love any sort of play if it's played for all its worth. It's a lark, and I do love Benrimo – so does Lewis.'

During the run the young Laurence Olivier came to see the play. The Casson and Olivier families had remained friends during the war years: as they grew up the three Olivier children – Sybille, Dickie and Laurence – had often played with the Casson children, with Sybille (who was named after Sybil) sometimes baby-sitting for the youngest ones. The two families had adjacent holiday cottages in Dymchurch – Athene Seyler was also a neighbour – and would spend summers there. When Sybil's father died, Father Olivier was one of those who had comforted her mother. Soon afterwards he was appointed rector of St Mary's in Letchworth, Hertfordshire. Agnes Thorndike acted as his organist, living for a while in the Queen Anne rectory (now part of St Christopher School), where Sybil would visit her with the children.

In 1917 Father Olivier had asked Sybil and Lewis to observe ten-year-old Laurence play Brutus in a production of *Julius Caesar*, and give their opinion of his performance. After five minutes, Sybil recalled, they knew he was a born actor, and told his father he'd never be able to keep him off the stage. Now thirteen, Laurence had come to a matinee of *The Mystery of the Yellow Room* with his father, and was taken round afterwards to see Sybil. This was his first taste of the professional theatre, and of Sybil as an actress. His mother, on whom he had been greatly dependent, had just died. Before long he was to look upon Sybil as 'my surrogate mother'.

Sybil and Lewis now needed a secretary, and took on Susan Holmes, who would stay with them for forty years. Within the family, Eileen had married a naval officer, Maurice Ewbank, and given up the stage to have children. Russell had married Rosemary Dowson, who now gave birth to their son Daniel. Rosemary was one of the twin daughters of Rosina Filippi, reputed to be the half-sister of the great Eleonora Duse, who had briefly directed Shakespeare at the Old Vic before Ben Greet. The twins were identical: Mary remembers Sybil having a long conversation with one, and refusing to believe it when told it had been with the other. The family legend is that Russell fell for Fanny, proposed to Rosemary by mistake, and realised his error too late. It was to prove a difficult marriage, during which Sybil and Lewis frequently had to come to the couple's rescue, usually over money or finding them a home.

Despite its poor reception, *The Mystery of the Yellow Room* ran for four months, bringing in some much-needed money. But to be stuck in such an inferior play was clearly a waste of Sybil's talent. Then she had a stroke of good fortune. Then unknown in England, Grand Guignol was a type of theatre of horror that had become hugely popular in France. Staged in the smallest theatre in Paris, the Théâtre du Grand Guignol in the Pigalle district, the plays featured blood-curdling stories of street life, crime, insanity and murder most foul. The management liked to measure the success of a play by the number of people who fainted during a performance. The producer Joseph Levy wanted to bring the genre to London. He was warned that, while it appealed to the morbid and unstable French temperament, it would not suit the solid and phlegmatic British character.

Ignoring this advice, he leased the Little just off the Strand, and hired for his project 'the most brilliant theatrical family now working upon the English-speaking stage'. He believed Sybil to be 'the best emotional actress' of her time; but he also took on Lewis, 'the most consistently excellent producer I knew', and Russell, 'an actor of undoubted brilliance and remarkable versatility'. This view was a reflection of Russell's recent work at the Old Vic, to which he had returned as leading man and co-director, playing Falstaff, Shylock, Brutus, Bottom, Malvolio, and Aufidius in *Coriolanus*. Sybil only agreed to be involved if her brother was too, telling Levy that 'if you want horrors, he's got a mind like a ghost story in a morgue'. Here, she saw, was a chance to play to a wider audience the kind of bloody melodramas they had acted with such relish in their childhood. For her and Lewis it was also an opportunity to work again with a permanent company in a challenging variety of plays and roles, though perhaps not quite the kind envisaged by Barker or Annie Horniman.

Also in the company were George Bealby, an excellent player of farce, Dorothy Minto, Nicholas Hannen and, later, Athene Seyler and Franklin Dyall. Each programme played for about ten weeks. A typical performance consisted of one main play, normally a melodrama, and four or five short plays or sketches. Several of them, daringly, were about the war. Lewis, who translated many of them from the French, set out to create fear rather than just horror. 'He used suggestion rather than blood-dripping props,' Russell recalled. 'We frightened our audiences rather than disgusted them.' Versatility was required, as the actors had to move from comedy to tragedy to fantasy to farce to horror in a single evening.

During two seasons Sybil appeared in three or four pieces in each of seven programmes, in a dazzling variety of roles: they included a street-walker, an aristocratic countess, a sixteen-year-old slut, a singer, a mad woman, a bereaved mother, a chorus-girl, and several unfaithful wives. She was variously murdered and stuffed in a trunk, had her eyes gouged out, was strangled, poisoned and asphyxiated, encased in plaster, and crushed with her lover under a moveable ceiling. In an effort to understand the unstable minds of some of the characters, she made several visits to the Bethlehem Hospital (the old Bedlam), then in Lambeth, where her sister-in-law Elizabeth Casson, a psychiatrist on the staff, enabled her to observe some of the mentally ill patients. The more decadent the character, the more she seemed to enjoy playing the part. 'She was a nasty, horrible, loathsome creature,' she said of the heroine in H F Maltby's *A Person Unknown*, 'but I adored the part.'

Although some thought the plays too ghoulish, they were a box-office hit and developed a cult following: Londoners came, saw and shivered. Most critics enjoyed the programmes, but a few took exception to the low life depicted, labelling the productions 'brutal' and 'bestial'. St John Ervine wrote loftily: 'Too much of the stuff given at the Little is concerned with neurotic prostitutes and lust and drink and general horror. This sort of thing may interest overfed voluptuaries and creepy-crawly people with flabby insides, but I cannot imagine that this fashion will continue to be popular.' Later Lewis persuaded him to write a play for one programme.

The critic of *Play Pictorial* was especially stern about *GHQ Love*, declaring: 'It is nasty without any redeeming artistic feature, save the acting of Sybil Thorndike. Its environment savours of the lavatory, and its morals of the brothel.' During one performance a woman shouted insults at Dorothy Minto for daring to play a *demi-mondaine*. On other occasions people simply walked out. Dion Boucicault went a step further, refusing even to go to the Little, arguing that Grand Guignol was a waste of the company's energy and talent. There were many objections to Maurice Level's drama *The Kill*, on the grounds that the sight of a man being thrown out of a window to a pack of wolfhounds was not a pleasant one. The play almost provoked a prosecution by the Society for the Prevention of Cruelty to Animals, until an inspector was shown that the agonised howling of the wolfhounds was Lewis and the stage manager blowing through lamp glasses in the wings.

The greatest controversy was caused by *The Old Women* in which, to the strains of a requiem mass, a trio of lunatic women (one played by Russell, another by Athene Seyler) gouged Sybil's character's eyes out with knitting needles. In order to avoid the expected trouble from the Lord Chamberlain, Lewis had deviously persuaded the vicar of Wrotham in Kent, where Russell lived, to apply for a licence for a performance in the village hall in aid of a girl guides' jamboree. It was duly granted for this apparently insignificant performance, after which the Little company was legally free to stage it in London. But there were violent reactions to its horrors. 'Even strong men sickened,' Archibald Haddon wrote, after a first night when several people walked out. During another performance a man stood up, shouted 'This is monstrous', rushed out and was sick in the foyer. Nurses were in attendance to deal with the casualties, and people wrote to the papers deploring the degeneracy of the theatre. Sybil as usual defended the play she was in, arguing in the *Daily Express*: 'It is a beautiful play, perfectly worked out. The only thing to which it can be adequately compared is the music of Mozart.'

Meanwhile, to Levy's fury, the Beardsley-style poster on the Underground was considered too much for the sensibilities of the public, and ordered to be withdrawn. In Oxford the Vice-Chancellor considered the plays unsuitable for students, and banned Sybil from bringing a selection of them to the New, on the grounds that while Elizabethan plays were bloody, they at least had tragic power, whereas 'in the Grand Guignol the morbid lusts of the shambles was unatoned'. His decision provoked outrage, not least that he should have the power to ban plays already passed by the Lord Chamberlain. Sybil wrote to Murray: 'I can't help admiring the VC – he does fight – it's a pity he doesn't fight for the things we all feel to be good!!'

She received excellent reviews, many critics suggesting she raised the melodrama to the level of tragedy. One wrote: 'Miss Thorndike's performance, in its tigress ferocity, has almost a Bernhardtian vigour.' But Hubert Griffith, while praising her in the *Observer*, asked: 'Ought Hecuba to be doing these things?' The question was answered by *The Times*: 'Miss Thorndike's wan face, her penetrating voice, her skill in presenting a gradual crescendo of "nerves", her general sense of style, lend these shockers an artistic dignity which they do not intrinsically possess. You feel that the actress is too good for the work, and yet so fine in it that you couldn't bear the thought of her absence.'

For Lewis, the seasons were immensely rewarding, giving him a rare chance to direct five completely different items in a single evening, and to work with an ensemble company. Sybil enjoyed them for other reasons. 'Horrors have been my meat and drink day and night since I was a tiny child,' she explained. When she read the plays she was terrified, in particular by *The Old Women*. But they gave her a chance to pull out all the stops, in a manner which few contemporary plays allowed. Playing such parts, she said, was 'like a confessional, only more satisfying'. Her nightmares temporarily vanished, as did her fear of the dark. In defence of the plays she asserted: 'Horror is one of the big emotions, and to rule out any emotion deprives the healthy, God-fearing citizen of a legitimate outlet for his violent nature. What wonderful churchwardens, parish councillors and justices of the peace we might have, were they able to enjoy a little more than they do the goodness that there is in this adventure of horror and other violences. But then they might begin to sympathise with criminals; they might begin to understand the unrespectable – the outcasts – and of course that would be bad for the world!'

Sybil confessed to a friend: 'Lewis is dead tired and we are working so fearfully at the moment. When we are late and have constant early rehearsals we get all bad-tempered and loathsome! I'm hopeless about being late at night, I *can't* get up to work.' She always did though, and proved her stamina by playing no less than 25 parts over the two seasons.

After the first season she reflected on the value of the experiment: 'We have had a most interesting time here, and I think a one-act play theatre has been established,' she wrote to Murray. 'It's of such benefit to have this sort of work occasionally – technically one needs it – it does require a more than ordinary concentration.' She added: 'I've been working at Hecuba all this time and I hope I'll be better if I do it again.'

During the Grand Guignol seasons she saw Sarah Bernhardt, now 76 and in London for the last time, in *The Trial of Jeanne d'Arc* and *Daniel*. She was struck by the 'golden bell' of her voice, which almost turned the plays into opera. 'She was always a little remote from the person she was playing, but very beautiful to the ear,' she recalled. After one performance she and a few other actors met her on stage, where she gave a speech. 'Then the glorious golden voice became real, intimate and personal.'

Russell now returned to the Old Vic where, in the space of five weeks, he achieved the astonishing feat of playing King Lear, Hamlet, Peer Gynt and Sgnarelle in Molière's *L'Amour Médecin*. *Peer Gynt* marked the first public performance in England of Ibsen's poetic play, and Russell gave what many considered the performance of his career. 'Russell *is* Peer Gynt, a born romancer,' Lilian Baylis told Sybil, who agreed that the role of Ibsen's great fantasist – 'Peer, you're lying' is the first line of the play – suited him perfectly.

She and the family now took a holiday at Dymchurch, spending their days swimming, exploring the marshes and picnicking in the fields. They joined forces with Athene Seyler and her family, who had a cottage further along the sea-wall: while the children played on the sands, the adults talked theatre. Sybil always warmed to other people's children. Jane-Ann Jones, Athene Seyler's daughter, recalls: 'I was an only child, and I felt she loved me as much as her own children.' They visited friends of Sybil's mother, the children's writer E Nesbit and her husband, who had a bungalow nearby in New Romney. One day Coward breezed in and talked entertainingly about the theatre, songs, music and plays – as John remembered it, 'without so much as pausing when his mouth was full of cake'.

Sybil now began to be active offstage for a variety of causes, a habit that would continue throughout her life. When a row between the government and the London County Council threatened to stop Shakespeare school matinees, she joined Shaw, Ben Greet, the Archbishop of Canterbury and others in protesting against the move. With Lena Ashwell and others she was involved in an appeal for the Winter Distress League, set up to help provide work and entertainment for some of the one and three-quarter million unemployed. Though always nervous beforehand, she often made speeches. Booked to speak before a performance of *Everyman* at the Old Vic, she told Lilian Baylis: 'I am thoroughly scared!! I wish I could speak entirely extempore but I doubt being able to. I'm worked to death and I need to be very fresh for speeches!! It's my last speech, I've made up my mind!!'

She soon changed it again. In a lively debate on censorship at a Church Congress, she argued that the theatre should be free to present all aspects of life – after which another speaker criticised her for telling her audience 'that a parade of evil and filth was good for people to listen to'. In the more congenial atmosphere of a dinner held by the theatrical OP (Opposite Prompt) Club, she took the London theatre-going public to task for its conservatism. 'It would rather go to the same plays over and over again than see its favourite actors in something different,' she complained. She raised the question of an honour for Ellen Terry, arguing to cheers that it was a scandal there had been no official recognition of her 'wonderful career and unique genius'.

In between the Grand Guignol plays she gave strong performances at the Lyric, Hammersmith in two productions by the Phoenix Society, both directed by Allen Wade and designed by Norman Wilkinson, and each staged just twice. An offshoot of the Stage Society, the Phoenix Society specialised in works by Elizabethan, Jacobean and Restoration playwrights, whose plays were then considered to be dull, unstageable and, in some cases, obscene. Its productions engendered great enthusiasm for the work of many neglected writers. They also created a stir in smart society, often drawing a more distinguished audience – Desmond MacCarthy called it 'the snob rush' – than weekday West End first nights.

The Witch of Edmonton by Rowley, Dekker and Ford was staged to celebrate its three-hundredth anniversary. Alongside Edith Evans, playing the small part of a raving madwoman, Sybil as Mother Sawyer was in her element: Archibald Haddon saw 'a deformed old hag – hook-nosed, toothless, ghastly…Bent nearly double, she croaked like a raven and hissed like a snake.' He also enjoyed the theatrical effect of the Devil, played by Russell, 'whose gaunt features recalled Henry Irving's Mephistopheles'. Sybil's other role was Evadne, the mistress of the libidinous king, in a revival of Beaumont and Fletcher's *The Maid's Tragedy*. Here, in a story full of murders and suicides, the critic of *The Times* labelled her 'a born tragedy-queen', writing that 'she has authority, style, ample gesture, "line", and superb elocution, helped by a voice that can send a thrill through the house….There are notes in Miss Thorndike's voice that send a cold shiver down your back.' He regretted that 'the modern theatre so rarely permits this fine actress to essay parts of this calibre'.

During these productions she and Lewis had long discussions with one of the Phoenix founders, Montague Summers, an eccentric Catholic writer and believer in the occult and witchcraft. 'We found him a most stimulating mind, a subtle piercing researcher, and we learned much from him,' she remembered. 'He fascinated us by his knowledge and intense interest in black magic and diabolism, and all forms of decayed religions and ancient beliefs. We always came away from him with a firmer belief in the Catholic faith.' This odd friendship with Summers was evidence of her ability to hold different, often conflicting, religious beliefs in her head.

Sometimes these matinees were true family occasions. In *A Christmas Carol* at the Lyric, adapted from Dickens' story by Russell and directed by Ben Greet, Russell played Scrooge, Rosemary Thorndike was Belle, Ann and Mary played Tiny Tim and Cratchit, Sybil featured as the Wife of Scrooge's Nephew, and even Mrs Thorndike made an appearance, as Mrs Fezziwig. For another matinee Sybil was with her other family, taking part with many leaders of the profession in the first act of a new play, *Shall We Join the Ladies?*, which Barrie had written for the opening of the theatre in the Royal Academy of Dramatic Art. The starry company included Johnston Forbes-Robertson, Gerald du Maurier, Fay Compton, Violet Tree, Lillah McCarthy, Irene Vanbrugh, Charles Hawtrey and Dion Boucicault; Sybil was, according to *The Times*, 'spectrally intense' as one of the dinner guests.

Charity matinees for good causes were then frequent, and Sybil was involved in several. Her stamina seemed extraordinary. With Lillah McCarthy and Constance Collier she was in a Pageant of Dress in aid of the People's League of Health. She played in two matinee performances in aid of the Old Vic Reconstruction Fund: one for the Shakespeare Association at the New, where she and Russell played a scene from *Cymbeline*; the other at the Palace, when she again played Hecuba in *The Trojan Women* – as she had done a few days before for the LNU.

As a leading actress, she was often asked for help by others keen to start or further their careers. 'Do please forgive me, being the plague I am, I am always asking help for people,' she told Leon M Lion. 'All the girls I ever knew think if I speak a word to you it will go well with them because you were the one who helped me!' She was writing about Winifred Oughton, who had been with her at the Old Vic. 'She is a very clever character actress – has done more period work than anything, but is awfully good in modern character. If you've got the tiniest thing you could give her I'd be so grateful. She has done such good work.' This was just one of many small acts of kindness she was to perform over the years.

Many stage stars took part in music-hall programmes, and Sybil was no exception. She played in Act 4 of *La Tosca* at the London Coliseum, in a 'prolonged engagement by general request'. Also on the bill were Grock the clown, the ballerina Tamara Karsavina, 'America's Songsters' Harriet and Marie McConnell, the Sutcliffe Family ('Scotland's Most Versatile and Popular Entertainers') and Norman Drew, Bass ('Ballads of Bygone Years'). In this 20-minute version of Sardou's play, *The Times* noted: 'Her wonderful voice could be heard in every corner of the vast theatre, and yet she never seemed to be raising it at all unduly.' Hubert Griffith was less impressed: 'There is no time for subtlety here, and Miss Thorndike does not attempt it;' he wrote. 'Each phrase fell on my ears like a note of doom.'

Sybil's breadth of experience in Shakespeare continued to impress. 'Forgive me if I direct your attention once again for the hundredth time to Miss Sybil Thorndike,' Archibald Haddon wrote. 'When the gods give us greatness, let us welcome it with glad hearts and open hands.' He had pestered Sybil to send him a complete record of her work in Shakespeare, but she had refused, saying she didn't want to be thought egotistical. 'Really and truly it is my art that I am in love with, not myself,' she told him. Eventually she sent him a list, detailing 107 parts in 25 plays. Lewis meanwhile came up with 60 parts in 23 plays, while Russell, an expert in the art of doubling – he had played 16 roles in *Macbeth* alone – totalled an astonishing 180 parts in 25 plays.

Sybil added to her tally in a gala performance of *Macbeth* at the Odéon in Paris in June 1921. It was organised by the French government to mark the eventual signing of the peace treaty, and to raise money for British, American and French charities. Sybil was invited to play Lady Macbeth opposite James Hackett, the famous American tragedian, who had recently played Macbeth in London opposite Mrs Patrick Campbell. The production was directed by the eminent actor Louis Calvert, and the company included John Drinkwater as Banquo, Leslie Faber as Macduff, and Miles Malleson as the Porter.

It was a tough assignment: Sybil had not played the part since 1915, and had to rehearse late at night after her Grand Guignol exertions. Edy Craig insisted she borrow the dresses Ellen Terry had worn, as they were 'now beautifully supple and will almost play the part by themselves'. One of these, sewn all over with real green beetle wings, had been a sensation at the Lyceum, and immortalised in a portrait by John Singer Sargent. 'The instant I put on Ellen Terry's dress something happened to me,' Sybil recalled. 'Not a tremble, not a quake.' When Hackett lost his way in the banquet scene, she hurled him across the stage, while whispering his lines in his ear. Afterwards she told him: 'Don't thank me, thank Ellen's dress.' Despite this hitch, it had been a satisfying occasion. 'I felt ten feet high that day,' she said later. 'Under great emotional stress I always feel enormously tall. It's a strange feeling: I seem to be on a higher plane, looking down on the audience from a vast height.'

While barnstorming at the Little, Sybil had made her screen debut. Like many stage actors she looked upon the burgeoning film medium, still silent, as inferior to the theatre. Her own film career began in 1920 with an extract from one of the Grand Guignol plays, *Progress* by St John Ervine. This was followed by a short silent film and a series of potted dramas. The short, *Moth and Rust*, was based on the popular novel by Mary Cholmondeley, and centred on fraud within a family. It was directed by Sidney Morgan, who specialised in cheap, unsophisticated melodramas. 'Sybil Thorndike conveys unrelieved tragedy in her interpretation of the erring wife,' *Kinematograph Weekly* noted, while *The Times* observed: 'She has a somewhat lugubrious part and dies very quickly, but she at least has time to give glimpses of her ability, and we look forward to her next appearance with interest.'

That came the following year in the silent anthology *Tense Moments from Great Plays*, which involved several other stage actors, beginning gingerly to dip their toes in the cinematic waters. The project gave Sybil a challenging range of parts, from familiar ones such as Portia and Lady Macbeth (with Russell as Macbeth), to Lady Dedlock in *Bleak House*, Marguerite Gautier in *The Lady of the Camelias*, Esmerelda the Gypsy in *The Hunchback of Notre Dame*, Hesther Prynne in *The Scarlet Letter*, Mrs Garland in *The Old Curiosity Shop*, and the title-role in *Jane Shore*. They filmed *Macbeth* during one week-end on a stage in a field in Teddington, while for *Jane Shore* Sybil recalled 'dying on the banks of the Thames with people in pleasure boats jeering at me as I died with a cross plastered on my bosom'.

The publicity for these 'one-reel masterpieces' described Sybil as 'England's Queen of Tragedy', then more dubiously claimed she had now 'established herself, unquestionably, as a star of the film world…and set her feet upon the ladder of Fame'. Sybil thought she was awful and, according to Russell, walked out of the trade show after the first film. *The Times* praised 'the genius of an actress who can undertake so difficult a task and emerge from her ordeal with such undoubted success'. Yet it was to be several years before she appeared on screen in a performance that merited the star label.

14

The Albery Partnership

1922–1923

'Everyone was against it. All our friends said we should be ruined'
Sybil on plans to stage Shelley's The Cenci

Writing to the critic Archibald Haddon in 1922, Sybil looked back on her eighteen years in the professional theatre. 'If my career so far has not been a howling financial success, at least it has been full of work and interest,' she reflected with satisfaction. This pattern now seemed set to continue: after her and Lewis' short foray into management with the Greek tragedies, they were hatching ambitious plans to encourage innovative work in the West End, as formidable a challenge then as now.

Most plays, she argued, were geared to appeal to children of twelve. 'The authorities have made the theatre wishy-washy, a milk and water sort of thing, and so today on the stage we see simple little stories that you can read every day in the newspapers,' she said in the *Observer*. 'You know the sort of stuff: charming and safe no doubt, but hardly stimulating to mind and imagination.' She put much of the blame on the Lord Chamberlain, citing an unnamed writer who wrote four 'brilliant and wonderful' plays for their Grand Guignol programme, which were banned by the censor. 'Any one of them France or Germany might envy, but there does not seem to be a chance of his work ever being produced in England, because he writes in very strong terms.'

The scheme she and Lewis now aimed to launch involved staging a popular play five nights a week, leaving Monday night free for an experimental play at reduced prices. 'We want to go as far as possible for the best,' Sybil explained, 'and on one night a week to produce other plays which may only appeal to a limited audience.' She realised the Greek plays were unsuitable for long runs, but criticised the public for being unadventurous. 'People are afraid of tragedy, and I am convinced that they are mistaken. Art, and above all dramatic art, offers an outlet for the tragedy of life. The sublime tragedy of the Greek plays gives expression and voice to the sorrows which otherwise remain hidden. It is far better they should find a way out.' She wanted their scheme to be available to a broad public, with no seat over five shillings.

Nothing came of this bold but risky scheme. But she and Lewis were soon given a chance to fulfil a long-held dream, after Sybil played Queen Katharine's death scene from *Henry VIII* at a charity matinee at the New. Her performance greatly impressed the actress Mary Moore, widow of Charles Wyndham, who owned the New. She told Sybil and Lewis that if they could find a good play to stage there, she would back them in their own management and underwrite any losses. Generously, she agreed to loan them £500, and let them have the theatre without a deposit for five months.

For women to be in theatre management was exceedingly rare; Gladys Cooper's spell at the Playhouse from 1916 was one of the few exceptions. *The Times* hailed the move. 'Everyone must be glad to see Miss Sybil Thorndike in command of a theatre. She stands in the foremost rank of our serious actresses, and it is in the general interest that she should have the opportunity of choosing parts for herself.' Initially they struggled to find a suitable play. Sybil received an astonishing 50–60 plays a week, of which she felt around 90 per cent were worthless. 'They've not a vestige of an idea, and their authors have not a vestige of talent for writing,' she complained. 'But you have to plough through them because of the possibility of finding a new author.'

Eventually she found Henry Bataille's social melodrama *La Scandale*, which was translated by Florence Bell. Sybil enjoyed a close and loving relationship with Florence, whom Elizabeth Robins described as 'the one person who, not of the theatre, yet loved and understood it beyond any other I had known'. When she had voice problems, she would sometimes stay at Rounton Grange, the Bells' spacious Yorkshire house near Northallerton. Part of the Murray circle, Florence wrote novels and plays for children in both French and English, and was very musical. She would arrive at Sybil's house in a beautiful chauffeur-driven car. Sybil observed later: 'She was like a second mother to me, and helped me in my theatre work almost more than any other woman. I loved her. She was my mental guide, and made me work at my French and keep up my piano-playing. She was a very fine pianist herself, and we used to play together constantly on two pianos.'

Sybil often inspired strong emotions in her women friends, and Florence

Bell was a supreme example, as is clear from a letter she wrote in this year. 'And now Sybil Thorndike – the incomparable – I wonder if you can realise what your friendship and affection have meant to me? How they have illuminated these years – these last years – for me?....Our music together Sybil – and our *wonderful* companionship! – don't forget me, beloved – but when I am gone where will you go for a rest cure? I've been so proud to be your friend.' She ended: 'Goodbye then beloved friend. I've lived to see you standing among the immortals.' In a further letter she wrote: 'Sybil beloved friend and companion, you must find someone else now....How divinely odd our companionship has been! And oh how much it has meant to me.'

But Sybil and Lewis decided to stage first a revival of *Jane Clegg*, in which she had achieved such a success in Manchester, and which she now described as 'a Greek tragedy in cockney, and not one word you could misplace'. Agate thought Ervine's play a small masterpiece of naturalism, and praised Sybil ('our most responsible actress') for shining in a very unshowy part. *The Times* felt it gave her only limited opportunities, but noted that 'what is required of her she beautifully accomplishes; she is earnest, wan, pathetic, scrupulously repressed, slightly hard'. Ervine himself wrote later that it was 'such a performance as a dramatist dreams of, but seldom sees'.

Set in the south of France, *Scandal* had run for three seasons in Paris, and was much sought after by West End managers. Here Agate was critical, observing that Sybil's 'persistent agitation' got on his nerves. The exhortations in rehearsal from her leading man, Leslie Faber ('Relax, relax, for goodness sake!'), seem to have gone unheeded. But Ervine defended her, saying the play would die if she didn't act in this manner, adding: 'I cannot pretend to like seeing Miss Thorndike exhibiting neurosis, but this does not alter the fact that she does it better than anyone else.' Though neither was an adventurous choice, both plays did good business, enabling the loan from Mary Moore to be re-paid, and allowing Sybil to play Medea for nine further matinees.

Before resuming her celebrated role, with Leslie Faber as Jason, she underlined Medea's more human side: 'Medea is Jane Clegg on a grander scale,' she observed. 'I shall most certainly not make her anything of a witch. She is a very human, lonely woman. Surrounded by foreigners who misunderstand her. Rather unreasonable at times: like Jane Clegg, she is too highly strung to be able to get on with her more commonplace partner.' She spoke of what she saw as the educative value of theatre: 'The whole tragedy is caused because neither can see the other's point of view. It is the cause of half the tragedies in the world today. The reason I think theatre-going so good is that it shows other people's standpoints.'

The writer Graham Sutton provided a vivid and detailed picture of her performance, observing 'the full sure gestures, the marvellous light and shade of that great deep heroic voice, the sneer and the anguish, the barbaric insolence and pagan despair; now loud and menacing, now crafty, suppliant, seductive, now deep again with the note of a great bell, the despair of mariners aghast on a lee shore. And always restraint, restraint…so much expressed, so much still left to the imagination.' For Ervine her performance highlighted defects as well as virtues. 'She is not always careful to preserve the distinction between queenly rage and the twisted sneers of a woman suffering from neurosis,' he wrote in the *Observer*. 'She is undoubtedly the most distinguished tragic actress on our stage, but she has not completely mastered her craft, or rather she has allowed certain mannerisms to grow upon her.'

The matinees were packed, and their box-office success and that of *Jane Clegg* and *Scandal* enabled Sybil to tackle a part she had long coveted, that of Beatrice Cenci in Shelley's dark tragedy *The Cenci*. That spring she had taken part in a reading of it at King's College in London. Written in 1819, Shelley's play, the story of a woman tried and condemned for murdering the father who has raped her, had been banned by the stage censor because of its themes of incest and murder and its horrific picture of evil. 'I regret that people would desire the public performance of this unspeakable horror,' wrote Lord Buckmaster, a member of the Lord Chamberlain's advisory committee. 'It can only sicken, terrify and distress.' Tree declined to play Count Cenci, believing no one would enjoy the play except 'impotent old men and nymphomaniac spinsters', and that the part of Beatrice required several Bernhardts rolled into one.

The centenary of Shelley's death meant the ban was about to expire. Sybil and Lewis decided to mount the first-ever public production in London (the Shelley Society had staged a private one in 1886). 'We hope to do four shows, and think that will arouse a great deal of interest,' Lewis told Murray. They checked with the censor's office, which formally lifted the ban, prompting one popular newspaper to announce that Sybil was to stage Shelley's 'dull and dirty' play. It was another bold, apparently foolhardy decision. 'Everyone was against it,' she recalled. 'Lady Wyndham said it would be an utter failure. All our friends said we should be ruined. But for us it was sink or swim: we just didn't care; we wanted to justify our existence.'

Shelley's gloomy poetic drama is not a great work, but it has some good dramatic moments. It appealed to Sybil politically as well as dramatically, as she explained to a journalist shortly before the first of 16 performances at the New: 'To me Count Cenci is not so much a villain as Shelley's protest against the world of organised society. He is the capitalist who can buy heaven and earth with his ill-gotten gains.' Asked how she intended to play Beatrice, she was unusually coy: 'That depends! Something may speak to me in the night, and I shall alter all my ideas at the last moment.'

The company included Robert Farquharson as the tyrannical Count Cenci, Brember Wills and Lawrence Anderson, with Lewis playing the Judge. The first performance was attended by many literary figures, and was hugely applauded. Sybil was in fact far too old and powerful for the part of the twenty-year-old Beatrice, described by Shelley as 'most gentle and amiable'; one admirer likened her more to 'Brynnhilde going into battle'. Many found it hard to believe that a woman showing such heroic strength in the later scenes would have been raped. 'She would have destroyed old Cenci in her cradle,' Graham Sutton wrote. 'She was too hefty and formidable.'

But her majestic and forceful performance under Lewis' direction drew appreciative reviews. In the *New Statesman* Maurice Baring described her as 'inexpressibly dignified, grave and moving, and at the end magnificent', while in the *Sunday Times* Sydney Carroll, after noting in the early scenes 'an indecision, a nervous eccentricity that marred much of the beauty of her performance', wrote that 'her final speeches were delivered with extraordinary purity and tenderness'. Agate however was not stirred, writing: 'I should as soon think of being sorry for a marble statue as of being sorry for Sybil.' But he then compared her to his idol Sarah Bernhardt. 'There is one matter in which Sybil not only beats her great rival, but is so immeasurably her superior that she disappears from view – that matter being the conveyance of moral grandeur.'

Beatrice was a gruelling part, and prompted another scare with her voice. 'I am so very sorry I cannot come to the ceremony on Friday next,' she wrote to the secretary of PEN, the newly formed international writers' association. 'My voice has been so bad this week that I am warned that, unless I keep almost entire silence during the day, it will not last out to the end of our season here. As we are doing *The Cenci* for the last fortnight, it would be a very serious matter if I could not play, so that I am cancelling every outside appointment.'

The Cenci was a commercial success, justifying the gamble of staging a difficult play in the West End. In celebration Sybil and Lewis took a two-week break in Italy without the children, their first proper holiday for eight years, and their first trip to Europe as a married couple. Walking was a supreme pleasure for both of them, and they spent happy days from dawn to sundown among the hamlets of the Ligurian Alps. Moving on to Amalfi, they stayed in a converted monastery where Ibsen had once been a guest, and where the previous year – though fortunately they didn't know this – Mussolini had planned his 'March on Rome'. 'Italy is simply gorgeous,' Sybil wrote home in ebullient fashion. 'We went to a funny little church yesterday and the priest was killing. The Italians are darlings. Tons of love.'

But work was never far away. In Rapallo they visited Gordon Craig, and, with hopes of being able to stage Shakespeare in the West End, talked about collaborating with him on *Macbeth*. But when they returned to London they could find no theatre to take the production. This didn't stop Craig turning up with the sketches and charging Lewis for them, an episode which inevitably soured their relationship with the notoriously unreliable designer. Meanwhile Sybil had been contacted by his sister Edy Craig, to see if Ann and Mary would appear in a children's play, *Between the Cracks*. 'I'm afraid Ann won't be any good,' she replied. 'She's very shy as yet and I don't want to make her unhappy.' She foresaw problems about getting a licence for Mary to appear – she was still only eight – but added: 'I needn't say how wonderful it will be for her to have such a start – I'm thrilled to death over it.'

The theatre in London was now in transition, with new playwrights and directors coming through. Pinero, Jones and their contemporaries were on their way out, Coward and the Bright Young Things were storming in. Basil Dean staged Clemence Dane's *A Bill of Divorcement*, Maugham's *Rain*, James Elroy Flecker's *Hassan*, and Galsworthy's *The Skin Game*. Barry Jackson brought the Birmingham Rep company to London, putting on Shaw's *Back to Methuselah*, *The Immortal Hour* with the young Gwen Ffrangcon-Davies, and the long-running *The Farmer's Wife* with Cedric Hardwicke. There were also foreign imports, including Capek's *RUR* and *The Insect Play*, and Eugene O'Neill's raw drama *Anna Christie*.

This was the scene in April 1923, as Sybil and Lewis teamed up in management with Mary Moore and her son Bronson Albery. A courteous, self-effacing but shrewd man – he had been a barrister – he combined a great interest in new plays with an instinct for the public's taste, which Sybil and

Lewis demonstrably lacked – indeed, they often fought against it. Albery's astuteness acted as a valuable buffer to Lewis' evangelism and Sybil's overflowing enthusiasms. In the West End, where there was little room for the classics or for radical experiments, he was the ally they needed. He was also a friend, inviting the family for Sunday lunch at his large Hertfordshire house. 'He was a very hale and hearty character, who used to play games with us,' Mary Casson remembers. 'He looked a bit like Gerald du Maurier, and Sybil and Lewis were very fond of him.' They were to be in partnership with him for five years, staging some of their finest work under his auspices, and sharing a desire to work for the good of the theatre as well as for their own careers.

Their first joint venture, staged at the Criterion, came as a shock to those who had seen Sybil only as a tragedienne. *Advertising April* was a lighthearted romp and a satire on the cinema, suggested by Albery and written by his friend Herbert Farjeon and the critic Horace Horsnell. Dressed in bright silk pyjamas, Sybil played April Mawne, a caricature of a glamorous film star, dubbed 'The Girl Who Made the Sunshine Jealous'. After the huge strain of playing Medea and Beatrice Cenci, she delighted in this switch from tragedy to frivolity, and the chance to send up the world of film. She was dismissive of those who wanted her only to play tragedy. 'I want to be lots of different people,' she told Russell. 'Isn't that what's acting is for?' To Farjeon she wrote: 'You needn't say I've done you both proud – it's you that's done it – the play is so good – I *like* the second act in spite of what you say. It's a bit knockabout – but then things *are* knockabout – at least I've found life so! Great fun too!'

The critics were astonished, but delighted by her vigour, high spirits and sense of fun. 'I have never seen her show such agreeable physical witchery,' Sydney Carroll wrote in the *Sunday Times*, enjoying 'a picture of feminine filmy magnetism that would make Euripides storm his tomb and Dr Gilbert Murray shed tears of ink'. 'She steps from the sublime to the ridiculous with an effrontery and a gusto that are positively entrancing,' cooed *The Times*. Even Agate approved of her change of mood. 'Let her who is already a great actress be wise in her time and generation,' he wrote. 'Let her look not on masterpieces only.' But Graham Sutton was not sure she was right for the role. 'The lamp of intelligence shone through the turnip-head too brightly,' he suggested. 'The player was helplessly greater than the part.' Sybil herself relished the change: 'April is an enormous relief after tragic parts – like taking a bath after a dusty day,' she said. 'I shall not find it necessary to be so desperately trivial in my leisure hours in order to counter-balance the horror parts I have been playing recently.'

Her so-called leisure hours were as full as ever. She gave a reading of Browning's *The Ring and the Book* for the Poetry Society, a recital for PEN, and a concert for the Theatre Girls' Club in Soho. She also laid the foundation stone of Shakespeare House, a block of flats built for working people in Shoreditch. As so often, her support for good causes took a practical form. For a sale of gifts to complete the fund-raising for the East End building, she agreed to run a stall, and set about soliciting theatrical mementoes from her friends: 'If you had one tiny relic of your time with your mother that you could spare, it would be a wonderful thing,' she told Edy Craig. 'It's a splendid house, and reasonable for purses that haven't anything beyond the dole.'

Her concern for others was also apparent in a letter to Lilian Baylis, who was facing an operation. 'This is just a line to say we're all thinking of you – saying a prayer for you – and cheering you on,' she explained. 'I'm going to Mass on Thursday so I'll be especially near you in thought. You're so wonderful and your spirit is so wonderful – you're an encouragement to everyone. God bless you darling, you'll be splendid and come thru' like the trump you are, all fit and jolly again.'

She also offered her support to the feminist activist Dora Russell, who was having a difficult second pregnancy. 'Poor you! I do feel so for you,' she wrote. 'And you are really so wonderful – you never give way – a born fighter – the new arrival will be born with fists, I'm sure!…If there's anything I can do for you, do let me – you must take such care of yourself now.' Dora was married to the philosopher Bertrand Russell, who was, Sybil explained, 'one of Lewis' gods'. He had recently stood as the socialist candidate for Chelsea, Sybil's constituency, and been heavily defeated. 'We can't all help wishing that he'd stood for a seat that wasn't so safely Conservative,' Sybil told her. 'It would be of such infinite value to have him in the House – but I expect you are a little relieved and his other work has to be considered!'

Advertising April had a successful eleven-week run, a month longer than originally planned. Sybil and Lewis then took it on a provincial tour with *Jane Clegg*, *Medea* and *Scandal*. Touring was, as always, a great pleasure to both of them, enabling them to play to different types of audiences. But occasionally Sybil wearied of the continuous work, as she confessed to Edy Craig. 'I am disappointed not being with you today – lovely Sunday in the country – curse Lewis and rehearsing!' She was in some despair about attitudes to theatre.

'We have plenty of actors and actresses who are doing great work, but we do not really appreciate the art of acting,' she observed, suggesting the English cared more for the music-halls than the theatre. 'I do not mean to deny that there is a genuine theatre-going public. But it is a small one, and it is not the public of the stalls. There is far more appreciation of the drama in the five-and-ninepenny than in the twelve-shilling seats.'

While on tour they tried out in Birmingham a new production of *Cymbeline*, which they then brought to the New. 'We chose it in a spirit of challenge,' Lewis explained to a journalist. 'We want to know whether Shakespeare as we want to do it will be acceptable to the London public.' It was another risky venture, since they had chosen one of the least coherent and plausible of Shakespeare's plays, described by J C Trewin as 'an odd and lovely collision of the Renaissance with Snow White and Lear's Britain', and often thought impossible to stage. At the Old Vic during the war Sybil had played the courageous and steadfast heroine Imogen, a part made famous by Ellen Terry at the Lyceum; now she wanted to attempt it again. Part of its appeal for her was no doubt the Grand Guignol moments, notably Imogen waking to find herself next to what appears to be the headless corpse of her husband.

Lewis' production was a bold, jazz-age one, heavily influenced by Barker's pre-war Shakespeare work at the Savoy, with a simple setting but vivid, abstract costumes. But like those earlier productions it failed at the box office, reflecting once again the West End audience's resistance to Shakespeare. Most of the critics gave Sybil a hammering, finding her mannerisms irritating. Desmond McCarthy drew attention to 'that perpetual lowering and then raising of her voice at the end of a sentence, which often destroys the verse, and over and above that suggests a false note, reminiscent of the business-like alacrity of a kind governess setting down her little pupils to their morning tasks'. In vain did Sybil argue that Ellen Terry's performance had been in a heavily cut version, which emphasised Imogen's charm and obscured much of the play's harshness. The production ran for just three weeks at the New.

Discouraged by the failure, the Albery-Thorndike-Casson partnership next staged *The Lie* by Henry Arthur Jones, a leading playwright of the late Victorian years, best known for his well-made drawing-room melodramas. At a time when the more naturalistic style of acting exemplified by Gerald du Maurier had begun to hold sway, this kind of piece had gone out of fashion. Written in 1913, it turned out to be Jones' last play. With Lewis directing her in a company that included Mary Merrall and O B Clarence, it gave Sybil another chance, as a wronged but noble woman betrayed by her sister, to unleash a torrent of emotion, and in the process, as Russell observed, 'do a little throttling'.

The climactic moment of the third act was an emotionally charged scene in which Sybil's character cries out to her devious sibling, 'Judas sister! Judas sister!' Hannen Swaffer in the *Daily Express* described the burst of applause that followed as 'the loudest enthusiasm I have ever heard in a theatre. Full-throated roars came from the stalls and gallery. It had been an intense scene, acted with a hurricane of genius, that forced tears down hundreds of faces.' Sybil had to take twelve curtain calls, and another fifteen at the end. Jones, who had not had a success for many years, was much moved by what he called 'the inflaming sweep' of her acting. Afterwards he thanked her for what she had done for his play: 'What words of praise can I choose to describe the patient tenderness of your quiet early scenes, swelling into stronger but still reserved and self-contained emotion, startled at last into the poignant and terrific fury of your great tragic abandonment? Take all the dictionaries, and pick out from them all their superlatives of eulogy, and I will multiply them again and again.' Hubert Griffith was also bowled over: 'In its restraint, its simplicity, and its beautiful understanding and rendering of each one of the emotions demanded, it was the most nearly perfect performance I have seen her give.' But *The Times* was cool: 'Miss Thorndike and Miss Merrall give able and lavish displays of emotional fireworks in parts that call for little else.'

Sybil's name was increasingly appearing in the press outside the review columns, where her views were sought about topics such as 'My Dream Home'. This proved to be an old house in Devon or Cornwall, 'comfortably large, but not too large, for I should not want too many maids, and I should never, never want stylish living'. There would be a little theatre and a music-room, equipped with a grand piano and a selection of instruments. She would keep lots of pets – horses, dogs, cats, goats – but 'anyone who hunted or wanted to hunt from my ideal home would be promptly turned out!' Would she miss London? 'No, I should want to keep in touch with my friends, but I should not want to go to parties, and I should not mind how isolated I was.'

In November she was awarded an honorary degree of Doctor of Laws by Manchester University, in recognition of 'a devotion to her profession which had had a profound influence on national art'. The only other actress to have received this honour was Ellen Terry. On the day, with the poet John

Masefield and the Archbishop of York Cosmo Lang, Sybil processed in bright scarlet robes and a golden hood through the streets of Manchester to the Free Trade Hall. Masefield, who hated publicity and was terrified by all the press attention, remarked: 'It's just like *Advertising April*.' During the eulogy, Professor Alexander noted: 'Miss Thorndike is dear to our hearts in this city since she first came among us in the great days of the Gaiety,' and asked: 'Dare I breathe a comparison with Signora Duse herself?' Sybil was seen to shake her head: though flattered by the comparison, she thought it quite inappropriate: 'I've always been so much rougher, much more experimental, absolutely different,' she said later.

She had seen Eleonora Duse earlier that year, and thought her the greatest actress of all. 'Her voice was not particularly melodious, but what she did with it made a miracle,' she remembered. 'Her beauty was from within; the movement of her body and those beautiful hands all significant.' Duse had been outstanding in Ibsen roles, and Sybil saw her play two of them: Mrs Alving in *Ghosts*, and Ellida in *The Lady from the Sea*. Duse was now 65, but this seemed irrelevant to Sybil: 'As Ellida, with hair quite grey and no touch of make-up, she was a young woman. Her struggles and strivings were those of a young woman. She had no age….I think she must have been the perfect actress – her art so controlled that her spirit could soar free.'

Sybil now made contact after a long gap with the American actor John Sayer Crawley, one of Ben Greet's company on the 1904 American tour. 'Master Rawdon', as she and Russell called him, had become a kind of elder brother to them. There had been some sort of jokey secret society in their friendship, with Sybil describing him as the 'Great and True Master of the Owls and Leader of all Choughs and Best and Bravest of Panthers!' Now she wrote: 'I'm a beast and a cad and a thief and a cur to boot!!', starting a correspondence with him and his wife Mary that was to continue for the next thirty years. As well as family news ('Russ is a film director and star and *loves* it… Lewis is kept at it very strenuously, but is well and splendid'), she held forth about the theatre: 'The West End here is curiously lifeless – we're waging war all the time and get the name of being mad enthusiasts – and I hate society – and the West End (typical) actor is society, and it's no good for work.'

During the run of *The Lie* she was in a single performance of Gordon Bottomley's verse play *Gruach*, directed by Basil Dean. The story of the young Lady Macbeth on the night before her wedding, it also featured Malcolm Keen, Felix Aylmer, Hermoine Baddeley and Walter Hudd. Dean, much feared by actors for his bullying methods, tried to stop Sybil standing on tiptoe when she became emotional. Agate, who disliked the play, was impressed, observing that Sybil 'looked so ineffably radiant, and spoke her lines with so communicable a quality of ecstasy, that I forgot all about the piece, and remembered only that in this kind of trance-like emotion, this suggestion of auto-hypnotism, she is without peer on stage'.

The Lie played to full and hugely enthusiastic houses for 188 perform-ances, and helped to restore their management's fortunes after the failure of *Cymbeline*. For Sybil its success was a mixed blessing. 'I do not believe in runs,' she had said before it opened. 'No actress can remain flexible if she plays one part for months at a time. And when flexibility has gone, everything has gone.' But during the run she was already hard at work on what would turn out to be the role of her lifetime.

15

Saint Joan

1923–1925

'It's a stupendous play, and says all the things that
the world needs to hear at the moment'
Sybil to Bernard Shaw

While attending a performance of *The Cenci*, Shaw had been especially
struck by Sybil's playing in the trial scene. Afterwards he told his wife
Charlotte that he was going to start writing his play about Saint Joan. This
greatly surprised her, as for some years she and others had been urging him to
do so, but without success. She had even been leaving books about Joan and
her trial lying around the house, in the hope that he would read them. When
she asked him why he had changed his mind, he replied that he had just seen
an actress who could play his Joan.

Shaw had been pondering the dramatic possibilities of her story for more
than a decade. He disliked the way she had been used as a vehicle for nationalism, romanticism or misogyny. His first notion of a play was far removed
from the final result. In 1913, while staying, aptly enough, in Orleans 'in Joan
of Arc country', he wrote to Mrs Patrick Campbell: 'I shall do a Joan play
one day, beginning with the sweeping up of the cinders and orange peel *after*
her martyrdom, and going on with Joan's arrival in heaven.' He added in true
Shavian style: 'English literature must be saved (by an Irishman, as usual) from
the disgrace of having nothing to show concerning Joan except the piffling
libel in *Henry VI* – where Shakespeare has a diabolic version of Joan who
conjures up evil spirits – and the 'extravagant decorum' of Voltaire's *La Pucelle
d'Orléans*. He ended: 'Would you like to play Joan and come in on horseback
in armour and fight innumerable supernumeraries?' Mrs Campbell didn't. In
1920 Joan's canonisation by the Catholic Church temporarily renewed Shaw's
interest in the idea, but he continued to blow hot and cold.

Sybil had risen in his esteem since she had first played Candida. He had seen her powerful performance as Hecuba: writing to Lewis from Ireland in August 1922, he had ended the letter 'Love to Sybil the Great'. Shortly after catching *The Cenci*, he had made clear his view of the Lord Chamberlain's banning of it in a speech on Censorship: '*The Cenci* was forbidden, yet it is now licensed, and has been performed by the great actress Sybil Thorndike, and no one is a penny the worse.' There is no doubt that, while others had suggested Joan to him as a good subject for a play, it was Sybil and *The Cenci* that provided the catalyst.

Shortly after seeing her as Beatrice, Shaw made inquiries about the where-abouts of the records of Joan's rehabilitation. But he said nothing of his plan to Sybil and Lewis. In April 1923 he started to write the play. Claiming to be guided by Joan herself, he said 'the words came tumbling out at such a speed that my pen rushed across the paper and I could barely write fast enough to put them down'. He finished it in September, writing to his fellow-Fabian Beatrice Webb: 'I've had no trouble writing it, the historical material being ready-made and interesting.'

Sybil and Lewis had been making their own plans. The rebellious, single-minded Joan had captured her imagination years before: she had read several books about her, as well as the historical documents. She had also read several Joan plays but, according to Russell, 'always hated the sort of church-window-saint that they invariably portrayed'. She and Lewis commissioned a play from the poet Laurence Binyon, today best remembered for his war poem 'The Fallen'. 'He was such a beautiful writer, and we had great talks about it,' she remembered.

But then they got wind of Shaw's play. Sybil was upset at the thought of missing such an opportunity, but unhappy about breaking the arrangement with Binyon. So Lewis wrote to Shaw, asking if the report were true, hoping he would consider Sybil if it was, and explaining their dilemma with Binyon. Shaw replied in May: 'Yes: I am at work on a Joan of Arc play, and have already finished the first act. I warned Drinkwater off, but forgot Binyon. Of course Sybil ought to play Joan – at least *my* Joan: Gladys Cooper will do for Binyon's. I daresay I shall be ready by the autumn.' Binyon, when told of the situation, generously withdrew from the commission, saying Shaw would write a better play.

Shaw claimed to have modelled Joan on Mary Hankinson, a tough, energetic feminist and committed suffragette, who ran the Fabian Summer

Schools for many years, and captained their cricket team. Another possible model was Elsie Fogerty: Lewis believed Shaw may have drawn on her unstoppable drive, and her ability to compel people, sometimes against their will, to join her enterprises. Whether Shaw was influenced by Sybil's personality is equally open to speculation; but there is no doubt that her vigorous, passionate nature, combined with her strong but not uncritical Christian belief, made her an ideal choice for Joan. Sybil said later, 'I was young for my age, and Joan was old for hers, so it was just about right.'

Shaw told Sybil that *Saint Joan* was the easiest play he had ever written, since all Joan's words were there in the records. 'Have you read the histories?' he asked her. 'Every single one,' she answered proudly. 'Forget them,' Shaw replied. '*I'll* tell you what to think.' He finished the play in August, then invited Sybil and Lewis to hear him read it at his home at Ayot St Lawrence, a secluded village in the Hertfordshire countryside. Three other people were present on that momentous day: Shaw's wife Charlotte, Bronson Albery and the Antarctic explorer Apsley Cherry-Garrard, a neighbour and close friend of the Shaws.

Writing next day to her son John, Sybil conveyed the excitement she and Lewis felt. 'He read it beautifully – he ought to have been an actor really – and from the moment he started we couldn't move! You know how I've always longed to play Joan of Arc and I'd been having the most awful quirks that I wouldn't like the Joan he'd written. But we needn't have worried. It's the most marvellous play and we're so excited we don't know what to do.' Shaw was a brilliant reader, and Sybil was enthralled from the first scene. 'So daring and true, with that girl exactly as I had imagined her,' she thought. After the moving scene on the Loire, when the wind changes by an apparent miracle, Shaw paused and said, 'That's all flapdoodle; now the real play starts.' He then launched into the tent scene, in which heresy, loyalty and nationalism are debated. This impressed Sybil mightily, as did Joan's speeches in the cathedral and trial scenes, which she thought 'sheer poetry'. When Shaw reached the Epilogue she and Lewis were in tears. 'It was the most amazing experience,' she recalled.

Though Shaw had used the historical records, the whole play, including the trial scene, was infused with the Shavian spirit, and some of it marked with an unexpected beauty. But Joan herself he consciously made unromantic. Sybil loved his tough, strong-willed, crafty and unsentimental heroine, and the fact that Shaw was using theatre in the way she felt it should be used, to shock people into awareness of political and religious matters. 'It's a stupendous play, and says all the things that the world needs to hear at the moment,' she told him. She admired his championing of the free-thinker within the Church, which echoed her own dislike of dogma, and his 'deep understanding of Catholicism', a faith that had always interested her. She also identified passionately with Joan's rebellion. 'Had she lived today, I would have followed her without question,' she remarked later.

She was temporarily alarmed when Elizabeth Robins spoke to her about the play. Did she realise the responsibility she was taking on by agreeing to impersonate a woman who was the ideal, indeed an idol, for so many people? 'Be sure what you are undertaking has nothing in it of self ambition,' she warned Sybil sternly, afraid perhaps that Shaw would simply scoff. 'This is not just another part in the theatre.' But when Sybil showed her the play, she was appeased, and full of encouragement.

Albery however had reservations, and was uncertain about risking a West End production. Shaw, now sixty-seven, had rarely proved commercial, and was not as popular as he had once been: although he had written *Heartbreak House* not long before, there were still those who remembered and hated him for his stinging 1914 polemic 'Common Sense about the War'. In this virulently anti-war and subversive piece, he had compared England and Germany to 'a couple of extremely quarrelsome dogs', and advised the soldiers in both armies to 'shoot their officers and go home'. This had provoked newspapers to tell their readers to boycott his plays, and libraries and bookshops to remove his works from their shelves.

To Albery his new play seemed a curious mixture of poetry, Shavian humour and unfashionable costume drama. He was also doubtful about the Epilogue, set twenty-five years later, in which Joan appears in a dream to the Dauphin, now King, and the principal characters return from the dead to reflect on their treatment of her. Yet the combination of Sybil's rampant enthusiasm and Lewis' flinty determination over-rode his doubts. They boldly offered to invest all their money in the play, Sybil feeling it was almost a duty to do so. 'If I have to go and live in the King's Cross Road,' she said dramatically, 'I shall be perfectly happy.' So Albery agreed to stage the play at the New. Sybil had told John Casson: 'Shaw says that he wants us to do it as soon as possible and we're going to as soon as the silly old *Lie* is finished.' However, *The Lie* continued to do excellent business for several more months, with Sybil still receiving rapturous curtain calls at every performance.

Shaw had promised his next play to the New York Theatre Guild, which had premiered *Back to Methuselah* and *Heartbreak House*, so the world premiere of *Saint Joan* was staged just after Christmas at the Garrick on Broadway, with Winifred Lenehan as Joan. Despite very mixed notices it caught on with the public, and ran for 215 performances before going on tour. Meanwhile in London there was a flurry of machinations behind the scenes. In January George Grossmith, the manager of His Majesty's, having heard about the success of the Broadway production, sounded Lewis out about the possibility of a big production at his theatre. Lewis, presumably with Sybil's approval, broke this news to Shaw, but suggested another alternative, asking whether Shaw might approach Barry Jackson about doing *Saint Joan* at the Regent or elsewhere. 'What I had in mind was, if we succeeded in working successfully together, to make it the opening play of a fairly permanent theatre for us, with a definite policy.'

Shaw passed the idea on to Jackson, explaining the arrangement with Albery and Lady Wyndham at the New, and the approach by Grossmith. He went on: 'But Lady Wyndham belongs to the 1880s, and Grossmith to the world of the stunt revue. Casson and Sybil Thorndike, both as modern as can be, and very nice people at that, would be happier at more congenial artistic moorings. I need hardly say that I should be much more at home with you than anyone else, so you may take me for granted if you are disposed to discuss the matter with Casson. I should in fact have offered you the play if it had not been clear that it should go to Sybil Thorndike, as the only possible Joan.' For whatever reason, neither of these alternatives bore fruit. Shaw persuaded Albery to withdraw the *The Lie*, which was still playing to full houses at the New, and start rehearsing *Saint Joan*.

London was seething with casting rumours for the English production. Shaw, who was co-directing with Lewis, wanted good Shakespearean actors, people who could speak 'bigly', as Sybil put it. In February he responded in skittish mood to Lewis' initial proposals: 'I think you may jump at Ernest Thesiger for Charles. Lawrence Anderson will be all right for Baudricourt if he can get over his obvious stage terror of the manager's wife. Miss Thorndike for Joan is quite a good suggestion. So that is three parts settled.' The rest of the letter is an engaging mixture of serious casting ideas ('Brember Wills, who is really a dreamy creature, has not the biting edge for the Inquisitor') and characteristically flippant remarks ('Milton Rosmer will say "My lord, the carriage waits" sooner than not be in the cast').

Lewis had suggested himself for Cauchon, the Bishop of Beauvais, but Shaw told him he was 'not wicked enough' for the part: 'I have an idea that you could do Stog (the Chaplain de Stogumber); and if you think you can, there can be no question about its being the sensationally effective part. It has been puzzling me more than any of the others: I had serious thoughts of asking Sybil to double it while she is being burnt.'

Lewis took his advice. The final company included Ernest Thesiger as the Dauphin, E Lyall Swete as Warwick, Eugene Leahy as Cauchon, and the mellow-voiced O B Clarence as the Inquisitor, with Raymond Massey and Milton Rosmer in smaller parts, and the 13-year-old Jack Hawkins as Dunois' page. As was then the custom, Lewis gave complete scripts only to the principal actors. The rank and file were given 'sides', pages which contained merely their own lines and the cues for them, a curious Victorian hangover soon to die out.

The sets and costumes were to be created by the versatile Charles Ricketts, a leading illustrator, painter, art critic and collector, whose work for the theatre rivalled that of Craig. A friend of Wilde, Yeats and Sickert, he was a pioneer in the theatre in the protest against naturalism, and favoured a mixture of clean lines and rich colours in his stage designs. The music was to be by Lewis and Sybil's friend John Foulds, whose *A World Requiem*, a plea for peace after the horrors of the First World War, had been played at the Albert Hall the previous November. As rehearsals loomed the house in Carlyle Square echoed to the sounds of Foulds experimenting with French peasant music, and Ricketts' piping voice contrasting with Lewis' deeper tones as they discussed the design sketches.

O B Clarence recalled the first day of rehearsal. The company sat in a circle on the stage facing Shaw, who read the play to them. 'His delivery was clear and emphatic; his exuberance and enjoyment of the lighter scenes was refreshing to see; he acted each part and, at times, and at tense moments, I expected he would rise up and tramp up and down the stage.' Immediately the reading was over, and without any discussion of the play, Shaw got the actors on their feet. He conducted the morning rehearsals, acting all the parts and fixing the characters' moves and positions, then watched the scenes right in front of the actors, gave detailed notes, and left Lewis to implement them in the afternoon. This method led to difficulties. Lewis had to translate Shaw's Irish intonations, and try to help the actors communicate effectively with the audience: Shaw, he believed, was skilled at helping them get inside their characters, but not so good at making their performances large enough in the theatre.

The play was long, but Shaw refused to cut a single line. Lewis tried to speed things up; Shaw complained that his lines were being 'gabbled'. In Shaw's absence Lewis, revealing his stubborn streak, patiently and skilfully cut each of the seven scenes by five minutes. Raymond Massey remembered the battle's climax: 'After two weeks of rehearsal Shaw came backstage with his clipboard and notebook, which he threw down on a prop table. "Lewis," he said, "I don't think much good ever comes from these afternoon rehearsals." "We must have more of them," Lewis said. I think Shaw accepted defeat at that moment.' Lewis boasted later: 'I was a much better coach than Shaw; I would learn from the morning and then teach the duller actors afterwards. I had more tact, and anyway I think I knew what Shaw wanted better than he did.'

One particular problem concerned the Epilogue, which one critic compared to 'jazzing in Westminster Abbey'. Shaw defended it unswervingly: 'Without it the play would only be a sensational tale of a girl who was burnt, leaving the spectators plunged in horror, despairing of humanity. The true tale of Saint Joan is a tale with a glorious ending; and any play that did not make this clear would be an insult to her memory.' Yet as he admitted, there was within him a conflict between the tragedian and the clown. His obvious delight in the idea of a Church canonising someone they had burnt for heresy, witchcraft and sorcery led him, in Lewis' view, to over-emphasise this point 'with overplaying and funny business'. Lewis feared this would shock the audience more than necessary, and spoil the shape of the play, but he and Thesiger were only slightly able to rein in the joker.

Always looking for the best in people, and ignoring or not seeing their faults, Sybil spoke during rehearsals of her admiration for Shaw. 'He knows exactly what he wants. That is why I think he is easy to work for in the theatre. He has such beautiful manners that he never hurts. It seems as though he feels it would be an offence against himself to say anything harsh or hard. If he has to, then the criticism is cloaked in such a way that nobody could be offended. He can lay you flat and knock all the conceit out of you without making you feel humiliated. That in a man with such a tongue, who can flay institutions and people alive, as he does, is, I think, very remarkable. It is part of his charm. At rehearsals he is always quiet, always courtly, but there is about him the suggestion of a volcano. If anyone sets himself against him it would be to discover the force in him, but nobody ever does.' She was pleased when he agreed to keep in a line she had inserted in rehearsal: after Joan says 'I might almost as well have been a man,' Sybil had added: 'Pity I wasn't.'

Shaw wrote to Kenneth Barnes, the director of RADA: 'Sybil will be all right, if she remembers that in the third scene Joan does not know that she is going to be burned in the sixth.' Shaw liked actresses who were obedient to his wishes –'I like an empty head for my ideas,' he once said – and Sybil was generally a model in this respect. 'We worked together like one person,' she remembered. The day after the opening night Shaw wrote pointedly to the notoriously uncooperative Mrs Patrick Campbell: 'Sybil Thorndike for a whole month never let me doubt for a second that she regarded me as far superior to the Holy Trinity as a producer.' Sybil was totally admiring of Shaw's latest creation. '*Saint Joan* is the biggest play since Shakespeare and, being more tightly packed with thought, greater than many of Shakespeare's works,' she declared. Later she observed of Shaw that, although 'he minded character, he paid more attention to the reading of the lines than to anything else. Speech was the main concern: one would get the thought through the language.'

Shaw reminded Sybil that Joan was not a child or an angelically sweet little girl, but a sturdy young woman, whom he likened to a suffragette. He took her through the script, indicating the intonation of each line, which she accepted without question – even when he asked her to say one or two like the chimes of the cathedral clock. She agreed that, to avoid too ladylike a Joan, she should invent an accent. She based it in part on her Cornish maid's speech, the result being 'a sort of Lancashire cum the West cum this and that – what Nigel Playfair used to call Lumpshire'. She tapped into her maid's attitude to life: 'When I was uncertain how Saint Joan would behave, I put myself into the mind of this girl,' she said. 'She had a very common-sense view of life, and yet she was hard – a realist full of fine ideals.' She also found inspiration from another source: a week before the opening she wrote to Lilian Baylis: 'I'm thinking such a lot about you, working on St Joan – she's so like you – the only woman who carries on a concern of the people by prayer and sure, certain faith.'

'Sybil walked on air during the month's rehearsal,' Russell recalled. Unlike Lewis, she seemed to see no flaw in Shaw's rehearsal technique or acting ability. She admitted later that he was 'quite fierce' with her, but that 'I worshipped him, and I would have done anything – crawled on my hands and knees – to do what he wanted.' Her obedience no doubt came more easily because of his approval. 'Yes, you've got it, just what I wanted,' he would say repeatedly. 'I don't have to tell you anything, you know it.' To the young actress Molly Tomkins he wrote: 'Become a hard-hammered actress like Sybil, who can do anything I want with a cock of an eye.' Sybil found him dynamic and stimulating; her empathy with him was complete: 'Almost instinctively I knew what he wanted me to say and how he wanted me to say it.'

Shaw left Lewis to supervise the sets and costumes, taking little interest in them beyond insisting that Sybil wore 'real chain armour which clatters as she walks'. But when it came to the dress rehearsal he suddenly announced: 'Scenery and clothes have ruined my play. Why can't you play it in plain clothes, as at rehearsal? Sybil is much more like Joan in her ordinary jumper and skirt than when dressed up like this, with her face all painted.' Was this just Shaw playing the jester, or was he, as Sybil believed, really in despair? His attitude echoed Sybil's preference for simplicity, though it never quite went as far as Russell suggested: 'She hates scenery, hates costumes, and always says she can act better with a towel round her head and her face ordinary.'

Among those at the dress rehearsal was Margaret Webster, whose actor-parents Ben Webster and May Whitty had been invited by Shaw. 'There were only a dozen of us in the dim, white-sheeted stalls,' she recalled. 'Above, in the front row of the dress circle, you could just catch the glimmer of a white beard, a hand, an eyebrow. Nobody spoke. The houselights went out. The curtain slid up revealing Charles Ricketts' beautiful painted medieval drop; trumpets, a haunting little oboe melody; footlights out; drop curtain up.... By the end I was so profoundly moved that I have no recollection of what happened. I think my father spoke to Shaw. I think we went round to say thank you to Sybil and Lewis. I only know that "glory shone around".'

This was certainly the feeling of the audience at the first performance the following night, 26 March 1924, attended by many theatre luminaries, including Ellen Terry, Johnston Forbes-Robertson, Arnold Bennett, A A Milne and Somerset Maugham. There had been two thousand applications for tickets, and the production had sold out three weeks earlier. People had been queuing for the gallery since five in the morning, so the management provided teas for them, and opened the doors an hour early. The theatre was packed, and by curtain time the atmosphere was electric.

Sybil had been to the early-morning service that day, seeing her playing of Joan as akin to an act of worship. For the first time, as she waited in the wings for her entrance, she experienced no stage-fright. 'I was exalted, that's the only word for it,' she recalled. 'God was there, and I didn't care a hoot for anything, except getting over what Shaw had written.' Her performance, driven by her fervour and showing an inner radiance, held the audience throughout. At the end of the trial scene the applause was tremendous, though it was less after the controversial Epilogue. The play lasted until midnight, Shaw and his wife leaving before the end to avoid any curtain calls.

Despite the extremely warm reception, the critics were divided. Desmond MacCarthy was not alone in thinking it Shaw's greatest: 'It is immensely serious and extremely entertaining; it is a magnificent effort of intellectual energy and full of pathos and sympathy,' he wrote. There was widespread approval of the portrait of Joan as a human being as well as 'a pillar of faith and fire', although some people would have liked more of the saint and less of the revolutionary. Many were surprised that the iconoclastic, Protestant Shaw had presented the Catholic Church's arguments so fairly. Others, expecting wit and irreverence, were impressed by the beauty and eloquence of the writing. There was no one opinion, except over the Epilogue, Shaw's moment to 'talk the play over with the audience', which was attacked for being wordy, fantastic, or simply an anti-climax.

Shaw responded to this criticism with a jibe: 'When disapproval of the Epilogue persists after witnessing a second performance, the case is one of mental defect, and is hopeless.' Today the Epilogue seems thoroughly modern, and Shaw's focus on Joan's posthumous rehabilitation and eventual canonisation, and his bringing the characters back from the dead, an integral part of the play. Sybil believed this from the first, arguing that Shaw didn't want to 'send the audience out in a bath of emotion' after Joan had been burnt at the stake. Barker, who saw the play soon after it opened, also defended it: 'I am all for the Epilogue of course – though there again, I could wish it had been done differently,' he told Shaw, in a critique of the play. He had reservations about Joan's character, but not about Sybil's performance: 'I don't believe Joan was as glib as that – peasant girls (even saints) aren't glib. And then suddenly she turned Candida (with the Bastard)! Her last speech though in that church scene is magnificent – and Miss T did it magnificently.'

Among the critics the response to Sybil's performance was generally positive. In *The Times* A B Walkley felt she played Joan 'quite beautifully, rather like a headstrong boy...she has the very face and voice for it', while A E Wilson of the *Star* thought 'all the simplicity, the sublime tenacity of faith and passion for a cause, was shown clearly and vividly'. Agate thought her excellently real, 'boyish, brusque, inspired, exalted, mannerless, tactless and a nuisance to everbody', but implored Shaw to get her to drop the dialect: 'Whatever the quality of Lorraine peasant speech, it cannot have been Lanca-shire.' Others thought she overdid Joan's gaucherie and heartiness, while the *Athenaeum* critic felt that' when ever she got on to the high pedal, she was intolerable'. Darlington, thirty-five years and many Joans later, reckoned she alone had been able to capture both the peasant girl and the saint.

The morning after the opening, as Sybil and Lewis read the notices over breakfast, he predicted that with Shaw's name they might if they were lucky manage a run of six weeks. He could hardly have been more wrong. Shaw wrote to Lawrence Langner at the Theatre Guild: 'The play has repeated its American success here: it is going like mad; and everyone, to my disgust, assures me it is the best play I have ever written. Sybil Thorndike's acting and Charles Ricketts' stage pictures and costumes have carried everything before them. I am convinced that our production knocks the American one into a cocked hat.' He told Mrs Patrick Campbell that with Sybil's success in *Saint Joan* and Edith Evans' recent playing in *Back to Methuselah*, 'Siddons and Rachel were never so praised and exalted as these twain'.

Sybil liked to hear the honest opinion of those whose judgement she trusted. One of these was Christopher St John, a lively, forceful personality whom Sybil found stimulating, especially as her criticisms of her work were not always favourable. A week after the opening Sybil wrote to her in response to an approving letter about her performance: 'Chris darling, I got your letter just before I made up tonight – I don't know how to thank you – you know what a help your criticism is to me and how much I care for what you think, so I feel all happy and encouraged by what you said. There's such a lot I'd like to ask you about it – do let me come and see you one day.'

Her performance drew praise from the younger generation: when Dora Russell went backstage one night she found seventeen-year-old Laurence Olivier 'sitting on the floor by Sybil and expressing great admiration for her performance'. Another on whom it had a great impact was Eric Johns, later editor of the *Stage*, but then a teenager on his first West End visit. 'Like a mighty bell Sybil Thorndike's rich voice boomed out and reverberated through the hushed theatre. Each line intensified my excitement and raised me to a state of emotional ecstasy.' Nineteen-year-old John Gielgud wrote on his programme after the first night: 'Sybil Thorndike gave a magnificent performance, imaginatively conceived and simply carried out, almost altogether without mannerism, and full of charm and sincerity.'

Standing in the gallery another night was the playwright Christopher Fry, then fifteen. Nearly eighty years later he still remembered vividly the vigour and simplicity of Sybil's performance: 'The strength of her voice, which at the same time had a lyrical quality, was so perfect for the part. Every word meant something, and there was a great feeling of youth about it. Her vitality was absolutely superb.' The playwright John van Druten, then unknown, had queued for seven hours to catch her performance, and saw it again half a dozen times. 'I have seen other Joans since,' he wrote later, 'but not one of them has ever moved me to the realisation of a blinding courage, and of an indestructible religious faith, as she did.' But although Tyrone Guthrie, then a fledgling director, thought her 'stupendous' in the trial scene, he felt she was too hearty, too much 'the New Girl's Nightmare about the Games Mistress'.

A more unexpected element in the audience came from Kingsley Hall in Bow, a desperately poor working-class district in East London. One of the founders of the settlement, Muriel Lester, brought groups to see *Saint Joan* from the gallery seven times that summer. As a result, Sybil established a close connection with Kingsley Hall, whose leaders were pacifists: she visited often, and later laid the foundation stone for a new hall. She gave instructions to the stage-door keeper in any theatre she was playing in to let anyone from the settlement up to her dressing-room. It was there she met George Lansbury, a future leader of the Labour Party, which had come to power for the first time in January, under the leadership of Ramsay MacDonald.

There were many other attractions in the West End at this time. Fred and Adele Astaire were dancing their way through *Stop Flirting* at the Strand, Somerset Maugham's biting satire *Our Betters* was drawing the crowds at the Globe, Tallulah Bankhead was playing to adoring audiences in *The Creaking Chair*, while Edith Evans and Gwen Ffrangcon-Davies were giving matinee performances of *Back to Methuselah*. But there was little doubt that *Saint Joan* was the most significant production of the year. It struck a chord with the public: Sybil received scores of letters from people who said they had been inspired by the play to carry on with their humdrum lives. Her picture appeared in the *Tatler*, with the caption: 'Great in Shaw, Superb in Shakespeare, Frightening in Grand Guignol!'

Seven months into the run the show broke the New's weekly box-office (£2,533 14s 6d) and attendance (9,268) records. It was only withdrawn the following month, after 244 performances, because Matheson Lang had previously booked the theatre. One reason for its success was Shaw's ability to straddle the religious divide: Catholics seemed to like it as much as Protestants. His insistence on showing both sides of the argument led people to wonder if he was converting to Catholicism. 'There's no room for two popes in the Roman Catholic Church,' came the reply. For one performance he arranged for the Carmelite nuns of Saint Teresa to have all the seats: Sybil remembered them 'rocking with laughter' at the comic elements. The Epilogue, however, offended many clergymen, and Sybil had to respond to 'biting arguments and bitter letters'.

She summed up her feeling about Joan to a journalist after the first night: 'To me she has always been a flaming spirit with the military genius of Napoleon, but with a spirituality that he lacked. Joan was another Abraham Lincoln.' She had read that Joan never had a period, that this was possibly the source of her visions. Her strength appealed to her as a powerful indication of women's potential. Just as she had enjoyed playing all those male parts at the Old Vic during the war, so she relished Joan's warrior nature: 'I love playing a woman who has a touch of masculinity. I can't be sheer femininity. Feminine wiles I can't manage at all – and I don't want to.' Shaw seems to have understood this: bumping into her in Leicester Square shortly after the opening, he said: 'We're a success. What shall we do now?' Sybil replied: 'A play about Elizabeth and Richard III – both together.' Shaw laughed: 'Very well. And you and Ernest Thesiger can play both parts turn and turn about.'

The play and the role brought her tremendous fulfilment. 'It's a glorious play to be in, and I'm very happy about it,' she wrote to Ellen Terry, after the great actress had sent her a first-night telegram. 'A word from you cheers us more than I can say.' To her friend the actress and playwright Inez Bensusan she reported after the first week: 'It is going too wonderfully, and I do love the part so.' She was intrigued to discover that her two Christian names were those of Joan's grandmother. Later she recalled: 'I have never had anything in the theatre which has given me as much as *Saint Joan* did. Something more than just theatre. It confirmed my faith...and all the things I had to say I wanted to say.'

Sybil's children – John was now 14, Christopher 12, Mary 9 and Ann 8 – found their lives taken over by *Saint Joan*. 'We lived, breathed and slept the play,' John recalled. 'No one talked of anything else.' Mary remembers its impact: 'Ann and I were too young to go to the first night, but we saw it soon afterwards, and after that we used to sneak off on Saturday afternoons, and watch it from a box or from the wings.' Soon all four children could recite the whole play, in the appropriate accent for each actor. Sybil would give them little tests, quoting a line and challenging them to continue with the scene. Eighty years on Mary still knows it by heart.

Sometimes John and Christopher filled in for any missing extras by dressing as monks and going on for the trial scene, occasionally roping in a friend to make up the numbers. Sybil's mother was involved more directly, having agreed to play the organ offstage at the start of the cathedral scene. One day she was given a ride in her car by Lilian Baylis, a reckless driver, and was horrified to hear her shout at other drivers: 'I'm the manager of the Old Vic, so out of the way, you bounders! I've got Sybil Thorndike's mother in the car, and she plays the organ in *Saint Joan*!'

Sybil was very popular with the company. O B Clarence felt that 'her generous nature and her innate honesty shine through all she does', and suggested 'she has something of the radiance of Ellen Terry'. She also got on with the younger generation. 'I like Sybil Thorndike very much, and all my scenes are with her,' Robert Donat, involved in a revival, wrote proudly to his parents. Most unusually for a star actress, she insisted on being on first-name terms with the company, extras included. Godfrey Winn, only sixteen when he played a page, remembers her stopping him backstage on Saturdays, still dressed in her armour, and asking: 'Godfrey, are you all right for your Sunday dinner? If not, come and have it with us.' Jack Hawkins, playing Dunois' page, remembered Sybil saying to him: 'Up, up, *up* with your voice.'

She became good friends with the eccentric Ernest Thesiger. 'He was a peculiar person, but oh what an artist, and what lovely speech,' she remembered. Thesiger called her the 'most loveable of enthusiasts', and pinpointed the qualities that had brought her success: 'No one but a very simple and charming woman could have survived the exaggerated publicity from which Miss Thorndike has had to suffer, and no one with less of an iron constitution could have achieved so much by sheer hard work. Holidays from work, rest from indefatigable kindnesses, are unknown to Sybil.'

This lack of starry behaviour also impressed journalists. Hesketh Pearson, who later wrote a biography of Shaw, noted after an interview with her that she was not at all like the popular conception of a famous actress. 'After chatting with Miss Thorndike for several minutes, and hearing all about her children and her home, you rub your eyes and begin to suspect that this quiet, unassuming, gossipy soul may after all be her understudy, the aura is of so domestic a quality.' He was struck in particular by a contrast between her onstage and offstage personality. 'Here is a person whose sole object in life seems to be the making of everyone round her happy and comfortable – and yet her artistic inclinations are all towards the unhappy and the uncomfortable.'

Sybil and Lewis had become good friends with Shaw, and were among a number of writers, actors, politicians and economists invited to the regular lunch parties presided over by his wife Charlotte at their London home, where meat and fish were served for the non-vegetarian guests. Others who came included H G Wells, Bertrand Russell, Rebecca West and Sean O'Casey. The latter boasted that he was now 'a great buttie of Sybil Thorndike, a very natural, kind and loveable woman'. Mary Casson remembers him coming to their house 'looking very disreputable in a rather old mackintosh'.

Shaw's relationship with Sybil was essentially a paternal one: he never fell in love or wrote passionate letters to her as he did with Ellen Terry, Mrs Patrick Campbell and several other actresses. 'Shaw took me under his wing,' she recalled. 'He was as fatherly towards me as I think he could be towards any other human being.' Their relationship was one of mutual admiration and affection, reinforced by her belief that he was a deeply religious man. 'He often talked about religion,' she recalled. 'Nothing abstruse or analytical – perhaps because I am not clever. But he had read a lot about it and was constantly thinking about it. He seemed to know the Bible almost by heart, and was always quoting from it.' Shaw seems to have removed his mask in her company, allowing her to observe the difference between the public and private man: 'In public he was a know-all, and tried to be so. In private he behaved like an ordinary person: there were things which he admitted he didn't know, and tried to understand. He was conscious of his shortcomings. There was at times a humility about him.'

She treasured a rough proof of the printed play, on which she later wrote: 'This is Sybil Thorndike's book, and anyone who takes it is a liar and a thief and a murderer to boot, and please return it as fast as you can.' Shaw gave her a copy of the final version, inscribing it: 'To Saint Sybil Thorndike from Saint Bernard Shaw.' He also gave her a postcard of himself dressed in a Chinese robe, which she used as a bookmark. Another gift was a red-leather-bound illustrated 1876 edition of Henri Wallon's *Jeanne D'Arc*, an account of her life and trial. Sybil decided she would hand it on to an actress whose playing of

Joan meant as much to her generation as her own had at this time. It was to be forty years before she would find the right person.

At one point there were tentative plans to put *Saint Joan* on film. In October 1926 Shaw took part in Italy in a short 'phonofilm' interview, which used synchronised film and sound. The following summer, while considering whether to allow one scene from the play to be filmed, he and Sybil and Lewis made a five-minute phonofilm, in which they talked about the English language. Shaw decided to allow the cathedral scene to be filmed as an experiment, agreeing that more scenes could be shot if it proved successful. In July, in a small studio under a railway arch in Clapham, Sybil became the first actor to be filmed in a Shavian role. But Shaw was still uncertain about the idea, Sybil felt she was dreadful, and no further scenes were shot.

Tyrone Guthrie later described *Saint Joan* as the outstanding theatrical event of the 1920s. The critic J C Trewin called it one of the overwhelming performances of the first half of the twentieth century. It was Shaw's biggest commercial success, and was soon being performed all over Europe. It brought him the Nobel Prize for Literature for 1925. 'I wrote nothing in 1925, and that is probably why they gave it to me,' he observed. For Sybil too, the play marked a significant change in her public reputation. While her performances in the Greek tragedies and her two Grand Guignol seasons had revealed her as an actress of great power and emotional strength, and put her right at the top of her profession, with *Saint Joan* she became a household name. She was to remain one for the rest of her life.

16

Top of the Tree

1924–1926

'You always make me go out wanting to do tremendous things!'
Sybil to director Edy Craig

On 16 October 1924, some 1,200 people crowded into Christ Church, Westminster, a building that normally held 700. They overflowed into the choir stalls and the Lady Chapel, and sat on hassocks blocking the aisles. The occasion was not a church service, but a lunchtime recital. Dressed in pale grey velvet and standing at the lectern, Sybil recited a series of dramatic poems, by Shelley, Walt Whitman and Tagore, to the packed 'congregation'.

The remarkable turnout was a striking indication of Sybil's popularity. Shaw declared that if a plebiscite were to be held to elect an absolute monarch, a handful of actors would be in contention, but 'Miss Sybil Thorndike would wipe the floor with the lot of them'. This prominence enabled her to make her views widely heard. She had begun to be active in theatre politics: at a recent meeting of the Actors' Association to discuss a new contract organised by the Stage Guild, she had protested against a deal that clearly put the needs of managers before those of actors. Urging loyalty to the AA, she said: 'Let us stick to our guns. There are a lot of us who are loyal members of the association, but we do not show ourselves enough. I stand for the actor and the rights of the actor every time.'

She also stood for the right of playwrights to explore the seamier side of life. New plays such as Noël Coward's *The Vortex* and Frederick Lonsdale's *Spring Cleaning* had been labelled decadent and depraved in the popular press, with Gerald du Maurier and Owen Nares among the actors who criticised these 'indelicate' works. One critic wrote: 'It is not the kind of drama you would wish intelligent foreigners or servants to witness.' Sybil, however, argued that such plays were 'showing up quite legitimately certain phases of life, and it is stupid to suppose that no one knows anything about the sort of thing they deal with. I believe the evils in our midst should be shown up in an amusing way. That is where Shaw is so great a force.'

Her fame brought with it new pressures. Although willing to be photographed at home and give interviews, she did so reluctantly, believing there was too much publicity about actors' private lives. 'I realise that our public likes to know all there is to know about us,' she told one interviewer. 'But personally I think it is a pity that we lost the mystery part of the theatrical make-up; that the days when the theatregoer did not even know what their favourites looked like off the stage were better for the theatre as a whole. However, we live in an age that demands publicity; our public must know even the very bath soap we prefer, our favourite brand of cigarette, where we purchase our shoes and stockings!'

As if to prove her point, as well as to make some extra money, she lent her name to various products, including Snowfire Cream, Bristow's Georgian Toilet Preparations and Pond's Cold Cream and Skin Freshener. At first she turned down any connection with the Pond's products, on the grounds that 'everyone who knows me knows that I'm careless about my skin and personal appearance as anyone could be – to my shame be it said'. But then a full-page ad for the product appeared, somewhat incongruously, in the programme for *Saint Joan*, with Sybil doled up in ermine and pearls instead of armour, and confessing: 'Coming back from the theatre at night, a good cleansing with the cold cream is very refreshing.' She also lent her name to the Mah Jong Society, of which she was made an honorary president.

In parallel with this relative frivolity, she became increasingly in demand as a public speaker, and involved in numerous women's and political causes. One of these was Women in Medicine, now celebrating its jubilee. She was one of a dozen public figures – they included Louise Garrett Anderson, Millicent Garrett Fawcett, Eleanor Rathbone, Maude Royden and Ethel Smyth – to appeal for funds for the London School of Medicine for Women. At the jubilee dinner she gave the main address, speaking of 'our pride in the place won by our countrywomen, and gratitude for what their success has meant to us'. That summer, along with Shaw, Wells, Russell, Maynard Keynes and Virginia Woolf, she was involved in the formation of a cultural society bringing together the people of the Commonwealth countries and the USSR.

In October 1924 she re-visited her childhood, returning to Rochester

Grammar School to give a Shakespearean recital, and signing three hundred autograph books and programmes. She was delighted to find her two music teachers still there, as well as many of her friends. One current pupil asked her in awed amazement: 'Is it true that you and your brother know all of Shakespeare by heart?' Russell was in fact continuing to establish himself as a writer with his second novel *The Slype*, set in Dullchester, 'a sleepy old Kentish town', and praised by the *Manchester Guardian* for its Dickensian quality and 'a whimsicality of manner and a sincere love of humanity which by no means distantly recall the great Victorian'.

John and Christopher were now naval cadets on HMS *Worcester*, a training ship for the merchant service moored at Rotherhithe in Kent. 'I can't turn them from the sea, and it's a very good training anyway – it makes them fit and self-reliant,' Sybil told Master Rawdon. Both boys had for many years wanted to become sailors, and been encouraged to do so by Sybil. John had joined the ship in April 1923. Two days later Sybil wrote to him while on tour: 'Daddy and I are wondering so much how you're getting on in your ship. It must be very exciting but I expect it's a bit strange to begin with....Oh, how I envy you doing such exciting things.' John stayed with the ship for three years before going into the navy, and Sybil and Lewis went to see him at least every three weeks. Later he reflected: 'Sybil was already seeing me as another Conrad-Masefield-Melville, with perhaps St Paul casting four anchors out of the stern. She was in a seventh heaven of delight.' After Christopher joined the ship the captain told Sybil and Lewis he would be more suited to the navy, so they enrolled him at the Royal Naval College at Dartmouth in Devon.

Sybil created a small moment of history this year when she became the first stage star to be televised, in a broadcast to a British Association meeting in Leeds shot in John Logie Baird's experimental studio in London. 'I just moved my head about and said a few words – thrilling!' she recalled. She was also one of the first to get involved in radio drama. The BBC began drama broadcasting in 1922 with scenes from Shakespeare, initially from different stations around the country. Lewis, along with Nigel Playfair and Milton Rosmer, was made a guest producer early on: seven of the eleven 'play evenings' broadcast from the London Station in 1924 were his responsibility, and featured Sybil. She made her debut in two short plays from the Grand Guignol seasons: *Columbine* by Reginald Arkell, and *The Tragedy of Mr Punch*, by Arkell and Russell. She was then in an abridged version of *Medea*. A reviewer in *The Times*, without mentioning names, hinted at a problem for actors in this unfamiliar medium: 'The voice that is suitable to the theatre is not always the one that lends itself to transmission by wireless, and that argument one felt to be rather underlined in listening to the *Medea*.'

Although she was now indisputably at the top of the theatrical tree, Sybil had recently been joined there by another actress. Just before *Saint Joan* opened, Edith Evans had attracted sensational reviews for her playing of Millament in Congreve's *The Way of the World* at the Lyric, Hammersmith. Agate wrote: 'Miss Edith Evans is the most accomplished of living and practising English actresses. Leaving tragedy to Miss Thorndike, she has a wider range than any other artist before the public, and is unrivalled alike in sentimental and heartless comedy.' Their careers from now on were to run in parallel.

Sybil had promised to revive *Saint Joan*, and in January 1925 she buckled on her armour for a further 132 performances at the Regent, a 2,300-seat theatre opposite St Pancras station. In her curtain speech on the first night she expressed the hope that she could make the Regent 'a home for artistic and interesting plays'. She wrote to Gwen Ffrangcon-Davies, who had recently played Juliet there: 'So far people don't seem to mind coming to the Regent. I expect you paved the way for us.' Sustaining such an emotional role over a long run was demanding, but as she wrote, she had done the emotional work already: 'I think the *feeling* of a part should be done at rehearsal and during the time of study, and as far as possible converted into stage language, so that one is free in performance to perfect small details – which is not a possible thing without an audience who play with one. Hence the slight differences each night – differences scarcely noticeable to an audience, but to oneself immensely different.'

By way of contrast, Lewis directed her at the Regent in a Stage Society production of the 'revolutionary-pacifist' drama *Man and the Masses*, a politically controversial expressionist work by the German poet and playwright Ernst Toller, written while he was a political prisoner in Munich. It was the kind of work rarely seen in London. Agate hailed the production as a fine 'gesture of intellectual brotherhood' – Toller was still serving his sentence – and praised Sybil's performance as The Woman, who stood for the soul of humanity, noting that 'she spoke exquisitely throughout'. E A Baughan of the *Daily Telegraph* thought 'she acted with great intensity and unflagging inspiration', but another critic complained that 'she chanted most of her words', making it 'sometimes monotonous like a litany'. Many people were staggered by her ability to play such contrasting parts as this and Saint Joan simultaneously.

1. Leading lady at the Old Vic during its first four Shakespeare seasons, 1914–1918

2. Sybil's parents Arthur and Agnes Thorndike

3. Sybil and her younger siblings: left to right, Russell, Frank and Eileen

The Young Performer

4. Sybil aged four, at the start of her acting career

5. Ready for the dance in Rochester

6. Dressed for a piano recital

7. As Rosalind (fifth from left) in *As You Like It*, on tour in America with
Ben Greet's Pastoral Players in Minnesota, 1905

With The Gaiety

8. The 1908 company in Manchester included Sybil (seated, second from left) and Lewis Casson and Basil Dean (back row, far left and third from right)

9. Annie Horniman, repertory pioneer and feminist

10. Sybil in 1913 with the company in London, where she made a hit in *Jane Clegg*

11. As Julia in *The Two Gentlemen of Verona*, with Ion Swinley, Old Vic Company, Stratford Festival, 1916

12. Brothers in war: Russell (left) and Frank, killed in 1917: 'He was my great pal, my belonging.'

13. As Medea, 1920: 'Miss Thorndike is comparable with the greatest of them.'

Greek Tragedy

14. As Hecuba, with Ann as Astyanax, in *The Trojan Women*, 1920

15. Gilbert Murray: 'He was one of the guiding lights of my life.'

16. *The Trojan Women*: 'It made us one with those who had suffered thousands of years ago.'

Grand Guignol

17. As Lea with George Bealby in *Private Room No 6*, 1920

18. As Carmen in *GHQ Love*, 1920

19. *Moth and Rust*, with George Bellamy, her first feature film, 1921

20. Part of a publicity brochure for *Tense Moments from Great Plays*, 1922

21. As Nurse Cavell in *Dawn*, 1928: 'I believe I think in many ways as she thought.'

The Children

22. With schoolboys
Christopher (left) and John

23. With her musical
daughters, Mary (right)
and Ann

24. On holiday in
Dymchurch in Kent

25. With Lawrence Anderson in *The Cenci*, 1921: Shaw had found his Saint Joan

26. As Lady Macbeth, 1926: 'I was trammelled by all the scenery and my dresses'

27. As April Mawne, 'The Girl Who Made the Sunshine Jealous', in *Advertising April*, 1923

28. As Shaw's *Saint Joan*, 1924: 'I was exalted, that's the only word for it.'

At this time there was an upsurge in activity within the amateur theatre, of which Sybil heartily approved. 'I have a sneaking feeling that all acting of value should be amateur, that is, for one's pleasure, not necessarily for a living,' she wrote in a preface to a new book, *Play Production for Everyone*. She believed everyone should have the chance to act, and that the reserved English in particular needed an outlet for their emotions. 'Those of us with murderous instincts can tackle the Macbeths! I can assure you from personal experience, the result on oneself is most satisfactory. We can work off instincts which are purely destructive, and express them on an imaginative plane, and so make beauty out of what is so often used for ugliness.'

She invariably applied this argument to the Greek tragedies, which she returned to whenever there was a demand. In the summer of 1924 two planned performances had to be postponed when Lewis, through overwork, suffered 'a bad breakdown'. He was ordered to rest completely for three weeks, and had to leave the cast of *Saint Joan*. 'I simply could not face *The Trojan Women* without him, with the time so short,' Sybil wrote to Murray. 'I am dreadfully upset about it. The only saving grace is if we can do them in September instead, as we shall certainly try to do, there will probably be far better audiences – the theatre is suffering all round. It is all dreadfully unfortunate, and I was so looking forward to the performances, but I have been so worried the last few days over Lewis. *Nothing* but his (or my own) illness would have caused such a postponement. I feel hateful having to do this.' By July Lewis had recovered, as Sybil told Elizabeth Robins: 'Lewis is well again – it was worrying and stupid – but it's going to be a lesson to him and to me to work less frantically!' The lesson was never learnt. As one writer observed: 'Miss Sybil Thorndike is one of those tireless people who find in a change of hard work the perfect recreation.'

The matinees of *The Trojan Women*, in aid of the Women's International League for Peace and Freedom, were staged at the New in October, the *Observer* noting 'the magnificence of Miss Thorndike's voice' dominating the Chorus 'like the voice of Fate'. One of the Chorus, Margaret Webster, later a leading director, thought her superb. 'Her Hecuba was informed by her heroic vision of humanity, her sorrow for the world destroying itself,' she recalled. 'It was of truly classic stature....Even when I was breaking my back and cracking my knee joints crouching under the shield which held the body of Astyanax...the emotion transcended the extreme discomfort.' It was Ann's turn to play Astyanax. Now eight, she had already settled on her career. 'I want to be an actress like mother,' she said. 'My sister Mary has the same ambition. I want to be a tragic actress. Tragedy is real acting. My sister and I do not care much for comedies.'

Sybil stayed with the Greeks to play Phaedra in Euripides' *Hippolytus*, for three matinees at the Regent. One newspaper dubbed it 'A Greek Play Some Would Call Unpleasant'. Lewis again directed, with Nicholas Hannen in the title-role. Phaedra is a less satisfying part than Medea or Hecuba – the story essentially belongs to Hippolytus – and Sybil seems to have failed to get inside it. Agate thought her interpretation 'a trifle bourgeois' and rather too sensible: 'Moral indignation and elder pathos are this actress' forte, and in this play they are implied rather than formulated,' he wrote. The critic of *The Times* observed with thinly veiled irony: 'Miss Thorndike assumes a well-studied series of graceful, statuesque postures and speaks her lines as though she meant them.' At one performance there was a scare: rushing off to commit suicide, she nearly did so, falling off a rostrum and nearly breaking her back. Rather than have orthodox treatment, she invited a healer into her dressing-room. Although bruised and feeling stiff, she continued to work without a break.

The following summer she played Medea again at Murray's request, for an open-air charity performance in aid of the League of Nations Union, staged in Christ Church College, Oxford. 'What a perfect theatre that was!' she wrote later. 'Perfect for sound, and the open air gave Murray's fine English words a breadth which one felt was akin to the Greek.' The playwright Emlyn Williams, then an undergraduate, had a walk-on part, and recalled: 'The audience, mostly dons, were sitting in the sun, when the library windows flew open, and there was Sybil with her daughter Ann in her arms, about to throw her out. I could see the dons' consternation, because she was playing it so marvellously: it wasn't her child, it was Medea's.' Afterwards he watched Sybil and Lewis 'as they streaked across to Canterbury Gate, the youngest middle-aged couple I had ever seen – "Lewis darling, the thermos!" – and into a waiting taxi'.

Actors and critics were then more likely to mix socially than they do now. At the annual Theatrical Garden Party in aid of the Actors' Orphanage, which Sybil regularly attended, there was for once a reversal of roles, when the Critics' Circle performed 'Smithfield Preserv'd, or The Divil a Vegetarian', a witty burlesque by Ivor Brown of a typical Phoenix Society production, directed by Irene Hentschel. Sybil wrote a review for the *Daily News*, and enjoyed turning the tables on the critics by parodying their tendencies to show off their learning, to take a while to get to the point, and to write half the review before they saw the show.

She and Lewis had become friendly with Agate, whose witty, learned and often unpredictable reviews Sybil admired, even when they were critical of her work. Agate had seen Irving, Bernhardt, Duse and Ellen Terry, and thought himself the best judge of acting since Hazlitt. After reading his book *The Contemporary Theatre, 1924*, Sybil wrote to him: 'I've never had a chance of talking over your book, which interested me tremendously and is clearing up for me the fog in which I seem to be about the theatre.' She admired in particular 'your tremendous enthusiasm, your fire, and above all your deep love of the theatre and fearlessness in expressing what you feel – all these jump at one. And do you know, Jimmy, that's what such a lot of us feel grateful to you for, and why you hold an affectionate place in us, because though we may want to get up and fight you often and may disagree, yet we feel you *belong* to the theatre, and I'd rather belong to the theatre than anything.' Agate returned the compliment soon after, in a piece he signed 'Sir Topaz', where he described Sybil as 'an enormous force for good in the English theatre, being really interested in her art as distinct from the business of actress-mongering', and as 'an artist to her fingertips, a loyal, generous soul, a woman altogether jolly and altogether sensible, a good mother and a trustworthy chum'.

As always Sybil found time to read, and not just books about the theatre. She had, she revealed, read Hardy's *Tess of the D'Urbervilles* 'more times than I can count'. It now seemed she might play Hardy's heroine in a stage adaptation, having secured the stage rights. Florence Hardy, the writer's second wife, wrote to Sydney Cockerell in March 1925, after seeing Barrie and Sybil. 'She would make a good Tess I feel certain, but she is dubious now about the play. Barrie is very emphatic about its merits, and he's emphatic about anyone but TH touching it. Miss Thorndike is calling here after Easter, and will talk the matter over.' Sybil's doubts evidently continued, and Gwen Ffrancgon-Davies eventually took on the role.

She was, inevitably, sent numerous plays to read, and tried not to disappoint their authors. Edward Garnett, who had furthered the careers of Galsworthy, Lawrence and Conrad, sent her *The Girl at No. 5*, a play by H E Bates, who had just had his first novel *The Two Sisters* published. Sybil replied warmly: 'It is a pleasure to read a play with a plot out of the common run – and well written too,' before adding 'There's something wrong with the first act, I wish I could put my finger on it – it's a mixing of methods somehow – *you* would know what it is – but very interesting.' She liked to encourage experimental work, as she made clear when the pacifist and suffragette Evelyn Sharp sent her a play: 'I did like it awfully – I'd like to do it – I don't think, personally, there's any success in it – but you never know, and I most certainly can *never* tell – I wish you'd let one of the societies read it, because with so experimental a subject and treatment I think the commercial managements are shy.'

Sometimes she would seek out a script, as she did with Lytton Strachey after seeing a Sunday production of his play *A Son of Heaven*. 'I wonder if you would allow me to read your play?' she asked him. 'There are not many such parts this year for women – men get all the tremendous parts (except in the Greek plays) – I want to play a Queen Elizabeth one of these times. I've read eight different plays and been offered them – Bernard Shaw says she's too successful for him to tackle with interest – I hope that somebody might do her.' She also tried to persuade Hugh Walpole to adapt one of his novels for the theatre, using an absurd piece of flattery. 'Why can't you make *The Old Ladies* a play?' she wrote. 'It's as big as Greek tragedy, and how you do that in the just ordinary outwardly commonplace people is very wonderful.'

She was now becoming a figure of interest to sculptors and artists. Dorothy Dick created six reliefs of her sitting in her dressing-room during the run of *Saint Joan*. Clare Atwood tried to paint her as Hecuba from *The Trojan Women*, but had to leave the work unfinished, as Sybil was apparently unable to retain the same pose for long enough. Jacob Epstein was commissioned to create a bronze bust of her as Joan, and portrayed her 'gazing skywards as if hearing voices'. Placed on a wooden pedestal in a corner of her sitting-room, the bust became, Sybil told a visitor, 'a perpetual stimulus and inspiration'.

One marked feature of her work was her continual willingness to study a large and exacing part in order to play it for virtually no money and only one or two performances. This happened now with the disturbing expressionist piece *The Verge*. Published in England in August 1924, the play was written by the American Susan Glaspell, one of the founders of the Provincetown Players in Massachusetts for which Eugene O'Neill wrote many of his early plays. A complex spiritual allegory, it told the story of a woman seeking a new kind of life through experimenting scientifically with plants, and in the end descending into insanity. It was an obscure, literary work, but Sybil was entranced by it, and convinced she understood every word. She immediately began badgering Edy Craig to stage it, and to revive the Pioneer Players, which had stopped in 1921 through lack of money.

'Edy darling, I adore The Verge,' she wrote. 'Are you really going to do it? We're mad about it – and I'm longing to play it. The Stage Society is sure to bag it if you don't, and that would be sickening…. *Do do it.*' Soon her impatience had increased: 'I've found out about The Verge, so scared was I that it would be collared!! – it's expensive – very – still I think it's got to be done, don't you?….Let's meet as fast as we can and talk about it – I've never wanted to play anything so much except Joan, and this leads on from that – Angel – won't it be glorious doing it – I'm so excited I can hardly wait.' Then she could wait no longer: 'Well, what about The Verge? I've bought it!! Because it was £100 and I knew the Pioneers only had that….People will think it entirely mad – but I'm longing to do it – aren't you? Oh Edy, can't you see wonderful awful things in that play? I'm thrilled about it.' To Elizabeth Robins, as she waited to go on in the trial scene in *Saint Joan*, she wrote: 'It's the first time I've ever found a woman who says what I want to say without twisting.' In America Susan Glaspell wrote to her mother about the London production, and about Sybil, 'said to be the most interesting actress at present….Isn't that great?'

When the play was staged at the Regent for three matinee performances in March 1925, some critics thought it more awful than wonderful. 'For how much longer will the public be gulled into mistaking for genius the merely pretentious and absurd?' wailed *Vogue*, while the *Daily Express* described it as 'a repulsive play, written in the worst jargon I have had to listen to for years'. But the more serious critics recognised its ground-breaking quality: Herbert Farjeon in the *Weekly Westminster* considered it a brilliant psychological study, while Agate thought it a great play, to be considered alongside those of Ibsen, 'the work of a fine and sensitive mind preoccupied with fine and sensible things'. In the *Manchester Guardian* R Ellis Roberts described Susan Glaspell as the greatest playwright writing in English since Shaw began, while the artist Gwen John wrote to Edy Craig: 'It is a marvellous performance and you draw everything out of both play and players.'

Sybil's performance was ecstatically received by the audience, with the critics not far behind. 'She was positively terrifying in her uncanny suggestion of evil and mental fury,' shuddered the *Lady*. The *Era* enthused: 'For the immense understanding and fine nervous force, Miss Thorndike's performance has rarely been equalled on the modern stage.' In the *Star* A E Wilson thought it greater than her Joan: 'The part of Claire might have been written for her, so closely did she enter into the mood and personality of this insane creature. Her own personality was absorbed in the part, and in her gesture, tone, facial expression, deportment, and everything that composes the art of acting she was precisely right. She delivered herself of the mad jargon with frenzied conviction. She permitted us an astonishing glimpse into a mind: no other actress could have created such an intensity of interest.'

The play, the last staged by the Pioneer Players, was too difficult for any West End management. In other circumstances Sybil and Lewis might have produced it themselves. Sybil recalled that Hugh Walpole 'wrote to me in fury after the first performance, saying the play was destructive, and did I realise what danger I was in to be tampering with such thought? We just laughed ourselves silly. Of course I knew he was completely ignorant of what the play was really saying, as I dare say lots of the audience were.' At the time she wrote him a typically emollient letter: 'I appreciate what you said enormously. I believe I was too swept up in the part of Claire to be able to look at the play straight. From the first moment I read the script it seized me, and every single line in it seemed to me significant, but the other side of the footlights *is* different. As I told you, I *had* to play it even if no one had come, and get it off my chest!' But she also did it because she loved to do plays that broke the conventional mould, and to work with Edy Craig: 'You are so stimulating to me,' she wrote to her afterwards. 'You always make me go out wanting to do tremendous things!!'

After *Saint Joan* finished, Sybil appeared in *The Round Table* by the Irish playwright Lennox Robinson, alongside Raymond Massey, Ada King and Eliot Makeham. The play was a comic-tragic fantasy about a woman trapped domestically with a hopeless family, who has a vision of the life she might lead, and makes a break for freedom. Albery thought the part not substantial enough for her, but Sybil insisted on playing it. 'I always try to like my parts, as long as they are intelligently written,' she remarked during rehearsals. Agate thought the play better than 99 per cent of West End successes, but most critics agreed with Albery. 'If Sybil Thorndike wants a holiday from *Saint Joan*,' the *Daily Express* suggested, 'why doesn't she take one, instead of playing this sort of part?' The play lasted just three weeks, and had to be replaced by the ever-popular *The Lie*.

In July, in recognition of her status within the profession, Sybil was invited to join Barrie, Shaw, Pinero, Forbes-Robertson, Ainley, Boucicault and Irene

Vanbrugh on the RADA council. She took on other responsibilities, organising an entertainment by the Actors' Church Union, joining the management committee of a new Greek Play Society headed by Robert Atkins, and with Lilian Baylis, Hugh Walpole and the novelist W H Davies becoming a vice-president of the Empire Poetry League.

In the autumn she embarked on a gruelling three-month tour of *Saint Joan* to the major cities. When the production reached Birmingham a local critic unashamedly hailed 'the greatest play by our greatest playwright with our greatest actress in her greatest part'. On her return to London, as a favour to Edy Craig, she took part in a single performance of the *Old English Nativity Play*, staged at Daly's in aid of the Children's Country Holidays charity. With Fay Compton as Mary and the stars relegated to small parts, Sybil merely featured in a 'tableau' – of, inevitably, Saint Joan.

Shakespeare had long been considered a sure-fire commercial failure in the West End, and with the notable exception of John Barrymore's *Hamlet* earlier in the year, revivals had met with little success. Apart from the ill-starred *Cymbeline*, Sybil had not appeared there in a full-length production, although she had played Queen Katharine's death scene in *Henry VIII* to great acclaim at several charity matinees. It was a part made famous by Sarah Siddons, and Sybil now tackled it in a full-scale production. The cast was distinguished, with Norman V Norman as Henry, E Lyall Swete as Wolsey, O B Clarence as Cranmer, Arthur Wontner as Buckingham, and a young Angela Baddeley as Anne Bullen. But the venue was controversial: the 1,500-seat Empire had been famous as a music-hall with a once-lurid reputation, and many people thought it an unwise choice for Shakespeare.

A sprawling chronicle of Tudor propaganda, *Henry VIII* is more of a pageant of processions than a drama, 'a thing of shreds and patches', and only some of it credited to Shakespeare. Ricketts as set designer, Winston with the costumes and Lewis as director produced a gorgeous feast for the eye, with the tapestries and stained-glass windows suggesting a series of Holbein pictures come to life, prompting comparisons with the celebrated productions of Tree and Irving. There were many stars at the first night two days before Christmas, including Ellen Terry, a previous Katharine, and Forbes-Robertson, a famous Buckingham.

While the other actors received mixed notices, at the emotional heart of the play Sybil, despite obvious first-night nerves and only three scenes, scored a triumph. Some critics considered her Katharine finer than her Joan: *The*

Times picked out 'a face that can render every shade of emotion', the *Era* saw her as 'magnificent in her stillness and grief'. Only the *Manchester Guardian* dissented: 'She has, it is true, a great tenderness at her command, but rage more becomes her than patience, and Katharine has too much of saintly resignation in her nature to let us see Miss Thorndike's particular qualities of mastery and her full sense of surge'. In the continuing debate as to whether Sybil was a great actress, Agate decided she was – when performing in a great play. 'Her features may not launch ships for light-hearted capture; let them show moral anguish, and whole navies will flock to her succour. Her voice is not for balconies and conquests, yet in suffering it moves you to shattering depths of spiritual pity.' He concluded: 'Anything more noble, more dignified, more womanly, or more truly heroic than this Katharine would be impossible to conceive.'

Jack Hawkins was again in the company, as was the future director Carol Reed (Tree's illegitimate son), one of two pages holding up Sybil's train. The other was Laurence Olivier, now a lively eighteen-year-old with thick, curly black hair, bright eyes and heavy eyebrows. Unemployed and hungry, in desperation he had approached Lewis and Sybil for a job, and they had hired him for £3 a week: to walk on, understudy if required, and be second assistant stage manager. One of his tasks, he remembered, lay in 'protecting my saint and heroine', as he described Sybil. As Sybil recalled it, he and Reed were in love with Angela Baddeley: 'They used to quarrel like mad over her. I had to tell them to shut up and attend to what they were doing.'

London flocked to this unexpected hit, seen by nearly 200,000 people during a run extended from six weeks to three months. While spending £6,000 to stage it, Sybil and Lewis took the risk of keeping seat prices low, and were rewarded with a healthy profit, the production covering its costs in its third week. Herbert Farjeon suggested that with her Joan and Katharine Sybil had captured the imagination of the people, and as an actress-manageress could if she wished ascend London's theatrical throne, left vacant since the death of Beerbohm Tree. 'She is the idol of a huge section of the public,' *Theatre World* noted, 'and as such there seems little she cannot attempt – and carry out with every success.' Sybil herself relished the experience, telling Edy Craig in March: 'We finish Henry tonight; I've loved it – but always glad of a change to something else.' Her performance crystallised the stage ambition of Rachel Kempson, then a schoolgirl: 'I was swept off my feet, and my growing longing for the theatre took shape into a determination to go into it myself,' she recalled.

Part of Sybil's public crusade was to break down the opposition against

theatrical innovation. Speaking at the annual prize distribution of the British
Empire Shakespeare Society, she argued that people in the theatre should
'get away from the idea that they must copy somebody else, follow tradition,
and keep to the broad path'. There was, she said, a need 'to be experimenting
all the time, and in the case of a thing as big as Shakespeare it was worth
experimenting and even risking failures with it'. In an editorial the next
day, the *Manchester Guardian* praised her protest for being 'both vigorous
and opportune'. At a time when plays by Maugham and Coward and the
Aldwych farces by Ben Travers were dominating the West End, the production of *Henry VIII* gave force to her argument.

Ellen Terry gave out the prizes, prompting the chairman Henry Ainley
to note that 'the Queen Empress of the profession and the Queen Katharine
of the moment' were sitting together. She and Sybil would meet occasionally,
once in Ellen Terry's flat in St Martin's Lane. 'How she talked about everything and everyone but never about herself,' Sybil remembered. 'So gay when
so old, she threw out a sort of spring sunshine.' Sybil and others had started
to make the summer pilgrimage to Smallhythe to perform scenes in the Barn
theatre in the garden. 'She would be sitting in the house, and we would go in
and have a yarn with her. She was always eager to know what we were going
to play, and would discuss the scenes as if she were our contemporary.'

In his book *Certain People of Importance*, published that year, the great
Liberal journalist A G Gardiner wrote approvingly of Sybil's aim to conquer
'the philistine West End to the brave music of the Old Vic'. In a perceptive
analysis of her art, he suggested her appeal was unlike that of any other star:
'She exhales an influence that transcends the stage, that relates the stage to
life and the things of the mind and the spirit that is quite new and individual....Her intelligence is not exclusively of the stage. Her life does not
begin with the footlights and end with the painted scenery....She hitches the
drama to the general activities of life...It is this sense that, behind the artist,
there is the spirit of a crusader, fighting less for a personal triumph than for an
ideal of the stage, that is the source of the interest she awakens in multitudes
of minds ordinarily indifferent to the acted drama.'

Henry VIII was the first successful West End production of Shakespeare
since Barker's ones before the war, and its success was due as much to Lewis'
direction as to Sybil's fame. Gielgud was directed by him this year in *The
High Constable's Wife*: at twenty-one he was terrified by his 'iron hand', and
his rigorous insistence on phrasing and diction. Lewis likened the task of

director to that of a conductor, and insisted the actors find the right 'tunes' for their words. Once, according to Wendy Hiller, he even directed the actors from behind a screen, to ensure the speech rhythms were correct. Sybil always needed a strong director, and in Lewis she certainly found one. In her biography Diana Devlin described a typical moment.

'Lewis' rehearsals were violent, storm-tossed affairs, during which he barked and growled and roared at his actors, while they seethed or yelled or quaked in their shoes, according to temperament. The loudest retaliation usually came from Sybil. Preparing to start a speech for perhaps the sixth time, she would summon up the approximate emotion, draw breath, open her mouth and get as far as, for instance: "Now I – " "No!" shouts Lewis. "But I haven't *started* yet," expostulates Sybil. "But you were doing it wrong." "Well, how can I get it right if you don't let me *do* the speech. What I was trying to –" "If you start the speech wrong it will be wrong all through –" "But you didn't even *let* me start. How could it be wrong?" "The way you took your breath." "Lewis! What does it matter how I take my breath? The important thing is for me to know what she *feels* like." "Rubbish! The important thing is that you say it so that the *audience* knows what she's feeling, and if you can't do that, we might as well pack up and go home!"'

Despite a gruelling eleven performances a week as Katharine, she found the energy during the run to appear again in *The Cenci*, which she and Lewis revived for four performances, also at the Empire. Shelley's play and Sybil's performance again divided the critics. Despite – or was it because of? – the playwright Clemence Dane's opening 'discourse' about the greatness of the play, *The Times* thought it 'one long oppression', and found Sybil wearying: 'Her voice is vibrant and penetrating, but monotonous. Her face is full of intellect, but can be hard.' But Agate insisted that Lewis and Shelley had created a fine piece, and Sybil's performance was sensitive and moving: 'I cannot imagine that Beatrice could be better played,' he wrote.

Sybil liked to help young actors struggling to make a living, and she now helped the young Olivier to further his career. Although he had only a few lines in the play, she saw again the sensitive talent she had spotted in him as a boy. He badly wanted West End success, but was not confident of achieving it, and was on the point of abandoning the theatre. In despair he went to Sybil, who told him to forget the West End and try his luck with the Birmingham Rep under Barry Jackson, for whom she gave him a reference. It was the move which kick-started his career.

Because she found it hard to turn down people's requests, she invariably took on too much charitable work. This was reflected in her decision not to stand for re-election to the council of the Women's Institute, having failed to attend any meetings because of her theatre commitments. 'I feel very guilty about the matter,' she wrote to the secretary. 'May I withdraw, and send my best wishes to your splendid work?' But the WI asked her to stay on, and she gave in. 'I feel such a fraud when I can do nothing at all for the Institute,' she replied. 'If however the committee still wishes for my name on the list, and will continue to put up with my shortcomings, or rather lack of any comings at all, I will fall in with their views.'

She often used her charity work to expound her strong beliefs about social conditions. After giving a recital in aid of the Manchester Babies' Hospital, she sent a cheque and a letter praising the nurses and their 'life of absolute forgetfulness of their own wishes and needs'. Soon after she was criticising the salaries and working conditions of nurses as 'a crying disgrace'. At another event to raise money for the hospital she observed: 'It is perfectly appalling that we should allow children to live in the conditions in which many live in our cities and towns.'

She was much in demand as a speaker, sometimes on church issues, as at an Anglo-Catholic Congress at Church House in Westminster, sometimes in schools, as with her visit to the Literary Society of St Paul's Girls' School in Hammersmith. But the prospect of addressing an audience as herself rather than as Saint Joan or Jane Clegg still alarmed her. A speech she gave on tour prompted Tony Atwood to invite her to repeat it. 'I'll do it of course,' she replied, 'tho' what I said up there in the north goodness knows – it was awful, I'm sure! Will 10 minutes really be enough? Oh! dear, oh! dear, words are torture to me, but I pray God something will come. Don't let Edy know I'm worried – if it's only 10 minutes the Lord will be with me!!'

In March she returned to *Saint Joan*, with Russell now playing the Dauphin. She was thrilled to be in the Lyceum, where Ellen Terry and Irving had created their famous partnership. According to the critic of *The Times*, she was still in top form: 'She dominates not only the stage, but the huge theatre, and never strikes a false note.' Her great popularity with the public was attested to by one critic: 'I can think of only six performers on the so-called legitimate stage whose personalities can attract in London good audiences to an indifferent play for longer than a fortnight – Sir Gerald du Maurier, Miss Irene Vanbrugh, Miss Gladys Cooper, Miss Sybil

Thorndike, Mr Ivor Novello and Miss Gwen Ffrangcon-Davies.'

Unfortunately the revival was cut short by the 1926 General Strike in May, called to give support to the miners in their dispute with their employers. Although most theatres closed when the Trades Union Congress (TUC) called the strike, Sybil and Lewis decided to carry on with *Saint Joan*. But with little public transport available, few car-owners, and street disturbances breaking out, few people risked venturing to the Lyceum; the handful that did was invited to move down to the front row, to make the actors feel more comfortable. The lack of transport created a problem for Jack Hawkins, who had to walk eight miles from his home in north London to the theatre. When they heard of this, Sybil and Lewis invited him to stay in Carlyle Square for the duration of the run. 'I became like one of the family,' he remembered. Finally they had to accept the inevitable, and the play closed after just six weeks.

Most actors were opposed to the strike, and many became volunteers in the government's efforts to keep normal life going: Olivier, for instance, worked on the London Underground. But as socialists Sybil and Lewis – and others such as May Whitty and Margaret Webster – were passionately in support of the workers. Both active members of the Labour Party, they numbered amongst their friends George Lansbury, Margaret Bondfield, who was to be the first female cabinet minister, Bertrand and Dora Russell, and other leading socialists. Lilian Baylis set aside seats at the Vic each night 'for men and women called out by their unions'. Maude Royden made a plea for understanding the miners' position and defending them as brothers, and Sybil spoke and gave a recital in her church. She told her children: 'We think they're right to strike, it's the only thing they can do.'

Lewis became deeply involved in the dispute. He drove the union leaders to meetings with the government in his Armstrong-Siddeley, with a large TUC sticker on the windscreen – though his daughter Mary remembers that 'he took any buses that were going, and he gave people lifts, which was regarded by the union as cheating'. Once *Saint Joan* had closed he drove to Carlisle to help as a courier, living for a few days with the striking workers. He wrote optimistically to Sybil: 'This strike will go on and on until the government comes to its senses. The spirit of the people is marvellous.' Like many others, he was bitterly disappointed when the TUC gave in to the government after only nine days, leaving the miners isolated.

Sybil continued to support women's causes. In June, holding aloft a banner on which was hand-painted a silver dove, she led a procession of Women Peace Pilgrims into Hyde Park, part of a demonstration of 100,000, one of the most significant London had seen since the war. 'Her sympathy with the ideals of progress and liberty has often been manifested,' one reporter wrote. 'If ever she should retire from the stage I can imagine her making her mark in public affairs.' Soon after she addressed a meeting at Kingsway Hall, chaired by Margaret Bondfield, on the question of a relief fund for the miners' dependents. Sharing the platform with miners' wives from four coalfields, she said it was a privilege to express publicly her sympathy for the miners' cause, and that 'the conditions of the workers in the coalfields were beyond a joke'.

She still managed the occasional matinee production, sometimes for a little-known organisation. For the Jewish Drama League she played in *Israel* by Henri Bernstein at the Strand, in a company that included Ben Webster and Abraham Sofaer. It was a dull play about anti-semitism in France, in which, according to Agate, she still managed to shine as the Duchesse de Croucy: 'Miss Thorndike, who could play half-a-dozen of these equivocating duchesses before breakfast, was in first-class trim, coming up fit as a daisy for one emotional round after another,' he wrote. She was also in Eliot Crawshay-Williams' *The Debit Account*, which she had been discussing with its author. 'I think the play is terrific – the part wonderful – we've been arguing about it all the week!' she told him. Soon she wrote again: 'I want to start rehearsing immediately!!!' While playing Joan, her impatience grew stronger: 'My dear Eliot, for God's sake come in and see me one night – then we can talk!!!' All this was for a single performance for the Interlude Players at the New, directed by Matthew Forsyth.

She described her next play under the Albery management in an enthusiastic letter to her son John, now sixteen and in the navy: 'We've just read a thrilling play, one of the great plays. It's called *Granite* and we're going to do it as soon as we can. We met the author the other day, and she's a darling. Winifred Ashton's her name, but she calls herself Clemence Dane for writing….The play is about Lundy Island and an awful man who comes out of the sea who is really the Devil. Lewis will play the Devil man and I'll be the wife of the man he pushes over the cliff.' She and Lewis spent a few days with Clemence Dane in Devon, learning their parts and indulging their love of walking. 'I've just this minute arrived home from a four days' tramp on Exmoor,' she wrote to a friend.

Clemence Dane was a large, erudite woman of unquenchable vitality, with a penchant for long flowery dresses. Once an actress and a novelist, 'Clemmie-the Dane', as Lewis labelled her, was now a painter and sculptress as well as a playwright. Her first play *A Bill of Divorcement* had been an overnight success, but her next, *William Shakespeare*, was a relative failure. A contributor to *Time and Tide*, the feminist magazine labelled 'The Sapphic Graphic', she moved in gay and lesbian circles. Coward, a close friend, described her as 'a unique mixture of artist, writer, games mistress, poet and egomaniac…she is warm and generous, but stubborn and conceited'. Sybil and Lewis had known her for a while, but she now became a good friend. She loved an argument, and since they greatly differed politically, there were plenty of them.

She had a passion for history, especially Nelson, and based Sybil's character in part on Emma Hamilton. A morality play with more than a whiff of Grand Guignol, *Granite* gave Sybil the chance to be intense and emotionally battered for four acts, and to play a violent, evil character as a useful antidote to Saint Joan. Her cry of despair at the climax, she recalled proudly, 'got tremendous notices'. Lewis, who directed, gave a powerful, eerie performance as the Nameless One. The play found little favour with the critics, and ran for just seven weeks at the Ambassador's, the loss of £1,000 eating into the *Saint Joan* profits.

One night the poet Rabindranath Tagore came to the play. Sybil had spent an hour in the morning talking with him about theatre, and after the show, with a group of Indian professors who also came, he talked on the subject to the company. Sybil and Lewis had met him when she had recited a poem Laurence Binyon had written to welcome him to England. Since then, whenever he visited, they had met and talked, so increasing her passionate interest in India and its growing struggle for independence. Gandhi had also been in England recently, staying at Kingsley Hall: Lewis had met him, but Sybil to her great disappointment had been away filming.

That summer she took part in Stratford in the re-creation of the Garrick Pageant of 1769, playing the Tragic Muse, with Irene Vanbrugh as the Spirit of Comedy, and Lewis as Garrick. In March a fire had destroyed the Memorial Theatre, and an appeal had been launched for money to rebuild it. A poem by John Drinkwater was read from sixty stages nationwide, and Sybil and Lewis were among the first to give a donation.

They then took the children on a motoring holiday to France, exploring towns connected with Joan of Arc, including Chinon, Rheims and Rouen. In the latter they visited the room in the cathedral where Joan had been tried, and Sybil spoke some of her lines there. They moved on to Port Manech in

Brittany, where she found relaxation in swimming long distances in the sea, and declaiming the lines of her next part at the top of her voice. She was about to embark on a sustained immersion in Shakespeare, during which she would play four of the major female roles, beginning with the one many people consider the most challenging of all.

17

Lady Macbeth and Edith Cavell

1926–1928

'I believe that in certain circumstances I should have acted as Edith Cavell
acted. I hope I should have had the courage'
Sybil during the filming of Dawn

Apart from *Cymbeline* and *Henry VIII*, Sybil had been only sporadically involved with Shakespeare since her Old Vic days, and then only for single performances. Two of these had been for the British Empire Shakespeare Society. In March 1923 at the Strand she had taken part in a 'Star Dramatic Reading' of *Romeo and Juliet* – not, as might be expected at the age of forty, as the Nurse, but as Juliet, with Basil Rathbone as Romeo. 'Miss Sybil Thorndike's reading suggested rather a grown-up Juliet,' *The Times* noted politely. 'But her glorious voice brought out the beauty of some of the passages in a way that must have been a revelation to many of the young students present.'

In April 1926, with Gwen Ffrangcon-Davies, Nigel Playfair and Athene Seyler, she had played five scenes from *The Merchant of Venice* in a mixed bill at the Haymarket on Shakespeare's birthday. 'Yes – Portia, right you are – rather fun in modern dress,' she had told its organiser Edy Craig, promising to run through her scenes with Bassanio 'between the acts of Joan'. There had recently been a vogue for modern-dress productions, and on the day, in what *The Times* described as 'perhaps the most diverting presentation of Shakespeare yet seen on the stage', Sybil appeared as 'a bobbed Portia in a green sports dress'.

In the birthday celebrations that year she had played Gertrude in an uncut *Hamlet* at the Lyceum, organised by Greet, Lewis and herself in aid of the Sadler's Wells Fund, with Russell as Hamlet and Fay Compton playing Ophelia. Unfortunately Greet, who was directing, was unwell, the dress-rehearsal was a mess, the musicians were proving a problem, and Lewis had to take over. He and Sybil, as was their custom, consulted the day's psalm: 'The Lord shall rehearse it,' it ran. 'The singers also and the trumpeters shall he rehearse; all my fresh springs shall be in thee.' Thus refreshed, they gave, according to Sybil, 'an electrifying performance'. St John Ervine thought her Gertrude 'the most striking interpretation of the part I have yet seen'. But Agate thought her miscast: 'There are parts for which Miss Thorndike's strong-mindedness and suggestion of Puritan atmosphere generously unfit her, and Gertrude is one of them,' he wrote. 'One felt that she would have set that court to rights in no time, and done it cheerfully.'

Returning from France in July, she and Lewis undertook a successful tour of *Saint Joan* and *Henry VIII*, during which Sybil continued to work on Lady Macbeth. It was a role she felt she had not yet mastered, and one she was keen to work on under Lewis' direction. For the production at the Prince's, into which they put a lot of their money, her Macbeth was Henry Ainley, a fine, handsome, instinctive actor with a magnificent voice. Basil Gill was Macduff, Lewis played Banquo, Jack Hawkins was Fleance, and John Laurie was cast as Lennox. The designer was again Ricketts, while the original music was provided by Granville Bantock. Ainley came often to Carlyle Square to rehearse, as John Casson recalled: 'That glorious, golden voice would thunder through the house when, after supper, he, Sybil and Lewis would run through their bits together.'

Lewis' methods disconcerted many actors, especially when he focussed on 'the tunes'. Margaret Webster recalled: 'He would give you an idea both of the tonal quality and the emotional content he wanted by pouring forth a stream of total gibberish, precisely scaled and cadenced and rhythmically exact.' His stern demeanour terrified less experienced actors. Sybil would often disagree with him, sometimes robustly. John recalled the final Macbeth rehearsals. 'He shouted, he snapped, he cajoled, he praised, he applauded (a little). At one moment Sybil said: "Lewis, will you listen to me for a minute?" "We haven't time for talk now," he replied. "Just get on with it." "Oh, he's impossible!" she said to Ainley, in a stage whisper that reverberated through the theatre. "I can't think why I married him."' Later Lewis revealed that Sybil 'got her way for once' about how to play the part.

At Lewis' suggestion Shaw sat in on rehearsals, taking notes from the circle to help clarify the action when Lewis was on stage. Bizarrely, he seems also to have been allowed to demonstrate how the characters should be played. He gave Sybil advice, notably on Lady Macbeth's 'Now screw your courage to the sticking point' speech: 'Don't soften, scold like a fury,' he told her. She recalled him playing every part 'with loving care and humour', but not everyone saw his behaviour so kindly. Jack Hawkins remembered: 'He lost little time in putting everyone's backs up with his comments and his way of uttering them.' It ended in a furious disagreement between the Scot John Laurie and the Irishman Shaw about the pronunciation of the word 'Skoon'.

As so often with *Macbeth*, the production was beset by problems. The dress-rehearsal lasted ten hours, ending at 2am. Sybil was unhappy with Ricketts' sets and costumes: 'I was trammelled by all the scenery and my dresses,' she remembered. 'I had a dress like a wasp and a huge cloak.' The opening, bizarrely, was on Christmas Eve, by which time the stage-hands had started celebrating, and had problems moving the heavy and complex scenery. According to Margaret Webster, who played the Gentlewoman: 'The waits between scenes were agonizing. At one point Lewis dashed up to the Fly Gallery and seized the ropes himself. Everybody was nervous, and neither Sybil nor Henry Ainley were anywhere near their best.'

With twenty-one scene changes, the first night ran for three and a half hours, leading one reviewer to dub it 'Macbeth with Intervals'. Ainley, prone to severe first-night nerves, gave an erratic performance, while the critics saw both good and bad in Sybil's Lady Macbeth. Farjeon praised her power and restraint, while Agate, who returned a week after the notoriously wobbly first night, again thought her Lady Macbeth the best he had seen 'and within the actress' physical means entirely perfect'. But *The Times*, while praising her technical faultlessness, felt she failed 'to stir the blood or freeze it'. The *Theatre World* critic wrote waspishly: 'No need is there for her to call on spirits to unsex her, for this was apparently accomplished long before the play began… It is hard to believe that this Lady Macbeth could incite a man to commit petty larceny, let alone murder.'

Matters were made worse when Ainley became ill. 'He had taken to drink and bad ways,' his daughter Patsy recalls. He also had a mental problem, and would wander off into dark corners of the stage, mumbling his lines and missing his entrances; Jack Hawkins was deputed to make sure he remembered them. This and other problems led to Lewis one night suggesting that the Devil was at work, and that he and Sybil should read the 91st Psalm ('Thou shalt not be afraid for the terror by night') in their dressing-room. 'This quieted and strengthened us,' she remembered. On another night

Ainley's voice went completely, he was taken to hospital, and was away from the theatre for three years. He was replaced by Hubert Carter, a strong, very physical man with a massive jaw, who nearly strangled Sybil, and bruised her by manhandling her in the throne scene.

According to Russell, Sybil was initially depressed by her performance, but after a while she gained more confidence. Always self-critical and ready to listen to advice, she wrote to St John Ervine: 'I'm getting better in Macbeth, I believe – one or two things you said put me more on the track – I wish I weren't such a rotten slow cooker – but one can't alter.' Later, when Fabia Drake was preparing to play the part at Stratford, she asked Sybil how she managed to get into Lady Macbeth's psyche. Sybil replied: 'I couldn't have committed murder for Lewis, but I could have done so for the children.' She felt she had not yet mastered the notoriously difficult role. Yet Gordon Crosse, a connoisseur of Shakespeare productions, who called her the greatest actress he had ever seen, later wrote of Lady Macbeth as 'the top of her achievement'.

No doubt due in part to Ainley's exit, the play ran for less than two months, proving again the difficulty of staging Shakespeare in the West End. Two leading critics chose this moment to define Sybil's achievement. St John Ervine penned a perceptive summary of her as a woman and an actress. He listed her lack of vanity, her unaffected piety, her gift for emotional as well as restrained acting, and her physical endurance. 'She has probably greater physical strength than any other actress alive. She seems to be intense and nervous, yet her nerves must be like steel, otherwise they could not endure the strain she puts upon them. Her industry is extraordinary.' Although not everyone liked her acting, and some worried about her mannerisms, he noted that no great actress, including Bernhardt and Duse, was liked by everybody. After *Medea* and *The Trojan Women* she had been acclaimed England's only tragic actress; now her position was unassailable. 'She moves steadily towards the place she will presently and soon occupy, the position of the greatest actress on the English stage. She has position; she has popularity; there is not a stage hand in any theatre where she works who does not love her; nor is there any actor or actress who has played with her who does not regard her with deep affection.'

Agate meanwhile considered where she stood among the greats of the English theatre, now placing her above Edith Evans and Marie Tempest, and bracketing her with Ellen Terry, Mrs Kendal and Mrs Patrick Campbell as an actress whose name would go down to posterity. 'Whenever the English drama of the first quarter of the twentieth century is mentioned, it will be in connection with Sybil,' he asserted. 'She possesses, in addition to her own prodigious memory and her husband's extraordinary brain, the *flair* not only for things of all time, but also for things of the moment. Her genius will mate with that of Euripides, but it will not scorn the talent of an Ervine when Jane Cleggs are the mode....She has shown herself to be wedded indissolubly to the best and most intellectual plays and playwrights of all the times and epochs there have been and are.' Soon afterwards he dedicated his book *A Short View of the English Stage 1900–1926* to Sybil and Lewis.

Perhaps seeking something completely different from Joan, Sybil appeared next in a romantic melodrama, *The Greater Love*, by J B Fagan, a story of plots and counter-plots in Tsarist Russia. The role of Nadeshda Ivanovna, the good revolutionary and saviour of her people, who was prepared to sacrifice herself to save her family from arrest, gave Sybil another chance to tear a passion to tatters. Although she was generally praised for her performance, Agate took her to task for being too homespun and reasonable in a part that his beloved Sarah Bernhardt would have played up to the emotional hilt: 'The swooning and the transports were not altogether convincing, and the part offered little scope for the actress' finer brand of spiritual magnetism,' he wrote. 'I was looking for a princess, and Mr Fagan and Miss Thorndike supplied a young lady who might be seen shopping in Kensington High Street any afternoon.'

The play was a success in the provinces, but only lasted six weeks in London. Fagan, better known as a distinguished director, co-directed with Lewis. During rehearsals he wanted to sack one shambling, ill-favoured actor playing a Russian general, who rehearsed in a dirty old mackintosh, wouldn't take direction, barely knew the few lines allotted to him, and when he did was virtually inaudible. Only a few months earlier, Sybil had presented Charles Laughton with the Bancroft Medal on his graduation from RADA. What had gone wrong? But Lewis saw something potentially interesting about his acting, and insisted he stay.

John Casson saw this as one of his father's strengths as a director: 'Lewis could be devastating to people who thought they were good and weren't. But he could wait and wait with astonishing tolerance when he believed that an actor had something original in him that was trying to get out.' After the first night Agate paused in his review to praise at length the skills of 'that very remarkable young actor Charles Laughton', who then quickly became a West End star. Laughton received a note from Sybil after the first night, asking him to see her before he made-up. Dreading her reaction to the contrasting reviews they had received from Agate, he was surprised when she simply hugged him and offered him her congratulations.

Laughton was with her again for two productions at the Prince's during the play's brief run. The first was *Angela*, a play about the Australian business world by Florence Bell, which was attended by Queen Mary, and raised £1,000 for the British Hospital for Mothers and Babies. In April she returned to *Medea*, playing to full and enthusiastic audiences. Although *The Times* thought her speech distorted, Agate repeated his belief in her greatness in the great parts: 'Whenever this actress reappears in roles of this order she abundantly makes good that title of greatness which, in parts of lesser worth, may conceivably be denied her,' he wrote. 'She declaimed the part magnificently, and the poses and gestures which she found for it were resolute, bold, and appalling in their justness.'

Russell was also appearing in the West End. He had adapted *Dr Syn* for the stage, casting himself as Christopher Syn, the eighteenth-century Smuggler Parson of Dymchurch. He went into management, presenting the play successfully at the Strand after a lengthy provincial tour. 'Mr Thorndike plays the chief character with urbanity and charm,' the *Observer* reported. Robert Morley was in the company: 'Russell was an immensely attractive and clever actor,' he recalled. 'He had a trick of throwing his voice about which people said reminded them of Irving, and there was a moment in the play when he turned his back on the audience, simulated the noise of scalding flesh, and apparently burnt a tattoo on his arm while singing "Fifteen Men on a Dead Man's Chest". He was larger than life, and towered above the rest of the cast.'

Sybil chose this moment, during a debate at the Gallery First Nighters' Club on the question 'Is the critic any use?', to speak scathingly of certain elements in theatre audiences. 'We want to fight the people who sit like lumps of suet and only want to be amused,' she declared. 'Food occupies too large a part in the majority of people's lives, and they think they ought only to go on to the theatre after a good dinner.' She also spoke defiantly about her responsibility as an actress: 'I am not a servant of the public. I am the servant of something much higher, much bigger than any person or public. To be the servant of the public means that I must do what the majority want, but that would be death to my art.'

Charity matinees were still popular at this time. One of these re-united her with Edith Evans who, having finally won over Lilian Baylis, was now a favourite at the Old Vic. Sybil was Mistress Ford to her Mistress Page, playing two scenes from *The Merry Wives of Windsor* with Balliol Holloway as Falstaff, in a matinee in aid of the Sadler's Wells Fund. She often lent her name to Lilian Baylis' fund-raising efforts: the previous year, together with Mrs Kendal, Forbes-Robertson, Matheson Lang and Ivor Novello, she had backed an appeal 'to establish the historic but now derelict theatre of Sadler's Wells as an Old Vic in north London…an admirable project that will confer a great and lasting benefit on thousands of people of all classes'.

In June she and Lewis were asked to take *Saint Joan* to Paris as part of a seven-nation international dramatic festival, and to stage special matinees of *Medea*. Other companies represented Holland, Italy, Denmark, Spain, Russia and Japan. 'I do feel that we should make the occasion a real help in promoting the good feeling between the two nations that we all so much desire,' Sybil said. They managed to recruit most of the original cast of Shaw's play, with Russell playing Warwick and Mary his page.

Tom Kealy thought it would be a good publicity stunt if the company flew to France. This was Sybil's introduction to flying, an experience she described with her customary exuberance in a letter to her son John: 'Well!! We've *done* it! We've *flown*! All the way from Croydon to Paris in a *huge* aeroplane, and the whole company came with us – except Lyall Swete, who has to have a cigarette every five minutes and so couldn't bear to go two and a half hours without one – so silly. Think what he missed! When the engines started and we raced across the field I thought I'd die with excitement and quirks. Did *you* feel like that when you flew? Oh, but you're so much braver than me. I was terrified, and thrilled, too, of course. Doesn't the earth look gorgeous from up there. All those lovely fields and comic little houses….As we got out we saw a huge crowd of French people waving flowers and hats at us. All those nice actors and actresses. I just had time to dash into the Ladies and be very sick – all my breakfast – put on some make-up and then come back and make a speech to them all – in French!'

Artistically the visit was a success, and increased Sybil's prestige, but it was a costly one financially. Unlike the companies from other countries, theirs had no government support. 'This country is, of course, behindhand,' she complained. 'We never have dared to think of asking for a subsidy.' As a result the actors agreed to work for little more than expenses. Audiences were enthusiastic but small in the cavernous Théâtre du Champs-Elysées. According to Russell, it cost Sybil and Lewis 'a small fortune'.

Back in England they took the children for a month's holiday in Bron-y-Garth, the large house on a hill above Portmadoc in North Wales where they had spent part of their honeymoon. They were entranced by the view over the Traeth to the mountains of Cnicht and the Arennigs, and the ever-changing light beyond Penryndaedrath. Sybil loved the wildness of the place, the lengthy walks with Lewis. They took the family up Snowdon by the pig track, sneering at those who took the little mountain railway. 'We climbed Snowdon yesterday, 3600 ft – and had tea at the top right in the clouds and thick fog,' she wrote proudly to her mother. 'But then a little lower down the view was simply magnificent. The children all climbed marvellously – we did the whole thing in five hours.'

During these months her offstage work seemed to intensify. She spoke at the Mansion House in support of the General Council for District Nursing, and opened a hall and club room in the East End. She was a judge, along with John Drinkwater and W A Darlington, of a Festival of Community Drama, and spoke at a dinner celebrating the Little Theatre amateur movement. She was made a member of the lay council of the Friends of Canterbury Cathedral, and became president of Isis Players, a society founded by former students of St Hugh's College, Oxford. She was specially active in peace issues: she joined in a women's disarmament appeal by the National Council for the Prevention of War, and in armistice week joined with Nancy Astor, Dora Russell, Maude Royden and Virginia Woolf in urging people to work for peace.

Perhaps unsurprisingly, she had further problems with her voice, and had to endure another spell of silence. 'I've been away curing my voice and selfishly thinking of no one else but myself,' she wrote to Evelyn Sharp in July. She stayed with Florence Bell in Yorkshire, taking what was for her a long break from acting. She suffered the same problem a little while later: this time it lasted a month, during which she stayed in a Surrey hotel with Christopher. 'She often went back to Elsie Fogerty, but I think there was permanent damage,' her daughter Mary says. 'I remember her getting into terrible panics about it, and feeling very miserable. It was a constant worry.'

By the autumn she was ready to return to the theatre. While the Old Vic was undergoing major repairs, Lilian Baylis persuaded her and Lewis to head a company for a five-month Shakespeare season at the Lyric, Hammersmith, owned by Nigel Playfair. The plays were *The Taming of the Shrew*, *The Merchant of Venice*, *Much Ado about Nothing* and *Henry V*; the salaries were predictably nominal; the company included Eric Portman, John Laurie, Hay Petrie and Rupert Hart-Davis. The director was Andrew Leigh, who staged the plays in the Elizabethan manner. Freed from directorial duties, Lewis played leading roles opposite Sybil in all four productions.

They opened with *The Taming of the Shrew*, then considered one of Shakespeare's poorest plays. Lewis made a lusty, swaggering Petruchio, impressing everyone with his energy and gusto. Sybil, in a red wig and flowing robes and a part she knew well, came up with a Katharina full of vivacity and zest. According to the *Daily Mail*, 'she found a new delight in her semi-burlesque moods of shrewish rage', while Horace Horsnell in the *Observer* insisted: 'When fun is afoot she can doff the tragedy queen and romp with the best of them.' The first night, from which many were turned away, was marked by the usual fervour of the Old Vic regulars, who enjoyed hearing Lewis vowing to woo the right woman, whether she was 'as old as Sybil and as curst and shrewd as Socrates' Xantippe, or worse'.

During the run Sybil wrote a piece in the *Radio Times*, commending the BBC's plan to broadcast Shakespeare to schools during the day, as well as to present a few evening productions. She spelt out the virtues for young listeners of the first plays to be heard, *The Tempest*, *Twelfth Night* and *Richard II*, stressing in particular the poetry contained in them. She argued that works like *The Taming of the Shrew* might be suitable for school performance, but not for broadcasting or reading. 'They are, in my opinion, too closely allied with the old Italian Comedy, with its clowns and broad visual acting, where the characterisation is embodied in the action more than the words.' She urged listeners to 'turn on the loud-speaker or put on the headphones for these broadcasts with a sense of mental alertness, determined to extract from them all the tension, colour, vitality and experience which the greatest English poet and dramatist so lavishly poured into his plays'.

In *The Merchant of Venice* she was for once overshadowed by Lewis: his Shylock was widely acclaimed, and even considered by one critic to be the greatest since Irving's. It was more realistic and less flamboyant than many recent interpretations, making the character more human. He had chosen, he said, to play Shylock as he felt Shakespeare had written him, 'as a mean little miser with glimmerings of good in him'. His performance of the trial scene was put on film, creating a moment of film history as the earliest surviving example of Shakespeare's words being spoken in a synchronised sound film.

Sybil was commended for her playing of Portia in the trial scene, but was considered less successful in the more romantic ones, one critic complaining she was too soft and girlish, as if she were playing Juliet.

She had disliked the play since childhood, when Russell had refused to let her play Shylock rather than Portia, but had since kept her views to herself. So it must have come as a shock when soon after she revealed the intensity of her feelings. In an article headed 'The Play I Loathe', she explained that *The Merchant of Venice* 'has dogged and depressed me through life, made me lose faith and interest in the universe, and roused in me feelings of violence which I hardly knew I possessed'. She railed against 'that quality of forced cheerfulness that bubbles through the play', and criticised Portia's 'continual facetiousness', arguing that 'if she were the noble lady we are told she is, could she not have recognised Shylock's quality, and behaved somehow in some larger way to him, if he also is noble as critics have told us?' For someone who always sought to understand and sympathise with the characters she played, however wicked, it was a strangely intemperate attack.

But she entered gleefully into the battle of wits between Beatrice and Benedick in *Much Ado about Nothing*, which one or two of the more prudish critics still considered unnecessarily coarse. Playing opposite Lewis' resolute and soldierly Benedick, she caught beautifully, *The Times* noted, Beatrice's gaiety, mischief and wit: 'Her brazen indelicacies fly from her tongue with astonishing assurance.' Others thought she overdid the merriment: Farjeon found her to be 'boundlessly exuberant, rather like a child after the ice has been completely shattered at a party', adding that she was 'inclined at times to confuse physical with mental horseplay'.

The final production was *Henry V*, with Lewis in the title-role, and Sybil playing the relatively minor parts of Chorus and Katharine. The former she played as a high-spirited, impetuous youth. 'The effect is irresistible,' stated the *Morning Post*. 'The picture she describes, whether grave or gay, stands out as though thrown upon a canvas.' Her playing of the French princess, according to the *Sunday Pictorial*, 'revealed an entirely new facet of her art... she was as enchanting and captivating as any ingenue'. Perhaps it helped, or provided an extra frisson for the audience, that she was being wooed by her real-life husband.

Rupert Hart-Davis recalled how Sybil always came to the first rehearsal knowing Lewis' words as well as her own, and how 'whenever Andrew Leigh left the room for a moment, Lewis would try to step up the tempo a little

– which indeed it often needed'. Sybil had mightily enjoyed sparring with Lewis and returning to lighter Shakespearean roles. She wrote gratefully to Lilian Baylis: 'I've been so happy working under you again. I can't tell you what the season has given to Lewis and me – yes I can – it has enabled us to play together, a thing I never thought would happen, and I wanted it so. Thank you, darling, for everything – it's been the happiest five months, Lewis and I said, as we drove off on Saturday night. Hasn't it been lovely? Not one word or thought that wasn't jolly and happy, and we are so grateful.' She invited all the Old Vic staff to tea, warning: 'It will be an appalling squash in my little house', and that all that was on offer was 'tea and talk and being pushed about'.

During the season she had received an intriguing film offer. Her first experience of film had made her critical and dismissive of the medium, and she had not made a film for five years. But as the industry began to develop, she began to see the potential of the cinema, and to modify her views. This year had seen the setting up of British Incorporated Pictures, with ambitious plans to build studios and provide quality films to compete with Hollywood. Sybil was on its first advisory committee, with a high-profile group that included Gordon Craig, Gerald du Maurier, Phyllis Neilson-Terry, the artist Edmund Dulac, Tamara Karsavina, and the writers Conan Doyle, Arnold Bennett, John Galsworthy and Eden Phillpotts.

The offer came from the producer Herbert Wilcox, who wanted her to play the lead in *Dawn*, a film about the life of Nurse Edith Cavell. The part was one that attracted her, and the film, which was to prove hugely controversial, reinforced her new attitude. She landed it by good fortune, mixed with a dash of serendipity. During the First World War Edith Cavell, a nurse working in a Red Cross hospital in Brussels, had helped over two hundred British, French and Belgian soldiers to escape to neutral Holland. Executed by the Germans, she had become a heroic national figure, commemorated by a statue in Charing Cross Road in London. Wilcox had been inspired by the statue to make the film, and was about to start shooting with his star Pauline Frederick, a *grande dame* of the American stage. Suddenly she was called back to America 'on urgent private business'. Wilcox soon discovered the truth: the German embassy had told her that if she played the part no film of hers would ever be shown again in Germany, and pickets would be placed on cinemas showing her films in the States. This was the first hint that the film would cause controversy.

In desperation Wilcox scanned the London theatre columns, and noticed that Sybil was playing Portia in Hammersmith. Rushing back to London, he offered her the part. Her response surprised him. 'Sybil listened, but said nothing,' he remembered. 'She then brought out a small black book. "Do you see this?" she said. It was Thomas à Kempis' *The Imitation of Christ*. When Sybil and Lewis were married, she was given the book. When Edith Cavell was executed, she left her copy of the same book to her cousin Eddie. She had annotated certain pages with comments reflecting her last thoughts. Eddie Cavell lent it to Sybil and gave her permission to annotate her own book in the same manner.' The annotated book not only recorded Edith Cavell's last thoughts, but her thoughts at other times, and the dates when she had read certain books. (Sybil would later lend the copy to Anna Neagle when she played the part in *Nurse Edith Cavell* in 1939.)

She had long wanted to play Florence Nightingale, and saw Edith Cavell as 'a step in the right direction' towards that goal. She knew of Shaw's admiring comment in his preface to *Saint Joan*, that 'Edith, like Joan, was an arch heretic: in the middle of the war she declared before the world that "Patriotism is not enough".' The chance to play another strong, defiant, gutsy heroine, and to promote values she strongly believed in, prompted her to speak more positively about film. 'I am tremendously proud at being offered the part,' she announced. 'Not a woman among us but reveres the memory of Miss Cavell, and I feel that through the medium of the screen it will be possible to convey the great lessons of self-sacrifice and patriotism that she taught.'

She was nervous about her first full-length film role, but she admired Wilcox, and allowed him to guide her technically. It no doubt helped that she identified strongly with her character. Noting a similarity in the structure of their faces, she added: 'I believe I think in many ways as she thought. I believe, too, that in certain circumstances I should have acted as she acted. I hope I should have had the courage.'

She quickly became fascinated by the demands of filming. 'I am being rather swept away by the film, finding it intensely absorbing,' she told Murray. 'I'd love to tell you about it some time, the actual technique is most enthralling, it's like tiny miniature painting compared to scene painting. The stage is so much broader and in a way rougher. The film is a taking away of everything but essential movements and far, far tidier and cleaner-cut than the stage. Doing the two together is more fascinating than I can express.' She felt she was really living the part, a claim borne out by a journalist visiting the

Cricklewood studios, who wrote: 'Nothing seen in a British film studio has awakened deeper feelings than this re-enactment by Sybil Thorndike of the final scenes in Nurse Cavell's life. Miss Thorndike herself was so moved that for a little while she wept without restraint.'

Dawn was extremely well received, as was Sybil's performance. *Kinematograph Weekly* thought it 'dignified and static, but conveying the character's personality with an overwhelming force'; the *Manchester Guardian* praised her 'beautiful and deeply considered acting'; while the *Observer* thought 'her power of suppressing herself, of hiding all indications of her own individuality, is astonishing'. Although the pace now seems slow, the film tells the heroic story simply, with captions emphasising its anti-war stance. Sybil conveys an air of calm authority with impressive restraint, avoiding sentimentality, and using her eyes to great effect – never more so than when she walks out to face the firing squad, conveying vividly the gradual shift in her emotions from serenity to suppressed fear. The moment when she half-smiles at her grief-stricken jailer was, for Wilcox, 'one of the great moments, conveying compassion and forgiveness, that only the cinema can achieve'. When he showed the film to the staff of the distribution company, 'the effect was overwhelming and disturbing: the woman in charge of publicity had hysterics and affected all the other women, and even the tough salesmen found it hard to take'.

The power of Sybil's performance was a factor in the subsequent diplomatic row. The German ambassador told the Conservative foreign secretary Austen Chamberlain that the film would do irreparable harm to relations between their two countries. Chamberlain persuaded the head of the British Board of Film Censors to ban it, even though neither of them had seen the film. There was an outcry in the press, which attacked the government for this act of censorship. In the House of Commons Chamberlain, 'speaking as an English gentleman', described it as an 'outrage on a noble woman's memory to turn for purposes of commercial profit so heroic a story'. Lord Birkenhead wrote: 'Does any one suppose that the woman who, at the very moment of her agony, could speak like this (Patriotism is not enough. I must have no hatred or bitterness for any one) would permit her death to be commercialised, with the certain result that the bitter memories associated with it would be kept alive and fertilized so as to prevent the sweet restoration of friendship and good relationship between the nations of the world?' Shaw leapt to the film's defence, arguing that 'it has been told by a young film poet who has been entirely faithful to his great theme', and adding: 'You have here a most moving and impressive incarnation of that heroine by our greatest tragic actress, whose dignity keeps the whole story on the highest plane.'

Sybil wrote at length to Murray, who had evidently received letters criticising her involvement in the film. Her detailed defence of it underlined once again the strength of her anti-war beliefs, and her desire to make the film's message clear. 'Before I accepted the Cavell film I made sure there was to be no stirring up of hostile feelings or ill-will towards another nation,' she explained. 'The film people assured me that their great idea was to present it quite fairly to both sides. "You see, we want to sell the film in Germany," they naively remarked! I think no one will be hurt at all because the true story that we are telling shows both sides very clearly and humanly....They say the feelings amongst the Germans was very strong against shooting her, and I am trying to show that it is not just one nation that is to blame, but war – and that Cavell obeyed a higher code when she refused to be bound by the war code, and that the German soldier did the same....It is not true to what Edith Cavell stood for if we do not make her words "Patriotism is not enough – I must have no bitterness or hatred in my heart towards anyone" the text of the film....I do hope it comes out as we are trying to make it. We are all so anti jingo patriotism that I feel it must come over on the screen somehow.'

Despite the ban, most local authorities gave the film a licence, and it was widely shown. The issue threatened Chamberlain's position and, according to some informed opinion, almost brought down the government. Sybil fiercely opposed any censorship, and not long after joined the protest against another example of it. The London County Council had opposed an application for film societies to show a group of Russian silent films, including *Battleship Potempkin*, *Mother*, *October* and *The General Line*, arguing that they would 'cause a breach of the peace'. Shaw, Bertrand Russell, Nigel Playfair, Laurence Housman and Winifred Holtby were among her fellow-signatories in a letter published in the press protesting against this fatuous idea.

She also entered the public debate about a new invention called 'the television-cinematograph', which some people felt could spell doom for the theatre. In a spirited article in the *Daily Mail*, she argued that theatre had not only survived the advent of the motor car, the gramophone, the 'pictures' and the wireless, but actually thrived on them, and was now more popular then ever before. Theatre, she suggested, was unique in its appeal, because it was live. 'It may be possible to reproduce the words, even the intonations and the actions of a play on a television screen; but that wave of elemental feeling which reaches out from the stage to every part of the auditorium, from the stalls to the gallery, is something that can never be faked.' The theatre, she said, is not just a house of entertainment, 'it is part and parcel of modern life, a part that is almost as necessary as food and clothing'.

This doughty defence of her art-form was one that she was to continue to make in many different circumstances over the next fifty years.

18

Into Africa

1928–1929

'In my part as Medea I was representing the Africans.
I'd suddenly seen a new meaning to the play'
Sybil on playing to a mixed audience in Johannesburg

'Darling, we're going to Africa! I've always wanted to go there,' Sybil wrote excitedly to John in February 1928. 'Mary and Ann will come too and they can be pages and things.' Mary and Ann were now nearly fourteen and twelve respectively. For the previous two years they had been at the Francis Holland School in Chelsea. Sybil's attitude to the girls' education had always been relaxed, not to say careless. Mary had become a pupil at twelve quite by chance. 'It hadn't occurred to Mummy that I might want to go there rather than stay on at Mrs Spencer's school,' she recalls. 'Then one day we walked past it on the way to church, and she said, "You don't want to go there, do you?" I told her I would like to; the mother of one of my friends had told me I should. So then and there she made an appointment with the headmistress.'

Now, so they could be 'pages and things' in South Africa, Sybil and Lewis removed their two daughters from the school. The plan was for them to continue their studies under their supervision. 'They can do lessons on the boat with me,' Sybil announced blithely. 'Anyway seeing all those marvellous places will be much better for them.' But her liberal attitude to her daughters' education had its limits: 'I *can't* let M and A hear marriage discussed freely *just* yet!!!' she wrote to Edy Craig, in response to a suggestion that they hand out leaflets at a performance of *The Fanatics*, Miles Malleson's passionate play about revolution, marriage and free love.

Both girls already had considerable stage experience. At six Mary had played Belinda Cratchitt in *A Christmas Carol*, at ten Helga in *Peer Gynt* for the Oxford University Dramatic Society (OUDS), and more recently

Rosalind in a school production of *As You Like It*. There was a fashion then for Christmas productions of classics with young casts from theatrical families, and she had appeared among 'promising juveniles' in two plays by Barrie, *The Admirable Crichton* and *Quality Street*, at the Children's Theatre in Covent Garden. Small for her age, she was sometimes compelled to play a boy's role: 'I didn't like that at all,' she remembers, 'except in *Saint Joan* when I took over from Jack Hawkins and played Dunois' page. That was a nice part, because you have that great moment when the wind changes.' She was often seen in Carlyle Square hearing her parents' lines, and when in front would notice any divergence from the text; after Lewis had missed out three words in the wooing scene in *The Taming of the Shrew* she had told him off.

Ann had been stage-struck from the start. At six she had played Tiny Tim in *A Christmas Carol*, at nine had walked on in the OUDS *Peer Gynt*, then had played with Mary in *The Admirable Crichton* and *Quality Street*. Recently, directed by James Whale as Daisy Ashford, the lead role in the delightful *The Young Visiters* (sic), she was commended by the *Observer* for a 'remarkable clearness of utterance'. She was already clear about her future: 'I am going to be a real actress in musical comedy, with lovely dresses and lots of singing and dancing to do,' she told a journalist. 'Not like mother, who has to go about saying "Woe is me" all the time.'

In the build-up to the South African trip Sybil's schedule was as crowded as ever. She once again played the title-role for Ben Greet in a series of performances of *Everyman* in the Rudolph Steiner Hall, the cast including Lewis, Russell and Eileen. She took turns, with Edith Evans, Greet and Andrew Leigh, to play the Prologue in *Romeo and Juliet* at the Old Vic, where Eric Portman and Jean Forbes-Robertson were the star-crossed lovers. And she shone in the cameo role of Queen Elizabeth in two performances of *The Making of an Immortal*, directed by Robert Atkins and written by George Moore, best known for his novel *Esther Waters*. According to Agate: 'Miss Thorndike cocked her eye over the part, and without rehearsal walked doughtily on to the stage and off again, but convinced us in something under five minutes that the greatest of all English women had passed by.'

Her next production proved an expensive flop. *Judith of Israel* by the American E de Marnay Baruch, the story of Judith and Holofernes from the Apocrypha, had been written for Sarah Bernhardt, but only completed after her death. Seeing Sybil at the peak of her profession, the author persuaded her and Lewis, against their better judgement, to stage the play. The original plan, with Cochran as producer, was to mount a spectacular production for three nights in the vast Albert Hall. When this proved too costly they staged it instead on the grand scale at the Strand, with Lewis and E Lyall Swete co-directing, incidental music by Granville Bantock, and a cast that included John Laurie, J Fisher White and Rosina Filippi. But the play was weak, and Sybil could do little with an insubstantial part, described by *Punch* as 'a mere vague moaning wraith'. It closed after just 29 performances, losing her and Lewis the substantial sum of £8,000, virtually all their savings.

The artist Graham Robertson was not impressed. 'La Thorndike as usual infuriated me,' he wrote. 'To me her acting is the merest pastiche, a series of stale, stodgy effects and poses, put together with little thought and no heart.' Agate argued that the truly great actresses achieved fame, as Bernhardt did, by also performing superbly in bad plays. Sybil, he contended, could not do this, and *Judith of Israel* was proof of this argument. Another critic and friend, Herbert Farjeon, put another view. 'She is inclined to be at her best when she is exercising a severe restraint on her emotions. When she holds herself in, she can be very fine indeed. When she lets herself go, she is less impressive. This is probably due to the fact that in real life she is so full of enthusiasm that restraint on the stage comes to her as the relief that is experienced by many other actresses when they perform parts that are emotional.'

Her enthusiasm extended to religion, and brought her a commission to write an essay for *Affirmations: God in the Modern World*, a series published by Ernest Benn 'to provide concise information upon all the problems that are troubling men's minds', with Hugh Walpole and A A Milne among the other contributors. In her spirited essay 'Religion and the Stage', she vigorously attacked the Church for its moralistic approach to the theatre, and its attempts to censor plays. 'A religious system that patronises art and claims to teach the artist what to see and what to say is on the side of darkness, not of light,' she wrote. 'The artist accepts life as it is and claims the gift of a clearer vision of it, and the power of so presenting it that others also may see his vision. The Church attacks life as it is, and claims the gift of precise knowledge – the power to judge and the power to reform it. The drama makes no such claim, and the nearer it gets to direct preaching, the worse it is likely to be as drama.'

She was now able to do a favour for Leon M Lion. The American actress Willette Kershaw was playing the lead in a comedy at Wyndham's, *The Stranger in the House*, by Michael Morton and Peter Traill. When she fell ill

Lion cabled Sybil, then at Dartmouth, and asked her to take over. Back came the reply: 'Yes. Send the script.' She received it the next day, studied the part on the train to London, and arrived at the theatre almost word-perfect. It was a striking example of her speed of study – she claimed she could read a page and then rattle if off immediately – and her unselfishness – she was willing to give up a short planned holiday to repay her debt to Lion. But both the play and the part of a distraught mother were inadequate: 'No playing could make this bloodless female interesting,' declared *Punch*. However she only had to make it interesting for two weeks, when South Africa beckoned.

It was Shaw who spurred her and Lewis into action, telling them he would have to give the South African rights to *Saint Joan* to someone else if they didn't take the play there right away. Their first major foreign tour with their own company was a phenomenally ambitious one. In addition to *Saint Joan* their planned repertoire included *Henry V*, *Much Ado About Nothing*, *The Lie*, *Jane Clegg*, and a domestic drama by Sidney Howard, *The Silver Chord*. Sybil had mixed feelings about her part in the latter, a woman described as 'a type of self-centred, self-pitying, son-devouring tigress': 'The woman in the play's awful, isn't she?' she observed to John. 'I get depressed sometimes that I'm like that, bossing everyone about. But it's still a jolly good play.' She also, having received many letters from students in South Africa, intended to play both Medea and Hecuba.

Before they left, she and Lewis were given a farewell dinner at the Mayfair Hotel by the British Drama League. Sybil spoke of the value for actors of getting away from the capital. Someone had told her she had found her niche in London, so should stay there. 'The time to find your niche is when you are dead,' she replied hotly. 'To get settled is one of the worst things in existence.' She also admitted: 'I am always biting off more than I can chew, for it is only by doing so that you can get anywhere in this world.' She had recently experienced a feeling of imprisonment in London, and wanted to get away 'to find a bigger vision'. Africa, which had fascinated her as a child, she hoped would supply it.

On 20 April, after three weeks of rehearsal, she and Lewis sailed from Southampton on the Royal Mail steamer *Windsor Castle*. Their company included Colette O'Niel, Carleton Hobbs, Walter Hudd and Winifred Oughton, while in South Africa they would be joined by Leonard Sachs. Looking forward to days full of sky, sea and air, she found the rest of the 17-day voyage 'a grand thing, and so refreshing to the spirit'. Stepping off the boat, she was asked which was her favourite part. 'Saint Joan gives me more pleasure than any other,' she replied. 'It appeals to me and stirs my imagination more, so that I am engrossed when acting it. It is, I think, the only part in which I entirely forget that there is an audience.'

The tour began with an eight-week season in Johannesburg, also taking in Cape Town, Durban, East London, Port Elizabeth, Pietermaritzburg and Pretoria. Sybil wrote to Edy Craig from Cape Town: 'The hospitality of the people is beyond belief, I've never met such kindness. We did a jolly season tho' nothing ran long (I was thankful!).' For two weeks she again played Medea and Jane Clegg in a double-bill. 'That was a pull – and the two plays paired well. We also did some special readings of *Henry V*, rather like an Elizabethan Punch and Judy – half reading, half acting – I did Chorus and comments – beat the drum and did all the effects – it was most exciting and went so well we've had to do it a lot. They are lovely audiences, especially away from Johannesburg – here in Cape Town it's like playing in Heaven – everyone sees every point and is quiet at the right moments.'

She and Lewis had been warned that South African audiences would prefer the lighter fare, but this proved spectacularly wrong. *Saint Joan* and *Medea* were the most popular productions. *The Silver Cord* went down well in Johannesburg, Sybil being commended for 'a superb character study' and labelled 'an actress of incomparable quality'. She also gained good notices for *The Lie*: one critic wrote that 'the quiet hiding of her histrionic art and the reservation of dramatic strength add to the superlative finesse of her acting'. But the demand for Shakespeare was so great that they had to have their *Macbeth* costumes sent on, with Lewis taking the title-role.

Sybil had been fired up for the trip by reading Olive Schreiner's passionate, anti-imperialist, feminist novel *The Story of an African Farm*. As ever she was hungry to get to know the people and the country, and filled every moment offstage with unstinting activity. She lectured in schools, opened flower shows, ventured down gold mines, stayed on farms, visited hospitals and factories. She learned to surf in Durban, and went horse-riding in the veldt outside Bloemfontein. She also attended endless social events at the weekends. 'Mother loved seeing all these different people, and she was very good at all that,' Mary remembers. 'So was Lewis, although it wasn't really his thing.' Russell complained that her letters home were one long hymn of praise, and that every place she saw and every person she met was 'most fascinating'. But she had mixed feelings about the country, as she told Edy Craig. 'Edy, I *love*

Africa – it's so large and simple and the sun is indescribable and the feeling of the air – Cape Town is the pick for sheer beauty, but I love the high bare veldt round Johannesburg. The people there are charming, but there's a fearful grabbing of life there of which one is conscious all the time – of getting, getting. I suppose it's the feeling of the mines and the thousands of blacks working for the whites underground that gives one such horror.'

Although the separation of the races was less rigid than later, she was clearly shocked by the reality of racial discrimination, and tried to make as much possible contact with the natives. In Johannesburg she and the family attended church services where they were the only white people, and visited the Bantu centre with a Mr Shastri, a leading Indian scholar with whom they became friends. On another occasion she witnessed a tribal dance, a spectacle which thrilled her. But such visits induced in her a guilt about her own relative comfort, mixed with admiration for the Kaffirs' simple lifestyle. 'The kraals were as clean as a new pin and very sparsely furnished. That impressed us a lot, because one always has too much, and we felt this really was the way to furnish.' She also admired the apparently informal way of living of the Dutch farmers .'They live exactly as I like. All eating off a huge table under the trees. Any old person dropping in, and everybody helping themselves out of huge dishes into vast plates.' She tended to romanticise or sentimentalise aspects of the natives' lives: the workers down the mine, she said, 'looked like Rodin sculptures', while the dancers were 'lovely laughing people'. Yet her feelings were genuine and ran deep, as was shown when she and Lewis got into a furious argument with the theatre management in Johannesburg.

When they realised that their audiences were all-white, they tried to persuade the management to let them be mixed. When this was refused, Sybil boldly suggested shutting the theatre to the whites so they could play to a black audience. Horrified, the management agreed to a compromise, shutting the circle and gallery to the whites, and letting the blacks sit there for one performance each of *Medea* and *Saint Joan*. 'They were the most breath-taking audience I've ever played to,' Sybil recalled. 'In my part as Medea I was representing the Africans. I'd suddenly seen a new meaning to the play. Until now it had been for me a war cry for oppressed people – now it was the blacks, as Medea, crying out against the civilised whites in the person of Jason, the Greek. And they felt it. You heard sort of deep-breathing sounds coming from the dress circle, and it was absolutely thrilling.' But their firm stance on the matter of mixed audiences aroused suspicions in some quarters, a retired general accusing them of being 'clearly in the pay of the Russian government'.

On All Souls' Day the company left Pretoria and headed north. 'Rhodesia they tell us will be roasting,' Sybil wrote to her mother. 'I'm sure there will be spiders and ghastly beetles which terrify me.' The long train journey through the parched lands brought out the same bursting enthusiasm and romantic feelings she had experienced in her trips across America as a young actress. 'We got out of the train every time it stopped, and we existed through the day very dirty and continuously passing native villages and natives in every stage of undress, but so beautiful,' she wrote to Russell from Bulawayo. 'When sunset came we all sung hymns of joy and watched with eagerness the lovely golden pink of the sun and the moon coming up at the same time, and you know a breeze comes with the sunset and clothes all come unstuck, and every one then can cheer up.' Bulawayo was just as she had imagined: 'Men in white and sun-helmets and all looking like Rhodesians in books.'

They continued on to the Victoria Falls, where the water tumbled spec-tacularly down into gorges in the Zambezi river. 'We none of us could speak we were so thrilled,' Sybil wrote. Reaching the main fall in the rainforest, she was soon in the water. 'You have to be very careful and cling on to rocks or you would be hurled into the abyss,' she wrote. 'Oh, the gorges. And oh the families of baboons with faces like lions who watched us, but when I bathed in the river they all shambled off, which I took as personal. The water was lovely, but you have to look out for crocodiles as they come up behind you and snap off your legs, and then they keep you under a rock till you get seasonable, and then they devour you.'

In Livingstone they performed *The Lie* at the Bioscope cinema in very primitive conditions, 'just like a parish entertainment'. The back of the cinema was taken out and chairs put across the road to accommodate the audience. Mary recalls the occasion: 'It was an extraordinary fit-up hall, and as there was no music available I was shoved in front of the piano backstage to improvise.' She did it 'jolly well', Sybil told Russell. 'No music. Making it all up and fitting it together just like proper overtures and *entr'actes*.'

In the New Year, having been away for nine months, they sailed for England and home. 'Won't we have some yarns, mother, and nice little lunches and teas together,' Sybil wrote. 'You have been an angel over this time and now it will soon be over and then jolly old England once more.' For Mary and Ann the trip was a turning-point: they concentrated on theatre and never went back to school. For Sybil it was an immensely interesting experience. 'The country has a tremendously strong appreciation of everything that is going to make for its future greatness, and there is a groping after all that is finest in art,' she enthused on her return. She had noticed a strong desire for theatre, even in the most out-of-the-way towns, with amateur societies springing up, and people travelling three hundred miles to see their productions. She made clear her intention to return to South Africa, when she would hope to appear in Shakespeare 'for the benefit of the natives', having been 'filled with wonder at their aptitude for learning and their natural acting'.

It had been a successful venture theatrically, but also one that whetted her appetite for travel and seeing new places. Over the next forty years she would indulge it to the full.

19

Shaw to Ibsen

1929–1930

'If any photographer can get a picture of Miss Thorndike lying in a
hammock, he should be able to command a high price for it'
Writer and critic Herbert Farjeon

While in South Africa, Sybil had spoken about the possibility of going
to America 'to take up film work'. Instead, on her return to England,
she took part in her first British talking film, *To What Red Hell*. She did so at
a turning point in British film history.

Following the lead given in America by Al Jolson and *The Jazz Singer*,
which had just been shown in England, there was a realisation that sound
was the coming thing, and a rush to install the necessary equipment in
studios and cinemas. Films in progress or recently completed were hastily
re-shot with sound added. Overnight, film stars who had the wrong kind
of voices disappeared into obscurity, and producers turned increasingly to
vocally more accomplished stage actors. Its impact on the theatre was
serious: many buildings were wired for sound and converted into cinemas.
In the next five years the number staging live drama would drop from 500
to 250.

'I'm back in London for four days, doing a filthy talkie,' Sybil wrote to
Master Rawdon. In interviews she was more positive about filming. 'It was
all so interesting from a technical point of view,' she explained as shooting
ended. 'It means working with more limitations than on the stage, and of
course there was all the technique of perfect synchronisation to get up. But
I love learning new ideas, so the whole experience appealed to me.' She still,
however, preferred the silent films: 'They are so restful, and one can exercise
one's imagination throughout in a fascinating way.' She rejected the idea that
the talkies would supplant the theatre, arguing that the boom would be short-

lived: 'People will very soon tire of looking at photographs talking, and want once again to see actors and actresses in their flesh.'

To What Red Hell was a melodrama based on a play by Percy Robinson. Heading a large cast, Sybil introduced the film, and played the mother of an epileptic man, whom she shields after he kills a girl in a fit. Initially a silent film, it was scrapped and re-made as a 'talkie', with '100 per cent dramatic dialogue'. The result was a bizarre confusion of styles, with mimed scenes interjected into the dialogue. Sybil, it was felt, had done the best she could in the circumstances, though the reviewers were otherwise divided: while the *Manchester Guardian* observed that 'her voice records well, and is extremely lifelike', the *Observer* suggested that 'Miss Thorndike seems a little precious on the talking screen'. John Casson remembered her giving her role 'the full dramatic treatment of Hecuba, Medea, Judith of Israel and Joan rolled into one, and she jolly nearly bounced clean out of the screen'. Then, as later, her vibrant personality often seemed too large for films.

After Africa, Mary and Ann continued their theatrical careers. Mary had come home early, at Barrie's invitation to be Wendy in *Peter Pan*, a role she was to play in the West End for six successive years ('with freshness and sincerity', *The Times* noticed), with Jean Forbes-Robertson often playing Peter, and Du Maurier once playing Hook. Lewis, as he often did, acted as her coach: 'He always helped us with our parts,' she says. 'I can still remember the inflections he gave me for Wendy.' Ann continued to write plays: at fourteen she became the West End's youngest playwright when *The Camwells are Coming* was staged at the Children's Theatre in Bloomsbury.

The two girls were now educated at home, in a distinctly haphazard way by a variety of people. They learned French with Alice Gachet, a brilliant teacher at RADA. For 'movement' they had Penelope Wheeler, a well-known dancer. Margaret Webster, a family friend, taught them French, although this, she recalled, 'resulted in my learning far more than I taught'. Lewis helped with mathematics, Sybil with poetry. They were also, thanks to the family connection with Elsie Fogerty, allowed to attend elocution classes at the Central School. Both were musical and played the piano.

Sybil's attitude, that her children were different from others, was one they sometimes found problematic. 'They never thought of you as being one of the mob,' Mary says. 'Under our grandmother's influence, who thought we shouldn't be like everyone else, Mummy always dressed us in unusual colours, and we hated that. She and Daddy always regarded us as special, and she did occasionally embarrass us by saying so in front of others – although Daddy never did. We didn't like that; that's why we had loved getting into school uniform. They used to arrange things specially, like putting me into a French play at RADA. But I wasn't part of the class, I knew hardly anyone there.' In retrospect she feels they should never have been taken to South Africa: 'We missed a whole year of schooling, and it was difficult to catch up.'

Their home was still invariably full of people: Lewis would take on someone for a production, and they would stay for weeks. 'It was a kind of open house, and you never quite knew who was staying,' Mary remembers. 'We used to have lovely Sunday evening parties, Eileen would come over, and close friends, and we'd have a cold supper and then music, and we'd all sing.' Daniel Thorndike and his siblings stayed with them on and off, when Russell was away, or in financial difficulties, which was often. For Sybil all this could be stressful. 'I can't get through domestic things,' she complained to Edy Craig. 'It's *awful*, house jammed with boys – sleeping on floors – anywhere!! Hectic!'

She continued to support many causes, great and small. She became a trustee of the Theatre Girls' Club in Soho, which provided accommodation for unemployed or low-paid actresses – two-thirds of the profession were reckoned to be out of work at this time. She was on the board of the Council for the Abolition of the Death Penalty, an issue about which she felt strongly. She opened sales of work and church bazaars, and made radio appeals for the Invalid Children's Aid Association and the Homes of St Giles for British Lepers. According to Emlyn Williams, when one of her daughters took a phone call from a family friend, she said: 'They're not in. Daddy is reading Shakespeare sonnets to the blind and Mummy's playing Shakespeare to the lepers.' The story may be apocryphal, but its tenor is certainly accurate.

Often she spoke up for the achievements and virtues of women. While presenting the prizes at a girls' school in Middlesex, she reminded the students of the courageous and energetic way women of previous generations had fought to open up the professions to their sex. 'Energy is a magnificent thing, and always better than a lethargic peace,' she said. 'It's pitiable to see people fat, happy, and just contented with the way things are, and with no energy.' She also responded vigorously to an article in the press by a Professor Low, who argued that men were superior to women. 'There is absolutely no question that women are every bit as good as men, and better, on the stage,' she asserted. 'I think women's dramatic achievement has even been the greater. No man on earth could ever compare with Duse, and even great actors of the past like Burbage and Kean can hardly rank with Mrs Siddons and Sarah Bernhardt. Women are temperamentally better suited to the stage.' She concluded firmly: 'The stage nearly always improves young women, but it often deteriorates young men.'

In March, after nearly a year's absence from the London stage, she returned to play the title-role in *Major Barbara* at Wyndham's. Labelled by Shaw 'A Discussion in Three Acts', the play had been first performed at the Court in 1905, making Shaw the most talked-about dramatist in London. The character of Barbara was inspired by the actress Eleanor Robson, but based also on the social reformer and co-founder of the Fabian Society, Beatrice Webb, a close friend of Shaw. Mary Murray was another inspiration, as was Gilbert Murray for Adolphus Cusins, the professor of Greek. The idealistic upper-class woman who joins the Salvation Army can be seen as a prototype of Saint Joan. This was undoubtedly part of its appeal for Sybil, as was its central theme of the battle between religion and capitalism. Lewis co-directed with Charles Macdona, and played Adolphus Cusins, while Balliol Holloway was Undershaft the arms manufacturer.

'I am up to my neck in rehearsals of Barbara,' Shaw told Mrs Patrick Campbell. Once again he inspired Sybil with his energetic interventions: 'He goes on the stage,' she reported, 'and not only tells the actor how the part should be played, but gets into the character and acts it himself...He throws himself thoroughly into the thing to such an extent that the other day he even imitated the trombone at the end of act two.' Shaw then caught flu, prompting rumours he was on his death-bed. He scotched these success-fully by turning up for the first night, and sitting prominently in a box with T E Lawrence. Nearing the end of his reign over the theatre, he had written a lengthy programme note, justifying the play's revival after 24 years, princi-pally on the grounds that poverty and unemployment had got worse since he wrote it. He had mockingly warned theatregoers that the play had 'no drama, no situations, no curtains, no feeling, no heart, no dramatic interest – in one word, no adultery'.

The critics certainly thought it flawed and over-long – 'Speeches No Shorter Than 24 Years Ago' ran one puzzled headline. But Sybil was highly praised for a performance full of quiet earnestness and burning zeal. Alan Parsons wrote in the *Daily Mail*: 'Miss Thorndike has never done anything finer than her Barbara – lovable, romantic, impulsive, the almost hysterical high spirits of the Salvation Army lass, with her big drum and Blood and Fire flag, closely allied to the deepest melancholy.' J T Grein, the founder of the trail-blazing Independent Theatre, wrote in the *Sketch*: 'She was all youth and fire; she spread balm and solace; she was strong in her convictions, in her efforts as a reformer; but she was entirely feminine in her breakdown when her principles came into conflict with her mission. Never – even as Joan – has she been so simple, so natural, so little prone to let her peculiar idiosyncrasies prevail.' Herbert Farjeon summed up the evening pithily: 'Very good Shaw. Very good Thorndike. Makes everybody argue while going home.'

A fortnight after the opening, perhaps prompted by being back in Shaw/ Barker territory, Sybil mounted a strong defence of the idea of a National Theatre, which had attracted a lot of words but as yet few deeds. In reply to an article in the *Morning Post*, she likened the idea to that of a public library: 'It is an organisation which stores, and continually provides, varied dramatic fare of a definite quality and standard, independent of the passing fancies and crazes which make a play (apparently quite independent of merit) a "success" or a "failure". An organisation which keeps a tradition of fine speaking and fine team acting. An organisation which gives reasonable security to the company, so that they can play independently of making a personal success. An organi- sation run on real repertory lines, where every play once performed is kept in store (on paper if not in the concrete), and can easily be revived. Where the bill is changed nightly and at least three plays mounted each week, so that full advantage can be taken of successes, while plays of less obvious appeal can be mounted without heavy loss under the best conditions, and possibly nursed into success by playing them (at first) only once a week.'

In order to fill her empty Sunday evenings, Sybil continued to work with the small stage societies. She had a single scene as Princess Halm Eberstein in a performance at the Palace of an adaptation of George Eliot's novel *Daniel Deronda*, staged by the Jewish Drama League, with Esmé Percy, Nora Nicholson and Marie Ney. She also appeared in *The Donkey's Nose*, a comedy by Eliot Crawshay-Williams directed by Lewis. Staged by the Sunday Play Society, again for one performance, it allowed her as a politician's wife a respite from tragedy, and she revelled in it. Herbert Farjeon, astounded by her energy, remarked: 'If any photographer can get a picture of Miss Thorndike lying in a hammock, he should be able to command a high price for it.'

Major Barbara closed after just seven weeks. She and Lewis had ended their partnership with Albery on going to Africa, though on amicable terms.

The revival, the first staged in the West End, had been a collaboration with Leon M Lion, now manager of Wyndham's. Sybil remained grateful to Lion for his early encouragement, as well as for his later hospitality. 'Oh such lovely parties!' she wrote to him. 'The wine always just the right one to loosen our tongues and set us going with our pet arguments, and our voices would get louder and more excited, and the affairs of the world would be put completely right, the Theatre itself re-made, and all of us feel good fellows and strong, with a renewed sense of the deep jolliness of life.'

Lion also managed her next major production, *Mariners* by Clemence Dane. It was a curious choice: a grim melodrama based on her novel, it had flopped two years before on Broadway. At Wyndham's, in a company that included Alison Leggatt and Brember Wills, and co-directed by Lewis and Lion, Sybil was a faded harridan in a dressing-gown, making life a misery for her saintly, henpecked rector husband, played by Lewis. Her climactic scene of grief after his death was described by Ivor Brown in the *Saturday Review* as 'the authentic death-rattle of human hope, a scream of the most shiversome melancholy'. But many of the performances were inadequate: several actors were inaudible, and St John Ervine thought the direction 'boneless'. From Wyndham's Lewis wrote to Murray: 'Mariners is entirely failing to attract the public. We have had a pretty disastrous time here with both Major Barbara and Mariners.'

The latter ran for just four weeks. By now Sybil seemed to have run out of challenging new roles. Hannen Swaffer wrote with feeling about her dilemma: 'Sybil Thorndike is herself a tragedy. She lives in an age where there are no plays for her. She is the only tragedy queen, but she has no throne, and Greta Garbo has stolen all her subjects. The universities pay her honour. Royalty has acknowledged her greatness. Yet where is the public? And where are the plays? When you see her in *Mariners* you see the only inheritor of the tradition of great tragic acting. You see a distinguished player who is not too proud to strip herself of every shred of good looks and decent manners, one who, if the scene demands it, will jabber incoherently in a paroxysm of grief, rend her soul in tatters, and expose the uttermost depths of feeling until they seem repulsive under the searchlight of genius....Now that her powers are at their height – well, who wants tragedy, and who is there to write it, even if the public wished to go?'

In May, as if to prove his point after the failure of *Mariners*, Sybil and Lewis hastily revived *Jane Clegg* and *Medea* under Lion's management: 'The double-bill went well in South Africa, but who knows what it will do here,' Lewis wrote gloomily to Murray. It was an absorbing mixture, pointing up both the similarities and differences between the two pieces. It gave Sybil the chance, under Lewis' direction, to play in one evening two formidable women cruelly wronged by self-seeking husbands, and to play each of them twice on matinee days. *The Times* critic was impressed: 'In the quietly felt tragedy of the commercial traveller's wife, no less than in the dreadful and insistent Medean clamour for revenge, her power of shedding a clear, unsentimental light on the complexities of character was equally effective.'

The critics preferred her as St John Ervine's restrained wife, in which she was deemed to be close to perfection, than as Euripides' woman of fire, where a tendency to rant and posture was observed. But beneath the passion she remained in control. During one of Medea's speeches a tooth flew from her mouth. One Chorus member recalled: 'Without a moment's hesitation she shot out an arm, grabbed it in mid-air, and gave an enormous wink, without a suspicion of disturbance reaching the audience. Another time she sauntered into the wings munching an apple. At her cue she flung it with a chortle of joy at a stagehand, and after going on and rending the house's heart to bits, came off to finish it.'

Both Mary and Ann received good notices as the Clegg children, Alan Parsons of the *Daily Mail* noting of Mary: 'This child is a born actress, with a sure and certain intuition far beyond her years.' Meanwhile Russell, who had appeared in several silent films as well as continuing his stage career, had been writing a biography of Sybil. He had shown her extracts before publication, but made use of letters and other material she had asked him not to include. This was her claim in an article she wrote in *Pearson's Weekly*, which however reads more like a puff for the book than an airing of a grievance. In it she refers to her brother's 'acutely vivid imagination and memory', explaining that 'Russell has always taken me as a joke, and always will'. The book, published in May to favourable notices, provides a detailed picture of their childhood and early days, and reflects in its bantering way their close relationship. Soon after its publication, Russell joined up again with Ben Greet, to play leads in his company touring America, which he did for the next three seasons.

In the autumn Sybil and Lewis embarked under the management of Daniel Mayer on a seventeen-week tour of a romantic comedy by Brenda Girvin and Monica Cozens, *Madame Plays Nap*. 'Sybil is the only English actress whom the provinces treat like a queen,' wrote Hannen Swaffer. As she fulfilled her customary demanding offstage itinerary, she was certainly treated royally. She opened bazaars, visited newspaper offices and hospitals, and spoke at luncheon clubs and society meetings. She found ways of praising the character of each city. 'Edinburgh people are of a very good type, intelligent and appreciative,' she told a local journalist, in a city which had recently awarded her an honorary degree. Where possible she would emphasise her local connections. In Southampton she recalled her holidays there as a child, and her activities as an amateur actress. But sometimes she strained to find suitable material: 'My hairdresser is always talking about Portsmouth,' she told one gathering there.

Madame Plays Nap, which Lewis directed and also starred in as Napoleon, was a light, insubstantial piece ('A dash of History, a spot of Fiction, and you have a Legend'). The provincial public delighted in Sybil's coquettish Madame de Beauvais, but the critics were less convinced. There were mixed views as to whether 'our greatest tragic actress' was wasting her talent on such 'kittenish antics and childish babble'. For Ivor Brown it marked 'the full expense of her spirit in a waste of Napoleonic nonsense'. When it reached London in December its reception was again mixed, and it lasted just a month.

Sybil vigorously defended her right to choose a variety of roles, including light-hearted ones: 'Playing a part like Joan can do you a lot of harm, so you must play other ones,' she said. 'I refuse utterly to be stamped as a tragedy actress, or any other sort of actress. I am tired of playing on one note: why shouldn't I play comedy if I want to? If there is one thing we actors have to fight against, it is getting into a rut. It is always assumed that I *must* play tragedy. It is suggested that the public always wants and expects to see me standing, hands across breast, declaiming deep, tragic, fear-raising stuff. And I won't do it! Why should I? I prefer to be versatile.'

While playing in Brighton in October she experienced 'the most thrilling day of my life so far'. In the ancient Guildhall in Rochester, with her mother, husband and brother in the audience, she received the freedom of the city of her childhood. Princes, peers, statesmen, soldiers and sailors had been similarly honoured by the ancient borough, but Sybil was the first woman to be so, and one of the youngest. In her speech she duly pressed the right buttons, declaring: 'I think to receive an honour from the city to which one belongs, from one's own family, as it were, is the greatest honour that can be done to anyone.'

A month later, in an article published just before Armistice Day, she donned her pacifist mantle, urging people to 'try to destroy the illusion of war as a grand and glorious thing'. One way, she argued, was 'to encourage the reading of literature that paints war as it really is'. She advocated reading books from different point of view, such as Erich Maria Remarque's recently published *All Quiet on the Western Front*, e e cummings' *The Enormous Room*, and *Under Fire* by Henri Barbusse, where 'we shall find the same human revolt against the madness and stupidity of war'. But the theatre too could help, especially through *Journey's End*, R C Sherriff's powerful anti-war play then running in the West End, which she called 'the most magnificent plea for peace of them all'. Welcoming the BBC's decision to broadcast it, and no doubt with Lewis' experience in mind, she added: 'Many a hard-bitten soldier, with varied experiences in France, has told me that in this play we have an exact reproduction of what took place.... *Journey's End* is a mighty blow against war, a heroic weapon in the spiritual struggle to ensure peace and tranquillity for all mankind.'

She and Lewis were now involved in an historic struggle concerning the pay and conditions of actors, which led to the formation of the union Equity to improve the lot of a grossly exploited profession. Previously there had been two organisations within the theatre, the Stage Guild and the Actors' Association, the former linked to theatre managers, the latter more trade-union minded, and the one to which Sybil and Lewis belonged. In October 1929, after a bogus manager had left a touring company stranded and unpaid, a packed meeting at the New heard calls for the two bodies to unite, to protect actors and prevent another such fiasco from occurring.

This they did in December when, at an emotional meeting at the Duke of York's attended by hundreds of actors, the British Actors' Equity Association was formed. Lewis, though more sympathetic with the left-leaning Actors' Association, was a moderating influence in the effort to find a solution that would suit both organisations. He and Sybil, along with May Whitty, Ben Webster, Godfrey Tearle, Felix Aylmer and Raymond Massey, were among the leading figures forming the first committee. They were also involved in working out a constitution. At a further meeting it was decided to press for a £3 minimum wage, Sybil declaring that 'anyone not worth £3 a week ought not to be in the profession at all'. When the issue arose of a closed shop, she and Lewis were among a group of leading actors who pledged themselves not to work with non-members. Later she was elected to the first council, and remained on it until 1951. Unusually for a union, Equity was begun by people

at the top of the profession, to help their colleagues. 'Let us give our souls
to the work,' Sybil said. 'Let us be witnesses, not profiteers.' Her and Lewis'
voices would often be heard in the years to come, with Lewis eventually being
elected the second president.

Meanwhile a new decade had begun. In the West End the 1930s were to
be filled with thrillers, musicals, revues, comedies, but few serious plays of
any depth. The popular playwrights were to be James Bridie, Clemence Dane,
J B Priestley, Dodie Smith and John van Druten. In 1930 Coward was at his
height, with *Private Lives* soon to be followed by *Cavalcade*. Maugham's *The
Sacred Flame*, a success for Gladys Cooper at the Playhouse, was still running,
as was Shaw's *The Apple Cart*, with Edith Evans and Cedric Hardwicke. John
Gielgud's *Hamlet* transferred from the Old Vic, setting in train a brief revival
of Shakespeare in the West End.

Sybil was in correspondence with the American playwright Paul Kester
– best known for *Nell of Old Drury* and *Eugene Aram* – who tried unsuccessfully to interest her in *Lady Dedlock*, his play based on Dickens' *Bleak House*.
Meanwhile she was again bent on proving her versatility. In the first four
months of 1930 she played the small part of an actress in a modern morality
play by Benn Levy, a dying mother in a sketch on a variety bill, the title-role –
in French – in a masterpiece by Racine, and an unfaithful wife in a translation
of a play by Georg Kaiser, the founder of expressionism.

In Levy's witty *The Devil*, directed by the author for two performances
at the Arts Theatre Club, all the characters were tempted by the devil
(disguised as a curate) to fulfil their dreams. Sybil played a vulgar but good-
hearted actress, who longed to play Lady Macbeth at the Albert Hall under
the direction of Granville Barker. The strong cast included Lewis, Ernest
Thesiger, Jean Cadell, Dennis Neilson-Terry and a young Diana Wynyard,
whose beauty and intelligence brought her glowing notices. Levy was in a
quandary about the order of the curtain call, so decided to put everyone on
stage at once. Sybil, however, told him that 'this new girl Diana, who is so
lovely, should have a bow all to herself'. The memory came from Levy's wife,
the actress Constance Cummings, who said of Sybil: 'She was very straightforward, she had no false pride. She had none of the attitude that some actors
and actresses have of thinking of the effect that they're making in the part,
and wanting to be centre stage.'

Her second venture was H G Stevens' psychic sketch *To Meet the King*,
part of a variety bill at the Coliseum. Also on the programme on different

nights of the two weeks were Zaidee Jackson with 'negro songs and spirituals', Phyllis Dare singing and dancing, the Houston Sisters, the Reno Brothers and the magician Victor Andre; the sketch was sandwiched between a chorus of Foster Girls and a Horse-Riding Novelty. Looking gracefully wan in an invalid chair, with Lewis and Jane Comfort in support, Sybil died happily at the end just before news was brought of her airman son's death. 'She loses none of her intensity, despite the milieu,' the *Morning Post* critic decided.

This slight piece led to her making her first record. With Lewis, Jane Comfort and Jack Hobbs, she recorded the sketch for Columbia Records on the stage of the Savoy. The record survives: among the clipped voices of the time, hers conveys powerfully the pride and sorrow of a mother living only for her son. Fortunately the part required her to sit throughout: just before the opening, while appearing in *Madame Plays Nap* in Lewisham, she had slipped and strained a ligament. A doctor who saw her in the interval forbad her to continue, but she insisted on doing so. 'I'm laid up with a bust muscle in my leg – such a curse,' she wrote to Edy Craig.

Fortunately she had recovered in time for the third play, a formidable challenge. Racine's *Phèdre* is a major work in the French classical canon, and its title-role, that of a woman consumed by an obsessive passion for her stepson, had given the great French actress Rachel her supreme success. The production at the Arts was staged by J T Grein's Cosmopolitan Theatre, which special-ised in mounting French, Italian and Russian plays in the original language, with mixed English and foreign casts. It was directed by Sybil's friend Alice Gachet, with a company that included a young Celia Johnson, yet to get her break in the West End. Sybil had kept up her French since playing Saint Joan in Paris, and was felt to have coped reasonably well with the language. Critical reaction to her performance was mostly positive: while Darlington felt her powers were muffled, the *Morning Post* thought she rose to great heights, and the *Daily Mail* noticed 'a perfection of beauty and power'.

However, during rehearsals she had experienced problems with both her director and her voice, as she explained to a friend. 'It really is a great and awful business. Gachet has just been in – she says Lord knows when she can rehearse – it's so bad for us all to do these things just like amateurs – it's hard enough in all conscience it being a foreign language....I'm so dreadfully troubled vocally. I can make a big noise and be quite enough or play in a quiet low entirely unmusical voice – but poetry and *French* poetry requires *light* head notes which I have not got! I feel it's just going to be nothing at all and

I so hate doing a thing badly. It wasn't a great performance of mine before, but now with a voice like a man's cracked bass it will be laughable.'

Finally in April she spent a fortnight at the Everyman, Hampstead in Kaiser's *The Fire in the Opera House*. Here she was Sylvette, an orphan married to a French nobleman (Vernon Sylvaine), who thinks she is chaste, though she is having an affair with a singer. Dressed in Chinese costume and a golden wig, she was one of the revellers who escapes from a fancy-dress ball at the opera house when a fire breaks out. Eric Johns, then the theatre's office boy, recalled her in rehearsal, constantly persuading the company to do a scene one more time, even if it was time to break. 'Bursting with energy, she zig-zagged across the stage to take her place, clicking her fingers like a Spanish dancer. "Let's go slap ahead," she cried. "Don't stop for a moment's rest."'

The play was directed by J T Grein but, hindered by a poor literal translation, it totally baffled the critics and, it seemed, the actors: *The Times* observed that Sybil's 'dash and outward brilliance' in the only woman's part failed to suggest that 'she knew any better than the rest of us whether she was on her emotional head or her intellectual heels'. S R Littlewood poured scorn on her attempt to portray 'a burning flower of seduction'; the play, he felt, was nothing but 'far-fetched nastiness, with which it is a pity so respected an actress should ever have been associated'.

There was some uncertainty about her next play. She expressed interest in Herman Ould's *Flames in Sunlight*, to be staged by the Masses Stage and Film Guild, a new organisation which included prominent members of the Labour Party. 'I think it a very fine play and should like to play the part immensely,' she told Edy Craig. But her next role was again at the Everyman. A former drill hall converted into a tiny theatre in 1920 by Norman Macdermott, it had gained a reputation for putting on bold and interesting new plays. It was now run by Malcolm Morley, an actor and playwright, known for his fine productions of works by Strindberg and Ibsen. It was he who now directed Sybil in the great classical role of Mrs Alving in *Ghosts*.

Ibsen's play, with its reference to the syphilis which Mrs Alving's son Oswald has inherited from his father, was no longer controversial. But when it was given its first performance in England, a private one directed by J T Grein in 1891 for the Independent Theatre, it provoked one of the most violent critical receptions in theatrical history, turning Ibsen overnight into a household name. In amongst the torrent of abuse, the most virulent was by Clement Scott in a *Daily Telegraph* leader, where he described the play as 'an open drain; a loathsome sore unbandaged; a dirty act done publicly', and, warming to his theme, 'bestial, cynical, disgusting, poisonous, sickly, delirious, indecent, loathsome, fetid and crapulous'. William Archer, Ibsen's translator and champion, concluded despairingly: 'Who can carry on a rational discussion with men whose first argument is a howl for the police?'

Considering Sybil's keen interest in Shaw, a great champion of Ibsen, and her friendship with Elizabeth Robins, it seems surprising that this was her first appearance in an Ibsen play. It was a part that had attracted many of the great actresses, including Mrs Patrick Campbell two years before, and Eleonora Duse, whom Sybil had seen in London in 1923: 'She was superb, I was bowled over,' she recalled. 'There she was, old and frail, without any make-up, with the sea in her veins, and there was Oswald's haunted mother.' She had coveted the role ever since she and Russell had devised the pastiche *Spooks* at the Old Vic, and it proved to be one supremely worthy of her.

Ibsen's mixture of realism and symbolism was a far cry from the Greek drama. The challenge for Sybil was to achieve a controlled performance that reflected the sensitive suffering and self-discovery of Mrs Alving. She largely succeeded, in a performance that most critics applauded for its masterly restraint and intense reality. While a small minority found her acting exaggerated or artificial, others felt her Mrs Alving was an achievement on a par with her Hecuba, Medea and Joan. *The Times* critic's response was typical: 'Miss Thorndike's performance is a beautiful one, with emotion in its depth that illumines the terrible tranquillity of its surface.' When the play toured to Oxford her performance inspired one undergraduate to change course. Terence Rattigan recalled: 'It conclusively transformed my vague theatrical aspirations into a firm resolve from that evening forth to give up the foreign service for which I was parentally destined and to devote my adult life to writing plays.'

Ghosts had to be limited to a two-week run, as Sybil had already signed up for her next engagement. It was a production that would enable her to tackle another meaty Shakespearean role, and at the same time ally herself fervently to a worthy cause.

20

Robeson, Guinness and a Dame

1930–1931

'You must read lots and lots of poetry. I learn a sonnet every day'
Sybil to Alec Guinness, aged sixteen and a half

Amy Johnson had just made her historic flight from England to Australia, the first female pilot to do so alone. 'You can't squash vitality,' Sybil remarked, in talking of her achievement. 'If there is a woman of enough vitality, she will always come out on top.' Much the same could be said of her own career. For ten years she had been a leading figure on the London stage. In a sympathetic but balanced summary of her achievements Ivor Brown, a self-confessed 'Sybillite', used the occasion to define her stature. 'She is a National Institution, a member of the Tussaud's class,' he wrote in the *Weekend Review*. 'She is "Sybil" in her own world as Mr Donoghue is "Steve", Mr Hendren is "Patsy" and Mr Churchill is "Winston" in theirs.'

He acknowledged however that her vocal tricks and boisterousness could be irritating. 'The Thorndike voice is not of gold; its strength can be harsh,' he wrote. 'It drags its monosyllables until they become as two (fi-er for fire). Sybil has rhetoric, a quality possessed by very few actresses of our time, but it is often spoiled by a rasping note, spoiled, that is, for those who care for preciseness in diction. In antic or vampish parts her touch has often been heavy. When she is set amid the muted, hush-hush, tip-toe methods of modern comedy, her art is too large and hearty for so slender a containing vessel.' Yet these criticisms, he suggested, dwindled in the face of her tremendous range and drive. 'Sybil has authority, and it is a power justly won. Her art has stature; it is positive and assertive and owes nothing to any accident of charm.' He observed how her fellow-actors saw her: 'I have never heard a word whispered against Sybil's stage manners. She is the finest of colleagues and would scorn to cold-shoulder a young rival. She will play any part that excites her, however small it may be.' Finally, he praised her social virtues: 'The actress as good citizen is a fairly new idea in the world, and Sybil has nurtured and matured it with the fullness of her mind and taste.'

It was her role as Citizen Sybil that drew her to her next production. The actor-manager Maurice Browne, founder of the Little Theatre in Chicago, had made money out of the success of *Journey's End*, and was planning to stage *Othello*. Shakespeare was enjoying a sudden renaissance in the West End: the year was to see three Hamlets – from Gielgud, Ainley and Moissi – and Balliol Holloway's Richard III, as well as *Othello*. The announcement that Paul Robeson would play the title-role provoked much lively discussion: no black actor had played Othello in England since the 1860s. Although Robeson had some acting experience, and had been a hit in Eugene O'Neill's *The Emperor Jones*, he was principally known as a singer, having recently scored a huge success in *Show Boat*, notably with the song 'Ol' Man River'. He had recently been refused entry on racial grounds to the Savoy Hotel, and there was a undercurrent of racism in the discussions about the casting. This was one factor in Sybil's offer to play Emilia, Iago's wife, a tacit show of support for Robeson. The plan almost went awry when the American director, Browne's wife Ellen von Volkenburg, began their first meeting by asking: 'Do you have much experience?'

For Robeson, Shakespeare's play seemed very modern, 'for the problem is the problem of my own people. It is a tragedy of racial conflict, a tragedy of honour rather than jealousy.' But he was apprehensive about playing Othello, and wanted a strong cast. In addition to Sybil, the company included Browne as Iago, the young Peggy Ashcroft as Desdemona, and Ralph Richardson as Roderigo. Robeson feared his American accent would show, and studied an edition of the play printed in Old English to help with his vowels. He also had to endure the inept direction of Ellen van Volkenburg, who had never worked on a Shakespeare play before, who liked to give instructions from the back of the stalls through a megaphone, and who, according to Robeson's wife Essie, 'can't even get actors from one side of the stage to the other'. He requested a replacement, but in vain.

Two weeks before the opening, worried about not 'feeling' the role, Robeson asked to be released, but was persuaded to stay. The actors rehearsed part of the time at Dartington College of Arts in Devon, where in the evenings Robeson sang spirituals by the light of a great log-fire. At other times he,

Peggy Ashcroft and Sybil held extra rehearsals in their own homes. 'His huge figure and even more huge voice completely filled our house,' John Casson remembered, 'and he had the most heart-warming, uninhibited laugh.' Sybil admired his deep, resonant voice, and his courtesy and modesty: in their big scene together she would say to him as they entered, 'This is *your* scene, take the stage.' Later she shrewdly pinpointed his limitations: 'He was potentially a fine actor, but he hadn't the technique of acting, so he had to do everything *really*. He poured with sweat with the effort of it all.' Peggy Ashcroft fell in love with him and, though married to Rupert Hart-Davis, began an affair with him.

On the eve of the opening in May, Sybil wrote to Elizabeth Robins: 'This week is all mixed up, all days and much of the nights spent in the theatre. How I love Shakespeare – last night those words of Othello before he kills himself seemed like all humanity – "perplexed in the extreme" – it is a great tragedy, isn't it.' On the first night Robeson received twenty curtain calls. The critics admired much of his performance, notably his majestic bearing, dignity and sincerity, and his fierce passion in the final act. But there were criticisms of his movement, which seemed to suggest the Negro rather than the Moor, and of his verse speaking, which was thought to lack subtlety. He was not helped by Browne, who proved a hopeless Iago and was given a critical drubbing. However, Peggy Ashcroft's Desdemona, her first professional Shakespearean role, was admired for its intelligence and beauty.

Sybil received uniformly glowing notices for her tough, decisive Emilia. Farjeon thought it the best performance of all, the only one with any real zest in it. George Rylands' review in the *Nation and Athenaeum* was typical of many: 'She played Emilia as comfortable and coarse, almost as the Wife of Bath, in rich tones redolent of plum cake and porter.' But the production was seriously flawed: the text was savagely and clumsily cut, the lighting was too weak (later, with the director gone, Ralph Richardson pointedly carried a torch up his sleeve to light up the stage and his face), and there seemed more concern with spectacle than character. A terrific noise accompanied Peggy Ashcroft's singing of the Willow Song – until Sybil told the scene-shifters: 'Don't start your work until I begin my speech – I can out-shout you!'

In the climate of the day racism occasionally reared its ugly head. Hannen Swaffer reported that 'coloured people were dotted around the house', and that one newspaper editor walked out after the third act, 'saying he did not like being near coloured people'. Peggy Ashcroft was frequently asked about the propriety of a white woman kissing a 'coloured' man: 'The colour question never occurred to me,' she responded. 'Mr Robeson is such a fine actor that I had no thought of any other question.' Both she and Robeson received 'lewd and anonymous postcards', while she and Sybil were sent letters saying essentially: 'East is east and west is west, and no more theatres where you play after this.' Sybil's reply was to pop back between shows with another actress to help give Robeson's little boy his bath.

Despite her crowded schedule, she still found time to see her fellow-actors at work, and to write extravagantly about their performances. After seeing her friend Gwen Ffrangcon-Davies in *A Doll's House*, she wrote: 'Gwen, honestly, no words I can find express what joy your performance gave me. I think you must be the perfect Nora of one's imaginings – one felt the whole thing as inevitable and moving with such truth and certainty. The beauty of your work moved me just absurdly – it was of such fine quality.' She was even more enraptured by John Gielgud's Old Vic Hamlet, which he was now playing in the West End: 'I never hoped to see Hamlet played as in my dreams. I go to it again and again for I love him beyond all people – he's more part of one than anyone who's ever been written. And one gets lots of loveliness to go on with – new leads, new bits of thought in shows one sees – but tonight it was Hamlet complete. When you spoke your first words I said to myself what I said when I read the first chapter of Moby Dick – "This is too good to be true." I've had an evening of being swept off my feet into another life – far more real than the life I live in, and moved, moved beyond words. Thank you, John, for an unforgettable evening.'

Gielgud soon afterwards declared his desire to make Shakespeare more popular in the West End by breaking with tradition and creating more modern interpretations. Along with Barry Jackson, Gwen Ffrangcon-Davies and Nancy Price, Sybil joined the debate in the *Era*, backing the idea of experimentation with Shakespeare, 'about which it is considered rather bad taste to think originally or for oneself'. She stressed the need for full-blooded actors to play his characters, arguing that there was a shortage of them in the theatre: 'We seem to get the anaemic ones,' she complained. She backed the idea of casting music-hall artists in the comedies, but attacked the critics, 'who damn all originality' and 'have such very definite opinions about Shakespeare's creations'. Once more she was lining herself up with the theatrical innovators.

She was much saddened at this time by the death of Florence Bell. It made her reflect again on the possibility of an afterlife, as she explained to Elizabeth Robins: 'I can't believe it at all, Lisa, that she's not here any more, can you? She gave me so much – her friendship was a very precious thing….and then so much that she loved in art and life that you and I have in common too – I hope there is another life after this. I was in church this morning and it seemed to me as if my father and brother and all friends I'd loved and now Lady Bell who were passed over must be living somehow, somewhere. So vivid living cannot just be wiped out. Well, no one knows.'

In July, in her role of his surrogate mother, she attended with Lewis the wedding of Laurence Olivier and the actress Jill Esmond. They also took part in the first annual summer event at Smallhythe Place in Kent. After Ellen Terry's death in 1928, Edy Craig had turned her house into a museum and the barn in the garden into a 100-seat theatre. The first programme there consisted mainly of excerpts from Shakespeare's plays, including *Hamlet* with Gielgud, and *Henry VIII* with Sybil, Lewis, Mary, Ann and John. The following year, alongside Edith Evans, Harold Nicolson, Vita Sackville-West and others, Sybil became a vice-president of the Barn Theatre Society. The annual event became an occasion supported by many actors, and she and Lewis would often take part in subsequent years.

Othello ran for a disappointing seven weeks in the West End, then played briefly in the London suburbs. Its week in Streatham prevented Sybil from opening a fete in the castle gardens in Rochester where, the local paper noted, 'she is rapidly assuming the importance in her childhood city of the Charles Dickens whose ghost so saturated her home in the precincts'. Lewis, Mary and Ann stood in for her, and offered a couple of scenes from Shakespeare. Sybil sent her apologies via a letter to the mayor, which ended in girlish fashion: 'I shall be thinking of you during the performance of *Othello* this afternoon, and you can all think of me weeping bitterly with disappointment. I expect when I am killed at the end of the play, instead of Shakespeare's words I shall say unconsciously: "I have much pleasure in declaring this fete open," and the audience will be very mystified.' She was to make up for her absence by taking part the following year in the city's historical pageant, representing the Spirit of Rochester.

'I sometimes think I have worked too hard,' she told *Theatre World*. 'But one gets caught up in this kind of thing, and it is difficult to alter life-long habits.' True to her word, in August she and Lewis set out for a lengthy provincial tour, starting in Southampton. 'We actors and actresses are paid too much,' she announced. 'We should all be rogues and vagabonds again.' The company included Francis James, Iris Darbyshire and Winifred Hare, and their repertoire consisted of four plays, all directed by Lewis: Jean Bart's *The Squall*, Clemence Dane's *Granite*, *The Matchmaker's Arms* by Ashley Dukes, and *Ghosts*, with Lewis as Pastor Mandes. This was the first UK tour during which they staged two plays in one week. Uncertain how Ibsen would go down, but determined to make his work available, they planned to stage the occasional matinee of *Ghosts*, and if it proved popular, play it in the evening.

The Squall was a run-of-the-mill melodrama set in Spain, in which the life of the Mendez family is disturbed by the arrival of a seductive gypsy girl. Sybil, in a huge black wig topped by an enormous comb and mantilla, played the mother who proves a tower of strength as everyone else falls apart, and eventually enables sanity to prevail. 'It is a bold choice,' the *Manchester Guardian* noted, 'because it means that she must discard all those flourishes in the grand manner by which she has made her great name.' The play pleased a Leeds audience, as the *Yorkshire Post* critic remarked: 'The enthusiastic reception she received at the close showed that here in Leeds, at any rate, a good deal is still thought of the sanctity of Family Life.'

The Matchmaker's Arms, originally titled *The Matchmaker* and set in the London of Hogarth's day, gave her a more humorous part. 'Miss Thorndike was triumphant in the splendours and subtleties of the finely drawn Miss Fortune,' according to the *Manchester Guardian*. 'She made the character vitally alive amidst the artificialities of her surroundings.' Ashley Dukes had adapted several European plays, was a consistent champion of new dramatists, and was soon to found the Mercury in Notting Hill Gate with his wife, the ballerina Marie Rambert. After seeing the play in Glasgow, he wrote to Sybil, criticising the current theatre for being purely intellectual or merely trivial, but adding: 'But when you take hold of a piece of work like this, and infuse it with so much tenderness, and give it so much life and wonder, I see that the theatre is really worthwhile.'

As they moved around the country, she made use of every opportunity to talk about the theatre. 'Build up your amateur theatres,' she told a gathering in Blackpool. 'All popular art must come out of the people themselves. You in the north have something to say to the rest of the country. You have something to give to the world. The drama and the love of the drama may go a long way towards making a world peace. It is a fine organ for that.' In Oxford she put the case for an arts theatre for the city, hoping that J B Fagan would make it happen. She also made another plea for a National Theatre, where 'it would be possible to have an extraordinarily varied programme. Drama of every age and from every country could be staged. There would be no haunting fear of poverty.' But she felt it was a long way off: 'We don't care enough. We have too many amusements.'

This was the first English tour on which she and Lewis had brought Ann and Mary. 'I think the stage offers as good opportunities for a clever girl as any other profession, and possibly better than most,' Sybil told one journalist. If she thought a girl had talent, she could be extravagant in their praise, as Mary told her friend Margaretta Scott, then 19: 'Mummy proclaimed your praises from the top to the bottom of the house,' she wrote. 'She completely went off the deep end about you being the only one of the younger genera-tion who had any "go" at all, and having explained to me in great detail why, when and how you were the greatest actress ever born, she started again at lunch....I got quite tired of you by the end of the day!!'

Mary, now sixteen, with long fair hair and blue eyes, had parts in *Granite* and *The Squall*, and received good notices for her role in the latter. 'Her tripping steps, her sweet low voice and her wondering eyes give a curiously complete impression of innocent girlhood', a Blackpool critic wrote. By now she was well established on the London stage, having recently appeared in *Charles and Mary*, a play about the Lambs. Barrie was her favourite playwright: she had been Wendy in *Peter Pan* three years running, had acted opposite Gerald du Maurier in *Dear Brutus*, and was keen to play all his heroines, especially the title-role in *Mary Rose*.

Ann, aged fourteen, was understudying her, and learning about stage management. As an actress she had recently appeared in Galsworthy's *The Roof* in the West End, in which Basil Dean, now working also in films, thought her 'an enchanting child performer', and cast her in a small part in his star-studded 'talkie' *Escape*, in which Lewis also took part. But her real passion was writing: 'She is always writing plays for the other children to perform,' Sybil explained. 'I am afraid they are very modern, and quite out-Noël Coward.' Bubbly and mischievous, with crisp bobbed brown hair and blue eyes, Ann had brought her portable typewriter on tour, to help with Sybil's considerable postbag, but also to write short stories. 'Mary ought to have lived forty years ago, while Ann is always ahead; she is in 1932 now,' Sybil stated.

Labelled by one journalist the 'Melba of the Drama', her kindness towards budding actors suggested the opposite of a prima donna. In Bournemouth, after seeing *The Squall*, a young man wrote asking how the rain and thunder effects were done. 'It is important for me to know as I want to be an actor,' explained Alec Guinness, aged sixteen and a half. In reply came a scrawled note from Sybil, inviting him to come to a matinee of *Ghosts*, then to ask for her at the stage door. 'Do you like poetry? I do hope so,' she concluded. In her presence Guinness was tongue-tied. 'She was wearing a blue and white flowered dressing-gown, was sweetly welcoming, and there wasn't the least condescension in her manner or conversation,' he remembered. 'To her statements, though, about the greatness of Ibsen – how he cleared the air, got rid of all the bed-fluff, gave women their proper due, and so on – I could only nod in a way I hoped looked intelligent. "You did like this better than *The Squall*?" she asked, rather suspiciously. I nodded again vigorously, but it was a lying nod.'

After she and Lewis had shown this odd young man with sticking-out ears how the thunder-sheet and rain-making device worked, they adjourned to Sybil's dressing-room, where Sybil continued: 'Do you know *The Cenci*? You must read lots and lots of poetry. I learn a sonnet every day.... And now we must have our tea. Ooh, boiled eggs! Thank you for coming to see us. Come again one day.' Guinness stood outside in a daze, 'wanting only to stop any passer-by with: "I've met Sybil Thorndike!"' He was evidently not the only one to fail to warm to *Ghosts*. 'If you want Shakespeare, Ibsen and what I call the fine art of the theatre,' Sybil advised at the end of the tour, 'you are in for a pretty rough time, because there is not a demand for it at all.'

During the tour she was delighted to discover that one of the young actresses was a Quaker. 'They are absolutely against war, and they're such wonderful people,' she wrote to John. Her pacifist beliefs had remained steadfast, but they had now affected Christopher. After his first term at Dartmouth he had become increasingly miserable, sometimes sending his parents three or four postcards a day, written 'like a lunatic', according to Sybil. She had wanted him to leave, but he was determined to stick it out, and though he was never happy, he completed his training and went to sea at 16. Both he and John had joined the Atlantic Fleet as midshipmen, he on HMS *Tiger* and John on HMS *Emperor of India*.

Then, in November 1930, he abruptly left the navy. His captain wrote to Sybil and Lewis, telling them their son had belatedly become aware that being in the service might involve him in killing people, and that he had no intention of doing that. He felt that remaining in the navy could ruin his life, and advised them to buy him out. This they did, at the cost of several hundred pounds. John Casson wondered if this would have happened without Sybil's own pacifist beliefs. 'It seemed so right to her that one of her sons should take a stand on this issue, especially as it meant that without question he would become an actor,' he wrote. 'I've often felt that there should have been at least one or two very pointed questions asked.'

Christopher started at once as a student at Central School, under Elsie Fogerty. But it was a while, as Eileen's daughter Phyllis Walshaw recalls, before he settled on a career in the theatre: 'He used to say, I've decided to give up everything for ballet. Then after six months he'd bring back all his ballet things and say, I'm going to be a painter. Six months later it was a writer.' He could be equally impulsive in his personal life, getting engaged several times. Once he proposed to Athene Seyler's daughter Jane-Ann, then dropped a note through her letter-box saying: 'I can't! I can't! I can't!'

Sybil had for some time been interested in the growing campaign for independence for India, as had Gilbert Murray. In March 1931, on the day Gandhi shook hands publicly with the Vicerory of India Lord Irwin, she attended a dinner given in Murray's honour by Indian students in London. 'He gave us a most wonderful sermon – amazing in an after-dinner speech – on the unity of nations and the need of ceaseless effort in understanding each other,' she recalled.

With 2.7 million people unemployed, this was not a good time for the theatre. Herbert Farjeon observed how remarkable it was that leading actresses of such talent and fame as Sybil, Edith Evans and Athene Seyler were not permanent fixtures on the London stage. They had to face an inbuilt disadvantage, with star parts favouring men over women in a ratio of 20:1. In this difficult time Sybil's response was to turn again to *Saint Joan*, which had so far earned her and Lewis £30,000. In April they brought Shaw's play to His Majesty's for five weeks, and a further three at the Haymarket. Only one other actress, Ludmilla Pitoëff, had played the role in London since Sybil. When Shaw was asked to compare the two, he said that while he had wanted to give Pitoëef a double whisky and soda, Sybil needed a soporific.

Despite having broadcast a radio version two years previously, and played Joan some six hundred times, Sybil had lost none of her enthusiasm for the part. On the 500th anniversary of Joan being burned at the stake, she proclaimed: 'If she were alive in England today, I feel sure I should follow her without question, and – if I were brave enough, which I doubt – to the death.' She also told a journalist: 'Joan stood for all the things I care for, and was all that I could never be....For me, *Saint Joan* is in the same magnificent plane of mind as Shakespeare.' Asked if she was changing her reading of the part – her country accent, suggested by Shaw, had come in for criticism – she replied: 'Perhaps the accent will not be quite so pronounced this time, and I think the whole reading will be simpler. The first venture must of necessity be somewhat elaborate, but technically a character can be simplified as one goes on.'

The company, directed by Lewis, was substantially different from the earlier ones, although Ernest Thesiger and O B Clarence returned as the Inquisitor and the Dauphin. Dunois was played by the young Robert Donat. Flora Robson, who was desperate for work after four years away from the stage, begged to understudy Joan, but Sybil and Lewis demurred; instead they persuaded an agent to see her in *Desire Under the Elms*. The role of understudy, and that of the Duchesse de la Trémouille, fell to Eileen Thorndike, who had returned to the stage now her husband had retired from the navy. But Sybil's mother had given up playing the organ backstage.

Years later in America, when Uta Hagen was worried she was too old for the part, Sybil told her: 'You can never be too old to play Saint Joan. Only too young.' But at 48 her age seemed likely to be an issue. Sybil argued somewhat disingenuously that 'what matters with Joan is her passion, not how she looks'. In fact she had had misgivings, and had asked Shaw if she shouldn't leave Joan to a younger generation. Shaw would have none of it; indeed, nearly ten years later he would write to her: 'You could carry off Joan still. No one else can.'

Once again she held the first-night audience spellbound. The critics commended her austere simplicity and natural command: *The Times* noted 'her vigour, her assurance, and the alertness of her intelligence', while Audrey Williamson felt that her 'drive and generalship were as vividly suggested as her child-like simplicity and raptness of vision'. The director Frith Banbury, then an actor, remembers being 'absolutely thrilled by her performance, in which she was simple and very moving', and returning to see it again two days later. But one young admirer was less sure: 'She was a little too old for the part,' Alec Guinness recalled, 'and her delivery had become rather richly vibrato.'

Apart from a charity matinee at the start of the war, this was to be the last time London would see her Joan. 'I feel so happy doing the play again,' she told Elizabeth Robins. 'My dear Saint – yes, she is being re-born.' Her friendship with the older actress continued to be important. 'I feel I must never let too long pass without seeing you, 'she wrote. 'You don't know how much you give out to people – and this is a real bond between us, Lisa, isn't it?' She also reiterated her intense fondness for their mutual friend Florence Bell. 'Isn't it wonderful to see a lovely person really cared for and appreci-ated – and this tribute to Lady Bell does gladden those who love her – and you who have been so close must be more than overjoyed.' A new friend was Jennie Lee, who had recently become the youngest member of the House of Commons, but was losing her voice from too much public speaking. The Labour politician Charles Trevelyan, who had married into the Bell family, brought her to Sybil's dressing-room, to ask if she could help. Sybil suggested some exercises, which enabled her to get back her voice.

Once again there was a provincial tour of *Saint Joan*, with Ben Webster coming in as Warwick and Walter Hudd taking over the Dauphin. Bernard Miles was also in the company, playing Brother Martin. He was one of many young actors who absorbed Sybil and Lewis' attitude to working in the theatre, as he later told them. 'You set my sights and aims once and for all at the very highest. You taught me, without ever saying it in so many words, that the theatre is a great and noble profession, worthy of the most strenuous effort and exercise of the imagination.' He also told a story, possibly apocryphal, of Lewis failing to return for supper in their digs after one performance. Sybil, noticing that he had been paying a lot of attention to a pretty young actress in the company, stood outside her digs and called out: 'Lewis, come out at once! No good will come of this!' Lewis duly descended.

On their travels she spoke with her usual fervour about the state of the theatre, the vital importance of the growing amateur movement (with Edy Craig she opened the Eyebrow Club Theatre in Leeds), and the cowardly approach of the commercial managers who were content to stage safe or inferior plays. There was no expression, she said, of the poetic side of the people. The theatre should not be a soporific, but a stimulant; it was a place for alert people, eager to be entertained by thinking. In Cardiff she deplored the fact that the Welsh were neglecting their heritage in relation to theatre. 'Express yourself in dramatic art,' she declared. 'Find your own writers, people who will show the world the beauties of Wales and Cardiff, their culture, their difficulties and their incomparable love.'

After *Saint Joan* finished, she appeared at the Embassy in *Marriage by*

Purchase by the French writer Steve Passeur, with a cast that included Lewis, Margaret Webster and Donald Wolfit, with Lewis again directing. For once she was unable to find a deep meaning in a play. Clearly miscast as the sex-starved wealthy wife, she failed to catch the character's boiling, frustrated passion. Darlington observed that, while her performance was full of force and intelligence, 'it is impossible to believe in this actress as a woman driven to abnormal deeds by uncontrollable sex impulses'. The play mixed farce and tragedy in a way that confused the English audience, and led Sybil into mischief. Wolfit remembered how, prompted by an unexpected laugh, she realised she was not putting over the tragic dimensions of her role. 'She swung down stage in a great sweep, looked me full in the face and gave the most wicked wink, and from that moment we played the rest as farce.'

It was a busy summer, for in addition to playing at the Embassy at night, in the day she was back on a film set. *A Gentleman of Paris* was one of two films produced by Michael Balcon in which she now took part. Based on the novel *His Honour the Judge* by Naranjan Pal, it was a typical melodrama of the time, telling the story of a philandering judge deeply involved in a murder case which he has to try. Sybil played the minor role of Madame Lola Duval. She returned to more familiar territory with *Hindle Wakes*, a film of the controversial play. Also starring John Stuart, Belle Chrystall and Edmund Gwenn, it was a big production with crowd scenes and location work at seaside resorts and factories. Directed by Victor Saville, who was to make some of the finest and most entertaining British films during the 1930s, it was a box-office success. Sybil was now playing the stern mother of Fanny, the mill-girl heroine. Her son John, who visited the set, recalled watching Saville 'admirably damping down Sybil's stage acting'. The result was a strong, very believable performance, in which she catches the essence of the tough, ambitious and domineering Mrs Hawthorn, and manages a convincing Lancashire accent; the *Manchester Guardian* called it 'a splendid display of vindictiveness'.

The previous summer, when the Order of Merit was given to three men, Sybil had been one of several prominent women who protested at the discrimination against their sex. 'It seems amazing that women of eminence in the arts and sciences should have been overlooked,' she argued. Now, in the King's Birthday Honours in June, she was made a Dame Commander of the Order of the British Empire, with the citation for 'our trusty and well-beloved Sybil Thorndike'. She was the fourth and youngest English actress to be given the title, following May Whitty (who was granted it mainly for her war work), Ellen Terry and Madge Kendal, and the first to receive it while she was still appearing on the stage.

Mary remembers her reaction to the news: 'She opened the letter at breakfast time, gasped it out, and ran straight up to tell her mother, who had become ill and was living with us. She was very thrilled.' It was a popular accolade, and she received countless congratulatory letters and telegrams. At the Embassy the night the news broke, Wolfit led her to the footlights to receive the audience's applause. She was nervous about the investiture, wishing she could wear her doctorate robes 'to give me a little courage'. Instead she arrived with Lewis at Buckingham Palace in a large dark hat, a pearl necklace, and an elegant brown and white voile dress – the first time she had bought anything from a fashionable dressmaker's house.

Afterwards Hannen Swaffer wrote that 'whatever dignity Sybil Thorndike might attain, she would always be "Sybil" to all the crowd, and everyone who knows her'. Such indeed would prove to be the case.

21

Australia and Beyond

1932–1933

'She has the enthusiasms and vigour of a girl of eighteen'
Australian journalist on Sybil

It was perhaps no coincidence, given her socialist views, that the honour was bestowed on Sybil by a Labour government, headed by Ramsay MacDonald, whom she knew. Two months later the Labour Party was torn apart when a financial crisis which took Britain off the gold standard led to MacDonald agreeing to head a National Government, and being branded a traitor to his party. Many socialists joined other left-wing parties, including the Communist Party, but Sybil and Lewis remained loyal. Like everyone else, as the decade wore on they became increasingly alarmed about the rise of fascism in Europe.

During the next six years, apart from when they toured, Sybil was only directed by Lewis for the occasional matinee. In the autumn he directed Gladys Cooper in Maugham's *The Painted Veil*, at the Playhouse. John Casson was convinced they had an affair, a belief reinforced by a gold cigarette case inscribed 'To Lewis Casson, in appreciation, Gladys Cooper', which Lewis would take out and look at when he felt depressed. If an affair did take place Sybil never spoke of it, though after Lewis' death she talked of their differing views on fidelity: 'I was jealous of his occasional involvements with other women....Of course I sometimes got slightly involved myself, but Lewis wasn't possessive. He rather approved of these incidents, he thought they would make me understand human beings better. He was always freer-minded than I was...Infidelity depresses me terribly. But it wasn't really that with us. I suppose it was a sort of overflow of vitality.'

Yet vitality was not the quality in Lewis that most struck younger members of the family. 'He always gave the impression of being very solemn,' Eileen's daughter Sybil Ewbank (known as Donnie) says. 'He was rather frightening, and shy: you had to break that down, which was quite difficult. But actually he was a sweetie, with a tremendous sense of humour.' Daniel Thorndike also found him initially frightening: 'He was very gruff, he didn't go in for small talk. But he was really a delightful man, and fascinating to talk to.' It was in his work that the strong feelings which he generally reined in with the family found an outlet, as many an actor discovered over the years.

Ironically, the months that followed Sybil's visit to the Palace were relatively quiet theatrically. Then in January 1932 an elderly woman climbed out of the orchestra pit of the Old Vic, and announced: 'By your leave, gentlemen, I am a stranger here; I was ne'er at one of these plays before.' The audience roared with delight at this blatant untruth: as the Citizen's Wife in Beaumont and Fletcher's exuberant romp *The Knight of the Burning Pestle*, Sybil had returned to her second home. It was Harcourt Williams, the theatre's director, who had invited her back to star alongside Ralph Richardson and George Zucco. 'Work was fun, and she was ready for any amount,' he recalled. 'The dust of the Old Vic was in her bones. She took us all to her heart, and we knew at once that we had found a long-lost sister.'

Richardson, now leading the company, had like many younger actors followed Sybil's career with admiration: he had seen her Grand Guignol performances, been overwhelmed by her Saint Joan, and was initially in awe of her. 'Five minutes before the curtain went up I wondered if I dared pay court and wish her well,' he remembered. 'I went to the door of her dressing-room, but I was afraid to knock in case she was communing with herself before that big part. Then I heard a buzz of talk inside, and tapped. "Come in, Ralph dear," Sybil said. "Won't you have a bun? There isn't really time for introductions." She was feeding half a dozen schoolgirls with buns a few moments before the start.'

The critics much enjoyed her jovial performance in this spirited slapstick, in which she sat on the stage, eating, sleeping and criticising the actors in the play within the play. 'Miss Thorndike brings all that warm-heartedness which she has at her command equally with Greek austerity,' Agate wrote. But sometimes she went over the top, eating an orange and throwing the pips into the front row, until this was stopped as being too vulgar. She was clearly enjoying herself to the full, as Harcourt Williams remembered: 'She made the Citizen's Wife something so of herself that one never could be quite certain whether it was text or Thorndike, and by the end of the run there was a deal of Thorndike. I am sure Messrs Beaumont and Fletcher would have been proud to accept it as their own!' Later Richardson observed: 'She can make an actor act. She could act with a tailor's dummy and bring it to life.'

The boisterous role offered her what she believed was too scarce in the English theatre. 'Give us not pale ghosts or shadows, give us creatures with greater life than we know,' she wrote in *Theatre Arts Monthly*, in a piece putting the case for more tragedy. 'Give us a larger-sized life than we actually experience, give us violence, shocks; beings that surge with vigour and electricity, that touching them in spirit we may be charged with that same energy, and our grasp and scope be larger.' She scorned with unusual fury those who said there was enough tragedy in real life. 'Every time this is said to me, with sickening, irritating regularity, it is only by the grace of God and amazing self-control that I am prevented from hurling myself on the speaker.' As she said later to a critic: 'I like to go bang-splash like the Greeks!'

In February she headed an all-female cast in *The Dark Saint* by François de Curel, first staged by Antoine at his Théâtre Libre in Paris, and now directed at the Fortune by Ellen van Volkenburg. De Curel specialised in stories of souls in torment, and in this morbid psychological tale Sybil played Julie Renaudin, who becomes a nun after her lover deserts her, then returns to the world to take revenge on his family. 'It's a tremendous and awful play!' she informed Elizabeth Robins, describing her role as 'an enormous part which teaches, if anything, the terrible lesson of inhibition'. Ivor Brown stated that, 'in the mood of eloquent quietism, which is the most powerful of all her moods, she drove firmly into the torture-chamber of Julie's passion'.

Also in the cast playing a small part was Sybil's sister Eileen. Over the Christmas holiday her husband Maurice Ewbank had died suddenly at the age of 42, leaving her and her four children almost penniless. As a widow she found it hard to cope, but the sisters had always been close, and Sybil offered her solid support. Eileen's children were already stage-struck, and at home, inspired by regularly seeing their cousin Mary playing Wendy, they would enact scenes from *Peter Pan* over and over again. 'I used to ask Mary how the flying was done,' Donnie remembers, 'but she would only say: "Didn't you see Peter giving out the fairy dust?" Sybil rather discouraged us from taking up a stage career, she said the theatre was not a good place any more. But we all three girls went in for it anyway.'

The lease on Carlyle Square now ran out, but they were unable to afford to buy the house. It was in any case becoming too small for a family with four grown-up children, and a mother who often visited and stayed overnight. Fortunately Agnes Thorndike had earlier taken on the lease of a house at 74 Oakley Street nearby, so the family simply crossed the King's Road and moved in with her. This enabled Sybil to keep a closer eye on her mother, who liked to keep the brandy handy 'for medicinal purposes', and had sometimes provoked complaints from the neighbours when she and the housekeeper sang hymns into the early hours. Daniel Thorndike often stayed with her: 'She became slightly senile after her husband died, but she played the piano well, and she would suddenly break out into patter songs,' he recalls.

The red-brick early Victorian house had five floors including a basement, and plenty of spare rooms for relations and the numerous guests that came to stay. 'Our home is such a tiresome place,' Sybil remarked soon after the move. 'Everyone is always arguing, the house is always full of people, and meals happen at all hours. So much so that when we moved into a bigger house not long ago, I insisted that the basement be made into what I call a restaurant.' The director Charles Hickman, then an actor, remembered suppers round the big dining-room table, 'Lewis with his jumbo cup of cocoa and biscuits, Sybil with her glass of Guinness and a plate of cream cakes'. Phyllis Walshaw recalled a Fuller's chocolate cake at one end of the table, and a walnut cake at the other, and all sorts of people like Larry Olivier came and went.'

Russell too was a frequent visitor, having returned from two years touring in America as leading man with Ben Greet's company. Though much in demand, he seemed to lack the drive and ambition that had got Sybil to the top. Yet his distinctive personality and croaking voice made him one of the most versatile of classical actors, suited to both comic and sinister parts. That year at the Kingsway he played an astonishing variety of Shakespearean roles, including Shylock, Macbeth, Jaques, Mercutio, Petruchio, Hamlet and Sir Toby Belch. The *Twelfth Night* production was a family affair, in which, according to the *Observer*, Russell 'irresistibly blended belch with blarney', Eileen provided a 'staunch, dependable Viola', while Mary 'prettily pretended to Olivia's estate'. Mary also played Juliet, Ophelia, Nerissa and Bianca in the season, and the following year, in Anew McMaster's company at Chiswick, was cast as Desdemona. Once again she was exposed to Lewis' rigorous method: 'He took me through one speech word for word, so I would get it just right,' she recalls.

Sybil and Lewis now prepared for another tour abroad, Shaw once again being the catalyst. Wanting *Saint Joan* to be seen in Australia, he told them to decide if they wanted to take it there, or he would let another company do so. Sybil confirmed her desire to play her favourite role in Australia and New Zealand. Unable to finance themselves, they found backers in the shape of three Russian musician friends, known as the Cherniavsky Bureau. In addition to *Saint Joan* they planned to take ten other plays. *Macbeth*, *Advertising April*, *The Silver Chord*, *Granite*, *Ghosts* and *Madame Plays Nap* were already in their repertoire. They added Shaw's *Captain Brassbound's Conversion*, originally written for Ellen Terry, a stage version of Somerset Maugham's *The Painted Veil*, and *Milestones*, a comedy by Arnold Bennett and Edward Knoblock about family tensions across the generations.

It was a hugely ambitious project, with the burden falling on Lewis as director, leading actor and administrator. During rehearsals he became unusually anxious and morose. One evening John came home to find Sybil in tears, worried that Lewis might be cracking up. Persuaded to see a doctor, he was told he was on the edge of a bad breakdown. The proposed cure was a fortnight's rest in Dorset with Ann – although this didn't stop him learning his lines as they strode around the countryside. On his return, John remembered: 'He plunged back into rehearsals like one possessed, and gave everyone hell for not having done more work while he had been away.'

The twenty-strong company included Norman Shelley (who outdid Sybil and Lewis in Shakespearean parts, with 127 to his name), Zillah Carter, Michael Martin-Harvey, Bruce Winston (who also designed the costumes and sets), Colette O'Niel, Albert Chevalier (nephew of the music-hall artist) and Atholl Fleming. Ann too was part of the company. She was now beginning to make her name in films. She was hired by Anthony Asquith for the lead in *Dance Pretty Lady*, based on Compton Mackenzie's novel *Carnival*. She had also had roles in the minor comedy *Bachelor's Baby*, and in Hitchcock's *Number Seventeen*, with John Stuart and Leon M Lion. Seen as a rising young film star, she appeared on the cover of *Picturegoer* magazine, and was now under contract to British International Pictures.

Christopher, after his time at the Central School, had been with Russell in a Ben Greet company in America, but been released from it for his parents' tour, to double as actor and assistant stage manager. Sybil and Lewis assumed that Mary would also join them, but discovered she had other plans. 'The tour had been mooted a long time before,' Mary recalls. 'All the time I had been thinking I didn't really want to go, I didn't want to get stuck in a family groove. It worried me for about a year, because I thought they might protest. But when I plucked up courage to tell them, they were slightly surprised, but didn't argue about it.' Keen to mark out her independence, she went instead with her aunt Eileen on a Ben Greet Shakespeare tour.

Her decision chimed in with Sybil's views on parenthood, which were liberal for the day. 'I am all for children having their own way, and following their own desires, provided they have marked preferences, and real reasons for wanting their own way,' she wrote at this time. 'It is a fatal mistake for parents to decide careers for their children early in life, and then to work steadily and increasingly for an end which may wreck the child's life and be a bitter disappointment to both.' Yet loving and tolerant mother though she clearly was, in her enthusiasm she was sometimes blind to what her children really wanted, or their need to get out from under her shadow.

The original plan for the tour included Canada and the Argentine, but, perhaps because of the pressure on Lewis, this idea was abandoned. Instead, supported by the British Council, they decided to make a preliminary tour of Egypt and Palestine on the way to Australia. They sailed from Tilbury on the ss *Comorin* on 26 March 1932. After a week in Port Said, they played for a fortnight in the beautiful, all-wood Cairo Opera House, then moved on to Alexandria. As on every trip abroad, Sybil loved to sight-see: she and Lewis visited the Pyramids on camels by moonlight. They also had an unofficial ambassadorial role to play. They met King Fuad, who came to a performance, and the Egyptian explorer Hassanein Pasha; and Sybil had lengthy discussions about the Sermon on the Mount with the High Commissioner Sir Percy Loraine. By contrast, they played *Saint Joan* to an audience of RAF airmen in a huge hangar in the desert at Ismailia, before crossing into Palestine.

While staying in Jerusalem they staged *Saint Joan* in a cinema outside the city. Offstage they visited the Wailing Wall and other famous sites, and went to Bethlehem and Nazareth. As usual Sybil cut through protocol: warned not to talk about religion when meeting the Grand Mufti in Jerusalem, she thought this a ridiculous idea, and promptly did so. But her view of community relations in the city was somewhat inconsistent: 'The Jews and the Arabs all seemed charming and friendly,' she recalled, before adding, 'although there were constant fights as to which had the most right to the holy places, and we saw a number of riots.'

Ann now returned to London and her busy acting life, while Sybil and company sailed in the *Oronsay* down the Suez Canal, Sybil marvelling at 'seeing Mount Ararat and the Old Testament unrolled before us'. At Aden, during a stop-over for sight-seeing, the company had a scare when the car carrying Sybil, Lewis and Christopher overturned and threw them into the road. Shaken but uninjured, they sailed on, arriving in Fremantle in May, as autumn was setting in. In Perth the company played the complete repertoire for several weeks at His Majesty's, opening with *Saint Joan*, with Lewis, in defiance of Shaw's opinion, now playing Cauchon. 'No other role has given me so much for myself inside,' Sybil confessed. 'It grows and grows on one; I see something new in it every time I play in it.'

They then sailed along the south coast, meeting terrific storms as they crossed the Great Australian Bight to reach Adelaide, which like Perth was not well served by visiting professional companies. Here they met a different kind of storm. At a meeting in Melbourne someone had suggested that when planning the tour Sybil had been advised to give Australia 'muck', and that she should have included a Greek play in her repertoire. She denied the charge emphatically, stressing they had no intention of playing 'muck' in Australia or anywhere else: 'People in England who know Australia have always advised us to give Australians the best,' she said, adding diplomatically: 'Melbourne has, we have always heard, one of the best play-going publics in the world.'

Arriving there in mid-June, she spoke of her preference for simple staging. 'The theatre is rich in artists at the moment, but it is not rich in money; but that is all to the good. Elaborate productions are going; the stage is returning to simplicity. There is more simplicity in design, and we are turning away quite a lot from realism towards symbolism.' She spoke to bodies such as the English Association and the Shakespeare Society about the value of theatre, especially in relation to films. The press soon warmed to her personality: 'Intensely vital, interested in everything and everybody, generous minded, and with a quick sense of humour,' one journalist wrote, 'she has the enthusiasms and vigour of a girl of eighteen, and the intellect and balanced judgement of a finely cultured woman of the world.'

She loved Melbourne's parks and gardens, she and Lewis walking round Albert Park Lake learning their lines. *Saint Joan* was a triumph, and brought her a tumultuous reception. 'She left an impression of abundant vitality, of life full and bubbling over,' wrote the *Argus* critic, 'of an artist who indeed sinks herself in her part and is for the time not even a great actress playing Joan, but Joan only.' But after a demanding fortnight in Melbourne offstage and on, her voice problem returned. She had treatment, did Elsie Fogerty's voice exercises regularly, and somehow got through the performances using a false voice. She and Lewis stayed with friends up in the hills behind Melbourne, where she managed to keep complete silence for four days.

They answered the calls for a classical work by staging two matinees of *Medea* at the King's, then four more because of the demand. '*Medea* lives again, a great tragic performance', wrote one critic approvingly, more accustomed to the 'faltering efforts at schools and universities of abominable dullness'. As a prologue to the performance, Sybil and Lewis enacted scenes or speeches from Shakespeare, Sybil somehow playing both parts in the scene in *Henry V* where Princess Katharine is taught English by her attendant Alice. She and Lewis also gave a recital at the university, with extracts from *Henry V*, *The Merchant of Venice* and *As You Like It*.

She had the usual round of social and speaking engagements. At the Trades Hall she expressed her surprise and admiration that Australia had been ahead of her own country in giving women the vote: 'You have been a beacon to us women in England,' she said, before explaining how Lewis had 'dragged me into Labour activities and I became a suffragette'. Elsewhere she talked about the need for people to surrender to their emotions in the theatre. 'We have become such perfect ladies and gentlemen that we consider it bad form to show the world that we feel deeply,' she said. 'There is nothing so enriching, so ennobling as to feel the surge of a great emotion – lifting you up, inspiring you, opening your eyes to a new ideal.'

In their final week in Melbourne she played Lady Cicely in *Captain Brassbound's Conversion*; according to the *Argus*, the part enabled her 'to display to the full her gifts of comedy and her unique charm of personality'. The company then moved on to Sydney. One member remembered her during a train journey 'dispensing chicken and Cliquot, and booming, "Isn't this exciting!", like a child organising a midnight feast in the dormitory.' In Sydney she returned to Mrs Alving and *Ghosts*, playing it on a set that reflected her credo about the virtues of simplicity. Lewis 'improved' Ibsen by making her son Oswald a sculptor rather than a painter, apparently to make him 'a stronger, more solid figure than he usually is, and consequently make the final tragedy greater'. The part was played by Christopher, now gaining valuable experience in more substantial roles: in Australia he played the Inquisitor in *Saint Joan* and the Messenger in *Medea*.

Sybil again became involved in controversy when she referred to the experiments being carried out in Soviet Russia as being of interest and worth watching; one paper referred to her as 'under the thrall of the master-minds of Russia'. She also gave offence by saying that she favoured married women as teachers. Apparently affronted by her remark, the Premier of New South Wales announced that *Saint Joan* was 'pretty poor stuff', and that Sybil's acting had sent him to sleep. This stirred up a storm in the press, causing the Premier to backtrack hastily: 'I was not speaking for publication,' he said. 'I regret if I have offended the lady.'

'We are loving Australia and the people and thoroughly enjoying playing to them,' she wrote to Murray, after visiting Frensham School in Mittagong, where he had been a pupil. 'We finished the Medea yesterday. I think we have never had such a quiet audience and it was a packed house – it was a joy playing to them. This is a glorious country, we are really in love with it.' Their last major stop was Brisbane. The actor John McCallum remembers her Saint Joan there: 'I was very young, but I still remember vividly the voice, the passion and the dedication.' The company then returned to Melbourne for a week, where they performed *Ghosts* and *The Silver Chord*, the first time Ibsen's play had been staged there professionally.

Sybil summed up her feelings about the tour. 'I fell in love with Australia,' she said: she loved its scenery, its wildness, its vastness, its sunshine, and the friendliness of the people. She felt fortunate to have had personal contact with so many people of different ages and interests. But as so often, what had interested her most had been the women's work. 'You have a band of excellent and able women in your public movements,' she said. 'I have been impressed by the real gift of public-speaking among many of your women in public life – particularly younger women.'

In mid-December the company sailed from Sydney to Wellington in New Zealand, which Sybil later described as 'heaven on earth'. During their tour of the North Island she and Lewis stayed on a sheep-farm in the earth-quake district, and bathed in the hot springs at Rotarua, the centre of the geyser country. Predictably, she found the Maori people delightful: 'They were gentle and laughing, with lovely manners, and their dances were beautiful,' she remembered. They crossed to the South Island which, with its towering mountains and spectacular lakes, she found even more stunning. They played in Oamura and Timaru, and in Invercargill at the southern tip Sybil, now 50, played Saint Joan in full for the last time.

'We sail next Wednesday and the number of things to be done is appalling me,' she explained to a group of students from Samuel Marsden Collegiate

School, near Wellington. 'I am very interested in schools and am only sorry I have no free time to come to yours.' She invited them to come round after a performance at the Grand Opera House, where they much enjoyed *Medea*. 'We were very thrilled,' one student wrote in the school magazine. 'Dame Sybil welcomed us so charmingly. "Don't you love the words," she said, "they are simply beautiful."' Her performance in Auckland impressed the writer Iris Wilkinson, who thought she 'revealed herself as an actress whose greatness will not soon be forgotten. In her smoke-red robes, their folds revealing an unexpected strength and beauty in her frame, she presented a figure of restless and hungry passion'.

But not all New Zealand audiences were appreciative of the company's work, as the same writer observed: 'The enormous difficulties of putting on Shakespeare – turning the clock of centuries back for an indifferent audience – became obvious in the complete failure of Sybil Thorndike and Lewis Casson to make *Macbeth* convincing. Sitting through that play – with many of the audience sniggering over the succession of violent deaths – they don't mind buckets of blood in the Edgar Wallace manner, but there has to be a six-shooter and a phoney detective in the picture somewhere – was a nightmare experience.'

In the spring, while the company left for England, Sybil and Lewis returned home in a leisurely manner, taking the southern route, having three weeks without sight of land, and coming through the Panama Canal. But in mid-Pacific Sybil received a telegram from Russell, telling her that their mother, now 74, was very ill, then another the next day to say she had died. 'That was a terrible upset for her,' Mary remembers. 'Her mother had had a stroke and was bedridden, but we hoped she would stagger on until Mummy got back.' One of Agnes Thorndike's last actions, on hearing that Sybil was on her way home, was to drink a large glass of port. She was buried, in Sybil's absence, in the churchyard at Aylesford next to her husband, from whose death she had never really recovered.

Sybil was shattered by the news. 'She and I had such fun together all my life,' she recalled. 'We had the same ludicrous sense of humour, and she made me laugh so much. She often irritated me beyond words, but she was such fun and so ambitious for us, and so lively.' John Casson noticed other similarities: 'They had the same devastating energy, the same enthusiasm, and the same way of cocking a snook at everything and everybody that remotely smacked of the pompous.' Phyllis Walshaw recalled her grandmother's vibrant spirit: 'She lit up the house with love and joy, it was a warmth which bound us all together. She handed this on to her children, and I think Sybil benefited hugely.'

For Sybil it was a sad ending to a tour that had increased her prestige internationally, fulfilled her continuing desire to see new places, and given her insights into a very different culture through an intensive round of social, artistic, religious and political encounters. It had also made her and Lewis a lot of money, 'at least enough for us to lose on more plays'.

22

Back in the USA

1933–1935

'I'm enthusiastic and devastated by this city and its fantastic proportions!'
Letter from New York from Sybil to Elizabeth Casson

The next few years were to be difficult ones for Sybil. Firmly established at the top of her profession, she failed to find or be offered any new plays of real significance or of an experimental nature. There were also no appearances in classical revivals, perhaps reflecting her disenchantment with the public's taste. To Lillah McCarthy she wrote: 'Life goes on just the same – struggling to do a little more than the public want us to give them, and having to buckle down and do quite a lot they definitely want!!' Only near the end of the decade did she re-establish her position, returning to Shakespeare with Olivier at the Old Vic, and finding a new play that allowed her again to show her talent to the full. But these comparatively lean years in London did provide some compensation, in the form of two trips to America and Broadway.

In April 1933, a few days after her mother's death, Lewis' Aunt Lucy died, leaving him the bulk of her £43,000 estate, and Bron-y-Garth. 'I do so love it there and feel it's a most wonderful shelter,' Sybil wrote to Lewis' sister Elizabeth. 'Aren't the mountains glorious, and that so perfect view from the terrace?' Lewis immediately engaged an architect to make substantial alterations to the large house, so giving his young nephew Hugh Casson his first job. The house had several large rooms, and was soon in use by Sybil's extended family for summer holidays. Donnie recalls 'lots of places to rampage around, a marvellous garden with a great lawn where we played croquet, a big terrace, and a huge vegetable garden'. During the summer Sybil and Lewis drove there in their new Wolsey Hornet, walking and climbing, tackling Snowdon and scorning to use the mountain railway. Phyllis remembers their different attitudes: 'When you climbed with Lewis there would be no stopping or slacking: you got to the top, looked at the view, and marched down again. With Sybil, when you got to the top you would rest and the chocolate would come out.'

Sybil worked on improving her Welsh, helped by the local shopkeepers, who refused to serve her unless she used their language. She was soon roped in to local events, such as crowning the carnival queen. In the coming years Bron-y-Garth was to become a much-loved refuge, a place of space and beauty where she could draw breath from her hectic life in London, and indulge her passions for walking, reading and music. But even here the theatre was not entirely forgotten. In August she saw *Everyman* at the Wrexham Eisteddfod, describing it with typical exaggeration as 'one of the most wonderful things, if not *the* most wonderful thing, I have ever seen in my life'.

On the journey out to Australia she and Christopher had studied the ideas of the Russian philosopher Ouspensky, and Sybil now met him. He told her the following parable: 'You go out in the morning with a basket on your arm, a poor little thing down here. And then you go up, up, up and you are there far above, looking down at that poor little thing buying your vegetables.' Sybil found this an arresting image for how an actor should work, and never forgot it. Meanwhile Shaw, who now called her 'England's greatest actress', wrote to say he would be 'within striking distance of Portmadoc' while attending the Malvern Festival. His real intention was to sound out Sybil about his new play *On the Rocks*, a political extravaganza set in 10 Downing Street. There were five parts for women, 'but the only one that is at all striking is a lady doctor who appears for ten minutes or so and is mistaken at first for Death. If you were at a very loose end you might create it for me; but I cannot pretend that it is not utterly beneath your notice.' Sybil was either unavailable or untempted, or both, but Lewis acted in and directed the play's first production later that year.

Eileen, who had branched out into directing, now set up with the actor Ronald Adam the Embassy School of Acting, attached to the Embassy theatre in Swiss Cottage; Russell's sister-in-law Fanny Dowson, after a spell at RADA, also joined the staff. An early prospectus explained: 'The school is planned on the principle of an apprenticeship. The course lasts a year, fees are not inexpensive, but only young people thought to have definite promise are accepted.' It was later to provide training for stars such as Herbert Lom, Dennis Price, Irene Handl, William Devlin and Patrick Troughton. Eileen's talents were different from Sybil's, as her daughters recall: 'She was a very good teacher, which Sybil wasn't, she didn't have the patience,' Donnie suggests. Phyllis describes their mother as 'a very good actress, and much more sexy than Sybil, although she didn't have Sybil's great presence and big voice'.

Sybil's return to the London stage after eighteen months away was keenly awaited. 'Seldom has so talented an actress earned so enduring, so deep, so merited an affection from so wide a public,' the critic Sydney Carroll wrote. 'We who watch her adoringly do so with a full appreciation of her ripe experience, her unerring technique, her full, rich personality.' Her chosen vehicle, *The Distaff Side*, was potentially promising, the first time she had played a truly modern woman. It was written and offered to her by John van Druten, who had made his name with *Young Woodley*, a story – initially banned by the censor – of a schoolboy's love for his housemaster's wife. His new play also starred Martita Hunt, Clifford Evans, Viola Keats and Haidée Wright, and was directed by Auriol Lee, who had co-written some of his plays, and was one of the few women directors of the period.

A relatively plotless comedy about three generations of a family, it proved a critical disappointment, though it ran for three months at the Apollo. Sybil's performance as the sympathetic mother at the centre of the story was widely praised: she was, one critic noted, successfully 'restraining and smothering her dynamic force'; another noted that all the old mannerisms had gone. Agate noticed a similar quality of sure-footed quietness: 'Miss Thorndike, with a mellow understanding of the character, made it glow like a day in late October. It is only fair that we should now recognise as a property of this actress, and as a possession in her own right, that beauty of mind for which Messrs Euripides and Shaw have too often bagged the entire credit.' To the grateful John Van Druten, her performance 'produced a tender radiant magic of unselfishness'.

The relationship between actors and critics is always a delicate one, but Sybil found no problem in being friends with those who had to judge her work. In a foreword to A E Wilson's *A Playgoer's Pilgrimage*, she referred to 'a real friendship between us based on our mutual love of and enthusiasm for the theatre'. But she risked upsetting her good relations with Agate, criticising him privately for his review of Clemence Dane's *Wild Decembers*, which starred Diana Wynyard as Charlotte Brontë: 'My dear Jimmy, I'm doing what I've no business to – and quite probably you will curse me. You're a critic, but as you insultingly say that I'm a "dear" before I'm an actress (!!), so I say you're my friend before you're a critic!! Quits now!' She then berated him for not understanding any other passion but love. 'I do think you might own occasionally that you don't understand certain types of women's minds – there are a lot of us who have other deep burning passions as well as the one that one gives in love, and I think none of you have been fair over the Brontë play that Diana Wynyard is doing so *beautifully*! I do think your criticism is so wonderful and we all welcome it and do try to learn from it, but you make this play sound dull, and it's not dull. It gave me one of the biggest kicks I've had since being home... Forgive this and don't answer. You're such a darling, and I do enjoy a yarn with you and I *never* get it, and I long to argue certain things because you love the Theatre and I love it beyond all things – nearly! This letter is too vague and incoherent but I shall send it. Don't curse me! Yours affectionately, Sybil.'

Among several Sunday-night or matinee performances, she was applauded for her Gertrude ('she rose to the full majesty and splendour of the verse' – *The Times*) in two performances of *Hamlet* in its entirety, directed at Sadler's Wells by Ben Greet, and starring a celebrated Hamlet, Ernest Milton. One matinee provided a classic example of her ability to improvise. During the scene preceding her entrance for the famous 'willow' speech, Laertes and Claudius had reversed their positions. Sybil swept on, began the speech, realised she was addressing the wrong person, exclaimed 'No, not you!', thumped the king on the chest, and continued the speech to Laertes.

There was also a single performance at the Apollo of *Mrs Siddons*. Naomi Royde-Smith, a biographer of the great actress, had written the play espe-cially for Sybil, who had a great admiration for her famous predecessor. It was directed by Bruce Winston, and featured Nora Nicholson, Eric Portman as the artist Thomas Lawrence, John Laurie as the actor John Philip Kemble, and Ann and Mary as the Siddons daughters. For once Sybil was bored, as Mary recalls: 'We were all also playing at night, and were exhausted and terribly bored with the play. We hated every minute of it – even Mummy did.' It was evidently thin stuff, but Sybil managed to hide her boredom from Darlington, who wrote: 'Sybil Thorndike is superb. Whenever one of these life-size-and-a-half women has to be played, she steps in and claims it as by divine right.'

She had another opportunity to go over the top in *Double Door*, written by Elizabeth McFadden, produced by H M Tennent, and directed by Henry Oscar at the Globe in March 1934. In a full-blooded melodrama she played a mother who cruelly schemes to wreck the love-life of the family around her, shuts her daughter-in-law in a safe, and ends up a gibbering wreck. 'Audiences want to be given a full dose of the horrors,' she declared gleefully after the first night. She found a new low register in her voice, and several critics were terrified by her performance, including the critic from *Punch*: 'Miss Sybil Thorndike, superbly made up, with her cruel twisted lips, and the hint of physical deformity conveyed by the slightly raised shoulder, was positively horrifying in the savage intensity of her passion.'

It was about this time that her personality and demeanour made an impact on a teacher in an Edinburgh school. 'I recall being recommended to walk with my head up "as did Sybil Thorndike",' Muriel Spark recalls, 'and later I repeated these instructions in *The Prime of Miss Jean Brodie*.' In the novel Miss Brodie tells her girls: 'Form a single file, now, please, and walk with you heads up, *up*, like Sybil Thorndike, a woman of noble mien.'

At the start of the year Sybil had told Elizabeth Robins: 'I think a good new year resolution would be "I will not do deeds of charity."' If she made such a resolution, she failed to keep it. During these months she opened a fair at Chelsea Town Hall in aid of unemployed parishioners, and supported a move to build a Sarah Siddons Memorial Theatre on the site of the actress' home in Willesden. She also laid the foundation stone of Shakespeare House, a block of affordable flats to be occupied by Shoreditch families currently living in unhealthy surroundings. In a good socialist speech she argued that others had no right to comfortable homes while their brothers and sisters had to live in places that were not fit for anyone. The housing movement, she suggested, was 'a sign that English people were awaking'.

Meanwhile, along with Lewis, she was re-elected to the Equity council. This was a difficult time for the profession, with the popularity of the talking films forcing many theatres to close, so increasing unemployment among actors, musicians and theatre workers generally. 'You are killing the living drama for a few thousand pounds,' John Martin Harvey told the government, as he led a deputation to the House of Commons to protest against the 20 per cent entertainments tax levied on theatres. The high-powered deputation included Du Maurier, May Whitty, Gladys Cooper, Edith Evans, Gwen Ffrangcon-Davies and Sybil, who made a plea for lower seat prices.

Sybil kept in touch with Murray. 'He is one of the few people in the world whom one would follow blindly and without question, knowing that what he advocated would have no self-motive, but would be founded on a search for truth,' she wrote. She had assisted him by reading extracts from the plays for his lecture on Euripides at the London School of Economics. 'I study your plays daily,' she told him. 'They teach me more about modern acting than anything else.' Murray asked if she would stage his translation of *The Choephori*, which he considered one of Aeschylus' best plays. 'Thank you so much for sending the book,' she replied. 'It is a glorious thing and would be most intriguing to do – perhaps a chance will come one day, and not too far ahead – I'm getting very tired of the proscenium stage – also the apron – Gordon Bottomley has written of late things made for a different form of stage – most entertaining and full of promise of exciting ideas.'

Always interested in innovative modern drama, she became president of the newly formed Play Society, which planned to stage *Marco Millions*, Eugene O'Neill's attack on commercialism, and D H Lawrence's *The Widowing of Mrs Holroyd*. There were also two BBC radio broadcasts. For Agate's 'Stars in their Courses' series she performed extracts from *Saint Joan*, *Medea*, *The Trojan Women* and *Macbeth*; and with Leon Quartermaine in the title-role she played Volumnia in *Coriolanus*, in a production to mark Shakespeare's birthday. Radio plays, now broadcast from Broadcasting House, had the luxury of eight rehearsals, each three hours long. *The Times* judged Sybil to be 'immediately effective as Volumnia, getting so much character into her voice that definite pictures began to form themselves on the mind'.

She also took part with Edith Evans and Peggy Ashcroft in a series of mock trials staged in the theatre at the London School of Economics, and fitted in five matinee performances in a week as the Empress in Dryden's tragedy *Aureng-Zebe* at the Westminster. One evening John van Druten took her and the family out to dinner at the Savoy. Mary remembers the occasion: 'He said to mother, "What on earth do you think you're doing with these little companies?" And she replied: "You know I *must* have an outlet." This was when she was also playing in *Double Door* every night! John collapsed – and she saw the joke herself. But that was so typical.'

In June Sybil played in *Village Wooing*, a piece Shaw called 'A Comediettina for Two Voices'. The play concerned a bearded writer (said to be based on Lytton Strachey), who is badgered, bored and finally bullied into matrimony by the candid, no-nonsense village postmistress. Shaw initially saw it as a part 'only Edith Evans could make tolerable'. Subsequently he offered it to Sybil and Lewis, but Lewis was already spoken for. ('Whatever does Lewis mean by taking another engagement?' Shaw thundered. 'I bargained for a Joint.')

Before he cast Arthur Wontner opposite Sybil, and persuaded Lewis to help him direct. Shaw outlined his rehearsal plans, but warned Sybil not to do her usual trick of committing herself to other work: 'If you love me don't take on six more performances all over the place during the week. An unfinished performance of VW would look like a tomfoolery or a charade; and it will take a week's whole time to get the varnish your reputation demands.'

Foolishly, Sybil learnt the part in Cockney, unaware that Shaw had based the character on Jisbella Lyth, the postmistress at Ayot St Lawrence. At the first rehearsal he told her he had written it 'in a much more beautiful English, without an accent', so she had to switch to using what J C Trewin later called 'vowels that are privet-clipped'. The combination of Lewis and Shaw was not always an easy one, as Christopher Casson remembered: 'Shaw always acted all the parts and directed the performances too. My father had to smooth the way and perhaps pick up the pieces.' Both he and John were used to witnessing battles in rehearsal, 'sitting quiet as mice at the back of the stalls while Mummy and Daddy fought it out', as John put it. Sybil 'could be very forthright and very much one to have her own way', but eventually she would 'become the humble actress quietly taking her orders from the producer'.

Village Wooing was staged for a limited run at the Little under the management of Nancy Price, as part of a double-bill with Galsworthy's farcical morality play *The Little Man*. 'Who would ever have thought that Sybil Thorndike – the Gloomy Dame – could have got away with playing a coy, pert, pyjamaed blonde!' exclaimed one critic from a popular paper. *The Times* was more measured, noting that the two actors' movements 'skilfully emphasise the light and shade of the dialogue. Miss Thorndike almost persuades us that the postmistress is a real person, though she has little support in this direction from Mr Shaw.'

On 25 August she sailed on the *Berengaria* to America for the Broadway production of *The Distaff Side* at the Booth. It was her first visit to New York for nearly a quarter of a century, and she noticed a difference: 'I return an aged woman and mature in my reactions,' she told a reporter. 'But I find you all amazingly changed too. Such grand manners! I've really had the most interesting conversations in shops. I remember when I was last here, people were so abrupt: not rude, exactly, but unpolished. Now you all seem so much more gracious.' She also expressed her anxieties about the rise of Hitler and Mussolini. 'If nationalism means being degraded by the force of ruthless leadership, then civilisation itself must be dying in Europe.'

She stayed in the Gotham Hotel on Fifth Avenue with the director Auriol Lee and John van Druten. 'I'm feeling so stupidly homesick, I hate being away from my clan,' she wrote to Elizabeth Casson during rehearsals. 'The way I keep from this idiotic longing for Lewis is to go on swotting at my Welsh grammar, and talking it a little with the Welsh young man in the company... I can't write a long letter as I am pushed with work. I'm enthusiastic and devastated by this city and its fantastic proportions! People are most kind and everyone talks far too much.' It was the first time she and Lewis had been apart since the war, and they wrote to each other every day during their seven-month separation, broken only by a visit he made at Christmas. In October he wrote her a passionate birthday letter: 'It's the first birthday for a long time that we haven't been together, and we've had them together in so many places of late years! The plane to Tasmania perhaps the oddest! But though we're not together as much as then, the hunger for you makes you even more in my thoughts all day than any of those other birthdays. Every day you are a more lovely person than last year, and I love you more even than the first birthday together at Leamington.'

Although she missed Lewis, she still managed to enjoy herself. She mixed with the cream of American theatre: Alfred Lunt and Lynn Fontanne, Katharine Cornell and Guthrie McClintic, Otis Skinner, and the writer Marc Connelly. She went to Harlem ('Such marvellous shows – the Negro people are born actors'), and attended Broadway matinees whenever she was free. Current shows included plays by Elmer Rice and Sinclair Lewis, an adaptation of Erskine Caldwell's *Tobacco Road*, and O'Casey's *Within the Gates*. Sybil saw Connelly's religious play *The Green Pastures*, and Lillian Hellman's hit play *The Children's Hour*, which she thought 'tragedy at its finest, clear and unsentimental'. She suggested that American companies should bring both plays to England, where they were currently banned by the Lord Chamberlain. She also found time to record Arnold Bennett's story 'A Letter Home', so becoming the first woman to record a Talking Book.

And then there was Tallulah Bankhead, who had the room below her in the Gotham. Sybil had probably met her in the early 1920s in London, when the American star was making her name in *The Dancers* at Wyndham's. Now, late one night, high on champagne, the Hollywood actress rang her and invited her down to one of her riotous parties. Sybil reportedly arrived in a dressing-gown with her hair down, at which Tallulah knelt at her feet, kissed the hem of her gown, and poured out a hymn of praise to her qualities as an actress, ending: 'Now, you fucking old miracle, what will you have to drink?' Sybil politely asked for a sherry.

After that, when she came in after her show, she often found a big bunch of roses in her room, with a note telling her to join the party. One night she found Tallulah, her friend Estelle Winwood, and the star actress Laurette Taylor there, when the group, according to the hostess, spent the time 'shredding a few reputations, and griping about the theatre'. Sybil was fascinated. 'These parties used to go on all night, but I could never stay to the end,' she recalled. 'Tallulah used to give some of the best performances of her life, excerpts from her parts, and keep us all in stitches. She was a darling, so generous, and she had no inhibitions at all.'

The American company for *The Distaff Side* included Mildred Natwick, Viola Keats, Clifford Evans (the young Welshman) and Estelle Winwood. Although considered quaint and old-fashioned in its values by some critics, the play received good notices, and ran for six months. Sybil thought John Mason Brown and the other New York critics 'immensely helpful', as they proved to be. In the *New York Times* Brooks Atkinson wrote: 'She won all our hearts, and the simplicity, quiet force and womanly beauty of her drew the audience close around her.' Another critic observed: 'Her superb technique, kept well out of sight, is used as a blower through which she pumps the quality and real sweetness of her personality across to her audience.'

As always, Sybil saw New York in an optimistic light. She believed the skyscrapers were a reflection of a nation 'always on tiptoe for experience, always alertly seeking some truth, or energetically pursuing that stimulating, intangible "something" which is just out of reach'. She was bowled over by the labour-saving devices in the homes she visited, which seemed to have eliminated domestic drudgery, leaving women 'more time to devote to the cultural side of life and the consideration of the broader aspects of existence'. She felt that the equality of the sexes was an accepted fact, that American women 'were not feminist in any aggressive sense', and that the young American girl was 'a splendidly alert, energetic and promising element'.

While in New York she came to the aid of a friend in great distress. Edith Evans had come to Broadway to play the Nurse in *Romeo and Juliet*. Early in 1935 she heard from England that her husband Guy Booth had suddenly died. The news was also cabled to Sybil, who immediately went round to her hotel, and spent the day comforting the devastated actress. Soon afterwards she wrote from Boston:

'Darling Edith

… I can say in a letter what I can't to your face – you're a very courageous *big* person, and you've got *huge* things to do in the theatre, and huge things to give and keep giving, and anything you suffer turns to blessings for others. Even in that awful time in New York you were *giving* to us all, making us *see* something. How proud Guy must be that you are starting work again and fighting for Equity and just holding banners high. Bless you darling, your loving Sybil'

From Boston she and the company travelled to Canada. They played in Toronto, where she gave a lengthy speech about the theatre to the Empire Club of Canada. At times it seemed as if the paternal gene had taken over, her words having more than a whiff of a sermon to them. Her text was the importance of theatre as a live, active art, in comparison to the passive, second-hand, mechanical nature of cinema and radio.

'The theatre exists to keep us always surprised, always enquiring, always wanting to find some new aspect, always wanting to see some new point of view, to keep our minds, our mentalities, flexible, not willing to be settled,' she thundered. She touched on the power of audiences to change a performance, the element of danger that makes it dramatic and exciting. She made her familiar plea for theatre as a weapon for peace. 'That is the great problem of nations at the moment, trying to find something which makes us understand our fellow-nations, our brothers and sisters of various kinds and colours. The theatre is one way, and a very deep, instinctive way, of being able to find something out about other people.' For someone who claimed to hate speaking in public, 'these vague remarks', as she called them, were a formidable achievement.

The company were then persuaded to do an extra three weeks at the Ethel Barrymore in New York. Sybil would have preferred to have gone home. 'Honestly, life has been too much for me!' she told Master Rawdon. 'Since going away on tour I've had two public functions with speeches each day, and sometimes three! I got simply *dead*.' Yet as usual she warmed to the people she met. 'Boston, lovely Toronto and Philadelphia, I really did enjoy those places immensely – what *lovely* people, they are so generous and kind, and I feel all thrilled with America.'

Returning on the *Manhattan* to England in April, she received a telegram from the actress/director Eva le Gallienne, mentioning the possibility of doing another play in America. For a moment, she told Master Rawdon, she was raring to go. 'I felt, "Hurrah, now here's fun, and I'll just have a grand time working with Eva", and got all excited, but then Lewis said I'd better remember the contracts I'd made!' She also, more coolly, realised she had been away a long time. 'I'm really anxious to stay in London for a few months to get the life of the family tidied a little!' she explained, adding: 'I could not bear to be separated again.' She was also glad to be in England for the jubilee celebrations for King George and Queen Mary: 'The jubilee was superb, it has made us violently Royalist. I'm the most violent Royalist-Socialist ever – the King and Queen have been so wonderful. How we all cried at the procession!'

She plunged back into the West End in *Grief Goes Over*. Staged in June at the Globe, and then at the Phoenix, the play was by Merton Hodge, the New Zealand dramatist and doctor, who had recently achieved success with *The Wind and the Rain*. Sybil described it as 'delicate and lovely; I'd like a bit more beef in it, but it's got a real appeal and is very well-written'. Cast again as a sympathetic mother, she proved the point of the title – a quote from Rupert Brooke – by stoically overcoming a series of tragic incidents within her middle-class Knightsbridge family. Once again the director was Auriol Lee, who had recently suggested that women directors had certain advantages over their male counterparts: they were more patient, more skilled at dealing with temperament, and better at working sensitively with actresses.

She certainly coaxed a fine piece of work out of Sybil: Agate praised 'the perfect justice of this beautifully restrained performance', while Darlington wrote that 'she brings a quiet sense of sorrow borne and mastered to everything she does'. Even Graham Robertson was won over: 'For the first time I was able to admire Sybil Thorndike,' he confessed. 'She gives a beautiful performance.' The playwright Gordon Bottomley wrote to congratulate her for 'taking an imaginationless skeleton and clothing it and making it live with your own vivid life and power and creative energy'. But several critics noticed the play's similarity to *The Distaff Side*. Was Sybil in danger of being typecast as Everymother in gentle family dramas?

Ironically, as she admitted, Sybil lacked many of the traditional female attributes. 'Domesticity has never excited me,' she said. 'I love the children part – being a nurse has great attractions, but I have no real love for a house and possessions. House-proudness, which is a womanly quality – and one that I admire so much in others – does not belong to me at all....I can be content with very plain, almost bare living, which is not the thing for a woman to be.

It is lovely to be *without* possessions, the whole world is one's own then.' The article was headed 'My Regrets that I am not a Man', and in it she confessed that the wish to be one 'has not diminished with the years; rather has it become more strong'.

The morning after the opening night of *Grief Goes Over* saw the wedding of her son John, who was marrying Patricia Chester Master, the daughter of a Shanghai solicitor, whom he had met on a blind date in Hong Kong. Sybil had been given carte-blanche with the guest list and, according to John, appeared to 'have asked the entire list of actors in *Who's Who in the Theatre*'. The couple were married in St Paul's Church in Knightsbridge, in front of a vast congregation in which rear-admirals and flying officers mingled with theatre people, including Paul Robeson, Godfrey Tearle, May Whitty, Lilian Braithwaite, Owen Nares and Ben Greet.

Sybil's daughter-in-law was coming into a close-knit, flamboyant, enthusiastic family, which could be overwhelming to an outsider. As Sybil wrote at the time: 'We are not a quarrelsome family; but our household is an absolute hotbed of argument. Meal-times are notorious as occasions for a violent clash of opinion, such as would have been unthinkable a hundred years ago.' In her biography of Lewis, their granddaughter Diana Devlin develops this theme: 'Music, theatre, religion, ethics and politics were the chief topics, with the last three burning most brightly. It was nothing to find yourself covering the nature of patriotism over the soup, the responsibility of democracy during the roast beef, the limits of pacifism while you attacked the jam tart, and the existence of God as you sank back with your coffee.'

That autumn Sybil's friend George Lansbury resigned as Labour leader, and Clement Attlee took over. The Abyssinia crisis loomed, with Italy invading the African country in October without a declaration of war, an action condemned by the League of Nations. 'The thought of war is too terrible to think of – what a long way we all have to go before we are Christian,' Sybil wrote. A week later she expressed her anxiety about Patricia sailing to Alexandria, where John was stationed: 'Another war is unthinkable – and then poor Abyssinia and the poor young Italians and their mothers etc – awful!' She was now a staunch pacifist, though her family were divided on the subject: Ann and Christopher shared her views, John as a member of the armed forces clearly did not, while Mary and Lewis were more inclined to compromise. It was Maude Royden who had convinced her that pacifism was the only answer to international disputes: 'She made me realise that the term pacifism was not the passive thing the name suggests, rather it was a positive, a new and Christian attitude towards other nations and people, and a recognition that war is a sign of weakness.'

She continued to maintain a high profile in public life generally, attending a garden party in Westminster, at which political leaders met high commissioners from the Dominions, and being invited on to the BBC Advisory Council, which included among its members Lloyd George and William Beveridge. Meanwhile, on the basis that 'everyone should go back to school again at 50', she had started to learn Latin. But though she continued to give interviews, the public's desire to know everything sometimes exasperated her. 'Revolting public!' she scribbled in a letter to a journalist. 'We honestly have damned ourselves telling them every detail about our lives!'

In August 1935 it was announced that 'Sybil Thorndike (engagements permitting) and Lewis Casson will accompany a special tour to the Moscow Theatre Festival in September'. But engagements prevented, as she agreed to play the relatively small but comic part of Lady Bucktrout in Robert Morley's *Short Story*, directed by Guthrie in his first West End production, and put on by the budding impresario Hugh ('Binkie') Beaumont. The starry company for this thin, mildly amusing piece was headed by Marie Tempest, playing a celebrated actress returning to the theatre, and included A E Matthews, Ursula Jeans, and two relatively unknown actors in cameo parts, Rex Harrison and Margaret Rutherford. Sybil's performance, as a Gaiety Girl who has married into the peerage and become a student of the occult, drew Agate's ire. In his diary he wrote: 'There was a time when, although utterly free from any vulgarity of mind, Sybil had certain provincial elegances, mouth-twistings, arm-wavings and the like, *to which she returns for her comedy*. It is this that I find deplorable – the renewal of something long and successfully put behind her.'

If the modest part was not much of a challenge, Marie Tempest certainly was. Now 71, an expert and much-admired light comedienne, she was a monstrous tartar of a woman. ('That's what comes of playing saints,' she was alleged to have said when she heard of Sybil's damehood. 'Nobody asks me to play a saint.') Imperious, vain and self-important, and a notorious bully, she wanted all the men in the company to pay court to her. She insisted on rehearsing in the evenings rather than the afternoons, when she rested, and would snap at the prompter if he gave her a line a second too early ('Are you acting this part or am I?'). 'What a horribly common little woman,' Guthrie observed to Beaumont. She needed people to stand up to her, and Guthrie eventually did. 'Miss Tempest, why are you being such a bitch?' he said after one row. After that she was better behaved.

Denys Blakelock, who took over from Rex Harrison, recalled the contrast between her and Sybil. 'I used to feel, when I saw them together, that Marie Tempest had a sort of grudging envy of Sybil's goodness; that deep down she knew that her career, her riches, her illustrious name, all the adulation she received – none of this could compare in value with the qualities of character and the spiritual gifts possessed by this woman whom everyone loved and nobody feared. Certainly you could not have found two women more dissimilar. Marie spent every penny she earned on purple and fine linen and the good things of this world. Sybil, on the other hand, hated living in style; and as regards food, she would not know whether she were eating peacocks' tongues or a hardboiled egg.'

Yet if Sybil lacked style, she certainly had steel. 'Marie could be a bitch,' she remarked later, with rare directness. 'She would try to make you her slave, and if you gave way she despised you and treated you like dirt.' She also hated other actors getting all the audience's attention, and would try to upstage them. She tried it on with Sybil, sitting at her desk making scratching noises with her pen at the wrong moment. Sybil countered this by placing blotting paper there at the next performance. Another night she played with a handkerchief downstage while Sybil had a scene upstage that got several laughs. Sybil responded the next night by playing a game of patience on the floor during Marie Tempest's scene, so bringing the attention back to her. As they went offstage together the older woman whispered: 'You're a very clever actress, aren't you!' To which Sybil replied: 'Not especially, darling, but clever enough to act with you.' They then became good friends.

During the run Sybil also appeared for the 1930 Players in a single performance of Noel Langley's *The Farm of Three Echoes*, a Boer family drama set in the South African veldt, directed by Murray Macdonald. In a cast that included May Whitty and Jessica Tandy, Sybil and Russell played an oppressed wife and sadistic husband, and did so, according to *The Times*, with 'vivid realism'. She also joined the leaders of the profession in a massive, four-hour Shakespeare Matinee at Drury Lane in aid of the National Theatre Appeal. In a scene from the last act of *Othello*, with Godfrey Tearle as Othello and Margaretta Scott as Desdemona, she reminded the audience of her skill in Shakespeare: 'Dame Sybil's magnificent Emilia would have roused the most jaded soul to something of her own vivid emotion and fearless power,' one critic wrote.

Lewis now had an offer from the producer Gilbert Miller to go to New York, to play Lord Melbourne in *Victoria Regina*, by Laurence Housman. Queen Victoria was played by the versatile Helen Hayes, dubbed 'the first lady of the American theatre'. Marie Tempest advised Sybil not to let Lewis go, suggesting it might be 'dangerous' for their marriage for him to be alone there. Sybil felt able to risk this, but being apart from him was a wrench: 'Oh! I miss Lewis dreadfully, but he's quite happy in spite of his homesickness,' she told Elizabeth. In fact Lewis did have a brief affair in America: there was a belief within the family that it was with Helen Hayes. But this remained speculation, as did his alleged affair with Gladys Cooper. Lewis' occasional straying may partly have been prompted by Sybil's ambivalence about sex. 'It's a bore and an excitement and a thrill but it becomes tiresome sometimes, very tiresome,' she confessed. 'There are such ghastly ups and downs and difficulties and unhappinesses and glorious happinesses.'

By the time Lewis returned to London after five months away, the affair was apparently over. John Casson observed later of his parents: 'Whatever storms and crises may have occurred in their married life, they always managed to rise above them with the minimum delay, and always managed most successfully to keep it from the children.' Sybil put it another way: 'We were held together by the children when things sometimes got difficult, though we never really thought of breaking up.'

23

On the Road

1936–1937

'This should be the beginning of plays expressing the voice of the workers'
Sybil when about to tour Six Men of Dorset

Sybil's family was now starting to expand. 'Mary is being married at the little RC church round the corner here,' she told her sister-in-law in February 1936. 'Only family – Devlin Casson Thorndike Ewbank etc. It's horrid without Lewis, but he agrees they better get married …he doesn't know for sure when he will be back.'

Mary had become disenchanted with the professional theatre, partly because of being in her mother's shadow. While playing at the Q theatre, she was asked by Jack de Leon if she would play Saint Joan. 'I said I couldn't possibly do it,' she recalls. 'I could remember my mother's performance so well, so it would simply be an imitation. I was having more fun doing amateur theatricals, such as playing in Tennyson's *Becket* in Canterbury Cathedral. That was more my cup of tea.'

In May 1935 she appeared at the Whitehall in Walter Hudd's *Snow in Summer*. Then, after discussions with Lewis, whom she felt would be both sympathetic and objective, she decided to give up the stage, but continue with her music. Sybil was happy with her decision, and arranged for her to have singing lessons with Dorothea Webb, a professor at the Royal Academy of Music, who would thoroughly train her voice over the next few years. Mary also admitted to a fondness for domestic life. 'I like cooking and sewing and looking after the house,' she said before her wedding. 'I make all my own clothes. When Mother goes away on tour I enjoy doing the housekeeping. The most important thing in life is a home to look after and enjoy.'

Sybil was delighted with her choice of husband. 'She is so happy and we are all pleased about it,' she told Elizabeth Robins. 'Bill is a dear, and so are all his family, and they are very much in love, and wanting to "settle down" and be domestic!' William Devlin, aged twenty-four, was already making a success at the Old Vic in roles such as Peer Gynt and Richard III. With a fine voice and great presence, he had made a great impact in London as King Lear straight after Oxford. He and Mary had first met in Oxford in the summer of 1931, when she was playing Hero in an OUDS production of *Much Ado About Nothing*, and had been friends for a long time. In contrast to John's wedding, hers took place quietly at the Church of the Holy Redeemer in Chelsea on 7 March 1936. A fortnight later Sybil became a grandmother for the first time, when Patricia Casson gave birth to a son, Anthony. 'I can scarcely realise it – life going on thinking up generations is almost too wonderful to contemplate calmly!!' she told Elizabeth Casson.

She now returned briefly to the screen. She had not had any film work for five years, and times had changed. There were now 4,500 cinemas nation-wide, and two-thirds of the leading stage actors had worked in film studios, attracted in part by the lucrative salaries, which were five or six times greater than those in the theatre. But she remained ambivalent about the medium, lamenting the fact that so many of the best English actors, actresses and play-wrights were 'wasting their talents in Hollywood on indifferent films'.

Tudor Rose was a strongly cast and well-designed film typical of Gains-borough Studios, billed as a historical drama about the short, tragic life of Lady Jane Grey, 'who died for England she knew not why'. It starred Cedric Hardwicke, Felix Aylmer, Gwen Ffrangcon-Davies, Martita Hunt, Miles Malleson and John Laurie, with Frank Cellier as Henry VIII. Now relatively experienced in front of the camera, Sybil played the warm-hearted nurse of Henry's young queen. Sixteen-year-old Nova Pilbeam, who gave a delicate performance as Lady Jane, remembered being scared of but 'very supported' by Sybil. A young John Mills was Lord Dudley. 'Sybil was such fun, and so humble,' he recalled. 'I idolised her.' The director Roy Ward Baker, then a production assistant, remembers: 'She had the feel of a star who really knew her business. But she was friendly to everybody, and very down to earth. She couldn't have been nicer to a mere 19-year-old dogsbody.'

Tudor Rose, directed by Robert Stevenson, was voted the second most popular film in a *Film Weekly* poll, but Graham Greene, film critic for the *Spectator*, was not impressed. He condemned the dialogue ('I have seldom listened to such inchoate rubbish') and the film's historical accuracy: 'This sentimental pageant in fancy-dress could have displayed no more ignorance of the period if it had been made in Hollywood.' It was to be another five years before Sybil, still not convinced, would appear in another film. 'To me the cinema is a kind of drug and an escape,' she stated. 'Its great sin is that it has killed the stage productions in the provinces, where a generation is growing up without any knowledge of the living theatre.'

Shaw was now pondering who to cast as Saint Joan in a production to be staged at the Malvern Festival. 'I should choose Sybil without a moment's hesitation if she's available,' he told Barry Jackson in April. 'She's the only one who has the right sort of steel in her. She knows the part, and her figure is brilliantly presentable.' Sybil was already contracted to do a play for Gilbert Miller, but was so keen to play the role again, she told Shaw she might be able to persuade him to release her for the Joan performances. Shaw was sceptical: 'All this sounds very pleasant, but what on earth is going to happen with rehearsals!' he asked Jackson. 'I think it would be most dangerous to shoot a Joan on to the stage who is entirely strange to the company.' Sybil's hopes were not realised, and the part was eventually played by Elspeth March. Shaw also toyed with offering her the part of Epifania in *The Millionairess* the following year, but nothing came of that either.

The play which prevented her going to Malvern was *Kind Lady*, a melodrama by the American playwright Edward Chodorov, based on Hugh Walpole's story 'The Silver Mask' and directed by Lewis Allen. The plot concerned a rich woman, who mistakenly lets a gang of criminals into her home, and is held prisoner by them while they ransack her art collection and subject her to mental cruelty. The terror of the piece when she read it apparently forced Sybil under the bedclothes again. *The Times* noted that in conveying the woman's terrified hysteria she was able 'brilliantly to communicate the suffering of the rack'. But the play, later filmed with Ethel Barrymore in the role, lasted just 11 performances.

She and Lewis now decided it was time for them to work together again. They did so in the form they loved best: touring with a small company and a repertoire of old and new plays. Sybil relished the chance to keep theatre alive in the provinces. Unlike many in the profession, who hated the long train journeys and the dreaded theatrical 'digs', she enjoyed playing to different audiences, and seeing different parts of the country. 'In the provinces they enjoy more colour than you get in the natural conversational style of the West

End,' she said. 'And so do I.' From August to December, travelling north, south and west, she toured under the management of Barry O'Brien. The plays, all directed by Lewis, were an intriguing mixture: two familiar ones, *Village Wooing* and *Hippolytus*; two short ones by Coward, *Fumed Oak* and *Hands Across the Sea*; and DH Lawrence's *My Son's My Son*.

The small company was very much a family affair: in addition to Nora Nicholson and Nicholas Phipps it included Christopher, aged twenty-four, and Ann, now twenty. Christopher had gained solid experience in repertory at Liverpool, Perth and York, followed by a season at the Old Vic where, alongside William Devlin, he had, according to critic Audrey Williamson, played various minor parts 'with a certain quiet skill'. Ann had also been there, as Perdita in *The Winter's Tale*. Elsewhere, beginning a lifelong passion for Shaw, she had played in *Pygmalion*, *Mrs Warren's Profession* and *Man and Superman*.

With *Village Wooing* Sybil reprised the role of the village postmistress, this time with Lewis as the writer. The Coward pieces offered different challenges. The plays were part of *Tonight at 8.30*, a portfolio of nine short plays in which Coward and Gertrude Lawrence had scored a hit earlier that year. In *Fumed Oak*, Sybil played a nasty, calculating suburban wife, who gets her come-uppance when her husband (Lewis) finally breaks free from a marriage of deceit and misery; the *Manchester Guardian* thought it 'brilliantly and wittily handled'. Her part in the witty comedy *Hands Across the Sea*, with its main characters supposedly based on Louis and Edwina Mountbatten, and half the dialogue taking place on the phone, could hardly be more different. Here she played Lady Maureen ('Piggie') Gilpin, a cruel bitch who causes mayhem to friends and family by her butterfly mind and whirlwind social life.

The boldest choice was Lawrence's play, written in 1911 around the same time as *Sons and Lovers*, and like that novel dealing with the intense, often bitter relationship between mother and child in a miner's family. Lawrence had completed the first two acts of *My Son's My Son*, but the third remained in draft, and had recently been completed by Walter Greenwood, author of *Love on the Dole*, for a production in the West End. Sybil played the miner's widow, with Ann in the title-role and Christopher playing one of her sons. Like the original production, Lewis' was not particularly well received, both having problems recreating authentically the Nottinghamshire dialect and the mining setting. Lewis suggested it was a play everyone in the mining industry ought to see, while Sybil thought it revealed the essential character of 'people who live eternally on the fringe of disaster, yet always treat their precarious position with humour, the humour of great courage'.

The most complex production was *Hippolytus*, which they played for matinees only. Sybil hoped the play would appeal not just to the intelligentsia, but to the ordinary playgoer. Because of the small size of the company, all the actors had to be part of the Chorus, masked and cloaked at the side of the stage, then emerge to play their parts. Sybil was Aphrodite and the Nurse, with Christopher cast as Hippolytus, and Ann as Phaedra and Artemis. Lewis, as the Messenger, based his main speech on how he remembered Barker playing it. In Sybil's Nurse there was, the *Manchester Guardian* noted, 'occasional hints of *Romeo and Juliet*'. At Streatham *The Times* critic was particularly impressed by the scenes between Phaedra and the Nurse, which he called 'alive, arresting, and full of detail'. Ann, who had been a comic hit in *Hands Across the Sea*, seemed to have inherited her mother's versatility.

The provinces received Sybil with huge enthusiasm. In Oxford she was described as 'a figure of almost legendary greatness'; in Edinburgh, where she was dubbed 'our Second Siddons', the *Evening News* suggested the plays were varied enough 'to illustrate the genius of this brilliant and charming actress, who seems to absorb the very blood of the characters she assumes'. Sybil was in her element: 'We've had a wonderful tour since August,' she told Master Rawdon, 'and are enjoying ourselves vastly!' But they ran into trouble in Bournemouth, where *Fumed Oak* and *My Son's My Son* were considered too strong meat for the citizens of that genteel resort, and were banned from the municipal theatre. 'Much as we should have liked Dame Sybil to come to the Pavilion, we could not allow anything that the family man could not bring his children to see and hear,' the manager announced. He failed to persuade Sybil via her agent to substitute two different plays. Lewis observed: 'Bournemouth perhaps is a little old-fashioned, and I suppose these plays are rather too modern. But if the provinces are to be served it is no good catering only for the old ladies.'

Murray came to *Hippolytus*, and complimented Lewis on having staged the most Greek of all his productions of Euripides. Meanwhile, in a book of essays published in Murray's honour, Sybil thanked him for giving her 'a new vision of life' as friend, scholar, and a man of the theatre after her own heart. 'He has the Greek conception of the theatre – a place for the best brains and the most live creative people to meet and express in play form the high emotion, the tremendous laughter, the tears, the crushing grief, the pity that all live creatures know, actors and audience all taking their share in the symbolic expression. How sublime such a conception of the theatre – how far away from the general conception of the theatre now!'

In early December the news broke of Edward VIII's intention to marry an American divorcee, Mrs Wallis Simpson. Although the political and religious establishment opposed the marriage, the public were on the King's side, as was Sybil. 'We are overwhelmed about the King and Mrs Simpson,' she confessed to Master Rawdon. 'One is literally *torn* here as we all love him and want him to be happy, but the feeling is very strong – the 2 divorces have done it! It would have been lovely if he could have wed an American, but then she doesn't seem the right one for the British public….it all seems very cruel and rather awful and a terrible blow at kingship.' Three days later the King decided to abdicate. Sybil and company were playing *My Son's My Son* in Blackpool, and began the performance early so people could hear his announcement. Nora Nicholson recalled: 'Sybil and I went up to the circle after the show, still in our shawls and curl-papers, to listen to the King's farewell broadcast. We were all in tears.'

There were never enough causes for Sybil to support. Along with her friend the poet laureate John Masefield, the architect Edwin Lutyens and others, she backed an idealistic scheme launched by a Committee for Verse and Prose Recitation, to encourage verse-speaking and drama events in pub rooms and community centres on housing estates. Together with the Labour politician Ellen Wilkinson, the Archbishop of Canterbury and several bishops, she was a patron and gave money to a scheme of Holiday Camps for Girls, which catered in equal numbers for girls drawn from public schools and working girls' clubs. And at a social services event in Manchester she suggested, well before Tony Blair was born, that the cure for many of society's ills was 'education, education, education'.

As the situation in Europe deteriorated and the arms race gathered pace, she became more active in the peace movement. A supporter of the Popular Front government in Spain during the Spanish Civil War, which began in June 1936, she joined Emma Goldman, Rebecca West, Fenner Brockway and C E M Joad in establishing the Committee to Aid Homeless Spanish Women and Children. At a meeting of the Spanish Medical Aid Fund she argued that 'we are all being engineered into wars that we do not want'. She also spoke at a memorial meeting for men who had fought and died for the International Brigade in Spain. She was one of the sponsors – Lansbury,

Murray and the Chief Rabbi were others – who through the National Peace Council circulated a document for signature by people in leading positions in the country, suggesting ways of relieving international tensions to avert the increasing menace of war. Natasha and Stephen Spender were among those involved in the fight against fascism. 'We were both totally charmed every time we saw her,' Natasha Spender remembers. 'She was the embodiment of the Christian idea of enthusiasm.'

She was a member of the British Peace Campaign, as was Hewlett Johnson, popularly known as the Red Dean of Canterbury for his left-wing views and his unyielding support for Russia, which had caused him to be watched by MI5 since 1917. In 1935 the Friends of Canterbury Cathedral had commissioned T S Eliot to write a play for that year's festival – *Murder in the Cathedral* – and during it Sybil gave a lecture on drama. She met Johnson there, and she and Lewis became friends with him. Sybil admired his courage: 'I feel no one has done more to make friendship with Russia more true and lasting,' she wrote. 'He has had much criticism – sometimes very harsh criticism – thrown at him, but he has never swerved from what he believed was true and right and worthy of England. I think his courage is most heartening when people seem quite afraid of expressing an opinion for fear they should be tarred with the wrong sort of brush!'

Politics was at the centre of her next play. *Six Men of Dorset* told the celebrated story of the agricultural labourers in Dorset known as the Tolpuddle Martyrs, who in 1835 tried to start a friendly society to protest against wage reductions, and were imprisoned and transported to Australia. The play had been written by a Dorset railwayman to mark the centenary of the event, generally seen as the birth of trade unionism. Miles Malleson had then re-written it and shown it to the Trades Union Congress, which agreed to underwrite the costs of a three-month provincial tour to industrial centres, and to help trade councils, cooperative societies and local branches of the Labour Party to obtain tickets. Its council argued that the provinces were starved of serious theatre, that 'during the present decade the cinema has almost entirely ousted the theatre as a source of amusement'.

Before the tour began Sybil declared: 'This should be the beginning of plays expressing the voice of the workers. I have always liked the provinces, and it gives me a thrill to tour through the country and see how the actual English folk are living. We want to help create a theatre which will represent the real England outside London and attract a public which is characteristically

English.' The London theatre, she said, was 'little more than an extravagant entertainment for those who are comfortably housed, dressed and fed', whereas this play 'means something to everyone who works for his living'.

The play was co-directed by Lewis and Malleson, and for once Sybil had a smaller part than Lewis: while he was the farm labourers' leader George Loveless, she played his wife Betsy. It was, she told Master Rawdon, 'a grand play with good social feeling (say the 2 Labourites!!), and we are most excited. It's rather like the two Macbeths only two very fine and simple people instead, and smelling of English soil.' On the road they visited the industrial towns and other places where unemployment was high. 'The tour involved us in a plethora of political meetings,' Nora Nicholson remembered. 'We were entertained at tea parties, were taken over all manner of factories, and caught the infection of socialism from the Cassons, who were in their element and often spoke at meetings. We belonged to the Left Book Club, and the *Daily Worker* was our daily bread.' The whole venture was meat and drink to Sybil. After a performance in Wolverhampton she observed: 'It was an utter joy to act in a play which says something, and every word of which is documented in history. We were voicing something which these people stood for, and which we too stand for.'

One highlight was in Nottinghamshire, where they chartered a bus and visited striking miners in Harworth. Alex McCrindle, a member of the company, recalled: 'I'll never forget the dust that arose from the floor of the local cinema as the miners and wives greeted Sybil as she rose to speak.' Sybil described the scene to Elizabeth Robins: 'We had a thrilling visit – Lewis and I did duologues from Macbeth to about 2000 miners and wives – and never have we had a more electric alive audience – in a cinema we did this – then we went outside into a piece of waste ground and with them all in a circle round we did a scene from The Six Men of Dorset – and they were a *terrific* audience – never missed a *point*. How I wish we could take the theatre to the workers, but they've not enough money for theatre pieces – and tho' people like us can fix these things, the local provincial theatre managers won't ever help.'

Her eyes were opened by a conversation with one of the strike committee: 'He'd been a miner since leaving school, and he said: "We want this sort of play – it makes you think and enjoy yourself." He said too that they were keen readers on the whole – this particular man had read all Shaw, all Wells, Thackeray, Dickens and Anatole France, as well as heaps of stiffer stuff – philosophy etc. I asked him how on earth he found time, and he said:

"Between shifts – and we mostly keep a book or two with us below." I was so *amazed* – and their keenness for poetry. I'm thrilled myself, and so hopeful somehow, because I should have thought their frightful life would have left them with no inclination for such pursuits.'

They performed in Tolpuddle itself, in front of an audience that included descendants of the martyrs, and Thomas Hardy's widow Florence. Two of the scenes were played under the Martyrs' Tree in the centre of the village, another at the door of the cottage where the men used to meet. In Wolverhampton, according to the local critic, Sybil 'gave a profoundly moving performance. The depth of feeling in her acting sent time and again a thrill through the audience.' The play was also staged at the Arts in Cambridge, from where Sean O'Casey wrote: 'Cambridge is doing well, apart from Tolpuddle, although God be with Sybil in drama.' Although it attracted good houses full of trade unionists, it was criticised for being episodic rather than dramatic, and hopes of a London and even a New York run gradually faded.

During the summer of 1937 Sybil was further involved in discussions about the Spanish Civil War. In the *Manchester Guardian* she and ten others – including Picasso, Matisse, Virginia Woolf and Vanessa Bell – urged people to make common cause with those fighting for democracy in Spain, arguing 'it is our liberty, not merely the liberty of one country, that is being attacked and defended'. She highlighted the plight of the Basque refugees in a letter also signed by Murray, Julian Huxley and Hugh Dalton. She lent her support to the Merseyside Left Theatre, which was attempting to publicise the horrors of the Spanish Civil War. 'I congratulate you on your enterprise,' she wrote to them. 'Do the best plays always, however ambitious the attempt, and something exciting is sure to happen.' When the British Battalion of the International Brigade returned from Spain, she was part of a delegation with Attlee and Ellen Wilkinson that met them at Victoria Station.

She loved to argue her socialist and pacifist beliefs, as the Australian novelist Patrick White found when he met her and Lewis in London: 'The conversation was mostly political,' he reported. 'They are very ardently Left. Sybil works herself into a frenzy....Lewis Casson sat there like a block of granite against which, occasionally, she cannoned, to quiver off again. By the end of the evening I was in a state of complete awe and exhaustion.' With Eileen and Christopher, and persuaded by Maude Royden, Sybil became a member of the recently founded Peace Pledge Union (PPU). Set up by the Reverend Dick Sheppard in 1936 to provide a platform for pacifist, anti-militaristic opinion, it encouraged people to sign a pledge renouncing war. Later she would become one of the PPU's sponsors. She joined the Left Book Club, which brought her the radical, orange-covered books published by Victor Gollancz 'to help in the terribly urgent struggle for world peace and against fascism'.

Following the May coronation of George VI, a Coronation Costume Ball was held, featuring a 'History of Drama from Sophocles to Shaw', a parade led by Sybil as Tragedy, Irene Vanbrugh as Comedy, Lewis as Garrick, and Ann as Saint Joan. Recalling their childhood arguments about kingship, Sybil wrote a quirky, somewhat incoherent letter to Russell, making it clear she was quite comfortable being a socialist and a royalist simultaneously. 'A grand Visible Sign of Democracy – Kingship – isn't it – He who serves His people and He who truly serves – rules – and don't ask me to explain – do you see what I mean? – The King is the Servant and the Servant is the King and all the Lovely ceremonies mean that don't they? So Hurrah for King and People and Down with the – what shall we Down? No, we needn't – it's Coronation week – let's make a new form where we don't Down people.'

She now had a brief run at the St James' in an American play, *Yes, My Darling Daughter*, written by Mark Reed and directed by Alfred de Liagre Jnr. This had been a success on Broadway, but Rodney Ackland anglicised it to no great effect. Sybil played a former suffragette now married to a banker, whose daughter (Jessica Tandy) wishes to have a premature honeymoon with her young man (Alec Clunes). The critics thought it mediocre, and Sybil, according to the *Manchester Guardian*, seemed to have caught her bad habits again, 'waving her hands about freely, quick to excitement, quick to a calm which is so natural as to be almost undramatic'. The play ran for just 59 performances. Once again Sybil's desire to keep working had affected her judgement.

She was approached by the American agency J B Pinker to revive *Jane Clegg*: 'It's a wonderful play – I'd love to do it,' she replied, but didn't. She was down in the intimate Barn Theatre at Ellen Terry's house in Smallhythe in July, to play scenes from the history plays with Ann, Lewis, William Devlin, Edith Evans and Violet Vanbrugh. Hearing Annie Horniman was unwell, she wrote to her the next day, underlining the pressures on her of work and family: 'Now I am home from such a long provincial tour – since last August – I would *so* like to see you if I might come and call. I hear you have been very ill in the winter, and I feel so neglectful and no friend at all to have known nothing of this – do forgive – I get my life so tied up with a now-vast family, and them and work make me a bit selfish, I fear. Do let me come.' She made the visit to Shere in Surrey, but in August Annie Horniman died.

Then came another sadness. Sybil had recently lent her support, together with that of Olivier, Gielgud, Edith Evans and others, to an appeal to fund an extension of Sadlers' Wells and to clear the debt of both the Wells and the Vic, and had spoken along with Guthrie at a fund-raising supper at the Dorchester. In November Lilian Baylis died suddenly of a heart attack. Not only had she been a key figure in Sybil's career, she had also become a close friend. Sybil at once wrote to Guthrie, now the Old Vic's director of drama: 'I feel I must write to you because I know how you will be feeling Lilian's death. I saw it in the paper coming here from Liverpool today and I feel heartbroken. I loved her so and in very difficult years…because of the struggle and the war-life then. My thoughts went straight to you in gratitude, that you have been the one helper who has fulfilled somehow her high hopes of the Vic….She was great and really simple and really good – I know you will feel it. God bless her, she was happy this last year, wasn't she, you understood her so wonderfully.'

She and Lewis attended a crowded requiem mass at St Agnes Church in Kennington. 'We were all there to say thank you for a free spirit,' she said. They also were present at the cremation at Golders Green cemetery in north London, for close friends only, and at the memorial service at St Martin-in-the-Fields. She and Russell put together a biography of their mentor, 'a humble tribute to the memory of the most courageous woman that was ever associated with the theatre'. It's a lively and vividly personal account of what Sybil called the 'happy, thrilling, adventuring work at the Old Vic' with this remarkable woman, who had helped to lay the foundation for both her and Russell's careers. In *Vic-Wells: The Work of Lilian Baylis*, a book of tributes edited by Harcourt Williams, she wrote of her influence: 'No one came near that white hot zeal without partaking of her element; none of us who worked with her, and later have gone into management ourselves, could make of our companies or theatres just a commercial concern.'

That winter, in response to a request from the LNU for her and Lewis to stage another matinee, she returned to Greek tragedy. 'We do want to help, it being the one way to teach folk what the LNU really means,' she wrote to Murray. 'May we do The Trojan Women? It would be interesting, as it was the performance at the beginning of the L of N, and studying it again freshly it seems to me much more the symbol – the real play to do. We want Ann to play Cassandra – she is studying her very hard and I think should give something really imaginative.' Having gained Murray's permission, she wrote: 'I think we should do it in the "old way", but – we hope – with added experience and more knowledge of "speech"….Oh! how glorious a play it is, I've been working on it this morning.' Her search for perfection is evident in a further letter: 'I *always* feel disappointed – I *never* seem to get what I'd imagined – in my own performances, that is – but I go on working – I do always some Greek play daily. Too big the plays are to get satisfaction in performance except by everlasting experiment.'

The matinee took place at the Adelphi in early December. 'I have made it a condition that the price of the seats should not be too high,' Sybil told Murray. 'I would rather, if necessary, do an additional matinee for the same cause. Lewis feels just the same.' Lewis was again the Messenger, with Ann as Cassandra, William Devlin as Menelaus, and Margaret Rawlings playing Helen. Sybil's Hecuba seemed as powerful as ever: *The Times* noted that 'the intensity and passionate conviction of her performance, particularly in its magnificent conclusion, remains the fire and substance of the present production'. Ann too made a strong impression, causing one critic to assert: 'Greek tragedy is in her bones.'

'That was a magnificent performance,' Murray told Lewis the next day. 'I really should become sentimental if I tried to tell you how much I owe to you and Sybil for your help in interpreting Euripides to the modern world during these 30 years. And perhaps Ann will carry on the tradition after we are gone? Her Cassandra was lovely, and Sybil's vitality and tragic power carried the thing through in a wonderful way. Some of the LNU's hard-boiled money-raisers seemed quite astonished to find that they had been moved and interested when they had only expected to be bored.' Lewis replied: 'Sybil and I were both thrilled that you were pleased. I do think Ann shows signs of carrying on what we have learned from you and William Poel and Barker. What a treat it always is to get back to the things that are too big ever to accomplish – the more one works with them, the further one can see the heights and depths one hasn't touched.'

It was a happy return for Sybil to the drama she loved best. She had spent much of the decade searching for a new play that would provide her with a role to really challenge her. Before the next year was out she would find one.

24

J B Priestley to Emlyn Williams

1938–1939

'She just turns on the Hecuba tap, and there you are!'
James Agate on Sybil as Volumnia in Coriolanus

As she passed her fifty-fifth birthday Sybil continued to hurtle at life non-stop. She was engaged to appear on Broadway in J B Priestley's new play *Time and the Conways*. Priestley was a good friend, who greatly admired Sybil and Lewis, and wrote of their contrasting personalities: 'Her natural tendency was towards expansion, enlargement, amplification, while he tended towards a rather grim contraction (though at heart amiable and generous-minded), a determined and highly concentrated dimunition.'

Sybil liked Priestley's plays, but she was not keen to go to New York. However, Lewis persuaded her it would be fun, and would bring in good money. It seemed likely he would follow her in another Priestley play, *I Have Been Here Before*, in which he was appearing in London. But that plan fell through, so Christmas Eve found Sybil sailing across the Atlantic with the company, desperately homesick and depressed, having missed celebrating her and Lewis' wedding anniversary. 'We sang carols and cried buckets,' she recalled. Once in New York, however, she dutifully talked up the play, relating it to the increasingly tense political situation in Europe: 'There is something big in *Time and the Conways*, bigger than the story it appears to tell about one English family,' she explained. 'My part is symbolic of the world as it is now – of Europe so torn and troubled and the Empire in disarray. It's about how we all muddle along, clinging desperately to things that have been, just wanting to keep things because we've always had them.'

There was a lot of quality competition this season on Broadway, including Thornton Wilder's *Our Town*, Steinbeck's *Of Mice and Men*, *Amphitryon 38* by Jean Giraudoux, and Clifford Odets' *Golden Boy*. Priestley had already achieved success with several plays in London, including *Dangerous Corner*, in which he played around with the time sequence, repeating one act twice, with different consequences to the middle-class family involved. *Time and the Conways* was a similar piece. The first act was set during a family birthday party in 1919, the second revealed the characters' loss of innocence twenty years later, and the third, a continuation of the post-war party, allowed the audience to observe them through the prism of later events. It had recently had a success in the West End, although it was criticised by some for its pessimism. In New York it opened at the Ritz in the first week of 1938, directed like the London production by Irene Hentschel, with Priestley present at rehearsals.

Sybil played the demanding matriarch of the family, described by Priestley as 'charming, easy and vivacious' and a 'full-blown Edwardian type'. She is also the root cause of much of her children's later unhappiness. Sybil received appreciative notices, as did Jessica Tandy as one of her daughters, but the play failed to repeat the success it enjoyed in London: the critics felt the family was dull, and that Priestley, whose novels were much liked, had 'written down' for the stage. Priestley, who thought Sybil's performance 'wonderful', attacked the critics for killing off his play, which closed after just a month. During the run Sybil broke her wrist, slipping on the ice while staying with friends. Characteristically she refused to miss a performance, but the resulting lump remained for the rest of her life.

When the play moved to Boston she visited Christopher in hospital: while playing there in *Murder in the Cathedral* he had had to have his appendix out. 'We've talked and dozed and been quiet and all is well,' Sybil told Mary Crawley, after spending a day with him. 'I found him going along beautifully.' Soon after this Christopher was recruited by Micheál MacLíammóir, who was now running the fashionable Gate in Dublin with his partner Hilton Edwards. Christopher was hired to play one of the twin brothers in *The Comedy of Errors*, the suicidal son in Eugene O'Neill's *Mourning Becomes Electra*, and other leading younger roles.

MacLíammóir, a Londoner whose real name was Alfred Wilmore, had re-invented himself as a flamboyant Irishman, sporting a black toupee and full make-up in public. He recalled Christopher's appearance at his audition, 'in fly-away tweeds and a butcher-blue shirt that made his eyes almost as dazzling as his mother's, and with an eager boisterousness of manner that gave charm and quality to everything he did'. Once Christopher arrived in

Ireland, complete with harp and a repertoire of Irish songs, the *Irish Times* stated that 'he might pass for an Irish boy'. Sybil told Elizabeth Casson: 'Kiff went to Ireland yesterday for several months in great spirits.' But his stay there was to be longer than she imagined: after just a week he announced he wanted to make Ireland his home.

After returning on the *Queen Mary* Sybil told Elizabeth: 'It is glorious to be home from the US! No place like England!' Of the plays she had seen on Broadway, she commended particularly *Golden Boy* and *Our Town*. Yet her trip had highlighted for her the running sore of the censors in the English theatre. 'They are a worry and a nuisance and a bore,' she argued. 'In America there is no censorship except the police censorship; and the plays, in consequence, are vital and provocative of thought. They discuss everything that the times demand, but from a specialised, individual point of view. The problems of the age are given an airing, and so escape the danger of being pored over in private.'

She and Lewis took a few days' holiday in Wales, where they were now familiar figures, their voices often heard from below the house as they went through their lines on the terrace at Bron-y-Garth. The actor Sam Beazley remembers them coming one day by boat into the harbour at Portmadoc, with Sybil in the prow. 'She said "I've come! By boat!", as if she was Iphigenia coming to Aulis. We all clapped.' After this break she returned to London and her beloved Old Vic, where she was to play Volumnia in *Coriolanus*, with Olivier in the title-role.

It was a strong part that many people, including Agate and Herbert Farjeon, had been begging her to tackle. Lewis was invited to direct, but according to Sybil only agreed to do so on the understanding that Olivier obeyed him. 'His orders were that Larry was to get rid of all of his experimental ideas and tricks, and act Coriolanus in a natural, straightforward way, with an emphasis on the text.' It was thirteen years since Lewis and Sybil had given Olivier his first break. Sybil, as his surrogate mother, and godmother to his son Tarquin, had made her views known about his decision to leave his wife Jill Esmond for Vivien Leigh. 'I gave him hell,' she recalled. 'I was furious. I was brought up in the Church, as he was, and I hate divorce. Once you've given yourself to someone, if things go wrong, you've just got to lump it.' But she had remained close to Olivier, who was now in his second season at the Old Vic and, despite some hostile criticism, showing an increasing mastery of Shakespeare.

According to Sybil, Olivier and Lewis got on well during rehearsals, during which Lewis tried to curb some of his extravagant technical effects: 'Of course they fought – naturally, because they were both so violent. But they only argued like fun.' Lewis's obsession with the sound of the verse was not to the taste of younger actors: a few months later he annoyed Guinness by telling him that his Hamlet was wrong because he had failed to 'sing' his lines. 'He believed passionately in what he called "the tune",' Guinness remembered. 'I could only believe in what I considered credible.' With Coriolanus, whatever their disputes, Lewis certainly helped Olivier to increase the depth and resonance of his voice.

Patricia Young, playing one of Volumnia's attendants, recalled that, with the arrival of Sybil and Lewis, 'something of the Baylis spirit seemed to have seeped back into the theatre'. She found Sybil friendly, despite her regal manner. 'She never seemed to walk anywhere – she swept; and her voice, even when asking if one would mind fetching her a cup of tea, had a royal ring....Holding court in the stalls bar at lunch-time with her family and friends draped around her, she would always have a very sharp eye for all that was going on at the other tables.' She was full of motherly concern for anyone whom she noticed to be off-colour, advising them to eat more to build up their strength, or to get an early night. One day, finding a student crouched in a corner, she stopped the rehearsal with a dramatic gesture: 'Lewis dear, do you mind if I send this poor child home? She's got a raging temperature and should be in bed.'

Coriolanus was then rarely performed; it had not been staged at the Old Vic since the 1923–24 season. Many considered it the dullest of Shakespeare's Roman plays, with a hero notable mainly for his snobbery, pride and contempt for the people. But Olivier by general consent played the part with magnificent vitality. Sybil thought he was superb. 'One could feel his perplexity, his uncertainty as to whether he was doing the right thing,' she recalled. 'There was real tragedy in his performance.' She herself was also praised for her interpretation of what one critic called 'that inhuman old harridan', even bringing a certain humour to a essentially humourless part. Audrey Williamson wrote: 'Both she and Olivier made their scenes together an exciting match of brain, heart and meticulously timed comedy.' The *Observer* felt she infused the character with 'her own warmth of heart and abundant vitality'; but according to Agate, it was a performance of two halves: 'In the first half she tries to establish, and indeed does establish, a cheerful relationship with the audience. This is delightful, but it is not quite Volumnia. But Dame Sybil has no difficulty with the second half of the piece. Wallowing in grief and trailing trains of crape is something this gracious actress knows all about. She just turns on the Hecuba tap, and there you are!'

The play seemed suddenly topical, with Hitler having just marched into Austria, and Britain's prime minister Neville Chamberlain pledging to defend France and Belgium against unprovoked aggression. 'Europe is so awful we can hardly bear thinking of it,' Sybil told Mary Crawley. 'But it's got to be done – the thinking, I mean – and there is no way to peace but the Chamberlain way – of that many of us are convinced.' Lewis had meanwhile landed another plum Shakespearean job. 'He has got a huge production for Ivor Novello,' Sybil told Elizabeth Casson. 'Henry V at Drury Lane – terrific!! He's in a blue funk, but it's just what he can do.'

On the eve of Shakespeare's birthday she and Lewis attended an event which seemed to offer fresh hope of a National Theatre being established. Both had been long-time supporters of the idea, and Lewis had recently become a member of the Shakespeare Memorial National Theatre committee, which also included Shaw, Barrie and Playfair. A site in South Kensington had been bought, and the country's leading architect Edwin Lutyens commissioned to design the building. At the handing-over ceremony, the deeds were passed to Shaw, who in his speech berated the English people for not wanting a National Theatre: 'They have got a British Museum, a National Gallery, a Westminster Abbey, and they never wanted any of them. But once these things stand…they are quite proud of them, and feel that the place would be incomplete without them.' The actors were invited to donate money for seats to be named after their illustrious predecessors. Martin Harvey donated one to Irving, while Sybil did the same for Sarah Siddons. She also made an emotional appeal for gifts of £100 units to help finance the scheme.

With John and Mary married, Christopher in Ireland, and Ann self-supporting, Sybil and Lewis decided to give up the house in Oakley Street. They moved to 98 Swan Court, a compact, two-bedroom flat on the sixth floor of an enormous barrack-like block in Manor Street in Chelsea. Sybil had watched it being built, and decided it looked like a monastery – 'and I've always wanted to live in a monastery'. Since her cooking skills remained minimal, she and Lewis took most of their meals in the restaurant on the ground floor. It meant a simpler lifestyle, without any staff, but one that they both found congenial. 'Sybil returns from Bron-y-Garth on Sunday,' Lewis wrote to his sister. 'I think we shall like this flat very much.'

They had generously given up their Oakley Street house to Russell and Rosemary, who now had five children, two boys and three girls. The younger boy, Dickon Thorndike, recalls Sybil's impact on their household: 'My abiding memory is of a whirlwind of joy and enthusiasm whenever she visited us. The volume of everyone talking became so loud, we all acquired the gift of projecting our voices.' Russell, having considerable success as a writer, was working on a series of prequels of *Dr Syn*. But his love of fantasy was greater than his ability to cope with reality. 'He liked nothing better than being in a pub surrounded by locals telling rapscallion stories, about the theatre or his own life,' his son Daniel remembers. 'They all believed him because he was such a good actor.' But his marriage was in poor shape, with he and Rosemary constantly quarrelling. 'Rosemary was difficult, while Russell was hopeless financially, and a bit of a womaniser,' Phyllis Walshaw says. Both of them had a drink problem, which once led Russell to attack his wife with the handle of a bayonet. The drink affected his career: he was seen as unreliable, and his parts dwindled both in number and importance. Having got into financial difficulties, the family were forever moving house, often helped by Sybil and Lewis: when Russell was due to tour with Ben Greet to America and the family were penniless, they had found them a cottage in Devon.

Sybil remained devoted to her younger brother, but his errant ways caused her immense pain and anxiety. 'I am most unhappy about poor old Russell,' she confessed to Elizabeth Casson. 'I feel so responsible to Mother and Father for him somehow!' Her sister-in-law, a psychiatrist specialising in psychological medicine, had founded and was running Dorset House on the Clifton Downs in Bristol, a residential clinic where she had developed a school of occupational therapy catering especially for women. Sybil wondered if she might take in Russell's fourteen-year-old daughter Jill for two weeks, as an unofficial nurse. 'She's had scenes at home which (tho' she's a very wise girl and has a sense of humour about Russell and Rosemary's fearful quarrels – and the drink!!) have tried her – made her too responsible…I'd feel so happy if I could get her with you – she won't be any good in the theatre, she's too good, if I make myself clear!!!…If you could get her to talk of home difficulties it might be a help – she is so loyal and shuts up everything inside, but Rosemary thinks it would help to talk to an outsider. She says she wishes you had a man's place; we don't know what to do about Russell.'

In the summer she made two brief appearances at the opposite ends of the theatrical spectrum. In May she took part in the grand Henry Irving Centenary matinee at the Lyceum, in which a starry gathering of the profession's leading lights appeared in extracts from his most famous productions, with Sybil leading the company in a grand finale. In July she was again involved in the annual event at Smallhythe. In a programme which included scenes from *Timon of Athens* featuring Ernest Milton, and *Othello* with Donald Wolfit, she and Margaretta Scott performed a scene from *Coriolanus*. She then, after a year's absence, returned to the West End, having at last been offered a role in a play of substance and originality, her first since *Saint Joan*.

Emlyn Williams, now 32, had achieved success three years previously with *Night Must Fall*, widely acclaimed as the best intellectual thriller to date. In writing his new play, *The Corn is Green*, it was of Sybil he thought of first. Based on his own schooldays and his teacher Sarah Grace Cooke at Holywell County School, the play tells the story of a crusading Englishwoman, Miss Moffat, who at the end of the nineteenth century sets up a school in a remote village in North Wales, discovers a potential genius in one of the pit boys, and helps him to win a scholarship to Oxford. There were hints in the story of *Jude the Obscure*, without the grim pessimism of Hardy's novel. Williams had decided to direct, and when Marius Goring, his original choice to play the fifteen-year-old pit boy Morgan Evans, was unavailable and no one else could be found, he agreed to play the part himself.

His description of Miss Moffat might also have been of Sybil: she was 'a healthy Englishwoman with an honest face, clear beautiful eyes, and unbounded vitality, which is prevented from tiring the spectator by its capacity for sudden silences and for listening. Her most prominent characteristic is her complete unsentimentality.' Not surprisingly, Sybil seemed to mesh with the part straight away. 'She was absolutely superb at the first reading,' Williams recalled. 'She didn't really need to put any more colour into the part at all, but, being Sybil, she wouldn't have considered she was earning her salary if she hadn't worked all-out at it.' Rehearsals went with 'terrifying smoothness', Sybil proving an ideal support. 'She got more like Miss Cooke every day, and was everything a nervous actor-author-director could have wished for – eager, friendly, and through all her enthusiasm and understanding of the play, never without one critical eye cocked at every detail.' A meeting during rehearsals with Miss Cooke, who lent Sybil young Emlyn's school exercise books, helped her to develop the character of the crusading teacher.

They were on the road for five weeks, before opening at the Duchess in

September. The play was an instant hit with both critics and public, who found it moving, amusing and authentic. It had, Barker wrote to the author, 'that great dramatic virtue of looking facts in the face'. Alan Dent wrote that 'both the chief players have an unusual range of emotion, and the skill and subtlety of their interplaying are fascinating to watch', while *The Times* noted that 'Miss Thorndike, while preserving Miss Moffat's intelligent common sense, allows her emotion and her humour to appear through it in a way that makes the schoolmistress at once firm and loveable'.

The play seemed set for a long run, but a week after the opening came the Munich crisis, bringing Europe to the brink of war. Fears had become acute with Hitler's demands over Czechoslovakia: trenches were dug in the parks, barrage balloons appeared in the sky, cellars and basements were requisitioned for air-raid shelters, and the government announced plans to evacuate two million people from London. At the Duchess the audiences were thin, or preoccupied. The actors gathered nightly in Sybil's dressing-room, listening anxiously to her radio. Finally the news arrived that Chamberlain was to fly to Munich to meet Hitler; then that he had returned promising 'peace for our time'. Like many others, she rejoiced, believing war had been averted. 'We've got a long way to go yet on the road to peace, but Chamberlain did a big thing in going to Hitler, and it's the beginning we hope of conference instead of killing.' For pacifists this inglorious peace, later seen as appeasement, was infinitely better than war.

Munich was a factor in the failure of Michel Saint-Denis' production of Bulgakov's *The White Guard*, part of the director's attempt to set up a repertory company at the Phoenix. With Gielgud, Edith Evans and others, Sybil wrote to *The Times* trying to drum up support for the play. Meanwhile *The Corn is Green* continued a run that was to last nearly a year and almost 400 performances. Two years later Ethel Barrymore would play the part on Broadway. Sybil was of course not content simply to be Miss Moffat eight times a week, so she took part in her daughter Ann's one-act piece *The Crooked Circle*, staged with four other short plays at the Vaudeville.

She meanwhile kept her hand in with radio. In a production by Barbara Burnham of a shortened version of *The Winter's Tale*, she acted with Lewis alongside Gwen Ffrangcon-Davies as Hermoine and Miles Malleson as Autolycus. *The Times* commented: 'Mr Lewis Casson raged superbly and wickedly as Leontes, and Dame Sybil Thorndike had a part after her own stout heart in Paulina, defender of the innocent queen and her babe, a pleading part, with fine speeches, finely delivered, that would have melted the heart of any husband but that of the jealous Leontes.' She was also in a broadcast of Murray's new translation of Aeschylus' *The Persians*, but was criticised by the *Manchester Guardian*: 'One found that without the help of either expression or gesture her voice was much too much keyed in the same tone, too attached to the same rhythm, and too little expressive because of its recurring and ultimately as it seemed almost automatic up and down intonation.'

Earlier, dissatisfied with the way Wendy Hiller was playing Joan at Malvern, Shaw had asked if she might be available for the forthcoming radio broadcast of *Saint Joan*. She was still his favourite interpreter of the part, despite it having since been played by Elisabeth Bergner and Ludmilla Pitoëff: 'Joan is always the impetuous, masterful girl soldier: even her despair is an angry despair,' he explained to the writer Thea Holme. 'She has also the ecstasy of the saint; but the blubberings of Bergner and Pitoëff are all wrong. Sybil was right.'

In a moment of self-analysis Sybil once remarked: 'I'm naturally happy, and when anything goes wrong I sometimes twist it so that I am happy.' Her optimism made her see the best in everything and everyone. 'Anything she didn't quite approve of she would sweep under the carpet, and concentrate entirely on the good,' her niece Donnie says. Such unrelenting cheerfulness could be endearing, but also irritating, as her niece Phyllis remembers: 'I had my first curry with her, and it was so hot, we had sweat running down our faces. She said: "Isn't it lovely, isn't it the *best* food you've ever had!" That's how it always was. Every party was always the best you ever had, and sometimes we used to think: "Why did she say that? It was a *horrible* party."' She also invariably looked for some saving quality in a person who seemed to have little to recommend them. She once described a cousin as 'the best person in the whole world at making crochet bags'; of another she said: 'I know he's awful, but he's absolutely brilliant at tying parcels.'

This desire to find good in people was also the basis for her interest in prison reform, sparked by her friendship with Ethel Cunliffe when she first came to London. It was reflected in the foreword she now wrote to Lady Carter's book *A Living Soul in Holloway*, in which she made clear her support for those who believed that 'the prisons exist not simply for punishment, but primarily for saving or helping a human soul – an unfortunate man or woman'. Having visited a women's prison twenty years before, she was now involved in a concert there. She also, with Nancy Astor, George Lansbury and

Ernest Bevin, wrote to the *Manchester Guardian*, arguing for the abolition of the 'inhumane and purely repressive' death penalty.

She and Lewis spent Christmas at Bron-y-Garth, but there she began to feel unwell. She returned to London and *The Corn is Green*, trying to ignore the discomfort. During a matinee Emlyn Williams told her she was a bit slow in the last scene, so she promised to quicken it up for the evening performance. Then she collapsed in her dressing-room. A doctor was called, who diagnosed appendicitis, and insisted she be operated on immediately. Sybil, for whom illness was almost a moral defect, refused to go to hospital, arguing furiously that she must complete the week's performances. Told she would be dead if she did, she asked for Lewis to be sent for, hoping he would back her up. Instead he made her see sense, and the operation, during which her appendix burst, was performed just in time. Her friend Athene Seyler took over her part in her absence.

Over the next three weeks, while convalescing in a nursing home, bulletins appeared in *The Times*, charting her recovery. She told the Crawleys: 'I've never been ill before so it's been a new experience and I don't want it again.' To Elizabeth Casson she wrote: 'I'm getting on, but the doctor won't let me leave here 'til the wound has stopped discharging, and I suppose he's right. Anyway I feel tons better.' Christopher had come over from Dublin for a day: 'Oh! how he cheered me up – he sang and harped to all of us for hours – the patients all kept their doors open, and the nurses most of them. I think they were thrilled to hear Irish Gaelic.' She looked forward to convalescing at Bron-y-Garth: 'No place is so dear and so beautiful to me, I suppose because it's mixed up with Lewis and walks and the glorious smells there.'

While she was convalescing Lewis was engaged to direct an Old Vic company on a European tour. On seeing Sybil off to Wales he wrote: 'When I come back we'll be together again, and all this time will be like a dream as so many of our partings have become, for in spite of the separations we *seem* to have been together almost always, don't we? How lovely this evening was! The dinner and the quiet and the reading, and just being together. I don't think we've ever been closer. I do love you so....Think of me when you get to Bron-y-Garth. I'll be there with you. I shall think of you always. I love you I love you. Lewis.' Esmé Church, director of the Old Vic's School of Acting and co-director of the tour, told Sybil: 'Don't you worry about him, I'll be his second wife.' Lewis later reported: 'I did not fall on her bosom.' Since she was a lesbian, she probably saw her task as to be sure he didn't fall on anyone else's.

Soon Sybil was well enough to go with a nurse to Wales, where the scenery did much to further her recovery. 'It's so lovely here, and I'm having some very good long walks,' she told Elizabeth 'We went up to Pen-y-Las by the old car today, and walked along the Snowdon path – real huge black clouds on the summit – all very forbidding – but the valleys below were in vivid sunshine. How glorious it all is. The Treath heals me, it's so beautiful. I had a little heart bother at first – but that's gone now and I'm healed up, but I do go carefully.' To Elizabeth Robins she was more candid, writing: 'I was very ill, and nearly went altogether, but it was a very interesting experience, and I'm *grand* now.'

On her return to London she stayed in Covent Garden with her old friends May Whitty and Ben Webster. After ten weeks she returned to *The Corn is Green* – but on the strict condition that she rested from 4.30 to 6.30. Soon after she had supper with Micheál Maclíammóir and Hilton Edwards. The encounter later brought from Maclíammóir a characteristically florid and poetic tribute to her talents. 'Essentially English, she is yet nationless; essentially of her period, she is timeless; a classic creature, golden and brave as a lioness, with a face to reflect every mood of human experience, and a voice poured into her throat by the winds of heaven….No one could describe Sybil Thorndike: you might as well try to describe the Parthenon. She, like it, radiates a sense of power, of sanity and poise, a kind of golden reassurance.'

The previous year she had made her BBC television debut, on a programme called *Picture Page*, made at the studios in Alexandra Palace in north London. Now in April she made her first appearance in a television drama. The BBC had started regular broadcasts from Alexandra Palace in 1936, but there were still only some twenty thousand sets in the nation's homes. Plays, under the heading 'Theatre Parade', often consisted of transmissions direct from the theatre. Other productions were performed live in the studios, where the cast often had to suffer cramped conditions, very odd make-up, and only short rehearsals. The first play to be broadcast was Pirandello's *Henry IV*; other early productions included *Journey's End*, *Hassan* and *Cyrano de Bergerac*.

Sun Up was a melodrama by the American Lula Vollmer, a pioneer of the American folk play. In a letter suggesting the play to Sybil, programme organiser Cecil Madden wrote: 'I have always looked upon it as one of the great masterpieces of the theatre.' The story concerned a pipe-smoking widow living in a cabin in the mountains of North Carolina in 1917, who discovers that the deserter she has taken pity on is the son of the man who killed her husband. The production featured Finlay Currie, André Morell and

Anthony Quayle, and was directed by George More O'Ferrall, the BBC's first television drama producer. For the two live transmissions Sybil was paid 60 guineas. It seemed an odd role for her to undertake, but *The Times* noted 'the exquisite pathos of her performance', and judged that it was that 'and the sincerity of the whole production which lifted it out of the common rut of television plays'.

Always keen to support political theatre, she took part in a BBC documentary about the People's Theatre in Newcastle, founded by the British Socialist Party. She was interested in the left-leaning Unity Theatre, which specialised in revolutionary dramas, with the aim of 'rebelling against the escapism and false ideology of the conventional theatre'. Other Unity members included Shaw, H G Wells, Sean O'Casey, Paul Robeson and Michael Redgrave. After seeing Robeson in *Plant in the Sun*, Sybil said she saw 'as the greatest hope for the stage in this country the rise of Unity Theatre, realising that the real art of the theatre always was, and always must be, bound up with the life of the people'. In August she wrote an article on theatre in the first issue of its *New Theatre* magazine, and a foreword to the new *Unity Handbook*, in which she argued that it was 'the most exciting movement in the theatre of our day'.

Meanwhile she expressed her delight with Ann's development. 'She is such a grand worker and is making strides with singing too and is a most independent, nice, good-thinking girl,' she told Elizabeth Robins. 'She has her own flat and runs her life most satisfactorily.' Other members of the wider Thorndike family were also being drawn to the theatre, and Sybil sometimes used her connections to their advantage. She was instrumental in getting Daniel Thorndike his first job. He had always wanted to be an actor, an ambition Russell had encouraged. He had played Hamlet and Richard II at King's School, Canterbury, and was now a student at Eileen's Embassy School. Sybil secured him an audition at the Old Vic, where he was taken on as Paris' page in a production of *Romeo and Juliet*.

As the threat of war grew, her offstage activities became more political. She was involved with leading church figures in an appeal for collections to be made in churches, to send a ship of food as a New Year's gift to the Spanish people hit by the Civil War. She and Lewis joined the Actors' Refugee Committee – other members included Llewellyn Rees, Godfrey Tearle, Leon M Lion and Felix Aylmer – which was appealing for funds to enable visas to be granted to seven German actors in Czechoslovakia, two of them Jewish, 'who are in imminent danger of being extradited to Germany, where the concentration camp and probable death await them'. She also, with Murray, Priestley, Julian Huxley and many others, actively supported the newly created Free German League of Culture, which aimed to preserve the culture of Goethe, Dürer and Beethoven 'while countering Nazi propaganda abroad'.

She was fierce in her opposition to the war: May Whitty recalled a lunch with her, Edith Evans and Gwen Ffrangcon-Davies, at which they 'talked treason loudly...and denounced National Service and vowed we would not take oaths to serve King and Country'. She reaffirmed her stance to the Crawleys in June: 'Don't let's talk of European affairs, I am *completely* pacifist – the time has come to say, To hell with war – let's be on the side of something better – some new and better way.' What that way was, beyond carrying on talking, she could not explain. Meanwhile, under the Foster Parents Scheme for Spanish Children, she and Lewis registered as temporary foster-parents of a girl called Elena, so enabling her to be moved out of a refugee camp in Spain and into a safe house. Sybil wrote to the *Manchester Guardian* with a plea for donations to help save more children.

The Corn is Green continued to draw the crowds through the summer. At the end of August war seemed imminent, and the company again gathered nightly around Sybil's radio. Audiences dwindled, and by Friday 1 September closure seemed inevitable. Emlyn Williams recalled: 'I went in front of the curtain before the play to ask the handful of people there to draw up to the footlights and we'd do our best to make them forget about Poland.' He did the same the next day. On the Sunday war was declared, all theatres and other places of entertainment were ordered to be closed and, like the rest of the profession, Sybil and Lewis found themselves out of a job.

25

A Pacifist at War

1939–1940

'Nothing can justify this slaughter of boys – of whatever nation'
Letter from Sybil to Gwen Ffrangcon-Davies

The outbreak of the Second World War created a crisis of conscience
for pacifists. Many disavowed their principles in the face of the evils
of Nazism. Others, such as Hewlett Johnson, only dropped their opposition
to the war when the Soviet Union joined the Allies. But like many other
Christian pacifists, Sybil refused to change her beliefs. On the other hand,
having talked to Lansbury, who believed it would be better to be occupied
than to fight, she realised she could not take such an extreme position. So
while she continued to oppose the war, in the company of public figures such
as Vera Brittain, the Bishop of Birmingham and the Methodist preacher
Donald Soper, she also helped to maintain civilian morale by doing what she
did best, putting her formidable energies into working in the theatre.

The men in her family were divided in their attitude to the war. John, who
believed in fighting it, was already with the navy in the North Sea. Mary's
husband William Devlin volunteered for the Wiltshire Yeomanry regiment.
As for Lewis, now 64, he would have volunteered immediately if he hadn't
been too old for active service. Instead he joined the motor transport section
of the Air Raid Precautions (ARP) services in Chelsea, but found little work
to do. In October Sybil, on tour, wrote from Aberdeen to his sister Elizabeth:
'All's well at home – Lewis is splendid the way he goes on with this boring
job of ARP – such a waste.' Christopher, who had joined the Peace Pledge
Union in 1931, had remained a convinced pacifist ever since then, though once
the war began he joined the Fire Brigade and Ambulance Service in Dublin
as a non-combatant. Sybil herself was not always rational in her arguments:

Frith Banbury, who had registered as a conscientious objector after Munich, remembers her telling him: 'John is really a conscientious objector too, except he's in the navy.'

A few days after the declaration of war, pressure mounted for the decision to close the theatres to be reconsidered. The government yielded, recognising that people needed entertainment in what quickly became known as 'the phoney war'. Initially only matinees were allowed, but by October the times were more normal. Acting was made 'a reserved occupation', which meant actors could carry on in the theatre or cinema as long as there was 'a reasonable demand' for their services. Stars and key performers could have their call-up deferred, and special cases were considered.

Sybil had been appointed to the committee of the Entertainments National Service Association (ENSA), which Basil Dean had set up to provide entertainment for the armed services. Meetings were held at ENSA headquarters in the Theatre Royal, Drury Lane, where the committee under the chairmanship of Seymour Hicks – Thomas Beecham, St John Ervine, Marie Tempest and Jack Buchanan were also members – allocated the entertainments. Sybil volunteered to help look after the Hospitals Entertainments section with Lilian Braithwaite. 'Lil Braithwaite and I are working fearfully hard at ENSA as the hospital work has grown hugely (and sadly),' she told Gwen Ffrangcon-Davies, who was working in South Africa. 'We are sending out touring parties all over the place.' Here her other talent came into play, as Basil Dean recalled: 'Whenever she was in London her keen musical appreciation was invaluable in the selection of new talent for the hospital parties.'

Money was now a problem, as Sybil admitted to Elizabeth Casson: 'Life is so difficult now that Eileen is only earning half salary – and mine is down very considerably – and Lewis isn't earning at all – his services are free.' Eileen was teaching and directing plays at the Sadler's Wells School, which was three schools joined together. She had recently visited and fallen in love with America, and was considering moving there with her children to live when war broke out, and she had to return. Sybil remained very fond of her younger sister. 'I think she's such a lovely person – inside of her – and has made a splendid thing of her life and her children and all the boys and girls she teaches,' she told the Crawleys.

Meanwhile she continued to protest against the war. 'Politics are more and more exciting – we all go to meetings and get very worked up!' she wrote to Gwen Ffrangcon-Davies. She spoke at a meeting at Central Hall in London, addressed also by Vera Brittain: the plan had been to march afterwards to Buckingham Palace, but the police prevented it. She was now a sponsor of the Peace Pledge Union, which was attacked in the press for being an underground political force that endangered the life of the nation: Rebecca West referred to it as 'that ambiguous organisation which in the name of peace was performing many actions certain to benefit Hitler'. Murray, no longer a pacifist, told her she ought not to be one 'in the face of this evil', but she stuck to her beliefs. In her PPU capacity she addressed a meeting in Manchester, where she urged the pacifist cause, arguing that 'war was much easier than finding the way of peace, the creative way', and that 'everything should be done to make the people of the world know that we do not want to go on with the slaughter'.

By now she numbered many leading pacifists among her friends. She knew and admired Sybil Morrison, a pacifist and founder of the Peace Pledge Union who went to prison for her views, and Myrtle Solomon, who became the editor of *The Pacifist*. She was one of the early subscribers to Vera Brittain's influential fortnightly 'Letter to Peace Lovers', in which its author discussed 'the ideas, principles and problems which have concerned genuine peace-lovers for the past twenty years'. She also read *Forward*, a radical socialist magazine edited by Keir Hardie's son-in-law and biographer Emrys Hughes which, she told him, was 'full of challenging articles and stimulating thought'.

Soon after war was declared, she was one of six women – the others included the novelist Storm Jameson, Maude Royden and Vera Brittain – who signed a letter to the prime minister Neville Chamberlain, urging that Britain should not bomb German women and children in open towns. During the phoney war, while members of the PPU were advocating peace by negotiation, Sybil, Gielgud, Shaw and others wrote to Chamberlain, urging him to 'give sympathetic consideration' to any proposal for peace sponsored by the neutral countries. She was a co-signatory of further letters: with Hewlett Johnson, J B S Haldane, Shaw and Beatrice and Sidney Webb, she urged the government not to attack Soviet Russia; along with Ivor Brown, H G Wells, Margery Fry and others she protested against the British placating of Japan by closing the Burma road to China.

In October John's ship HMS *Southampton* was hit by German bombers. Sybil saw him in Edinburgh the following week, and found him sharing her hatred of the conflict. 'He says it's all so awful, it's not describable,' she wrote to the Crawleys. 'The young ones hate it more than the middle-aged – they find the acceptance of war shocking – it's been most illuminating talking to the young navy boys. John feels very miserable about the whole thing. I think the men who are imaginative *do* feel terrible. John says it's the prostitution of knowledge – science being used to destroy instead of heal and create. It seems as if our brains and cleverness had gone so far beyond our spirit – our mind – which have let powers of destruction seize the world and the only way we know to combat it is doing the same thing. It's Christianity we've got to find now.'

Lewis, Sybil explained, was 'feeling the war very, *very* badly': it represented a failure of his generation. Meanwhile Christopher's refusal to fight found support in an unexpected quarter, his brother John writing to Sybil: 'Tell Kiff to stick to his principles – it helps us all to know that there are some who won't have a hand in this hellish killing.' Sybil's protests against the war sometimes got her into trouble, as she told Rawdon Crawley, in a letter opened but passed by the censor: 'Life is being increasingly difficult over here, and one is worse if one keeps one's mouth shut – for on the occasions when one feels impelled to speak, words are twisted and one's true feeling is given a wrong flavour!' She suggested he contact Vera Brittain, now lecturing in America: 'You may not agree with all she says – she is strongly and magnifi-cently pacifist – positively Christian – and is a big writer.'

Once the theatres re-opened, *The Corn is Green* went on tour, playing to full houses, before moving in to the Piccadilly in December. Sybil still found time for good causes. She recited two speeches from *Saint Joan* at an international concert at Sadler's Wells in aid of the Relief and Refugee Council, where she appealed for funds to help Spanish refugee children living in distressing conditions in camps in France. She supported the Little Theatre club run by a group of Germans who had fled from the Nazis, and regularly attended their productions, and she was on the national committee of the Free German League of Culture in Great Britain.

At Christmas time the whole family, except for Christopher in Dublin, came together. Sybil still believed the war might be stopped: 'I feel something good may come if we keep from thinking badly about it all,' she told the Crawleys. 'There is a great woman's movement here to stop hostilities and see if there isn't a possibility of some other way – so many lives being wasted – and such lots of innocent lives – if only us older ones could give *our* lives – it's the young that are being sacrificed – it's heartbreaking – even here in fairly comfortable England – and Europe is a waste.'

Life became harder in the new year as meat and other basics were rationed, and in April 1940 the phoney war came to an end. Germany invaded Norway, and by the end of May its forces were close to the English Channel, forcing the retreating British army to be evacuated from Dunkirk. 'Wasn't the evacuation of troops amazing? ' Sybil wrote to John. 'Eye-witnesses say it was like a sort of regatta. All those tiny boats.' Many theatres had closed again, but the Piccadilly was one of the few still open. Another was the Old Vic, where Lewis was playing Kent alongside John Gielgud's Lear. 'Lewis' Kent was just real Kent – honest, sincere, and a darling person,' Sybil wrote to Gwen Ffrangcon-Davies: 'John was superb – always exciting…what he didn't get in huge power he made up in other ways, and moving – oh! so moving – he is a thrilling actor.' She passed on news of mutual friends, including Edith Evans. 'Edith just as ever – a grand girl! We have pleasant times together.' Meanwhile the West End was in a bad way: 'Such a lot of plays off. Those that are on are playing only because we've all come down to the minimum salary. It's worth keeping on just for morale, for life is quite frightening.'

Invasion, she explained, was a real threat: 'We are in the midst – or very near – awfulness now.…We are all waiting anxiously, all of us who have boys fighting, or near fighting – my John has got a very dangerous job – he's now Lt Commander, and we just pray – that's the strongest thing to do.' To Rawdon Crawley she wrote: 'London isn't too appetising just now – tho' the parks with may and laburnum and bluebells and chestnut look so glorious – one wonders why this insanity is allowed to go on. We feel very anxious – naturally – tho' why we in England should expect to escape when our poor allies have suffered so *terribly* – this week has been very wretched – but one mustn't say much in writing!'

Lewis was now with Gielgud in *The Tempest*, while Sybil had just finished in *The Corn is Green*. On 19 June, alone in Swan Court, she received a phone call from the Admiralty, telling her John, who was in command of a dive-bomber squadron stationed on HMS *Ark Royal*, was missing, believed killed in a raid over Norway. Stunned by the news, she went to the theatre to tell Lewis before the matinee. He just stood there with tears streaming down over his make-up. In his grief he had to go on as Gonzalo, the counsellor who comforts Alonso the king after his son Ferdinand is supposedly drowned. Guthrie wrote to his mother that Lewis managed to get through the performance, until at the end Alonso and Ferdinand are reunited, when he 'just broke down and wept on stage'. Offstage in private, he was near to total collapse.

Sybil of course was equally devastated. For six weeks they heard nothing. Every night she and Lewis would say the 91st Psalm together. Then a vague telegram came to Geneva, suggesting Lieutenant-Commander Casson was a prisoner. Confirmation came when a friend heard a propaganda broadcast from Germany by William Joyce ('Lord Haw-Haw'), in which he boasted that the son of Dame Sybil Thorndike had been captured. 'We both burst out crying,' Sybil remembered. 'Then we drank everything in the house there was to drink.' John, it transpired, had led an attack on the German battleship *Scharnhorst*, which was moored in Trondheim during the opening days of the Nazi invasion of Norway. Several of the planes in the raid were shot down, but he had been able to crash-land his in one of the fjords, and he and his gunner had survived. After being picked up he had been taken to a prisoner-of-war camp near Frankfurt. In August Patricia received her first letter from him. The next day Sybil wrote to Gwen Ffrangcon-Davies: 'I can't begin to tell you the relief, and curiously enough it has made me feel more intensely the suffering that so many wives and mothers have now – I never want to have a month like July again.' Her own suffering continued: though she wrote to John regularly, she was not to see him again for nearly five years.

In August 1940, with Hitler occupying Belgium, Holland and France, she wrote despairingly to Gwen Ffrangcon-Davies: 'The whole thing doesn't bear thinking of. Nothing can justify this slaughter of boys – of whatever nation, and there's winter in Europe – all those nations wanting food. It's on such a huge scale now. I do blame a lot of people like myself who believed that war is wrong – Pacifists and Socialists – for not being more energetic, and *making* ourselves heard – if we English don't find a way with our sort of experience and our humour, then I think we are in for many years of grave disquiet and misery. I think England could do it – I pray every day we shall – and it's a bigger way than military victory we've got to do it.'

On 7 September the Blitz began, and the London theatres closed down for several weeks, though the provincial ones remained open. The Old Vic was damaged by fire, and considered unsafe to use; the following May it received a direct hit, and remained closed for the duration. Its sister theatre Sadler's Wells was commandeered as a rest centre for air-raid victims. Meanwhile Wolfit, condensing the plays to just an hour, defiantly staged lunchtime Shakespeare at the Kingsway and the Strand, despite a bomb hitting the theatre and destroying all his costumes the day after he opened ('Shakespeare beats Hitler!' ran one headline). Even in the air-raid shelters theatre continued, with performances by the Adelphi Players. In the middle of this death and destruction, Sybil retained her belief in the value of theatre: 'I often feel the Communist Party has tried to jump over one of the steps and get to international by despising national,' she wrote to Gwen Ffrangcon-Davies. 'To love passionately your own land should make you realise others' passionate love for *their* land, and I believe the Theatre can teach this better than any other way – newspapers won't – just friendliness won't – it's got to be an imaginative *leap* that will show us the way.'

The public's imagination was caught during the war not so much by theatre as by film. People went on average once a week, with some cinemas during the worst of the raids offering shelter for the night and five films. Hollywood films such as *Mrs Miniver*, *The Wizard of Oz* and *Wuthering Heights* were hugely popular, as were the Gainsborough Studio pictures; there were also the Humphrey Jennings documentaries, and realistic films such as *Millions Like Us*, *Waterloo Road* and *In Which We Serve*. *Pygmalion* had also been a success, and as the Battle of Britain got under way, Sybil joined the cast of another Shaw vehicle.

Having played the title-role in *Major Barbara* on stage a decade previously, she was now cast as Mrs Baines of the Salvation Army. Wendy Hiller was Barbara, Rex Harrison was Adolphus Cusins (Leslie Howard had turned down the part) and Robert Morley was Undershaft. Shaw warned Wendy Hiller that for Barbara, 'all the other characters are her rivals professionally. Sybil Thorndike can do a tremendous lot with half a dozen lines, especially in a religious part, which suits her own saintly temperament.' In an affectionate tribute to her stature, he informed Sybil: 'I am changing Mrs Baines to a General, nothing less being good enough for you.'

The director was the Hungarian Gabriel Pascal, who had bounced Shaw into selling him the film rights to all his plays for ten shillings. He now persuaded him that *Major Barbara* should be shortened and in places entirely re-written for the screen. This was Pascal's first film, and on the set at Denham Studios, according to dialogue director Harold French, it was David Lean, nominally the editor, who really directed it. The unpredictable and essentially incompetent Pascal, described by Harrison as 'a marvellous gypsy rogue... as open as a baby and ruthless as a tiger', would greet the actors each morning with the cry: 'You are ruining my picture – you are crucifying me!' He bullied everyone, called Deborah Kerr 'a constipated virgin' – it was her first film – and sacked (and then reinstated) several of the actors, including Marie Lohr. Wendy Hiller was called in more than once to calm him down.

The filming at Denham Studios just outside London proved a nightmare for other reasons. Exterior shots were filmed one day in locations that became rubble the next. Railways lines were bombed and landmines made roads unsafe, so the actors had to stay as close to the studio as possible overnight, in dressing-rooms, pubs and friends' houses. Spotters on the roof sounded a klaxon when enemy aircraft were sighted, and the cast and crew ran to the shelter beneath the concrete floor of the sound stage. Donald Calthrop, told that his two sons had been killed, embarked on a drinking bout, and died of a heart attack, leaving his remaining scenes to be shot with a double. Pascal claimed 125 bombs fell in the vicinity during the filming, which took six months instead of the scheduled ten weeks. Shaw visited the set in his trademark Norfolk jacket, knee breeches, brogues and a woollen tie, and complained to the director that 'the cast is exhausted and sulky; and you have lost your head'. But Sybil, a hardened veteran of bombing from the First World War, seemed unbowed: Deborah Kerr remembered her as 'a positive hurricane of enthusiasm, carrying all along with her'.

Sixteen new sequences were added for the film, though only six could be included, and Shaw recorded a 'visual prologue' to accompany its planned showing in America. But the film, which suffered from cuts made by the distributors, received mixed notices when it opened in April 1941, many critics being baffled by some of the arguments in Shaw's play. Sybil plays General Baines as young and impish, flirting with Undershaft, and grasping the Salvation Army flag as if she were Joan leading her troops. She seems especially at ease in one of the added scenes in which, in a speech full of fervour and good humour, she addresses a revival meeting in the Albert Hall.

During the filming she was able briefly to escape the bombs. 'I am down in Wales for a few days, in between film shots,' she told Herbert Farjeon. 'We are all so very happy that John is alive and safe, and that we shall hear from him soon. I'm on the lawn looking at the mountain and sea – and John's children are giving me croquet balls telling me they are sardines, which seems a bit far-fetched! But I accept anything in this peaceful glory – I adore Wales!'

She soon returned to the theatre, this time on a unique venture which would prove to be one of the most satisfying of her whole career.

26

Shakespeare for the Miners

'I found myself a Conservative when we were with Communists,
and a Communist when we were with Conservatives'
Sybil on touring Macbeth *in the Welsh valleys*

S oon after war began the Council for the Encouragement of Music and
the Arts (CEMA) had been formed, with government support. Its aim
was to protect the arts 'at a time when they may mean more in the life of
the country than they have ever meant before', to 'carry the arts to areas
which are cut off from their enjoyment,' and to 'give encouragement and
refreshment to populations suffering from the strain and anxiety of war'.
Fearing the principal cities would be bombed, CEMA (which later became
the Arts Council) argued that the arts must be made available wherever they
were most needed. Starting early in 1940, under the slogan 'the best for the
most', CEMA helped artists to bring entertainment to workers in mines and
factories, and to those who had been evacuated or stranded away from home
by air raids. It supported concerts in churches, cathedrals and chapels by
orchestras such as the Hallé, and took art exhibitions 'to minor villages and
suburbs which have no cultural roots'.

Lewis was made CEMA's honorary drama adviser in April. The aim was
for 'companies to give worthwhile plays at popular prices where only the
cinema is available'. As a start CEMA backed the Pilgrim Players led by
E Martin Browne and his wife Henzie Raeburn, who toured *Murder in the
Cathedral* and James Bridie's *Tobias and the Angel*. Asked to come up with a
programme, Lewis approached Guthrie, who was running the Old Vic, and
suggested it seek support from CEMA. The result was a guarantee against
loss of £6,000 for two companies.

One, to be led by Esmé Church and to include Alec Clunes, Sonia Dresdel and Renée Asherson, would tour the industrial towns of the north-west with *She Stoops to Conquer* and Sierra's *The World is Yours* (renamed *The Kingdom of God*); the other, headed by Sybil and Lewis, would tour the mining villages and towns of south Wales, in a production sponsored by the Miners' Welfare Commission and the local education authorities. The play originally chosen was André Obey's *Noah*, but Lewis suggested *Macbeth* instead. When CEMA suggested it would be too heavy for mining audiences, Lewis said: 'I know my countrymen. They like a tragedy.'

In early September, before they could leave for Wales, the Blitz on London destroyed the Shaftesbury, Little, Queen's, Royalty and Kingsway theatres, and badly damaged the Saville and Drury Lane. Sybil and Lewis suffered two devastating blows. First, the warehouse in south London where they kept their scenery, costumes, scripts and papers was hit, and everything destroyed. Then, returning one evening from a rehearsal of *Macbeth*, they found that Swan Court had been bombed, and their flat made uninhabitable. As a temporary measure they moved into Eileen's house in Pembridge Villas in Bayswater. Others in the company had also been made homeless by the bombing, so Guthrie decided the last ten days of rehearsals should be in Wales. 'We'll be leaving Paddington at noon – if Paddington's still there,' he announced. The bombing was widespread: on their first night in Newport, where they were to open, the house of the couple managing the tour, in which Sybil and Lewis were going to stay, was destroyed by a bomb, and their two children killed. Throughout the tour their journeys and performances were to be interrupted by raids on nearby cities.

With Sybil as Lady Macbeth and Lewis as Macbeth, the cast included Ann as Lady Macduff, and Mark Dignam and his wife Georgia MacKinnon. Another company member, Kenneth Griffith, recalled the occasion: 'The tour was rather like the old actors used to travel, with us in the bus, and the costumes, scenery and props following us in a large furniture van.' The company played occasionally in theatres converted to cinemas, but mostly in miners' institutes and parish halls, in works canteens, and on one stage 'no bigger than a tablecloth'. Lope de Vega once said that all you need for a theatre is four planks, four trestles, two actors and a passion, and this was the spirit in which they operated. The costumes were minimal; Sybil described them as 'a sort of battledress for the men and unadorned robes for the women. Then we can add cloaks, hats, gloves, swords and things as we need them. Much easier for us and jolly good too for all of us, including the audience, because we have to use our imaginations.' The scenery was equally basic: a couple of screens, a bench, two throne-style chairs, and some drapes.

The day after the opening night Sybil wrote to Elizabeth Casson: 'Lewis and I agreed we'd never enjoyed *Macbeth* so much!' For her, this was what theatre was about, and she was in her element. 'I always want a bare board, no scenery, no lights – that's my greatest joy!!' she told Gwen Ffrangcon-Davies. 'We are playing *Macbeth* in rather a new way.' Their version included a chorus linking the scenes and explaining the action, and a didactic prologue, written with the critic Lionel Hale. The surviving script shows how they tried to engage the audience's interest, and justify staging *Macbeth* at this sombre moment in the country's history.

The prologue begins with Sybil and Lewis walking on to the stage, followed by two actors (Kenneth Griffith and Georgia MacKinnon) carrying a hamper.

1st Actor   We're going to do *Macbeth*, aren't we?

Lewis   Yes of course.

2nd Actor Why 'of course'?

Sybil   It's up on the posters; can't you read?

1st Actor No, we don't mean that. It's like this. We've come a long way to do a play here. Why *Macbeth*? Why not *Hamlet* or *Othello* or one of the historical plays?

Lewis   Well, that's a fair question. Now I'll ask you one. What sort of play do you think we ought to do?

1st Actor It has got to be Shakespeare.

Lewis   Yes.

2nd Actor But this particular play?

Sybil   I'll tell you. We want a good play and this *is* a good play. But we want something more than that. Though it was written over three hundred years ago it has got to mean something today. It has got to be true for 1940.

1st Actor Yes I see.

Sybil   Well when did this Macbeth live?

1st Actor That's just it. It's about a thousand years ago in Scotland and I still can't see what that's got to do with us in 1940.

Sybil   Just go on a bit. What do we know about him?

1st Actor Well, it's a legend about a savage time –

2nd Actor Macbeth was a chieftain. He murdered Duncan and made himself King.

1st Actor He had to go on murdering to keep himself in power.

2nd Actor With a spy in every house in Scotland and so on.

Sybil And you still don't see what this has to do with 1940?

1st Actor No.

Sybil Don't you? You've just given a perfect picture of a dictator.

1st Actor Yes but...

Lewis You needn't always think of dictators in terms of concentration camps and tanks and aeroplanes. Men don't change in a thousand years. What Macbeth wanted, what all such people want, is power. This is a play about a tyrant, a dictator.

Sybil Yes, and his wife too. Macbeth isn't the only part in this play, remember.

Lewis Sorry.

Sybil There's Lady Macbeth – that's me! She's the sort of woman who encourages this sort of man. You can meet her anywhere. The wife who wants her husband to get on in the world, always pushing him along from behind. And then when he *has* got on, he grows beyond her and above her. So that's the woman's side of this power business.

Lewis Well, let's get on with the play.

With only a handful of actors Sybil, in addition to Lady Macbeth, played one of the witches, and the cream-faced loon; she also led the 'Cries of Women' heard offstage during the battle scene. She had one other role. Because of the problem of taking a young boy on tour, in each town they recruited a Welsh lad to play Macduff's son. Because the boys struggled to say their words, they were asked to face upstage and mime them, while Sybil spoke them in a treble voice from the wings.

Almost everywhere the company went they were greeted with huge enthusiasm, full houses, and great appreciation by the mining families, who were, according to Freda Gaye, another company member, 'fairly ravenous for the play'. Afterwards the actors asked the audience to sing hymns, and the evening would end with a rendering in Welsh of the national anthem 'Land of my Fathers', which the company quickly learned by heart. Sybil was ecstatic. 'We've never played to such audiences,' she wrote to John. 'None of them moves a muscle while we're playing, but at the end they go wild, and lift the roof with their clapping. This is the theatre that we like best – getting right in amongst people. Afterwards they all come round and talk to us. How I love those lilting Welsh voices.' But her delight could be tempered by realism. One night the audience seemed rather noisy beforehand. Sybil was heard to say, 'Lewis, tonight let's just *do* the play, let's not try to *teach* them anything.'

The schedule was a punishing one: in just ten weeks they played in 37 small towns and villages, usually for one night only. It was a cold winter, and they often worked in unheated halls with only the most basic lighting and minimal scenery. Even this could not be relied on: at one performance Sybil had to lean against a couple of hefty flats that were in danger of collapsing upstage, while Lewis continued the scene downstage, apparently talking to himself. But the production made a huge impact. The director Patrick Dromgoole, then a ten-year-old evacuee, recalls the stir it caused in Garnant, near the Black Mountains: 'It was a huge occasion for the village, it was talked about for weeks beforehand. To me it was absolutely electrifying and terrifying. I believed every word of it: for weeks afterwards I couldn't go upstairs to bed in the dark. But I knew then that I wanted to be a part of theatre.'

Much had to be left to the audience's imagination. The critic Eric Johns saw Sybil's performance in a drab hall in the seaside town of Porthcawl. 'The banquet scene had all the suspense of a thriller, even though one saw only Sybil and Lewis seated at the end of a table which stretched away into the wings. They convinced the audience there were scores of guests seated just out of sight, horrified by Macbeth's hysterical outbursts. It was a superb perform-ance in the grand manner.' He also got a glimpse of Sybil's remarkable stamina, and the strain the tour put on Lewis, who shouldered the burden of stage management. 'The next day at tea time I saw them in a modest café in the town. Quite exhausted, Lewis was asleep with his head on the table, while Sybil, cheery and chirpy as ever, was sitting opposite him coping with correspondence.'

As there was rarely a hotel available, the actors often stayed with mining families, whom Sybil described as 'wonderfully hospitable'. As always, she looked on the positive side. From Ebbw Vale in Monmouthshire she wrote to Athene Seyler's daughter Jane-Ann Jones: 'Ann, Lewis and I are all together in a very nice house looking up at a coal pit.' The actress Freda Gaye recalled her ability to get on with anyone: 'All the company had to learn to be good companions whatever the conditions, and the art of being good guests. In this we had the perfect example of the Cassons, who always showed a genuine interest in the households they joined.' After one performance Sybil made an unexpected confession: 'Dear, dear miners,' she said. 'I've always wanted to be a miner. When I was young I used to burrow down to the bottom of my bed, and I'd say, "I'm a miner! I'm a miner!"'

The CEMA report on the tour, by its organising secretary Ivor Brown, highlighted their offstage work and its missionary character. 'The devotion of Dame Sybil Thorndike and Mr Casson to the social side of the tour was of great value. They not only faced the continual hardships of moving on, but found time and energy to meet all who wished to see them. They spoke often and most acceptably on the relation of drama to life, and their presence, as well as their performances on the stage, have been enormously appreciated.' The actor Ian McKellen's step-aunt was present one night when Sybil came forward at the end and said: 'Now we've done something for you, we'd like you to do something for us. Will you just sing?' The audience obliged with hymns and songs. 'That evening she couldn't sleep,' McKellen relates. 'She was so excited she got up and went into the streets, where she found other people still walking around, unable to come down from this climactic evening.'

Although there was plenty of radicalism in this part of Wales ('As you may guess, this is a very Red place!' Sybil told Murray), there was also plenty of argument, which she relished. 'I did manage to behave with discretion,' she claimed later. But her determination to see good in all things occasionally caused embarrassment. When she observed to a vicar in the Rhondda valley how wonderful it was for the miners to live in such beautiful countryside, he replied that the beauty wasn't much use to them when they got silicosis from being down the mine. There were lighter moments. Once, when the actors were emerging from their bus, a young boy asked: 'Which is the Dame?' His friend replied scornfully: 'They're all Dames.' In one miner's hall Sybil accepted a bouquet at the end of a performance, with tears in her eyes – only to discover that one item in the bill for hiring the hall was 'Flowers for the Dame'.

'Good business, *Macbeth*,' Shaw wrote approvingly to her in December, at the end of the tour. These visits to towns which had seen no live theatre for years showed there to be a hunger for serious theatre at a time of crisis. This was mirrored in the rise in demand in libraries for good literature, and in the enthusiasm for touring productions by Sadler's Wells in places not known for any particular interest in opera and ballet. The CEMA policy of 'the best for the most' was working, not just socially but financially; the *Macbeth* production finished in the black. Although it meant turning down better-paid work in easier conditions, Sybil and Lewis readily agreed to carry on their theatrical missionary work.

By the year's end, with the Blitz still going strong, only eight theatres remained open in London. 'The bombing was horrible – it is now,' Sybil told Rawdon Crawley. 'There is great bravery – London people are amazing. There aren't words to tell you what it's really like.' They now decided to move out of the city: 'Lewis and I are in town for three days getting the flat packed up, as we're giving it up,' Sybil wrote to Elizabeth Casson in December. 'I don't relish being in London a bit.' The war dampened her usual Christmas spirit: 'I'm not doing anything with presents this year, as life is just a bit too difficult,' she admitted. The disruption to her family had been considerable, with both Eileen and Russell having been bombed out of their houses. Eileen had taken her children down to Devon, while Russell and his family had joined Mary, now pregnant with her first child, and Patricia and her three children Anthony, Jane and Penny at Bron-y-Garth.

In January 1941 the *Macbeth* tour was extended for a further ten weeks, first to Lancashire towns, and then to north Wales. In total they played in 28 venues. Ivor Brown described the response to the play in Burnley: 'The theatre was packed with people who, I suddenly realised, were not just waiting to see what a famous player would do with a familiar speech. They were gripped with curiosity, wanting to know what happened and how it ended. They were the counterparts to Shakespeare's own audience.' In his *Observer* review he wrote: 'Shakespeare not only stands up to improvised staging: he thrives on it. For my part I have never seen *Macbeth* grip tighter or make more sense.... Dame Sybil's Lady Macbeth is beautifully strong, clear work which really serves the story, and is not an isolated star performance.'

Reporting on the success of the Old Vic's first two tours, Guthrie wrote: 'They evoked great local enthusiasm, and artists were greeted everywhere with the greatest kindness, which found expression in many ways – hospitality, splendid houses, and in Wales in particular a definite desire to repay in the same emotional coin. I shall never forget the moment when in a mining village not far from Swansea a packed audience, about a thousand strong, rose at the end of the performance and fairly lifted the roof off with a hymn – a magnificent, thrilling gesture of appreciation and thanks.' Sybil meanwhile was keen to show her commitment to the Welsh language. From St Asaph she wrote to Professor Glynne Jones: 'I feel very honoured that you are giving me a copy and I shall set to work to get Lady Macbeth into my head in Welsh!'

At the end of the tour Sybil was in Portmadoc, in time for the birth there of Mary's daughter Diana. She then slipped over to Ireland for a couple of recitals, but also to see Christopher, who was getting married to Kay O'Connell, a set designer from Kerry whom he had met at the Gaiety. According to their daughter Glynis: 'My father was in the Celtic mode, and determined to marry an Irish woman. He was always proposing to people; he almost proposed to an actress from the Abbey, it was between her and my mother. Eventually he proposed to my mother over beans on toast in the fish and chip shop opposite the Gate. Her response was, "Don't be daft!" But she came round.' Christopher had recently converted to Catholicism, and the wedding was held in Cardinal Newman's Church on St Stephen's Green, with Maclíammóir acting as best man. Two months later Sybil reported gleefully: 'Christopher's marriage is completely blissful!'

Lewis now resigned as CEMA's drama adviser in favour of Ivor Brown, then became its honorary drama director, supported by a panel that included Ashley Dukes, Herbert Farjeon, J B Priestley and Emlyn Williams. Sybil meanwhile played Saint Joan in full for the last time in London in a charity matinee at the Palace. Her ability still to conjure up the fire and vigour of the Maid of Orelans, even in the wrong surroundings and costume, was remembered by Paul Scofield, then a student in London. 'One morning she burst into our studio in Ebury Street like a breath of sunny cold air. She wore a hat and her customary tailored suit, and carried a large shopping bag. She relinquished the shopping bag and, still in her hat, launched into a speech from *Saint Joan*. Her tones were clear and ringing, her enunciation was incisive, her passion was undimmed by the school-room background. Those words reverberate for me still.'

In May 1941, the Blitz on London ending and Hitler turning his attention to Russia, the theatres began to revive. It was now considered safe for the Old Vic companies to play in the capital. Guthrie decided on the rarely staged *King John*, with Ernest Milton in the title-role, Sybil playing Constance, Ann cast as Prince Arthur, and Lewis as Cardinal Pandulph and, later, Faulconbridge. Before the two-week run at the New in July, the company toured by bus through Lancashire and the Lake District to Scotland. A warning ARP note in the programme for the Lyceum in Edinburgh reminded everyone of the dangers of life outside: 'The nearest shelter from this theatre is the Usher Hall. We recommend that patrons should carry gas masks with them when outside their homes. Above all, keep calm and keep smiling.'

Laurence Payne, a young actor in the company, remembered Sybil at rehearsals: 'I was unprepared for this relatively tiny and compact bundle of joy and energy which erupted into the rehearsal room like an unexpected land-mine, preceded by a cracked laugh, almost a cackle, a huge, almost masculine voice, and looking exactly like everybody's mother.' He recalled too the contrast between husband and wife: 'Lewis grunted and grumbled and stumped about, ever with his bright blue eyes fixed on the ground, and a heavy thoughtful frown on his face. Sybil, his antithesis, swept everywhere, trailing, it seemed, a rich and lengthy train behind her, though she actually favoured tailored skirts and rather dinky little, slightly out-of-fashion hats. Her hands and the poise and carriage of them were quite beautiful.' He also noticed 'little tiffs' between them, when Sybil became 'quite short' with Lewis, and how she had to keep a close watch on his appearance. 'He never cared much how he looked, and one would catch glimpses of Sybil brushing him down and straightening his tie, or pushing his hair back behind his ears. As Faulconbridge all this came to a head. Always in too much of a hurry, he never appeared to have a moment to look into a mirror; his belt was invariably twisted, his jerkin caught up at the back, a glove would be missing or a prop forgotten, and on one desperate occasion he stormed on to the stage with his wig on back to front. Eventually Sybil would field him in the wings before the curtain went up, to check him over.'

Renée Asherson, playing Blanch of Spain, remembers the younger members of the company making fun of Sybil: 'We knew of the way she did the Greek tragedies in what seemed to be an exaggerated manner, and we did rather mock it.' Guthrie directed the play with his customary originality and flamboyance, using stylised costumes and rug-wool wigs, giving the Dauphin blue hair, and having the main opposing characters enter on hobby horses. Lewis co-directed, concentrating on voice work. 'He used to try to help us to get the shape and the tune of a phrase right by humming it,' Renée Asherson recalls. 'He and Sybil would argue, though in a friendly way: he was very firm with her, he kept her under control.'

Sybil was nevertheless at full throttle: 'She went into top speed the moment the flag fell, and kept it up till the finish,' Agate wrote, while *The Times* critic observed more politely: 'Constance offers Dame Sybil Thorndike chances to act in the grand manner, and she takes them grandly.' According to Audrey Williamson, 'she lashed about her with vitriolic scorn…and in her distraction there sounded that note of deep and heart-shaking grief our stage rarely hears nowadays.' For the director Tony Richardson, then at school, 'she seemed the spirit of mysterious tragedy'. But Sybil felt she had been unable to connect up the emotions of the different scenes. 'My fault,' she wrote to a fan while on tour. 'One should be able to sympathise even with a tiresome, ambitious, over-temperamental woman like Constance, but somehow I've failed in it!'

While playing in London she found the energy to give a matinee performance of *Medea*, with Abraham Sofaer as Jason, and Lewis as the Messenger. 'How marvellously symbolic it is now,' she told Murray. 'I think the speeches are almost unbearable in their terrific feeling.' Now in her sixtieth year, she could still do justice to a part into which, as *The Times* put it, 'she can fling all the generous emotionalism of her art'. But the reviewer was also critical: 'Her voice has tricks of its own, and at times they tend to distort rather than clarify the language.' Ivor Brown wrote of her performance: 'It is a tremendous role, containing both the woman wronged and the woman wronging. In the first aspect Dame Sybil has the russet majesty of a tremendous oak through which the winds of tragedy are sighing; in the second she blazes into vengeance like a forest fire.'

In the autumn of 1941 she and Lewis returned with their own company to south Wales for two months, starting in Newport and Monmouth, playing one or two nights in the mining villages, and ending up in Llanelly. Sybil played Candida and Lady Macbeth yet again, but also Medea, which Lewis had suggested would appeal to his countrymen. In giving permission to stage his translation, Murray told Sybil: 'Your symbolic interpretation is extremely interesting – Jason as civilisation and Medea as the wild forces savagely rebelling against it because it has done its work so badly.'

Sybil found it richly rewarding that, as with Lady Macbeth, most of the audience were seeing a celebrated part played for the first time. 'The very mixed audience lap it up – the mining communities especially,' she told Murray. The passionate response of the Welsh people excited her. 'We were playing in one little place, and the audience was electric,' she recalled. 'They were sitting on the edge of their seats, playing the parts themselves.' The villagers would walk several miles across the valleys to see the play. One miner in the Neath Valley said afterwards: 'This is the play for us. It kindles a fire.' Lewis reported to

Murray: 'The big emotional sway and the beauty of the poetry really do give these Welsh people what they want. An old miner said after a performance that if he hadn't known a word of the English, the music of it would have made him understand it.' This being wartime, Sybil felt she had to be careful how she played Medea's offstage mourning of her murdered children: 'I mustn't wail too loud,' she remarked. 'They can't see me, and they'll think it's a siren.'

They hit audience trouble with *Macbeth* in Tredegar, where they had to complain about a group of people chattering in the front row, and ice-creams being sold from an illuminated tray during the murder scene. Sybil also had to defend their production against some serious criticisms from one member of that audience, who wrote complaining about their prologue, and the way they had cut and adapted the text, giving speeches by minor characters to a Chorus. 'A "straightforward" Macbeth as you suggest is rather a difficult thing to find!' she replied. 'I have played in about 10 different versions all claiming to be the authentic version – it's the most corrupt text of all the tragedies.' She also replied in more frivolous vein to criticisms about the First Witch's audibility. 'I think the First Witch *did* have adenoids – nasty old woman, she was! But she must be heard. It was *I* that played her....I love playing that hateful old crone – she's just like an old governess I knew with adenoids who I always felt *was* the First Witch, and I never heard a word *she* said either! Still that's my excuse.'

The Welsh audiences were less enthusiastic about *Candida*, which seemed too frivolous for the times. So when Sybil and Lewis returned to Wales in January 1942 they performed only *Macbeth* and *Medea*, prefacing the latter with a short discourse on Greek drama. 'Medea is being a riot!' Sybil reported to Murray. 'By some taken as a fairy story, by some as a real indictment of war and our present life – by some this and by some that – it's so big it stretches to give a solution to every problem.' They then crossed to the north-east coast, and played in several small mining towns around Durham. While there they saw Gielgud's production of *Macbeth* in Newcastle. Gwen Ffrangcon-Davies, playing Lady Macbeth, wrote to a friend about them: 'They play in funny little halls and sleep in miners' cottages when necessary! Sybil is a grand person, hates wars, a crime against humanity – has been a pacifist of course for years on religious grounds, so is dedicating herself to the cause of "construction", and not to making money out of the general calamity.'

During these months Sybil spoke publicly for the Red Cross, encouraging people to send money and food to be forwarded to John and other prisoners-of-war in Germany. The Crawleys sent several donations, and bars of chocolate for John to distribute among his fellow-prisoners. With rationing in force, they also sent food to Sybil and her family. 'Such a parcel came this week,' she replied. 'Oh! Oh! All the things we can't get! The *dates*! We revelled in them and the egg powder! But *all* was welcome.'

Meanwhile she had started to learn Greek, as she explained to Murray: 'I meant to wait until I was 60, but as our son in prison camp has just started I thought I'd wait no longer – I'm so thrilled, I don't know what to do. I have to ration myself vigorously on orders from Lewis, and he says I forget every other duty when I'm engrossed in my Greek grammar. I have hopes of reading the New Testament in a year – and then pray that I'll be able before 70 to do the plays.'

The CEMA company now had several new members, including Douglas Campbell. A young red-headed Glaswegian, a socialist and a pacifist with a fondness for violent arguments, his father had been a friend of Keir Hardie. According to Sybil: 'He came to see us in our bedroom at Tenby, and we became involved in tremendous arguments. When he left, Lewis said: "That's an opinionated young man. But I like him and I'm glad he's with us."' Douglas Campbell remembers their life on the road: 'Sybil was a very big star, so the houses, which ranged from 150 to 300, were always full, and very enthusiastic. She and Lewis were in a fairly constant bicker, and notes on performances were always to hand, as Lewis was never satisfied – the moment you got used to something he would change it, mainly to keep you fresh and on your toes. I think Sybil thoroughly enjoyed touring: she loved mixing the theatre and social life, and her interest in everything and everybody was completely genuine, though expressed rather larger than life, and therefore thought by some to be insincere – which was not the case.' However, her ringing tones could sometimes be mistaken for imperiousness. The cultural historian Richard Hoggart, then stationed in Llandrindod Wells, recalls hearing her 'booming-bittern voice' as she sat in a tea-shop with Lewis. 'The fluting voice asking for a scone as though for the documents of accession was unmistakeable. The two had the air of faces and presences which expect to be looked at, which are always on public duty, for whom there is no easily apparent separation between the public and the private personalities.'

Sybil's inexhaustible energy and fierce commitment often made it difficult for her fellow-actors: 'She insisted that we all keep up with her,' Douglas Campbell remembers. 'Neither she nor Lewis could bear to have anyone sick

– it just wasn't done, you always had to "rise above it", as Guthrie would say when people were sick.' Just occasionally even Sybil found this hard. The actor Richard Bebb, then a teenage evacuee, remembers her visit to Aberystwyth. 'It was a cultural desert, like all of Wales in war time, so the King's Hall, which was normally used as a ballroom, was packed. The play began at 6.30, which was not unusual during the war. At the end Sybil came out and thanked the audience for their generous reception. Then she said, "I hope you all heard what we were saying, because before the curtain came up we received a request from the council to get a move on, as they have a dance starting here at 8.30." She was in a towering rage, and there was a stunned silence. It was so typically Welsh.' But there were also humorous moments. Kenneth Griffith recalls a lunch given for the company at Colwyn Bay. 'The mayor, without meaning to be either amusing or provocative, referred to Dame Sybil as "a member of the oldest profession in the world".' As Sybil recalled it, 'nobody dared smile, let alone laugh'.

For this fourth tour Paul Scofield was recruited to play the Messenger in *Medea*, but after rehearsing for just one day he contracted mumps, and had to withdraw. He did however see a performance: 'It was gut-shaking,' he recalled. 'I will never forget Sybil's power and her combination of malevolence and shining goodness. It was shot though with human regret and helplessness, as well as burning anger and bitterness. It was great acting, and I was shaken by it.'

Of these tours among the Welsh people Sybil later observed: 'I found myself a Conservative when we were with Communists, and a Communist when we were with Conservatives.' It was a remark that reflected her love of argument for argument's sake. But there was no doubting her pacifist commitment. When Eileen's daughter Phyllis, another convinced pacifist, refused to be drafted into war work, Sybil went as a witness to her tribunal, and continually interrupted the hearing with her opinions. 'I was a little annoyed, because she took the whole thing over,' her niece remembers. 'I hardly said a word, because she answered the questions on my behalf. "Don't be silly, of course she's a devout Christian, she always has been," and so on. No one tried to quieten her down, which would have been impossible anyway. But she obviously helped my case, because I was allowed to work on the land.'

Sybil's pacifism faced a different test in the autumn. 'I had a very fiery and exciting meeting with Scottish ministers of many sects last Friday in Glasgow,' she told John Middleton Murry, wartime editor of the pacifist *Peace*

News. 'The pacifists present were the most lively, and almost violent! I found it hard to sit still at all!! We yelled at each other!' She confessed to being 'perplexed and bothered about pacifists being so aloof and away from the real struggle', and their 'denial that there is any good in those who cannot quite see the pacifist policy'.

As a pacifist she was criticised for remaining in the Church of England, which officially supported the war. In an open letter published by the Anglican Pacifist Fellowship, she robustly argued the case for tolerance and for staying in the Church: 'I can no more dissociate myself from the Church in which I was born and brought up than I can dissociate myself from my family or my country. I do not agree with all the views of my relations, my husband or my children, but they are the people I love and the people among whom God has chosen that I should belong; therefore I must find out where I can be in accord with them, for that is the place of friendliness....I cannot just say "I won't belong to England any more;" I'd be a deserter. This is my country that I love and must work for, even if I'm perplexed and distressed at what is being done in her name.' She liked the apparently contradictory qualities of strict discipline and freedom that characterised the Anglican Church, stressing that 'my roots in my own church go deeper than official pronouncements'.

She had always had a broad interest in different faiths, finding much to admire in the Catholic Church, in the Quaker faith, and even Christian Science, which numbered Edith Evans, Margaret Webster and Freda Gaye among its adherents. Although she had no belief in psychic phenomena, she had had one startling experience just before the war, while helping Patricia and John to move house. After the van had gone she was left alone in the garden. 'I caught sight, in a flower-bed, of a bright-coloured ball, which suddenly made me cry, and all at once I seemed to be in a changed atmosphere. It was a little alarming at first. Everything looked the same but seemed changed with something more real. It was as if suddenly, for a flash, I was seeing the significance of things – material things being just symbols – like seeing familiar things on another plane of existence. This curious feeling lasted about ten minutes, and then I was back to normal – but in those few moments I had sensed great happiness and a sureness of something that I felt was eternal life.'

Early in the war Eileen Thorndike had opened a drama school in Bideford in Devon. One of her students was Paul Scofield: 'I owe much to her, she was a wonderful teacher,' he recalled. 'She once recited the opening of *Genesis* for me, with the Thorndike voice strikingly reminiscent of Sybil's. She was a more reserved person than her sister, and I think happier as a teacher.' When her business partner ran off with the money she had closed the Devon school, formed a company from among her students, and moved to Cambridge. Their first production was André Obey's *Noah*, with Paul Scofield in the title-role and Eileen as Mrs Noah. Suddenly she wired Sybil to come to Cambridge, as she wasn't well: she had experienced a breakdown, and been advised by a psychiatrist to stop work.

'She reaches a point where she's over-worked or over-worried, when she ceases to think reasonably and dashes at anything,' Sybil explained despairingly to Elizabeth Casson. 'We are going to Newport tomorrow and open there on Monday, and Lewis says I can't break contract and leave and strand the company. He wondered if somehow you could get her to Bron-y-Garth – we'd hire a car if it's possible – she'd be looked after there and be with Pat and Mary and Nancy and be quiet – I don't want her to go away from her own people because she gets in such awful depressions, and Mary is always a help to her. I'm so sorry to worry you, Elsie, but I feel so impotent….Lewis takes this all in a very worried way, poor sweet, I don't want him to go cracking up….Do forgive me – I write in rather desperation, feeling I want to go myself but I upset so many people if I do – in South Wales they won't accept an understudy – nor will the Old Vic….I feel so despairing about her.'

After a spell in a nursing home Eileen stayed at Bron-y-Garth, and by December Sybil could report to her sister-in-law: 'Eileen tons better – she still looks on the dark side, but it's not quite pitch dark now.' When Sybil advised her sister to take life quietly, she said that would be a dull way to live. Sybil replied: 'Of course your life will be deadly dull unless you snap out of it.' The next morning Eileen was up and scrubbing the floor. Her daughter Donnie, who was with her, describes her mother as essentially a strong and happy person: 'The breakdown was a one-off. She pulled herself together and went on in the world.'

During this time Sybil observed: 'I feel I want to pack up and go to Bron-y-Garth and never move. I will one day too!!' The house had become an invaluable refuge for members of her family. She and Lewis also used it as a base when their tours brought them to north Wales, sometimes inviting the company to join them. Guthrie and his wife Judith, a couple who shared their simple tastes and indifference to money, were guests for a couple of nights, as Judith Guthrie explained to a friend: 'It's unbelievably beautiful and I think the situation of the house is the loveliest I've ever seen, and of course it was heaven warming one's hands at the dear Dame, who's in terrific form. The house is quite full – ailing relatives, healthy grandchildren, maniacal PGs incarcerated above stairs, and Sybil contending wildly with the housework, dashing madly under the beds with a carpet sweeper calling out "Horrid blanket fluff" and emerging the other side calling out "Have you read the New Testament in Basic English?" *Wonderful* woman.'

27

Red Army to White Queen

1943–1944

'It's the old splendid acting we miss these days in pulpit and theatre!'
Letter from Sybil to Celtic scholar J Glyn Davies

Like everyone else in wartime London, Sybil and Lewis had to make severe adjustments to their everyday life. Food was severely restricted and rationed, so that items that were normal in peacetime now seemed luxuries. 'It's funny how we revel in absurd bits of food – a prune can send us quite drunk, and a bit of honey faint straight off!!' Sybil wrote to Mary Crawley, thanking her for a food parcel. 'However, when one thinks of the people in Europe, one feels very humbled at all *we* have of good food, even if dull! Oh! would it might end.'

During the first three years of the war the London theatre was dominated by comedies, musicals and revues. The most popular plays were Coward's *Blithe Spirit*, Rattigan's *Flarepath* and *Arsenic and Old Lace*. The Blitz and the bombs inevitably affected audiences. Those who went often stayed on afterwards if a raid was in progress, to be entertained by sing-songs or turns by the actors. This also happened outside London, where touring companies were doing an important job in maintaining morale. Ivor Brown suggested that the Old Vic was now effectively a National Theatre. 'No theatre is really national or really popular unless it gives the nation and the people a chance to see if they like it. The essential conditions of such a theatre are excellence, mobility and cheapness. Hard enough to realise at any time, these become exceptionally difficult during a long, bitter and exhausting war.'

His words appeared in the programme for Laurence Housman's *Jacob's Ladder*, Sybil's final wartime touring production with Lewis, and the first new play to be staged by the Old Vic under the CEMA banner. Housman had achieved an international success with *Victoria Regina*, and was considered skilful at bringing historical characters to life on the stage. The publicity tried to emphasise the play's freshness: 'Here is the Bible story, brought close to us by a master of craft, and seeming as modern in its actuality as any fable that you may see upon the films.' Sybil doubled as Rebekah and one half of the Chorus, Lewis being the other. The play, directed by Esmé Church, was liked by the critics: the *Manchester Guardian* commending the nobility of Sybil's 'ruggedly intense portrayal of Rebekah'.

In the autumn Lewis was engaged for a further provincial tour with the Old Vic. Sybil meanwhile linked up with Russell, in a play he had written especially for her. *The House of Jeffreys* was a macabre echo of the blood-spattered melodramas they had created in their childhood. Sybil's role was that of Georgina Jeffreys, a descendant of the notorious hanging judge. She has returned from missionary work with a converted cannibal who, when the moon is full, reverts to his bad old ways, a habit which eventually drives her insane. 'A terrifying play, but full of interesting things – and a wonderful part for Ethel Barrymore,' Sybil told Mary Ward. 'Oh! a gem to play!'

But as in Rochester, brother and sister didn't always agree. From Brony-Garth Sybil wrote to Elizabeth Casson 'Russell is coming here tonight to re-write his last act – which I would do as it is!' A week later she reported: 'I'm working on Russell's play, very hard. It's been a real problem.' Patricia told John that they sang their way through the missionary hymns with great gusto. 'They rolled about the place in helpless giggles that grew farther out of control as the horrors grew more horrifying.' But there were also massive arguments, 'when it appeared that the only thing that prevented an outbreak of fisticuffs was their vicarage training'.

Once on the road Sybil began to enjoy herself. In August she wrote to Herbert Farjeon from Glasgow: 'I've always wanted to play a missionary wizard gone askew somehow. I'll enjoy the mad, diseased and abnormal – it releases such a lot of misery over the awful world war!!!' A month later she was in Cardiff: 'The play goes apace – I adore my part – I love playing the Religious Gone Awry!!' Russell, who also played a leading role, felt her part 'gave Sybil ample opportunity to ring the changes – and whether she was playing the travelling harmonium and singing hymns or smacking her lips over a cannibal feast, she gave to each side of a split personality the horror of a saint turned devil'.

When the play, directed by Henry Oscar, reached London and the newly restored Playhouse, the critics thought it preposterous and too full of arbitrary horrors, but appreciated Sybil's performance. Agate thought it incredible she should take on such a role, but admitted that 'the skill and tact of Sybil's performance are to be gathered from the fact that we did not laugh at Georgina once, not even when she came back from the wine-cellar clutching a bottle of Amontillado with which to wash down Roberta'. But Farjeon in *John O'London's Weekly*, while relishing her 'limping fanatically about the stage, dominating, riding the whirlwind, contorted, perverted', thought she should be marking her return to town after two years with something more worthy of her talents.

Sybil clearly appeared in this macabre thriller/shocker partly for the sake of Russell, who had a leading role in it. Offstage he remained the supreme fantasist, a beguiling storyteller who not only made up tales, but was the cause of them for others. In his unpublished autobiography Christopher recalled an example of his uncle's eccentricity. 'On tour he went missing – Burnley I think it was. The management were worried, they searched the digs and the pubs, then came down to the theatre to organise the understudy. There was Russell in the gallery queue, waiting to see himself act: "They tell me he's awfully good, so I wanted to see what he was like."'

As always, Sybil was being sent several scripts to consider. 'Oh! plays – plays – plays, too many and none very good,' she complained. But at Christmas she heard that *The Lion and the Unicorn*, a play about Queen Elizabeth which Clemence Dane had planned to write for her 15 years ago, was suddenly nearing completion. 'This is the one I desperately want to do,' she told Leon M Lion. 'I didn't think it was going to be brought to birth, but something set her going.' She thought it 'a beautiful play', and planned to appear in it in the spring, with Lewis as Lord Burleigh.

Sybil was a frequent visitor to Clemence Dane's rickety, untidy flat in Covent Garden. Mary recalls the family being asked to dinner. 'She would provide the most extraordinarily exotic food, that wasn't on the ration. One night I remember we had roast swan. She used to make the most disgusting drinks with gin and Lucozade, which we would surreptitiously pour into her fish tank. She was very extreme, but wonderful.' The flat was a favourite meeting place for theatre and film people, who relished their hostess' innocence about double meanings. Once she invited Noël Coward to lunch, booming down the phone: 'Do come! I've got such a lovely cock.' 'I do wish you'd call it a hen,' Coward replied.

It was she who wrote the script for *Cathedral Steps*, 'an anthology in praise of Britain' designed officially 'to impress upon the people our glorious heritage of freedom'. Directed by Basil Dean, it was performed in September on the steps of St Paul's Cathedral to a vast lunchtime crowd, and simultaneously broadcast to America. According to Dean, the original script needed little alteration, 'save to restrain a certain predilection for Queen Boadicea that might have involved Sybil Thorndike in a chariot race round St Paul's Churchyard'. It was a lavish, unashamedly patriotic occasion, with trumpets, drums and banners, and a procession of dignitaries. Sybil led the Men and Women of Peace, Lewis was The Warrior, and together with Henry Ainley, Leslie Howard, Edith Evans, Eric Portman, Marius Goring, Margaretta Scott and Cathleen Nesbitt they recited pieces by Shakespeare and many other writers, recalling great moments in British history.

Sybil had been concerned about their living arrangements with Eileen in her Bayswater house, telling Elizabeth Casson: 'I think we should get a small flat really. Unless I can make these rooms bearable – bearable for Lewis. I hate for him to be uncomfortable.' Their two rooms had been at the top of the house, furnished with what they had been able to salvage from Swan Court. The house was somewhat tatty, falling to pieces, and not always spotless. Eileen's daughter Phyllis remembers: 'We had a big hall covered in dark green lino, and Sybil would say: "Two spits to clean it all!" and get down on her hands and knees.' The two sisters would share the cooking, with Sybil favouring stews, as she claimed Lewis never noticed what he was eating, and would usually, to Eileen's annoyance, read a book during their meals.

Sybil was also having problems at Bron-y-Garth, where the housekeeper was thought to be playing fast and loose with the rations. She and Lewis decided to help with the war effort by giving the house over to shell-shocked children from Greenwich. 'I am desperately working now to get our house here turned into a Children's Home,' Sybil informed Vera Brittain. 'We will take 40 – and they come in next week with matrons and nurses – all from bombed places. I'm so excited for them to use this darling house. I keep one room so that I can come on occasions and say Hey to it all.'

Vera Brittain had sent her a copy of her new book *Humiliation with Honour*, which set out the pacifist cause in the form of letters to her son John. Some weeks later Sybil also read her friend's pamphlet 'One of These Little Ones', a personal plea for food relief for children in Europe. Her revulsion towards the war was exemplified in her letter to Vera Brittain. 'Your pamphlet is simply wonderful. We have done most of the things you ask us, except hold a meeting – which I simply cannot do at the moment. But if there is any way in which I can help you in any of your schemes will you please tell me. So many of us feel grateful to you for the work you do. The seeming hopelessness of relieving the ghastly suffering makes a lot of people *so* appalled that they hide their heads and pretend not to see – it's an easy way but I don't think it's a way any of them *like* – your concrete suggestions were a great help.'

There was a substantial demand for poetry during the war, which Peggy Ashcroft and Natasha Spender tapped into when they founded the Apollo Society soon afterwards; other founders included Jill Balcon, George Rylands, John Laurie, Stephen Spender and Maynard Keynes. The society's programmes, backed by CEMA, were a judicious mixture of poetry and music, and were performed all over the country, in army camps, factories and schools. Initially the participants were paid just £10. 'We felt like missionaries, we created an appetite for poetry,' Jill Balcon says. Sybil would take part in several of its recitals.

In the new year her ability to mix patriotism with pacifism was reflected in two events. *Salute to the Red Army* was staged by Basil Dean in the Albert Hall in February 1943 to mark the army's twenty-fifth anniversary. A mixture of pageantry, drama, poetry and music, based around an ode by Louis Macneice, it involved a cast of two thousand service men and women, paying tribute to Britain's new ally, and many leading actors, with Sybil and Ralph Richardson narrating the achievements of the Red Army. *The Times* described the spectacular scene: 'High up on pulpits painted a battleship grey stood the Spokesman (Lieutenant-Commander Ralph Richardson) and the Spokeswoman (Dame Sybil Thorndike) in cloth of gold and gold helmets, erect, heroic beings.' Soon afterwards Sybil presented Mrs Maisky, the wife of the Soviet ambassador, with a book of messages and pictures from British artists, as a tribute to their Russian counterparts.

She and Lewis now returned to Swan Court. The changes brought about by the war had compelled her to learn a new skill. 'I'm having to cook in my old age,' she told the Crawleys. 'We can get no help now, you see. It's very good for us all.' Like other Londoners she had also adapted to the bombs. 'Life seems very odd these days – we get raids and one gets used to them and it's all very horrible to think of – but we are lucky compared to poor occupied countries. It may be over sooner than we think. God grant it may – it's unbearable to think of the young lives gone.'

In the spring she went again to Dublin, invited by Micheál Maclíammóir and Hilton Edwards to appear with their Gate company in a six-week season at the Gaiety, as Mrs Alving in *Ghosts* and Lady Cicely Waynflete in *Captain Brassbound's Conversion*. Dublin acclaimed her performance in *Ghosts*, as did Maclíammóir, at 42 a somewhat elderly Oswald. 'The matchless austerity and fire of her Mrs Alving filled me with the deepest excitement,' he recalled. 'Essential truth is the secret of her acting. In *Ghosts* this was the lesson she taught me: that to be completely and faithfully oneself is the image to be held constantly before the eyes.'

With no blackout, very little traffic, and only the occasional plane in the sky, Dublin provided Sybil with an agreeable if brief respite from the war. But it also gave her a chance to see more of Christopher. Tall and spindly, and much cherished for his wit and erudition, he had been playing with Maclíammóir's company since arriving in Dublin. With his great vigour and fine voice, he was seen as a sound, reliable and unshowy actor. He was now doing voice work with a class of priests and monks at a Dominican monastery, and also at the Sacred Heart convent, and gaining a reputation as a harp-player and singer of Irish ballads. Sybil told Lewis' niece Peggy Reed: 'His voice is beautiful now. He does quite a lot of work on civic committees and all sorts. He lives very simply, almost like a religious.' To the Crawleys she wrote: 'It's queer the way he has become completely Irish, but he's a good boy and a hard worker and lives usefully.'

According to Glynis Casson, Christopher's eldest daughter, he and Sybil had a wonderful relationship. 'They wrote letters every week after he came to Ireland. I think he was her favourite in a way, because he was the more religious, and also very like her father.' There was, however, one topic on which they differed. While Christopher refused to have anything to do with the war on grounds of conscience, Sybil believed he was wrong to hold that belief from a safe distance in neutral Ireland, and that he should be working more actively for the pacifist cause. 'They were very, very close, but they didn't always see eye to eye,' Mary Casson remembers. 'She used to get very het up in her arguments with him.'

That feeling is evident in a letter she wrote to Vera Brittain the day after her return from Dublin: 'Do you ever get *very* disheartened? I'm fighting desperately hard – but it *is* hard to see how the *awful* problems are to be settled. In Eire life doesn't seem on our plane at all – they are a strange lovely people and I'm glad a *few* small nations have kept out of the horror, but I wish it were more positive, their non-fighting.' There was feeling of another kind, however, when Christopher mentioned in a letter that he and Sybil had met the German ambassador at a cocktail party in Dublin, and that Sybil thought him 'a darling man'. This letter was sent to John, still a prisoner of war, who was naturally annoyed with his mother.

John had made good use of his three years of captivity, moving from the camp near Frankfurt to Stalag Luft 3 in Silesia. Initially he had wondered about becoming a parson, and decided to study theology. Evidently delighted at the thought of her son carrying on where her father left off, Sybil immediately sent him several books. He had learnt German, and was now studying Russian, philosophy, semantics, logic and history. With other prisoners he had designed and built a combined church, library and theatre, where a new show was staged every three weeks: the repertoire ranged from Shakespeare to Shaw, farces to revue, orchestral concerts to band-shows. His first production was *Macbeth*, with Rupert Davies, the future Inspector Maigret, in the title-role, a six-foot-two Kenneth Mackintosh as Lady Macbeth, and he himself playing Macduff. Later he would direct *King Lear*, *Saint Joan*, and Priestley's *I Have Been Here Before*. In each case, he remembered, Sybil and Lewis 'sent me pages and pages of priceless theatrical wisdom'.

Although he was only allowed to send the occasional postcard to his parents, even this meagre contact was a huge comfort to Sybil: 'His letters have been very exciting,' she told Peggy Reed. 'He said there were great debates and discussions, always about politics etc, and the Germans take a great interest in their activities! Do them good, I expect! One of the ex-patriots from Stalag Luft 3 saw me last week, and said he is always in good spirits and keeps them all alive, never "down".' Clearly John had inherited not only the Casson qualities of determination and organisation, but also Sybil's optimism and cheerfulness. She herself, addressing a meeting in Manchester of hundreds of relatives of prisoners, was able to report that the books sent to the POWs 'had turned their time of exile into a fruitful period of study, so that after the war, when we had got to make the peace and set an example to the world, these boys would be able to make a really valuable contribution to the new world'.

In May she took part in a unique event. The Theatre Royal in Bristol, built in 1766 and the oldest in the country, had played host to most of the greats, including Sarah Siddons, Kemble, Kean, Macready, Irving and Ellen Terry. Situated close to the docks, it had miraculously survived the heavy bombing of the city, some parts of which, one visitor observed, 'were reminiscent of

Ypres in 1918'. It was now in danger of being pulled down to make way for a warehouse. Horrified at this prospect, a group of determined Bristolians raised enough money to save the building. CEMA then stepped in and took on the lease on behalf of the people of Bristol, and it became, almost by accident, the first subsidised theatre in Britain.

The play chosen to re-open the beautiful, intimate and restored theatre was *She Stoops to Conquer*, first performed there in 1773. In a makeshift Old Vic company directed by Dorothy Green, Sybil again played Mrs Hardcastle. The performance was preceded by a witty prologue, written by Herbert Farjeon and performed by Sybil, in character and full costume. 'She spoke Farjeon's ode most roguishly and prettily,' Beverley Baxter wrote. 'Then, to show her versatility, she gave a high-spirited Grand Guignol interpretation of Mrs Hardcastle in the play itself, which must have interested Goldsmith himself if he was present with other ghosts.' But for Agate, her performance confirmed his view that she was not a comic actress. 'She clowned Mrs Hardcastle tonight like an adenoidal – always her refuge in comedy,' he wrote in his diary. 'But I suppose Sybil couldn't resist being in at a "do" like this, seeing that it is so praiseworthy a "do". She has the heart of a fire-engine, and should be protected against herself.'

She stayed on to appear a fortnight later for another Old Vic company in Judith Guthrie's *Queen Bee*, an eccentric comedy set in an Anglo-Irish household in the Edwardian era, and directed by Hugh Miller. This failed to make the move to London, and perhaps for good reason. One of those who had helped to save the theatre, Veronica Lyne, described it as 'the worst play I have ever seen…my husband slept peacefully through the last two acts, but knows as much about it as the rest of us'.

For the rest of the year Sybil again showed her remarkable versatility as well as her hunger for the new, playing a sympathetic mother in a new West End play, plunging into a Greek comedy for one performance, and playing a part at Christmas that involved flying across the stage.

The new play was *Lottie Dundass* by Enid Bagnold, directed by Irene Hentschel and produced by C B Cochran. It was the story of a young actress on the edge of insanity, who kills her rival understudy when she is prevented at the last minute from going on for the indisposed star. 'It's a change after the coal mines!' Sybil told the Crawleys. The play, which ran for a solid four months, gave young Ann Todd in the title-role her first break in the theatre. She was offered it on condition she found a star to play her mother. Several leading actresses turned down the role, unwilling to play second fiddle to a relatively unknown actress. For Sybil this was not a problem. Here was another part demanding restraint, and she rose to the challenge: the critics wrote approvingly of her 'finely controlled acting', 'a subdued study of restrained emotion', of her 'subduing her imperial furies'. For Renée Asherson, making her West End debut, her performance was a revelation: 'I had only thought of her in terms of great pronouncements, and suddenly she was transformed, and utterly modern.'

During the run Sybil and Lewis took James Agate to supper at the Savoy. The critic afterwards captured the occasion in his diary. 'Sybil enormously tickled at Ivor Brown's statement that her performance as the mother in *Lottie Dundass* out-ranges her Medea. I say, "I suppose you could play Mrs Dundass and count the washing at the same time?" Sybil nods: "I wonder how much Ivor has thought about breath control." She wants to play Mrs Borkman to Flora Robson's Elle Rentheim. Do I think it a dull play? I say: "Yes. If Ibsen could ever be dull, he was dull there." Lewis is a delightful host who plies you with lots of food and drink, and just the right amount of wise, balanced comment to keep the conversation on an even keel.'

Sybil then appeared for one night only in *Rape of the Locks*, staged at the YMCA's Queen Mary Hall in Great Russell Street in aid of the International Voluntary Service for Peace. Murray had pieced together and translated fragments of the *Perikeiromene* by Menander, the Greek dramatist and leading figure in the 'New Comedy' of the third century BC, and added conjectural fragments of his own (the title was suggested by Shaw). Sybil made only a brief appearance as the Goddess of Ignorance, her main contribution being a recital before the play of English poetry from the fifteenth to the nineteenth century. This, according to *The Times*, 'delighted as much by the subtlety of the choice as by the range and sensitiveness of her elocution'.

The hunger for serious drama didn't prevent wartime audiences delighting in comedy, and at Christmas time in more traditional delights, such as *Alice in Wonderland* and *Alice Through the Looking Glass*, in which Sybil was now cast as the White Queen and the Queen of Hearts, in adaptations by Clemence Dane. She wrote to Leon M Lion: 'I'm working so hard I've only had time for the daily chores and getting a few things for the many children all around in intervals of rehearsal. I'm "flying" and so thrilled on the end of a wire – most exciting!!' Directed by Esmé Church, the shows had music by Richard Addinsell and designs by Gladys Calthrop, and played twice daily, packing the Scala for seven weeks. Sybil was in her element as the White Queen, as W MacQueen-Pope noted: 'To see Dame Sybil fly – on wires – as if to the manner born and as if she had been flying in ballets all her life, was breathtaking!'

The show was presented by Tom Arnold and Ivor Novello. Soon afterwards Novello was charged with the misuse of petrol coupons, and sentenced to eight weeks in prison. It was considered a harsh sentence: he had been foolish rather than intentionally law-breaking. Many friends tried without success to pull strings on his behalf with people of influence, including Churchill. Sybil and Lewis gave evidence of his character at his appeal. MacQueen-Pope was also in court: 'Dame Sybil gave her statement with shining enthusiasm and answered her questions like the wonderful woman she is, and one felt she carried the crowd with her. Lewis Casson was firm, unshakeable and clear, a perfect piece of integrity.' Novello's appeal was dismissed, thought the sentence was reduced to four weeks. When he was taken out of court, Sybil was among those who talked to him before he left for Wormwood Scrubs.

John of course remained constantly in her mind. 'He is in a huge camp, three and a half years of it,' she told Murray. 'More blackness to go through before the end of it all.' Her continuing despair about the war, and her frustration with the Labour Party, was reflected in a letter to George Caitlin, Vera Brittain's husband, in which she agreed to give an annual donation to the Chelsea Labour Party. 'I wish we could be sure that the Labour party was really out for *socialism*, for I think and believe – with many others – that this is the only way of making the world run at all with any hope of peace. One gets awfully tired of the Conservative attitude and the Labour party in Parliament, and the Cabinet!!! So let's keep one real socialist Labour faith alive – or we shall all turn Communist, and that would be a pity I think.'

She now spent several weeks giving solo recitals, many of them in Scotland and the Orkney Islands for the Army Education Corps. 'I've been doing mainly poetry,' she told Murray. 'There is such a new interest in verse, but then among quite unexpected people.' She also related another surprise. 'On the spur of the moment I tried the troops out with some Greeks – I was thrilled the way it held them – they'd only been given variety of the cheapest, and lectures! So I was a change at any rate!' Proud of her Scots ancestry, she gained a particular thrill from a visit to Elgin, the home of her grandfather John Bowers. 'I got up early and walked through the snow to see where the family post office had been,' she remembered. 'And that night I recited some of the lovely old poems my grandfather had read to me as a child.'

On her return from Scotland she was invited to re-join the Old Vic company. In doing so, she signed up for two celebrated seasons that would restore the morale of the London theatre, and provide an explosion of brilliance amid the darkness of war.

28

Triumph at the New

1944–1945

'I felt this little body go. I thought she was dead'
Ralph Richardson on Sybil's death scene in Peer Gynt

Looking back over his career as a director, Tyrone Guthrie drew a perceptive parallel between Sybil and Olivier. 'Of the actors whom I have seen, the two who best combine protean skill with star quality are Laurence Olivier and Sybil Thorndike. Both are more than equal to the long haul and are able, when required, to assume immense nobility, majesty and grandeur. Both excel in the expression of powerful passion. Both can be hilariously funny. Both almost take too much pleasure in the farouche and grotesque, and an endearing, almost childlike delight in looking, sounding and behaving as unlike their real selves as possible.'

Now, for the first time since *Coriolanus*, he brought them together again. Although the war was continuing, London seemed to be returning to a kind of normality. It was time for the Old Vic to return. Guthrie set up a company headed by Olivier, Richardson and John Burrell, a young BBC drama producer. Olivier and Richardson, friends but also rivals, were released from the Fleet Air Arm. The Waterloo Road theatre was still damaged and in use as a shelter, so Albery allowed the company to use the New. Olivier and Richardson would share the leading roles for five seasons, while Burrell would direct and be administrator. Mounting a repertory season in the West End was a revolutionary move, although Gielgud had also decided to stage a classical season, with plays by Shakespeare, Maugham, Webster and Congreve at the Haymarket. Londoners starved for years of top-class theatre were suddenly faced with an embarrassment of riches.

The Old Vic's repertoire was challenging. It consisted of Ibsen's difficult masterpiece *Peer Gynt*, adapted by Norman Ginsbury, Shaw's *Arms and the Man*, and Shakespeare's *Richard III* – and later *Uncle Vanya*. The company included Nicholas Hannen, Harcourt Williams, George Relph and Sydney Tafler; while the leading women were the young Irish actress Joyce Redman, and eighteen-year-old Margaret Leighton. Sybil – 'the Old Vic's staunchest champion', in Guthrie's words – was invited to play Peer Gynt's mother Aase, Catherine Petkoff in the Shaw, and Queen Margaret in the Shakespeare.

In June 1944 rehearsals for all three plays began in a large hall in an empty National Gallery in Trafalgar Square – the precious paintings had been sent into the Cheddar Caves in Somerset for the duration. The opening production was *Peer Gynt*, with Guthrie directing, Reece Pemberton as designer, and Robert Helpmann assisting with the movement. Richardson played Peer, and Olivier had the small but vivid part of the Button Moulder. Guthrie treated Sybil with easy affection: Peter Howell remembers him calling her 'that silly old Dame'. His skilful way of restraining her was to ask her to do a certain thing, 'but not as much as you'd like to'.

Early in the ten-week rehearsal period the V1s, Hitler's deadly flying bombs known as doodlebugs, hit London. During June and July almost 3,000 Londoners were killed, many more wounded, and hundred of buildings destroyed by the 8,000 pilotless bombs. 'We rehearsed in a spirit of cheerful enthusiasm, tinged with real misgivings,' John Burrell remembered. 'When as often happened a bomb seemed to be headed straight for the gallery, rehearsals would stop while everyone lay on the floor.' Guthrie recalled: 'It was shaming how relieved we all felt when a bang, and the ensuing shattering of timbers and glass, would proclaim that someone else had "had" it.' As the actors rehearsed, the London theatres began to close all around them, until only six out of 36 remained open. But Harcourt Williams had consulted the tea-leaves, which showed that the doodlebugs would stop before their first night. They did so, just three days before *Peer Gynt* opened on 31 August.

Sybil had loved Ibsen's picaresque poetic drama ever since Russell had played Peer at the Old Vic. Now it was a triumph for Ralph Richardson who, after years away from the stage, was terrified of tackling the title-role. His performance as the dreamy, romantic, cynical, ultimately hollow Peer was greatly admired; Agate called it 'heroic'. Olivier shone bright in a short but disturbing appearance as the Button Moulder – 'so ordinary, but so frightening', Sybil observed. But some of the most vivid memories are of Richardson and Sybil playing Aase's death scene.

Peter Howell, one of the trolls, recalls that 'she and Richardson had that same extraordinary quality, total reality, and at the same time great actors' feel for it'. Bay White remembers: 'I used to creep down night after night into the wings to listen to them play the scene. The house was so concentrated, you could hear the silence.' Joyce Redman, playing Solveig, believes 'there will never be another Aase like Sybil, she broke your heart'. Richardson himself found Sybil's playing almost too real, claiming: 'When she died my heart was in my mouth every time. I felt this little body go, I thought she was dead.' And while *The Times* detected 'an element of falsehood, some characteristic of sentimental motherhood' in her portrait, J C Trewin described the performance as 'her meridian....Aase's dying voice would have melted marble'.

Sybil was a big influence within the company, especially with the young actresses. 'People were very deferential to their seniors,' Bay White recalls. 'It was very much Mr Olivier and Mr Richardson, and I was completely overwhelmed. But with Sybil there was immediately personal contact and warmth, and that gave me confidence.' Margaret Leighton was impressed by her selflessness, notably on days when she was playing different parts at the matinee and evening performances: 'I would go into her dressing-room between shows and ask her to hear my lines. Without batting an eyelid she would sit down and work with me on my silly little part all through the tea-break....She never shooed me out, never even demurred, and behaved as if she had all the time in the world to worry over *my* problems.'

Joyce Redman also had reason to be grateful. 'Maggie Leighton and I were so frightened of Larry and Ralph; to us they were gods. I could hardly talk at rehearsals, I was so nervous of them. I wrote to John Burrell asking to leave the company. Sybil heard about this, took me aside and said, Now come on, we're all feeling like that. You'll find it strange and horrible, but if you want to be an actress you've got to brave it through. – She knew what I was going through, how frightened I was. If it hadn't been for her I think I would have left. She was wonderful, terribly *simpatico*. I would never have got through that season without her.' Richardson was also an admirer, but saw a side of her few others did: 'Although Sybil's well-known warmth of heart is true indeed, she has a stiletto – a stiletto for fools, whom she does not suffer gladly. But she keeps it carefully concealed, as stilettos should always be.'

Next came Shaw's delightfully anti-romantic comedy *Arms and the Man*, directed by Burrell. The company tried this out in Manchester and Glasgow, as Olivier, who had not been on stage in London in a major role since the

1938 *Coriolanus* with Sybil, wanted to ease himself back gradually. Harcourt Williams wrote later: 'In Manchester I came to appreciate the amazing vitality of Sybil Thorndike. Every day she seemed to be speaking here, giving a recital for some good cause there, attending early service, dealing with correspondence, and acting at night with undiminished vigour. And always in such good spirits and high humour.'

Sybil, in a colourful tea-gown, played the 'imperiously energetic' Catherine Petkoff, with a jet-black wig and heavily made-up eyes. 'One would not have foregone Dame Sybil's agonised bustlings,' noted *The Times*, while the *Manchester Guardian* wrote of her performance: 'It has experience, it has gaiety, it has gusto.' Olivier as the priggish and cowardly Sergius adopted the first in a long line of false noses – Sybil thought he was 'frightfully funny', but the audience didn't – while Richardson was brilliant as the phlegmatic 'chocolate-cream soldier'. Shaw's anti-militaristic jibes added an extra sting for wartime audiences.

The third play to open was *Richard III*, directed by Burrell. According to Joyce Redman, 'He was a very laid-back director, he didn't tell you very much, he let you do your own thing.' Yet he managed to tone down Sybil's work in one respect, as Athene Seyler recalls being told by Nicholas Hannen, who played Buckingham. 'She had what we used to call her Queen's Walk, rather a stride and holding her head up, a bit theatrical and not very good. When she made her entrance, John Burrell stopped her, whispered something to her, and the next time she came in perfectly naturally. None of us had been able to say that to her, even though we knew her well.'

Olivier, with his thin reptilian nose, his shoulder-length black wig streaked with red, and his voice based on imitations he had heard of Irving in the role, gave a bravura performance of hypnotic power that is still remembered by many over sixty years later. Darlington described him as 'malignity incarnate'; and such was the evil he gave off, Harcourt Williams gave him a wide berth in the wings. Sybil, in the minor part of the mad Queen Margaret, was back in Grand Guignol form. The critic Audrey Williamson wrote: 'Sybil Thorndike played Margaret with an agued intensity; her hands, quivering with age and a nervous passion, gave the half-mad queen an added terror, and she delivered the curse as if the woman's wandering mind had become transfixed, for a moment or two only, with a poisonous and prophetic hatred.'

Sybil wrote to John van Druten: 'The season is a huge success – Larry is a wonderful Richard – he really is evil....Oh! the theatre is all doing well. The real excitement is Larry's Henry V film, it's so beautiful – we have just seen it.' Olivier had invited her and the rest of the company to the trade show. Shakespeare on film Sybil generally thought 'the last word in frightfulness', but this she saw as an exception. It proved a huge draw as the V2 rockets fell on London. But by the end of the year all the London theatres had re-opened, and capacity audiences at the New again became the rule.

On Boxing Day Sybil returned again for a month to the *Alice* double-bill, now at the Palace. 'She flies through the air with the greatest of ease, and orders off heads with abandon,' reported the *News of the World*. Asked if playing 15 performances every week in the two theatres was too much, Sybil replied: 'Life can be exhausting everywhere but in the theatre. The more I work there, the better I feel.' Sonia Williams, a student at RADA who had a small part, remembers: 'I was stunned by her, she was the most amazing, rumbustious, wonderfully full-blooded person.' The matinees of Ibsen, Shaw and Shakespeare at the New meant she could only do the morning shows, so Margaret Rutherford took over in the afternoons. Esmé Church, comparing the two, suggested 'Sybil was quite special because her timing was exact and precise', but Margaret Rutherford 'was the essence of the White Queen'.

With long, overnight queues a common sight at the New, *Uncle Vanya* was added to the repertoire; a fifth, a new play by James Bridie about Lancelot and Guinivere, was planned, but failed to materialise. Because of the demand for tickets for the first three productions, the opening of the Chekhov, with Richardson as Vanya and Olivier as Astrov, was briefly postponed. Burrell had the company sitting in Sybil's dressing-room for several days while they read the play, which caused the actors great frustration. Richardson felt uncomfortable in his first Chekhov part, and Harcourt Williams – as well as some critics – felt he and Olivier should have swapped roles.

Sybil, dressed in shawls and a white mob cap, gave a simple, touching performance as Marina, the gruff but tender family nurse. Audrey Williamson thought her 'gnarled and luminous as a picture by Rembrandt', while Beverley Baxter noted: 'Miss Thorndike was so convincing she almost raised the samovar to a principal part.' Tanya Moisiewitsch, who designed the scenery and costumes, thought 'she was born to play the part, she was perfection'. But although the production had beautiful moments, it found little favour with the critics, and was dropped after 21 performances. It was, surprisingly, to be Sybil's only Chekhov role.

The season at the New restored two great actors to the theatre, provided much-needed stimulation both to civilians and men and women in uniform, and was hailed as a fine example of how a National Theatre might operate. Harcourt Williams noted: 'Perhaps the most startling thing about the venture was that the British public (for the first time, I think) had accepted and supported a real repertory of classic plays presented with a constant change of bill.' Although Sybil's parts had been relatively small, there were some who felt her Aase established her once again as the country's foremost actress. It was a role she repeated soon afterwards on the radio, one of her rare wartime drama broadcasts. She had already recorded Housman's *Abraham and Isaac*, to which she now added *Jane Clegg* and Guthrie's play *Matrimonial News*.

Ann, meanwhile, was about to take a bold step. 'She is doing Saint Joan after Christmas, taking it out round the country first,' Sybil told the Crawleys. 'She's a worker!!' After wartime tours with E Martin Browne's Pilgrim Players and with Sybil and Lewis, Ann had joined Wolfit's company, playing Regan to his Lear and Olivia to his Malvolio. In 1943 she had set up her own company, Curtain Theatre, touring Scotland and the Orkneys and Hebrides for the Army Education Corps. Having converted to Roman Catholicism in 1944 – but 'a Protesting one' she told Shaw – she was eager to tackle Saint Joan. 'I am approaching the part after a study of Joan's life, and not with memories of my mother's performance,' she stated firmly. 'My mother created the part, but this is my own interpretation.'

Shaw strongly approved of this idea, believing Ann looked the part and was the right age. 'She looks just the goods for Joan,' he wrote to Sybil, who had sent her a picture. 'She has the authentic Saint Joan tradition, and I look to her to rescue the part from the snivelling Bergners and Pitoëffs, who do nothing but cry and leave out all the strong lines.' He sent Lewis detailed suggestions for casting, warning him that he wanted 'as many new people as possible, to avoid making Ann an Infant Phenomenon and you a Crummles'. He told Ann: 'You are in exactly the right humour for it; for Joan is a volcano of energy from beginning to end, and never the snivelling Cinderella, born to be burnt, that all the others – except the first – made her.'

Lewis, who directed, declared: 'Sybil is a dominating force in our family circle, and I've encouraged Ann to be a rebel.' The prompt book for his original production was used again, as was the sword. Ann recalled: 'I was able to go straight to Joan myself, and Father wisely directed me without reference to Mother.' Miriam Karlin, an understudy in the production, saw things differently. 'Lewis directed in a way that would now be regarded as outrageous;

he gave you a reading on every line. He directed Ann to do it in exactly the same way as Sybil. I think she was constrained by him: she took his direction, though occasionally she would question something.'

Janet Ritchie, the daughter of Ann's cousin Owen Reed, watched a dress-rehearsal from the wings of the Theatre Royal in Bristol. 'Ann looked incredibly like Sybil, both in voice and personality,' she says. 'She was very outgoing and enthusiastic about everything.' While it was impossible for those who had seen Sybil's Joan not to be struck by similarities of accent, inflection and movement, Ann's performance was generally judged on its merits. 'This was no imitation,' Darlington wrote, 'but a fresh and vital reading of a great part.' Sybil herself, seeing the play for the first time, was delighted: 'I wish you could see her,' she wrote to Elizabeth. 'I went to Bristol on my off night and *loved* her.' A week later she caught the play in London, and told Elizabeth Robins: 'It was such a thrilling experience for me, it was quite her own performance, and I had nothing to do with her while she was working at it!'

Ann gained different things from her parents: penetrating and sometimes devastating criticism from her father, praise and encouragement from her mother. 'I had to face the challenge of Father's hurricane force as a director, and if you can survive that you must get somewhere,' she said later. 'Father was always extremely hard to please, so if he thought anything good at all about one's performance, it was most deeply valued.' Sybil, by contrast, was 'completely biased in our favour', seeing 'the good in people first, in everyone, but in her family most of all....She is quite marvellously generous in her appreciation of other people.'

As the end of the war seemed imminent, Sybil made a plea for the continuation in peacetime of the morale-boosting National Gallery concerts. 'What these concerts have meant and will mean to many thousands of people is constantly being brought home to me,' she wrote to *The Times*, 'and all sorts and conditions of men and women want an assurance that this music shall continue to be available in their lives. The part these concerts played in sustaining the morale of London through all the trials of war is incalculable....We Londoners have lost so much that can never be replaced: surely we can hope to retain one of the few real benefits that have been given us during these dangerous, difficult and nearly always uncomfortable years?'

One of her losses at this time came with the death of her friend Herbert Farjeon. Sybil wrote immediately to his widow Joan: 'You have always been such a good thing to think of – your home – the aliveness of you all – and

Bertie so courageous and never just taking the popular way. Integrity counts for so much – he will be such a loss to the theatre – the press – and the new things that are building.' As so often, she expressed the sentiment she hoped would be a comfort in such circumstances, adding: 'Somehow I think he may be doing something more creative where he is now; more and more I believe they aren't far away – those who have died here.'

During the war she had supported several small theatre companies. Along with T S Eliot, Dorothy L Sayers and Marie Tempest she was a vice-president of the Oxford Pilgrim Players. She gave constant encouragement to the Adelphi Players, a company with socialist and pacifist ideals which included many conscientious objectors. She also regularly attended productions at the Little Theatre in Islington, run by refugees from Nazi Germany: 'They always conveyed the content of a play, its essence and its main concern, in a way often lacking in West End productions,' she recalled. She also found time to read plays, as Peter Howell noticed while they were at the New. 'I had to fire-watch in her dressing-room, which was absolutely full of scripts. One knew that she was going to plough through them and write long letters to everyone, which is what she did.'

The Old Vic company now embarked on a short provincial tour to Glasgow and then Manchester, where they were when the war ended. On VE Day bonfires were lit and the crowds danced in the streets. Sybil wandered up and down Deansgate, wondering whether John was safe, and if so where he was. In fact he was already on his way home. During his five years as a prisoner-of-war he had established communication with London by coded messages in prisoners' letters home, an achievement for which he later received an OBE. He had also helped in preparations for the Great Escape; several of his friends were among the 47 caught and shot.

About to go on for the evening performance, Sybil received a phone call from him: he was already in England. She wept uncontrollably, with Olivier by her side, then pulled herself together for the play. Two days later John received a note from Olivier. 'How lovely it must be for you to be with your family again,' he wrote. 'Your mother's joy since you phoned is a delight to behold. It shines out of her.'

29

The Aftermath of War

1945

'London is a smart lovely town beside this devastation'
Letter from Sybil to Lewis from Hamburg

Two weeks after VE Day, sitting aboard a troop ship at Tilbury Docks on the Thames, Sybil wrote: 'Oh Lewis! to see those masses of soldiers and know that it's not for slaughter they are going over – it's wonderful!... Oh darling, if you were here it would be glorious, but I keep holding on to our deep deep blessing having John home – and all being fit and well and all having work.'

Dressed in army uniform, Sybil, Olivier, Richardson and 62 other members of the Old Vic company were about to undertake a tour of post-war Europe. Under the auspices of ENSA they were to perform *Peer Gynt*, *Arms and the Man* and *Richard III* to the Allied troops remaining there. One of 60 companies to go to Europe in the aftermath of the war, they travelled first to Antwerp, Brussels, Bruges and Ghent, then flew on to Germany, where they played in Hamburg and Lubeck, as well as Belsen concentration camp, before ending up at the Comédie-Française in Paris. Missing Lewis desperately, Sybil wrote to him every day, pouring out her thoughts and feelings about the pitiful plight of the people in these countries.

From Ostend they travelled through Bruges to Antwerp, where they began with *Arms and the Man*. The theatre here had been out of action for five years. 'Last night was a really wonderful opening,' Sybil reported. 'Crowds turned away, and such a *thrilling* audience got every point.' She recorded a similar response to *Richard III*: 'Crowds pouring in – it's wonderful – turn hundreds away each performance – and so responsive...that massed audience sitting like mice, but getting every bit of humour.' *Peer Gynt* was equally popular:

'Oh! the theatre tonight for Peer, jammed to the ceiling,' she wrote from Brussels. She relished the idea of bringing theatre to new audiences, but with the troops there was an added purpose: 'All the soldiers and sailors I meet make me feel humbled. As if we can't do enough to make up in some tiny way of stimulant and imagination what they are needing and have missed – their homes and their own life in their own country.'

Despite her love of bare boards and simplicity, she found the large European theatres impressive. 'The theatre is a *dream*!' she wrote from Antwerp's majestic Flamisches Schauspielhaus, where they played for a week. 'Very like the Bristol sort – only large – all gold and a beautiful shape – a real *theatre*….I felt glad to be an actor, it was a real *temple* feeling.' From Brussels, where they played in the Théâtre Royal de la Monnaie, she enthused about 'these beautiful, dignified theatres…what repose and culture seems to cling to the walls'; she confessed they made her 'sick of the awful places in England and America'. But she feared their size created problems. 'It looks lovely, but honestly I found it hard to hear,' she told Lewis, after watching part of *Richard III* from the back of the Staatliche Schauspielhaus in Hamburg: 'I think it's slovenly speech most of the time – I really don't think big theatres are any use to present-day actors. Larry hates them, so do they all.'

Working under the ENSA banner, the company was under the control of the army; the actors were given the honorary rank of lieutenant, so they had to wear uniform at all times offstage. They lived in some comfort in hotels, ate well, and Sybil, Olivier and Richardson were often taken out to lunch or supper by high-ranking forces people. Sybil enjoyed it all hugely, but felt guilty about their comfortable life, and the contrast with the deprivations of the local population. 'The starvation in Holland is ghastly, we hear pitiful tales,' she wrote from Antwerp.

After a stay in Holland they flew on to Germany. At first Sybil hated flying, but tried not to show it, as Margaret Leighton recalled: 'She would keep upright in her seat, green as a pea and praying for us to land safely, but all the time she pretended to be loving it.' She had an early glimpse of the effects of the bombing on Germany when the pilot took them on a diversion over the Ruhr country. 'He banked down over Essen to show us,' she reported. 'Such devastation it made one feel horrible. I got the most awful emotional crisis and I couldn't stop crying. Over the Rhine, such emotion again – all places one knew in one's newspaper.' When they landed they were told by the army authorities not to speak to any German: when she and Harcourt

Williams complained they were told they would be sent back to England if they broke the rule.

A few weeks earlier George Orwell had written in the *Observer*: 'To walk through the ruined cities of Germany is to feel an actual doubt about the continuity of civilisation.' One of the grimmest pictures was in Hamburg where, according to Basil Dean, 'the streets stretched endlessly through acres of desolation'. During the immense firestorms that hit the city, some 45,000 people had died in one night. Remarkably, the Staatliche Schauspielhaus was one of the few buildings still standing in the centre. Accompanied by Peter Copley and Sydney Tafler, Sybil walked round the town 'in the depths of misery at the sight': hundreds of buildings were flattened, and many people were living in cellars or under rusty, corrugated sheets. 'It just has to be seen to be believed, London is a smart lovely town beside this devastation,' she observed. 'I don't know where the people live, it's all destroyed. I'm just bowled over with it. I think English people should see it – and the senselessness and waste of war and the hatred engendered.'

Even in the theatre it was hard to forget the war. 'The crowds are going in past my dressing-room window, most of them with guns,' she wrote, as she prepared to perform *Arms and the Man*. 'Oh! it's a beastly feeling, war, isn't it?' As in Belgium, the company played to packed houses. 'The success of the visit exceeded our expectations,' Basil Dean noted. 'The troops came in from places fifty miles away, driving in their jeeps and lorries through a countryside still encumbered with the surrendering enemy. The fine old theatre was so packed that, in the words of one exuberant reporter, the troops seemed to be hanging on to the chandeliers. Never has classical drama been performed to greater enthusiasm.' But Peter Copley had a slightly different view: 'They packed the theatre every night, and we thought, Ah, this is the young audience of the future. But they had absolutely nothing else to do.'

Throughout the tour Sybil was struck by the unaffected areas of country-side: 'The scenery is charming – very flat but so beautifully cultivated,' she observed as they drove through Belgium. 'The way the trees are planted and the shape of the various fields make a sort of Paul Nash with Corot colours – such order and comeliness.' In Germany, when the ENSA bus broke down one day, she found solace and comfort after a picnic in the woods. 'I and two of the boys (both pacifists) went off for a lovely walk thru cornfields and pine woods. We sat down in a lovely cool place – and such a vista, no hedges or walls, just rolling country, and copses, and here and there a farm. Suddenly I had such a feeling of peace, and all the destruction and horror seemed unreal. The fields looked so tidy and rich and simple, and I felt suddenly happy, as if all these eternal growing things would put the horrible destruction right.'

One day she and some of the company were taken into the countryside in an open car, accompanied by an army officer. Peter Copley recalls the occasion: 'As we passed a small forest, along the track came this enormous cart piled high with hay, drawn by four big horses, with an old farmer sitting on the top. Sybil said: "It's so beautiful, this is what we fought the war for, a free and a decent and an open life like this, this is wonderful, this is our future, we must preserve it." Later she was visited by a security officer, who gave her a dressing down. He said it was totally improper for us to be heard speaking in such favourable terms of the enemy. Sybil understood, but it distressed her, because what she was saying was really a wonderful truth.'

Because of the volatile situation, none of the company was allowed out after eight in the evening. The rules against fraternising with the German people were strict, and no German was allowed to see the plays. With her natural instinct for engaging with people and finding out about their lives, Sybil found these rules hard to bear. 'The awful thing is, the people look just like us,' she wrote from Hamburg. 'Extra-pretty fair girls and lovely children – one can't imagine how they got landed in this foul Nazi regime.' Keen to make contact with ordinary people, she disobeyed the rules in small ways, talking to shopkeepers, her room maid, girls working in the fields, and the hotel receptionist. She tried to improve her knowledge of the language: 'I swot at my bits of German for I feel this in some way is a sign of friendliness – or rather a desire for peace'.

Within the company she was seen as a mother figure, and sometimes had to step in to resolve a conflict. Some of the younger actresses broke the rules by going out to champagne parties with British officers in the evenings. Joyce Redman remembers Sybil's intervention: 'The manager wanted one of them sacked, but she prevented it. She said to him: "Don't be stupid, she's back now, she's safe and sound, she's young." She had everything in the right proportion, she was a centre of sanity, and everybody would go to her if something happened.' She also had time for late-night talks with Olivier and Richardson. 'Larry is very interesting when one really gets him talking – he is very loveable – he's thrilled with cinema work – not as an actor but as a director. I think acting makes him bored after a week! Ralph is very interesting too, particularly on painting and all that entails.' But she was not impressed when

Richardson missed a performance: 'Ralph is off – a cold, and afraid of his voice – when I *think* of the awful voices I've played big parts in – so as not to be off!!'

Sometimes she forgot this ban on mentioning their whereabouts in letters home. When she remembered, her coded descriptions of places were none too subtle. Brussels, for example, she called 'the place that's part of the vegetables you have with turkey at Christmas'. The enemy code-breakers might have had more difficulty with Ghent, which she described as 'the place Joris and I galloped to', a reference to a Browning poem. But the coded messages were not just going in one direction. In mid June she received a letter from Lewis saying: 'Remember our black spaniel? That's what's coming to me. But not a word.' It took her a moment to recall their dog's name, and to realise what he meant – the dog was called Knight. Her reaction to this news of Lewis' knighthood was ecstatic: 'I'm so thrilled I don't know what to do,' she wrote. 'I cried when I got your letter, it's so wonderful. Oh darling, darling, I feel so happy for you – and for myself and all the children…I can't get over it all, it's like a glorious bit of warm sunshine in my inside….I'm not sure it isn't the biggest thrill of my life…I'm just singing with glee and dancing and capering!'

Inevitably she found it hard to keep the secret over the next few days, and when the news finally appeared in the papers she couldn't contain herself. 'I flew off to the lounge panting and trembling – and there in *The Times* was your face, looking immensely pleased, like at a Welsh tea before a show – completely satisfied that the Welsh have the cream!! Then Billie [Harcourt Williams] came in and I told him, but I couldn't tell anyone else at that moment, for I was "filled as the morn at the full". Then I met Beau [Nicholas Hannen] coming downstairs and I shouted "Lewis is knighted", and Beau very nearly did a cartwheel he was so excited, then Ralph, and one by one everyone chased me up, and dear Sydney Tafler who I love devotedly was the most thrilled of all almost, for he is a socialist and hails you as the saviour of the stage etc, etc. I was so bucked at everyone being so bucked.' Olivier was one of the last to hear the news. 'He rushed over and hugged me, calling out: "Cheers for my old boss, he turned up trumps – now the young 'uns must bestir themselves!"'

Lewis wondered if becoming a Knight Batchelor might go against his socialist principles. Sybil made her view clear immediately: 'Of course it's right, and against no principles, and it's just to show how splendid you are, darling, and you work quietly and never think of yourself, and your own comfort, but always of the work in hand….You never ask for any chocolates or pats on the back – everyone has said this today.' There was another, more parochial consideration. 'I adore being Lady Casson,' she confessed, 'and won't all Portmadoc be thrilled!'

The following night there was a small celebratory supper party, at which Olivier made a suitably theatrical speech: 'It was Larry and Ralph and Joyce and Margaret and Beau and I – and just as we were starting Larry said, "Charge your glasses and drink to our dear, dear friends Sir Lewis and Lady Casson" – then he went on, "Nature made her a lady, her parents made her a lady, her acting makes her a lady, the king made her a lady, we made her a lady because we love her, and now crowning all this her husband has made her a lady." *Such* a fool – everyone yelled and I made a silly little speech, and all felt fine.'

But that same week she came face to face with the human consequences of Hitler's regime. The concentration camp at Belsen had been liberated by the British army two months previously. They had found 15,000 dead, with mass graves, some holding as many as 800 corpses. Robert Collis, the head of the Red Cross medical team in the camp, and a friend of Sybil's son Christopher, asked if she and the company would stage a matinee there for the staff. The camp still had 40,000 inmates, 10,000 corpses rotting in the open, and 500 British and French troops stationed there. Gerald Sim, a company member, remembers the day: 'They had burnt all the huts down, but there were signs saying Beware of Typhus all over the place.' Dr Collis asked Sybil to come round the camp with him, which she agreed to do, together with Joyce Redman and Margaret Leighton. The letter she wrote to Lewis the next day conveys the full horror of the suffering endured by the Jewish children, and the effect it had on her.

'Dr Collis wanted me and the two girls to go and see the children's hospital – it was utterly pitiful to see these children – nearly all TB and such little skeletons – we saw all the ones that are going to get better first – all perfectly grim tho' – then we saw those who were hopeless – poor little skeletons – the mother of one was there – there was another mother too and I managed with my halting bits of German to get out of her what had happened – she was a German peasant – she'd seen her husband shot and a daughter – and two sons, she didn't know where they were – and the other little daughter was dying – a poor little girl like a ghost with a shaven head. Both women were crying and they clung on to us and as we went said "Danke, danke" – I just couldn't stop crying. There was a wonderful Russian girl in her twenties who had seen her husband tortured (Dr Collis told me this) and her baby burned – and she just turned to and made up her mind to save as many children as she could. She saved 67 – and 58 of these she took back to Holland last week. She was such a darling, so jolly and bright. She spoke very little English, only Russian, but she conveyed a lot – and the poor little children just adore her – her name is Inpar – they call her Sister Inpar. Then Dr Collis took us round the burial hut. A horror place – you can still see quite a lot – they buried 23 thousand – we were so overcome by it all – how brutal and calculating it all was…I am so full of admiration for the heroism – Dr Collis told me as I went round the hospital, "You're meeting some of the greatest heroines in the world." The death rate has gone down now to 15 a day – so they have hope – I didn't see the adult hospital, didn't have time. Typhus, TB and dysentery is the scourge there.…I'd like everybody to go just to see how much humans can stand and how brave and good people can be, but no wonder it made the soldiers feel blind with rage when they saw it.'

Joyce Redman still remembers the visit clearly. 'It was so terrible, I couldn't believe what human beings could do to each other. I remember one little woman with matchstick arms, she was up in the bed, she had no hair at all except a strand, and on this strand there was a red bow – she was still trying to look her best. Sybil was wonderful to everyone, she kissed and patted and talked to the dying children, while I just trailed after her. Nothing mattered to her but love. She was the most gutsy woman I've ever known, a woman for all seasons.' Afterwards no one could eat their lunch, but in the afternoon they somehow managed to perform *Arms and the Man*, in a vast echoing cinema near the camp. Actress Bay White recalls that 'when they came back Sybil and Margaret were crying all the time, I remember how terribly shocked they were, and trying to stop because they had to do *Richard III* that night'. Sybil got through the performance, but wrote to John afterwards: 'I was in a haze, a nasty evil-smelling haze. I'll never forget this all my life. Oh, war turns people into monsters – though some heroism comes sometimes, doesn't it? I'll never get over today – never.'

Horrified by the war, she was also much concerned with what would happen after it. 'I wish I didn't feel so awfully unhappy about the world,' she wrote. 'I just can't see how we're going to tackle it with the old methods. I feel Russia gets nearer to some sort of working way than we do. …Same old things starting again – same old grab and greed. The Wells story keeps coming back to me, when God shook us all out of his sleeve and put us in a new place and said, "Now try again." It's such a chance.' Like most people, she expected Churchill and the Conservative Party to win the forthcoming British general election. Frustrated at the idea of missing it ('I'm *mad* at not being back for it'), she spent much time offstage in vigorous political arguments. 'I was alone as a socialist, but put up a fight,' she declared proudly, after a lunch with Olivier and Richardson with the Consul-General in Antwerp.

Within the company she was not quite isolated politically: her allies included Peter Copley, Sydney Tafler, the composer and conductor Herbert Menges, and George Relph, who was that rare creature, a member both of the Communist Party and the Garrick Club. They and Sybil argued often with Richardson and Olivier, trying to persuade them to vote Labour in the imminent general election, without success. Her main antagonist was her great friend the debonair Nicholas ('Beau') Hannen. 'We have *such* arguments here, but I don't think Beau will ever change – "Old English" is him,' she wrote. 'He thinks we've gone completely red, so I disabused him of much of his nonsense!' Soon after she told Lewis: 'Beau and I had a pass about the election – he says just what the Conservatives want him to say.' In Germany they received their proxy voting cards, and the debate continued. 'We have much talk with the younger people, and it's very amusing – Beau is such a darling, but he is living in a completely unreal world.' Once the discussion became heated: 'We had a hideous argument at supper last night with Beau. I felt sorry after – it's really no good talking to him, he's a bit unbalanced over politics, the Conservatives are the Voice of God.'

In Hamburg she found some fellow-spirits in the shape of a group of young Quakers, working in a Friends' Ambulance Unit 'Oh! it was a lovely change to be with about 12 splendid boys who have been doing fine work all the war and all helping instead of destroying,' she wrote. 'All of them have been out here following the main armies – and they are a fine crowd and all very definitely Christian, and so intelligent and steady. I felt a sort of balm to my very perplexed and not very happy spirit. You can't be happy here, it's too devastating – you can only help to assuage somehow the awfulness that war has made. These boys had a lot to do with the camps, and they said that was horror beyond belief.'

Though she could more than hold her own in an argument, her opinions sprang from her humanity and easily aroused emotions, and could often lead her into wild inconsistencies. It was Lewis who provided the more measured arguments, the more detailed, realistic political analyses. Once, in giving a speech, she had talked vaguely about 'building bridges'; afterwards Lewis asked 'between what and what?' Now she wrote to him on a question relating to relations with Russia. 'I can't quite make out what it is. Perhaps you'll give me one of your illuminating paragraphs to pass on to Beau and others in this company!' Yet while she clearly missed Lewis' support politically, it was the emotional deprivation that caused her the most anguish.

Every letter she wrote included a declaration of her love, and how much she missed him – sentiments that Lewis also expressed when he wrote to her. After a fortnight away she told him: 'I *can't* find things perfect if I haven't got you with me to share and discuss.' After thirty-seven years of marriage her passion seemed undimmed. From Hamburg she wrote: 'We are so close. I can feel your hands – and the side of your eyes – such strength you have. I do love you so, and more and more I miss you terribly.' A few days later she wrote: 'Oh! Lewis darling, I can't bear not seeing you – you are the peak of the world to me.' But their separation, and Lewis' tendency towards depression, sometimes made her anxious and insecure: 'I get awful quirks sometimes that you'll get down and then ill and won't like me,' she wrote. She also worried about her violent temper: 'I wish I'd always been nice, and never cross!!'

When they reached Paris, the contrast with Belgium and Germany renewed her spirits. 'Paris! I'd forgotten how perfect it is,' she wrote. 'It's so beautiful, beyond belief. After all the shabby towns and misery, to see this beauty....No bombs seemed to have touched it.' Yet she was aware of the problems facing the Parisians, more than half of whom were underfed, living mainly on dried beans and boiled potatoes, and coffee made from roasted acorns. 'No war on the outside, but no food – or very very scarce,' she noted, after seeing girls turning over dustbins to find something to eat. 'No transport at all, no buses, no trams....Oh Lewis! how the people suffered here. When I think of the anonymous letters I had and the non-anonymous ones, saying why fuss about the French and Dutch etc, look at the starving at home first!'

She stayed in a small hostel in the poor part of the city, and with no transport available, indulged her love of walking. 'Oh! Paris is heavenly, just walking the streets is a stimulant,' she observed. 'The space is so beautiful and those glorious bridges, I just walk over one and back over the next for the sheer pleasure of bridges.' She walked for hours, sometimes feeling dizzy under the hot sun, but reciting poetry to keep herself going, aware she might appear odd, but determined to see everything: 'One goes on and on, it's so lovely you feel "I'll just go round the next corner."'

For the first week the company performed *Arms and the Man* for the American troops in the small Théâtre Marigny on the Champs-Élysées. Then for a fortnight they staged all three plays at the Comédie-Française, the first foreign company to perform in France's ornate national theatre. The actors, used to the cramped and shabby conditions in English theatres, were astonished at the facilities, which included 42 dressing-rooms. 'Sumptuous was not the word, it seemed more like a museum than a theatre,' Gerald Sim remembers. 'I had a room to myself, with busts, and chaise longues to entertain my visitors, and windows that opened out on to a balcony overlooking Paris.' Sybil was stunned by hers: 'It's not believable. Each French actor furnishes their own room, so they are beautifully furnished like a drawing room, with carpets and books and pictures. What would they think of the New!' Some of the rooms were decorated with great lushness and many frills, prompting Olivier to exclaim in mock horror: 'I can't act in all this, I shall end by playing Richard as some effeminate woman.' Sybil, though impressed by the architecture, was not attracted to the working conditions of French actors: 'Personally I'd find it a bit boring to be in,' she told Lewis. 'No one is a bit free, and they have their special types and roles and must not go outside. I think it's a very cramping place, and they stay there for years and years and then are pensioned off!'

The opening play was *Richard III*. The theatre was packed with the fashionable elite of Paris for the first night. Sybil reported: 'Our opening was tremendous! At the end the very distinguished audience was all on its feet, shouting – and Larry made a very fine speech in French – just learnt by heart – he can't speak a word! Wasn't it an achievement!' For the second night, after *Arms and the Man*, she was asked to do the same. Normally she preferred to speak off the cuff, relying on the inspiration of the moment, but here she was asked to prepare something more formal. 'It made me nervous all evening, they all made such a do about it being the right thing,' she wrote. 'If I could have just said it out of my head it wouldn't have worried me.' In fact she felt the speech went well, and was pleased when the celebrated director Michel Saint-Denis flatteringly told her 'it was like a poem – in the grand style and delightful!'

One night she attended what she called a 'beano' at the theatre. At one point she turned to a quiet man sitting next to her. 'We'd all been talking of Thornton Wilder's *The Skin of Our Teeth*, and I asked him if he knew Wilder, and he said: "Very well, he translated a play of mine about Lucrece." I said

"What!!" and snatched the card by his plate. "You are André Obey," I said. "Oh! Oh! Oh!", and I practically fell on his neck. After that we talked and talked – he doesn't speak one word of English but his French was not hard to understand – he told me of a play that when he saw me he said "She is the one to play it."…He delivered the play today – it's very exciting and very queer and it's never been played….We got home at 1.30 and today he writes me a sweet little letter, *J'ai été bien ravi de passer ces deux heures près de vous hier soir!* So we'll have a lunch or something (if I like the play!).'

The month in Paris was hectic, a seemingly endless round of parties and receptions. But she also found time for less glitzy activities, taking tea with the local Quakers, going to an exhibition of the Impressionists, sitting in the Palais Royal Gardens to write a foreword to a book by Patrick Figgis, Vera Brittain's secretary, and travelling to Lille to do a recital. She visited several churches, and went to High Mass in Notre-Dame with Olivier and Richardson ('Ralph is a Roman Catholic, but not a good one'). She also, reluctantly, agreed to a more dutiful task: 'They want me to lecture to French students next week. I suppose I'd better – everything disagreeable ought to be done, it makes me feel I'm doing something to pay for all this. I may be able to get in a word of international cheer to the young people.'

For several weeks she had been desperately hoping to meet up with Lewis, who was touring Europe with his production of *Saint Joan*, with Ann as the Maid. It seemed like a lost cause, until it was arranged for her to stay a few days longer. 'I shall do a British Institute reading with Bobbie Speaight to salve my conscience,' she told Lewis, explaining that she would have to back out of the annual Barn Theatre event at Smallhythe. A few days later her joy was unconfined when she was reunited with him for a week. One evening, after her show finished, she dashed round to the Théâtre Marigny and caught the end of *Saint Joan*. Another day Miriam Karlin, a walk-on who was also doing the wardrobe, made a suggestion before a matinee: 'I said to her, "I've got a spare habit and tonsure. Why don't you come on as a monk in the trial scene?" She said: "Ooh, shall I, Lewis? Perhaps I will." And she did.'

The family reunion was a happy ending to a physically and mentally gruelling tour, crowned for her soon afterwards in July by the Labour Party's unexpected victory in the general election. 'Am so thrilled about the election,' she wrote to Lewis soon after her return to England. The result seemed to offer her and millions of others the promise of a new dawn after the upheavals of six years of war.

30

A New Age

1945–1946

'Sybil lambasted Larry, she gave him a real dressing-down'
Actress Joyce Redman

For a brief moment in Paris Sybil seemed to have tired of the theatre. 'I've finished wanting the old theatre, I'd rather live in Wales and just study and do a little bit of ordinary good,' she told Lewis. But reading Obey's play had revived her passion. 'It's very queer – it has outward likenesses to Wilder, but it's near Pirandello too. I'm very excited about it – it's the sort of way I want to move in my old age, which is a young and new age that I'm beginning. This sort of play *lifts* me.'

After the emotional strain of the last few weeks, Sybil spent ten days in August with Christopher and his family in their Dublin flat. 'I'm shedding my worries because there are too many of them,' she wrote to Lewis, who was still touring Europe. 'Ireland is so perfect, and I'm enjoying the quietness here.' Apart from broadcasting a poetry recital on the radio, she was able to relax, meet friends for lunch, browse in bookshops, go swimming, visit the theatre – Steinbeck's *The Moon is Down* at the Gaiety, Lennox Robinson's *Is Life Worth Living?* at the Abbey – and talk politics, notably with the Abbey actor F J McCormick and his wife Eileen Crowe. 'We had terrific discussions,' she enthused. 'They are great friends of de Valera, and I find him very sound and good Left! I didn't want to stop talking with them!'

She spent many hours with Christopher, and felt she understood him better. During the ENSA tour she had been anxious about him. 'I had an early morning panic this morning,' she told Lewis from Belgium. 'I was panicky about him being away from us all, and feeling if I died no one would talk to him.' From Hamburg she added: 'Odd though he may be, he is so dear a specimen! I've never really got it out of him re war etc. I think it goes awfully deep with him. I do so badly want to see him again – so much to get talked over and readjusted somehow. Funny odd boy he was, I think of him a lot. I often wonder what it was that made him cut right away – some need that we didn't realise.' Once in Dublin her anxieties seem to be eased: 'Kiff is of another world, he is such a saint. He and I had a tremendous talk and I feel much happier.'

Recently she had also been reflecting on John's future: 'Has John heard any more from the Admiralty?' she had asked Lewis in June. 'I wonder what use they will make of him. I long for him to be working in some re-building way. I *wish* he could have been a parson, I think he'd have had enormous influence as a leader, but I think he won't be able to stomach that. I see him as head of a settlement – with a live theatre etc.' In fact John was appointed to a naval post, but not long afterwards confessed to Lewis that his thoughts were turning to the theatre. Lewis advised caution, but mentioned the idea to Sybil who, as John remembered, immediately assumed the matter was settled. 'I was bound to succeed in the theatre whatever I did because she had always known I was a good actor – and perhaps I would be a great director into the bargain.' She advised him to contact their friend Matthew Forsyth, now running the Glasgow Citizens', started by the playwright James Bridie. John took her advice, was offered a job as an assistant stage manager, and resigned from the navy. The pay was low, just £7 a week, so Sybil and Lewis frequently helped him and his family financially, as they also did Christopher and Kay, who would never be well off.

Once Lewis returned from Europe, John and Mary and Sybil accompanied him to Buckingham Palace, where he was to be knighted for services to the theatre. As he walked away from them Sybil said to John: 'Doesn't he look sweet? I bet he hasn't got a handkerchief.' She was right to be concerned: that morning Lewis had been caught wearing odd shoes with his morning suit. It was not his first moment of forgetfulness at the palace. At a garden party in the 1920s, he had walked up the stairs with a price label trailing from one shoe, and been saved by Sybil, who stooped and snatched it off. Now, at dinner that evening at the Savoy, Lewis threatened to make a speech to the whole room, outlining the need for the new Labour government to make Britain the kind of country they and others had dreamed of and fought for.

Sybil became involved with the publisher Victor Gollancz's 'Save Europe

Now' campaign, involving an appeal for the millions of homeless refugees in Germany, Austria and Hungary. Numerous meetings were held around the country to raise the money. Unable to attend the London one herself because of rehearsals, she gave Gollancz a list of names of star actors who might help, including many leading Equity figures, adding: 'There may be ways I can help as I saw Germany and felt so desperate about it.' To the scholar and musician Edward J Dent, who had told her what he planned to say at one of the meetings, she replied: 'You have been such a help – and one feels so discouraged at the attitude towards German culture.'

In September news came through of the discovery of Hitler's 'blacklist' compiled by the Gestapo, indicating the 2,300 people to be automatically arrested when England was invaded. Ranging from Churchill to Jewish refugees, it included figures such as Freud, Vera Brittain and Bertrand Russell and, from the world of arts and literature, Coward, Robeson, Epstein, Forster, H G Wells, Virginia Woolf, Aldous Huxley, Rebecca West – and Sybil. It was, perhaps, a compliment of sorts. Rebecca West telegrammed Coward: 'My dear, the people we should have been dead with.'

The triumphant wartime season at the New was followed by a second repertory season there, which was to prove equally successful in peacetime. The Old Vic company, led again by Olivier and Richardson, now also included Harry Andrews, Miles Malleson and George Rose. For Sybil it was the ideal set-up, in which she and Olivier and Richardson played both small and large parts in true ensemble fashion. In addition to repeating her roles in revivals of *Uncle Vanya* and *Arms and the Man*, she was cast as Mistress Quickly in the two parts of *Henry IV*, Jocasta in *Oedipus Rex*, and the Justice's Lady in *The Critic*.

Before the season began she received an angry letter from Wolfit, who characteristically accused Olivier and Richardson of including *Oedipus Rex* in the season so as to thwart his own plans to do the play. 'I feel very upset about this,' Sybil replied diplomatically. 'I don't believe anyone could feel this is deliberate "getting in first". It's just very foolish not to make enquiries as to what you are doing and what John G is doing.' She pointed out that they were using different versions. 'The Old Vic's is the Yeats prose version, not the splendid one that Jack M Harvey did. I think they won't hurt each other at all. Yours is the larger-size play and the true Greek one. Theirs is a version made by Yeats for the Abbey – much smaller in conception tho' very exciting prose. It has not the ritual of the complete play, therefore I think it will be no rival. I shall talk to Larry about all this, but I know he'd not mean to do a hateful think like you suggest.'

The Henry plays, directed by John Burrell with sets and costumes by Roger Furse, were chiefly notable for Richardson's magnificent and dignified Falstaff, considered by many to be the best interpretation they had ever seen. Olivier doubled with characteristic versatility as a virile, stammering Hotspur and a rascally, wizened Justice Shallow, while Sybil made for a lively, eager Mistress Quickly at the Boar's Head ('I love the bawdy old bitch' she said), though her accent appeared to place her well west of Eastcheap. 'Her performance wasn't quite as low as it might have been,' Frith Banbury remembered. 'It didn't quite smell of the stews of London.' The director Peter Hall, then a theatre-mad schoolboy, concurs: 'Her Mistress Quickly was rather genteel, in striking contrast to Joyce Redman's Doll Tearsheet.'

The second production, a double-bill of Sophocles' *Oedipus Rex* and Sheridan's *The Critic*, featured Olivier in another deeply contrasting pair of roles, Oedipus and Mr Puff, quickly dubbed 'Oedipuff'. Sybil robustly defended the decision to stage such a stark piece so soon after the war. 'Now is the right moment for Greek tragedy,' she said. 'It is symbolic of great moods of crises, and we are living in a world of crises. *Oedipus Rex* is a perfect reflection of our own world....Drama exists to kindle the fire, and that is why Greek tragedy is always topical, even in a world as unsettled as ours. Lads in the forces are eager to see it. We have proved over and over again that they do not necessarily demand that their theatre provides obvious escapism. They prefer plays that give them a point of view and lasting food for thought.'

Originally Guthrie was to direct *Oedipus Rex*, and since it was a relatively short play, it was thought Aristophanes' *Peace* might make it a good double-bill. But Olivier then came up with *The Critic*. Guthrie thought this a vulgar notion, so Michel Saint-Denis was brought in to direct the Sophocles. Jane Wenham, playing Antigone, remembers the French director's method as being 'to break people down so they had no mask, which was often a very painful process'. Sybil was, as usual, well behaved, though she didn't like her mauve costume, and was generally unhappy with her appearance. According to the composer Antony Hopkins, who wrote the haunting, dissonant music: 'She seemed rather lost in rehearsal, though very willing to do what was wanted. She was always asking Saint-Denis for guidance, very much wanting to please him. But she was very good at the wailing, she could do that at the first rehearsal.'

Olivier revelled in the opportunity to play the extremes of tragedy and comedy in one evening. His Oedipus was a powerful and moving interpretation, memorable especially for his blood-chilling scream when he discovers his dark secret. In total contrast, his foppish, be-wigged Mr Puff was a camp dandy that delighted some, and was condemned as showing-off and even sacrilege by others. But while the critics frowned at the pairing, the public loved it. Sybil thought his Oedipus perhaps his finest performance to date. 'He wanted to be down-to-earth rather than poetic, but his performance took on higher qualities,' she recalled. But she also felt 'there was a hysterical thing which took charge, rather than the big tragedy'. She later confessed to finding Yeats' translation pedestrian, preferring the lyricism of Murray's version. 'I like flight, and Gilbert Murray was always in flight.'

Her notices were predictably mixed: 'statuesque' was all *The Times* could manage, while a fledgling Kenneth Tynan proclaimed: 'Sybil Thorndike played Jocasta…with the traditional blazing intensity which, so far from illuminating the personality, strangles it into a sort of red-hot anonymity.' Others were more positive: Audrey Williamson praised her for having 'the courage which these plays need from the actor – the courage to let out the emotional stops'. But she had problems with a costume for *The Critic*, as designer Tanya Moiseiwitsch remembered: 'Miles Malleson was directing, but Olivier took over quite a lot of it. Miles had said, Don't you think it would be fun if Sybil came on for one short scene as Mrs Siddons? So we did a fitting, I thought she looked marvellous, and so did she. Then her five-minute scene was ruthlessly cut. We cried on each other's shoulders.' Sybil had to be content with her brief appearance as the Justice's Lady.

Joyce Redman had reason to be grateful to Sybil. 'She had no nonsense with either Larry or Ralph,' she recalls. 'In *The Critic* Miles Malleson had suggested a way of playing the lady's maid which on the first night provoked uproarious laughter, and a tremendous ovation at the end. Larry called for me, and said, "How dare you ruin my evening?" He really went for me. Just then Sybil came in, and asked why I was crying. I told her I had only been doing what I was asked to do. Sybil lambasted Larry, she gave him a real dressing-down. "How dare you, what are you doing to this child?" she said. "Just because someone else gets an ovation! For goodness sake, pull yourself together." From then on she was my great champion.'

The second successful season at the New closed at the end of April. 'It has been the greatest joy working with you,' Sybil wrote to Olivier. 'Thank you darling for your affection and consideration to me during these two years – I appreciate it all *very* much. Good luck, oh! good luck to you in the USA.' Although Olivier and the Old Vic wanted her to stay with the company while they took the plays for a short season to Broadway, to the surprise of many Sybil turned them down.

She was now 63, but her enthusiasm remained strong. 'I don't want to "settle down" now – horrible idea!' she told the traveller and explorer Rosita Forbes. 'I want to help create some better world for us all. It'll take all our work and patience and faith – but it can be done…And I do think we must not be afraid of our future. We must be adventurous – in our religion, in our government and of course in life.'

31

Cavalcanti, Hitchcock and Powell

1946–1950

'I *loathe* filming, but enjoy doing it every now and then,
just to show myself that I don't like it'
Sybil after filming Nicholas Nickleby

When Sybil had said: 'I want to be lots of different people: isn't that what acting's about?' she was defending her decision to play a greater variety of parts than people expected of her. In this post-war period, during which she largely left behind the great barnstorming roles, she successfully extended her range and style, creating what Darlington described as 'an astonishing gallery of portraits of contemporary ladies, all subtly varied and minutely observed'. She complemented them with several film roles, some of which allowed her to continue to mine her Grand Guignol seam.

Her decision not to go to America was prompted both by self-interest and family loyalty. She had begun to feel there were not enough parts for older women in the Old Vic repertoire. She wanted to work with her family, and when Olivier tried to change her mind, she remained steadfast: 'I can't desert Lewis and Ann,' she told the Crawleys. 'I couldn't turn them down, tho' the Old Vic did want me to re-consider. But it will make a big difference to Lewis and Ann's plays (they're doing a very interesting repertory of six plays) and *not* so much to the Old Vic….I love the Old Vic, but I do want to get back to some other work.'

The season at the King's, Hammersmith, was for the Travelling Repertory Theatre (TRT), run by its founder, the Canadian actor and director Basil Langton. The company included Renée Asherson, Esmond Knight and a young Eric Porter. For two years they had been touring blitzed towns, playing in church halls, hostels and tents. It was Sybil and Lewis' old dream of a season of classical and modern plays, in which two or three would be staged each week. The six were Shaw's *Man and Superman*, *The Wise Have Not Spoken* by Paul Vincent Carroll, *Romeo and Juliet*, *Saint Joan*, and two in which Sybil would appear directed by Lewis, *Electra* in the Gilbert Murray translation, and *In Time to Come* by Howard Koch and John Huston.

The latter, about the American president Woodrow Wilson and his efforts at the 1919 Peace Conference, appealed to Sybil because of her and Russell's earlier friendship with him. Based on Wilson's sayings and letters, it was a chronicle rather than a drama, and essentially lacked any sparkle. Lewis played Wilson in one of his home-made false noses, while Sybil, for once playing the lesser part, did according to *The Times* 'the little there is to do with comfortable ease' as his wife.

Rarely performed in London, Euripides' tragedy *Electra* had Ann in the title-role, Sybil playing her mother Clytemnestra, and Basil Langton as Orestes. With Murray's agreement, they altered some of the more obvious archaisms, such as 'Woe is me'. Hugh Manning was also in the company. 'Sybil was electrifying,' he recalls. 'But Lewis would go on and on about inflections. He thought some of we younger actors were too self-indulgent, and inclined to wing it.' According to Rosalind Boxall, another company member, this had a negative effect on Sybil. 'She had a magnificent voice, and at the first reading she took this great speech, and the cast were in tears. Lewis made her lose all that emoting, and I thought that was wrong. We watched him hammer it out of her. He was a disciplinarian, and a lot of people felt he squashed her instinctive feeling.' *Electra* was his last production as director. His autocratic method, especially his emphasis on 'stage speech' and 'tunes', was now seen as distinctly old-fashioned, and intimidating to young actors.

Ann had many of Sybil's vocal and facial qualities, but was a more controlled actress. To Sybil's annoyance, some critics argued that she was copying her style of acting. 'Ann has never copied me, but you can't help certain family likenesses,' she argued. She told Elizabeth Robins: 'It was very exciting playing it with Ann, who is very strong and vigorous, with a lovely voice and real fire.' Audrey Williamson thought her Electra 'remarkably fine: savage, intense, yet torn unwillingly by conscience', but *The Times* felt she lacked power and stature. Ivor Brown summed up: 'She has inherited the Thorndike intensity and tragic mask, yet she lacks Dame Sybil's enfolding sweep.' The audiences were enthusiastic, but small: Greek drama remained a minority taste, even within the theatre-going public.

CEMA had supported the TRT on its tours, and had guaranteed to cover any losses incurred at the King's. The season had begun well and attracted favourable notices, but audiences had gradually fallen off. After a matinee of *In Time to Come* before a half-empty house, Langton learned that the TRT was broke. Seeking the promised CEMA support, he was told it had been withdrawn: economic problems meant that theatre money would now only go to the Old Vic and Sadler's Wells. Later he was told Bronson Albery had argued that CEMA should stop giving money to 'that pacifist organisation TRT'. That evening Lewis and Sybil arrived at the theatre with a cheque for £5,000, to save the company and the season. This was a substantial sum for the time, and a striking reflection of their generosity and commitment to repertory theatre.

At the season's end Sybil was a guest at a party at Penguin Books to celebrate Shaw's ninetieth birthday, and Allen Lane's decision to issue ten of his titles with a total print-run of a million. Shaw wondered if Sybil might play the Empress Catherine in his 1913 play *Great Catherine*, to create a double-bill with his new play *Buoyant Billions*, but nothing came of this idea. Meanwhile she was missing the Old Vic company, who had scored a huge success on Broadway. But as Olivier and Vivien Leigh flew back from America, they narrowly escaped death when the engine of their plane caught fire, compelling it to make a forced landing in Connecticut. '*So* glad you are home and *safe* – what an escape,' Sybil wrote. 'And what a triumph you've had. I've purred with joy to think I'd had a hand in the re-starting of all this two years ago. How I thought of you all over there, and rejoiced – tho' homesick for the lovely family time we'd had – but I had another sort of nice family time with Ann and Lewis to console me.'

Within the family it was a time of mixed fortunes. Eileen joined the Central School as a teacher, and in these post-war years continued to appear on stage, often in the smaller London theatres such as the Q at Kew, prompting her to label herself Queen of the Outer Circle. Christopher remained in Ireland, as he was to do the rest of his life. 'He played the Irish harp, had a lovely singing voice, and sang in many Shakespeare productions,' his fellow-Irishman Milo O'Shea recalls. 'He was a very sweet and kind man, a wonderful character, and a damn good actor.' But according to his daughter Bronwen, there were similarities in the theatre to his mother's behaviour. 'Like Sybil, Daddy needed a strong director,' she says. 'He could create a performance standing on his head. The problem was to stop him.'

In February 1947 Ann married Douglas Campbell at the Church of the Holy Redeemer in Cheyne Row, Chelsea. This surprised many who knew them both. 'I was staggered they got together, because they were so different,' Miriam Karlin says. 'Ann was a gentler version of Sybil, and quite a thinker. Douglas was a totally different class, a real rough and ready Scot, a tub-thumping kind of character, but with a great sense of humour.' Now established as an actor, after working with Sybil and Lewis he had been a member of Ann's wartime company, and when *Electra* went on tour he had played Orestes. He was seven years younger than Ann, and at first Sybil was horrified: when Ann phoned her to break the news, her response was 'Oh no!' Douglas Campbell remembers: 'Sybil was furious to begin with, because she had better plans for Ann than marrying an actor. But we soon became great pals. Yet I found her difficult to love: admiration and wonder were what she commanded.'

Mary was finding work singing, playing the virginals, and undertaking lecture-recital tours playing mainly Elizabethan music. Her marriage, which had been shaky for some time, did not survive the war: she and William Devlin separated by mutual consent. 'No quarrel, but five years' separation and they both have changed very much, and in utterly different ways,' Sybil told Elizabeth Robins. 'It's sad, and makes me very unhappy, but we must just hold on and trust that a right way will be shown them both.' She found it hard to come to terms with the break-up, as Mary remembers: 'She was very upset, she couldn't grasp it at all. Being very bound up with her church, she thought people should stay together.' Meanwhile she was making sure her own marriage remained solid. 'Lewis is in fine form,' she told Mary Crawley. 'But I have to watch him not to let him get too wildly involved in life! How glad our husbands must be to have such loving wives taking care of them!!! Tra-la!'

This was a time of austerity, with Britain returning to rationing. Like others, Sybil was grateful for food parcels, which the Crawleys continued to send from America. After one parcel arrived she enthused: 'So exciting to unpack – Lewis and I yelled – and so very welcome for our store cupboard. Every packet that appears seems to be the one thing we have been wanting.... The bacon!! We both said we hadn't tasted bacon before – we get *awful* stuff here.' That Christmas there was a breakthrough on the kitchen front. '*I* cooked the Xmas dinner,' she told the Crawleys proudly. 'I nearly had a nervous breakdown, but it all turned out just perfect.'

Sybil continued to give poetry and dramatic recitals: sometimes with

Lewis, sometimes alone, with several programmes organised by the actor Laurier Lister. The programme invariably featured works by Whitman, Keats, Browning and Hopkins, with the occasional surprise item, such as 'Sunset from a Prison Camp' by John Casson. She was increasingly in demand to read at memorial services for her fellow-actors. She and Lewis arranged the one for May Whitty. 'We've just come from the service in St Paul's Covent Garden for my darling May,' she wrote to John van Druten. 'It was so lovely, and we felt you there…and these two decades gone over. I think we were all crying at the end. We had such lovely hymns. Oh! Johnny how wonderful friendship is.' More happily she, Edith Evans and Peggy Ashcroft each read a Shakespeare sonnet at a celebration service to mark the centenary of Ellen Terry's birth. Sometimes she and the other theatrical Dames sat together. 'Are we a Pride?' she wondered, 'or perhaps a Gaggle? Finally it was decided we were a Tangle of Dames.'

She was now taken on by Christopher Mann Ltd, an agency that also had Anton Walbrook, Carol Reed and, later, Michael Redgrave on its books. Her agent was Aubrey Blackburn, a shrewd and charming man, and one of the few able to outface Binkie Beaumont. He had been a casting director in films, to which Sybil now returned. In *Nicholas Nickleby* she was cast as the violent and revolting Mrs Squeers, wife of the cruel Wackford Squeers running the appalling school Dotheboys Hall. The director was the Brazilian-born Alberto Cavalcanti.

Derek Bond, who played Nicholas, was at the start of his career. 'Sybil was extremely kind to me, and helped me with my character,' he recalled. 'She was an amazingly good listener.' But her relationship with the brilliant but excitable Cavalcanti was a difficult one. 'On the surface he was very strong, but if someone stood up to him, he would give way. He was quite overawed by Sybil. It was a battle of wills, but she got her way with most shots, and her judgement was usually accepted.' Bond himself had a problem in the scene in which Nicholas beats Squeers, and Mrs Squeers intervenes. 'I had been trained as a commando in the army, but I had a hell of a time trying to stop Sybil overcoming me. With every take the scene became more and more violent, and she seemed to get stronger and stronger. Cavalcanti danced around us, saying, "Dame Sybil, *he* is supposed to win!"'

Sadly, the tussle was cut from the final version, which left Sybil with very little screen time. Coming soon after David Lean's masterly screen version of *Great Expectations*, the film met with only mild enthusiasm. *The Times* noted that Sybil 'administers brimstone and treacle with an impressive relish', but she herself found the experience a frustrating one. 'I don't think the film a bit good – it was flat-footed, not nearly extreme enough in acting, and over-done in clothes,' she told the Crawleys. 'I felt mad – I wasn't allowed to do anything. I could have been really horrible if they'd let me, but they were so afraid. I *loathe* filming, but I enjoy doing it every now and then, just to show myself that I don't like it.'

In her public speeches she continued to compare the cinema unfavourably with the theatre. Films, she argued, had taken over 'the dead end of purely realistic drama'. People went to the cinema to relax, whereas the theatre was 'a cooperative ritual act' in which the audience 'came to be impressed but also to express themselves'. Warming to her 'proscenium-busting' theme, she advocated a return to the open stage, criticising the isolating influence of the footlights, and citing the way the open stage was used to good effect in Russia to bring audience and actors into intimate contact.

During these post-war years plays by Arthur Miller and Tennessee Williams were seen in London for the first time, the verse dramas of Christopher Fry and T S Eliot came into vogue, as did translations of French works by Anouilh and Giraudoux. None of these impinged on Sybil's career – although she was offered Cocteau's fantasy *The Eagle Has Two Heads*, but declined it. She was looking for something different. 'How good it is to see new ground dug up,' she wrote in a foreword to Philippa Burrell's play *He Was Like a Continent*. 'This play belongs to the theatre of experiment which many of us are welcoming now, for in our topsy-turvy world there is need in plays for a daring approach to human and world problems.'

Disappointingly, she eventually opted for *Call Home the Heart*, a mediocre, whimsical play by Clemence Dane about love in wartime. There were problems immediately. Early in the pre-London tour Judy Campbell discovered she was pregnant. 'I decided to confide in Sybil, who said: "Splendid! I had four before I did *Saint Joan*!" It was a wonderful reaction, and made me feel less foolish. From then on she took me under her wing, insisting I put my feet up after lunch and read a book. Eventually I was replaced by Celia Johnson, but then she too became pregnant, so Valerie White took over. When I finally had my daughter Jane, Sybil came to see me in the nursing home with a blanket for her, saying: "It's only utility, because I'm a socialist."'

As usual Sybil defended her choice of play: 'Very fine it is', she told Elizabeth Robins. But it appealed to few others: when it reached the St

James' in April 1947, Coward thought it 'completely scatty with all values, both psychologically and theatrically, wrong'. But Sybil was praised for painting a realistic portrait of a woman living in a failed marriage. Ivor Brown commended her 'superb presentation of a tiresome old dear, mothering, dithering, managing', while the director Peter Cotes thought 'she subjugated herself and played as a member of a team, which few other members of the cast appeared to be doing'.

During the tour Judy Campbell heard her speak in Glasgow at the local Socialist Association: 'She contradicted herself left, right and centre, but the whole thing had such a generosity and warmth and life and inspiration, the fact that she made a lot of mistakes didn't matter. It was a splendid, rabble-rousing speech.' It was also reminiscent of the self-description she offered a journalist: 'I am madly English, being Scottish. I am madly everything I believe in; I hate apathy and indifference. I am wholeheartedly socialist and internationalist and religious and pacifist.'

Her internationalism was not merely theoretical, as Vera Brittain's daughter Shirley Williams recalls: 'She was very supportive of my mother's attempts after the war to effect some reconciliation with Germany, to raise money for Feed Our Children, which was directed at Germany and other parts of blockaded Europe where people were suffering serious malnutrition. She shared a platform with her more than once.' She also joined other leading women in protesting about destitute families in Germany being evicted from their homes to provide space for the wives of British officers. 'We read of young women with babies, old people, invalids, victims of Nazi horrors, all indiscriminately turned out at a few days' notice,' ran their letter in *The Times*. 'Sometimes twenty people (including families with one room each) are evicted to provide the rooms for one officer and his wife.'

During the *Call Home the Heart* tour she found she was missing the Old Vic. She wrote to Vivien Leigh, who had just opened in Thornton Wilder's *The Skin of Our Teeth*. 'I loved the notices – and how lovely again you sound – and I love to see George Devine, for I always enjoy his acting,' she told her. 'How's darling Larry? I look forward to his Lear more than I can say. Give him a hug from me. I'm enjoying the play hugely, but I miss all the darlings at the Old Vic.' Fortunately, her next production was to prove immensely satisfying, for Lewis as well as for her.

This was J B Priestley's *The Linden Tree*, directed by Michael MacOwan and financed by Priestley. Set in the new welfare-state Britain in a climate of hoped-for social revolution, the story centred on the Linden family living in a drab northern town, and the fight by Robert Linden, a man of integrity and liberal ideas, to resist the efforts of the university and his family to compel him to retire. It was to be Lewis' last major role in the West End, and the last time Sybil, as his wife, would take a smaller part than he did.

Priestley claimed to have deliberately cast Sybil as a weak petulant woman. 'When you are dealing with an actress of great talent, with a superb sense of character,' he suggested, 'it may be best to cast her dead against her familiar type and real personality, presenting her acting with a sharp challenge.' Later he shrewdly added: 'Lewis could just be this character not unlike himself, for there really was something a bit professorial about him, but Sybil had to act a woman utterly unlike herself, and so give a *performance*, and that's when she's at her best.' Sybil told a different story, recalling Priestley bringing her the play, saying there was nothing in it for her, but asking her to read it on Lewis' behalf. She saw that the part fitted him perfectly. 'I was terribly moved, and I knew at once that I must play his wife, though she filled me with misery.'

Priestley attended rehearsals, during which, Sybil remembered, 'we all worked happily together'. But this was less than the truth. MacOwan, a competent though not brilliant director, told John Casson: 'Lewis wanted not only his own way with his own part, but with all the other parts as well, and they had quite a few fights.' Sonia Williams, playing one of the Linden children, has similar memories. 'Lewis was prickly, but Sybil was a controlling influence. When he blew up she would put her arm round him.' For MacOwan one problem was to stop Lewis acting 'old', when at 72 he was older than his character. 'He needed confidence just to be himself, and Sybil was a fine ally. She was nervous and excited for him and watched him like a lynx, urging me to tell him when I thought anything should be changed....It was safe to feed Sybil anything, knowing that everything would be absorbed. "Let me do it. Let me try it," she would say, the moment I suggested anything. Directing her was like a lighting rehearsal. "Bring up number 3 full. Now take it down to half. Up a third. Now set." The only thing I had to do was to stop her making faces.'

The play opened in Sheffield in June 1947. Sybil was still a great draw around the country, as the Shakespeare scholar Stanley Wells recalls: 'The news that she was coming to Hull amazed me: it was as if a legendary figure such as Sarah Siddons were to swim within my ken.' Arriving in London at the Duchess in August, *The Linden Tree* played there for over a year, winning the Ellen Terry Award for Best Play of 1947. It was a piece about hope and sadness, full of ideas and debates, 'a tonic to the mind and a bath to the spirit', as Alan Dent observed. Lewis was applauded for his dignified and gently passionate performance, while Sybil was praised for the sincerity and quiet emotional force of hers.

It was their most successful partnership for several years. 'We are both so happy being together in such a lovely play,' Sybil told the Crawleys. ''Lewis' is a wonderful part – mine not so important but it's beautiful to play.…It's a deeply symbolic and deeply moving play.' She was pleased to be in one that dealt with contemporary conditions under a new Labour government. 'It shows the way that England should, and can, go and makes it clear that we are doing a wonderful thing, even if not in a wonderful way,' she told a journalist. 'We are in the throes of a bloodless revolution, every bit as far-reaching as the Russian Revolution, but being English we have accompanied it without secret police, and with so little fuss that people don't really know it is happening.'

Before the end of the run Sybil asked Priestley if she and Lewis might do *The Linden Tree* at the Glasgow Citizens'. 'It's a *very* good company, and my son John is producing and he's very good,' she explained. John had made quick progress at the theatre, where Bridie treated him like a son. He had made his directing debut with O'Neill's *Anna Christie* and Patrick Hamilton's *Gaslight*, and was now resident director, working with some of his fellow prisoners-of-war. Hard-working and well-liked, he was considered best at directing plays demanding ingenious staging and pageantry. According to Sheila Ronald, an assistant stage manager: 'He ran things a bit like a sergeant major. It was efficient, but not very cosy.'

Priestley agreed to the plan, and after a brief stopover at Bron-y-Garth, where they just found time to climb Snowdon again, Sybil and Lewis joined John in Glasgow. Inevitably, Lewis tried to interfere with his direction, forcing John to bawl him out publicly before he would stop doing so. Sybil, on the other hand, he found a joy to direct. 'She would try anything I suggested and always seemed grateful for it,' he remembered. 'She never had the slightest concern about her own dignity.…She would take an idea of mine, try it out and then add her own ideas, finally transforming it all into something much more exciting. No other actor that I ever directed made me feel less of a director and more of a catalyst.'

Always quick to champion playwrights whose work she admired, Sybil wrote appreciatively to John van Druten about his new play *Voice of the Turtle*, which had flopped in the West End: 'We were both enthralled with the play and your production. We felt so mad about the critics, the lukewarmness, the non-awareness of what a splendid job had been done....Oh! what a beautiful play. I think you are a terrific playwright!' She was also excited by Ted Willis' powerful play *No Trees in the Street*, which dealt with violence in London's East End brought on by the appalling living conditions. 'Thank you for an afternoon of real stimulation, I was glued, couldn't move even an eyelid, so held was I,' she wrote to Basil Dean, its director. 'I found it horribly alive and beautifully played.....No one who ever reads the papers can say it's untrue, and lots of us who have lived in slum parishes (as I have with a parson father) know it's true. I can only think that the West End audiences don't like to think such people live in this country – or that they are worth saving.'

Her socialist beliefs continued to compel her to give practical support to the Labour Party. During 1948 she spoke at by-election meetings for two candidates, in Epsom and Croydon North. The latter event, where Harold Nicolson was standing for Labour, shocked Nancy Astor, the first woman to take her seat in House of Commons: 'Sybil Thorndike went down to speak for the socialist candidate,' she told Shaw's secretary Blanche Patch. 'I was horrified: I had no idea she was Red.' A newspaper dubbed her 'one of the rosy-minded daughters of Actors' Equity', while within Equity during elections the actor Ralph Truman circulated a blacklist that included Sybil and Lewis, saying in effect: Don't vote for these people, because they're communists.

Despite accusations that the British-Czech Friendship League, started during the war as an anti-Nazi organisation, was now 'a stooge of the Comintern', Sybil remained a member while others were resigning. Yet she was already disillusioned by events in Russia: at a wartime meeting with the Soviet Ambassador Ivan Maisky she had asked him why the Soviets had marred a great experiment by totalitarian methods and practices. After the war Peter Copley, a Communist Party member, asked her to give money to some Russian cause: 'She said, "I'm sorry, I can't, I do feel it's all so wicked." It was the only time I heard her say No to something.' For similar reasons she turned down the offer of the presidency of the British Peace Council.

She returned to the cinema as a blackmailing harridan in *Britannia Mews*, an Anglo/American film made in English studios (its US title was *The Forbidden Street*). Set in Victorian London, based on the novel by Margery Sharp, it starred Maureen O'Hara and Dana Andrews, but also a clutch of

British stage stalwarts, including Fay Compton and A E Matthews. Perhaps frustrated at not being allowed to make Mrs Squeers horrible enough in *Nicholas Nickleby*, Sybil persuaded the make-up department to create a suitably hag-like face for her. When she came on to the set the place went silent, until the Romanian director Jean Negulesco said: 'It's wonderful. It's superb. But of course you can't use it. It's too terrifying.' The softer version was terrifying enough: the *Manchester Guardian* thought her 'a fearfully lifelike old hag', while *The Times* noted her playing 'with rollicking delight in make-up and virtuosity'.

She and Lewis now persuaded Gielgud to appear with them in St John Hankin's *The Return of the Prodigal*. The company included Irene Browne, Nora Nicholson, Rachel Kempson, Richard Goolden and Walter Hudd, with Sybil playing Gielgud's mother. The story concerned a charming wastrel returning from Australia to cause mayhem among his respectable, wealthy and philistine family, whom he shocks with his cynicism and disillusionment, and his scathing comments about snobbery and industrialism. A radical play in its time, full of neo-Wildean epigrams, it lost much of its sting in Peter Glenville's production, which opened at the Globe in November 1948. The central speech in which the hero bitterly attacks society was cut, and the play was fatally softened by a series of sumptuous Cecil Beaton sets, which drew more attention to the drawing-room than to the comedy.

'We love the play,' Sybil told Mary Crawley, but later she criticised the production: 'It got too smart, too over-dressed, and it should be just ordinary middle-class northern people.' Many critics felt the same: Beverley Baxter labelled it 'the best dressed and best acted bad play in London'. Harold Hobson thought Sybil 'gentle and endearing' as the fussy, dithering mother, but *The Times* critic felt the actors too often burlesqued the play, to avoid it seeming dated: 'Even Dame Sybil Thorndike – whose portrait of the prodigal's warm-hearted mamma is otherwise so right in feeling and in unconscious humour – cannot help giving the impression that she is deliberately over-playing at some point.'

She continued to find stimulation in books on the theatre, including one by Herbert Farjeon, of which his widow Joan had sent her a copy. 'I have already dipped in and found such joy in that beautiful imaginative writing and his really constructive criticism,' she told her. 'He writes as one who loves the theatre and loved acting, and when we know how he could write a play himself, it adds to the joy of reading him.' She also, while on tour in Cambridge, enjoyed meeting the Greek scholar and Provost of King's College, John Tresidder Sheppard, who translated and directed Greek plays. 'I am *thrilled* to have your two translations and have already begun browsing in them,' she wrote. 'The talk to you yesterday was a real thrill, kick, and stimulation – thank you, thank you. I came away on air with resolves about Greek and lots of things!!'

She lent her support to more theatrical schemes. Along with Paul Robeson, Miles Malleson, Michel Saint-Denis and Flora Robson, she helped as a tutor at the Unity Theatre School, taking part in a reading of Gorky's *The Mother*. She and Lewis agreed to become joint presidents of the New Yiddish Theatre in the East End, to help them raise funds for a new theatre building. They did so, she explained, 'because of the excellent work they are doing in the cause of the theatre and the Jewish culture'. She also sponsored and helped raise funds for the mobile Century Theatre based in Leicestershire, which planned to tour to towns and villages in a convoy of converted wartime military trailers and tractors.

After a disappointing run of just two months for *The Return of the Prodigal*, she spent the next five months at the Duchess in *The Foolish Gentlewoman*, based by Margery Sharp on her own novel. Her role was that of a garrulous, feckless but good-hearted woman, who many years previously had intercepted a love letter to a poor relation, so condemning her to spinsterhood, and who now wanted to atone for her guilt by handing over her own fortune to the woman. The company included Mary Merrall as the cousin, Lewis as a tough-minded solicitor, Isabel Dean and Mona Washbourne.

Despite rows between Lewis and Mary Merrall which spilled over from rehearsals into performances, the play was liked, though mainly for the acting. The critic of *The Times* wrote: 'Dame Sybil Thorndike has been provided with a part which no other living actress could play half so persuasively. Nobody else could be so naturally quixotic, could induce so much fun and sunshine to play on a surface of simple goodness, could strike so surely notes foolish and tender, comic and pathetic, without letting a finger touch a single false note.'

One visitor to the Duchess was the playwright Arnold Wesker, then just eighteen. Hoping to raise money to attend the first World Peace Congress in Paris, an event inspired by the Soviet Communist Party, he wrote begging letters to Sybil, Sean O'Casey and others. O'Casey sent him ten shillings ('All I can afford'), while Sybil invited him backstage, where she suggested he contact her again when he'd raised what he could. 'I was summoned to her flat,' Wesker recalled, 'told to wait at the front door, where she reappeared within seconds, thrusting two pound notes into my hands, and good-luck-bon-voyage-and-thank-you-for-fighting-for-peace-on-everybody's-behalf into my spirit.'

One regular visitor to her dressing-room was her niece Donnie, who enjoyed her performance there. 'At her first nights we would sit around like courtiers while she welcomed everybody in,' she recalls. 'She was very actressy. It would be: "Darling, how lovely to see you!' and then to us, "Who on earth was that?"' In John Casson's view she never really stopped performing, and always on a large scale. 'To be with Sybil is to see everything through an enormous emotional magnifying glass,' he wrote. 'Her unflagging enthusiasm can, at times, be as exhausting as a prolonged exposure to the sun. When you work or live with Sybil you must develop a kind of "enthusiasm tan".'

During these post-war years she continued in radio drama. Some plays – *The Trojan Women*, *The Cenci*, *Coriolanus*, *The Corn is Green* – she had already appeared in on stage. She was in Webster's *The White Devil*, and made a rare excursion into Ibsen in *Brand*, in which Richardson as Brand and Sybil as his mother were directed by Val Gielgud. However, the *Manchester Guardian* felt that, 'for all the force of their acting, they could not make the thing real'. These were relatively early days at the BBC, when broadcasts were live, and actors had to think quickly. David Spenser recalls a broadcast of Maeterlinck's *The Blue Bird*: 'Hermione Hannen forgot she had a scene at the end, put on her veiled hat and left the studio. Sybil, with a warm, peaceful smile, came up and played the scene, giving a most convincing imitation of Hermione.'

As ever, she supported causes, made speeches, opened fetes and exhibitions. Sometimes her enthusiasm ran away with her. In May 1949 Barry Jackson organised a major British Theatre Exhibition in Birmingham, which she and Lewis opened. One critic, Claude Westell, recalled: 'She worked herself up to a fine flight of histrionic rhetoric such as had us all surging with the tide of her enthusiasm.' She waved her arms about so excitedly that she knocked her hat off and, with the whole national press in front of her, announced: 'Never mind the critics: they don't count.' She was often fierce on this subject, defending Tyrone Guthrie's expressionist play *The Top of the Ladder* by declaring that it had failed because of the 'stupid, asinine critics who went to the play with their intellects – those valuable things which are not very imaginative'.

She now teamed up again with Gielgud, this time under his direction.

Treasure Hunt, by M J Farrell (the pseudonym of novelist Molly Keane) and John Perry, was a gentle farce set in an Irish country house. The company included Milo O'Shea, Marie Lohr, Terence Longdon, and Lewis as a paying guest. Sybil played the central character, a demented aunt who spends her days in a sedan chair, which in her imagination can become a car, train or aeroplane when she wishes to travel. 'It provides me with an escape,' Sybil explained, 'being so unlike those tragedy queens who have appeared so frequently in the course of my professional career.'

Milo O'Shea remembers her behaviour offstage: 'She was very kind and maternal, she just adopted me, making sure that I got digs on tour. And in rehearsals she was a rock, full of tremendous enthusiasm.' She would, however, have been anxious about Lewis' increasing deafness, which forced the actors to face him to give him his cues. His memory, as Terence Longdon recalls, was also a problem. 'He wasn't terribly good on his lines, even after three hundred performances, so if he forgot a word he would sometimes mumble and come out with, Oh for a muse of fire!' Both he and Sybil had difficulties with Gielgud's notoriously mercurial style of direction. 'They were devoted to him, but they couldn't cope with his continual changes of mind,' Mary Casson recalls. 'They always liked something very structured.' Gielgud for his part found Sybil 'professional to her fingertips, disciplined, punctual and kind'.

The critics thought her Aunt Rosa a joyous and subtle creation. *Theatre World* hailed it as 'the comic performance of the year', while J W Lambert in the *Sunday Times* observed: 'She pursues her imaginary voyages with mischievous gaiety. Never, even at her most vagrantly absurd, does she abate her poise; eyes, shoulders, hands and chuckle summon up a whole world of long-lost cosmopolitan delights and private pleasures.' Some were dubious about insanity being treated as comic, but Sybil was quick to defend her character, and give the discussion a political context: 'There is nothing particularly insane about this attitude of mind,' she argued in the *Stage*. 'So many people today refuse to listen to facts about Russia and conditions in Germany simply because they dislike having their minds brought up against realities. They have no sedan chair, but that doesn't prevent them from drawing imaginary rose-pink curtains across their mental windows.'

The play ran for ten months until July 1950, first at the Apollo, then at the St Martin's. Sybil used her time hidden in the sedan chair to learn her lines for her next role. At one performance the company had a visitor, as Milo O'Shea remembers: 'Sybil used to go to Marlborough House to have a glass of sherry with Queen Mary. One day she told us she was coming to a matinee, and that we would meet her in the interval – but not to worry, she wasn't going to talk to anyone. We lined up, all very nervous. I was last, and Queen Mary said to me, "Where are the jewels hidden?" Quick as a flash Sybil said: "Don't tell her, she won't come back after the interval!"'

At this time her sister Eileen was supplementing her work at the Central School with private lessons. One of her pupils was Claire Bloom, aged 14, who came to her house, and remembered 'that great Thorndike voice' and 'those strong English faces' of Eileen and her daughters, and having to recite 'an awful lot of the Bible in addition to Greek drama'. Donnie meanwhile was a student at the Central School. While there she was invited by a teacher training college in Egham to play Saint Joan. 'Sybil showed me how to do one of her speeches,' she remembers. 'But when she and my mother came to see it, all she said afterwards was: "A good try dear, but don't wear lipstick in the trial scene."'

Sybil was now beginning to make an impression on the next generation in the family, as John's son Anthony remembers.'Throughout the war, when my father was in Stalag Luft 3 and my mother had to cope with the vicissitudes of rationing and shortages, she was always there as a comforting backstop. She always seemed to be able to lay her hands on some impossible-to-obtain treat at just the right moment. After the war the headmaster of my boarding school in Surrey would invite her down on a Sunday night to read ghost stories to the boarders, about 50 of us. She was immensely popular, and most of the boys and girls couldn't get enough of her.'

Her life was as packed full as ever: while playing in *Treasure Hunt* at night, by day she spoke at election meetings for the Labour Party, and worked on another film. Alfred Hitchcock's *Stage Fright* was a thriller set in a theatre, starring Marlene Dietrich as a musical comedy star, Richard Todd as her lover, and Jane Wyman as a student at RADA. Hitchcock, who was in a slump in his career, saw it as a good opportunity to use some leading British actors, and the film is notable less for its suspense than for some fine character playing, with cameo roles for Miles Malleson, Joyce Grenfell, Irene Handl, Lionel Jeffries and Kay Walsh. As Wyman's eccentric parents, Sybil and Alastair Sim perform with delicious comedic timing and humour. 'Hitchcock was not an actors' director, he was more interested in his camera angles,' Todd remembers. 'But Sybil was marvellous to work with. She had a great sense of humour, and was wonderful to watch.'

She was back in front of the cameras again in and around Much Wenlock in Shropshire, where Michael Powell and Emeric Pressburger were filming *Gone to Earth*, the popular novel by Mary Webb set in the Welsh marches. Showing the green and brown hills of the English countryside, the film is visually stunning, with a touching performance from Jennifer Jones as the child of nature Hazel Woodus. Sybil, in an impressive range of hats, shawls and blouses, and constantly knitting and pursing her lips, catches effectively the prim, haughty respectability of his Victorian mother. But she disliked Powell. 'Everyone hated working with him,' she told John later. 'He was horrid to *small* people.' She disliked his autocratic methods, and was frustrated by his insistence that she do a piece of business many times over, but each time differently. Eventually she told him to make up his mind what he wanted.

Both *Stage Fright* and *Gone to Earth* were released in 1950. In February that year the Labour government under Attlee won a general election, but with only a tiny majority. Sybil continued to speak publicly on behalf of the party. During the election campaign she addressed a women's meeting at Kenilworth Hall in Warwickshire, where she stressed that no one party had a monopoly on virtue: 'Every person in the Labour party is not a perfect angel with silver wings,' she said. 'But that goes for all parties. We are all human beings trying to do our damnedest – failing many times, but always trying to get further on.'

The time had now come to sell Bron-y-Garth. While Sybil loved the place, Lewis was finding it increasingly depressing to be there; at one point he considered having the house exorcised. As Diana Devlin put it: 'It had a powerful and brooding atmosphere, which either enveloped you in a romantic attachment to the place, or drove you to black, despairing moods and melancholy.' Mary and Patricia had left during the war and moved to Surrey, and with the family using it less frequently, they now sold it for £5,000, and instead bought Cedar Cottage, near Wrotham, in Kent.

A charming, secluded and somewhat ramshackle early seventeenth-century cottage with ancient beams, it stood on a hilltop overlooking a heath and fields. It had three bedrooms, and a 'sunroom' where the grandchildren could camp out. Within reasonable distance of London, it became a convenient family weekend and holiday bolt-hole for many years. Sybil even had visions of making it their permanent home while they continued to work in London. They got to know the local people, and when Sybil heard that £600 was needed to repair the church tower at nearby Stansted, she gave a recital to raise the money. 'She came in flowing robes, and held us absolutely spell-bound for two hours,' one villager remembered.

She and Lewis now distributed the proceeds of a life endowment policy to their children, which helped them all to buy houses in the next few years. Meanwhile their modest Chelsea flat in Swan Court remained a comfortable, convenient and simply furnished home. Although she used the bedroom as a study for writing and learning Greek, life centred on the sitting-room. Its shelves were overflowing with books and family photographs, its walls hung with paintings and drawings collected on their travels, one of sunflowers by Clemence Dane, another by Hugh Casson, now a thriving architect who had been given the job of designing the 1951 Festival of Britain. In one corner was the grand piano, on which Sybil practised a Bach prelude every day. Another corner was Lewis' 'workshop', where he kept his tools for mending pottery and sundry other objects – including his own teeth. Sybil would joke that their cleaner would break objects on purpose, so he would have the fun of mending them. Because of his practical skills and her support for good causes, they were labelled the carpenter and the joiner.

At home they adopted conventional roles, as Diana Devlin recalls: 'When I was young I would ask to get down, Lewis would leave the table too, I would sit under the piano and he would read the paper. Sybil would clear the things away and wash up, always singing while she did so, or doing her Elsie Fogerty vocal exercises.' Now without staff, they lived very simply, taking meals in Betty's restaurant on the ground floor, or at the local Bar-B-Q. Sybil made breakfast (usually bread and butter, marmalade and tea), the occasional lunch, and Sunday supper (typically cold ham, salad and tinned fruit). Buns, biscuits and cocoa were often her staple fare. She had a sweet tooth, as Douglas Campbell remembers: 'Once she was eating raspberries covered in syrup, and adding sugar to it. When I remonstrated with her, she said: "I love the crunch!"' He and Ann were vegetarians, and for a while she became one too, though not entirely consistently: she continued to enjoy turkey, arguing that they were so stupid they deserved to be eaten.

She disliked cooking, which she had not had to do until the war. 'She found it a terrible trial, although she eventually got quite good at it,' Mary Casson says. 'I used to congratulate her on her rice puddings, but she would never believe I wasn't being nasty.' Her lack of culinary imagination is clear from her slapdash recipe for stew that featured in *Our Favourite Dish: The Theatre Recipe Book*: 'Take anything that's left over, fry it all up with more vegetables of any

29. As Shaw's Major Barbara, 1929

30. As Mrs Alving in *Ghosts*, 1930

31. Lewis, Sybil and Shaw discuss a phonofilm of *Saint Joan*, 1927

32. A publicity postcard for Ann

33. Mary as Wendy in *Peter Pan*

34. Sybil, Ann (left) and Mary in their Carlyle Square kitchen

35. Agnes and Eileen Thorndike (far left) see off Mary, Sybil, Lewis, Ann
and company to South Africa, 1928

36. Russell in the film *The Roof*, 1933

37. Lewis, Christopher, Sybil in Australia, 1932

38. As Volumnia with Laurence Olivier in *Coriolanus*, 1938

39. As Miss Moffat with Emlyn Williams in *The Corn is Green*, 1938

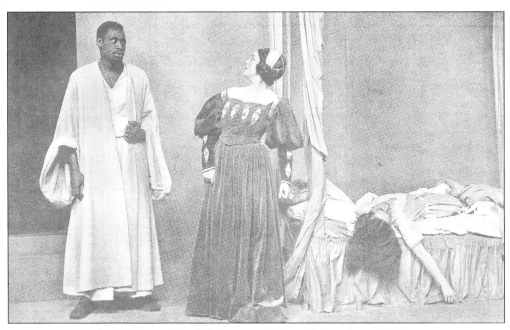

40. As Emilia with Paul Robeson and Peggy Ashcroft in *Othello*, 1930

41. Lewis rehearsing Sybil, Ann and Christopher in Coward's *Hands Across the Sea*, 1936

42. As Jocasta with Laurence Olivier, in *Oedipus*, 1945

43. As the White Queen (left) in *Alice in Wonderland*,
with Roma Beaumont as Alice, and Zena Dare as the Red Queen, 1943

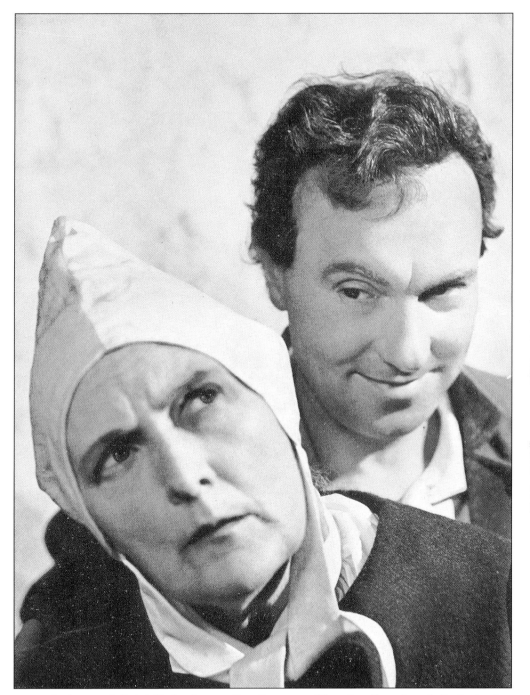

44. As Aase with Ralph Richardson in *Peer Gynt*, 1944: 'Peer, dear, I can hear bells ringing.'

45. As Mrs Whyte with Edith Evans in *Waters of the Moon*, 1951:
'When Edith forgets she's a grand actress and a dame, she is superb.'

46. As the Queen Dowager with Marilyn Monroe in *The Prince and the Showgirl*, 1957: 'Marilyn was perfect, and I was the old ham.'

47. As Mabel Wicks with Athene Seyler in *The Weak and the Wicked*, 1953

48. Reciting the prologue to the Dickens Pageant, Rochester Castle, 1951

49. As Saint Teresa, with Lewis as the Father-General, in *Teresa of Avila*, 1961

50. As Marina with Laurence Olivier in
Uncle Vanya, 1962

51. Rehearsing the Toy Symphony for a concert
in her honour, Festival Hall, 1963

52. Celebrating the building of the Thorndike Theatre in Leatherhead, completed in 1969

53. Farewell to the stage, in the title-role of
There Was an Old Woman, 1969

or every sort, put in any flavouring you like, cook and cook and cook until it's a gorgeous mess.' But she had little incentive to be a domestic goddess since, as she put it: 'Lewis couldn't tell a mutton chop from a butterscotch toffee.' Mary confirms this verdict: 'She never had an audience in Lewis. Neither of them thought food very important.'

Sybil's next stage role was in John Home's *Douglas*, an eighteenth-century play that Sarah Siddons had made famous, Lady Randolph supposedly being her favourite part. The play, once hugely popular, had not been staged for sixty years: a fustian, sentimental piece, with an absurdly creaky plot, it was written in a high-flown blank verse. It told the story of a mother who suddenly meets her long-lost son from a secret marriage, only for him to be killed the following day, prompting her in her grief to throw herself off a cliff. Sybil admitted in a programme article that the writing 'is consciously a little pompous' and that it needed to be played 'in the grand manner'. She likened its style to that of Greek tragedies, and to an opera rather than a play, hoping that 'if we actors succeed in creating figures large enough and heroic enough to speak and act the play with sincerity, it will move our audiences today'.

James Bridie had asked John Casson to direct it at the Lyceum as the Glasgow Citizens' contribution to the fourth Edinburgh Festival. The company included Douglas Campbell as Lady Randolph's son, Lewis as Lord Randolph, and Stanley Baxter and Fulton Mackay among the soldiers and servants. Baxter recalls rehearsals: 'Lewis would walk up and down in the wings, grumbling about people's speech. Once Sybil said to him: "If I were a better actress I'd do what you want, but I'm not, so go away."' Bruce Sharman was an assistant stage manager: 'The style was all very declamatory – Sybil played it as if she was hailing a taxi. But she was full of jokes and charm; there was no grandeur or fuss. With Lewis you could never be sure if he had dried, but she just said "Let him find his own way." At the dress rehearsal, when he at last got his long speech right, she came out of character and said, "Well done, Lewis!", and everyone collapsed.'

Sybil's gamble paid off: treading a fine line between the sublime and the ridiculous, she mesmerised the first-night audience by her high-octane playing. She also mesmerised many of the critics, notably J C Trewin, who wrote: 'Dame Sybil, speaking and acting as if *Douglas* were new, governed the stage in attitudes beside which a picture of the Siddons waned to a cardboard cut-out. The most buoyant mockers were watching, stilled. No noise, no bluster: she created the woman in our minds without apparent effort

– the passion, the power, with never a hint that this was an exercise in faded theatrics, in histrionics lacking heart.'

But Derek Monsey, writing in *Picture Post*, was both admiring and scathing: 'To prove one can hold a modern audience in their seats with nonsense, speak impossible lines with conviction, and assume the exaggerated gestures, facial contortions, mannered walk and vibrant voice of tragic acting of a bygone age, is a clever, even a magnificent Sunday Theatre trick for an actress of Dame Sybil's standing; but it is no more creative art and worthy of her than if she had played Juliet, imitating the accents and gestures of Jean Simmons.' Bridie commented afterwards: 'One hopes that the thing will now be decently buried after such stylish obsequies.'

Sybil's performance re-kindled Cochran's interest in her, and he agreed to fulfil her long-held desire to play Elizabeth I by staging Clemence Dane's *The Lion and the Unicorn*. There was talk of John Mills playing Essex and Anthony Pelissier directing, but finally Lewis took on the latter task. Once again there were lengthy discussions and arguments with the author, so plans were not finalised quickly enough. Sybil and Lewis went off for a rare and long-delayed holiday in St Jean de Luz in France, but while they were away Cochran was badly scalded in his bath, and died a few days later. Sybil mourned the loss of the man who had given her a start in the West End; but she was also bitterly disappointed not to be able to play a woman of such a strong, independent nature as Elizabeth.

Cochran's death came almost immediately after Shaw's, which occurred on 2 November 1950. His ashes, mixed with his wife's, were scattered in the garden at Ayot St Lawrence, some of them around the statue of Saint Joan. The British theatre paid no formal tribute, but both Olivier and Sybil paid personal ones. Her admiration for 'his humanity, his deep goodness and his god-like exuberance' remained undiminished. She made a broadcast to America about *Saint Joan*, and wrote to thank Nancy Astor for a newspaper article she had written about Shaw. 'He has been in our minds for these weeks since his fall – oh! how much – and you seem in a way nearer to him than anyone else.' The death of one of her mentors made her think again about an after-life: 'How one wonders what happens – where Charlotte is – where he is – all that vital personality can't just go out.'

Shortly before he died she and Lewis had visited him at Ayot St Lawrence. Perhaps suspecting his life was ending, she wrote a fervent and lengthy 'vote of thanks' to Shaw. She remembered the huge influence he had been, both in her formative days amongst the socialists in Manchester, in her experience of working with him on *Saint Joan*, and on her whole outlook on life. 'Reading the prefaces, reading the plays, acting in them, what an experience!' she wrote. 'How he wakens one to the sense of one's responsibility to one's fellow men, to one's own country, to any country! Consider the way he uses every period, every story of history or imagination, as a comment on things of the moment, and more than a comment – a direction pointed. In my young days they said he was destructive. Yes, of course, but never destructive without reason, or without a signpost to another way of going.'

It was a worthy tribute to one of her mentors, whose faith in her talent had played a significant part in shaping her career within the theatre, and inspiring her thoughts outside it.

32

Sybil and Edith at the Haymarket

1950–1952

'If one accepts that Edith is only interested in Edith,
one can be quite fond of her'
Sybil on Edith Evans

In the early 1950s few new home-grown playwrights were in evidence, the West End theatre being dominated by imports from America and France, or classic revivals. One rare new work of quality was *Penny for a Song*, a second play by the promising young writer John Whiting. Sybil was furious at its poor reception from critics and audiences. The encouraging letter she wrote to him was typical of her desire to help struggling new writers: 'I meant to have written to you before to tell you how thrilled I was with "Penny for a Song". I went to it just a bit swayed by some of the notices, but was completely carried away by it. So was my husband. I had read it before and been extremely interested in your "Saint's Day" – I hope you aren't *too* discouraged by your short run – I think in many ways it was beyond the critics! I think the public would have liked it if they had been encouraged, but the public are fearful, and won't risk if the critics have not praised. I am completely mystified and disappointed at its non-commercial success – I made several lots of people go to it, among them Dame Edith Evans, who was completely carried away with the pleasure of it and the "meaning". The meaning of the play was so exciting I really jumped in my seat with joy. Please go on writing and don't play down because of stupid critics. "Penny for a Song" will live, but of course you have to live too, which is a worry!!'

Soon afterwards she was involved in the next step towards the dream of a National Theatre. The proposed site was now on the south bank of the Thames, between the newly built Festival Hall and Waterloo Bridge (it was later moved again, to its final site on the other side of the bridge). In July the foundation stone was to be laid by the Queen, and Sybil was booked to speak an ode by the Poet Laureate, John Masefield. Concerned to get it absolutely right, she wrote to him. 'I am thrilled, and have put the beautiful words already in my heart and my head, and I hope they come out properly! One problem, for which I want your help please, you who speak the English tongue so exactly and finely.' She explained how two words in one line were difficult to speak, and asked if he would accept a small change. '*You* say it over and over to yourself, and see my difficulty – if I leave out the *s* in poets', I'm a completely happy woman and reciter of verse!!' Masefield bowed to her experience, and changed the line.

The stone-laying was preceded by speeches in the Festival Hall, where Oliver Lyttelton spoke of a building 'where drama past and present, native and foreign, might be set before audiences with taste, distinction and discernment, and played by actors and actresses of the highest accomplishments'. Sybil's speaking of the ode moved the critic Claude Westell: 'Her voice pealed forth like a trumpet note,' he remembered. 'Queen, princess, prelate, statesmen, all were forgotten as the voice of Thorndike declaimed the lines, making them sound infinitely richer and more melodious.' For Sybil the royalist, the occasion had special delights. 'Before the stone was laid about twenty of us went with Her Maj and Princess M to have drinks and be presented,' she told John. 'I had quite a nice talk with the Queen with Lewis.' She continued to revere the royal family, and they seemed fond of her: earlier that week she reported proudly 'a long talk with Princess Alice – she came up to me – not me to her!!' This was at the Buckingham Palace Ball, during which she had 'a long dance with the home secretary Herbert Morrison, and settled the Labour policy!'

During the 1950s, although he acted with Sybil in America and Australia, Lewis rarely shared a stage with her in London. He returned to Shakespeare, appearing at the Phoenix in Peter Brook's production of *The Winter's Tale* (where he exited pursued by a bear) and Gielgud's revival of *Much Ado About Nothing*. Margaret Wolfit, playing Ursula, recalls Lewis trying to get her to ignore her notes from Gielgud: 'He would say, "Don't do that," and try to direct me. It was very difficult.' She also remembers mischief of another kind: 'He was a bit of a wicked old devil. During the run he took me to a matinee of *Coriolanus*, and held my hand the whole way through. I was dying of embarrassment. Alec Guinness, who was sitting in front of us, turned round and asked him: "How is Sybil?"'

Sybil was also attending matinees whenever she could, especially if friends or family were involved. 'Donald dear, what a terrific afternoon we had!!' she wrote ecstatically to Wolfit, after seeing him in the title-role of Guthrie's production of *Tamburlaine the Great*. 'You really do give us something huge – how frightening it is – and so close to something we've known in the world – what a power to sustain that gigantic role, I don't think there's another actor who could have touched it – Chaliapin I expect – the end – that speech to Mahomed and God – wonderful – Thank you again for a stimulating afternoon, and what a pearl for the eye.' She was equally moved by Douglas Campbell's' performance as Othello at the Old Vic, telling John: 'He had real star quality, such authority and poise; he has real passion, hasn't he, and looked really beautiful….I got all sorts of new meanings out of it.' Donald Sinden remembers her being quicker than anyone else to grasp a point. 'She always came to see whatever play I was in. She sat on the edge of her front-row seat with her wonderfully alert face, bright and eager, and at the curtain calls applauded louder than anyone else.'

In her offstage role as grandmother she enjoyed weekends in the Kent countryside, taking the grandchildren on adventurous outings. 'We had a jolly weekend at Cedar,' she told John. 'Jane, Diana and I did one of my awful walks when we all came home bleeding from scratches and brambles! Great fun.' She and Lewis would take long walks along the lanes and across the hills, she striding a little way ahead of him. One local man recalled: 'They would learn their lines as they went, and stop and admire the animals, which she loved, especially the pigs and cows. They invited us into their cottage, where she would sit on one side of the fire and he on the other. You never had to talk, she did all the talking. He'd fall asleep, and she'd say: "Look at Lewis, what *is* he doing!"' A woman who let Sybil and her family use their swimming pool remembered the first time she saw her famous neighbour: 'She was standing on the garage roof, saying how beautiful the view of the pool was, and reciting Shakespeare.'

Her public duties continued thick and fast. There was a primary school to be opened in Hammersmith, a fete in aid of British prisoners-of-war in Malaya and Korea to be opened in Mayfair. She unveiled a bronze bust of Ivor Novello by Clemence Dane in the Theatre Royal, Drury Lane, and a renovated statue of Sarah Siddons on Paddington Green. She gave a talk to the Marriage Guidance Council, during which she remarked: 'Don't try to be sweet all the time: there is great refreshment in a good, loud explosion, provided you can kiss and make up afterwards.' On such formal occasions she was generally seen in what she called her 'floweries', the busy floral or chintzy two-piece outfits run up for her by a local dressmaker. Depending on the occasion, she also favoured capes, and accessories such as brooches, strings of pearls, long gloves and scarves, and hats with veils over them.

Public speaking remained a trial to her, at least until she got going. 'I've been to Canterbury today, talked one hour on Theatre and Everyday Life,' she told John. 'I hate speaking but could have talked for two hours easily – "filled as the moon at the full I were".' This seemed to have been the case when she spoke at a lunch to celebrate forty years of the Birmingham Rep, as Claude Westell remembered: 'She persuaded the Lord Mayor to allow her to support the toast of The Theatre. This she did in her usual irresistible style, with a magnificently delivered peroration which mounted on a crescendo of high passion, and she finished in a blaze of glory, to make a spectacular exit – down stage right – to catch the train to London.'

She and Lewis joined a Society for Theatre Research committee, chaired by Edith Evans, which organised a matinee at the Old Vic commemorating Poel's work, in which Russell appeared in a scene from *Everyman*. She gave the first British Drama League lecture for children, exhorting them solemnly not to go to the theatre just for a lark, but 'in a proper frame of mind, determined to find something there; it is a form of research into other human beings'. But she declined to appear on a BBC religious programme, telling the producer: 'I refuse many invitations to "preach" – it is looked on as a form of publicity and I *do* hate this so – I get in a message when I have things like luncheons.'

Throughout this period she was appearing at the Haymarket in N C Hunter's cosy, middle-brow drama *Waters of the Moon*. Set in a hotel on the edge of Dartmoor, where the life of the residents is disturbed by the arrival and departure of a rich, volatile and flamboyant woman and her family from the outside world, the play had certain echoes of *The Cherry Orchard*. Edith Evans was already cast in the lead when Sybil, against the advice of Lewis and John ('Edith will be able to swamp you. Don't do it'), agreed to play Mrs Whyte, a lonely, snobbish, aristocratic widow living in reduced circumstances on a small pension. Unfazed by the notion of playing a supporting part full of silences, she did so because she thought it 'a compassionate play', she admired Edith Evans, and, perhaps crucially, it contained a scene in which she played the piano.

Frith Banbury directed a cast that included Wendy Hiller, Kathleen Harrison, Cyril Raymond and Nan Munro. 'Sybil and Edith were chalk and cheese in their artistic attitudes,' he recalls. 'Sybil was not in the least difficult, whereas Edith wanted to get it right, and didn't have much patience with people who didn't do it quickly.' She could also be imperious, as Donald Sinden, an understudy in the company, recalls: 'During rehearsals Edith was telling the younger actors where to stand. From the stalls Frith called out, "Dame Edith, what am I here for?" "Don't worry," she replied. "We'll find something for you to do."' But she sometimes needed her director's help. After she engaged him in a long, nervous discussion one day, Wendy Hiller asked Sybil: 'Is Edith always like this?' Sybil replied: 'If one accepts that Edith is only interested in Edith, one can be quite fond of her.'

The play received mostly lukewarm reviews, but the acting was hugely admired. Sybil's performance was all the more impressive because it consisted largely of expressive silences. Yet many critics wondered why two such formidable actresses were squandering their considerable talents on such a thin play. Hobson summed up the feelings of many: 'Tennent Productions have taken our Titian and our Rubens, set them in a palace, furnished them with exquisite paints and brushes (for the play is staged enchantingly), and put them to designing Christmas cards. They do it so beautifully that our breath is taken away and the protest dies on our lips.' Tynan, however, writing in *Harper's Bazaar*, deemed it 'opulently shallow', 'insistently derivative', and unworthy of its stars.

The public saw it differently: the play ran for over two years, with neither Dame, each paid £800 a week, missing a single one of the 835 performances. Those who knew nothing of Sybil's musical background were astonished by her beautiful rendering of Chopin and Schumann. Few tributes meant more to her than that offered by the celebrated pianist Myra Hess, who came round one night to tell her she was 'a great artist'. St John Ervine wrote to tell her that her performance was 'the finest display of pure acting that I have ever seen'. But she quite soon tired of the play. 'I'm weary of *Waters of the Moon* – I feel like screaming!' she told John, after four months.

There were, inevitably, rumours of rivalry between her and Edith Evans, mostly unfounded. One story had Edith complaining that Sybil was playing the piano too fast while she was doing a little dance, and Sybil retorting irritably that she could play it even faster, and was going home to practise doing so. This sounds extremely unlikely. But Sybil did indulge in a spot of scene-stealing. Her ability to draw the audience's attention while doing nothing but knitting on a sofa was noticed, but she was not always so restrained, as Frith Banbury remembered.

'Sybil's tendency to indulge herself got up Edith's nose, it was something she would never do herself. Sybil was over-flowing with love, and that included the audience, so at times, unless controlled, she allowed the audience to dominate her.' Once, when he heard that Sybil's behaviour at a matinee had reduced Edith to tears, he sat in on a performance, then sent a note to each actress. 'Why ruin a lovely performance by pulling too many faces?' ran the one to Sybil, while to Edith he wrote: 'Please understand that Sybil's over-playing is due to enthusiasm and *joie de vivre*.' Their responses were in character. Edith replied acidly: 'I will not discuss people's *motives* for over-playing because I have not yet arrived at your kindly Christian estimate. But I'm progressing.' Sybil's reply was apologetic and disarming: 'Yes, I was a bit highly coloured on Saturday, I had two grand-children in front & was very anxious they should know just what everything meant – consequently much underlining – but I took your sweet rebuking to heart & and it's better again I think.' Another well-worn story verified by Banbury occurred after a year, when Beaumont decided that Edith, originally dressed by Hardy Amies, should be re-dressed by Balmain. Pleased with her outfits after a trip to Paris, she said: 'And Sybil must have a new cardigan.'

Despite Sybil's unprofessional moment, the two of them remained friends, though they were never close. They were both on the Equity Council, and often shared a point of view. 'I am taking it to show Edith, because we are so at *one* in this,' Sybil told Margaret Webster, in connection with a particular Equity policy document. But they disagreed about the new trend for an open stage. 'Edith doesn't like to see the audience, but I love to,' Sybil explained. 'I love to be *with* them.' Publicly she described herself as a lifelong admirer of Edith: 'Larry and John, Peggy and Flora are all great, but for me Edith Evans tops everyone,' she said. 'We have played a lot of the same parts, and she has always been much better than me.' But privately she was critical, telling John: 'Edith is living on her past work and hating every minute of her present existence, refusing to take part in the world of theatre or life it seems to me – I'm *so* fond of her, but she *is* a comic – a sort of governess-spinster, often kittenish in life – and on the stage, when she forgets she's a grand actress and a dame, she is superb! Yes, I'm quite devoted to her and have all sorts of games inside myself when she tries *her* games on me. She is fond of me too, in a way as fond as she can be of anyone – she being a complete egoist, in quite a kind way too!'

Outside the theatre they led very different lives: Sybil the warm centre of an ever-expanding family, Edith the aloof, independent, self-confessed loner, known as 'the mistress of disdain', and lonely outside the theatre. 'I envied Sybil for having all those relatives,' she confessed some years later. 'She had the dressing-room above me, and all I ever heard was the tramp of children's feet.' But she was generous about Sybil's appearance and voice. 'From the beginning Sybil has been a great beauty, with that fine bone structure and those exquisite features, the eyes perfectly set in that lovely forehead. And her voice is wonderful with that magical diction.' She also acknowledged her pioneering work. 'She came into the West End with a hatchet. She destroyed the notion that the leading lady must be a conventionally beautiful woman. It is her work that has made it easier for such as I to achieve success.'

Harold Hobson shrewdly summed up the difference between the two formidable actresses: 'Edith has never had that enormous moral force, touched here and there with a most moving tenderness, that in Sybil makes goodness so positive a reality that in its presence everyone is uplifted.' The actor Robert Flemying supported this notion. 'Edith is a wonderful artist, and greatly admired,' he told a fellow-actor, 'but she doesn't have the same chemistry with the audience as Sybil does. Sybil is loved, even when she goes over the top. She has a completely different sense of comedy.' He added: 'One is a selfish lady, the other a great human being.'

Sybil's desire to help all and sundry sometimes backfired. During the run of *Waters of the Moon* the Ballet Negres did a season as the Playhouse. 'Because they were black dancers, out of the goodness of her heart Sybil invested money in them,' Frith Banbury remembers. 'But it wasn't on the level, it was a dicey management, and she lost it all. That was very like Sybil.' But at other times it was her fellow-actors who suffered. 'All kinds of people came into her dressing-room,' Wendy Hiller recalled. 'She gave the needy not only her own husband's trousers, but my husband's too.' Despite this lapse, she admired Sybil greatly. 'If she'd been the grocer's wife or the archdeacon's wife or the prime minister's wife, she would still have been a great woman, with her generosity of spirit, wisdom, common sense and vision. She was a good woman, but never dull or po-faced.' Sybil, she said, helped her with her stage-fright: 'One night at the side of the Haymarket stage, trembling with fear, I said to her, "How lucky you are not to be nervous." – "Don't be stupid," she said, in that beautiful veiled voice, "it gets worse as you get older." And now, when I'm pulverised with fear, I always think, What would Sybil do? And it's, Do the best you can.'

Waters of the Moon finally closed after two years, breaking every record at the Haymarket. Frith Banbury wrote to Sybil thanking her for her beneficial influence on the company spirit. 'My dear Frith, how very sweet and like you to write,' she replied. 'It's not only me that kept us all free of friction. I will mention specially Kathleen [Harrison], Cyril [Raymond] and Nan [Munro] – but all of us have been very happy together. I think it is partly too the atmosphere of the Haymarket. Yes, I'm sure I shall enjoy the tour. I believe Irene will be very good, tho' of course Edith will be an incalculable loss – especially financially!!!'

An eight-week provincial tour had been planned, with Irene Browne replacing Edith Evans. To John she wrote: 'I go on with the bl----- play til July – Edith won't – she doesn't like the provinces. I do, only I wish I had a larger part!!' She was critical of her friend's refusal to tour. 'No actor has any business to say they won't tour, it's part of our work. I can't talk to her about it – it makes me mad.' She was totally uncomprehending of Edith's attitude to life on the road. 'She loathes the provinces and says, "There's nothing to do there and I'm bored all day long." Now isn't that dreadful for an actor of all people to say? I *love* the provinces and touring, and even if Lewis isn't with me, I find an infinite number of things to do and study – philosophy, Greek, religion, all sorts of oddments....But Edith hasn't a *thing* – she's a genius at her job but not really interested *objectively* in anything – oh yes, Christian Science, but that's so very personal.'

On her single free day between finishing at the Haymarket and starting the tour in Oxford, she squeezed in a recital in Bath, she and Lewis rehearsing their pieces on the train. But she was becoming increasingly anxious about his health: 'He gets very very tired, and then comes over him the "What's the use?" attitude,' she wrote to John. 'I get a bit too "urging" with him, and have to watch my step a bit more now. Even the doing of recitals, which I find stimulating and exciting beyond words, gets him a bit tired.' But Lewis' moods were unpredictable. 'I wish he didn't get so abysmally depressed. I do get so worried about him – and then suddenly he perks up and is only 50 years old!' Her message to herself was: 'Be positive – away with negativeness!!'

While at the Haymarket she made brief appearances elsewhere. She visited her home city to appear in the Rochester Dickens Pageant. She and Lewis took part with other leading players in 'No Hurry, Ifor Davies', a fantasy by Emlyn Williams written for a *Salute to Ivor Novello*, which was staged at the Coliseum, and featured Richard Burton as Novello. She performed scenes from *Ghosts*, *Medea* and *The Trojan Women* for an entertainment for the Free German League at the Embassy, Swiss Cottage. There was also a Shakespearean programme at the Old Vic, in which she and Lewis performed a scene from *Macbeth*. Norman Tozer, then a drama graduate student, was in the gallery: 'Their energy was revelatory. Some hurricane blew them excitingly close, so they seemed to be acting at the front of the gallery rather than on the stage.'

Sybil also took part in many radio broadcasts. One that gave her special pleasure was when, directed by Raymond Raikes, she spoke three of Hecuba's speeches from *The Women of Troy* – in Greek. For 'The Stars in their Choices', a series in which leading actors and actresses chose a role they had always wanted to play, she selected Ivor Novello's *Comèdienne*, which provided her with the part of a famous actress modelled on Mrs Patrick Campbell. She suggested Ibsen's *John Gabriel Borkman* to the BBC's head of drama Val Gielgud, with Eileen and her playing the two female leads – 'I could play the Duse part as Eileen is very strong' – but this intriguing idea was not taken up. She at last managed to play Queen Elizabeth in a Clemence Dane work, *The Saviours*, but disliked her performance. She was aware of her limitations in radio: 'I've not got it, Lewis is far better than me,' she told John. 'The theatre and theatricalism is my medium, I see that very clearly.'

She was reported to be working on a film about the history of the Old Vic, in which she would play Emma Cons, but it seems not to have materialised. She broadcast talks on Lilian Baylis and Annie Horniman, and memorial tributes to James Bridie and Elizabeth Robins. The celebrated actress died in her ninetieth year, and Sybil provided a eulogy of her long-time friend. She ended it by suggesting the way in which the theatrical baton can be passed on: 'The actor's art is ephemeral, nothing tangible remains; but we, who loved Lisa Robins and recognised her power, have something of her spirit in us, which we in turn pass on. The actor's art, by its very intangibility, may have an unconscious life, which is as powerful and durable as the arts that are materially indestructible.'

Sometimes she felt overwhelmed by all the claims on her. 'He is *so* nice and so good, but what is one to do?!' she wrote to Victor Gollancz, after passing on a member of the religious Bruderhof Community who had asked her for money. 'I get despairing at all the Causes – don't you?' These causes were taking their physical toll. 'I'm having a too hectic time with schools and bazaars, and not enjoying them one bit,' she confessed to John. 'After next week I am really going to rest, but so difficult it is, people and causes swarm on one!' There was also the financial pressure: after sending Gollancz a small sum for one of his peace initiatives, she added: 'I can't do more as I'm on all the Peace things and more subscriptions than I can pay honestly!!'

But she liked to help young actors where she could. Alfred Lynch, the son of an East End plumber, was keen to get into the theatre but had no money, and was unable to get a grant to train because he had left school early. Sybil paid for him to attend a theatre course at Toynbee Hall, and before long he was working with Joan Littlewood and her Theatre Workshop. It was a kindness to which he frequently referred as he established himself as one of the new breed of working-class actors.

At the Royal Court she spoke at a midnight matinee about Shaw's influence during the famous Barker-Vedrenne seasons in 1904–7, and of the special affection in which the theatre in Sloane Square was held by Chelsea residents. The theatre was then being set up as a club, with Sybil, Lewis, Giles Playfair and Joyce Grenfell on its council. Later, when George Devine was trying to raise sponsorship to take over the theatre, he enlisted Sybil as a go-between in talks with the John Lewis Partnership, whose founder, Spedan Lewis, was one of her admirers. When Devine outlined his repertory plans, Sybil replied: 'Awfully good – not wildly original, as you say, but there is no theatre in London with these aims in view, is there?'

In January 1952 she was Roy Plomley's guest on *Desert Island Discs*. Her choice of music reflected her love of Bach, whom she described as 'the next thing to God Almighty': she chose three of his works, the famous Toccata and Fugue in D minor, the Brandenburg Concerto No 5 in D, and the Fantasia in C minor. Her other selections were César Franck's Symphonic Variations, an aria from Mozart's *The Shepherd King*, On Hearing the First Cuckoo in Spring by Delius, Beethoven's Kreutzer Sonata, and the Shakespeare sonnet 'Shall I compare thee to a summer's day', spoken by her friend John Gielgud. As her luxury object she chose the blue vase which Lewis had given her when they discovered she was pregnant with John.

John had accepted a job for two years in Australia, as resident director with J C Williamson Theatres, who then owned most of the theatres there and in New Zealand. Sybil was in no doubt about her son's abilities: 'You're the boy who's going to set the continent ablaze!' she told him. 'You are Lewis with an extra dynamo, with something of your Ma's extreme enjoyment of life.' That enjoyment embraced the next generation in the family. 'Our nine grandchildren have certainly altered my life and all for the better!' she told Margaretta Scott. There were other pleasing family developments: 'My Mary is going to marry again,' she wrote to Mary Crawley. 'I am so happy. Her marriage had been such a frustrating thing, and now she has no bad feeling, just feels all is well.' She and Ian Haines, her daughter Diana's class teacher at her primary school, married the following April. It took him a while, as he recalls, to adjust to Sybil's tendency to puff up her family's achievements. 'If she introduced me to anybody, you would assume that I was running London's education service. It was a little embarrassing, but I got used to it.'

With an offer of publication from Harrap, she had started to write her memoirs. But she also agreed to help with a biography to be written by J C Trewin for a series of monographs published by Rockcliff. His son Ion Trewin recalls: 'She came to my parents' house in Hampstead to talk about it. I remember her infectious laugh. Apparently she was very cooperative, and flattered to be in the series.' His father had been watching Sybil for thirty years, and was a great admirer of her achievement. Later he wrote: 'For me she was always high above other actresses, because her range was so great. Others would be tremendously successful in a single line of parts. But when Sybil appeared in something new to her and offbeat, I think she was sometimes under-valued, because she made it all seem so easy. I still think she was the greatest actress I've ever seen, and am likely to see.'

33

Gielgud and a Jubilee

1952–1954

'I hope to go on for a little longer yet'
Sybil in a curtain speech after the last performance of A Day by the Sea

In October Sybil reached 70, an event that prompted many tributes. *The Times* noted: 'As the years have passed there has been no decline in Dame Sybil's art: indeed, it has deepened in feeling and technical assurance, grown wider in delighted virtuosity.' A profile in the *Sunday Times* observed how she and Lewis had shown 'that dignity in the theatre can be combined with abundant vitality', and that while her interest in politics had 'led her sometimes far from the convictions of her multitudinous admirers, their admiration for a great actress remains undimmed'. Victor Gollancz wrote to her: 'I am told that you have just celebrated your twenty-first birthday…I hope you live to be as old as Methuselah.' To a letter from St John Ervine she replied: 'Years aren't anything really. It's fun saying 70, knowing one has more energy than one had at 50!' She ascribed her vitality to 'good health, liking work and loving life'.

In a letter to Equity members she reflected on the changes she had seen, as the profession had evolved from one of 'rogues and vagabonds and rebels to obedient trade unionists with the ideal of dignity and security'. She wrote about the revolution brought about by Barker and the Ibsenites, and the poor use to which she felt Stanislavsky's ideas had been put: 'We in this country, being far more bred on the ideal of perfect ladies and gentlemen, instead of violent, living, moving human creatures, have let this commendable principle of reality develop into pale photography.' Elsewhere she regretted the passing of the grand manner, and the scornful talk of 'ham' acting. 'But ham is only a form of cliché acting, and to lounge through a part, mumbling your lines and trying to make it all look as un-theatrical as possible, is cliché acting at the other end of the scale.'

Although she now retired from the Equity Council, she still attended meetings with Lewis, speaking out passionately against regulated entry to the profession. At one meeting, wearing 'a startling green hat and beating the air', she declared to sporadic heckling: 'We must have freedom! The great bother about the whole profession is that we have become too darned respectable and everybody wants to get into it....We don't want standardised acting, standard actors with standard-shaped legs. Acting needs everybody, cripples, dwarves, and people with long noses. Give us something that is different.'

She continued to be critical of the English theatre: 'Everywhere the theatre is bad, except a few in the centre of London, but the country will only go with film stars or a recognised London success,' she told John. 'The failure of plays in London is frequent, and the general taste isn't a very high one.' She bemoaned the lack of new work: '*Where* are our Picassos – our Matisses or Nashes – our equivalents in the theatre? The leaders like John G and Larry don't seem to do anything *new*. I suppose because all interpretative arts have to *pay* now.' The growth of television worried her. 'TV has usurped so much – that and the BBC are more important in the country than the theatre, which is *so* depressing.'

During this time she made further ventures into film. She was in Herbert Wilcox's worthy but dull biopic *The Lady with a Lamp*, starring Anna Neagle as Florence Nightingale; Sybil appeared as Miss Bosanquet, who accepts the Order of Merit on behalf of Florence Nightingale. She was glimpsed for thirty seconds as a haughty aristocrat in *The Magic Box*, the story of William Friese-Greene, a British pioneer of the cinema. Chosen as the film to mark the Festival of Britain, it featured cameo roles by most of the leading actors. And in *Melba*, a conventional account of the great soprano directed by the American Lewis Milestone, Sybil played a humane and imposing Queen Victoria, reassuring Melba that she too knows about the conflicts between love and other demands. 'The film is a bore,' she wrote afterwards. 'How I dislike love and kissing.'

Her continuing discomfort with the medium was amply demonstrated in *The Weak and the Wicked*, an uneven, didactic film about the lives of women prisoners. Directed by J Lee Thompson, and starring Glynis Johns and Diana Dors, one farcical story involves a plot by two old ladies (Sybil and Athene Seyler) to murder Sybil's husband. Sybil blatantly over-acts with a series of funny faces and shifting accents, her defects highlighted by Athene Seyler's natural, more subtle playing. Yet she appeared at least to be gaining confidence before the camera: 'Got thru' wonderfully, everybody bucked at my speed of work,' she boasted to Val Gielgud. 'Athene and I work very quickly (*too* quickly for our pockets – we save the film folk *days*!!).'

Meanwhile there was intense competition between the leading West End managements to hire Sybil. Henry Sherek wanted her to play Lady Elizabeth Mulhammer in Eliot's *The Confidential Clerk*, Donald Albery was trying to cast her in Graham Greene's first play *The Living Room*, while Binkie Beaumont made great efforts to retain her for his next production. She was ambivalent about Beaumont, the most powerful and most feared manager in London. 'Talk about Machiavelli!!' she wrote to John. 'We've had churns up all this week – machinations and Binkieisms – so little that's honestly real and straightforward, but it's an amusing game if one doesn't let oneself get downed by it in spirit. Really life in the theatre is almost an absurdity. Lewis and I sit back and say, "Mad – the whole thing!" If you could see the ridiculous comings and goings. It's like a farce – being rung up by one or the other all the time.'

Eventually Beaumont persuaded her to do another N C Hunter play, *A Day by the Sea*, to be directed by Gielgud, with Richardson, Irene Worth, Megs Jenkins, and Gielgud himself. Rehearsals before the pre-London tour began well, as Sybil told John: 'We both rather dreaded having John G after our experience in Treasure Hunt – but we are finding him immensely stimulating and we *love* the play – it's very delicate, very funny and quite moving. Ralph Richardson as a drunken doctor is superb.' But she was, perhaps for the first time, experiencing memory difficulties: 'I get fussed with learning words now, so it makes everything doubly hard,' she admitted. But after four weeks' rehearsal she was still appreciating Gielgud: 'I like John G, he never alters – never gets bucked with himself – takes hints from anyone – he's a real dear, and it's simply his homo-sex that has stopped him being a very great actor.' She also observed: 'He's been a very selfless worker in the theatre – but it's odd he's so very feminine – the best work is done by homos!! It's very sad I think.'

Three days later Gielgud was arrested for 'importuning male persons' in a public lavatory in a Chelsea mews. His court appearance the following morning was noticed by a reporter, and the incident got into the press. After great soul-searching, including momentary thoughts of suicide, Gielgud agreed to continue with the play, and arrived at rehearsals the same day. The story goes that Sybil broke the ice by telling him he had been 'a silly bugger'. But Mary Casson believes this is apocryphal: 'She wrote him a letter of support immediately, they met in the theatre that evening, and there was a hug and a quiet sympathetic word,' she insists. This is supported by Sybil's letter to her son that day: 'We've had a difficult time,' she wrote. 'John G has been a bit indiscreet again and it's a great worry – homo-sex is a perfect nuisance – it's an illness. In some ways he isn't grown up – still at the schoolboy stage. I had to tell you in case it hitches up all our doings – we hope not, and we went on as if nothing had happened today!'

On tour she defended Gielgud solidly. She gave the company a dressing-down for talking too much about the incident. She and Lewis received several abusive letters, asking how they could work with 'this filthy pervert'. Sybil answered them all personally. From Liverpool, where the play opened, she wrote to Gielgud's mother: 'It has been an anxious time, but John has been splendid – and he has played beautifully. Please don't worry too much about him – he is surrounded by people who love him.' Lewis told John about her support of Gielgud: 'Sybil went on stage first and fixed the audience with one of her looks, as though she were saying, "I don't think it matters; do any of you?" and daring anyone to think otherwise. Apparently nobody dared.'

At the London opening at the Haymarket, where protest demonstrations were predicted, Gielgud stood in the wings paralysed with fear at his first entrance. Sybil, already on stage, walked over and whispered to him: 'Come along, John darling, they won't boo *me*,' and led him on. Cheered and applauded, he stood there in tears. Gielgud wrote to friends: 'The friendship and loyalty that has surrounded me has almost made up for so much vileness – but I wish I had not caused distress to so many dear friends.' Many people were hostile, or simply evasive. When the conductor Malcolm Sargent came backstage to see Sybil, she asked him to see Gielgud as well. Sargent replied: 'I don't think I can: you see, I mix with royalty.' Nor was Edith Evans sympathetic, remarking in true Lady Bracknell style: 'When I consented to become a Dame, I gave up the privilege of going on the streets when I felt like it.' The contrast with Sybil's reaction could hardly be more startling.

The play itself was poorly received: Tynan labelled it 'an evening of unexampled triviality', but he was not alone: the critical consensus was that this was English Chekhov without the Russian writer's mystery, but a play that gave the opportunity for fine acting by its starry cast. Stephen Williams approved of Sybil's 'perfectly delectable study of a dear, crafty, feather-headed, sharp-witted widow and mother', while Derek Granger thought her 'radiant with querulous humour and most affecting in her moments of regret'. Lewis, now 78, also had splendid reviews, though when he was supposed to fall asleep in his chair, he occasionally did so, forcing Richardson to bellow his cue at him.

Philippa Astor, the assistant stage manager, remembers Sybil's zest backstage. 'She thrived on people, and used her dressing-room as a green room. Alison Colvil, our stage manager, tried to lock her in between the matinee and evening show, but it didn't work. If someone wanted to see her, no matter who they were, she would always give of her time.' Irene Worth especially admired her courage: 'She was wracked with rheumatism at this time, and being kept awake at night by cramps in her legs, but she never complained. She and Lewis would refuse all offers to fetch taxis for them, and go off home by bus – to have their favourite meal of bread and milk.'

Just before the play opened in London, Dylan Thomas had died in New York. Early in 1954 Sybil took part in a memorial programme at the Festival Hall, along with Emlyn Williams, Peggy Ashcroft and Michael Hordern. She was also involved at the Old Vic in two rehearsed readings of *Under Milk Wood*, Thomas' 'Play for Voices', for which she, Richard Burton and Emlyn Williams joined the BBC company of Welsh actors who had recently taken part in its first broadcast. 'Wonderful stuff it is too, very queer though,' she commented. In a lighter vein, she and Lewis took part in a matinee in aid of the Actors' Orphanage at the Palladium, where they played two old tramps singing in a theatre queue. 'It's great fun but oh! I could sleep for a week!' she told Patricia.

For her first television work since before the war she began filming *Mr Sampson*, the first of two episodes in the series 'Douglas Fairbanks Presents', which also starred Joyce Carey and Joseph Tomelty. She found the director Lawrence Huntington very unsympathetic. 'So much to learn – and keep one's head,' she wrote. 'And a director who just looked at us as bits of furniture – no feeling for any sensibility on our part.' Judy Campbell was with her in the second episode, *The Heirloom*, directed by John Gilling, and featuring Nora Swinburne: 'Sybil was very professional in rehearsal,' she recalls. 'She knew her words, never made any difficulties, and was helpful without being a clever boots and taking over the directing.'

By now Sybil and Lewis had planned a further overseas trip. Leaving in June, under the auspices of the British Council and the New Zealand entrepreneur Dan O'Connor, they were to tour Australia, New Zealand and Tasmania, giving recitals of poetry and scenes from plays. Sybil could hardly contain her excitement, but as usual was taking on too much in the weeks before her departure. 'Life is so full, I wake in the morning agonised at what is left undone!' she confessed to her daughter-in-law Patricia.

Then at Easter her sister Eileen, now 63, had a brain haemorrhage and died. 'She has gone! I can't believe it,' Sybil wrote to Patricia that night. 'I love Eileen so and have been so close to her always, and she's been so steady and strong. Oh! I hope she's with Maurice and not lonely any more.' Her sister's death hit Sybil hard. She and Lewis and the family attended the cremation at Golders Green. 'A lovely quiet service, and somehow we were comforted, the words were so beautiful – but oh! Pat, it's all been so sudden and such a shock to us. I can't get straight about it yet.' She and Lewis at once took over the mortgage of Eileen's house, and gave it to her family.

John was present at the service, having returned to England to find work after coming to the end of his contract with the J C Williamson management. Sybil's delight at seeing him again after nearly two years was tempered by the departure a fortnight later of Ann and Douglas to Canada, where they were to join Guthrie and Alec Guinness at the new Festival Theatre in Stratford, Ontario. Not knowing when she would see them again, she was distressed. 'I can hardly bear partings now,' she told Patricia. 'Something dulls in one if one isn't careful to keep one's thoughts creative. I shall miss the children, as I see them daily. It felt like you going to Australia all over again.' But she thought it a good career move for Douglas. 'He is very happy with Guinness and Tony Guthrie, and Tony has handed over a little of the production side to him – and of course all the fights. I often feel Douglas would do well in a place like Canada – the West End drives him crazy, and the Old Vic has become very West End.'

It was now fifty years since she had begun her career, and there were many events and tributes to mark the occasion. On Shakespeare's birthday she was invited to unveil a stained-glass window in Southwark Cathedral, containing figures from Shakespeare's plays: at the ceremony she described it as 'fitting for a poet through whose work shone the light of God, the light of truth'. The Gallery First Nighters' Club held a dinner in her honour. 'About 350 people and all very jolly,' she told Patricia. 'One's whole life surveyed and one felt 180!' The BBC broadcast a 90-minute radio adaptation of *Henry VIII* by Clemence

Dane, with a cast from the theatre's top drawer: Gielgud, Richardson, Scofield, Donat, Vivien Leigh and many others, including Lewis and Russell, with Olivier as the Porter. Appropriately, they all donated their fees to charities of Sybil's choice. She herself played Queen Katharine and, *The Times* critic wrote, 'lavished on it all the rich resources of her humanity and her art, a performance the more effective for never striving merely for effect'.

The big occasion was an all-star matinee attended by the Queen at Her Majesty's, to mark jointly Sybil's and RADA's jubilee, and the centenary of the birth of Beerbohm Tree. Sybil asked Vivien Leigh if she might play the screen scene from *The School for Scandal*: 'You know it will make all the difference in the world to us and the success if you can. I spoke to Paul Scofield about playing Charles Surface – and he's thrilled to do it. Richard Burton will be in Newcastle and is dreadfully disappointed, and we've written to Alec Guinness. Have you any idea whom you'd like for Joseph Surface? Is Denholm Elliott enough – or not as lively as he should be?'

Virtually all the leading stage stars turned out for the occasion, which opened with a prologue written by Alan Herbert, beginning:

> Just fifty years ago, a glorious age,
> A girl called Sybil pranced upon the stage.
> In that year too they had a happy thought,
> That little actresses were better taught.
> But then, could six academies of arts
> Prepare a Thorndike for a thousand parts?

After touching on highlights of her career, it continued:

> And then, dear Sybil, you were never one
> Who went on acting when the play was done.
> A public friend, a very private wife,
> A star not only of the stage but life,
> Who else could cope with all the parts you bore –
> Medea, Lady Macbeth – and Mother of Four?
> You've shown – and here you earn our best hurrahs –
> That mummers, after all, can be mammas.
> Let us salute the youngest of the old –
> Her golden jubilee – our heart of gold.

The programme consisted of acts from four plays, acted by the cream of the profession. It was the last item which meant most to Sybil. Directed by Lewis, in a cast that included Russell and his son Daniel, with Mary playing on the virginals, she finally achieved her ambition of playing Queen Elizabeth in the theatre, in Clemence Dane's *The Lion and the Unicorn*. According to *The Times*, 'she gave a most touching study of greatness turning gradually to dotage'. Sybil herself was delighted: 'Our scene went terrifically – yells and yells at the end, and Larry made a lovely speech about me,' she told Patricia. 'Such a crowd outside, and when we came out, John, Lewis and I, they all yelled in the street and practically carried us to the Haymarket.'

Among the numerous press tributes and profiles, the writers picked out her flaming zeal and supernatural energy, her warm humanity, her love of her work, her total dedication to the theatre, and her 'happy belief in the importance of being earnest, to which she had added a radiant disbelief in the necessity of being glum'. While noting her greatness as a tragedienne, they praised her versatility, and her ability, as shown with CEMA during the war, to go anywhere, with comforts and stardom forgotten. One tribute gave Sybil special pleasure: 'I was so bucked by the Observer profile, cheered and helped by it,' she told George Caitlin. In it the anonymous writer asserted: 'In her warmly human performances the decent humdrum of our lives, so difficult to make appealing on the stage, has acquired the radiance of romance and the emotional pressure of a great adventure. The speech of common use becomes as moving on her lips as any poetry or rhetoric.'

After the matinee, she made her final appearance that evening in *A Day by the Sea*, though the play continued until October. When the performance ended she took the last curtain call on her own, and was presented by the Gallery First Nighters' Club with a statuette of herself as Saint Joan. There was a tradition that no speech should be made from the stage of the Haymarket, but she proceeded to ignore it. She spoke of the wonderful life the theatre had given her. She then walked down to the footlights and added: 'I hope to go on for a little longer yet.'

Leaving the stage door that night to begin her fifty-first year on the stage, she declared: 'I want to go on, not hark back.' She then took off to the other side of the world.

34

Far Horizons

1954–1956

' If I was asked to open a theatre in the North Pole, I would be off'
Sybil in an interview

On 25 June 1954, together with John Casson and Dan O'Connor, Sybil and Lewis set sail from Southampton on the *Dominion Monarch*. Their first overseas recital tour had originally been planned to last three months, but they were to be away for nearly two years, performing in Australia, New Zealand, Tasmania, India, Malaya, Hong Kong, South Africa, Rhodesia, Kenya, Turkey and Israel. It was another testament to their remarkable energy and stamina, and their curiosity and determination to see how other people lived, rather than drift into a comfortable old age in Chelsea.

But there was also, aside from their burning desire to see John and his family, another motive for their journey. For some time now they had, as Sybil put it, grown 'weary of the over-emphasis in the English theatre on décor, on over-production of lights, costumes, etc which the public seems to want, being more ballet-conscious than theatre-conscious – wanting to see rather than to hear, and enjoying the extraneous things of the theatre more than theatre itself'. They were concerned that less and less importance was being given to the spoken word, and wanted to see if theatre could be reduced to 'the bare bones – just the actor, the audience and the words'.

They had devised six different programmes of poetry and drama for the tour. There was generally a long excerpt from Shakespeare, and a selection of poems stretching from early English to the modern era, from Chaucer and Spenser to Dylan Thomas and Edna St Vincent Millay. They would perform some lyric poems, but mostly concentrate on dramatic ones that required them to act: Browning remained Sybil's favourite, because of the dramatic, first-person nature of many of his poems. They would also perform scenes from the Greek tragedies, *Saint Joan* and *The Lion and the Unicorn*. There would be no scenery, just a simple platform, two chairs and a table.

Their first three recitals were in Perth, an oasis of culture in the vastness of Western Australia. The first, in the Government House ballroom, seemed set to be a disaster. At the rehearsal they discovered the acoustics were dreadful: nobody could hear a word, and they were in despair. But with the ballroom full every word was audible, and the applause tumultuous. The local critic picked out especially their playing of scenes from *Macbeth* and *Much Ado About Nothing* ('Dame Sybil's sparkling Beatrice was an especial joy') and her rendering of Browning's 'Up at the Villa', which was 'a brilliant tour de force of colour and vivacious, witty characterisation'.

In Melbourne they were re-united with their grandchildren Anthony, Penny and Jane at John's home in the fashionable suburb of Toorak. Their recitals were a huge hit, compelling an extra thirteen performances to be added to the original seven, each one a sell-out. Sybil wore a simple blue dress and a long green stole, Lewis a blue dinner-jacket. The critics were enthusiastic. 'Dame Sybil was elegant, mannered and gay,' Geoffrey Hutton wrote in the *Age*. 'She put her hearers in the mood with a slight and vivacious fluttering of the hands, a joke or two, an informal aside….We were all completely under the spell.' It was noticed what a good listener she was, an important ingredient of their performance. There was the occasional hitch, as when Lewis forgot his lines one night: Sybil simply sat him down and gave him a glass of water, and the show went on.

In between the recitals Sybil opened bazaars, spoke at luncheons, attended women's tea parties and receptions. 'People hugely admired her in Melbourne,' recalls Brian McFarlane, then theatre editor on the student newspaper *Farrago*. 'She was genuinely interested in the amateur and student theatre in Australia, and had a real and infectious interest in what other people were up to.' Interviewing her for his paper, he was impressed by her warmth and vitality. 'She had that way of making you think nothing is more important in her life than talking to you at that moment.'

After Melbourne they flew over the snow-covered Victorian Alps to Canberra, the capital, where their status as artistic ambassadors brought them the royal treatment. They dined and spent the night at the house of the British High Commissioner, and were guests of the governor-general Lord Slim and the prime minister Robert Menzies. Sybil delighted in it all, reporting to Murray: 'Very grand here in Government House, surrounded by blue mountains and *glorious* scenery. We feel quite elated. We gave a recital last night for Members of Parliament. Mr Menzies and the Slims were there – we did some Medea which they all loved. We've had a superb time. It's a country of great contradictions, but oh! how fascinating.'

In Sydney – which Sybil found 'spectacular and wonderful, everyone lives at great speed – all most exciting and at times Broadwayish!' – they gave recitals in the Conservatoire of Music, before flying on over the Tasman Sea to New Zealand. In Auckland and Christchurch they found audiences hungry for theatre: 'What a joy to play to, and to speak such fine words to avid crowds,' Sybil enthused. They moved on to Dunedin and Wellington, where the Cabinet adjourned so that the Conservative prime minister and his colleagues could join their wives at a tea-party held in their honour – with Sybil making it clear they were long-standing members of the Labour Party. One recital was in St Paul's Cathedral, where the audience included students from Wellington Girls' College. One of them, Barbara Laurenson, was inspired by Sybil: 'I felt I had been touched by grace, and decided that somehow or other I would become an actress,' she remembers.

They toured the length and breadth of New Zealand's two islands, Sybil constantly exhilarated by the beauty of the mountains and glaciers, the drama of the geysers and volcanoes. 'It all seems a little too near paradise to seem quite real,' she noted. They took a few days' holiday in Dunedin, hired a pilot and a small plane, and went for hair-raising trips over the Southern Alps. Here, as elsewhere, they found time to walk and climb. In Auckland they met Edmund Hillary, who had conquered Everest the year before, while at Rotorua, the centre of the geyser country, they met again Rani Guide Rangi, whom Sybil described as 'a remarkable Maori woman who had known kings and queens and leaders of all sorts'.

Back in Australia by late October, their next stop was Brisbane. 'The audiences were perfect – our exhilaration knew no bounds, and we could hardly drag ourselves off the stage!' Sybil reported. They were received with huge enthusiasm wherever they went. They flew on to Tasmania, where in Hobart they played in a theatre built by convicts, and Sybil was reminded of the Tolpuddle Martyrs, who had been transported to Australia. Back in Melbourne they gave further recitals, Sybil tactlessly telling the audience they had 'improved' since she had played to them a few weeks ago.

In January 1955 they moved on to India and the Far East. The British

Council, which was again sponsoring them, were worried this would prove a journey too far. Sybil's response was: 'What does it matter if we do crock up – better than going to sleep and retiring.' Besides, they had long been fascinated by India, a country whose people and struggle for independence they had been involved with since meeting Tagore in the 1920s. They knew India's first prime minister Jawaharlal Nehru and his sister Mrs Pandit; and they were old friends of Krishna Menon, India's representative at the United Nations, whom they knew as 'dear tricky Dicky'.

They performed recitals in Bombay and New and Old Delhi, in Madras and Calcutta, to attentive audiences in colleges, universities and elsewhere. They were following high-powered cultural delegations from Russia and China. 'Without Turkmeni acrobats or the Chinese variety of comic opera, and with no props, the visitors filled every house,' a local journalist wrote approvingly. 'Thousands of young men and women have come to realise that Shakespeare is not only an examination subject.' A Bombay vernacular paper wrote of Sybil, 'Her voice is like a tinkling temple bell,' while the English-language papers ran long laudatory reviews, and detailed reports of their movements and offstage remarks.

"The recitals have been a huge go, and we are adoring every minute,' Sybil wrote to Patricia from Delhi. 'We are in a *dream*.' They had been told Indian audiences would be fidgety, that it was their custom to chat and move about. 'But the silence was lovely, not a sound, and then terrific applause. Such gratitude from all the Indian people.' They found the students of St Stephen's College in Old Delhi among the best. 'The undergraduates were so quick – they got some comedy points in Shakespeare which I'd never known got over before.' As well as performing, they saw a great deal of Indian theatre, of plays acted in Hindi, Bengali and other languages, by students and professionals. 'It didn't matter not being able to understand the words because the acting was so expressive,' Sybil noted.

Like most westerners they were shocked and distressed by the slums and the poverty, especially in Bombay and Calcutta, where whole families lived on the street. But they loved the beauty of the countryside, and the elegance and warmth of the Indian people. Again they stayed mostly in government residences, being welcomed as unofficial ambassadors of their country. Nehru had left instructions that everything possible should be done to make them comfortable, which resulted, Sybil reported, in their being 'treated like Dresden china!!' One highlight was a lunch at the home of the health minister

Raj Kumari Amrit Kaur, who flew with them in Nehru's plane to Agra and the Taj Mahal.

'I can't find words to say what we felt,' Sybil reported from Delhi. 'It was one of *the* days of our life.' She loved the vastness of the Taj Mahal, and the tiny mosaic flowers set into the marble. She was also deeply moved by visits to the Gom monastery, to Kalimpong in West Bengal, where they watched the Tibetan caravans come in, and saw the room where the Dalai Lama had taken refuge after his exile from Tibet. They saw the old temples on the sea shore around Madras, 'feeling ourselves going back centuries into another century of thought, with a sense of others being present'.

She and Lewis were both fascinated by mountains, and had read widely about the Himalayas: they had 'been on every journey that had been made, gone up foot by foot with the climbers'. Before they left England she had told Nehru that her greatest desire was to see the sun rise over Everest. Nehru had promised to arrange it, and now did so. They were driven up to Darjeeling, 7,000 feet up – only to be met by fog. They had tea with Tenzing Norgay, the co-conqueror of Everest with Hillary, who had a mountaineering school there. The next morning they were woken at 4am, and driven up Tiger Hill, fearing the fog wouldn't break. But as they watched, hand in hand, they saw Everest and the surrounding Himalayan peaks slowly turn pink in the sunrise. Speechless at first, Sybil eventually said to Lewis: 'I don't care if I never see anything beautiful again. We've reached the top.'

Their experiences in India, Sybil observed later, seemed to bring them closer together. 'Lewis and I were in a special and even more complete harmony during this time, which was the fulfilment of so much we had thought about and yearned for, and which was now completely shared. We were gloriously happy.' The next day they flew to Hong Kong, where they stayed with family friends on the Peak overlooking the harbour. 'We're here not to rest, but to enjoy ourselves, which means to work,' Sybil told a reporter, neatly summing up her philosophy. They gave several matinees for children and two for adults. The press were loud in their praise, picking out the extract from *Saint Joan* as the highlight of the programme. A review in the *South China Morning Post* suggests Sybil could still inhabit the part: 'She was again the young French girl who dared defend her vocation against the challenge of an interested Church. In those few and moving and simple words, Dame Sybil re-created the eternal and essential youth that only an actress needs and only a great actress may ever possess.'

One visit was to the leper colony on Hay Ling Chay Island, which had several hundred patients. Sybil had kept in contact with lepers since the days when Lilian Baylis took the Old Vic actors to the colony in Essex. Here she and Lewis gave a recital to a mixed-age audience, after which the leper children performed a mime, and the older patients staged a Chinese play in honour of their guests. They were accompanied by Patricia and her daughter Penny, who recalls the occasion: 'Granny talked to all the lepers, and told the nurses how wonderful they were to be coping, with all the dangers involved. She had such empathy with people; she inspired them by just being herself.'

As in India, they were feted and feasted everywhere, though the delicacies were not always to Sybil's taste: one dish she likened to 'old vests, boiled', only to see Lewis eating it quite cheerfully. But for a moment they seemed to be flagging. 'I think deep down we're both getting a bit tired of the continual racket,' Lewis wrote to John. 'There's too much to take in too quickly in beauty and interest and new people and different peoples.' But there were still more recitals to be given. In Singapore, then a British colony, they stayed for several nights with the commissioner-general for South-East Asia, Malcolm MacDonald. 'I was enchanted by their visit,' he recalled. 'They never talked about what they were doing themselves, but were genuinely and unflaggingly interested in our concerns. This was a critical time in Singapore, when Britain was doing her utmost to weld together the hostile factions – Chinese, Malay, Indians, Eurasians, Ceylonese – and Sybil and Lewis helped us, for about them at least there was a united opinion.'

Finally they reached Kuala Lumpur, the Malaysian capital, where they gave three further recitals, and continued their relentless sight-seeing, visiting gardens and a rubber plantation. While in Singapore they had to turn down an invitation to visit Communist China, but Sybil expressed the hope that they could visit Peking before the end of the year. She had recently, together with Laurence Housman, Augustus John, Moira Shearer and Compton Mackenzie, been a signatory to a goodwill message which Hugh Casson, Stanley Spencer and A J Ayer had taken to China, advocating closer cultural relations between the two countries, to try to stop 'all the dissensions which at present threaten to separate us'.

They flew back to Melbourne in March, to begin rehearsals for their next project. Beaumont had arranged for them to return to Australia and New Zealand with two Rattigan plays, *The Sleeping Prince* and *Separate Tables*, in which they would co-star with Ralph Richardson and his wife Meriel

('Mu') Forbes, under the direction of Lionel Harris. Rattigan had written *The Sleeping Prince* 'as a little nonsense for a great occasion', the 1953 coronation. and admitted it to be 'a very slight piece'. *Separate Tables*, by contrast, was a work of substance, set in a dingy hotel on the south coast, its characters a sad collection of English misfits and losers. When Rattigan attended rehearsals Sybil, who had always liked his writing, warmed to him: 'He has a kind of witty sympathy,' she observed. 'You never have to explain anything.' The liking was mutual, Rattigan later writing of his delight in 'making friends with one of the most enlivening and enchanting spirits of our age'.

The company alternated the plays as they toured the country, playing in all the big cities, every state and many country towns. They opened with *The Sleeping Prince* in Perth on 20 April. Sybil played the outrageous, bombastic Grand Duchess in Rattigan's piece of Carpathian froth and bubble. She had spoken often of her desire to act with John's daughter Jane, whom she was increasingly seeing as the one to pick up the theatrical baton. Jane, now fifteen, had secured the small part of the Princess, and also acted as Sybil's dresser. She recalls with pleasure her grandmother's odd ritual preparations: 'She looks at herself in the light-encircled mirror and says: "Sybil, you look *awful*." As she dresses she twinkles at me like a naughty girl and recites one of her childhood rhymes: "First me coit, then me petticoit, then me shimmcombobs, then me shallicoumdiddles…"; no one mentioned undergarments in her youth.'

Sybil was thrilled by the positive reaction to Jane's performance, telling Patricia: 'She got a huge round on her exit. Rattigan came round to our dressing-room and said to her: "You are splendid, I see myself writing plays for you in the future." Lionel Harris said: "Well, the die is cast, there's no doubt what *you're* going to do, Jane." And Ralph and Mu kissed and thanked her.' Amid the euphoria, Sybil was still able to assess Jane's abilities more coolly. 'I think the actual *tone* of voice will develop – it's very carrying and very light – but the theatre is huge, and she has *very* good diction.' But John Sumner, then director of the Melbourne Theatre Company, recalled: 'Jane tried to imitate Sybil vocally, but was unable to show her own talent.' The situation was difficult for Jane, who bore a strong resemblance to Sybil. Often they had rows, as Sybil acknowledged to her shortly after leaving Australia: 'I feel so sorry that I used to get cross sometimes, you don't hold it against me, do you? I've got a beast of a temper and I get so mad. But you and I are awfully alike in lots of ways, that's why we scrapped. But we did have some fun, too, didn't we, and hopeless giggles!'

In Melbourne, reviewing *The Sleeping Prince*, the *Herald* critic praised Sybil's 'warm vigour as the Regent's shrewd old battle-axe of a wife – a clear-cut and joyous job', while the *Age* saw 'a magnificent figure with just the touch of burlesque needed to raise this cardboard comedy to uninhibited laughter'. Brian McFarlane recalls: 'Meriel Forbes was charming as the chorus girl, but Sybil bestrode the dull play like a colossus.'

In *Separate Tables* she played the snobbish, bullying widow Mrs Railton-Bell. She felt she had a feeling for this bitchy kind of woman, but her performance provoked a family row. John believed she was breaking one of her basic principles about acting by showing her disapproval of her character, thereby satirising her. He said so on the radio while reviewing the production. 'When I got home we had a high old dust-up and much temper whirling around,' he remembered. 'Sybil said, "I loathe Mrs Railton-Bell!" And I said, "That's what I'm complaining about." Of course we ended up the best of friends and vowed undying love and affection, but I noticed that thereafter with great skill and subtlety she changed her performance.'

Sybil and Lewis stayed with John and his family throughout the six-week run in Melbourne. 'She had a huge sense of fun and of the ridiculous,' Penny recalls. 'One night after they had gone to bed – this was the time when people still had chamber pots at night – she appeared holding hers, saying, "Who lies in the second chamber?" It turned out there was a huge spider in it. Another night, while we were having cocoa after a recital, we heard peals of laughter from their bedroom. Granny had taken her teeth out and was making faces in the mirror, seeing how awful and grotesque she could make herself. Granddaddy was in fits of laughter.'

In Sydney the company opened the refurbished Elizabethan Theatre in the suburb of Newtown, playing *The Sleeping Prince* to a capacity audience. The press reported that 'Newtown people stood with babies in arms and barefooted boys brought their dogs to see the Bentleys and Cadillacs and the Anglias and other baby cars bring a capacity audience of more than 1,500 people.' 'Splendid acting matched the fanfares, movie lights and brilliance of the historic opening,' the *Daily Mirror* reported. Although the lights failed twice, Sybil was exultant: 'A terrific do last night – all went swimmingly,' she told Patricia. During the ten-week run the company were surprised by the number of young people that came to see the plays, but even more surprised to hear the sound of babies in the audience. The management put up notices saying No Infants in Arms, but soon after at a matinee another one was heard, its wail turning into a ghastly rattle. Confronted by the manager, the mother admitted: 'I did bring my baby, but I also brought this rattle to keep him quiet.'

There was a marked contrast between the Cassons and the Richardsons in their attitude to attending functions. 'I don't really think they've enjoyed this country very much, I don't think it interests them,' Sybil confided to John. She respected their unwillingness to meet people, without sharing it. Richardson later put his hand up, admitting: 'I rather shirked my duty. Ill at ease, packed tightly among people, I felt I was the worst possible advertisement both for my theatre and my country. But Sybil and Lewis possessed brilliant social gifts, and gave themselves with the utmost generosity, swallowing each cup of tea to the last with grace and apparent appetite.' John McCallum, touring at the same time with his wife Googie Withers in Rattigan's *The Deep Blue Sea*, confirms their diligence: 'Sybil's enthusiasm and warmth enveloped everybody with whom she came into contact, and Australian audiences loved her. She and Lewis were full of vigour, and indefatigable in their promotion of the theatre. They must have spoken at hundreds of English Speaking Union lunches, Victoria League lunches, Commonwealth Society functions, and so on. Both of them were a pleasure to listen to, Sybil's big round voice giving double value to every vowel, and Lewis' deep Welsh growl always accompanied by a twinkle in his eye.'

The New Zealand tour didn't quite live up to expectations, at least at the box office. But Sybil continued to seek adventure. Googie Withers recalls a car journey she and John McCallum shared with her on the South Island: 'Sybil said: "Look at that tremendous mountain over there. Lewis, we must climb it!"' She was now seventy-three, he was eighty, their birthdays falling while they were in Auckland. 'The party for both of us was a riotous success last night,' she wrote to John. 'They did it beautifully. Lovely eats and every sort of good drink. Lovely cake and masses of flowers. At 12 o'clock it became Lewis' birthday so we all sang and we both made speeches and we stood in the middle while they sang Auld Lang Syne – very gay – and Lewis kissed me there and then to cheers from the stage-hands.'

Back in Australia, Sybil lent her name to a scheme to set up a Gilbert Murray Fund in England to mark his ninetieth birthday. Sponsored also by Churchill, Masefield, Bertrand Russell and others, it would be used to promote the study of ancient Greek literature and Hellenic culture, and provide travelling fellowships to spread the values of the United Nations with which Murray was deeply concerned. But Sybil had been planning to mark the occasion in her own way: 'I made up my mind that by your ninetieth birthday I'd know the whole of the Shield speech of Hecuba in Greek,' she told Murray, 'and yesterday morning I got the last lines in my head! I feel quite elated, and tho' I find it very difficult, yet the sound is so glorious, and anyway it is in my head and I can speak it in my bath, if nowhere else!'

Their time in Australia was, according to John Casson, 'a period of astonished excitement for them both. They steeped themselves in Australia's energetic and bustling life, and they did almost everything it was possible to do.' They had, he felt, 'made ordinary people feel that their lives and what they did with them really mattered. It didn't matter what they were doing, visiting a university, having a picnic, seeing over a steelworks, lunching with a bishop or shopping, they devoured Australia and Australia devoured them, to their several and mutual advantages.'

They left Australia on 25 January, aboard the *Southern Cross* with the O'Connors, for Africa and Europe. As they sailed away Sybil took stock. 'Lewis and I have a sort of feeling that this eighteen months has been a transition into another beginning of life,' she told John. 'At our age we could easily have rested on past achievements and been just "comfy", watching the world pass us and only "living" in our minds.' On board ship her hopes for a welcome break from work were soon shattered: 'Very nice people, but we feel a concert in the offing!' she reported after a fortnight at sea. 'You simply can't be stand-offish on a ship, can you. We can use it as a rehearsal!'

Arriving in Johannesburg, they gave a fortnight of recitals there in the Brooke Theatre, directed by Brian Brooke. They were then driven hundreds of miles through Natal to Durban, to perform in East London, Grahamstown and Port Elizabeth, before moving on to the Hofmeyer Theatre in Cape Town. 'It's a lovely country to live in, if one could shut one's eyes to the big problem,' Sybil wrote. 'I'd not like to live here for there is bound to be a bust-up one day. I'm still quite horrified at apartheid and all its implications.' She and Lewis were keenly interested in seeing the living conditions of the native population, and visited several townships. One of these was Sophiatown outside Johannesburg, home to many different races, who were now being 'removed' under an extension of the apartheid laws. Sybil told John: 'We had been warned by someone we quite respect to be careful not to take an interest in the state of the natives – which advice Lewis and I completely ignored, and glad we did, although we were both vicar's-family tactful.'

In Johannesburg and Cape Town they managed to play to native and Cape Coloured audiences as well as to all-white ones – 'a great score!!' Sybil noted gleefully. But by now even she was beginning to tire. 'We've just had a deadly boring matinee,' she wrote from Cape Town. 'I feel for the first time that I've had enough, but I dare say I shall perk up in Rhodesia – and certainly in Israel, if we get there without being shot at!' They gave further recitals in Bulawayo and then Salisbury, where to Sybil's pleasure they again were able to do a show for the native Africans only. They moved on to Nairobi, where they visited Kikuyu orphan schools and hospitals, went down a copper mine, and finally saw a family of lions in Kenya's National Game Reserve.

Their first European stop was Greece, where they spent hours in Athens on the Acropolis, and visited what was believed to be Medea's house in Corinth, where Sybil was unable to resist declaiming the 'Women of Corinth' speech from the play. They flew to Turkey to give two recitals in Istanbul and one in Ankara, then went on to Israel, where their initial reception was the most fervent yet. 'Everyone very glad to see us,' Sybil wrote. 'Cheers at the airport from a crowd – really it was most touching. Apparently we are the Great Friends of Israel!'

She found the land much changed since their last visit, and was moved to see the trees that had been planted for her then now fully grown. They fitted in some theatre visits: 'The acting here is the best we've seen in years,' Sybil told Jane. 'Absolutely first-class professional. Lewis said it gave him great hope for the theatre again.' With her usual interest in a country's affairs, she attended meetings on the position of women and Jewish issues. She and Lewis went to Haifa, Acre ('a town of 500 BC – wondrous!'), Nazareth and Tel Aviv. 'The theatres here are big and need real tone,' she noted. 'Very good for us.' Their last recital was a special performance for artists and actors in the Camera Theatre in Tel Aviv. 'We had a terrific send-off tonight,' Sybil wrote. 'The audience yelling and shouting, and a presentation to us of a first-century goblet dug up here – thought to be in use when Christ was alive.'

They finally returned to London at the end of April, having travelled some 40,000 miles and covered four continents. They were, and had been, on top of the world.

35

Waiting for Marilyn

1956

'Are you helping her or bullying her?'
*Sybil to Olivier, on his directing Marilyn Monroe
in* The Prince and the Showgirl

As Sybil and Lewis arrived back in London, John Osborne's *Look Back in Anger* opened at the Royal Court. The play, as the writer Alan Sillitoe later observed, 'set off a landmine' under the genteel British drawing-room theatre.

It made it possible for playwrights from more varied backgrounds to emerge, so opening up the theatre to younger audiences. They were able to create working-class characters who were not just servants or 'characters'. This in turn opened up the theatre to a new breed of working-class actors and actresses, many of them from the regions rather than London and the Home Counties. Joan Littlewood's Theatre Workshop was reinforcing this trend at Stratford East, where Brendan Behan's *The Quare Fellow* opened a fortnight after Osborne's play. While Beckett's more iconoclastic *Waiting for Godot*, staged by Peter Hall the previous year at the Arts, would usher in the experimental work of Harold Pinter, N F Simpson and Ann Jellicoe, *Look Back in Anger* would open the door to writers of the calibre of John Arden, Edward Bond, Shelagh Delaney and Arnold Wesker.

Look Back in Anger brought a new kind of passion and language to the English stage, which in the West End had been dominated recently by expensive Tennent productions: plays by Coward and Rattigan and, in translation, Anouilh and Giraudoux. Its tone and content shocked the theatrical Establishment: at the opening Beaumont walked out at the interval. Rattigan suggested afterwards that Osborne was merely saying: 'Look, ma, I'm not Terence Rattigan', while Olivier observed to Arthur Miller: 'It's just a travesty on England, a lot of bitter rattling on about conditions.' Sybil, however, gave it a warm welcome, as she did the new regime at the Royal Court: 'We were completely fascinated by it,' she told Patricia. 'It's a very moving and odd play and a great success.'

That visit was part of an orgy of theatre-going, in which she and Lewis tried to catch up with the London scene. They saw *Separate Tables*, followed by supper with Rattigan, who was trying to persuade them to do the play in America. They took in Coward's *South Sea Bubble* and Enid Bagnold's *The Chalk Garden*, and enjoyed being feted when they went to see Guinness in *Hotel Paradiso*: 'We had such a welcome as never was,' she told John. 'The whole theatre clapped us and we held a kissing reception in the stalls! Great fun and very exhausting.' During this time they were also regulars at the Old Vic, as Paul Rogers remembers: 'The production changed every four weeks, but they seemed to see everything.' At the Royal Court they saw Arthur Miller's *The Crucible* and Angus Wilson's *The Mulberry Bush*, and thereafter, according to George Devine, would come to all the new plays, and Sybil would write him vivid and constructive criticism as soon as she got home.

She and Lewis very familiar figures in and around Chelsea, which still had something of a village atmosphere. Nora Nicholson would often meet Sybil at the grocer's, where 'we would hold impartial discussions about cheddar cheese and the church, and strolling home argue amiably over politics'. The actor Ian Burford would bump into her in the post office: 'She would say: "Did you see that programme about Tagore? Wasn't it marvellous?" Nothing dimmed her enthusiasm.' Donald Sinden, also a resident, recalls another sight: 'Lewis would come out of Swan Court in his carpet slippers to buy a paper, cross the King's Road never looking to right or left, with traffic screaming to a halt. It's amazing he wasn't killed.'

Their next venture was T S Eliot's complex and mysterious verse play *The Family Reunion*. Set in a northern country-house, it uses the techniques of Greek drama (notably Aeschylus' *The Oresteia*) to tell a story about sin and redemption within an aristocratic family. Sybil was cast as Amy, Dowager Lady Monchensey; a selfish, arrogant and dictatorial mother. Her eldest son Harry was played by Paul Scofield, and the company also included Gwen Ffrangcon-Davies, Nora Nicholson, Patience Collier, Cyril Luckham and Harry H Corbett. Lewis was content with the small part of the doctor, explaining in a broadcast: 'If I'm billed rather less than Sybil, I console myself with the fact that I am Svengali to her Trilby.'

During rehearsals, as she wrote to her family, Sybil blew hot and cold over the play and its director.

'First rehearsal today –and we *adore* the play. Peter Brook producing and very good….

We're very thrilled with the play and think it's coming out finely….

Peter Brook *will* get so fussy and over-elaborate….

Paul is a big actor, he is breaking new ground, and Gwen is a lovely actress, I'm liking her more and more….

It's a damn difficult play. Lewis itches to get at them all – make them *speak* – only of course Paul and Gwen are very good in this way….

We are in the worst stages of production – all feeling suicidal, and also that the director knows nothing about the play. Lewis is itching to take over the whole production from Peter Brook, leaving him the lighting and the ballet side and Lewis to do the vocal….

We work all day, it's such a darn difficult play….

We open tonight, it's all very much under-played, which maddens Lewis, and makes *me* feel depressed….

Last night was a terrific success – we were astonished – very depressed about it at the first dress rehearsal, but P Brook has got a sense of magic and it came over – it looks very beautiful – it was listened to breathlessly!….

Business is very good, and we do enjoy the play.'

Nora Nicholson remembered that 'for all his cherubic appearance and soft voice, Peter Brook was quite a disciplinarian, and the rehearsals were Herculean'. Both Sybil and Gwen Ffrangcon-Davies found him difficult to work with, and there were several arguments. Scofield suggested the two actresses may have 'wished for more joy in the production, more emphasis on the passages of potentially uplifting spiritual belief, whereas Peter, I think, wanted to avoid sentimentality at all costs, and wanted Eliot's bleakest intentions to be realised'. Sybil's work was made more difficult, according to Cyril Luckham, by the fact that Lewis would take a prompt only from her, so that she had to learn his part as well as hers, and be in the wings whenever he was on stage and she was not.

 The production, which ran for 100 performances at the Phoenix, received mixed notices. Many critics who were unable to warm to the play were full of praise for the quality of the production. Alan Dent thought it 'magnificently directed and flawlessly acted'; J C Trewin noted a production of 'absolute mastery, with acting to match'; while *The Times* observed that Sybil 'once again uses silence as the principal element in the making of yet another of her wonderful old ladies'. Even Tynan wrote that Sybil and Gwen Ffrangcon-Davies 'perform magnificently'. Eliot, who had previously turned against the play, feeling he had failed to integrate the classical and modern elements, approved of the production. Lewis' view is not recorded.

Sybil remained involved with Equity, often speaking passionately on matters about which she felt strongly. In June she and Lewis attended the annual general meeting, which was urged to 'instruct all members not to work in any theatre in which any form of colour bar operates'. Sybil spoke strongly against it, describing her recent experiences in South Africa, and arguing that the job of actors was to go 'into every blooming country we can' and preach the gospel of the theatre. Paul Rogers remembers the meeting being hostile, and Sybil being booed. But according to one press report: 'Her harangue, delivered breathlessly and obviously with profound conviction, moved the meeting to cheers and sustained applause.' A crucial extra clause was added, specifying 'unless some performances can be given to persons of any race, creed or colour'.

A quarter of a century after her involvement in the founding of Equity, she was still an influential figure. Richard Attenborough, who shared her opinion about visiting countries that operated a colour bar, admired her courage: 'She and Lewis were the most stalwart, dedicated members of Equity,' he says. 'With her passionate socialist principles and enthusiasm for life, she was nevertheless very pragmatic and committed. Even if she found herself in a frightening minority, she stuck absolutely to what she believed. She was a star player, a major figure. I think if she had been primarily involved in politics, she could have done anything.'

Her oratory was also in evidence during the centenary celebrations of Shaw's birth. Speaking at a Society of Authors lunch, she suggested Shaw should be remembered for his spiritual exuberance, and for 'a tremendous, gorgeous levity that brought him nearer to sainthood that even his serious-ness did'. Afterwards she couldn't resist telling John about the reaction: 'I really *felt* the speech. Lewis said it was the best he had heard me make – he said it was real oratory with a good shape. Eric Linklater was there, and said: "Yours was the best speech I've ever heard – I admire you!"' She took part in two television discussions about Shaw as a playwright, and a celebratory film directed by Robert Hamer, which featured interviews with her and other friends, including Wendy Hiller, Barry Jackson, Anthony Asquith and Esmé

Percy. But the incessant demands on her time tried her patience: 'TVs nearly every day – this GBS centenary is getting me down!' she told Patricia.

That summer she was at Smallhythe for a special Ellen Terry Anniversary Performance, to mark the centenary of her first stage appearance. She and Lewis acted as narrators for a programme of Shakespeare excerpts, in which Edith Evans also appeared. 'Edith had supper here this week,' she told Patricia. 'We're spending Sunday week at her new old lovely home in Kent – she's thrilled and happier than she has been since Guy died.' Sybil had admired her performance in *The Chalk Garden*, which was still running. But then Edith was taken ill, and Gladys Cooper flew over from America to replace her temporarily. Sybil agreed to take over the part thereafter, but doubted it would be necessary: 'Edith has left hospital and has gone home – she's still pretty weak but I think she'll be OK – she has such resilience.' She was right, explaining to John with no trace of sarcasm that Edith had made 'a miraculous recovery – a triumph for Christian Science!'

Her next film proved a difficult but absorbing experience. The screen version of Rattigan's *The Sleeping Prince* was to feature the intriguing combination of Olivier and Marilyn Monroe. Olivier was to repeat the role of the Prince Regent of Carpathia which he had played in the stage production, and also direct the film, while the American star would play the chorus girl. (The press quickly dubbed them the Knight and the Garter.) Warner Brothers insisted, against Rattigan's wishes, that the title be changed to *The Prince and the Showgirl*, while, under pressure from the American film censor, Sybil's role as the Prince Regent's wife was changed to that of his mother-in-law, to make his pursuit of the chorus girl more acceptable.

The film meant Sybil had to turn down other offers, including the chance to play in Rattigan's *Separate Tables* on Broadway. But the blow was softened by her fee: £2,000 for ten days' work at Pinewood Studios. 'I've got the most gorgeous clothes and corsets from neck to knee!' she told Patricia. 'I long to see Marilyn Monroe – it will be a lark.' It turned out rather different from that. Even before Marilyn arrived in England with Arthur Miller, her husband of just two weeks (the press labelled them the Hourglass and the Egghead), Olivier saw trouble ahead. 'Larry in a spin because Marilyn is so difficult, and he's afraid he may want me longer,' Sybil wrote to John. But when she met the American star she was much taken with her.

'I was being made up and Larry brought her in. She had dark specs on and face covered with grease – she said in a tiny voice, "Do forgive my horrid face."

She's very sweet and young in manner. Larry tells me she'll have to have a lot of help, but she is a very nice girl, and no side or stardomness at all.' After watching her work for a few days she concluded: 'She's very slow – very sweet – shy, seemingly shy. But I see why Larry can't hurry the film. Yesterday she was the same, but she has got allure – even with no make-up, and very untidy and messy! She has a coach here from NY who teaches her every night. It's an amazing phenomenon....She has a ravishing smile – no airs and graces at all – simple and quite fun – I like her awfully.'

However, the filming proved a nightmare. Olivier, at first besotted by Marilyn, was soon brought down to earth. She invariably turned up late, often forgot her lines, and needed numerous takes for even the simplest scene. She started to rely on barbiturates, was thought at one stage to be pregnant, and soon discovered that Miller already had doubts about their marriage. She relied increasingly on her coach Paula Strasberg, the wife of the head of the Actors' Studio Lee Strasberg, both purveyors of a version of Stanislavsky's 'Method' quite opposite to Olivier's 'work from the outside in' approach. Marilyn had what Miller called 'a nearly religious dependency' on Paula Strasberg, and insisted on having her on the set, while also making transatlantic calls to Lee Strasberg every evening, thereby doubly undermining Olivier's authority.

Olivier made the mistake of over-directing her, and making tactless remarks such as 'All you have to do is be sexy, dear.' He demonstrated how a scene should be played instead of just allowing her to play it instinctively, which other directors such as Joshua Logan, who had directed *Bus Stop*, told him was how she worked best. Sybil agreed, stressing that she was an intuitive actress who was best left alone. Olivier ignored all this advice, there were rows, and the working relationship between star and director steadily turned into one of mutual hostility and suspicion.

Amid this artistic mayhem and bruised egos, Sybil invariably took Marilyn's side. Colin Clark, the third assistant director, who kept a diary throughout the filming, saw the calming, reassuring effect she had on her. 'Dame S radiates love and good fellowship so genuinely that even MM could not resist her,' he observed early in the filming. 'She was warm and welcoming to MM, as if really glad to see her, as a human being.' She once sat with Marilyn and helped her when she had problems remembering her cues, and even managed to welcome her when she arrived seriously late. When one day Olivier insisted Marilyn apologise for keeping Sybil waiting in full costume on the set, she responded silkily: 'My dear you mustn't concern

yourself. A great actress like you has other things on her mind, doesn't she?'
Marilyn beamed.

Sybil was stern with Olivier over his treatment of Marilyn. After she
forgot yet another line Olivier exploded with anger, and Marilyn was taken
aback. Sybil then publicly berated Olivier: 'Don't you realise what a strain this
poor girl is under? She hasn't had your years of experience. She is far from
home in a strange country, trying to act in a strange part. Are you helping
or bullying?' Colin Clark (he dubbed Olivier SLO, for Sir Laurence Olivier)
described the aftermath: 'Poor SLO, who naturally thinks he is the injured
party, was stunned. MM was radiant. "Oh thank you so much, Dame Sybil.
But I mustn't forget my lines. I'll try to remember them from now on." And
she was as good as gold for the rest of the afternoon.'

Despite everything, Sybil continued to admire Marilyn, and the sympathy
seemed to be mutual. 'Marilyn is well again – such a sweet loveable girl,' she
told Patricia. 'She was very tired yesterday: after we'd run up and down an
immense staircase at least 18 times; we were walking up together again, and
she looked so fragile as if she could be blown away. She slipped her hand
under my arm – me the old tough who doesn't mind staircases, mountains,
ships, hills – and said "You mustn't get tired" – I felt it so touching….She is
so utterly unaffected and kind, everyone from the top to the bottom of the
picture loves her.' In reality most people, from the electricians to Olivier, were
tearing their hair out at her erratic behaviour.

So was it tact, good fellowship or a lack of awareness that prompted Sybil
to suggest all was sweetness and light? Initially she thought little of Marilyn's
ability, finding her acting too small-scale and understated. But when she
looked at the early rushes she changed her mind. 'She was perfect and I was
the old ham,' she decided. 'Everything she'd done that I'd thought was a
muck-up came over beautifully.' She expanded on this another day, as Miller
recalled in his memoirs: 'In a momentary lull in the talk and noise as a new
shot was being set up, the voice of the venerable Dame Sybil Thorndike,
a very great actress over many decades, was heard saying: "This little girl
is the only one here who knows how to act before a camera."' It was not a
remark that would have pleased Olivier, who was coming to loathe Marilyn.
Meanwhile Sybil was endearing herself to Colin Clark. 'Dame Sybil treats
me as if I were her grandson,' he told his diary. 'She bought me a lovely thick
wool scarf to keep me warm while I waited outside the studios at dawn to
welcome the stars. Come to think of it, Dame Sybil treats the whole crew

as if they were her grandchildren, and would buy each one of them a woolly scarf if she could.'

Off the set, Sybil was aware of Olivier's personal problems. As filming of *The Prince and the Showgirl* began Vivien Leigh announced she was pregnant, then immediately suffered a miscarriage. It was perhaps the one hope of rescuing her faltering marriage to Olivier, and keeping at bay her manic depression. Sybil wrote her a sympathetic letter: 'Vivien darling, Lewis and I feel quite heartbroken about you – we were so thrilled at the coming of your baby and the shock and disappointment we feel for you so much.' Suggesting that, like her daughter Ann in a similar situation, she would be able to become pregnant again very soon, she added: 'You're such a darling and so courageous, and you and Larry are so much loved. All of us will be holding on for you. God bless you darling, and Larry too.'

The film received mixed reviews, and was not a commercial success. Heavily made up and wearing her richly coloured costume, Sybil played the Grand Duchess with authority and wit, even bringing a touch of Edith Evans' Lady Bracknell to the role. Her performance won her a Best Supporting Actress award from the National Board of Review in the USA. Olivier, considering the problems he had, was surprisingly subtle and funny as the Prince Regent, while Marilyn confirmed Sybil's view of her talent, giving a delicious performance, skilfully suggesting her character's mixture of vulnerability, impudence and sexual power.

Like Sybil, Russell had worked in a few films since the war, including *Caesar and Cleopatra*, and three of Olivier's screen versions of Shakespeare: he had played the Duke of Bourbon in *Henry V*, the lugubrious Priest at Ophelia's burial in *Hamlet*, and another priest in the recently completed *Richard III*. With his cane, his bow tie and flowing hair, he was now very much the Old Actor, still telling his peculiar, macabre stories. The historian Tom Pocock described him as 'the best raconteur I've ever heard, terribly theatrical, always rolling his eyes, with terrific bohemian panache'. Recently he had made a niche for himself as Smee in *Peter Pan*, a part he was to play throughout the 1950s, providing, the *Manchester Guardian* noted on year, 'a bewildering mixture of the genial and the sinister, the whimsical and the unkind'. According to playwright Ronald Harwood, who was Donald Wolfit's dresser when he played Captain Hook in 1953: 'Russell was drinking, he had rheumy eyes, and his nose was just red at the tip. He had these little make-up bottles in which he kept gin. He was an English gent who had drunk too much, but he was never incapacitated on stage.'

That October the Suez crisis erupted, followed immediately by Russia's crushing of the Hungarian revolution. Like so many others, Sybil was angry. 'We are all completely laid low by the news of Suez today – and our sinking of an Egyptian ship; we all think Eden has gone mad,' she told John. ' We couldn't be so crazy as to get into another war, could we? It's so dreadful, the way we've lost prestige.' A week later she wrote: 'We are all very anxious about this b----y mess of Suez – it seems most awful for us to go slap against the United Nations….Oh the world! What is Russia up to – perhaps Eden did know something.' And a few days on: 'Hungary and Suez occupy our thoughts all the time. The bother is we can't say much to the Russians about Hungary now that we've destroyed so much in Egypt.'

At home she continued to play the piano daily, though not always to her satisfaction. 'I'm working half an hour a day on a lovely Bach partita,' she told Jane. 'I feel a bit down about the way I play.' She was booked to take part with Peter Pears in a performance of William Walton's *Façade* at the Scala, with Charles Mackerras conducting the English Opera Group in a work with words by Edith Sitwell. 'I'm rather quirks as the music is very modern and strident, but awfully good practice for me,' she told John. For a performance ten days earlier Edith Sitwell had recited her own verse but, according to Mackerras, she was not very good. 'When Sybil Thorndike took over reciting the poems, it was more clearly spoken and much more professional,' he recalled.

She re-entered the world of television, which now included a commercial channel. She was not a fan of television, and rarely watched any. 'I like to go to a theatre and *feel* an audience all around me,' she told an interviewer. She felt television encouraged laziness: 'People sit by the fire and doze, when they should be on the edge of their seats at the theatre.' She was also critical of the standard of drama. 'Television must make plays to please a Woolworth's audience. Don't misunderstand me, I like Woolworth's – love it – but I don't want to shop there all the time.'

She was engaged to introduce scenes from *Cymbeline*, performed by Barbara Jefford, Derek Godfrey and the Old Vic company, and directed by Michael Elliott. The theatre's publicity manager wrote anxiously to the BBC's head of television drama Michael Berry: 'How do you suppose that you and I can hope to canalise the glorious Thorndike exuberance? I am perfectly willing to try, but what we need is some muted structure like the Asswan High Dam.' Sybil herself was uncharacteristically nervous before the broadcast: 'It made me jumpy, I really had a bad attack of nerves,' she told John. 'However it went very well, and I felt as if I'd had a baby!' She was also in *Waters of the Moon*, re-creating her stage role alongside Edith Evans, but directed now by Lionel Harris. 'It's all quite different,' she told John during rehearsals. 'I don't really like it, it's so non-vital, and all the company speak in undertones and carelessly at that. I just can't hear what they say!' Once again she was surprised by the result: 'We did the play last night and all said it was a triumph.'

For a brief moment she had some leisure time. 'You can't believe what fun it is to meet my friends and have *dinner* at night,' she told an interviewer. 'I'd almost forgotten what that word means.' After a meal with Alec and Merula Guinness she told John: 'It was so lovely having a real yarn with Alec – he's not a bit spoilt, and he's really about the highest paid actor, stage and screen.' She enjoyed Dylan Thomas' *Under Milk Wood* ('a wonderful play, bawdy but full of beauty and tenderness'), and after seeing Richardson in Robert Bolt's *Flowering Cherry* decided: 'He's wonderful, a superb performance. I now *know* he is my favourite actor – even if bad (as he can be).' Mostly she avoided parties. 'I didn't go to Binkie's party last night – I couldn't face that ghastly professional crowd – all friends of one too!' She found time, however, to help persuade a highly promising student at RADA not to leave prematurely. 'I had lost my sense of judgement, and she was wheeled in to bring me to my senses,' Siân Phillips recalls. 'She was really quite tough and severe, telling me I shouldn't squander my talent.'

She now arranged to spend a fortnight in Canada with Ann and her family. After the war Ann had taught at the London Academy of Music and Art, while Douglas had been at the Old Vic, playing, among other parts, Othello and Macbeth. In 1953 he had acted in Guthrie's first season at the new theatre in Stratford, Ontario, and the family had moved there the following year. He and Ann then founded the Canadian Players, touring platform-style productions without costumes or scenery to theatre-starved areas of the country; they once staged *Peer Gynt* with just two ladders and a plank. One of Ann's first parts was Saint Joan; later she too would become a member of the company in seasons at Stratford, Ontario.

Their children, all of whom started out wanting to act, believe their parents moved to Canada because of the pressure on them to succeed from Sybil. Ben Campbell, now a leading actor there, says: 'Mum loved Sybil very deeply, but she had to cut out on her own.' His sister Teresa Campbell adds: 'I think Dad found part of the family quite daunting. He adored Sybil, but found her energy quite difficult to deal with.' Tom Campbell, now an artist, suggests that 'life was a bit of a competition. You had to keep up, you had to have wonderful ideas and zest. Granny would be sure that Mum was keeping her end up.' Dirk Campbell, now a television director, concurs: 'Dad said that Sybil didn't understand that other people didn't have the support network she had. When I was a baby, and Mum and Dad were living on this little boat on the Thames near Swan Court, Mum was doing all the shopping and washing nappies, and was completely exhausted. Yet Sybil was still putting a lot of pressure on her to do things.'

Her visit went down well with her grandchildren, as Tom Campbell recalls: 'She would play the piano, and we would all stomp around in a circle. "Be monsters!" she would shout, and we would all make the worst faces we could. She liked trolls and goblins and scary things over sweet and sentimental ones.' In the theatre she watched Douglas directing *Othello*, with Ann playing Emilia ('very strong'). Just before she left Canada she was entertained by George Caitlin and Vera Brittain. 'It all seems to me quite fantastic, this flying business – I can almost understand the 4th and 5th dimension because of it!' she wrote on her arrival in England. 'How kind you and George were to me, I will never forget it – when I might have felt so blue and alone, leaving my Ann. You made me all cheered, and not only the wondrous whisky. The lunch was such fun and getting a real yarn with you, Vera, which as you said is so idiotic, having to come to Canada to get a real talk.'

Another prominent pacifist, Maude Royden, had died in July. Sybil broadcast a radio tribute to a woman who had greatly influenced her. 'It was Maude who made me convinced that pacifism was the only answer to international disputes,' she said. 'She made me realise that the term pacifism was not the passive thing the name suggests, but rather a positive, a new and Christian attitude towards other nations and peoples, and a recognition that war was a sign of weakness.' She also credited her for persuading her that public speaking would be a good discipline. 'I often think of her words when I'd prefer to say no to something I *ought* to speak about.'

In December she wrote to Murray: 'We've both had a very hard-working year – but it's good to be working when one is old at something to which one has been devoted all one's life.' Another hard-working year seemed in prospect, for by Christmas they were in New York, ready to rehearse the world premiere of a new play on Broadway.

36

Fifty in the Sun

1957–1959

'We get fed up with this amateurishness which is called The Method –
it's a travesty of Stanislavsky'
Sybil on rehearsing The Potting Shed *on Broadway*

Soon after Sybil and Lewis arrived in America, Tyrone Guthrie wrote a lengthy article about her in the *New York Times Magazine*. His perceptive summary of her skill as an actress reveals the impact she made on one of the century's great directors.

'Unlike most stars, she has never been content to find a kind of role that expressed her personality and pleased the public, and then go on playing it year in, year out. Her great quality as an actress has always been her range; she will tackle anything, and she has the technique to play almost anything.... Personally I like her best in roles in which she can, so to speak, tear a cat – rampageous parts. So few actors and actresses have got what it takes to tear a cat – the muscle, the gusto, the self-confidence, the childlike desire to tear and rage and stamp, disciplined and organised with adult mentality and sublimated to constructive purpose....Her art is the expression of a truly great woman, of a person whose violent energy has always been directed outward with an amazing disregard of self-interest; whose considerable intelligence has controlled but never overwhelmed the capacity for emotional reactions, not only to persons but to events, places, ideas; whose deep religious conviction and high sense of mission have always been suffused with humour.'

He also paid tribute to her and Lewis' adventurous attitude, exemplified by her latest venture. 'Instead of returning to a fashionable theatre under the sponsorship of the principal Moguls of Showbiz, they will appear at the tiny Bijou under a youthful and adventurous management that has made its mark off Broadway, in a play that bears few of the stigmata of the pre-fabricated,

gift-wrapped, homogenized Smash Hit....No anxious casting about for
insurance against risk; no prudent concessions to that figment called Popular
Taste; no surrender to bourgeois preconceptions of what is or is not distinguished and fashionable. No, just to defy all that and wade in with what you
yourself admire and respect and want to do.'

The play was Graham Greene's *The Potting Shed*, a kind of religious thriller
about metaphysics, psychiatry, the loss of faith, and a Lazarus-like resurrec-
tion. Sybil thought it a delicate and moving piece, better than his first play
The Living Room, and full of original parts – including hers of the mother, 'a
handsome upright figure in spite of her seventy years', as Greene described
her. She and Lewis had met him in London to discuss the script. But the trip
might never have happened if she hadn't resisted pressure from Beaumont, as
she explained to Patricia: 'Binkie, very naughty, tried to make us back out of
the American contract (which isn't signed yet, but our *word* given) by doing
a new play about Catherine the Great – he and Peter Glenville were on and
on at me – but the play isn't anything like as distinguished as the Graham
Greene, and anyway we're bound: even if contracts aren't signed, one's word
should count unless something catastrophic happens.'

They stayed initially in New York with their old friends E Martin Browne
and his wife Henzie Raeburn. Once again Sybil was stunned by the city:
'New York is amazing, the buildings are quite terrifying in height – it has
grown a lot since we were last here in '37, but it's very stimulating,' she wrote
to John. Before rehearsals began at the tiny Bijou, run by Carmen Capalbo
and his partner Stanley Chase, they met the company, which included Robert
Flemying, Leueen MacGrath and, in her first Broadway role, Carol Lynley.
Capalbo, whom Sybil described as 'very intelligent and eager', was directing.
But a clash soon occurred between the American and British ways of working,
notably over the discussions which began each rehearsal. 'Lewis says he never
remembers being bored with a play before he knows it!' Sybil wrote. 'It's
been these long Stanislavsky rehearsals – talk, talk, and very little *do* – and
much as we like Carmen Capalbo and find him sensitive as a person – it's all
underdone.'

By the first night she was near despair. 'We've been doing previews all the
week – and hoping vainly that these would settle us in the play but oh! no!
worse than John Gielgud – every day alterations, new speeches put in – new
moves – new approaches – all very good, but we've been rehearsing five weeks
and these things ought to have been done during that time. We both think

these young modern directors don't think anything out – it's trial by error all the time. A certain amount of experiment is good and necessary during rehearsal time, but not when the show is supposed to be finished and all ready to stage – all experiment then should be the actor's with the audience. I'm afraid Lewis has lost his hair quite a bit with Carmen and there has had to be smoothings down and saying it's Welsh temperament and so on – simply to keep him from going completely haywire. We get fed up with this amateurishness which is called The Method – it's a travesty of Stanislavsky, who had violent temperamental actors to deal with – not like the American and English half-bakes!'

There was, inevitably, the question of audibility. 'At the third rehearsal we said "Surely more voice and clean speaking is needed", but we were smiled at! Then it's the dress rehearsal and Guthrie McClintic (the best and most exciting and experienced director) comes round and says: "I only heard you and Lewis – not anyone else" – then frantic efforts to make them all speak up – when it's too late – just being loud is no good. It's clear phrasing and articulating. Oh! we get so *mad*. But we're too old to get in tempers!' But four days later she reported: 'We're a success, packed business, and lovely notices. We're quite astonished at its success as it's such a queer play – but people seem very moved.' *Time* magazine noting approvingly that 'Dame Sybil Thorndike displays an almost vanished grand manner'.

The play, getting its world premiere, ran successfully for four months, transferring to the Golden for its final weeks. It gained a Tony nomination for Best Play, and Sybil was nominated for Best Actress. Graham Greene, who attended rehearsals, wrote of 'the delight of working with players interested not only in their own parts, but in the play as a whole'. But Sybil felt the play was flawed. 'We still play to full houses,' she told John van Druten. 'I love the first act, but after that I feel it's a brilliant man writing amateurishly because he doesn't know the "form" – the shape of a play.'

She and Lewis were in great demand, both for interviews and other plays. 'We've piles of offers for next year – we're the Old Age Wonders!' she reported gleefully. Capalbo tried unsuccessfully to make them stay on longer. Their shared dressing-room was as full as ever, often with celebrity friends. 'Noël Coward came in last night, with darling Marlene Dietrich,' Sybil wrote. 'Now there is beauty and goodness and loveliness and skills! Noël loathed the play – he was killing about it – loved Lewis and me in it – but said it was just careless and unformed.' Her success meant a heap of fan mail: 'I get 20 or 30 a day and all so personal. I'm developing a telegraphic form of letter – very matey but swift.'

They gave their first recital in America in the Theatre de Lys, a matinee described by one critic as 'one of the most memorable events of the season', and one that led to many requests for them to repeat it elsewhere. They made a record of poems by Tennyson, including 'The Revenge', which 'Lewis did so beautifully I simply sat and blubbed'. Sybil also spent a morning with Charles Laughton, who was directing and appearing as Undershaft in a Broadway production of *Major Barbara*. 'I really am devoted to Charles – success has done him a power of good,' she wrote. At his request she read the title-part to Anne Jackson, who was about to replace Glynis Johns; he asked her 'to show her what religious ecstasy is – she thinks it's looking holy'.

They spent a day in the country at Katharine Cornell's house, and another at Helen Hayes' on the Hudson. They dined with old friends such as John van Druten and Michael Redgrave, but failed to warm to Tennessee Williams: 'We were put off by his looks and his manner!' Sybil told John. They sat through Wagner at the Met (*Parsifal*), and visited the Picasso Exhibition at the Museum of Modern Art. But the highlight for Sybil was a morning at the United Nations, where they heard a debate, and attended a lunch given by Krishna Menon in their honour. Sybil revealed that 'Krishna explained about India and Egypt, so that I didn't have time to eat the most delectable lamb chop I've ever tasted.'

As ever she made a strong impression on people. After meeting her at John van Druten's home, Christopher Isherwood noted in his diary: 'Sybil Thorndike was even more wonderful than I'd expected. She *is* a sort of saint – if only because, as an actress, she still doesn't seem to give a damn what sort of an impression she creates.' She scored a hit on the Mike Wallace Show on television, skilfully handling the notoriously tough host; for days afterwards she was stopped in the street and congratulated on 'fixing that interviewer'. Henzie Raeburn enjoyed having her and Lewis as guests. 'We have made a lovely job of living together,' she wrote. 'Sybil generally gets up at 7am, has tea, and then reads her Greek testament for an hour. Her strength is wonderful. She is very gay and we all laugh a lot.'

Returning briefly to England, they set off again in July to Australia, where they were to tour in *The Chalk Garden*, directed by Lionel Harris for the J C Williamson management. The play had been a success both on Broadway with Gladys Cooper and in London with Edith Evans, where Tynan, surprisingly, felt it 'may well be the finest artificial comedy to have flowed from an English (as opposed to an Irish) pen since the death of Congreve'. Its story revolved around the arrival of Miss Madrigal, a governess with a past, to look after the granddaughter of the eccentric Mrs St Maugham, 'an old, overpowering, once beautiful ex-hostess of London society', in whose house there lived a pacifist butler. Sybil thought there was more depth to the play than was evident in Gielgud's production at the Haymarket, a feeling that had been confirmed when the producer Irene Selznick had read it to her and Lewis in New York: 'I'm playing a woman who's a combination of six people I know,' she told a reporter. 'I don't think she's an admirable character, but she's very interesting.'

Lewis played the Judge, while the granddaughter was played by Jane Casson. Sybil had made it clear, contrary to what she said later, that she would not embark on the play unless Jane was cast in the role. More than ever she saw her as the theatrical white hope of the family. 'She has got it in her to be a first-class actress,' she told Jane's parents, 'but she must work not just at a particular play – but at poetry, philosophy, etc. *She must enrich her mind*!' To Jane she wrote light-heartedly about their difficult relationship: 'We'll be so sweet to each other – butter won't melt, or will melt in our mouths, and we'll always smile at each other in every sentence…and by the time we've smiled all that we shall be ready to sock each other over the head!!'

She and Lewis had endeared themselves to the profession in Australia by insisting, against the management's wishes, that the key supporting roles of Miss Madrigal and Maitland the butler should be played by Australian actors, who should share their billing. Patricia Kennedy, who played Miss Madrigal, recalls Sybil in rehearsal as Mrs St Maugham: 'She was full of energy, always on time, ready to laugh, ready to listen. She was invariably supportive, never overwhelming, which she could easily have been. She got on famously with Lionel Harris, who was quiet but firm.' The actor Gorden Chater remembered her generosity to the other actors: '"This is their scene," she would say. "I should really play with my back turned, and not be too well lit."'

They opened in Melbourne, playing at the Comedy for three months, then toured to Sydney, Adelaide, Brisbane and Perth before going on to New Zealand. 'Once we opened she never altered her performance,' Patricia Kennedy says. 'She didn't upstage, play tricks, or any of that nonsense. And she always kept an eye on Lewis: if he dried she would leap in with a whoop and a gurgle and some waving of arms until he got back on track.' If Lewis strayed beyond his acting role into that of director, Sybil would say to Lionel Harris: 'Remember he is 82 and Welsh.'

Business proved excellent, and the notices positive. Bruce Grant of the Melbourne *Age* suggested the play suited Sybil because of her skill in conveying the 'undertow of emotion'; she was, he thought, at her most appealing 'in the touches of ordinary feeling later in the play'. Jane, he observed enigmatically, 'played the abnormal grandchild with a rather intransitive charm'. Sybil herself described it as 'a delicate and moving show'. At Christmas she wrote to Olivier and Vivien Leigh: 'We are enjoying our time here *awfully*. Sydney is glorious, but too hot. The audiences are wonderful, so quick and alert, and we are feeling full of beans.'

She was delighted with Jane's performance: 'Jane gave a lovely show last night, had several people round after, all praising her sky-high,' she told John from Sydney. 'She is good too.' Later she remarked, perhaps a touch generously: 'It was really rather a remarkable performance. She wasn't in the least a stage ingenue. She played it with great reality. She gave me a new view of the character, and in a way dominated the play.' Lewis was less happy with her performance, and after Lionel Harris had departed he re-directed one of her scenes. 'All this pressure was troubling for Jane,' Patricia Kennedy recalls. 'She was a friendly, intelligent girl, but disadvantaged by having her grandparents towering over her.' There were tremendous rows between her and Sybil. Surprisingly, John Casson suggested that neither of them was consciously aware of the rivalry between them. Margaret Wolfit, a friend of the family, was in Australia at the time. 'Jane was a younger version of Sybil: she looked like her, she spoke like her, and had the same kind of vocal mannerisms, which made it very difficult for her.'

Sybil still liked to play the occasional trick on stage, such as crossing her eyes at Jane as they were about to play a scene together, or tickling the palm of her hand as she held it, making it difficult for her not to giggle. Patricia Kennedy recalls: 'Once or twice she crossed her eyes at me – but always in the middle of one of her own speeches.' But Lewis' playfulness was much more extreme. One night, having heard that someone thought him 'a bit past it', he came on at the next performance in full juvenile make-up – fair hair, blue eyeshadow, doll cheeks and cupid-bow lips – and flounced about the stage, while the other actors tried desperately to carry on normally. Sybil was furious at this unprofessional conduct, and was heard raging at him in the dressing-room afterwards, forcing him to apologise to the management and company.

The playwright Ben Travers came round to Sybil's dressing-room on the hottest night of the Sydney summer. Sybil had done two shows that day: 'She was skipping around in her dressing-gown,' he remembered. 'She told me that her morning had been spent in visiting a girls' school, speeding off to keep a date at a film studio, where she rehearsed and shot a scene in a picture, and getting through with it just in time to arrive at the theatre for the matinee.' The film was *Smiley Gets a Gun*, a story of a boy living in the Australian outback, directed by Anthony Kimmins, in which she played a grandmother. Writing to Olivier, she mentioned the 'grilling' he had given her in *The Prince and the Showgirl*, which 'has had some effect – tho' in this film I can make as many faces as I like, which is a comfort to me!!' This lack of restraint was picked up by the *Picturegoer* critic, who noted: 'The adults – particularly Chips Rafferty as the local law officer and Sybil Thorndike playing a miserly granny like a grotesque pantomime dame – ham it up shamelessly.' Lewis thought she was 'like Russell at his most Russell-ish', which probably amounted to the same thing.

In Melbourne, as world vice-president of the Save the Children Fund, Sybil spearheaded a World Rice Bowl Appeal, to help sick and hungry children, including needy young Australian aborigines. She also visited the city's Blind Institute, where the children presented her with a large string bag. 'Nobody's ever thought to give me one of these before,' she said with her customary tact. Her personality again made a strong impression on Patrick White when they met at a lunch party: 'I sat next to Sybil and was burnt up by that wonderful personality,' he reported. 'She is ablaze with everything that is vital, and so beautiful, one had not realised.'

Sybil turned 75 during the Melbourne run. But to some she seemed younger than on the previous visit. One interviewer caught her returning to John's home after a shopping trip. '"Dear Melbourne", she exclaimed in rich resonant tones, rushing into the sitting-room and flinging down an armful of parcels. In about two minutes she'd called loudly for afternoon tea ("No cake dear, remember the calories"), asked her grand-daughters Penny and Jane a dozen questions in three breaths, talked to Sir Lewis, and given vent to four of her expressive "Ahhhhhs" which she utters whenever anything specially excites her interest.'

When they moved on to New Zealand in the New Year, Patricia accompanied them as their manager, secretary and personal assistant. Sybil found it impossible to understand why the company didn't fill their day as full of

activity as she did. From Wellington she wrote to John: 'Pat is very upset at
the life of the touring actors and I must say I agree – it gets me mad – they
don't get up until midday – never want to see the country – go to cinemas,
and the life of just parties drinking and club-chatting seems to me very bad.
None of them seems to do any study or be in the least interested in the theatre
apart from stage gossip.'

In one town the amateur group invited the company to supper. Patricia
Kennedy's memory of the occasion captures well Sybil's mixture of idealism
and practicality. 'She gave a lively speech in praise of such groups, saying
how valuable they could be, how they could do the rarely seen classics, and
Pinter and Beckett, and how the word amateur meant love, and they were
the true lovers of the drama world. She asked the director what the next
production was. "It's *See How They Run*," he replied (a classic farce featuring
four vicars). "Oh well dear," said Sybil, patting his arm. "We have to think
of the box office."'

An emotional highlight of their stay was the evening she heard that the
first Russian satellite was due to pass over Melbourne minutes before the
play began. Hugely excited, she persuaded the company to watch it from the
theatre's flat roof. Patricia Kennedy was with her at the critical moment. 'Face
uplifted, she threw up both arms in a gesture of welcome and embrace. "Oh
you dear little thing," she said, her voice ringing out over the neighbouring
street. Her eyes were moist, she was deeply moved. "What Man can do," she
said with great feeling.' Afterwards Gordon Chater heard her say: 'Oh Lewis,
if only we could be the first ones to play on the moon!'

One apparently trivial incident was later to cause major problems in their
lives. While spending a day by the sea with friends of John and Patricia,
Lewis tripped and fell on the cliff steps, hitting his head a nasty crack. The
doctor who was called said he had mild concussion, but would be all right if
he stayed still and quiet overnight. After he had gone, Lewis said this was all
nonsense, that actors 'knew how to fall without hurting themselves', and that
he must return to John's home that night. A few months later he began to
have problems with his eyes.

The tour ended in June, after which they flew to Canada for a short
holiday with Ann and her family. Douglas was now well established in the
Shakespeare Festival Theatre in Stratford, Ontario, and playing Falstaff in
Henry IV Part 1. Sybil and Lewis went to a dress rehearsal. 'We were mad
about the theatre – absolute perfection!' she wrote to John. 'I must say the

production looked quite magnificent – Lewis and I were greatly enthralled with the sort of heroic set-up. It's a very spirited colourful production with heaps of swing. But still – we don't really hear the words – and they are *such* words too. Lewis is deaf, but I am only very slightly and I know the play so well. We noticed when Michael Langham gave the notes after that it was all on movement and lights – not one word of criticism of the speaking, which was very spirited too, but not *clear*. I think I shall give up going to the theatre, I never hear anything.'

On their return to England she experienced a rare black moment, brought on by Lewis' depression and a visit to Cedar Cottage. 'It left us both suicidal,' she told John. 'The garden was a wilderness and the house looked dark and boring....I have not had such a depression for years, and I wanted to pack up and go off on the boat to Australia, where we never felt that sort of depression....As for Lewis, he was in Hell's own depression. His eyes are too bad to risk driving, besides his deafness and age. In his own work he is only 60, but cars, cottages, any sort of responsibility and he's 83 at once.' She wondered about getting a smallish house in Chelsea. John suggested they sell the cottage and simply enjoy living at Swan Court, and a year later they did so.

She now began filming *Alive and Kicking*, a whimsical story about three elderly women who, fed up with their monotonous lives, escape from an old folks' home, hop on a boat to a remote island off the Irish coast, and set up a successful knitting industry. With Kathleen Harrison and Estelle Winwood as Sybil's fellow-fugitives, Stanley Holloway and Joyce Carey in supporting roles, and Richard Harris making his screen debut, it was directed by Cyril Frankel. Sybil was looking forward to a madcap film, and was surprised by the final result: 'It's done much more delicately than I'd imagined, but very charming and not a bit Marx Bros, no exaggeration at all as I'd hoped,' she wrote to Jane. 'I think old people will like it – they'll feel there's a chance to have a bit of an adventure, even if they're 70!' She was unsure about her own performance: 'God knows I'm a bore in this film, it's not nearly as mad as I'd hoped.' *Films and Filming*, though finding it over-sentimental, thought it 'as fresh as *Genevieve* in its day'.

The location scenes were filmed on an island near Oban off the west coast of Scotland, in between the mist and the rain. 'The clouds is a raisin' and the sun a peepin' and we're off to the island,' Sybil told Jane. It was an area of rugged beauty which, like all wild places, affected her profoundly. 'Isn't this country like magic?' she wrote to John. 'I really think Scotland is the most beautiful place in the world. One feels something else behind everything.' Lewis joined the unit for a few days, but then became tired of hanging about, and allowed Sybil to find tranquillity in solitude. 'Even when it's misty and we're not able to do any takes I scramble about in hills and rocks and little beaches, it's so lovely. I find a lot to think about. I've enjoyed sitting on a rock and not even thinking, just brooding.'

Soon after she and Lewis were off to Ireland for a very different film, *Shake Hands with the Devil*. Directed by Michael Anderson, whose father Lawrence had been in their company in the 1920s, it starred James Cagney as an eminent Dublin surgeon leading a double life as an IRA leader. Sybil told John: 'It's a really beautifully written though terrifying film about the Irish rebellion – done very fairly – cruelty and goodness on both sides – it's a very compassionate film.' A strong cast included Michael Redgrave, Don Murray, Dana Wynter, Glynis Johns, Cyril Cusack and Richard Harris. When Anderson asked Sybil to play Lady Fitzhugh, an aristocratic Irish rebel, she asked him if Lewis could play the judge, explaining that she fancied the idea of him sentencing her to prison for treason – although really she just didn't want to leave him behind.

The film shows both the cruelty of the Black and Tans and the fanaticism of the IRA as exemplified by Cagney's ruthless character. Sybil has just three brief scenes, but conveys strongly the steadfast nature of the loyal Irish aristocrat, whose hunger strike in prison leads to her death. Her work and attitude on set impressed Michael Anderson. 'Like most great and talented actors she was unassuming, undemanding and brilliant,' he remembers. 'She had a quality of dignity and command that shone through on the screen.' But there were difficulties with Lewis: because of his deafness, Sybil had to shout her lines off camera to him during the court scene. 'Their affection, care and protection for each other off set and on was a shining example of team work and team love.' He also has a recollection of one particular moment: 'In clear and ringing tones she said: "What is an English judge doing in an Irish court?" Her delivery, and his reaction to it, would bring the house down in the cinema both in England and Ireland.'

Christopher was also involved, playing a brigadier in the Black and Tans. There was a party in his new house in Sandymount in Dublin, at which he and Cagney exchanged stories about playing small-town America. 'We love it here,' Sybil told Patricia. 'Kiff and I have tremendous talks walking along the sea front – he is such a darling, and so deeply good.' But she was concerned about his life and marriage: 'I wish I didn't feel Kiff wasted. Sometimes I don't know where he and Kay meet, what they've got in common. A love of theatre, and affection – but Kiff's real life seems to me to be quite alone.' This anxiety was a continuing theme in her letters to the family, as was the couple's financial state, which was often precarious.

She and Lewis had advanced them half of the £2,000 needed to buy this virtually derelict house, which they were to pay back gradually as rent. 'Lewis thought this sounder than just giving – it's more self-respecting,' Sybil explained. 'It's an enchanting house, with a little front garden on to the sea front and the whole stretch of Dublin Bay, which is a mixture of Dymchurch and the Traeth, and a glorious beach.' But there was not enough to pay for the furniture, which meant Sybil had to bypass Lewis, as her granddaughter Bronwen remembers: 'When they came over to Dublin she had to slip some money quietly to Mummy, as Lewis would have been horrified at the extra expense. These things were generally kept from him.'

Despite all her filming, Sybil managed to fit in other work. On television she played the Nurse for the first time, in scenes from *Romeo and Juliet* for the BBC's Women in Shakespeare series. But television she still felt was not her medium, as she told Jane after working on Rodney Ackland's *Before the Party*: 'The good words we had to speak were made to go too fast, and lots of essentials cut – it's all done to the split second and I find it maddening. It went very well according to everyone except Mary, who thought it awful – and I agree with her!' Soon after, in a spirited speech to the Gallery First Nighters' Club, she complained that stage plays on television 'have all the meat taken out of them so as not to offend those dear, darling, lazy people who like to sit back after a good dinner'.

In the autumn she and other prominent women, including Nancy Astor, Mary Stocks and Helen Pethick-Lawrence, formed a committee to raise funds for a memorial to Christabel Pankhurst, in recognition of her fight for Votes for Women. Soon after, in a speech at the new Belgrade Theatre in Coventry, she made the case for the theatre as a reflection of contemporary life. 'As long as there are things like Teddy Boys, the theatre's business is to show them.' It also had a role to play in bringing nations together. Speaking in the wake of the Stratford company's visit to Russia, she suggested that theatre could give people 'a deep knowledge of their oneness with every other human being', adding: 'Our differences should make us entertained with each other, our sameness should make us friends.'

In London she attended Emlyn Williams' one-man show on Dylan Thomas, enthusing afterwards to her old friend: 'Your artistry is beyond words – we were electrified! What superb words and humour and touching quality in his writing. I only know the poems, which I love – even those I can't fathom!' There were the enjoyable arguments with Clemence Dane: after a visit to her home at Pendean near Midhurst in Sussex – she shared two caravans with her companion Olwen Bowen – Sybil told John: 'We all got so argumentative the welkin rang with us shouting at each other "Let me speak" and "Shut up, it's my turn". Philosophy, religion, we touched everything. Such fun.' The writer herself approved: 'God how you do stimulate me!' she wrote, referring to late-night debates in her sitting-room, 'all four *raving*, with broad swords clashing'.

But their long friendship was strained to breaking point over *Eighty in the Shade*, which she had started writing for Sybil two years ago, but only finished recently. Loosely based on the relationship between Ellen Terry and her Craig children, the story concerned an elderly actress who is bullied at home by her daughter, and escapes to Italy to be with her son and daughter-in-law. Neither Sybil nor Lewis were happy with it, and Lewis wanted to re-write the whole play. But Clemence Dane refused to make a single change. 'She's awfully pig-headed, as stubborn as five mules, and thinks she's written a masterpiece,' Sybil complained to John.

The play opened on a pre-London tour in Newcastle, where it seemed to have settled well: 'We are going strong here and are delighted the way the play has turned out,' Sybil told Patricia. 'There's lots more comedy than we thought – it goes with a bang. Binkie says I am a cross between Marie Tempest and Gladys Cooper! Ha ha!' But when they reached Blackpool the arguments continued: 'We've had to alter and re-write and Winifred thinks she has written the Bible – but hasn't – too exhausting – she argues the toss about every "but" and "and", but we're now doing what we like.' Unfortunately the playwright then had a heart attack, so Lewis and the director Lionel Harris worked on the script, the latter visiting the writer during her convalescence: 'We send Lionel rather than Lewis or me,' Sybil explained. 'She goes up the pole with us. We excite her.'

Having been persuaded to re-write the piece, Clemence Dane recovered enough to attend further rehearsals, a picturesque figure reclining grandly on a chaise-longue, dressed in a kaftan and sticking cloves into an orange. But again there were continual arguments between her and Lewis about the script, with Lionel Harris hard put to be the peace-keeper. The cast included Valerie Taylor, Robert Flemying, Helen Lindsay and Mary Peach. Valerie Taylor was known for playing 'mother died yesterday' parts, often involving tears (she and her first husband Hugh Sinclair had been known as 'Hue and Cry'). Helen Lindsay recalls: 'She twisted her part to be sympathetic, then would weep to get the audience on her side. This meant Sybil was not getting enough opposition, there was no tension, and she was obviously greatly tried.' Privately Sybil was unusually blunt: 'Valerie is being a b------ nuisance,' she told John. 'She is an hysterical idiot and talks and talks until you long to be a Trappist!'

Lewis remained pessimistic, suggesting that if the play succeeded it would be purely on Sybil's performance. Things came to a head on the opening night in Brighton, after Clemence Dane had written to Lewis to complain about changes he had made 'to clarify the action'. In particular she objected to a speech he had added without reference to Lionel Harris or herself, which she felt such a serious matter she had sent his letter on the management. She reminded him of the different roles of actor, author and director, adding: 'Any attempt to exchange these roles obviously spells disaster, and I am sure when you think this over you will realise it.' The letter was ill-timed, arriving on Sybil and Lewis' golden wedding anniversary, causing Lewis to fly into a rage which nearly ruined their party.

Eighty in the Shade was a sell-out at the Theatre Royal, and an extra matinee was required. 'The audience *eat* it!' Sybil reported to John. 'If we can get through the critics then we may have a success. It's not a good play – it's muddled – but it's very well played, and it has charm and originality. There's a fine acting part for me and a b------ awful one for Lewis.' The critics were indeed lukewarm about the play when it arrived at the Globe in January, but admired Sybil's performance. 'With her gales of energy and splendid heart and style, she is delightful to watch,' Philip Hope-Wallace wrote in the *Guardian*; *The Times* critic felt she skilfully breathed 'the spirit of her own bracing personality' through the play's sentimentality.

Thelma Holt, who was understudying Mary Peach, admired her refusal to play the star with the younger cast members. 'There was then an enormous hierarchy in the profession. Yet she was a huge friend to everyone. Instead of a star, you got someone who would talk to you about religion, about RADA, about training for the theatre. She used to say, whatever you get out of it, you must put back. She saw it as a very important profession, she believed it mattered. She had a big heart and spirit, and amazing generosity. I was newly married, and she gave us a dining table for our flat. She came in when it was delivered, and when I told her the carpets were coming the next day, she insisted on taking a bucket of water and scrubbing the floor.'

It was assumed that the play was written to mark Sybil and Lewis' golden wedding anniversary, a misconception that nevertheless helped to publicise it. They were now the longest husband-and-wife partnership among leading players in the history of the British theatre. The day itself reflected their immense popularity with both the public and the profession. Sybil reported ecstatically to John: 'We've had a thousand wires and letters from all over the world. Bottles and bottles of champagne. A jeroboam from Binkie, and presents galore. Lewis said it would have been better to live in sin, then there wouldn't have been such a fuss. But it was a *lovely* fuss.' The family gave them a large globe to enable them to re-live their travels from their sitting-room. 'There it was on the grand piano – the globe of globes,' Sybil told John. 'We nearly fainted at the beauty. It's the most perfect present we have ever had.'

When Sybil had previously been asked the secret of their long-lasting marriage, she had replied: 'We have argued until we can't see out of our eyes, but we have always liked the same things and wanted the same things. But I've been personally more ambitious than Lewis. He has given in to me.' Now widely seen as the theatre's best-loved acting team, they received intense press attention, which Sybil relished. She had a neat sound-bite for her first meeting with Lewis at Dublin Zoo, explaining: 'He was there to mesmerise the animals, and ended up mesmerising me.' Stressing that marriage was never easy, she suggested that, apart from luck, you needed the same type of humour, upbringing and religious training, 'to give a sense of values and to teach you to know that you are not always in the right'.

Pressed to comment on future plans, Sybil mentioned South America and Russia as two of the places she still hoped to visit, adding: 'There's quite a lot of China I'd like to see.' She revealed that she read the gospels in Greek every morning 'as Lewis doesn't like talking at that time'. The journalists were impressed by their apparently happy and stable personal life in a notoriously unstable profession. The television personality Gilbert Harding, once an actor himself, observed: 'I admire them both enormously, because neither of them has ever been greedy, ever wanted flashy motor cars, press publicity or other people's wives or husbands. Fifty years together. The thought of it is like a breath of sane, cool, fragrant air, isn't it?'

Guthrie, who knew them well, summed up the key elements in their partnership: 'He gave to her violent and farouche temperament a stability, a constancy, a sense of direction which might otherwise have been lost. Moreover he was able to yield to her the leading public position in the partnership without the slightest loss of manly dignity. She would stand in the limelight, he in the shadow. Her name would be in large type, his in small. Her roles were usually flamboyant, his were quiet and inconspicuous...He was never a nonentity; that he never even seemed to be so is an extraordinary tribute to their mutual affection, tact, and good honest horse sense.... Together they have what is to me, especially in eminent seniors, the wildly endearing trait of valour that is forever outrunning discretion.'

37

Noël Coward and Saint Teresa

1959–1961

'It's the first time Noël has shown real *heart*,
and none of the critics has noticed this!'
Sybil on Waiting in the Wings

'I'm not one for much putting my feet up,' Sybil admitted to the director
and academic George Rylands, just before giving a recital at Cambridge.
After years of use her recital book was falling to pieces. But instead of taking
this as a sign from above, she immediately had a new one made. Recitals and
readings were now an increasingly frequent feature of her life, taking her all
over the country – to Stratford, Hastings, Coventry, Oxford and Harrow in
the next few months. The formula remained the same: a carefully chosen
selection of poems – lyrical, witty, tragic – mixed with scenes from a Greek
tragedy and other plays in which she had appeared.

She took particular pleasure in a recital in March 1959 at the Royal Court,
telling John. 'It was so exciting – an audience of largely followers of the Court
and the Angry Young Men type – but they were wonderful. We did a lot of
the old stuff, but it gets newer each time.' Cecil Wilson in the *Daily Mail*
felt the same: 'It was more than a recital; it was a vivid performance in plain
clothes fluently embracing comedy and tragedy and ranging through the
ages.' But Sybil was clearly anxious about Lewis' contributions. 'Even when
she was not performing in her own electrifying and at times radiantly girlish
way, Dame Sybil was mouthing Sir Lewis' words and punctuating the lines
with rapt little nods.'

Although now often suffering from rheumatism, her energy and will-
power remained formidable. She described to John how she started one day:
'I've just done my voice work – and learnt a poem (nearly) of Sitwell, and
practised me Bach and me Mozart, and my fibrosytis in neck and shoulder is

hell and Lewis has just massaged me.' She suffered from frequent nightmares, in which she found herself on stage with no idea what the play was about. But she believed firmly in the power of mind over matter: 'Sorry you've had a temperature,' she wrote to Jane. 'Say all sorts of positive things to yourself like "I am in perfect health, my muscle is superb, my tummy angelic, and in fact I am supremely and everlastingly well", and something will happen.'

Undaunted by her aches and pains, she plunged into another film. *Jet Storm*, directed by Cy Endfield, was set in an aeroplane in which the passengers discover that one of their number intends to blow them all up. The part was played by Richard Attenborough, who thought it a dreadful film, but who remembers Sybil in action: 'We were sitting on this bloody aircraft for god knows how long, doing virtually nothing in terms of performance. Yet she knew almost intuitively that, though the camera was yards away, her head would be the size of the entire screen, so that all she had to do was mentally think the thoughts that the shot would require her to illuminate. She understood that absolutely.' She also revealed once more her capacity to get on with all sorts, enjoying the company of stars such as Marty Wilde ('the rock an' roller boy I've been hobnobbing with') and Harry Secombe ('we got on terrifically, he's a sweet man, and as absurd as you could wish'). She also reported proudly that the Cy Endfield said: 'I've never had anyone work as quick as you, Sybil, you and Harry save the film people hundreds!'

Meanwhile *Eighty in the Shade*, bolstered by excerpts shown on television, continued until the middle of June. As with any long run, Sybil looked for ways to keep her playing fresh, something she found harder to do in lighter fare than in tragedy. 'I find I have to be so relaxed for this play or it doesn't gell,' she told John. 'One can do hugely dramatic stuff if one is dropping – but not this "radiance" business! I'm radiant fit to bursting!' She also blamed the play, explaining to Jane: 'One has to be so relaxed and un-tired because the play doesn't hold on its own – and it's inventing, inventing all the time – little new ways of saying things – and bits of absurd tiny business – and dear Winifred thinks she's written the Bible!'

She remained very open to the work of the new writers, even when they seemed obscure. 'What a wonderful play,' she told John after seeing Pinter's *The Caretaker*. 'Didn't know what it meant – it was like a modern Picasso – and as thrilling!' She admired Whiting's *The Devils* and Wesker's *The Kitchen* – 'wonderful, terrifying – the kitchen is the world'. She was also intrigued to see Barbara Jefford playing Saint Joan at the Old Vic: 'We liked her awfully – much less positive than Shaw's idea – much more modern and introvert.'

Meanwhile she was becoming increasingly worried about Lewis' physical problems, which forced him to be ever more dependent on her, both in their work and at home. Now eighty-four, and mentally alert as ever, his vision had started to be affected by the fall in Australia. A clot behind one eye meant he could see very little with it, while seeing double with the other one; this meant he was no longer able to drive. His deafness had become more pronounced, and Sybil had finally persuaded him to wear a hearing aid. Yet he continued to do work around the flat. 'Lewis painted the bathroom, while I meditated,' Sybil told Patricia one day. Encouraged by her, he started to go once a week to meet friends at the Savage Club. But this induced in her a rush of guilt. 'I have failed socially,' she confessed to John. 'I can't be a real hostess or leader of a salon (which Mother always wanted me to be), I am a boring, very hard-working student, and I've never got further on than that! We've met such thrilling people in life together, and yet we never have them in our home.'

She remained active in the cause of peace and other issues. Within the Campaign for Nuclear Disarmament (CND) she joined a group of Christians on a committee chaired by the novelist Pamela Frankau – it included Donald Soper, the Bishop of Southwark and the writer John Braine – set up to gain the support of churches for the CND campaign. Along with several leading literary and artistic figures –Augustus John, J B Priestley, Michael Redgrave, Stephen Spender, Leonard Woolf – she signed a letter to *The Times* protesting against the death sentence passed on an eighteen-year-old. She also pressed with others for the liberalising Wolfenden Report on homosexuality to be implemented. But she was becoming disenchanted with the Labour Party, which in opposition she felt 'just creep about no better than the old dyed-in-the-wools. What we need is a great leader, but ou est-il?'

When the comedian Tommy Trinder accused members of Equity of being a bunch of communists, she replied forcefully in the press. She also became worked up about a familiar subject at Equity's annual general meeting, as she told John: 'A lot of riff-raff actors got together and carried through a resolution about regulated entry, which we fight and have fought for ten years. But hardly any of the best actors were there, and I do blame stars for not attending. We were about the only two with real reputations – and those who were for keeping out actors were themselves actors we wouldn't think of employing – awful. I fairly yelled my head off when speaking and shouted down interruptions, and Lewis said I got more votes than he'd expected.' On this occasion, with the backing of Richard Attenborough and John Neville, she again spoke out passionately against a boycott of South African theatres, arguing that a 'foot in the door' approach was best, and that 'if we refuse to go no one will know what we feel'.

In her abiding thirst for knowledge she continued to read widely. 'Isn't reading a terrific stimulant? I find I depend on it almost too much,' she told John. She was particularly gripped by Teilhard de Chardin's *The Phenomenon of Man*, opting to read the Conclusion first, 'before I could do such a fearful plunge as the beginning was'. After finishing *George*, the first volume of Emlyn Williams' autobiography, she wrote to Miss Cooke, the teacher who had inspired *The Corn is Green*: 'I think it's a wonderful book. I find it quite tragic – but oh! how entertainingly written, and true – that craze for the theatre – isn't it amazing? – the sort of *fan* side of it. He is so brilliant an actor, but his writing is bigger I think.' She read *Moby Dick* for the third time, 'the greatest novel in the world'. No book seemed too obscure to enjoy: 'I'm reading an entrancing book about Ants,' she revealed.

Once *Eighty in the Shade* had closed and she had fulfilled the annual engagement at Smallhythe, she and Lewis took themselves off for a week's rest in the Bernese Oberland in Switzerland. They stayed in a hotel directly opposite the spectacular Jungfrau mountain range. 'We are absolutely bowled over with the splendidness of it all,' Sybil wrote home. But her idea of 'rest' was not the same as other people's. 'We're having a terrific time,' she reported. 'We did 12 miles' climb and walk round the mountains, Eiger, Mönch and Jungfrau, and the snow and sun have burnt us up – I think we overdid it, so we only strolled up in the hills today – and learned our lines.'

The lines in question were for *Sea Shell*, a play by Jess Gregg. Lewis disliked it, so for the first time since *Waters of the Moon* Sybil appeared without him. The story concerned a tyrannical, possessive American woman living an illusory life in rural British Columbia with her brood of daughters, until her son returns to break the spell. 'It's almost Ibsenish in its real tragedy, thought there's lots of comedy too,' Sybil informed John. 'I play a mother who won't let her girls look at or talk about anything disagreeable or controversial. It's a wonderful part, like Mother in lots of ways (so many of my parts are like different aspects of her).' Directed by Henry Kaplan, the cast included Ursula Howells, Patience Collier and Heather Sears. But Sybil was especially impressed by the one man in the company. 'We've a wonderful young man from Edinburgh, real male looking and a bit like Larry and a bit like Paul Scofield – but taller and tougher than either, with a deep full voice,' she wrote. His name was Sean Connery.

The play toured for a month in the provinces, where Sybil was still immensely popular. 'She is one of the few who remain loyal to touring, and whose coming is heralded quite as loudly as the latest popular singer,' one critic wrote. Privately Sybil confessed to George Rylands that 'touring the north in fog and sleet is not so good'. Publicly she continued to support the idea, arguing that without touring no one in the provinces would see the theatre, so they wouldn't bother to come to London, and the theatre would lose three-quarters of its audience. Looking back Dulcie Gray, another touring regular with her husband Michael Denison, remembers supporting this argument: 'We thought that was very true, and she and Lewis inspired us to tour.'

While waiting in vain for a West End theatre to be available Sybil resisted pressure from another scheming impresario: 'Peter Bridge loves me and wants me to chuck Sea Shell and Stephen Mitchell,' she told Patricia. 'I couldn't, for I felt loyalty to Stephen and liked the play….Oh! the Machiavellis – it's a foul profession, but never dull.' One morning she had a scare, waking up in a Coventry hotel hardly able to speak. 'I'm feeling like a used stamp with no voice and a cold sent from Hades!' she told John. Her fear that she had damaged her vocal cords proved unfounded, but the doctor insisted she avoid speaking for two days.

The tour included Dublin, which enabled her to prepare for J M Synge's one-act tragedy *Riders to the Sea*, directed by George Foa for BBC Schools Television. In this she played the old mother Maurya, with Sean Connery cast as her son. She worked with a member of the Abbey Theatre to perfect the accent and intonation of Synge's language, which used a lot of Gaelic and idiom. According to one reviewer: 'Dame Sybil gave us a superb glimpse of the grand tragic style, playing with that complete simplicity of which only the highest artist is capable.' She also starred in *A Matter of Age*, a play written and directed by Rex Tucker, about the conflict between a Summerhill-type libertarian school and an old woman stuck with Victorian values. 'I'm the old aristocrat on whose land the school is – great fun,' she told John. She appeared again in *Waters of the Moon*, cut and updated by N C Hunter, with Lewis now joining the cast. Another newcomer was Margaret Tyzack, who recalled Sybil's quality of directness: 'During rehearsals we had lunch in a local pub. Sybil said very strongly and very clearly: "Lewis! I'm out tonight. Get yourself a pie!"'

While the London theatre was featuring notable plays about working-class life, such as Wesker's *Roots* and Shelagh Delaney's *A Taste of Honey*, Sybil opted for the more comfortable kind, making her one and only appearance in the West End in a Coward play. *Waiting in the Wings* was a tragi-comedy, full of humour and pathos but not much drama, about a group of actresses living out the last act of their lives in The Wings, a retirement home. Probably his most sentimental work, filled with characters for whom he clearly felt great affection, Coward believed it contained 'the basic truth that old age needn't be nearly so dreary and sad as it is supposed to be, provided you greet it with humour and live it with courage'. Sybil accepted her part without reading the script. Having done so, she wrote gleefully to Jane: 'It's got a lot of most moving stuff in it as well as Noël Coward real bitchery!' But she was anxious about Lewis, who had been offered a part in Robert Bolt's *The Tiger and the Horse*. 'Could he play the small male role?' she asked Margaret Webster, who was to direct. 'I know if he's with me he'll be OK and not get in the doldrums as he's apt to!!'

So Lewis turned down the Bolt play and joined the company, Sybil and Marie Lohr had the principal parts, old stagers such as Edith Day, Mary Clare and Maureen Delaney were recruited, and Michael Redgrave and his partner Fred Sadoff took over the management. As rehearsals began Margaret Webster was impressed with Sybil's restraint and subtlety. 'She was very quiet, very simple. At the first walking rehearsal she came into the room and paused for a second, looking round. The expression on her face was so totally revealing that pages of dialogue could say no more. "Oh," I prayed inside myself, "if only she can keep it." She did.' But she worried about Lewis' interventions. 'Sybil is quite beautiful, literally and figuratively,' she told Coward. 'Lewis made a couple of IDIOTIC suggestions yesterday, bless him, about the last scene. I pray she will not be shaken by them. I don't think so.'

Sybil's son was played by the Canadian actor William Hutt, who remembered 'the generosity of her patience with my constant interruptions searching for "motivation", for the "Whys" and the "Hows". If she was ever irritated, she had the compassionate grace to hide it completely.' Margaret Webster also remembered these discussions. 'Sybil looked peaceable but far away. Bill would make quite a long speech and turn to her eagerly – "Don't you agree,

Dame Sybil?" She would start slightly and say, "Oh yes, dear, yes I do."…After a while I would detect a faint "I wonder what time it is?" expression on her face, and presently she would jump to her feet and say briskly, "Yes, well, shall we rehearse now?" She was deeply sympathetic towards Bill's problems, but she wasn't really interested in all that introspective bit. She knew by instinct, deeply and wholly, who her character was and what she was thinking and feeling; all she needed was the mechanics of doing it.'

The company included the music-hall stalwart Norah Blaney, who was also a first-class pianist. She and Sybil were soon doing four-handed Bach jam sessions during rehearsals, news of which filtered through to a BBC producer of the show *London Lights*. The result was Sybil's only broadcast as a pianist, the pair being engaged to play a jig from a Bach suite and a Khachaturyan waltz. But while rehearsals were generally harmonious, there were occasional flare-ups. One involved Coward, as Margaret Webster recalled: 'He and Lewis raged at each other in strangulated politeness. Noel turned purple and Lewis turned bright crimson and they both swelled up till I thought they would burst; but that night Sybil and I defused the two bombs and they returned to their normal shape and colour.'

Coward's lover Graham Payn was also in the company, and recalled Sybil's professionalism and leadership. 'She was a tower of strength. She was word-perfect for the first rehearsal, took direction, and even spurred on the other ladies to greater effort. She would prompt them discreetly when they faltered, without any attempt to score points. Her example as a team player shamed anyone who might have been tempted to throw a temper tantrum. She was particularly kind to some of the very senior ladies, who spent more time in their own world than in the one we were trying to create.'

In private Sybil was less than happy with her old friend's work. 'Rehearsals OK,' she reported to Patricia, 'but I find Peggy Webster a bit forthright, unsubtle and stage managery! Disappointing.' But after the opening in Dublin she was on her best behaviour: 'Peggy, darling Peggy,' she wrote. 'Can't thank you enough for all you've done – the help you've given me – and the wonderful way you have "managed" us all!' The play then visited Liverpool and Manchester, and was greeted in both cities with great enthusiasm and positive notices. There was a similar audience reaction at the Duke of York's at the London opening in September, where each actress got a round on her entrance. 'A terrific affair,' Sybil told Patricia, 'it went with a bang and shouts and bravos.' But the notices were quite different.

Coward's resurgence as a playwright was still to come: partly because of his unpopular decision to live abroad for tax reasons, he was at this time regularly attacked in the press. Now, though some critics were kind – Hobson thought the play would 'give a great deal of quiet and legitimate pleasure to many theatregoers' – others were savage, accusing him of tastelessness, vulgarity and sentimentality. The *Daily Express* called it 'A Play About Nothing At All', the *Daily Mail* 'Just Timeless Rootless Prattle', while T C Worsley in the *Financial Times* wrote: 'There is a lot of old shop talked and a lot of old songs sung, and it gets more nauseating as the evening wears on.' Sybil thought their criticisms untrue and unfair. 'It's the first time Noël has shown real *heart*, and none of the critics has noticed this.' But she accepted that 'Noël doesn't make it easier, the things he says about critics and about himself'.

Coward was upset by the notices, not only for himself – 'I have never read such abuse in my life, to read them was like being repeatedly slashed in the face', he wrote in his diary – but for the company: he thought their performances very fine, but several reviews failed even to mention them. Soon afterwards he recalled the opening night: 'Sybil Thorndike, to my mind one of the few really great actresses of our time, played the part I had written with such unswerving truth, restraint, lack of sentimentality and sheer beauty that I saw much of it through a haze of grateful tears.' Some critics agreed: *Theatre World* thought she gave one of her finest performances, while the *Guardian* reviewer stated: 'Dame Sybil Thorndike has never spoken more superbly…and her superb technique, lit by a temperament combining humour, sweetness and mobility, makes even some obvious bitter-sweet sentiment richly moving.'

The play ran until February, then toured for several weeks. Legend has it that at one performance one elderly actress dried, the prompter gave the line, then gave it again, after which someone said: 'We know the line dear, but who says it?' William Hutt remembered Sybil on stage: 'She was never any place but *there*, attentive, listening, responding, supporting, and staunchly leading that lovely gaggle of not-yet-quite-forgotten stars.' But offstage the stars didn't always want to be led by Sybil: according to Marie Lohr, they would hide from her on train journeys, to avoid being drawn into exhausting word-games. Margot Boyd recalled one incident when her enthusiasm became insensitivity. 'Before the curtain went up Marie Lohr would come on stage and sit quietly in her chair and think about her performance. Sybil would come rushing on, full of beans, and tell Marie all about her day, which seemed to involve a funeral or memorial service at least once or twice a week. Marie said: "Remind me to add a codicil to my will, saying that Sybil is not to come to my funeral.'"

In fact two of the cast died during the run and the ensuing tour, necessitating further funeral attendances. Recalling her role in the play, Sybil later remarked: 'It was a beautiful piece of characterisation, and so tender. It was modern with a beautiful shape – that was Noël's musicianship. All his plays have perfect shape.' But she occasionally had problems with her lines: 'I used to be frightfully excited when I knew Noël was in front. And every blessed time he was there I dried. The first time he came round he said "Fluffy Damesy", and that's what he always called me from then on – which is a pity, because I'm not a fluffy actress.' Despite this lapse, Coward dedicated the published play to 'Sybil, with my love, admiration and gratitude'.

While the play was in Dublin she performed one of her many acts of kindness. The director Peter Gill, then an actor, had watched Coward give notes at a run-through, and then had suffered an accident in the hills and landed up in hospital. 'A note arrived from Sybil, asking if she might visit me,' he remembers. 'It was the most charming thing to have happened. She came and sat beside me. She was a remarkable woman.' Often she would give money to out-of-work actors or others who came to her flat, as Ann's son Dirk Campbell remembers. 'She was always very warm, and genuinely concerned about others. At Swan Court there were always people coming to the door. "Darling, oh dear, how terrible, have five pounds." She never turned anyone away.' He and many others were amused by Sybil's habit of seeing them to the lift, then as it descended saying in very audible tones: 'Aren't they darlings!'

John's daughter Penny stayed at the flat for six months while training to be a midwife. 'She and Grandaddy were endlessly helpful and kind,' she recalls. 'I was never chastised or made to feel I was irresponsibly young. But Sybil was extremely sensitive about people not being up to the mark. She didn't do it bitchily, but you knew when you were being criticised, and it made you feel you had to do better. I think she had an enormous ego, but she overlaid it with this huge interest in everybody.' Teresa Campbell, then eleven, was there by herself for a week. 'I found it quite frightening being with her,' she says. 'Although there were lots of hugs, she wasn't really a cuddly granny, or someone you felt wanted to hear that you were a bit frightened.' Daniel Thorndike offers a similar perspective: 'My children were a bit frightened of her to start with, because her gestures were so much bigger than other people's. She would envelop them with love and affection, and some children shy away from that.' Other grandchildren point up the contrast between her and Lewis. 'If you wanted advice you went to Lewis, if you wanted cheering up you went to Sybil,' Diana Devlin says, while Ben Campbell suggests: 'Lewis was a more real person, you could sit down with him and talk about a personal problem I think his love was more profound, rooted in something more solid, whereas Sybil's was more bubbly and on the surface.'

She remained deeply interested in the state of the theatre. At a lunch at the Dorchester she unveiled a model of the proposed Yvonne Arnaud Theatre at Guildford, using the promotion of a provincial theatre to criticise the London scene. She continued the attack in a preface to Malcolm Morley's book on old London playhouses, praising him for 'bringing to the mind of the people of London the history and romance that once belonged to us, and which we have exchanged very largely for the Mechanical – the Machine Theatre'. Her enjoyment of the theatrical past brought her into contact with Raymond Mander and Joe Mitchenson and their vast collection of memorabilia. In the succeeding years she gave them gifts and donations, describing them as 'my dear detectives', and their collection as 'the profession's passport to posterity'.

She was also in demand for the centenary celebrations of the birth of Tagore, taking part in a dramatised reading of his play *Sacrifice* at the Old Vic. It was performed by members of the resident company, including John Stride, John Neville, Barbara Jefford in a blue sari of Sybil's, and Judi Dench in a orange and black one. The director Patrick Garland, then an actor, remembers 'rather a ponderous work, full of high-flown phrases'. He also recalls Sybil refusing to go down on her knees in front of the High Priest, played by Lewis, because she feared she might never get up again. 'After all, I am 77 years of age,' she told Lewis, who replied: '*I* always go down on my knees.' Sybil responded: 'You may, but *you're* only 84.'

During this time, when the Old Vic was staging *Saint Joan* with Barbara Jefford in the title-role, the Vic-Wells society held a sherry party there, inviting people, including Sybil and Russell, who had been involved in past productions to meet the resident company. It was another chance for Sybil to demonstrate her capacity to always look on the bright side, as Daniel Thorndike remembers: 'Father asked Sybil what the sherry was like, and she replied: "Cough mixture!" One of the organisers who was behind her said:

"Oh I do hope it's all right, Dame Sybil." Without a pause Sybil replied: "Oh but I sometimes think cough mixture is absolutely wonderful!"' The Old Vic was also the venue for *So Richly Spun*, a programme of poetry arranged by John Carroll, which Sybil performed for Shakespeare's birthday. Her partner on this and several later recitals was Barbara Jefford. 'Sybil had terrific passion, and as much energy as I had,' she recalls. 'Her spirit never dimmed. We'd rehearse at their flat, and Lewis was always very particular about emphases and inflections. I remember Sybil saying once: "Don't pick me up so much Lewis, you'll frighten the life out of her." She knew a lot about the poems. I felt she had a special affinity with Browning, especially "My Last Duchess", perhaps because it's a dramatic piece. She seemed also to have a very proprietorial feeling about Hopkins' poems. Lewis was her sternest critic: he would come with us to the performances, and she was always trying to live up to his expectations. They were a very sparky and vigorous couple.'

During the run of the Coward play she was the subject of a *This is Your Life* programme. 'Oh crikey!' was her response when, having recorded some scenes from Shakespeare in a studio, the programme's presenter Eamonn Andrews suddenly appeared and broke the news to her. Among all the usual tributes from family and friends, the most striking moment came when, after shots were shown of Ann and her children in Canada, Ann suddenly appeared in person, flown over especially for the occasion. This shocked Sybil, who thought at first it was some new form of three-dimensional projection. She was also initially aggrieved that Lewis, who had been consulted beforehand, had kept the secret from her. But the programme raised her profile with the public, who now took to stopping her in the street or talking to her on buses, still her favourite form of transport in London.

Her children were leading very varied lives. Christopher was still acting in Ireland, but supplementing his meagre income by teaching deaf and dumb children in a convent. Mary, a first-class musician, was specialising in playing the virginals, while Ann and Douglas were now a permanent presence at the theatre in Stratford, Ontario. John had left his job as resident producer for J C Williamson after differences over production policy. After achieving some fame by giving late-night Bible readings on television, he had moved to a firm of management consultants in Melbourne. He had also had a small part in the film *On the Beach*, in which, in a cast that included Gregory Peck, Ava Gardner, Fred Astaire and Anthony Perkins, Sybil told him 'yours was the only really satisfactory performance'.

Her letters of this period reflect a constant anxiety about her children's progress in life. 'We find that you are the only one of the four that has ambition,' she told John. 'Kiff has none in the world what ever – Ann has transferred what she has to Douglas – and Mary prefers a quiet jog-trot life, which is full of interesting things, but she has no wish for anything startling.' She seemed unable to understand that people could be fulfilled without having to 'startle' in the way that she very publicly had done. Meanwhile her desire for her children to succeed was filtering down to her grandchildren, several of whom she tried to put off going into the theatre.

'Thank God the stage is being swept out of her ken!' she wrote to John about Glynis – who would later establish herself as an actress in Dublin. Mary's daughter Diana, academically successful at school, had become mad about the theatre. This Sybil thought undesirable. 'She's in love with Larry and John G and heaps of others,' she complained. 'We all think university is her metier, and just curse her!' But a few weeks later Diana applied for a state scholarship to Cambridge. 'I'm glad to say she's going to work for her scholarship to the university, and then we hope the theatre craze will pass over.... She's quite reconciled, as we've pointed out all the advantages.'

With Jane the pressure was in a different direction. Sybil had long been telling her parents she should come to England. 'We think she is *the* hope of the theatre!!' she had told them after *The Chalk Garden*, telling Jane herself: 'You'll be top of the tree before much time is past.' Once Jane arrived in England in autumn 1960, Sybil used her considerable influence with people such as Binkie Beaumont and the Old Vic's director Michael Benthall to try to obtain interviews or auditions for her granddaughter. 'It's only a question of waiting – she's bound to get to the top – she's so full of talent,' she blithely informed John and Patricia.

Her belief in Jane quickly became counter-productive, for when no work was forthcoming, Jane began to resent her interference. 'Jane is very against me putting a word in with any managers,' Sybil explained. 'She must do it herself, and not get labelled Granny's little girl!' Despite this rebuff, Sybil continued to 'put in a judicious word when I can without telling her'. Soon after she concluded, apparently without irony: 'Jane might do anything – if she's not pushed. One can't force her, or she gets into a tangle. But it's a touch of the mad something that is Jane's asset, I feel.' When Jane's interest in the theatre appeared to evaporate, she decided this was the theatre's fault, that Jane was 'too good for it', and that maybe her future lay in music. But Jane now put her foot down: 'Jane won't talk about her future, and we think she's quite right,' Sybil explained.

After another holiday in Switzerland with Lewis, she worked on two more films, one British, the other American. *Hand in Hand*, directed by Philip Leacock, was about the friendship between a little Catholic boy and a little Jewish girl, and gained several awards for promoting international understanding. *The Times* thought the acting unremarkable, except for Miriam Karlin as the girl's mother, and 'a bizarre but quite fetching appearance by Dame Sybil Thorndike as an eccentric old lady the children run into during their wanderings'. In the *Observer* Penelope Gilliatt suggested that 'no one in England says "gel" as prettily as Dame Sybil'.

Her last film was *The Big Gamble*, an adventure story directed by Richard Fleischer, starring Stephen Boyd and Juliette Greco. Filming took her to Paris, from where she wrote gleefully to John: 'Paris has been a big pleasure – it's the most lovely city in the world! I'm in great luxury here, treated as a first-class film star, cars everywhere, and people looking at me as if I was the Queen.' She liked Fleischer, who made severe demands on her. 'I get nervous with these long speeches and a director who is meticulous – every syllable has to be exactly as he wants.' *The Times* critic enjoyed her performance as Stephen Boyd's aunt, 'dominating a scattering of relations with a thump of her stick and a gleam of humour in her eye'. Fleischer thought her performance 'magnificent', recalling that 'the only conflict we had was about whether a word should be pronounced in the British or American way – and Sybil won'.

She still did the occasional radio play. *The Sunday Market*, a comedy by Caryl Brahms and Ned Sherrin with music by Johnny Dankworth, was a new departure. Her role was that of an elderly upper-class woman selling off the family silver. 'Sybil Thorndike Sings Johnny Dankworth is an LP that the authors have long looked for,' Caryl Brahms wrote in the *Radio Times*. 'Although Dame Sybil will only speak-sing in this play, who knows what it will lead to?' Directed by Charles Lefeaux, the cast included Miriam Karlin, James Kenney and Perlita Nielson. Johnny Dankworth recalls: 'As a composer you're always worried about whether an actor can handle the music, but she dealt with the number well, she had the rhythm.' Waiting to rehearse her number with the orchestra, Sybil wrote to Patricia: 'As it's very modern and jazzy I have to be on my toes – but it's a charming play, and I've a delicious part.' *The Times* agreed, noting that 'she provided a personality of majestically overpowering gentility'.

In December a proposed major television interview with Sybil by Derek Prouse caused anxiety within the BBC. 'She is old and not fit, and I do not want it to be an obit!' wrote Cecil Madden. He needn't have worried. 'To younger viewers she may have appeared strangely extravagant,' wrote the *Listener* critic when the programme was screened in January 1961. 'But even they must have been taken with her generosity of spirit, the warmth with which she spoke of Dame Edith Evans and Marilyn Monroe, and the vigour of her response to contemporary questions.'

She and Lewis now sold Cedar Cottage. 'I feel the most enormous weight off me,' she admitted to John. 'It's a new start we'll be making.' With the rent at Swan Court suddenly increasing substantially, she wondered if they should consider a move. She liked the idea a house with a small garden in Chelsea, Hampstead, Kensington or Richmond. Sometimes she yearned for the ultimate simplicity: 'I'd like to live in one room and just work – and me piano! And Lewis!' There were other dreams, as she wrote to John after a visit to Bron-y-Garth: 'We feel if we don't settle in our later years in Australia, we shall in Wales.' But Lewis' condition was worsening. 'He gets a bit collapsed sometimes and then gets the wind up and thinks he's finished!' she wrote. As he became increasingly anxious about money, she found it hard to convince him that the income from her film work meant they were comfortably off. She was also worried about his loss of vision. 'You know how he loves reading and it is extremely difficult now, even with a large magnifying glass.'

Lewis' problems didn't prevent them from still having rows. One of their most violent came at the end of an evening at Swan Court, during which Lewis had continually criticised what he saw as a left-wing guest's very idealised view of life in Russia. After she had gone, Sybil in a fury kicked the glass umbrella stand, which shattered into pieces, then threw a vase at the wall. Lewis coolly said to Patricia: 'Go and shut the kitchen door or we shan't have any crockery for breakfast!' Sybil exploded again, but finally burst into tears, and was comforted by Lewis. This was often the pattern of their arguments.

They were both still in demand in the theatre. 'Lots of plays coming in for us to do, but I don't like any of them,' she told John. But there was one brewing for which she had high hopes. Three years earlier she and Lewis had met the historian and playwright Hugh Ross Williamson, a former Anglican priest who had become a Catholic. He had just started work on a play about Saint Teresa of Avila. 'My life will be complete if I can play that terrific old girl,' Sybil wrote; she thought it 'the most thrilling part I've been offered since

Saint Joan'. She had read everything by and about Saint Teresa, but Williamson's first draft disappointed her: it was, she decided, too uncritical of the
saint's life, while Williamson was 'an RC and therefore too credulous!'

She and Lewis invited him to dinner 'to go slap bang with us into the
arguments and pronouncements necessary for the play to be challenging'.
The scheme clearly failed to work. 'Hugh Ross W is lazy and Lewis has
practically written the play for him,' Sybil reported. The cast included Rachel
Kempson, Richard Pasco, Nicholas Hannen, Veronica Turleigh and Ernest
Milton, with Lewis playing the Father-General of the Carmelites. Richard
Pasco remembers the first reading, held at Swan Court: 'I got three or four
lines out, and Lewis said: "No, no, no! It's not *tong te tong te tong*, it's *tong te
tong tong* tong *te*." I said: "Forgive me, I'm just reading it at the moment." But
he went on interrupting people all the way through.'

As part of their research Sybil and Lewis visited the Benedictine nuns at
Stanbrook Abbey near Malvern, where they were shown the correspondence
between Shaw and the former abbess Dame Laurentia, a woman Sybil greatly
admired. They discussed Saint Teresa with the present abbess, and the actors
read the play to an audience of sixty nuns who, this being a closed order, were
separated from the actors by a grille the width of the room. 'You should have
heard the laughs,' Sybil told John. 'I hope ordinary audiences get the comedy
the way the nuns did.' Dame Felicitas Corrigan, who helped them with the
music for the play, wrote from the Abbey the next day: 'The whole community
is smiling and uplifted.' They also went to the Carmelite monastery at Ware
in Hertfordshire, where they had further discussions about Saint Teresa with
the nuns, and Sybil was allowed to don one of their habits.

She was often in great pain at this time. She had recently had a fall while
trying to board a bus in the King's Road, which brought on acute sciatica.
'We had the first Teresa rehearsal yesterday, so of course I was in despair,' she
told John in early August. 'I just can't *act*! I really find the Theatre exhausting.
I'm bad with rheumaticism, sciatica, the palsy and all other sorts of music, so
a bit groggy on me pins.' Yet according to Ian Burford, playing a lawyer, this
was not apparent. 'She and Lewis and Nicholas Hannen were all around 80,
but they exhausted me in the first scene,' he remembers. 'They just went full
out all the time, vocally and physically. It was like trying to run up hill after
three sprinters.'

Though Sybil liked the director Norman Marshall – 'he has real *style*, and
is not just fussing with scenery and lights – Lewis likes him too, which is rare!'

– to others he seemed weak and insecure. The script also remained a problem: 'It's a complete mystery what it's like and what it will do!' Sybil admitted to John. 'The author has not done his homework, which gets me mad.' She was nervous before the first night at the Dublin Festival, telling Ian Burford: 'Don't think it gets easier, because it gets worse. When I was a girl I did things and didn't worry about it. Now I know what I can do wrong.' Afterwards she wrote to John about the problem-filled opening: 'The devil did all he could to bitch everything up – my voice nearly gone – very bad sciatica in one leg and the other one with a slipped bone – Lewis on the verge of a nervous breakdown – a strike of dockers, so no scenery or props or lights. But Teresa's own method worked. I made a long nose at the devil and jeered at him, and I could hear our Lord laughing and saying, Go it, Syb and Lew, see how much you can stand, and I'll be there to give you a push! And it all went wonderfully. Lewis improved – my voice returned – my legs both hell but copeable – audience wonderful – and life holds out hope.' Rachel Kempson felt that as Teresa 'she was very good, she had a sort of inner beauty'. Ian Burford recalls one special moment: 'In one scene she just stood there, and she looked as if she was made of silver. She started shining, she looked radiant and lit up. Yet you couldn't see what she was doing.'

By the time they reached Brighton she was temporarily lame, and had to use a stick to prevent herself from collapsing. For perhaps the first time she was forced to avoid taking on anything outside the play. She and Lewis had supper with Olivier and Joan Plowright, now his wife, and Olivier insisted she visit his physiotherapist. She noticed a positive change in him. 'For the first time in years he is relaxed and like the old dear Larry that we've not seen for the last ten years,' she wrote to John. 'Joan is a darling, you couldn't have anything more unlike poor Viv. She's a very good actress – she'd be a very good Saint Joan from what I've seen of her work.'

Hugh Ross Williamson had a small part in his play, which in Brighton prompted a typically sharp remark from the actress Coral Browne. On his entrance she said: 'Oh look, here's the author. He looks pregnant. Perhaps this time it's a play!' The London opening at the Vaudeville in October produced the familiar audience/critic split. 'Our first night was a riot – yells and bravos and curtain after curtain – and then stinkers of notices,' Sybil told John. The play was variously likened to a friendly chronicle, a lantern lecture, and an elementary propaganda pamphlet, its language compared by one critic to that of a Women's Institute Civil Defence meeting. But Sybil, in the longest part of her career, was widely praised for making the best of a poor offering.

'There is very little for Dame Sybil to do but deploy her own qualities of imagination, sensitivity and theatrical brilliance,' the *Stage* critic commented. Norman Shrapnel in the *Guardian* rhapsodised about her voice, 'a fine instrument, still remarkably youthful, charged with humanity, and above all a speaking voice: no great-actressy viola-playing, nothing forced or over-pitched'. Robert Muller in the *Daily Mail* noted that 'Saint Teresa is presented as a determined, jolly, brave, and spiritually beautiful Anglo-Saxon lady, i.e. as Sybil Thorndike, and Dame Sybil achieves an impeccable projection of her own loveable personality.'

The reviews were a great disappointment for Sybil, who desperately wanted the play to succeed. 'It's a pity the critics crabbed it so, for that keeps a large public away,' she wrote to John. 'All the people who know anything about Teresa love it, because it's a real portrait. It's not a first-class play, but if one waits for that would never act at all, or just do classics, which isn't what one wants.' Her only compensation was the huge number of letters she received from people who had been moved by the play and her performance. But her pain made it harder to deal with the droves of friends who came round. Ian Burford remembers: 'As they went she would say, "Aren't they marvellous!" but when the door closed you would hear "Aren't friends hell!"'

The play ran for just six weeks, closing in early December. 'I have no ambitions any more, I just want to go on acting for a little longer,' Sybil told a reporter. In reality she was preparing for yet another ambitious expedition to the other side of the world. She was also about to take part in what came to be seen as a landmark production in British theatre.

38

Olivier and Chekhov at Chichester

1962–1963

'Sybil could pour trust into you; it was like a message from God'
Olivier on the first night of Uncle Vanya

Preparing for their fifth and last visit to Australia, sponsored by the Australian Elizabethan Theatre Trust, Sybil and Lewis planned to give a full programme of recitals. But for a moment the tour was in serious jeopardy.

'I'm in a blue funk about Lewis,' Sybil wrote to John and Patricia. 'He's deteriorated badly in the last two weeks, and this morning I had the worst crise with him – crying and gasping for breath and saying he wants to die – I don't know what to do – when he saw the itinerary of the tour he just fell to pieces. He can't do it.' After consulting a doctor, who diagnosed a depressive illness that would eventually run its course, they decided to risk going ahead. Sybil hoped the long sea voyage and the prospect of seeing John and family in the Australian summer would revive Lewis' spirits.

As a precaution they agreed she would do solo recitals until he felt well enough to join in. Once on board the ss *Canberra* in January 1962, she did her best to bring him back into action. The film director Muriel Box was a fellow-passenger: 'The sight of her sitting close to him on the upper deck rehearsing him in the various roles for the two-hour show they were to give in Fremantle will always remain with me,' she recalled. 'Her patience and gentle encourage-ment as he misheard cues or dried on his lines moved me to tears.'

Sybil was now in her eightieth year. Yet despite her acute arthritis and Lewis' vulnerable state, the two of them performed twenty-five recitals in three months, beginning at the Perth Festival, where the temperature was 106° in the shade. The heat was often intense in the other cities and townships where they played, and their resilience astonished everyone. After a recital in Melbourne's Assembly Hall one critic wrote: 'For sheer vitality and range of effects this famous team has never been better. They seem to grow younger with the years.' Sybil told a Melbourne reporter: 'We are strong physically, but I suspect that if we stopped working we would crumble.'

They returned home in leisurely fashion on the ss *Orcades*, taking in Singapore, Bombay, Aden, the Suez Canal, Naples, Marseilles and Gibraltar. The tour had been shorter than previous ones because Olivier, in his first season as director of the new Chichester Festival Theatre, had engaged them to appear in *Uncle Vanya*, with Michael Redgrave in the title-role and Olivier playing Astrov. Rehearsals started in June while they were still aboard ship, with Peter Woodthorpe standing in for Lewis as Telyegin, the old retainer, known as Waffles. Olivier wrote to Sybil: 'Rehearsals are going very well and I thrill to the work. I think Michael is going to be the most wonderful Vanya: it turns out that the part is just one of those definitive ones for him, and he is quite amazingly right for it.' But he wondered about Lewis' ability to cope, and cabled the ship, suggesting he might like instead to be advisor to the company on matters of diction. Sybil's reply was uncompromising: 'Nonsense,' she said, 'he knows the lines, he'll be all right.'

They arrived in England in mid-June, and within a few days were settled in a thatched cottage in Fishbourne, just outside Chichester. Jane Casson joined them, having gained a job as an usherette at the theatre. The Chichester company was a formidable one, featuring Joan Plowright, Keith Michell, John Neville, Robert Lang, Alan Howard, Rosemary Harris, Athene Seyler, Peter Woodthorpe, André Morell, Joan Greenwood and Fay Compton. *Uncle Vanya* was the third production of the season. By the time it opened on 16 July a great many hopes were riding on it. For the first two plays Olivier had chosen two relatively obscure Jacobean works, *The Chances* by John Fletcher, and *The Broken Heart*, a lurid melodrama by John Ford, in which he also acted. Both had received a critical roasting. Tynan wrote Olivier an 'Open Letter to an Open Stager' in the *Observer*: 'Something has clearly gone wrong: but how?....Does the fault lie in the play, in the theatre, or in you, its artistic director?…Tomorrow *Uncle Vanya* opens. Within a fortnight you will have directed three plays and appeared in two leading parts. It is too much.'

Sybil was furious with Tynan. 'KT's notices were beastly about Larry and the whole set-up,' she told John. 'Just a smart-aleck sort of thing.' The attack cast a shadow over rehearsals for *Uncle Vanya*, but Sybil, playing again the small but important part of Marina the Nurse, was a steadying influence. Olivier was relaxed with her, as Peter Woodthorpe recalls: 'At one rehearsal she was sitting on the stage knitting, and from the stalls came Larry's voice: "Sybil! No bloody knitting!" "All right," she said, and put it down.' In general though, according to Robert Lang, 'Larry pretty well left Sybil alone – but to a large extent he did that to everyone.'

In choosing *Uncle Vanya*, Olivier was throwing down the gauntlet to those sceptics who suggested Chekhov's naturalistic drama wouldn't work on Chichester's 'arena' or 'thrust' stage, which ran out into the auditorium with the audience on three sides. It had been inspired by similar ones in Stratford, Ontario and Minneapolis, both of which owed their success to Guthrie's pioneering spirit. Sybil loved the feeling of it, of being in closer touch with the audience. But it presented problems, as Robert Lang recalled: 'If you went too high you couldn't be heard, if you used a lot of chest tone it disappeared, and if you gave it too much volume it didn't carry. You also had to move a lot more than on a conventional proscenium-arch stage. But Sybil was bell-like, you could always hear her, and also Lewis, who had a big, chesty voice.'

Privately they both nursed doubts about Olivier's way of working on the open stage. 'The theatre work depresses us a bit,' Sybil told John. 'Larry is producing it like the cinema – everything thrown away – and honestly I can only hear a *quarter* of what anyone is saying! I can't bear the over-intimate acting…everything underplayed! It's a lovely theatre – Michael Redgrave beautiful as Vanya – but I hear about *half* of what he says. And Larry's wife…I can only hear one quarter, and that only if I'm near!!!' This was becoming a familiar theme: apart from a very slight deafness, Sybil seemed increasingly unwilling to value acting less exuberant than her own.

The dress rehearsal, which continued into the early hours of the morning, was a disaster: cues were missed, and the sound effects went chaotically wrong. Watching one scene from the back of the stalls, Olivier suddenly exploded: 'For fuck's sake Lewis, I can't hear a bloody word!' Lewis looked up slowly, and said: 'If you can't hear me Larry, why don't you come a little closer?' At the end Joan Plowright, pregnant with her second child, burst into tears. Olivier feared Chekhov was not going to work on Chichester's open stage. 'My heart was full of lead,' he remembered.

He had reckoned without Sybil, as Peter Woodthorpe recalled: 'On the first night Larry called us together and said: "Here's to the next flop!" Sybil replied, "Nonsense!" – and hit him in the face. Afterwards he said that moment woke him up.' Olivier later wrote how, when Marina hands Astrov tea from the samovar right at the start, he looked into Sybil's eyes. 'She had her own very special gift with them: just when the occasion demanded it, she could pour trust into you; it was like a message from God.' She also poured trust into Lewis, as Robert Lang recalled: 'Lewis dried at the start, but Sybil fed him every line, not in a whisper but a normal voice, which he then repeated. This went on for about six lines, until he found his feet.'

With its single set by Sean Kenny designed to cover both the indoor and outdoor scenes, Olivier's production is still remembered today as a definitive version of Chekhov's tragi-comic masterpiece. Yet though it was a commercial hit and hugely popular with audiences, not all the critics admired it. Robert Muller complained: 'We saw the play in fragments which never gelled to an emotional whole.' Others thought it didn't suit the open stage. Yet the vast majority loved it, describing the production as faultless, near-perfect, and a marvel of ensemble playing. *The Times* thought it doubtful if the Moscow Art Theatre could improve on it, while Hobson saw in it 'something miraculous… something beyond the order of nature'. Even Tynan – who had turned up in a pink suit for the first night, to be roundly booed by his fellow-critics – wrote admiringly of Olivier's and Redgrave's 'superlative' performances.

Sybil's earthy Marina drew universal praise: Clive Barnes called it 'a tiny masterpiece of naturalism'. Robert Lang remembered: 'She had the common touch, so she could play peasants. I thought that was extraordinary, as she didn't have a peasant type of voice or vowels. But you had no doubt her Nurse was a worker, and you could feel her strength.' Joan Plowright was also admiring: 'She was very simple, she threw away the grand manner, she had that ability to be ordinary if she had to. You felt a warm buzz from the audience when she came on.' From out front Janet Suzman was also impressed: 'Her Nurse had something so bustling and vivid about it, a ringing presence,' she recalled. The audience were unaware that her arthritis prevented her from climbing the stairs to her dressing-room, so she had to sit throughout on a chair in the wings. Adam Rowntree was the assistant stage manager: 'One of my duties was to help her gently to her feet for her entrances,' he recalls. 'She didn't make a noise, but I felt she was groaning inwardly. Yet once on, she was like a young girl.'

Lewis continued to have problems, as his dresser Brian Glanvill recalls: 'He was practically blind, and if I didn't get to him on time he would stick on his beard, moustache, and toupee in the wrong places. One night Dame Sybil told me to make sure that his flies were done up, as they were having cocktails with the mayor of Chichester after the performance.' Yet Lewis' downtrodden Waffles was widely enjoyed: *The Times* critic described it as 'an oasis of peace in the discordant atmosphere'. But his increasing deafness was a handicap. One night Sybil called to him to leave the stage with her: 'Come on, Waffles.' When there was no response she said sharply, 'Lewis!' Sometimes he missed his cue when required to strum the guitar to a background tape, or was uncertain when to stop. Eventually a buzzer was fitted to his base of his chair, to be activated by the stage manager when necessary.

Though he completed the run, to Sybil's consternation his condition was slowly deteriorating. Outwardly she tried to remain cheerful as she undertook more public duties. Interviewing her for Southern Television, John Gordon recalls: 'When she came into the studio it was like the sun coming out.' When the news broke of the death of Marilyn Monroe, she obliged Olivier by standing in for him in a television tribute. 'We've been so shocked and sorry about Marilyn's death,' she wrote to John. 'Poor bitter soul – very lonely – no discipline – colossal charm and no stability – it's a tragic thing.' She also spoke at a CND meeting to the hundreds who had marched from Portsmouth to Chichester. 'I'm not such a good speaker as you, not so tidy-minded,' she told John. 'But I enjoyed it, they were so responsive.'

She was still obsessed with getting Jane going in the theatre. Lewis added further pressure, telling John he felt 'she would be able to take up the torch of making people think of speech as an art in itself, when he had to drop it'. Although Sybil had apparently backed off, she privately talked to the Old Vic about Jane, and had a long talk with Olivier, whose views on actresses differed from hers. 'I was depressed,' she wrote. 'He said they want thin girls – but I said, All parts don't require these "little bits" of girls….I convinced him of the need of another sort, and he's writing to Michael Elliott about Jane – I'll write too. She is a big girl with a resounding bottom and a good *sweep*, not one bit like one of these "darlings" they all seem to want.'

In August Olivier was appointed the first director of the National Theatre. The success of *Uncle Vanya* had not only secured the future of the new theatre at Chichester, but provided a springboard for him to take on his new role. Sybil's delight was mixed with reservations. 'We are all quite thrilled at Larry being made the director – it was to be expected I think – we only wish he'd care a lot more for words, but he has broad and effective ideas which are really wanted. I think he's a bit tired of acting, and wants directorship – a wider scope.'

Soon afterwards, on holiday in France, Olivier wrote a remarkable letter to Sybil that confirmed the power of their long relationship.

'My darling, I can never tell you what it has meant to me to have you and Lewis helping me in this venture, it has just made all the difference in the world to me for so many reasons. Nobody in the world will ever do for a venture what you do, or for a company, or for me personally; I suppose that last one goes back a long way – long enough to be almost pre-natal, one might say! Your Nurse will always be for me one of the most perfect things I shall ever know, and as you probably surmised I most dearly needed that most definitive of performances, not only for me to present it proudly, but to give one a feeling of such utter safety and comfort....Our first moment on the stage together was like a little sacrament that I looked forward to every time, and even between times when I would be worried, depressed or overwrought, I would think, "Never mind, tomorrow afternoon Syb is going to give me that look straight in the eyes, and all will be so wonderfully alright again for a time." I shall borrow from the memory of it all my life when things are bad.'

Although Lewis was not too keen on the idea, preferring a new role, he and Sybil returned to Chichester and *Uncle Vanya* the following summer. There were cast changes, with Rosemary Harris, Max Adrian and Robert Lang taking over from Joan Greenwood, André Morell and Peter Woodthorpe. The season also included John Arden's *The Workhouse Donkey* and *Saint Joan*, directed by John Dexter, with Joan Plowright in Sybil's original role.

As before, Sybil had mixed emotions about the production: 'We've been rehearsing all day,' she wrote to John. '*Vanya* is a *perfect* play and it's beautifully played, but it's rather like watching a perfect foreign company, for neither of us get the words, alas. I'm waiting to see if Mary and Ian get them – then I'll know if it's just deafness!' As the dress rehearsal approached Lewis became worried about his costume, as Rosemary Harris recalls: 'Sybil came in and said, "I hope I'm not ponging dreadfully, darlings, but I've not been able to take a bath for the last three days: Lewis is soaking his suit in it to make it look less new."' Later he was spotted outside the theatre, jumping up and down on it to make it look more worn.

The revival quickly settled down with its new cast. Once again the notices were excellent. T C Worsley in the *Financial Times* described it as 'a living work so perfect in every conceivable detail', while for Hobson it was 'the master achievement in British twentieth-century theatre'. Sybil's own notices were equally fine: typically, Caryl Brahms thought her nurse 'wonderfully right and heart-warming'. Her performance and those of the rest of the company were preserved on film, when Stuart Burge directed a television version of the stage production.

Within the company Sybil was again the benign matriarch. 'She was very approachable – we called her Syb,' Rosemary Harris recalls. 'She was the mother of us all, including Larry, who treated her with great respect.' During rehearsals Sybil told John: 'Larry is being sweet to us both – rather hanging on to us as parents!' But she was anxious about how the National Theatre job would affect him: 'He's got very middle-aged and gout bothers him. We get a bit scared about him taking on so much responsibility.' But as Olivier began forming the National company, her concern turned to annoyance: 'I think Larry has got a rather dull company and the only girls are tiny and small-boned with untidy hair! I feel a bit dismayed about the whole thing.'

Her jaundiced and distorted view of a company that included actresses of such different shapes and sizes as Maggie Smith, Joan Plowright, Lynn Redgrave, Sarah Miles and Joyce Redman was explained by her determination to promote Jane. According to John: 'Sybil's very enthusiasm to all theatrical authorities had firstly made Jane unhappy about herself, and caused the managers to regard her rather as "Granny's pet".' Her belief in Jane's talent reached alarming heights when, after she had been turned down by the Glasgow Citizens', a problem with Joan Plowright's voice forced her to miss a performance of *Saint Joan*. 'If Jane were here she'd have known the part and could have done it. So few of the girls have any guts as Jane has. I don't know what it is – if she's too strong for the rather soppy rep producers...but she's deeper than all the little modern bits.'

Sybil was more balanced, however, about Joan Plowright's acting. '*Saint Joan* is being vigorously rehearsed – Larry's wife Joan will be awfully good,' she wrote, adding on the eve of the play's opening: 'Joan is lovely – a real peasant – I think she misses a bit of the largeness – but it's true and sincere and you can feel she "sees" things.' Three years earlier, after seeing her in Wesker's *Roots*, she had told her that she must play Saint Joan. At Chichester they had supper together, as Joan Plowright recalls: 'She didn't give me notes, because she knew it was a different generation. She just talked about the character. When I told her I was never satisfied with my performance, she said: "You never will be."' On the opening night Sybil gave her the edition of Wallon's book *Jeanne D'Arc* which Shaw had originally given *her*, and which she had decided to pass on to the next memorable Joan.

In June the Old Vic company staged its final performance, of *Measure for Measure*, before handing over its building to the National Theatre as a temporary home. The audience was packed with scores of those who had appeared there since Shakespeare had become the resident playwright and Sybil the leading lady almost half a century before. The box where Lilian Baylis had sat was filled with flowers. Under the television lights, the entire company came on stage at the end of the performance, to be joined by Sybil, who received, according to J C Trewin, 'what must have been the loudest ovation in the memory of anybody there'. She then gave a speech 'of shining enthusiasm', recalling the theatre's past and looking forward to the future.

'Let us say, Glory be to the Old Vic, that is taking a new shape and a new life,' she exhorted everyone. 'We've waited a long, long time, and now – the last country in Europe – we've got a National Theatre. Nobody's to think of this as a sad event at all. Nostalgia, get away!' She wrote to John two days later: 'It was a great occasion, everyone though was being a bit nostalgic and sad, and that got my goat, for it's a bigger thing and one to be proud of, from that small rather Mission Room atmosphere doing good to the poor, to have evolved into the National Theatre.'

At the start of the second Chichester season she and Lewis appeared in a newspaper photograph of the sixty-strong company, described as 'the men and women who will form the nucleus of our new National Theatre'. But this was not to be. Olivier, who had decided to make *Uncle Vanya* part of his first season's repertoire at the National, tried to persuade them to join the company. 'Lewis went up the pole and said he *couldn't*, he'd be too bored doing nothing but Vanya again,' Sybil told John. Yet there must have been a sadness for both of them, two of the doughtiest campaigners for a National Theatre, at not being present when that long-held dream was finally realised.

39

Vanity Fair to TW3

1962–1963

'I don't care if I don't have another television engagement or another film,
as long as I can traipse the country and act'
Sybil at 80

Between her two visits to Chichester, Sybil had made her debut in a
musical, and embarked on another recital tour with Lewis. As she turned
eighty she showed no sign of stopping. Asked about the secret of her youthfulness, she said: 'I take everything that comes as an opportunity to grow,
instead of something that will get me down. You see, life is an experiment,
the whole time one is trying new things out.'

The musical was based on Thackeray's novel *Vanity Fair*. The lyrics were by
Robin Miller, the music by Julian Slade, composer of the long-running *Salad
Days*. Sybil told John: 'I have the fine part of the peppery, aristocratic old aunt
Miss Crawley, who is a bit of a terror and very funny. It's a very gay script
and very spectacular.' Despite her fine musical ear and talent as a pianist, she
lacked a proper singing voice. This at first made her doubtful about taking
the part, which involved 'one very good number towards the end, and I sing
little bits in between with the chorus'. The director Lionel Harris suggested
she speak rather than sing the song. Julian Slade recalled: 'She wrote to me
saying she was thrilled to hear I was writing a song for her, but that nowadays
vocally she had very little up top, although down below she was a good strong
bass. So Robin and I set her song in the lowest key imaginable. She put the
number over perfectly all right; her voice was very strong for her age.'

The company consisted of Naunton Wayne, Joyce Carey, Michael Aldridge
and George Baker, with Frances Cuka as Becky Sharp. The working day lasted
ten or twelve hours, and Sybil needed to do an hour of exercises every morning
to get herself going. 'When I wake up I'm like an old woman, absolutely

bowed down,' she told Frances Cuka. 'I get out of bed and I crawl to the window, I open it and I stand there and I take deep breaths, and then I stand up straight and I feel much better. The elaborate production – George Baker calls it 'the maddest in which I've ever been involved'– was beset by technical problems. It was due to open at the vast Bristol Hippodrome, but the ice from the preceding ice extravaganza took longer to shift than expected. The delay caused chaos to the schedule: scenery was being flown in and out during the technical rehearsal, which went on until three in the morning. George Baker remembers the moment of Sybil's first entrance: 'She swept out of her dressing-room and said: "My dear, God is going to have to put a hand on our shoulders this evening."' He did so in one respect, as journalist Guy Thomas recalls: 'It all looked quite pretty as the curtain went up, but soon the scenery started to wobble, lighting cues were missed, and a tension swept through the theatre. Some quarter of an hour into the show Dame Sybil, heavily rouged, mob cap and Georgian frills everywhere, made her entrance spread on a *chaise longue*, which was pushed towards the footlights on a trolley. Unfortunately someone had pushed it too hard, and the audience gasped as it rolled onwards. By sheer luck it stopped just before it would have tipped her into the orchestra pit. Seeming oblivious to all this, Dame Sybil sang on. She was in full sail as the evening continued, the voice carrying to the back of the gallery. It was a definitive performance in how to galvanise a show.' Afterwards he and Lewis went backstage, where Sybil greeted them with: 'Oh God is so good to actors. He got us through.'

The play overran badly, and at the end Lionel Harris collapsed backstage. He then ordered a taxi and disappeared to London. This left Julian Slade in charge of rehearsing the urgently needed cuts and re-writes. 'The process went on for days,' he recalled. 'Sybil was constantly having to learn new lines, rehearse them with Lewis, and go on and speak them that night. She never complained, she was a model of professionalism. Her performance was a bit over the top, but then Miss Crawley was too – a very commanding woman who buried everybody in sight, and Sybil was very good at doing that.' Her technique surprised George Baker: 'She played everything out front, so I did the same. I had been very doubtful about this, but she taught me that as long as you looked at each other occasionally to establish a link, it worked. "They've come to see our faces, dear," is how she put it.'

The morning after, she had a television interview with Guy Thomas, who asked her whether she enjoyed being in a theatre audience. 'Yes, yes, yes, I love it!' she replied. 'I'm the best audience in the world – I believe it all.' At the end he asked what else she would like to do in the theatre. 'Oh, something on ice perhaps,' she said. 'I rather fancy that, skating around to music.' Thomas remembers the aftermath: 'Over sherry and sandwiches she and Lewis treated us to another performance, with tales of their travels and taking *Medea* to the miners during the war. They were lovely together: she urging him to tell a story, which she would finish; he wanting to let her enjoy the limelight, and she pushing him forward. Occasionally he would admonish her for some exaggeration or other, and she would defer to him.'

Vanity Fair moved to the Brighton Hippodrome, from where Sybil reported: 'We are in a vast theatre and packed and it's jolly hard work. We keep altering and fussing and it's all nerve-wracking, but getting better.' But when they reached the Queen's in London the company endured another buffeting from the critics. 'Terrific reception, numbers of calls, everyone rapturous – and the notices this morning all awful!' Sybil wrote. 'We were utterly flabbergasted as there was such cheering and excitement....We felt very let down by the notices. I think the critics don't like a classic being "musicalised".' One critic called it 'a musical full of stars who couldn't sing'; Irving Wardle in *The Times* thought the show old-fashioned, the score banal, and most of the characters dummies, but felt Sybil made Miss Crawley the 'one blazingly theatrical figure', who 'stamps every line with comic authority'.

The show remained popular with the public, and with Sybil, but it suffered from external as well as internal problems, notably a sudden spell of dense fog in its second week, and then at Christmas one of the severest winters on record, with snow continuing for weeks on end and people dying in snow drifts and being frozen to death in their cars. Robin Miller visited Sybil in her dressing room just after the notices had gone up. 'She was lying on a *chaise longue* with her hair down. I must have looked like death, because she said: "This is the theatre, my dear: you win some and you lose some. We lost this one – I'm so sorry."' In public she put on a brave face: 'Never be sorry to attempt something new – never, never, never,' she declared.

The company marvelled at her youthful quality. 'It was wonderful how she was still able to be so thrilled by everything,' Julian Slade remembered. 'Although she was a very clever woman, she had this child-like quality.' She also retained a kind of innocence, which received a jolt when she had a long talk about religion and morals with Jane Casson, who had been taken on to play three small parts and help with the stage management. 'She opened my eyes,' she admitted to John. 'I am shocked at the morals of our company, I sat aghast. Jane is wonderful – they all respect her because she is a virgin and intends to be so until she's really in love – and that to them is quite extraordinary!' Meanwhile her religious belief remained strong but pragmatic: 'I can't swallow churchy teaching, but I go regularly for a discipline and a communal act!'

Her eightieth birthday brought visits from several journalists. Irving Wardle was one of many struck by her vigour and optimism: 'Everything about her – her powerful hands and robust movement, the indestructible voice, the clear-sighted sympathies and irrepressible explosions of fun – express an inexhaustible appetite for life.' Asked by Taya Zinkin for the secret of her youthfulness, she ascribed it to her love of work, her faith, and her continuing curiosity about the world. She felt the passing years had enabled her 'to become more myself', that she was now 'the same person who danced in a charity musical when I was five and a half'. She remained optimistic about the future, believing that 'the world today is a far better place than it was in my youth'. Her next ambition, she revealed, was to be able to read *The Iliad* in Greek by the time she was ninety.

In a lengthy interview with Derek Prouse in the *Sunday Times*, in which she looked back candidly at her lengthy career, she underlined her love of new challenges. 'I think I've always tried to do more than I'm capable of – you might say my spirit is larger than my capabilities. I've not got the right face for the things I've always wanted to do – but that hasn't always stopped me doing them….Whenever a critic talks about an actor's meticulous style, that's the moment, it seems to me, when he should break the mould and throw it away. That's what often slightly bores me in the French theatre – the neat perfection of the actor's style. I feel I would like to see them do something ugly; break up the smooth surface.' She ended by emphasising her favourite medium. 'I don't care if I don't have another television engagement or film, as long as I can traipse the country and act.'

On the birthday itself she was overwhelmed by congratulations. 'Near 500 wires and things and flowers and we dunno where to turn and are exhausted with the tremendous kindness,' she told John. There was also a surprise. At the end of the matinee that day of *Vanity Fair* Lewis secretly donned a hooded cloak and joined the chorus. When Sybil took her bow, he stepped forward and offered her a birthday cake. 'Lewis! What are *you* doing here?' she shouted. The audience roared with laughter, and joined in the singing of

'Happy Birthday' and 'For She's a Jolly Good Fellow'. In response Sybil said, 'What can I say? Well it doesn't matter what I say, because at my age you don't give a damn about anything!'

This was of course far from the truth, as her life outside the theatre showed. She spoke, with Peter Hall, at the inauguration of a new, all-purpose theatre at the London Academy of Music and Dramatic Art. She was a guest at a *Theatre World* luncheon, where she was reported to have delivered 'a deliciously amusing and even pungent speech containing some timely advice for drama critics', berating them for 'making the theatre sound so dull!' She made a similar attack on the critics when she appeared as the mystery guest on the television panel game *What's My Line?*

She admitted her enthusiasm for certain kinds of such charity occasions was waning: 'I'm finding cocktail parties, lunches etc a bore – not exactly a bore, but effort!' Yet her love of argument had not diminished. 'We're going down to Canterbury tomorrow to see Hewlett Johnson,' she told John. 'Longing for a good argument.' She remained passionately interested in world affairs. 'We are in the throes of the Common Market – we get swept this way and that. I suppose it will be a great benefit our having a real say in European affairs, tho' it's a real gang-up against Russia, which seems an added aggravation – and the Commonwealth *is* something fine....America wants us in as she is so scared of communism. Oh! fear is so destructive.'

She had now 'got pretty fed up with the "gentlemanly" theatre', and greatly welcomed the new breed of playwright, although she felt the 'kitchen-sink' label 'a very silly description of the exciting drama of today'. But she disliked Barry Reckord's *Skyvvers*, a hard-hitting piece set in a comprehensive school. 'It's a sordid, filthy but sincere play,' she told Patricia. 'I felt like having a bath after it. All the young generation are not as foul as these modern writers say! I long for a play showing decent youth.' Yet though these new plays, both in form and content, subverted those by Rattigan, Hunter and Priestley which she had been playing in since the war, she embraced them with zest. 'I'd love to work with Joan Littlewood, or play in something by Wesker or Osborne,' she said.

Peter Woodthorpe, who played Aston in the original production of *The Caretaker*, recalled her coming to see it twice. 'When she came round afterwards she told me she had learnt my speech about the brain operation by heart. She wanted to get into the modern theatre.' However, perhaps partly because of her age, none of the new wave of writers and directors offered her a role during the 1960s. She herself admitted that given the choice she would really rather return to Greek drama, to play parts yet unexplored. 'I should like to play in the *Ion* of Euripides, or Hecuba in the play of *Hecuba*. But I'm pretty old now, you know, to go bouncing about.' She made no mention of Joe Orton, perhaps understandably. He and his lover Kenneth Halliwell had recently been caught stealing and damaging a number of library books. One of his creative paste-ups was of Sybil as Nurse Cavell, locked in a cell and staring at the mammoth genitalia of a superimposed Greek torso.

She remained very critical of the speech of actors. 'I think the modern writers are most exciting, in a way I think they have gone ahead of the actors. I'm thinking of speech: half of them don't work on their voices. They can act with their bodies and their faces, and express with their voices, but not with the words….I think it's a blemish on the whole of modern acting, not just classical playing.' She underlined her preference for 'solid tragedy and immense feeling', arguing after seeing *Porgy and Bess* that 'the future of the big theatre is with the Negroes; they don't mind pouring down with tears and saying banal sorts of things that would embarrass an English actor. We like reticence too much.'

As always she was deeply interested in the work of young actors, and their training. David Horovitch remembers her and Lewis visiting RADA, where they attended several classes, including one where two students were improvising carrying an imaginary piano up an imaginary staircase. 'She watched the exercise with rapt concentration, then suddenly jumped to her feet, exclaiming: "No, no, you'll never get it round the corner like that!" Then, with absolute seriousness, she issued a series of commands: "To you", "Take the strain", "Lower your end", until the corner had been negotiated.' Later, when the students met them on stage, John Theocharis was talking to Lewis: 'I was rather flattered by how intently he seemed to be listening to me, nodding his head in agreement as I enthused about their work in Greek tragedy, when I heard Sybil's voice rise above the din, saying: "Don't waste your breath, my dear! He's stone deaf, he couldn't hear you to save his life." She had a way of saying the brutally honest thing without making it sound cruel or insulting.'

Her relationship with Jane was still volatile. 'I had a bad flare-up with her on Monday,' she told John. 'She was really looking a frump – she was very annoyed at my mentioning it, and I went up in the air, because I said Lewis and I were very responsible to you for her.' Later she wrote: 'Jane and I are at the moment in complete accord. She's going to be all right – she will never have too easy a time with her temperament, and in some ways she and I are alike. But I wonder where she gets her very odd complications from – she has got a real touch of genius somewhere, whether theatre or writing or what I can't yet see, but we must be gentle with her.' Soon afterwards she was seeing the situation more clearly: 'I think from now Jane will manage her own life and won't want any help – not that she's had much, for all the intros I gave her were no good – so keep out of the way, Sybil!'

John Casson later wrote: 'Sybil cannot see any of her relations as other than babies to be controlled and directed.' Certainly Jane was not the only grandchild to be irritated by her tendency to pigeon-hole them, or insist they were destined for great careers. Glynis Casson, now an actress, remembers: 'When I was in my teens she gave us all a role, and made us all swans. This was annoying for me because the other ones were such good swans – Diana would be so clever, Jane was going to be a wonderful actress, Penny was the sensible one, whereas I was going to be a secretary to some nice man, whom I would marry. But then I got my voice trained, and suddenly for Sybil I was to be the great singer, which annoyed the hell out of all the other grandchildren.' Her sister Bronwen, who became a stage designer and worked at the Abbey in Dublin, backs up this view. 'When we heard about our cousins in Canada who were so wonderful, we absolutely hated them. It wasn't until Dirk and I compared notes later that we found they had the same feeling about us.'

In the spring of 1963, after *Vanity Fair* closed, Sybil and Lewis undertook a three-week recital tour with their programme *Some Men and Women*. Sybil wondered if Lewis would cope. 'I can't help feeling it's a bit much for him – but if I reject these offers he gets much more troubled,' she wrote to John. But work proved a good medicine: 'On the stage he is wonderful – better than this time last year.' His desire to preach his favourite gospel was seen by Stanley Wells at the annual Stratford poetry festival: 'Sybil was pretty infirm, but read 'The Lady of Shalott' in her great swinging voice. Lewis tried to give another reader advice about Poel's method of verse-speaking, and was unkindly snubbed.'

Despite being constantly in pain, Sybil continued to be remarkably active publicly. The critic J C Trewin, astonished at her off-stage life, wrote a paean of praise about her: 'Always she is opening this, speaking at that, writing a preface, lending her name to a cause, learning Greek or playing the piano, helping, soothing, suggesting, challenging. When she speaks she persuades with heart and soul and mind and voice. If she is on the platform, we feel that before long she will be taking wing into the audience....There is something blessedly immoderate about her. She is an idealist, a splendid crusader for all the things she loves, the causes she admires, the people she cherishes; by a crusade she means a crusade, not a mild hint. Her faith is with the present; her eyes are on the future.'

That Easter Sunday she took part in a matinee concert at the Festival Hall in London, organised by the Pro Arte Society in her honour, and to raise money for mentally handicapped and invalid children charities which she supported. 'Such a lark playing in the Toy Symphony of Haydn!' she reported. 'I am the drum and the quail!' The piece had Léon Goossens on trumpet and Millicent Martin on bird whistle; *The Times* music critic thought her 'a spirited virtuouso on the drum, not only bursting with rhythmic brio, but also commanding a wide dynamic range right down to the most delicate pianissimo'. The programme, conducted by Antony Hopkins, also included her favourite D minor concerto by Bach, and Peter O'Toole reading extracts from Haydn's diaries and letters. 'The most wonderful party I've ever had,' Sybil told the audience. 'Can I have a similar one when I'm a hundred?'

Despite being in her eighties, she retained her enthusiasm for travel and new experiences, as Christopher Fry recalled: 'She and Lewis came to tea with us in Little Venice, by the Grand Union Canal. She saw a boat go by, and suddenly said to Lewis: "We must do that for a holiday next summer, we must go down all the canals."' That summer they spent a week with Mary and Ian at a farmhouse near Ambleside in the Lake District. Although Lewis could scarcely see the rocks and stones at his feet, they ventured on to the slopes of Great Gable and Langdale Pike. But even amongst the lakes and fells work was not far away, as Mary recalls: 'They sat on the banks of Buttermere and rehearsed a scene from *Henry VIII*.'

In May Sybil took part in an evening to celebrate the re-opening after a closure of 133 years of the Georgian Theatre in Richmond, Yorkshire. Some while before she had launched an appeal for £15,000 to preserve and renovate the beautiful theatre. The prologue and epilogue to the programme of music and dramatic excerpts, both written by Ivor Brown, were spoken by Edith Evans and Sybil. Two days later she joined Lewis for a week of *Some Men and Women* at the Haymarket. She was nervous beforehand: 'I rather funk it, tho' what the hell does it matter at our age!' But her anxiety was unnecessary: 'We were a bit scared thinking London would be sniffy and not as warm as Australia, but the notices were splendid – even the ones who always crab everything – and we've never had more wonderful letters, which has cheered us a lot.'

The notices were indeed mostly glowing. Felix Barker enjoyed the rapport between 'these two fine artists, he sturdy of speech, she with her sweeping gestures, bird-like pounces and comic sniffs....See how they follow each other's words, partly with adoration, partly with anxiety, lest the other fluff.' The critic of *The Times* described the atmosphere as 'less that of a recital than of a drawing-room entertainment, with Sir Lewis as the genially grizzled host giving rock-like support to his bubblingly impulsive partner'. Only Tynan dissented, writing: 'When the Cassons seek to move us, the meaning gets lost in a blur of brandished words, and all we get is generalised grief.'

In the autumn they appeared in Judith Guthrie's *Queen Bee* which, according to its director David William, 'aspired to a Chekhovian texture, though in that respect it didn't get much beyond Dodie Smith'. Sybil had the central role of Lady Cuffe, the matriarch of the family, who 'carries the art of knowing what is best for her children to almost unprecedented lengths'. Isabeal Dean and Margot Boyd were also in the cast, while Lewis played the butler. It was his first new part since he had been unable to read. 'I record it on tape and he repeats it over and over,' Sybil explained.

David William recalls an incident in rehearsal: 'Occasionally Lewis would nab Isabel and start giving her notes. One day she had a bit of a weep, largely strategic. Sybil noticed this and gave him a talking to, after which he stopped doing it, and was completely professional.' As so often, once she had committed herself to a play Sybil tended to praise it, but not always wisely. Before rehearsals began she thought *Queen Bee* 'a good tale and wittily told', a play that was 'going to be great fun', and one that 'we do like so much'. Once it was running she saw other elements: 'The play is very interesting taken not quite in the comedy way – there is a macabre feeling in it...it is quite subtle and can be translated symbolically with peoples and countries.'

But she was now having difficulty with her lines: although she learned them as fast as before, she had to keep refreshing her memory. 'We're in the worst stages now and I'm all hair-fluffy with words,' she confessed. A week before opening in Windsor she wrote: 'I don't know where I am – it's so difficult and I get so tired'. Yet the play was well received there and elsewhere. In Brighton Jack Tinker noted 'a brilliant performance by the indefatigable Dame Sybil... sweeping around in grey chiffon and being amusingly eccentric with a string of worn-out slang'. But the producer Murray MacDonald decided not to risk the play in the West End.

Bronson Albery once said of Sybil, 'She's magnificent, if you can keep her arms below her shoulders.' But it was not always easy to do so, or to keep her from overdoing it vocally. The director Hugh Wooldridge, who knew Sybil through his mother Margaretta Scott, recalls a story of her proclaiming to the Gods during a matinee on tour in Westcliff-on-Sea. 'The manager came up afterwards and said: "That was a marvellous performance, but there was no need to act for upstairs, because this afternoon all the audience were downstairs." Sybil replied: "Young man, *you* know there's no one sitting upstairs, *I* know there's no one sitting upstairs, but the people in the *stalls* don't know that."'

Before *Queen Bee* Guthrie had told David William: 'Don't let Damie overact!' But sometimes he found her doing so. 'Sybil on form was very strong and charismatic, but she could be erratic,' he says. 'After one excellent performance, the next was full of excess and grotesquerie. Round I went to her dressing-room, which she shared with Lewis. Something like the following dialogue took place. *Sybil*: Hello darling, went well, don't you think? *Me*: I'm afraid not, Sybil. *Sybil*: What do you mean? *Me*: Not a patch on last night. *Sybil*: Oh well, we can't be the same every time. *Me*: Granted, but there was so much over-acting and exaggeration (*then desperately*) – wasn't there, Lewis? *Lewis* (*glumly putting on his trousers*): You mean all that hooting she was doing? *Sybil* (*bright as a button*): Oh lord, sorry! Better luck next time.'

Her latest television appearance was on the popular, ground-breaking satirical programme *That Was the Week That Was*, in a sketch by Keith Waterhouse and Willis Hall about an agony aunt replying to letters supposedly written by Cabinet ministers about their marital problems. Ned Sherrin, the show's producer, recalled: 'She hadn't appeared before a live studio audience before, nor used a teleprompter, but she quite liked it once she got used to it, especially when we started rehearsing and her lines got big laughs. She told me to bring her down if she went over the top. When it came to the live transmission she was obviously quite nervous, her hand was trembling as she held the dictaphone to dictate her letters. So she slapped it with her other hand, and everything was all right.'

Her second appearance on the show that year was in very different circumstances. On the evening of 22 November 1963 she was at the Dorchester Hotel, helping to present the Guild of Television Producers awards. As dinner was about to begin the president broke the news that President Kennedy had been assassinated. Ned Sherrin was there to accept an award from Sybil for *TW3*: 'We had to scrap the next night's programme and write an entirely new one,' he remembered. 'Caryl Brahms wrote a sonnet about Jackie Kennedy. I rang Sybil to ask if she would do it. She said: "Yes, as long as it's not funny!" In she came and magisterially delivered it.'

Like the rest of the world, Sybil was shocked by Kennedy's assassination. 'I felt simply bowled over,' she wrote to John that Sunday. 'What a lunatic country America is, and so violent. Thank God for the monarchy, and politics not being so violent here.... We've just heard the six o'clock news that the man who shot him has himself been shot. – Isn't the waste awful? That poor little wife – a young man like that, and doing such splendid work.' Like the world in general, she found it hard to come to terms with the traumatic event. 'I had to read a poem last night on television written for Mrs Kennedy. It nearly did me in. What a world – we are all shattered.'

40

Later Stages

1964–1966

'It's not a masterpiece, but if one waits for a masterpiece
one would never do a thing'
Sybil on Season of Goodwill

The British theatre in those years was about to see the emergence of a new group of playwrights, most notably Edward Bond, Peter Nichols, Christopher Hampton, Tom Stoppard, Joe Orton and Charles Wood. Although Sybil remained interested as a theatregoer in much of this new work, the plays she chose to appear in during her last years on stage, sometimes on the advice of Harold Hobson, were mostly conventional pieces, and generally of a poor quality. Now more than ever, with Lewis less able to help, she was at the mercy of her first instincts about a script, which were not always sound.

In October 1963, in the wake of the Profumo affair that fascinated the country and rocked the Conservative government, Harold Macmillan resigned as prime minister. He was succeeded by the Earl of Home who, renouncing his peerage, became plain Alec Douglas-Home. His brother William immediately sat down and wrote *The Reluctant Peer*, a thinly disguised version of the real-life events within his family. It was the kind of play that was becoming increasingly rare in the West End – it had a French window and a butler who answered the phone – but Sybil as so often jumped at it impulsively, accepting the leading role the day she read the script.

The plot hinged on the attempts by the family of an earl to stop him giving up his peerage on becoming prime minister. Sybil played his mother the Dowager Countess, in a company that included Naunton Wayne, Frank Pettingell, Helen Horton, Imogen Hassall and Bette Bourne. The latter recalls his fear as the London first night approached: 'During the dress rehearsal there was a pause to solve a lighting problem, and she said wearily, "Will I ever know it?" She was genuinely terrified. But when we opened there was not a moment's hesitation. She tore the wallpaper off the walls, she shook the whole play, she was a real leading lady, she led us out into the sea. Her energy made it a success.'

Her vehement performance was praised, notably by Bernard Levin, who wrote: 'As the prying old woman she gets her fangs deep into the meatiest part she has had for years, and the gravy fairly drips down her chin with the relish and zest she brings to her playing.' But the notices were generally poor. *Theatre World* derided the play for its 'stereotyped characters, hollow action and political name-dropping', while Irving Wardle in *The Times* stated bluntly: 'Sybil Thorndike's association with the play is a saddening mystery.' She was once again baffled by the critics' apparent short-sightedness, complaining to John: 'The play's humour is so subtle and I enjoy it more and more. The critics didn't get it at all – but they only want avant-garde and classics now, so boring they are – or rather bored.'

The play was a commercial success despite the critics, running for eighteen months at the Duchess. Having committed herself to another play that autumn, after six months she reluctantly left the cast, and was replaced by Athene Seyler. The new play was Arthur Marshall's *Season of Goodwill*, adapted from the novel by the American Dorothea Malm. It told the story of three elderly Americans, two sisters and a brother, whose home is invaded at Christmas time by younger members of the family. Lewis was offered the role of the brother, but turned it down, feeling there was not enough time to learn it properly. 'It's a very distinguished play so we do hope it will go,' Sybil mused with her usual optimism.

It was a severe challenge for her physically, as she would be on stage virtually all the time. The director was Vivien Matalon, with Gwen Ffrangcon-Davies and Paul Rogers playing the other principals. 'I was frightened that these three wonderful actors wouldn't be interested in my ideas,' he recalls. 'But it was quite the opposite. Sybil was an angel to work with. She had a habit of turning out front when she had a really good line. It was her end-of-the-pier instinct and I tried to stop her. She said she had to do it, and I said: "I do wish your taste matched your talent." Lewis was there and applauded. After that I could see her about to turn, and then she would remember. She was a wonderful talent. I'm a gay man, but I found her very sexy.'

Her closeness to Lewis was very apparent. 'He was waiting for her in the hotel in Oxford,' Matalon recalls. 'When she came in he jumped up like a little boy, and kissed her. They were obviously still in love.' Paul Rogers remembers them on train journeys: 'Sybil treated him with such tender loving care, spending the entire journey reading to him. Her hugeness of heart was wonderful, but it created problems for others when you were touring: if you stayed in digs she and Lewis had been in you never heard the end of it, because landladies throughout the country adored them.' But according to Arthur Marshall she was bored with people calling her saint-like. 'She would say, I'm not a saint, ask Lewis. And he would say, No, no, she's not, she sometimes throws things at me!'

The pre-London tour began at Brighton, where Olivier and Joan Plowright came to see the play. Olivier was critical of the accents and other elements of the production, and told Sybil so. This made her uncharacteristically cross. 'Larry's a pick, he just loves to criticise,' she told Marshall. 'With him it's pick, pick, pick all the time.' The question of accents came up in unexpected form at a performance in Newcastle, when Gwen Ffrangcon-Davies fell and disappeared behind the sofa. Sybil, in very English tones, cried out: 'Are you all right, dear?' to which she replied: 'Ah sure am, honey! Ah didn't hurt mahself none' – thus, as Marshall observed, 'smartly removing the action to somewhere in the Deep South'. However, the play received some good notices on tour, although Peter Preston for the *Guardian* described it as 'the theatre of the nothing-in-particular, theatre of the genteel yawn'.

The London critics were unenthusiastic. The Theatre of Cruelty based on the ideas of Artaud was then in fashion, but Martin Esslin in a withering review argued that there could be nothing crueller than subjecting two distinguished actresses to such a pointless piece: 'What Roman gladiatorial contests or public executions on Tyburn could compete with the cruel obscenity of having an eighty-two-year-old actress deliver obscenely trite and meretricious observations about death?' he asked. The *Theatre World* critic thought the play slow and over-literary, but praised the two actresses, who 'brought their consummate acting skills to the rescue, and brilliantly succeeded in creating two entirely different women out of a torrent of words'.

The play closed after less than three weeks. As always, Sybil remained stout in its defence, and furious with the critics. 'Very stupid notices, no one critic seeing below the surface,' she complained to John. 'But the people that come *do* – Noël Coward, John Gielgud thrilled with it. It's too delicate for the Theatre of Cruelty, which the critics now praise so.' She also defended her decision to get involved in a play that, at least in retrospect, she realised was flawed. 'It's not a masterpiece, but if one waits for a masterpiece one would never do a thing.'

Having some unexpected spare time, she and Lewis spent it seeing the plays in London that the critics praised. What she saw often depressed her. 'The whole theatre is musicals or the *Who's Afraid of Virginia Woolf* type,' she complained. She hated Osborne's *Inadmissable Evidence* ('boring and ugly') and Joe Orton's *Entertaining Mr Sloane* ('amusing but intolerably vulgar and dirty'). After seeing the latter she observed: 'I hate this extreme sex emphasis – playwrights ignore other aspects of life – ignore the problems that aren't sexual or drunkenness. I get so fed up with drunks!'

Yet she was open to a truly challenging work such as Peter Brook's production of *Marat/Sade*, which was certainly Theatre of Cruelty: 'tremendous' was her verdict. She also thought Brecht a wonderful writer: 'I think his underlying idea of simplicity has done a lot. He's given a sort of cosmic feeling to the theatre that is very fine.' She loved Shakespeare productions with a difference. She was impressed with David Warner's modern Hamlet, feeling that Peter Hall's RSC production 'gave a very new outlook on the play'. But like many others she had reservations about Olivier's Othello at the National: 'Larry is wonderful – tho' he hasn't fulfilled one as Othello, in spite of his superb notices. It's a terrific impersonation of a Negro, but not Othello.' Olivier, she felt, was a greater comedian than tragedian.

At home she played her grand piano for at least an hour each day, always keen to try out new works. 'I shall start on them this morning,' she told composer Herbert Howells, after he sent her some of his music. 'Some will be beyond me I'm sure, but I always loved your music.' She liked to play around with hymn tunes, adding her own choruses to them. She retained her love of Bach, aiming to play one of his 48 preludes and fugues every day. 'My piano is a great joy and stimulant,' she said. She also loved to play Mozart, although her appreciation of his operas was unusual: writing about the Promenade Concerts in the *Radio Times*, she stated: 'That's one of the wonderful things about Mozart, isn't it? You never have to worry about the story, but just sit back and listen to all that lovely music.'

For the 400th anniversary of Shakespeare's birth she gave a recital for the Poetry Society, and on the actual birthday a reading in Westminster Abbey – 'a lovely little thirty-minute service in Poets' Corner just by his statue' – when she spoke two sonnets and a quartet of celebrated speeches from the plays. In July she attended a party at Buckingham Palace for leading actors, writers and critics, where she met some old friends. 'La Reine had just a long friendly chat with us, and we had a very matey, jolly one with Princess Marina. I had a lovely new hat and a white-figured frock and Lewis was in a lounge suit and good tie. I'll never be surprised if he goes to one of these affairs in his pyjamas – he hates tidy clothes!'

She was probably the only guest there to be a regular reader of the Communist Party's *Daily Worker*. The following month her photo appeared in advertisements for the paper, together with her view that it was 'an entertaining, honest and courageous' paper. The comment had been taken from a tribute she had given the previous year in an anniversary edition. Confronted with the advertisement by the journalist Hunter Davies, she explained: 'I'm not a communist. For a start I'm religious. I'm an Anglo-Catholic. But I've always been a red-hot socialist. As I've got older I feel things stronger than ever. One also sees other people's points of view more clearly.' Told that someone had called her praise of the paper an insult to the Crown and demanded she renounce her Damehood, she replied spiritedly: 'What rubbish! All Dames should read the *Daily Worker*.'

When the paper was re-launched later as the *Morning Star*, Sybil set the presses running, and was made a temporary member of the printers' union. In her speech she explained that she was an old-fashioned socialist, an Anglican and a pacifist, 'a mixture of which Mr Marx might disapprove'. Meanwhile she polished her Labour credentials by campaigning for Hugh Jenkins, the candidate in Putney, during the October 1964 general election, which the party won narrowly, with Harold Wilson becoming prime minister. Her loyalty to Labour was reflected in a lunch held in her honour at the House of Commons by the Society of Labour Lawyers, with Attlee, Jennie Lee and Bernard Levin among the guests.

She returned to the theatre in the spring of 1965 in *Return Ticket* by William Corlett. The play was directed at the Duchess by Joan Knight, with Megs Jenkins and Ursula Howells starring alongside Sybil. Set in a northern guest house, it was a weak, old-fashioned piece, in which she played a curmudgeonly grandmother joyfully putting the boot in to her daughter's messy love life. The play came off after three months, Peter Saunders rejecting an offer from Sybil to work without salary to keep it afloat.

For once she was not happy with the play. But nor was Corlett keen on her playing. 'She was from a different world, she was bringing Grand Guignol into the present,' he remembered. 'She wasn't curbable, she had that soaring tone. Joan Knight was nervous of her, and pretty much left her to get on with it. She needed someone she already trusted.' Heather Stoney, also in the company, could see the director's dilemma: 'Sybil was playing this elderly woman, yet she would skip about the stage like a spring lamb. It used to drive Joan mad; she couldn't slow her down.' She remembers a note she received from Lewis. 'He was sitting in the front row for the dress rehearsal. Sybil told us: "Lewis says you should speak up, you need to be heard right at the back." And I thought, it's just dear Lewis, he can't hear us!'

In fact Lewis was so low one day Sybil said to Corlett: 'Do say hello to Lewis, he's nearly dead.' He had just come through a crisis, possibly linked to his depression, or his continuing guilt at having been unfaithful to Sybil. Whatever its cause, Sybil was keen to put it behind them, and be positive: 'Sometimes a crisis or a trouble enlarges one,' she told John. 'We've had a wonderful life together, if somewhat turbulent and over-emotionalised! But we've been very happy together and have passed through one crisis – and at least given it its right proportion – so no more need be said.'

She gave yet more recitals – in her local Chelsea church, in Southwark Cathedral, at the National Book League. With Lewis she did readings for the Apollo Society, and recitals at the annual event in Smallhythe and at Benenden School in Kent. Occasionally she worked with an orchestra, as when she narrated Poulenc's 'Babar the Elephant' at the Kensington Town Hall. She went further afield, to Newcastle, Middlesborough and to Richmond, Yorkshire. Sylvia Craythorne, whose mother had raised the money to refurbish Richmond's beautiful Georgian Theatre, recalls her recital there: 'The audience included Bright Young Things and country, sporting types. They were all spellbound, it was absolutely magical, she was so moving and beautiful.'

She still took great pains with her voice, which could sound surprisingly young, as the actress Margaretta Scott remembered: 'As I went to ring the bell at Swan Court I heard a young girl singing. I thought it was Sybil giving someone singing lessons, but when I asked her who this wonderful singer was, she said: "Darling, it was me, doing my voice exercises."' Her vocal versatility is impressive in the many recordings she made in these years. She could capture the dark mournful quality of Tennyson's ballads, the vibrant alliteration of Gerard Manley Hopkins' verse, and the speed and wit of Browning's narrative poems. She also recorded some of her best-known Shakespearean roles, notably a strong, earthy Emilia with Dorothy Tutin as Desdemona in the willow-song scene from *Othello*, and Queen Katharine in her favourite scene from *Henry VIII*, in which she subtly demonstrates the queen's dignity and simplicity, but also her inner power.

The artist Claude Marks was one of many who persuaded her to sit for him, in this case at Swan Court. It was not a straightforward task. 'Although most cooperative as a model, she was not easy to draw,' he wrote. 'She had the kind of face that needed to be seen in animation. Dissatisfied with my first efforts, I found that I was more successful when she was listening to music on the radio. Then her features had a gentle inward quality, for music appealed to her deepest sensibilities. But even that was a different look from her expression when responding to people or to an amusing situation. An American actress friend of mine said of one of the drawings: "She has the eyes of a sixteen-year-old girl."'

Her youthful gaiety appealed to her grandchildren. When the Campbell family came to England all six stayed in the Swan Court flat, while Sybil and Lewis moved temporarily to another one downstairs. Tom Campbell loved her company: 'She was a deliciously warm grandmother. She was so elegant, but so easy to be with and talk to. She was always pulling faces and making us laugh. She had a great gift of playfulness, which made children love her.' But sometimes her enthusiasm could be embarrassing, as Teresa Campbell recalls. 'I was in an art class at my primary school in Fulham, painting in the corner, and suddenly there was Granny Sybil at the other end of the room – "Teresa daaaahling!" – and rushing across to greet me. I just wanted the earth to swallow me up.'

In March 1965 Sybil told John: 'So many of our friends now are dying, but that's because *we* are so old – and we feel it more.' She was present at several memorial services, including those for Donald Wolfit, Diana Wynyard and Ada Reeve, often giving the address. She read a poem and a psalm in a memorial concert for Myra Hess in St Paul's Cathedral. Afterwards she wrote to Joyce Grenfell to thank her for the tribute she had written about their friend. 'Oh! what a beautiful thing to have done, and so true and big somehow. What a gift to her and to all of us who love her – I shall put it in one of her books to remember always.' Another death that deeply saddened her was Clemence Dane's. 'Lewis and I feel a bit of our life has gone. She was such an exhilarating friend – always one of my stimulants she was. I had to do a reading last night at the Lyric Hammersmith, and some stanzas of Shelley's "Adonais". It was hard not to cry – it all suggested Winifred.' She and Lewis later attended her memorial service: 'It was glorious, perfect, no address, lovely hymns and music.'

For what proved to be her last appearance on a London stage, Sybil opted for a truly archaic vehicle. The American writer Joseph Kesselring's black comedy *Arsenic and Old Lace* was about two elderly spinster sisters living in Brooklyn, who poison their lonely gentlemen lodgers with doctored elderberry wine as an act of charitable kindness. The play had been a huge hit during the war, with Lilian Braithwaite and Mary Jerrold in the lead roles. Sybil had seen it twice in a week and roared with laughter. Now, for its first London revival, under the direction of Murray MacDonald, she and Athene Seyler played the sisters. The cast included Richard Briers, Julia Lockwood and David Andrews, with Lewis playing the superintendent of the mental home who appears at the end of the play.

Simply to appear on the stage at ninety was clearly a risk for him, especially as he had to negotiate his way down a flight of stairs carrying a pile of luggage. 'I just pray he can do it, as it will give him a great kick. He should bring the house down,' she told John. David Andrews remembers how she looked after him. 'He was nearly blind, so she recorded the whole play on her tape recorder. At the read-through, by which time she already knew her part, Lewis would intone the stage directions in his scene: she had taught him these as well. She ministered to him the whole time. He wouldn't have been able to do it without her.'

After the first performance at the Vaudeville she wrote gleefully: 'The play went with a bang last night – never had such curtain calls. Lewis fine – we're feeling very jolly about the play.' The critics thought it little more than a one-joke farce; one or two even thought it tasteless. But the partnership of the two much-loved stars was much enjoyed. Darlington called it 'a real acting treat'; Wardle praised 'an exquisitely comic relationship…superbly played'; and Levin thought Sybil splendid: 'Clearly enjoying every wicked moment, she floats effortlessly up and down, in and out of innumerable impossible situations, with a calm, majestic certainty of her own rectitude.'

Richard Briers, playing the sisters' nephew Mortimer Brewster, remembers the production clearly. 'Before the audience arrived, Sybil used to sit with Lewis reading the Bible: it was touching, they were very nervous. But when the curtain went up, she and Athene were like two old warhorses, they smelt the audience. They each got a huge round on their entrance. It was all so dated, all rather grand mannerly. But they couldn't half act, and they really enjoyed themselves.' They also occasionally misbehaved: 'Twice we got the giggles on stage,' Sybil confessed. 'I can pull myself together with anyone in the world except Athene.'

Athene herself told Richard Briers: 'I love Sybil dearly, but she does drive me mad, everything is so *positive*!' The two of them so enjoyed having arguments in the wings, they sometimes had to be pushed on at the last minute. Once they were talking so animatedly they missed their cue, leaving Richard Briers to carry on expressing horror at greater length than usual at the discovery of yet another corpse. Lewis played his part by numbers: he would count six and then someone would shake his hand, then three and a chair was there for him to sit down, and so on.

This turned out to be his final London stage appearance as well as Sybil's – and nearly his last anywhere. At one performance his head suddenly dropped to the table, and he started to make funny sounds. Briers, standing by the prompt corner, was terrified. 'I said to the stage manager, "Get ready to take the curtain down, he's going to die on stage." He remained conscious, but unable to speak. Sybil said all his lines, the curtain came down, and she helped him off. We took our bow without him, but then Sybil turned up stage and bellowed "Lewis!" He came on, bumped his head, staggered over and took a bow. Afterwards Sybil said: "I'm terribly sorry, I forgot to feed him!"'

Sometimes she found her pain almost unendurable. One night the producer Peter Saunders found her contorted in her dressing-room, and suggested she shouldn't appear that night. But she would have none of it: as she frequently said, 'I shall carry on as long as I can stand up.' Briers recalls people coming round to see her between shows on Saturdays. 'She was so tired, but she would always see them, she'd just lean against the wall in the corridor. She was so patient and a real trouper, always giving, giving, giving.'

41

E M Forster and Adam Faith

1966–1968

'It's women like that who built the empire for England'
Adam Faith on Sybil during Night Must Fall

Sybil's love/hate relationship with television continued until the end of her days. She accepted the work because it was well paid, but she often hated the experience. The small screen, she felt, was too restrictive for her sort of acting. Yet in one play at least, an adaptation of E M Forster's *A Passage to India*, she gave an exquisitely restrained and memorable performance.

Sybil knew the novel well, and thought it magnificent. She wrote to Forster of her delight in being cast: 'Yes, to my joy I *am* playing Mrs Moore in the TV. I've missed playing her three times in the theatre owing to other playings – and now I'm so very delighted I've the chance. I'm a very old girl now, though I don't feel it.' The play also starred Zia Mohyeddin as Dr Aziz, Cyril Cusack as Mr Fielding, and Virginia McKenna as the young and earnest Adela Quested, whose visit to the famous Marabar Caves with Dr Aziz destroys several lives and severely damages Anglo-Indian relations. Hugh Whitemore had been commissioned to adapt the novel for the BBC, but it was then discovered that Forster wanted the original stage adaptation by the novelist Santha Rama Rau to be used. The director Waris Hussein paid him a visit, and persuaded him to let him use some scenes from the book, including Mrs Moore's meeting with Aziz in the mosque. 'Knowing his fondness for India, I used my Indianness to sit at his feet, putting on a look of adoration, so that he would grant some of my requests.'

Shooting was mainly done in Ealing Studios, from where Sybil wrote: 'This film part is sheer hell for hanging around, but I'm enjoying very much all the Indians and Pakistanis – I'm getting a lot of light on India from them.'

Hussein was impressed by her interpretation of the part. 'She was born to play Mrs Moore,' he suggests. 'She was the right age, because she's dying, and at the same time she has the wisdom of life. There was a dignity about Sybil, but it wasn't a grande dame one. She got the slightly mysterious quality in the mosque scene, and her mixture of awe and fear when she wakes from her sleep. She was spot on with every take, and word perfect. She just did it wonderfully. She was exactly as Forster had written the character.'

For Virginia McKenna acting with Sybil was a delight. 'You were never intimidated, because it felt so real and genuine, you felt you were talking to Mrs Moore. It all came from within, she never superimposed; it came from a deep understanding of the character. She was very economical, which a lot of actresses aren't.' The morning after it was shown on television, to widespread praise and good notices, Sybil told John: 'I dislike myself on TV more than I can say!' She pursued a similar theme in response to a letter of congratulations from Forster: 'I'm glad if you were pleased. I felt it was nothing like the power of the book, but in 60 minutes it's not possible, and if it makes a few more people read the book, then that is well. I loved Mrs Moore, but I am not wild on TV as a medium to express her! She's bigger than that.'

After this success she appeared in two Armchair Theatre productions for ABC Television, both directed by Paterick Dromgoole. *Man and Mirror* by Robert Muller was a Gothic horror story, also starring Richard Pasco and Denholm Elliott. 'I found Sybil mesmerising,' Dromgoole recalls. 'It was her sheer presence, the fusion of her voice and authority. You knew you had her complete concentration, even though she was gazing at you quite fondly. It was difficult when directing others not to be aware of her. She had a considerable intellect, although she pretended not to have. She also had a wonderful sense of humour, she was endlessly taking the micky.'

Dromgoole also directed *Don't Utter a Note*, with Peter Bowles, Athene Seyler and Sid James – who spent much of rehearsals on the phone to his bookie. 'She and Sid got on like a house on fire, even though their backgrounds couldn't be more different,' Dromgoole recalls. Her unstarry demeanour also appealed to Bowles: 'I didn't feel any grandeur from her at all, she was just a friendly working actress; you could have been in rep with her.' But he did pick up a little competitiveness between her and Athene Seyler. 'If they were called individually to rehearsals, they would each be very sprightly. When they came together, each would try to appear older than the other – that was the act.' Peter Copley noticed a contrast between them: 'Sybil was looking old, she was a bit slow, and didn't always remember her lines, whereas Athene was prompt, brisk and keen, and would prompt her when she forgot.' At the end Sybil wrote: 'I dislike TV more than I can say, and I don't want to do it again. It's a hateful medium and ruinous to real acting.'

Radio, however, was a different matter. As always, many of the plays were ones she had appeared in on stage, such as *The Women of Troy*, *Henry VIII*, *The Linden Tree*, *Waiting in the Wings* and *The Potting Shed*. John Powell, who directed the latter play, tried to set up a production of *Peer Gynt*, with Richardson, Sybil and Olivier repeating their 1944 stage roles. 'Sybil couldn't wait, I kept having letters from her asking when I was going to do it,' he remembers. 'It was all arranged, then at the last minute Olivier said he couldn't do it. He was very sensitive about his voice, and felt he couldn't get it on radio. I asked Richardson if we could try Scofield, but he said he couldn't do it without Olivier. But Sybil said, Any time, any where, I'll be there.' On *The Potting Shed* she brought Lewis with her to the studio. This was a mixed blessing, as actress Jane Wenham recalls: 'One day a hum was detected, and everyone tried to find the source. Finally they realised it was Lewis' hearing aid turned up too high. Sybil said: "Wake up Lewis, you're creating a disturbance!"'

Lewis was increasingly reliant on his family. As well as Sybil on the piano, he loved to listen to Mary singing folk songs, especially the old Welsh ones. 'His favourite was "David and the White Rock",' Mary's husband Ian Haines remembers. 'He used to sit there on Sunday evenings with tears trickling down his cheeks.' He also loved classical music, as was clear when he was Roy Plomley's guest on *Desert Island Discs*: his choice covered works by Bach, Mendelssohn, Mozart, Schubert, Stravinsky, Eric Coates and Peter Warlock. His final choice was 'Now Thank We All Our God', which he and Sybil would always sing at key moments of their lives – at the end of a tour, a run of a play, or as a farewell after a visit to their children abroad. Music, he said, 'has always been a hobby and an inspiration'. Poignantly, he confessed that his blindness meant he would have to do without a book on the island; instead he chose to take a miniature portrait of Sybil, painted in their Gaiety days.

Yet his mind was alert as ever. He and Sybil took part in the radio programme 'The Lively Arts', prompting *The Times* to comment: 'Anyone who thinks this incomparable couple belong to history must pretty soon have realised their error, for here they were giving us some of the shrewdest dramatic criticism we could ever hope to hear.' Sybil also gave some shrewd if unexpected advice to Olivier, then creating his controversial Othello at the

National. In his diary he wrote: 'Stage fright – painful tautness.' The next day he sought Sybil and Lewis' advice. 'Take drugs, darling, we do,' she told him, though she was apparently referring to valium rather than anything harder. Perhaps even that was not needed for her brief appearance at the Royal Court that summer. Her old friend George Devine had died in January, and along with Olivier, Coward, Osborne and many others, she took part in a gala performance to raise money for the George Devine Award for helping new writers. Appearing as an elderly waitress in a scene from Wesker's *The Kitchen*, she had to drop her plates on the line 'I'm not used to this way of working.'

The year was a mixed one for her and Lewis. The death of Susan Holmes, their secretary for 48 years, hit Sybil hard. 'She was like a sister, and one of the most selflessly good people I have ever met,' she wrote in a tribute. 'Lewis and I have lost our dearest friend – a most shrewd critic both in the theatre and in daily life.' There was pleasure at the return of Wilson's Labour government. But there was also a very special day in Oxford. She had already received honorary doctorates from the universities of Manchester, Edinburgh and Southampton, and would later receive others from Surrey and Durham. But nothing could match the occasion in June when, along with the artist John Piper and four others, she and Lewis were made doctors of literature by Oxford University, hers also being for her support for good causes.

Speaking in Latin in the Sheldonian Theatre, the Public Orator called her 'an artist of true nobility, who captivates our eyes, our ears, our hearts… for so many years you have moved us by your supreme art both to tears and to laughter'. Sybil wrote John and Patricia a lengthy, blow-by-blow account of the occasion, delighting in its theatricality and her costume of scarlet and grey robes: 'We processed through crowds (who clapped Lewis and me and called out our names – *our* public!), right up the Broad we went at funereal pace – but all scarlet and looking fine…and into this glorious Sheldonian Theatre where great ceremonies are held….One by one we were called up by the Public Orator to stand beside him while he read out a long bit about us in Latin (I was cheered to hear Sybillimus Thorndike and Lewis Ludovico Casson). Then we went up six steps and were shaken by the hand by the chancellor, Harold Macmillan, and told we were now Doctors of Letters – all in Latin.' She ended ecstatically: 'It's been the Crown of our Life and we feel at the Top!'

Meanwhile another honour was on the horizon. Many theatres have been named after actors, but fewer after actresses. In 1967 Sybil was asked by Hazel

Vincent Wallace, the director of Leatherhead Theatre in Surrey, if she would allow a proposed new theatre to be given her name. 'I'd be honoured – oh very much – to have the new theatre with my name attached,' she replied. 'Yes, thrilled. I'll be able to come down and perform one day if I'm still on my legs.' It seemed appropriate that, for such a life-long advocate of touring, the building should be situated outside the West End.

She and Lewis were involved from the start, inspecting the model, witnessing the signing of the building contract, and taking part in the inauguration and topping-out ceremonies. Sybil recorded the message asking the audience to return to their seats after the interval, while the space to be used as a base for a youth theatre was named the Casson Room. The actor Clive Francis was present at the inauguration, to start the demolition of the cinema standing on the site. 'Without the aid of a microphone Sybil made one of her impassioned speeches. Then she swung the bottle of champagne attached to a rope, aiming to hit the wall. After her third failure to reach it, Lewis grabbed it, and smashed it first time. "That's why I married him!" Sybil intoned with great glee.'

As the project got under way, Sybil began work on *The Viaduct*, by the French writer Marguerite Duras. Suggested to her by Harold Hobson, the play was based on a famous real-life murder case in France, when a railwayman and his wife killed a deaf-mute cousin without any obvious motive. Sybil found it obscure and difficult on first reading, but felt it had 'something I wanted to express'. A production was arranged at the Yvonne Arnaud in Guildford, with Max Adrian cast as her husband, and Laurier Lister directing.

It was another role where she had to be on stage throughout. 'I have to get it in my head slowly, it's so difficult,' she told John. But just as she had done so, a crisis arose: Duras decided the play wasn't good or modern enough, and completely re-wrote it. When she received the new version Sybil was shattered. 'It was *awful* – not the same play at all – horribly boring, and I said I wouldn't do it,' she fumed. After a lot of argument Duras agreed to revert to the original script. Glad to have stood her ground, Sybil found rehearsals exhausting but rewarding: 'It's a *hell* of a part, though I like it very much and find it in some odd way a releasing of lots of emotion,' she wrote. She thought it a profound piece, telling George Rylands: 'It's not Grand Guignol at all, but I think a very important play. I haven't enjoyed anything so much for years.'

Once again she was at odds with most of the critics, who found the play undramatic, the dialogue unreal ('Nothing remains but the memory of having forgotten' was an example), and the characters unconvincing: 'cardboard cutouts who would seem two-dimensional in an Agatha Christie thriller', wrote Alan Brien in the *Sunday Times*. Sybil and Max Adrian chose to play it as melodrama: 'Eyes bulge, jaws quiver, and tables are clutched with ferocious intensity,' Michael Billington observed in *Plays and Players*, while Philip Hope-Wallace saw them 'radiate sparks of madness and the right gibbering for this kind of intellectual Grand Guignol'. But Hobson, who perhaps had a special interest in its success, judged Sybil to have given 'one of the most riveting and creative performances, both beautiful and terrible, of a long career studded with memorable achievement'.

The Viaduct played to packed houses for three weeks, but the adverse notices ruled out a London run. Sybil was hugely disappointed: 'I've not loved a play so much since the Greeks and Saint Joan,' she told John. 'It's been a rewarding experience – I've been able to "cast off" something in this play – and I have had some very wonderful letters expressing the same thing – letters of such depth I've never had before.' Loyal to the last, she felt her performance would have been better opposite Lewis. 'Max Adrian is a character actor and plays like a French character actor – Lewis would have been true and symbolic and we'd have played as *one*.'

In the summer of 1967 they stayed for two months with Ann and her family in Minneapolis, Minnesota, their first decent holiday for years. Douglas was acting and directing at the open-stage Guthrie, which Sybil thought 'a gem of beauty…much nicer than Chichester or Stratford'. He was about to open in Guthrie's stunning masked production of Aeschylus' *The Oresteia*, which Guthrie had re-titled *The House of Atreus*. Douglas was playing both Pallas Athena and Clytemnestra, the latter in a manner apparently modelled on Sybil. She and Lewis attended rehearsals: 'We're waiting for the dress rehearsal of the big Greek masks play to begin – it's tremendous, and so applicable to the time.' She wished, she told Tanya Moisiewitch, the play's designer, that she and Lewis had been able to do a production in masks.

Ever the tourist, she paid a visit to Lake Minnetonka where she had played with Ben Greet's company in 1905, and took trips with the family down the St Croix and Mississippi rivers. 'It was a glorious trip with friends,' she wrote after one expedition. 'We loved every minute, getting back by bright star night. We saw a satellite moving across the sky – a thrill.' But there was also a moment of great emotional upset, as Diana Devlin remembers: 'A former lover of Lewis made contact; she was having trouble with her child, so the question arose, Was it Lewis'? It wasn't.' Their grandson Dirk Campbell was there at the time: 'I think Granny knew about most of Lewis' affairs, but on this trip she found out about this one, with a friend of hers that he had previously denied. I slept along the corridor, and heard this terrible wailing: "Darling, of *course* I love you!" – "Oh but Lewis, how *could* you!"'

Inevitably it was not purely a holiday. Sybil taught a week's acting workshop at the University of Minnesota. One participant, Kathleen McCreery, recalls how she helped another student work on Juliet. 'She didn't talk down to her, she tried to enthuse, to inspire. Her warm smile, her infectious laugh, made us feel that she trusted us to understand and to share her passion. Suddenly, without warning, she bounded up on the stage, and we watched spellbound as this elderly woman was transformed into a young girl in the throes of first love. Her Juliet was the most believable I've ever seen.' She and Lewis also gave a recital, which Teresa Campbell recalls. 'I remember thinking before-hand how tiny and incredibly small she seemed walking down the corridor, but on stage she was this extraordinary tall woman, with amazing arms and beautiful drapery.'

She found Ann's family 'very lively, tall and clever', she told John. She also met another grandchild: 'Jane is coming over from Canada on Sunday, and we're living for it.' As she told George Rylands not long before: 'Jane is being splendid – went off into the blue from Australia for Canada, and has found lots of work, and does a cabaret and shows on her own between whiles – musicals and all, she's doing – she's a grand gal.' She had joined the company at Stratford, Ontario, where she would stay for five years, starting with walk-ons and understudies, and eventually playing major Shakespearean roles such as Beatrice and Helena. She also toured a programme of poetry, sketches and songs all over Canada. Though never a major star as Sybil had hoped, Jane's career must have given her some satisfaction.

Once back in London she and Lewis continued to go to the theatre. 'Oh! Lewis, I do love a play!' was a remark heard more than once in the front stalls in the West End or the Royal Court. Because of her arthritis she liked to have a seat on the aisle. They went to an eclectic mixture of productions, including *The Cherry Orchard*, with Lila Kedrova ('a lovely Russian actress') as Madame Ranevskaya, Peter Terson's exuberant *Zigger Zagger*, staged by the National Youth Theatre ('most impressive'), Galsworthy's *The Silver Box*, Alan Bennett's *Forty Years On*, and Stoppard's *Rosencrantz and Guildernstern Are Dead*. Stage censorship, which she and Lewis had strenuously fought against all their lives, would be abolished the following year. Surprisingly, the Lord Chamberlain gave a licence to a piece by the controversial American company La Mama Troupe at the Gate, about a man in love with a pig. In one scene a woman mimed graphically having sex with two men: 'That was awfully good, don't you think?' Sybil observed. 'They fitted each other so well.'

She now decided to do something about the pain in her arm and neck. Deep-ray treatment failed to help, and in December she was confined to bed, which made her unusually gloomy. 'I'm in bed with bronchitis, having to put off a recital, which makes me mad,' she told John. 'But I couldn't get through it, choking as I am. It's so awful for me to be ill, because it sends Lewis right down to the depths! I am not able to read to him – I get very down about my own inadequacies. I've not stood up to life enough – perhaps we both should have gone before this – but we have had some great happiness in the last few years, so I ought not to say things like this.'

She was soon back in harness, starting rehearsals two weeks later for *Call Me Jacky*. Enid Bagnold's play centres around Mrs Basil, a rich woman with a servant problem who is considering who should inherit her 30-bedroom house, which symbolically represents Britain. 'It's a very odd play with a very silly title, but I hope that may be changed,' Sybil wrote to Diana Devlin. She was keen to work with director Frank Hauser ('he's so intelligent and so alive'), and make her debut at the Oxford Playhouse, where the play would run after visiting Guildford and Brighton. It was another demanding part, Mrs Basil being offstage for just four minutes.

Also in the company were Sheila Burrell, Paul Eddington, Heather Chasen and Derek Fowlds. Problems soon arose in rehearsals: ten days before the opening Fowlds decided he was not suited to the leading male part, and was replaced by Edward Fox. Sybil was, Frank Hauser later admitted, much too old to play her part, and this affected rehearsals. Heather Chasen, playing a homicidal, dipsomaniac lesbian cook, recalls: 'She was put centre stage, and she stayed there like a great galleon floundering, so she didn't have to move about. So we all had to move around her, which made it less interesting than it was.'

Although Sybil knew her lines before anyone else, she found it increasingly hard to retain them. 'The brain is a box, and all the words are in it,' she would say. 'The trouble with mine is that it's got holes in it, and they all fly out.' Sheila Burrell remembers 'You always knew when she was going to dry, because she immediately gave a hearty laugh. But despite this, she would sail on through it.' Sometimes she would disconcert an actor by improvising, so that 'Go and fetch my three-quarter-length gloves' became 'Go and fetch my middle-age-length gloves', or instead of asking 'Is there a corridor to this hospital?' she would say 'Is there a stalk to this tomato?' After the Guildford opening she confessed: 'I'm not a bit certain in it yet. Such a long part and I have to go over and over again with it – but I'll improve!'

During the run Lewis sometimes sat watching in the wings, and Sybil would say: 'I *must* be good tonight.' Enid Bagnold was impressed by her gusto, humour and intelligence, her delight in cooperation, and her ability to keep her temperament in check: 'Whatever Sybil has – of Celtic impetuousness, of sentiment, of a quick rise to anger – she watches over it like someone who owns a lion and must keep it in order.' Her performance in this weak, static play was enjoyed by most critics: Stephen Wall in the *Guardian* noted her 'marvellously audible authority…she burnishes her lines until they shine greatly beyond their worth', while Hobson thought her 'very much at a delightful ease in this play, which utters so many opinions one fancies alien to her progressive nature'. But Ronald Bryden felt Sybil's talent was wasted in this 'Tory attempt to re-write *Heartbreak House*'.

The poor notices prevented the production going any further than Oxford. Sheila Burrell recalls how Sybil received the news. 'Lewis was there when Frank Hauser told us the show wasn't going into London. He was sitting there with tears running down his cheeks. I think he was upset for Sybil, because he thought this would be her last big part. She didn't give anything away, she was very brave, she just smiled.' But a few days later she confessed to John: 'I was very disappointed, because I'd put such work into the darned thing. The West End is tricky now, except for musicals and very light plays – and this one is a bit obscure.'

She was next offered the female lead by Emlyn Williams in a revival of his celebrated 1935 thriller *Night Must Fall*. May Whitty, who originally created the part of Mrs Bramson, described her as 'an old beast in a wheelchair', who is charmed by a young schizophrenic. The young pop star Adam Faith was a surprise choice for the role first played by Williams himself: hugely popular as a singer, he had ambitions to be a straight actor, but his stage experience was limited to a season in Blackpool and a couple of pantomimes. 'To help Adam is the main reason I am doing this play,' Sybil told a reporter. 'I believe we veterans of the profession have a responsibility to the young ones to help them along.'

The cast also included William Lucas, Polly Adams, Helen Cotterill and Gretchen Franklin. Having signed the contract, Sybil got cold feet: 'Adam Faith is a darling fellow, but I'm scared of doing another tour with Lewis,' she told John. 'He gets so dreadfully tired and worried and sometimes I think a little unbalanced! When I read to him that snaps him out of it – but it's quite exhausting, for both of us. I'll see Aubrey Blackburn this week and see if I can get out of it.' Lewis was to play the small part of the Lord Chief Justice, with just one long speech at the beginning of the play. 'I think he ought to do it, but he gets into such a tiz over it – tho' deeply I think he wants to.' Finally it was decided he would record the speech, then mime to it on stage.

Faith was deeply impressed with Sybil: 'She was always complaining that she wasn't good, that she couldn't do the job, but of course she was stunning and wonderful.' He was astonished to find that she and Lewis, as they had always done, came to work by bus. The next day he called for them at Swan Court in his black Rolls-Royce, then offered to do so every morning. Sybil declined, saying he had to come out of his way, and anyway the bus conductors might wonder what had happened to them. But when he secretly organised and paid for a car to bring them in every morning, telling them it was courtesy of the management, she was delighted to accept.

Director Charles Hickman observed: 'Her enthusiasm for youth was one of Sybil's most endearing qualities: today and the future always meant more to her than the past.' Her cast agreed: 'She was always interested in us all, and so communicative,' Helen Cotterill remembers. 'She wanted to know what jobs we might be going for, how we had got on at interviews. She was totally un-damey, totally down to earth. She had this ability to find joy in small things. On tour in Birmingham she came in one lunch time, and said: "We're off to buy a biro in the Bullring!"' Gretchen Franklin noticed that she and Lewis used to pray together before each performance.

During the long provincial tour Sybil and Faith did a double-act for the local papers, he describing her as a 'goddess' and a 'smashing person', she calling him 'a wonderful and talented boy', and taking quite seriously his desire to play Hamlet one day: 'I shall be there looking down on you from up above, cheering you on,' she declared. During performances she gave him constant encouragement, whispering 'Lovely, Lovely!' whenever he came off stage and passed her in the wings. Later he wrote: 'She was an incredible woman, who had a big impact on me. As a person, if you met the Dalai Lama or any of those Indian meditators, you couldn't get calmer than you could with Sybil.

It's women like that who built the empire for England, the sort that would drive through the African jungle and get out the tea with all the silver.'

The original plan had been to bring the play into the West End, where she and Lewis had already beaten the record for the most appearances by a married couple. But the cast were told in mid-tour that, despite good business, this was not to be. The reason was never quite clear. There may have been fears that Lewis would have to withdraw – and Sybil would therefore do so too – for his deafness was creating problems. In Oxford the recorded speech started without him, so Sybil then had to nudge him with a broom handle for his cue. Then in Cambridge early in the speech the tape ran down, then started up again, while Lewis continued miming the words at the correct speed.

Charles Hickman observed later: 'I believe we all knew this would be the last time the Cassons would be seen together in a play. In their own minds they saw it as their final bow together on the stage, taking it as they wanted to, giving their blessings to another generation.'

42

Losing Lewis

1967–1969

'We've always been able to communicate on every level,
professional, domestic, emotional and political'
Sybil on her sixty years with Lewis

In her final years, as her appearances in the theatre became fewer, Sybil gained a great deal of pleasure from working in radio. Graham Gauld, a BBC producer who worked on a dozen plays with her, believes she stood out among her generation as a performer in the medium: 'She was one of the few great stars who could handle it. Some of them just couldn't cope; Ralph Richardson for example was too big. But Sybil could usually be quiet and restrained if need be.'

He first directed her in Somerset Maugham's *The Sacred Flame*: 'As the mother she was marvellous, it was a superb performance,' he remembers. He then set up a 'Sybil Thorndike Festival', inviting her to perform in her six favourite plays, which he would direct. She chose a wide variety, including *A Passage to India, Jane Clegg, The Foolish Gentlewoman* and *The Distaff Side*. There was also a cut version of Shaw's *Captain Brassbound's Conversion*. Her other choice, *Saint Joan*, created a flutter at the BBC. 'The planners couldn't see her playing the nineteen-year-old Joan in her eighties, even on the radio,' Gauld recalls. 'But Sybil was adamant. She said to me: "That was the greatest moment of my life, and if I can't do *Saint Joan*, I won't do any of them." I then suggested a compromise, in which she would do the four great scenes, and write a linking narrative, and this was accepted.' Asked how she felt about returning to the role, she replied: 'Although I'm ancient, I hope the voice isn't.'

Gauld remembers watching her from the control room while she recorded the *Saint Joan* extracts: 'Her face was lit up, she was shining, she was eighteen again – and her voice was astounding. Everyone was spellbound.' Ian McKellen, playing the Dauphin, remembers a characteristic intervention from Lewis: 'He beat out the rhythm of the lines as Sybil was speaking, but she seemed to like that.' The critics were hugely impressed: the *Sunday Times* thought her performance 'totally convincing' and 'quite incredible'. The public was equally appreciative, as the BBC audience research showed: the scenes gained unusually high appreciation figures: 'superb', 'magnificent' and 'perfect' were common individual responses. 'She received many letters, including one from Clement Attlee, her friend and contemporary. 'I listened to you yesterday with great pleasure,' he wrote. 'It carried me back many years to that wonderful stage performance. I admire very much how you are able to speak your lines so well at your age. Wish that I was so fit.'

Not all her radio work was drama. She introduced and read *Man's Quest for Truth*, a selection of poems about pilgrimage. In *Your Loving Sybil* she read a selection of her letters to Russell from America in the Ben Greet days, with Russell acting as narrator. There was *The Captain's Log*, an account of a sea voyage round Cape Horn, based on the log of one of Lewis' ancestors, a sea captain. 'It was a little bit over the top, I think in that instance I should have quietened her down,' Gauld recalls. She agreed to take part in a programme he compiled about Flora Robson, but her contribution was not used: she stopped in the middle of the interview, telling Gauld she couldn't go on, because 'Flora has been a great disappointment to Lewis and me: we thought she was going to be one of our great tragediennes, and she hasn't been'. To Frith Banbury she was more outspoken, telling him: 'Flora was a sentimental bore!'

Encouraged by the BBC's head of drama Martin Esslin, she starred with Janet Suzman and Joan Matheson in *Peace*, by the Hungarian novelist Magda Szabo. There was also *The Son* by the young German playwright Gert Hofmann which, according to Esslin, 'contains a splendid part for an actress of Dame Sybil Thorndike's depth of feeling and sense of the tragic and the comic…it is a great part for a great actress'. She was also in radio versions of *The Father* and *Night Must Fall*. All this time she kept her voice in trim, doing 15 minutes of vocal exercises twice a day, and humming a lot – in the bath, walking along the road, everywhere she could.

On television she worked on Strindberg's *The Father*, with Patrick Wymark in the title-role. 'It's a wonderful and terrible play,' she told John. 'I'm playing the Nurse – a beautiful part and quite a wonderful cast – Dorothy Tutin is the wife and awfully good – she has made me understand the play more than before. But oh! it's not like the theatre.' Yet she recognised the discipline the smaller screen imposed on her. 'Television is good for my personality, because it keeps me quiet, it cuts me down to size.' Sometimes it apparently failed to do so, as with her contribution to the ABC series 'The Actor and the Role', about which Stanley Reynolds wrote in the *Guardian*: 'There was something exceedingly charming about Dame Sybil's theatrical manner, all eyes and hands, when she was merely sitting in the studio chatting, but the grand manner seemed only ridiculous when she appeared as Medea.'

Yet in her live recitals she could still startle as Medea or Hecuba. In Nottingham she included the final scene from *The Trojan Women*, using her green silk stole to create the impression she was holding her dead grandson. 'I thought it was the greatest piece of acting I'd seen in my life,' teacher Megan Jones says. 'She didn't seem like a little old lady but a young woman back in the 1920s.' Sometimes she performed with a musician, occasionally still with Lewis. At a recital in Bath he was slow to pick up his cue. 'Now come on, darling, it's your turn,' she said, explaining to the audience: 'Lewis is going to read this, and I'm going to find it for him because he's a bit slower than I am.' But just to perform often demanded a supreme effort. Teresa Campbell was present at a recital she gave in the Orangery at Kenwood, Hampstead: 'I saw her sitting beforehand, looking very shaky, very small and frail and bent. I thought she wasn't going to be able to do it. Yet on she came, glowing, and did it with such power and energy. She absolutely transformed herself.'

Her public activities were beginning to get her down. 'I am working very hard – charities to speak at (ugh!!),' she complained to Diana Devlin. Nevertheless she continued actively to support many charities, especially those involving children and old people. She also kept up the political activities. After the Russian invasion of Czechoslovakia, she was among those who helped Czech actors to obtain visas to enter Britain. At a large public meeting at Friends' House to celebrate the centenary of Gandhi's birth, she read from his memoirs, in what Gandhi's friend Richard Symonds described as 'a wonderful booming voice, like a bell sounding over a silent lake'. But she withdrew at the last minute from opening a charity event at the Wimbledon home of the Vietnamese ambassador in aid of his country's war orphans, declaring: 'I might let forth something they wouldn't have wanted to hear. Being a complete pacifist, I'm something of a liability when it comes to speech-making.'

The actor and writer Ronald Hayman recruited her and Lewis to help launch his floating barge theatre, a scheme to provide children's theatre in the afternoons and experimental theatre for adults in the evening. 'They came along to a press stunt, and were piped aboard at Little Venice,' he remembers. 'She was terrifically supportive, exhilarating and exuberant, and got everyone's spirits up.' The barge she sat in sailed along the Regent's Canal to London Zoo, where it was to be moored. On board for the *Guardian*, Terry Coleman wrote: 'Dame Sybil, immediately at full dramatic pitch – as is her gift – announced to Regent's Park that she was so thrilled she could hardly speak, that this was wonderful, that this was the first time since the old showboats of America that London had had a theatre on the water.'

She gave many younger actors and actresses the benefit of her experience. Bette Bourne recalls: 'During *The Reluctant Peer* she used to coach me in her deco suite at the Duchess. She taught me a lot about diction and phrasing. I was 20 and didn't know anything, but she was full of sympathy.' Some young actors she influenced in another way, as Ian McKellen remembers: 'I heard her say on the radio that it was very important for young actors to go and work in repertory companies, as that was the best training you could get. That impinged on my consciousness, and when I left university I deliberately spent three years in rep.'

Isla Blair, then 24 and playing Nora, remembers her advice after a dress rehearsal of *A Doll's House* in Leatherhead. 'She led me to the sofa on the set and said: "My dear, you are good, but there is an element of Nora you are not playing. She is not sad or self-pitying, she is *angry*, and has been for years, but through all that baby acting and little-girl stuff, she has kept a lid on it. During the play she lifts the lid, not in an explosive way, but in a much more dangerous way. She is coldly angry, so she is able to make her decision to escape. But don't ever let us see her anger, just think it, feel it, and we in the audience will pick it up. Nora may not even be aware she *is* angry! A thought in your head, a feeling in your heart is all you need, without demonstrating it." Her words gave me a little core of steel, which became the basis of my interpretation.'

She liked to talk about Shaw and the original production of *Saint Joan* to young actresses cast in her famous role. Barbara Leigh-Hunt remembers one particularly helpful note: 'She said, "Don't get all holy and talk about God in inverted commas, talk to him on a level, as in, Now look here God, this isn't good enough." That was so like her, she always had this directness.' Anna Calder-Marshall recalls: 'She was like a Life Force, even at eighty-six. She had this wonderful bubble, but also a serenity.' She and Lewis also went round to see Siobhan McKenna after she played the part in London. 'She was so warm and generous,' the actress remembered. 'Sir Lewis then suddenly went down on one knee, took my hand and kissed it, and said: "The greatest Saint Joan ever." Dame Sybil took her programme and smacked him on the head and said: "Too much!"'

In 1968, shortly after playing Saint Joan on television, Janet Suzman met Sybil for a feature for *Drama* magazine. 'She loved talking to young people, and I found her a complete charmer,' she recalls. During their conversation, chaired by Eric Shorter, Sybil stressed her liking for Brecht's plays: 'The first thing you get out of Brecht is a humanity, you don't get political ideas first.' She felt her socialism had helped her as an actress: 'It makes you much freer, you have a much deeper understanding of all sorts or people.' But she confessed that she had had enough of the stage: 'I don't want to work in the theatre again unless I find something that really gives me a kick.'

Meanwhile John and Patricia were back on her doorstep. After several years as a communications consultant, John had returned to England to lecture as a freelance to industrial, banking and commercial management training courses. He and Patricia bought a small Georgian house in Lawrence Street in Chelsea. 'It's heaven having them home,' Sybil told Gwen Ffrangcon-Davies, though she admitted to sometimes finding their energy tiring. 'Their life is *beyond words* lively! But I hold my breath and count ten and am grateful for their stimulation!!'

Many of her grandchildren were now in their twenties, with John's son Anthony being the first to marry. 'All the grand girls are slow about marrying – too many boyfriends and interesting work,' Sybil complained to Colette O'Niel. So when Mary's daughter Diana became engaged to Will Grahame, a fellow teacher of drama in Minnesota, she could hardly restrain herself: 'Diana darling!' she wrote. 'Oh! Oh! Oh! What a thrill! Oh! it's wonderful – being married is so much nicer than not – I hope you will have a beautiful life together.' But she was caught on the hop later, when Penny Casson became engaged to a family friend and distant relative of Sybil, the historian Tom Pocock. 'We went to Swan Court to tell them,' Penny remembers. 'When I said, "Granny, I would like you to meet my fiancé," she said, "Penny, you mustn't joke about these things." Lewis said: "Don't be silly, Sybil, she *means* it!"'

She was mostly encouraging about her grandchildren's ambitions, as Tom Campbell, now a painter, remembers. 'When I was at art school I would have dinner with her every Thursday. She encouraged me to become a painter, and not get sidetracked into stage design or something similar just for monetary reasons. She loved painting and talked to me about the paintings she had bought, and why she loved them.' His brother Dirk recalls: 'She encouraged people to do what they wanted – except to go into the theatre, when she was always discouraging. She would say, "Unless you have a burning desire, don't do it."' Jane of course was an exception. Ben Campbell, now a leading actor in Canada, says: 'I think Jane could have been a star, but the enormous pressure of expectations from Sybil and also from her parents destroyed that hope.'

In the autumn Sybil's sciatica forced her to pay another visit to the nursing home, and by November she was suddenly feeling her age. 'I am very ancient, and life is not at all easy,' she wrote to Diana. 'Everybody wants me to do things – radio and TV and interviews.' She turned down four plays – 'they bored me so, and one was just not intelligible; I won't be bored at 86' – and a film to be shot in Cyprus: 'I can't cope with it – it's too great a responsibility with Lewis too, though it would have been quite exciting – a lovely and very odd part of an old Greek woman of 104 – right up my street!' When Gwen Ffrangcon-Davies told her she had been offered a part which involved being in bed the whole time, she said: 'That's just what I'd like now, a lying-down part.'

In December she and Lewis celebrated sixty years of marriage. Two parties were held to mark their diamond jubilee. The first, in a Kensington flat, was a full-blooded theatrical occasion for 90 people. Seated on a dais as if enthroned Sybil, in a gold dress, and Lewis received their friends, drawn from different eras of their lives: Ellaline Terriss, Basil Dean, Gladys Cooper, Jack Hawkins, John Gielgud, Bronson Albery, Michael Redgrave, Athene Seyler, Paul Scofield, Richard Attenborough, Joyce Grenfell, Margaret Rutherford, Anthony Quayle and many others, including Cardinal Heenan, in full costume. 'My God, if a bomb fell on this lot there would be no London theatre left!' Emlyn Williams remarked. 'What a cast!' Sybil observed. Soon after, a family party was attended by over a hundred Thorndikes and Cassons.

Sybil talked about their marriage with zest, humour and candour. She pointed out that many actresses had been married for sixty years, but not to the same husband. The secret of a successful marriage, she said, was deep friendship as well as love. 'Idyllic love that brings you together obviously cannot continue for a lifetime.' She admitted she and Lewis had colossal rows. 'If you've got tremendous tempers, as we have, you can't help flying off the handle. But it's better than holding it all in. Our arguments are real ding-dong ones, the roof goes off – and what an enormous stimulant that is! I can't think of anything more boring than being married to a nice complacent husband!' She cited a sense of humour and shared interests as key elements in their long relationship. 'We've always been able to communicate on every level, professional, domestic, emotional and political.'

In Leatherhead the Thorndike theatre was taking shape. Sybil was keen to do a modern piece there, perhaps with Lewis: 'Is there a play for two old dodderers?' she asked. Three of the scripts sent to her she denounced as 'lavatory plays'; a fourth, a 'nice well-made play', bored her to tears. But as soon as she started to read *There Was an Old Woman*, the story of a bag lady reminiscing about her past, she wanted to do it. 'Very modern and odd, but I love it,' she told Diana. 'I am always interested in these old girls who just walk about and sit on park benches. I always wonder about their lives, what they talk to themselves about. The play is a great challenge, because it has tragedy, and courage. It's about facing whatever comes with no self-pity at all.'

Lewis encouraged her to do the play, which was actor John Graham's first stage work. At Sybil's request he went to Swan Court to read it with her before she started to learn her lines. 'She read it perfectly,' he recalls. 'Lewis came in to listen, looking very frail. Sybil said: "Sit there Lewis, and don't interrupt!" While we were reading I suddenly saw him slump sideways. I thought he'd died. I could see the headline, Sir Lewis Casson Dies during Play Reading! But suddenly he woke up and said: "A change of lighting there, I think." He was absolutely right.'

But Lewis' condition was deteriorating. He had been suffering for some time from anaemia, which contributed to his depressions. Bronwen Casson stayed at Swan Court for a few weeks in 1969, and was upset to discover he was unable to play chess because he couldn't see the pieces. Sybil continued to read to him, and to play one of Bach's 48 preludes and fugues for him each day. He was well enough in February to see Nicol Williamson's tortured Hamlet at the Roundhouse. In April Sybil reported that he was 'a bit piano, but really very wonderful for an old'un'. Early in May she and John gave a recital at Kenwood House, with Lewis in the audience, having rehearsed the programme with them with his usual critical eye and ear.

He and Sybil continued to have the occasional row, notably one about voice production. Two days later his health became a cause for great anxiety, the doctor was called, and he was taken into the Nuffield Nursing Home for tests. Sybil had two engagements that week, a Dickens reading at Rochester and a recital in Ayslesford for schoolchildren, but Lewis refused to let her cancel either of them. She then was told that he was very seriously ill, and unlikely to recover. She spent much of the next two days with him, but on the following day, 16 May, he seemed calmer and more peaceful. They talked for a few minutes before the specialist arrived. Soon afterwards he collapsed and died, with Sybil holding his hand.

Soon after she returned to the flat, Olivier arrived to console her for her loss. Later that day she wrote to Emlyn Williams: 'Only this morning he went. Oh! I can't tell you what I feel – we've had such a lovely life – stormy, wild, loving and sympathy always.' In the following days she received hundreds of letters and telegrams from all over the world and all walks of life, from India's prime minister Indira Gandhi to a fan representing the Gaiety gallery of 1912–13. Friends in the profession wrote admiringly of Lewis' qualities, of his integrity, courage and dedication. Joyce Grenfell picked out 'his humour, warmth, kindliness, unselfishness, and generosity'. Several remembered how they owed their start in the theatre to his help and encouragement. Anthony Quayle echoed a common sentiment when he wrote of 'the radiant influence of you two great people…You have been, by being your remarkable selves, a compass by which younger people could set their course.'

The obituaries centred on Lewis' great contribution to the theatre and the profession, and his remarkable personal and professional partnership with Sybil. They described him as a courageous fighter, a key figure in the founding of Equity and the improvement in actors' living standards, and a pioneer in his work for CEMA. They praised his abilities as a director, a role in which he was felt to have achieved even more than he did as an actor, where he had often been overshadowed by Sybil. Gielgud wrote to her: 'Even in these last years he still radiated humanity and warmth. He never seemed to lose his enthusiasms and his generous judgements. What a fine life, what a rich career, what a dear unforgettable friend.'

The official cause of his death was a non-functioning of the kidneys. After viewing his body, Sybil wrote to Gwen Ffrangcon-Davies: 'He looks so lovely now – quite young again.' The day before the funeral she was taken to Harrods, and ordered masses of flowers, observing: 'I've spent an absolute fortune. Lewis will be simply furious, and he can't do anything about it.' He was cremated at Golders Green, and his ashes scattered around a tree planted there. The Dean of Westminster Abbey asked Sybil if she would like his thanksgiving service to be held in the Abbey. At first she hesitated, as she explained to Emlyn Williams: 'I thought it a bit grand – but then the other thought came – in honouring one whom you call that "fine and modest man" it was honouring the theatre which, not according to popular ideas, does not like "show-off" – and Lewis didn't, and nor I – and I couldn't help feeling he'd be so bucked, for he never thought a lot of himself.'

Lewis became only the second actor after Henry Irving to be so honoured with a service in the Abbey. Because he had loathed mourning, and couldn't stand Sybil in black, she asked people to wear white or colours, and wore white herself. She asked Paul Scofield, Richard Attenborough, Emlyn Williams and Michael Denison to be the family ushers. Charles Hickman remembers 'Sybil's tiny figure dressed in white, with a flowing matching scarf, gently smiling greetings to her friends as she walked slowly up the nave'. In the packed Abbey, surrounded by her family, she maintained an impressive dignity throughout the service, which she and Lewis had planned together. John Casson read Lewis' favourite poem, W E Henley's 'Margaritae Sorori'; Gielgud spoke Prospero's speech from *The Tempest*, 'Our revels now are ended'; and the service ended with Bach's Toccata and Fugue in D Minor.

Gielgud wrote to Mary Casson: 'How wonderfully Sybil graced the strain that it must have been for her. But I know she must have been touched by the unanimous love shown to her and Lewis in that huge congregation. Her life and genius are such an inspiration to us all.' Sybil wrote again to Emlyn Williams: 'Yesterday was unforgettable. I did love it so, that splendid music – the Toccata, we often played it, me on the piano stumbling through, but it made us love it – and "A Late Lark", which Lewis only said to me a week before he went – and we both said, "Let's have that at our funerals" – little realising.'

One notable absentee from the abbey was Olivier, who was ill. Shortly after the service he was astonished to find Sybil at his bedside in the Nuffield Nursing Home. 'I shall never forget her coming in to see me,' he wrote to John Casson soon after. 'I think it is the most wonderful, remarkable thing I have ever known.'

43

A Bag Lady at the Thorndike

1969–1971

'These ruddy words to be learned nearly finish me'
Sybil in a letter to Diana Devlin

After their sixty years together, Sybil inevitably found Lewis' loss extremely hard to bear. Right until the end they had slept together in the small double-bed they had bought in 1908. A week after his death she confessed to her grand-daughter Diana: 'It has all happened so suddenly I can't quite take it in – but he went so *quickly* and peacefully after 2 or 3 trying days – I can't quite pull myself together yet – I can't get used to not actually having him with me – I wish I could stop crying – I keep going over things he said to me – but I'm lucky to have had him for so long.'

She wrote to Gwen Ffrangcon-Davies about the subject that now worried her more intensely than ever. 'He was more than my husband, he was my great friend and help, and I *wonder* where he is just now. I'm sure he's close, even if I feel alone.' Before he died, they had talked about life after death, and Lewis expressed the belief that it existed. Mary Casson remembers how after his death Sybil talked about him all the time, but only rarely broke down. 'We took her to see Edward Albee's *Tiny Alice*, in which someone dies alone on stage at the end. She got terribly upset, and we found her sobbing in the car afterwards. She said it was the thought of someone going off in the dark all on their own.'

In his will Lewis left £17,321, most of it to her. Her remedy for her grief was to throw herself into work. 'I get a holiday in beautiful words,' she said. Within a month she gave a poetry reading with James Roose-Evans at the Hampstead Theatre Club, which had been arranged before Lewis' death. 'She insisted on going ahead,' Roose-Evans recalls. 'All went smoothly until she reached a poem by Andrew Young. On the line "And leave me here alone" she suddenly broke down in tears. I held her hand and waited quietly, as did the audience, until she was able to continue. In the interval she apologised, saying: "Those words suddenly made me realise how Lewis and I had always read together, and now he is no longer here."'

Generally she kept up a courageous front. In August she saw Marlowe's *Edward II* in Edinburgh 'with a remarkable young man, who is also playing Richard II' – this was Ian McKellen. Afterwards she went backstage to meet the company. McKellen remembers her fortitude: 'None of us knew what to say because she had just been widowed – but there she was, full of enthusiasm, talking about the play.' The director Toby Robertson also met her at this time. He talked of Lewis' visit to one of his productions, and how interesting he'd been about it. 'Oh good, you're talking about Lewis,' she said. 'People so often don't like to talk about his death.'

In living alone she found both solace and inspiration in the Bible, which she read in bed with her tea at the start of each day. She read The New Testament in Greek, with a lexicon and translation by her side. She had by now mastered the St John's Gospel, but was finding Matthew 'a bit of a trickster over the Greek'. She would dip into *My Daily Light*, to find texts for the day, and finish up with a psalm. 'This starts me off the day feeling I'm being looked after,' she said, 'that there's something bigger than I can understand, but there's something in charge of me.'

Work was the great consolation. She resumed her recitals, giving three at that summer's Edinburgh Festival in St Cecilia's Hall and, according to one critic, 'held a full house clutched firmly in the palm of her hand'. Her success delighted her: 'Edinburgh went finely,' she told Patricia. 'I had packed houses and scores turned away. I could have played a week there – such friendly, expressive audiences.' Tanya Moisiewitsch remembered a reading she gave at the Royal Society of Literature in London. 'I heard many people read poetry there, but she was the most entertaining. She said she found Milton a bit of a stodge, and he was horrid to his wife, then read most beautifully lines from *Samson Agonistes*. She arrived with someone carrying a lot of shawls and scarves, and said to the organiser: "I don't want you to let anyone sit in the front row, because I want them for my things." These things turned out to be her grandchildren, who came in hordes. It was very lively.'

Despite her arthritis, she was determined to carry on with the play at the Thorndike: 'This is a theatre after my own heart, which changes its bill frequently, and belongs to its community,' she stated. She was present on the opening night for a production of *The Lion in Winter*, as Hazel Vincent Wallace remembers: 'Princess Margaret came in first with Lord Snowdon. Everyone stood up, and there was silence. Next in was Sybil, who looked around and said, "Oh! it's just like church." It was too solemn an occasion for her, she had to break the silence. She got a big laugh.' Bryan Forbes was there with Edith Evans, and remembered that, after she and Sybil had chatted, Edith said in a piercing voice as the lights went down: 'Why does Sybil always wear blue? Such an unsuitable colour for her.'

At the end Sybil came on stage and gave a speech. 'It was very moving,' Virginia McKenna remembers. 'Her voice was so strong, and she reached everyone.' Tom Pocock recalled the scene afterwards in the Green Room, with Olivier and Jennie Lee present. 'Princess Margaret came in and talked to the younger actors. Sybil wouldn't sit, even though she was very tired. Olivier came over and told her to sit down, but she wouldn't. Then he came over again and said, Sit down or I'll knock you down! And then she did. Finally Jennie Lee came over and said, Well I'm going home anyway. She was very concerned about Sybil, whereas Princess Margaret hadn't noticed.'

The cast for *There Was an Old Woman* included George Cole, Nicholas Jones, Valerie White and, as a young version of Sybil's character, Virginia Stride. As rehearsals loomed Sybil was in considerable pain in her leg, arm and back. A session with a faith healer failed to help, although some injections did: 'The doctor said I should go to bed for a month, but that is nonsense!' she told Diana. By the read-through she seemed word-perfect. She had noticed a bag lady in Chelsea, 'an old terror with two whopping bags', and had been watching how she walked.

After a week she complained to the director Philip Grout that he never gave her any notes. When he told that this was because she was perfect, she said: 'No, no, I've been on the stage for years, but I'm still learning.' Grout was struck by her openness. 'She would ask me to help her, and when I suggested something, she would say, "Oh yes, what a good idea." I did an experiment I had learned from Joan Littlewood, where the actors speak their lines to each other from the four corners of the theatre. Every single word Sybil uttered was bell-clear, she was the only one who immediately got the measure of it. She had a tremendous effect on all of us: her incredible spirit, and the warmth she gave out to everybody.'

Another cast member, Barbara Laurenson, recalls: 'There were no histrionics, no displays of ego. Sybil was dignified, undemanding, almost unassuming.' There were humorous moments. At the point where a stage direction read 'Old Woman hovers in the background', Philip Grout saw Sybil making strange hand movements. When he asked what she was doing, she replied: 'I'm hoovering.' She also had problems with her lines, telling Patricia: 'I'm worried about the play. I love it, but such speeches I've got. These ruddy words to be learned nearly finish me.' She would hit herself and say, 'Silly bloody fool, can't remember anything!' She would exercise her memory by trying to memorise the names of the shops in the street. Grout recalls another method: 'I went to her hotel before the opening to hear her words. She had six coins laid out in a row, and she would only move a coin away if she got a page or a section perfect. I was amazed by her desire for perfection.'

There Was an Old Woman opened in the Thorndike in October for a three-week run. The theatre had 530 seats, and exactly the kind of thrust stage Sybil favoured. Sadly, with its unreal characters and bizarre sub-Pinter dialogue, the play was little more than a succession of sketches, of dream scenes from her past intended to illuminate the old woman's descent into the gutter. Wrapped in a bundle of coats, her hair tied up with an old scarf, clutching her bulging carrier bags and swigging gin, Sybil was a remarkable sight. The critics once again celebrated her ability to rise above inferior material. 'Dame Sybil is a marvel,' Felix Barker wrote. 'Not a syllable do we miss. Not a point is lost.' Irving Wardle enjoyed her 'inextinguishable energy and charm…she warms up the theatre like a bonfire'. Another critic wrote: 'Dame Sybil constantly sweeps the sentiments away from slosh; the voice is as strong and fascinating as ever; she is gentle but far from frail; and still full of beauty.'

The audience that night demanded a dozen curtain calls. She played to full houses throughout the run, receiving a huge ovation after each performance. In Grout's view she gave the part all the life she could. 'She got to the heart of the character, she really inhabited it,' he says. 'I just wish it had been written more vividly: there were not enough shadows, no highs and lows, it was too episodic.' Sometimes Sybil struggled with her words. 'Once she missed a page, panicked, and then went back and made it up,' Nicholas Jones remembers. Behind the set an assistant stage manager kept as near as possible to her, ready to give her a prompt she could hear. Usually she covered up well, unfazed by any lapses, buoyed up by the obviously supportive audiences: Barbara Laurenson remembers 'waves of love for Sybil coming from the auditorium'. George Cole recalls the penultimate performance, a matinee:

'She stepped forward to take her bow, and her white silk knickers fell down round her ankles. She stepped out of them, waved them in the air and, roaring with laughter, continued to take her bow.' When another actor, John Crocker, asked at the curtain call for the last performance, 'Are your drawers OK?', she told him: 'I took no chances, I left them off.'

The plan was to bring the play into the West End, to the Duchess, but this had to be abandoned, as Sybil was clearly struggling. Although her pain ceased the moment she made her entrance, it gripped her again as soon as she stepped into the wings. 'I'm beginning to think I'm too old to be bothered any more,' she told Diana. 'It's the most nervy and difficult play I've ever done. I love it, but I'm past it now, and I shan't do any more.' One night in her dressing-room she said wistfully to Amanda Saunders, who was about to become a student assistant stage manager: 'How I envy you, to be seventeen and going to Birmingham Rep.'

At the end of the run she agreed to spend a week in bed 'to get rid of aches and tiredness'. John Graham believes she was relieved to have finished. 'She had such energy mentally, but technically she was flagging,' he recalls. Soon she was writing to Patricia: 'I've had two offers of plays to go on at once, and I've refused with joy!' After sixty-five years, she had made her farewell to the stage. Yet in spite of her frailty and lack of mobility she carried on giving recitals, appeared several times on television as herself, and was involved in more radio broadcasts, though now mostly readings. 'I'm not giving in yet, though I'm old and infirm!' she declared.

That autumn a 'heart bother' forced her to cancel her engagements, which she hated to do. She believed it was a delayed reaction to Lewis' death. 'I feel so lost sometimes without him,' she confessed to Gwen Ffrancgon-Davies. But she took comfort in her tentative belief in an after-life. When Emlyn Williams wrote to her of his wife Mollie's death, she replied: 'That warm, jolly and lovely personality *can't* be dead – she's alive and perhaps having a slight argument with Lewis! I shall read the account of her going again and again, for it's so brave, and helps me to be more brave than I am....I think of all the times I've been impatient and non-understanding and feel so unhappy.... But I'm like you, having a loving family who help me – not to forget – but somehow to put things in a right perspective.'

Remarkably, by the summer of 1970 she was back in action and, in the space of a few weeks, closing one theatre and opening another. The closure was of the Theatre Royal in Bristol, which was shutting down temporarily for re-development. After the last performance of *As You Like It* she spoke an epilogue written for the occasion by Priestley, part of which featured her link with the theatre's history:

> 'As long ago as May of Forty-three
> I spoke a piece to set this Theatre free
> Of darkness, dust and silence, so that we
> Players and patrons both, might then enjoy
> A playhouse like a marvellous old toy:
> Now I'll confess – though everybody knows it –
> I come back to our Theatre Royal to close it.'

The opening was of the Young Vic, a new offshoot of the National Theatre, built in The Cut near the Old Vic, and created to present plays for young people. Olivier, knowing the pain she was in, tried to persuade John not to let her undertake the task. Predictably, Sybil insisted on being there. 'She was terrific at the opening,' the theatre's first director Frank Dunlop recalls: 'She said, "I know all you young people like to protest about things, but if you're going to do so, you must be HEARD" – this with her biggest voice, that shook the timbers. She also said, with an upward sweep of her arm, "My dear husband wanted to be here, but of course he's up there watching us!"' Thereafter she was thought of as the Young Vic's godmother.

In June, on the day Olivier was given a peerage, she was made a Companion of Honour, a rare accolade for a woman; only Lilian Baylis and Annie Horniman within the theatre had been similarly honoured. Frederick Ashton, director of the Royal Ballet, who joined this select club on the same day, wrote to her: 'I cannot think of a more charming and distinguished companion to be honoured with.' Coward sent a typically terse telegram: 'Darling Fluffy Damesy How Absolutely Lovely.' She also received congratulations from existing Companions, including the conductor Adrian Boult, and the art historian Kenneth Clark, who wrote: 'You are, and have long been, an inspiration to me. If I was ever tempted to be tired of life, I would think of you.' The only other woman on the list was the politician Edith Summerskill, who told her: 'You deserve the honour not just for your contribution to the theatre, but because you have had the moral courage to proclaim your political beliefs irrespective of whether it was expedient or not.'

Her political allegiance remained steadfast. For the June 1970 general election campaign she contributed a pamphlet on 'Why I am Labour'. She wrote about the roots of her socialism, stressing the pioneering work of the early Labour leaders, 'to whom we owe the fact that the workers of our country are treated as human beings and not slaves'. She also wrote of the Party's achievement in bringing greater equality for women. Arguing that an international outlook was essential for world peace, she ended: 'My basic social and political belief is that the vital necessities of life should not be the means of individual person's profit. They should be the people's profit.' The election was a surprise victory for Edward Heath and the Conservative Party.

In December, together with the sculptor Henry Moore and the travel writer Freya Stark, she was made a doctor of literature by Durham University, her sixth honorary degree. Unable to attend at the last minute because of her health, she wrote despairingly to the new chancellor, her friend Malcolm MacDonald. 'Oh Malcolm, dear dear Malcolm. I've failed you! I feel utterly miserable – and I've failed beautiful Durham, which cuts me to the soul.' Throughout her life she had seen illness as a weakness, both in herself and in others.

One autumn day, leaving her flat to see *Saint Joan* at the Mermaid, she slipped and fell on a wet pavement., and broke her elbow. The next day she was in the Nuffield Nursing Home, where the actress Pauline Jameson visited her: 'She told me that all her life she felt impatient with other's illnesses or depression, but now she was so grateful for her physical pain and sadness at her husband's death for giving her compassion and understanding.' But the fall had taken its toll, as she told Colette O'Niel: 'I'm mended now – but the fall has waked up *hell* of arthritis – back legs and arms, and it makes me mad!'

Yet work remained her drug. 'Even now she cannot sit and relax in an armchair without feeling guilty,' John observed. Recitals were still manageable. 'All I need is a table to put my books on in case I forget my lines, and something to lean on in case I faint,' she told Hugh Manning, before appearing at the Hampstead Theatre Club. She performed also at Bryanston School in Dorset, for an Indian audience at the Royal Commonwealth Institute, and in Plymouth during the celebrations of the Pilgrim Fathers. Vi Marriott, who started the Young Vic with Frank Dunlop, remembers her recital there on 'Shakespeare's Heroines'. 'She arrived in a smart gold suit, a white chiffon scarf covering her immaculate white hair, and went through the whole evening without looking once at the script.' Dunlop was staggered by her versatility: 'She became all the characters: Rosalind, Juliet, Cleopatra, Queen Katharine, Lady Macbeth, and Katharina in the *Shrew*. When she did Juliet she became a girl again. She just suddenly bloomed. It was an electric moment.'

Her memory remained remarkably intact. 'I don't ever forget poems, at least not good ones,' she said. She returned to the Thorndike for 'An Evening of Words and Music' with the oboist Léon Goossens. She performed, with Richard Pasco and Gabriel Woolf, in 'Adonais and Ariel', an Apollo Society commemoration of the 150th anniversary of Keats' death. Her voice was still resonant, as Kitty Black recalled: 'When the actors arrived in the Purcell Room, and a technician came up to the stage with a microphone, Sybil said: "You know what you can do with that!"' She appeared at the London Academy of Music and Dramatic Art with Hugh Casson, for 'a personal and family choice of poetry and prose', which was broadcast on BBC2. Another family occasion was 'An Evening with Sybil Thorndike' at the Shaw, with supporting contributions from Jane and John. 'Jane collared the show,' she said afterwards. She gave an evening of Masefield poems at the Greenwich Festival, and two warmly received recitals at the Stratford Poetry Festival. The director Richard Digby-Day attended one of them: 'I've never met anyone who created such a strong spiritual presence,' he says. 'And the range of voices produced by this very old lady in extracts from the Greek tragedies was astonishing.'

At the King's Lynn Festival in Norfolk she was on the programme with singer Cleo Laine and her musician husband Johnny Dankworth. Later they persuaded Caryl Brahms to bring her down to Wavendon in Buckinghamshire, to give a poetry reading in their village church. In her memoirs Caryl Brahms wrote: 'I was astonished that, waiting to enter the church, she clutched my hand to give her confidence. I should, of course, have known that like the true artist she was, she would be nervous no matter how often she had given poetry recitals.' Her manner charmed her two hosts. 'Although as a young jazz upstart I wasn't part of her scene, she was very gracious, respectful and cordial,' Johnny Dankworth recalls. Cleo Laine appreciated her informality: 'She had no airs and graces, you didn't feel you had to dip a knee.'

To mark the centenary of Dickens' death in 1870, Sybil and Emlyn Williams read extracts from his work in Westminster Abbey, prompting John Betjeman to thank her for 'your sublime reading of Paul Dombey's death'. Dickens also provided her with her last television role. Caryl Brahms and Ned Sherrin had devised *The Great Inimitable Mr Dickens*, a biography based largely on autobiographical scenes from the novels. It had Anthony Hopkins as Dickens, and a host of stars in cameo roles, including Sybil as Dickens' grandmother. Ned Sherrin remembered. 'She had a small scene, and when she fluffed a line I told her we'd have to do it again, because of a technical fault. – Ah, she said, you're a liar, but I like you!'

Her longevity inevitably meant she outlived many friends and colleagues. She was often seen at memorial services at St Paul's in Covent Garden or St Martin-in-the-Fields, remembering friends such as Robert Atkins, Binkie Beaumont, Miles Malleson, Vera Brittain and Jack Hawkins. Alec Guinness recalled: 'Sybil managed by her presence to bring a certain gaiety and spiritual confidence to the proceedings. Often, in old age, she would read a sonnet with heart-rending clarity. She would always arrive, in white wool, with clockwork punctuality, and be led by the presiding priest to the front pew. She would be the last to arrive and the first to leave, acknowledging all and sundry.'

She still had the power to move people. She read a lesson at St John Ervine's service which reduced the congregation to tears. At Margaret Webster's she read passages from Teilhard de Chardin in a voice which the actress Eva le Gallienne described as 'younger and more resonant than most voices of people at 20'. But sometimes she showed her age. Alan Bennett remembers her frailty at Nora Nicholson's service. 'She was in the front pew with various other elderly ladies. When she had to stand up to recite the 23rd Psalm, they hunched together and squeezed her like a rugger scrum, remained supporting her while she spoke in her ringing tones, and then allowed her to subside.'

After the service for Gladys Cooper, whom she described as 'a bright and dazzling friend', Cecil Beaton spoke to her. 'I told her how beautiful she had become, more so now than at any time in her life. "Don't be such a fool! Don't be so silly!" she said, but was pleased. Then she said: "I hope my service will be as gay as this one. It won't be long now; you know I'm nearly ninety."'

44

The Oldest Working Girl Around

1971–1976

'I do like speaking on the air like this, because nobody can see me'
Sybil on her final radio broadcasts

It was said that the only way Sybil could convey old age was by acting it. Her nephew Hugh Casson was one of many who felt she became beautiful in her later years. 'She was like one of those wood-burning stoves you find in Scandinavia, which glow. As she got old that glow didn't leave her, she got increasingly beautiful, and in her last years she was outstandingly so.'

In August 1971 it seemed the end might be near when she suffered a heart attack in Dublin and spent three weeks in intensive care. She was taken in an ambulance on the ferry to Liverpool, and then to London, where she was put to bed in Swan Court with a nurse in attendance day and night. Yet within a month she was better, and welcoming visitors to the flat. A week soon after with Christopher and his family in Dublin was clearly restorative, as she told Patricia: 'Kay made me go to bed – wot I done – and I had no pain – not the heart one I mean – but did we *talk*. Bronwen in the throes of Macbeth and looking very sweet – and Glynis, the real sane one of the family, was a love.' About Christopher she concluded: 'I don't think his work actually means a lot to him. He's caught up in religion deeply – we were very soon in discussion and he brings me very wonderful and profound books. He really is a monk, I think.'

Lewis was constantly on her mind, as she confessed to Brian Glanvill, his dresser at Chichester: 'I miss him more than ever, but I'm very old and shall be joining him some time!' In October she unveiled a plaque to him in St Paul's Church in Covent Garden, inscribed with lines from Euripides: 'What else is wisdom – / To stand from fear set free,/ To breathe and wait.'

On another day she visited the grave of her brother Frank in France with her granddaughter Penny and Tom Pocock, who recalled: 'I took a photo of the headstone, had it blown up, and took it to Sybil. She looked at it for a long time, and then just said: "Oh Frank."'

She still went regularly to the theatre, though now in a hired car. At the Royal Court she admired David Storey's *Home* and *The Contractor*, and Paul Scofield in the title-role of *Uncle Vanya*. Often she surprised herself: expecting to hate *Jesus Christ Superstar* and *Godspell*, she loved them both. But she remained doggedly opposed to the trend towards naturalism in Shakespeare. 'I don't want to see Macbeth scaled down,' she said. 'I can't *bear* conversational Shakespeare. They're such gigantic words that you've got to play them bigly. It's no good playing it as if you were walking into a drawing-room.'

She also disliked what she saw as an unnecessary emphasis on sex, arguing that 'the theatre should be a platform to express what is going on in the world, but they talk about a lot of things we all know about....Sex is not new after all.' She disliked nudity on stage. 'I find it such a bore. When a girl is made to take off her clothes on the stage it robs her of all her innate modesty and decency. The problems in life are not always concerned with bare bodies.' Yet she could accept nudity in an appropriate context. Emlyn Williams recalled that when she was asked why she had gone to Storey's *The Changing Room*, where actors walked across the stage naked, she said it was a marvellous play, and she 'didn't mind a bit them showing their little arrangements'.

Now in her ninetieth year, she continued to support causes about which she felt strongly, and write letters to the press on political matters. On the twenty-fifth anniversary of Hiroshima, together with 40 other eminent CND supporters – including Michael Foot, Canon Collins, Trevor Huddleston, James Cameron and Cecil Day-Lewis – she signed a plea for the abolition of nuclear weapons. She also protested against the imprisonment of a Soviet dissident, and against the severe treatment by the Russian authorities of the Bolshoi Ballet dancers Valery and Galina Panov. But by now one long-standing campaign had been won: hanging had been abolished in 1969.

At the age of 60, and then again at 65, she had started writing her auto-biography, but had become fascinated by her family history, and 'never got beyond the great uncles'. Eventually she had accepted an offer from Elizabeth Sprigge to help her. The book then turned into a biography, for which she and Lewis spent many hours digging up the past. Now published, it had a foreword by Sybil in which she described her biographer as 'a generous friend who sees few faults where there are many'. It was a disappointingly superficial and uncritical work; Kenneth Allsop in the *Evening News* called it 'unabashed idolatory'. The family too were disappointed: Diana Devlin suggests the writer missed 'Sybil's sharp intellect and the steel within her character', while Penny Pocock remembers 'she was so doting Granny found it exhausting'.

In May 1972 Sybil returned to Rochester as a guest of the local paper, and spent a day visiting all her childhood haunts: the cathedral, the castle, the Vines, and her home in Minor Canon Row. 'I owe everything to this place,' she said. She went into St Margaret's Church where her father had been the vicar, and where she promised later in the year to read an epistle for the church's seven hundredth anniversary celebrations. There were now plans for her to become a tourist attraction, for her voice to echo round the castle battlements as part of the city's Son et Lumière show.

She appeared at the Film and Television Arts Awards ceremony at the Albert Hall, where she caused a sensation in front of millions of television viewers by ignoring protocol and going across the platform for an impromptu chat with Princess Alexandra: 'I wasn't supposed to be talking to her,' she admitted afterwards. 'But I just had to because of her mother, the late Princess Marina. She was so good to me, and her grandfather too.'

She was still able to work in radio. She read *The Viceroy's Daughter*, a selection of letters from India in the 1920s written by Alice, Countess of Reading. She and Athene Seyler repeated their roles in *Arsenic and Old Lace*, supported by Prunella Scales and Dindsdale Landen, and reminisced with Basil Dean about their Gaiety and Grand Guignol days in *Three's Company*, a discussion directed by Hallam Tennyson. By now it was difficult for her to get to the studio, so recordings were done at Swan Court. Here, directed by Graham Gauld, she chose the period of *Saint Joan* for 'A Time of My Life'. 'I do like speaking on the air like this,' she said, 'because nobody can see me, and I look an awful sight now.'

In another broadcast she and John Casson read extracts from his book *Lewis and Sybil*, an affectionate, perceptive memoir about his parents. Full of vivid detail about their personal and working lives, it also provided an honest portrait of their strengths and weaknesses, and the impact of their fame on their children and grandchildren. According to Dirk Campbell, Sybil was not entirely happy with the first draft. 'Because John was in the navy and Christopher was a conscientious objector, he was quite nasty about Christopher, he gave him a very bad press. Sybil was very upset about his treatment of him, and had long talks with John about it.'

The celebrations for her ninetieth birthday in October 1972 reflected the great esteem and affection in which she was held. First came a party thrown by Collins, jointly to celebrate her birthday and the publication of *Lewis and Sybil*. Then came a concert at the Queen Elizabeth Hall by the Philomusica of London. Sybil chose the programme, which included pieces by Handel, Bach and Mozart. For Haydn's 'Toy Symphony' her soloists were Léon Goossens on toy trumpet, Joyce Grenfell on drums, and John Casson on triangle, with Millicent Martin imitating a nightingale and, less predictably, Jeremy Thorpe a quail. The Liberal Party leader said in a speech that Sybil 'had enlarged and enriched the lives of millions in many lands', after which, according to Philip Hope-Wallace, 'booming and joyous and saying she had never felt less like ninety, the Dame thanked us from the bottom of her heart and then – with a very characteristic touch – had second thoughts and observed: "What am I thanking *you* for?", which got one of those laughs which you remember for years.'

Finally came a tribute from the profession. Called simply *Sybil*, directed by Murray MacDonald, George Rylands and Wendy Toye at the Haymarket, it aimed 'to show how deeply the British theatre loves this elder stateswoman of the stage', with all profits at Sybil's request going to the actors' home Denville Hall. The cast recalled dramatic and light-hearted moments from her 68 years on stage while, sitting in a box with Princess Alexandra, Sybil lent forward, calling out 'Yes! Yes!' at the reminiscences. The actors then spoke lines from scenes they had shared with her. The last reading was from *Uncle Vanya*, with Joan Plowright turning to Sybil's box on the line: 'You ought to be in bed, nurse darling. It's late.'

In the second half the stars performed pieces linked to illustrious figures from the theatrical past – Olivier and Kemble, Edith Evans and Sarah Siddons, Scofield and Edmond Kean, Gwen Ffrangcon-Davies and Ellen Terry. Then, as Wendy Toye remembered: 'Sybil hobbled on with her stick, and halfway across the stage stopped using it, and waved to the audience with it.' After a huge standing ovation, she said: 'I feel so awfully moved and touched. It has been such a real joy tonight, a tribute to the theatre because I am the oldest working girl around.' When the national anthem was played, none of the 80 people on stage or the 900 in the audience joined in – until Sybil's clear voice rang out, and then they did. Afterwards, during a party on stage, Guinness re-enacted his first meeting with her. Later Priestley wrote: 'Never had the famous old playhouse been so warm with affection. That night her unwearying art and her enthusiasm for everybody and everything brought gigantic dividends.'

A few days later Sybil wrote to Cecil Beaton: 'I'm in bed after driving 300 miles yesterday to see my dear old brother Russell, who is *very* ill – he's two years younger than me, but older physically.' After the death of his wife Rosemary, Russell had gone to live in a former pub in Foulsham, Norfolk. Invariably short of money, much of it spent on drink, forever moving house but never owning one, he had lost a fortune by selling the film rights of his Dr Syn books, which were subsequently sold to Disney. He had only recently gained a discharge from bankruptcy, for which he had blamed his 'unbusinesslike ways over income tax returns'.

This was Sybil's farewell to the great companion of her childhood and youth, to whom she had remained close, and given frequent moral and financial support throughout his chequered life. He died a couple of days later, on 7 November. Despite his long acting career, the obituaries were generally headlined 'Dr Syn Author Dies'. Sybil wrote to Gwen Ffrangcon-Davies: 'My darling old Russell was so full of fun, though feeble – well, God rest him.' She helped to organise his service of thanksgiving, held three months later at St Paul's in Covent Garden: it included readings by Daniel Thorndike and John Casson, and the anthem 'O for the Wings of a Dove', which as a boy soprano Russell had sung at Queen Victoria's funeral.

Sybil was always quick to console others for their losses. Jill Balcon, married to Cecil Day-Lewis, recalls: 'When Cecil was dying she wrote to me constantly. I was very touched.' After his death Sybil wrote: 'You will learn to live with your sorrow, but it doesn't get any better – but perhaps that's as well – for we can then go on as they would have us.' She was still uncertain about there being an after-life. Following the death of Margaret Rutherford she wrote to her husband Stringer Davis: 'God rest her, the darling woman – Oh! Stringer, I do so wonder where they are – our beloveds – Are they near us? I do hope so.'

While others of her age were critical of the younger generation, Sybil used the inevitable birthday interviews to speak positively about them: 'Today youngsters are more honest, more kind, more considerate. Thousands of them work hard at helping others. My generation never gave a hoot about people worse off than themselves.' She praised them for their political commitment.

'It's a good sign that they are interested in politics, and problems of the world, and they take up cudgels for so many things that are cruel and unkind.' She had become more tolerant of couples separating when their marriage broke down. Earlier, when Diana Devlin had told her of problems with hers, she replied: 'I can't think how you are so angry with each other....One must not think of oneself all the time – there are duties!!... One must think of other people and one's obligation to them.' But now her view had mellowed, and she decided that 'when people really can't get on together in a marriage, they should part'.

Olivier was one who had been on the sharp end of her views on the subject. As an intimate friend of his for more than 50 years, Sybil was an obvious person for his latest biographer, John Cottrell, to interview. Her assessment of Olivier's character was wildly contradictory: 'Larry has a tremendous temper and a sharp tongue too,' she said. 'Anybody who's supposed to be cock of the walk, he can strip down very nicely. He can make you feel a real fool.' She then went on to describe him as 'the most loveable man in the theatre', a far from common view clearly influenced by their close relationship. 'I can't tell you what a friend he has been to me – the best friend I know, because he's deeply, deeply sympathetic and genuinely emotional. He's got such enormous sympathy for people, and that's what makes him such a tremendously good actor.' More interestingly and shrewdly, she agreed with Agate's opinion that he is 'a comedian by instinct and a tragedian by art'. She accepted that he could be terrifying and sinister, and could make villainy attractive: 'He could do the awfulness. It's just the big parts like Lear that he couldn't quite compass. He got a lot of the humour in Lear, but I don't think he has the stature for great tragedy.'

She continued to miss Lewis. 'I haven't coped with his death really,' she told journalist Lynda Lee-Potter. 'I just talk about him as though he's here. It's so awful when you've been such tremendous pals for 60 years. He held me up somehow.' She did however feel able to be more open about their professional differences: 'We argued the line of every play I was in, and about their interpretation,' she told Russell Harty on his chat-show. 'He used to make me mad. I used to spout out something I thought was so good, and he would say: "Oh dear, that's awful."'

The arthritis continued, but publicly she managed to be stoical about it: 'I've been so healthy all my life, I feel it's due to me,' she said. 'I've jolly well just got to lump it.' Not long after she remarked: 'I don't feel 90 in my head, but I feel 180 in my body.' She fell over now and then, but remained calm, observing: 'When I'm down I don't panic, because I think God wants me to have a little rest.' In October 1973 she turned down an invitation to the launch of Michael Denison's autobiography *Overture and Beginners*, telling him: 'I think I'd be idiotic to come, in case of collapse, which would be very awkward, and I'd be accused of "stealing the thunder".'

Eventually it was arranged for an Irish woman, Kathleen Dell, to live at Swan Court as a housekeeper/companion. 'I love having her here, we can have a good row!' she told Graham Gauld. To Mary she confessed: 'Thank God I'll never need to cook again!' Now forbidden to travel, she was increasingly confined to the flat, and restricted in her activity: 'I read and read and do my poems and learn new ones,' she explained to Colette O'Niel. 'I struggle with a few exercises on the piano – since Lewis went I've not been able to play – fingers all gone awry!!' She still learned a few lines of verse every day, but had to give up the Greek. She found herself enjoying television, especially talks, news programmes and discussions, *Upstairs Downstairs*, *Coronation Street* ('my favourite programme – I never miss it') and, more surprisingly, *Basil Brush* and the wrestling. One day she suddenly thought she saw herself on screen, but it proved to be Stanley Baxter impersonating her.

With John and Patricia in Chelsea and Mary and Ian in Ealing, there was no shortage of family support. Christopher remained in Ireland, gaining new popularity in his role as a church canon in the long-running serial *The Riordans*. Ann and Douglas had recently come over from Canada, and were now leading a company at the newly opened Crucible in Sheffield. They had planned to work there with Guthrie, but he had died before the season began. Susan Wooldridge, a young company member, remembers Ann's power as an actress: 'As a person she was very open, generous and modest, and yet on stage she could produce real fury. She was a wonderful Aase in *Peer Gynt*, and of course looked very like her mother.'

Among Sybil's visitors was Basil Langton's daughter Jessica Andrews, who remembers: 'She was in bed, but still very lively and alert, very sharp in her memory and passionate about the theatre.' Another was Megan Jones, who showed her two scrapbooks she had made of her career. Sybil read her some lines from the Greek text of *The Trojan Women*, and they talked about music. 'She said she no longer played the Bach preludes and fugues, but could still hear them in her head,' she recalls. Soon afterwards her fingers became numb, with two of the right hand eventually sticking together. Her back pain made it difficult to play, so she was propped up with cushions in her wheelchair. One hand was fine, so she could play duets with Mary.

In January 1973 at Covent Garden she featured in *Fanfare*, a celebration in words and music devised and directed by Patrick Garland and John Copley to mark the UK's entry into the European Community. While Olivier, Max Adrian and Judi Dench took on most of the readings, Sybil again spoke her favourite 'Up at the Villa', and filled the Royal Opera House with her huge voice. John Barber wrote in the *Daily Telegraph*: 'Outshining them all, speaking more clearly and firmly than the others, was Sybil Thorndike. Leaving her nonagenarian's wheelchair in the wings, she leaned on her stick to recite her Browning poem extolling city life, but brandished it magnificently on the line "The procession sweeps by". She alone used no book.' The audience stood and cheered, thinking it would be the last time she performed in a theatre – as indeed it was. For once she was overcome, and in tears.

The following year – with Gielgud, Peggy Ashcroft, Joe Melia and Margaret Rawlings – she took part in a recital *Salute to the Chile of Pablo Neruda* at the Royal Court, held to raise money for persecuted artists all over the world, but most immediately for the Chilean artists suffering the consequences of the previous September's coup. She was also involved in a festival to celebrate the centenary of Lilian Baylis' birth, with a reading at a commemorative service in Southwark Cathedral. She watched *Tribute to the Lady* at the Old Vic, with Peggy Ashcroft impersonating the lady in question, and Barbara Jefford playing her. Barbara Leigh-Hunt was in the audience: 'Larry introduced her, and she was wheeled on by John. She stopped him, put her hands on the arms of the chair, got up, and walked to Larry, who caught her. From the front row Ann cried out: "She can't do that, she can't walk!"'

Unwell again in November, she stated: 'I am 92 and no longer a child. I really don't expect to act again.' In fact she did one more radio play, *The Evening is Calm*, a verse documentary about life in an old people's home by the Norwegian Paal Breeke. Its director Martin Jenkins recalls her initial difficulties: 'It was a dark and sombre piece, and she had quite a problem finding that, she was so ebullient and effervescent and outgoing. I said I felt the character was more inward-looking, and reflecting on the end of her life. "Oh I don't like to think about that," she said. But all the antennae were still there, and she eventually found a simplicity and a beauty, and a quiet, controlled sense of power.' Val Arnold-Forster in the *Guardian* was impressed, suggesting 'Sybil Thorndike at 93 has enough charm and verve to justify a wavelength to herself'.

That autumn she had to spend three weeks in Dovehouse Court, a council old people's home, as Katherine Dell was on holiday, and her children not able to provide the level of care she needed. She still went to church on Sundays, 'but as I fidget so much, they put me in a corner where no one can see me. It's murder getting down on my knees.' She insisted on going even when her housekeeper/companion was not available. On one such occasion she fainted, an ambulance was called, and she landed up in hospital: 'She's quite all right, but a little "piano" still,' John reported. On her 93rd birthday she received some good news, the Queen having awarded her an additional £100 Civil List Pension to add to her previous pension of £500.

On the National Theatre's last day at the Old Vic in February 1976, *Tribute to the Lady* was revived. Sybil was wheeled down the aisle to the front of the stalls by Jane, smiling and waving for the last time in the theatre that had meant so much to her. Peggy Ashcroft, repeating her impersonation of Lilian Baylis, announced: 'We've got our dear Sybil with us tonight.' Simon Callow recalls her response: 'Dressed in what appeared to be swathes of muslin, she turned round in her wheelchair and cried out "Hello everybody!" in a voice that shook the theatre to the very gods.' Peter Hall, who was taking over from Olivier as director of the National, received a letter from Sybil. 'She wrote to say how sad she was that she and Lewis were too old to be there at the start of the great adventure.'

She now spent most of her days at Swan Court, and was eventually confined to bed. One of her last visitors was Frances Cuka. 'She was propped up in bed, but very lucid,' she remembers. 'She looked so beautiful, her skin was like porcelain.' Claude Marks was with her: 'Her voice was faint, but she did not seem to be in pain, and her eyes were as bright and responsive as ever. As she looked at the sunshine outside and then considered her bed-ridden state, she exclaimed: "Oh it's such a *damn* nuisance!"' Tom Campbell remembers when he and Ann's other three children came to say good-bye to her. 'She was in a dreamy state, and not quite there. But even then she made a joke, and started acting the part of a grand duchess holding court, and laughing.'

Patricia had acted as her main family carer in recent months, but now Ann came to stay at Swan Court. Later she described Sybil's last days to Tanya Moisiewitch: 'I saw her every day and nearly all day. We had some really marvellous times, reading favourite books and plays too, Mother going through lots of parts, and of course remembering all kinds of odd people. It was a wonderful re-living of things. She still had great zest for anything.... Even when it was difficult to have the energy to speak, her voice came back when she read *Saint Joan*, and she would read a lot of poetry. Although she was in a lot of pain, she insisted she wouldn't be given anything that would get her fugged up. She wanted to keep her mind alert, and it always was.'

After her ninetieth-birthday gala someone had said they were sure there would be a celebration at 100. Sybil had replied: 'I do hope not.' But she did want to live longer than Lewis had done. When Mary told her she had achieved her goal, she rose slowly from her chair, looked upwards, and made a 'sucks-to-you' gesture to the heavens. After that, Ann remembered, 'she set about methodically doing the things she wanted to do. She went often to the river in her chair, and John took her for drives to all her old haunts. Her timing was beautiful to the end, she just decided when she was to go.'

As she weakened a nurse was employed to be present along with Katherine Dell. The end was peaceful: one day her breathing became less and less frequent, and then just stopped altogether. She died on the morning of 9 June 1976, with Ann at her bedside. She was cremated at Golders Green, which she had visited every year on the anniversary of Lewis' death. She had wanted her ashes to be scattered there with his, but when it was suggested there might be a request for them to be placed in Westminster Abbey, she had accepted the idea happily. In her will she left £10,345, her theatrical treasures, including the prompt books for *Saint Joan* and *Henry VIII*, to the Theatre Museum at the Victoria and Albert Museum, and £100 each to the Save the Children Fund, International Help for Children and the Actors' Charitable Trust. Among her papers was a list of the charities she supported: it ran to five pages.

On 2 July 1976 her long life was rounded with the service of thanksgiving and internment of her ashes in Westminster Abbey. Later there was the dedication of the tombstone where her ashes were buried in the south aisle. Finally, in the actors' church of St Paul's in Covent Garden, a memorial tablet was erected just below the one created for Lewis. Above the motto 'My head was in the skies and the glory of God was upon me', the simple inscription read: 'Sybil Thorndike, Actress and Musician'.

Epilogue

What was the essence of Sybil Thorndike's achievement as an actress? Why was she so admired and loved by her profession, as well as by the public at large? It seems fitting to end this biography with a mosaic of thoughts from some of those who helped me compile it, who knew or worked with her in various phases of her life.

Peter Hall   In her enthusiasm she represented so much that is important in the English theatre: the absolute love of Shakespeare and the classical tradition, but also a very progressive attitude to life. She believed theatre should reflect current living. I think her lasting influence is as an inspirer of the high seriousness of theatre. She really believed in it as a branch of the Workers' Educational Association.

Paul Scofield   She was a glorious actress, who suggested immense power. She aimed at the big targets, and used every ounce of her being to do justice to great classical themes. She was never melodramatic, because there was a steady reality in her being, a kind of sensible centre which precluded effect for its own sake. She was both commonsensical and poetic.

Joan Plowright   As drama students in the 1950s we held her in great affection, as an example of what was the best in acting. We were aware of being in the presence of a great and very powerful actress with a whole lifetime of experience behind her. Her later performances showed great humanity; it radiated from her. I always thought of her as having a kind of goodness, but not at all a pious one.

Frith Banbury   The best of Sybil was her wonderful vitality and her wonderful voice. The worst was her tendency to give the customers too much of what they wanted. From time to time she was self-indulgent, she was inclined to enjoy herself too much.

Prunella Scales   She was a tremendous actress, and always very truthful. Her stillness is what I remember. She was a good listener, and that's to do with artistic manners. She had a wonderful sense of timing, and a tremendous enjoyment of the work.

Patrick Dromgoole   She could be naturalistic if she wanted to be. But once you gave her a stage, a proscenium arch and an audience, she wanted to lift things, to take them above the ordinary.

Donald Sinden   She could project herself, as that generation could. But it was not just a matter of voice, it was personality, and Sybil had that in abundance. She was also the most wonderful member of an audience. She would sit on the edge of her seat, her eyes darting, watching everything, and always be the first to laugh.

Renée Asherson   I thought of her as embodying the dignity of the theatre. No one was quite such an emblem for its serious side. She was unique. But she wasn't solemn, she had great humour.

Hallam Tennyson   Offstage she was incredibly interested in other people and their work. She gave you an unalterable feeling that she enjoyed your company. But on stage she over-elocuted: she was the last trace of the Irving-Terry era, in which the important thing was to speak beautifully and clearly and be heard throughout the auditorium.

Frank Dunlop   She had this serene assurance on stage. When she came on she took charge without doing any excessive work. You were absolutely under her control straight away, you just wanted to be with her.

Dulcie Gray   She was a very strong person with very strong emotions, which was one of the reasons why she was such a good actress. She was probably the best-loved of anybody in the theatre.

Ronald Harwood   I'm not sure she was the greatest actress of her age, but she captured the imagination. What I liked was that she treated everyone the same. She had beautiful manners.

Richard Pasco   She was a great leader of a company. But there was no side to her, she didn't do the great actress thing. She was humble, and hyper-sensitive to other people, very sympathetic and wonderful to work with.

Christopher Fry   She had an enormous sympathy with human beings generally. You felt she was open to you, and you naturally fell in beside her. She gave you a feeling that you had known her for much longer than you had.

Rosemary Harris   I liked her shrewdness, her astuteness, her no-nonsense kindness and gentleness. I can't think of anybody kinder or warmer, especially to the young.

Tarquin Olivier   She had a tremendously magnetic character. You always felt she saw more deeply into you than anyone else had. You certainly were aware you were being appraised, but also that she was exercising a very forgiving perceptiveness.

Joyce Redman   It didn't matter what you were, rich or poor, she was a great humanist. She didn't care a damn except for what was right. She was the most gutsy woman I have ever known.

Corin Redgrave   Her shining spirit came through almost everything she did. She never wavered in her humanitarian Christian socialist beliefs. In the 1960s we tended to smile at her legendary enthusiasm for causes, not realising what an astonishing thing it was that a lady of that age could be so committed.

Julian Slade   You felt you couldn't behave badly in front of her, but she wasn't remotely autocratic. She had this ability to be thrilled by everything, a child-like quality in one sense, and yet she was very clever.

Judy Campbell   She wasn't loveable in a cuddly sense, but something about her made people want her advice, her backing and her approval. She could be inspiring and brave, and make other people brave. If I had to go into a gas chamber, and could choose someone to hold my hand, it would be Sybil.

The final word goes to *J B Priestley*, a version of whose sonnet for Sybil's ninetieth birthday was reproduced on her memorial in Westminster Abbey.

'When in *Who's Who* we reach the crowded page
Of Thorndike, Sybil – why, the world's your stage!
How far you've travelled – Lewis by your side,
Your own Glendowered Cambrian rock and pride –
Acting all womanhood from rags to riches,
Saints, Queens, wronged wives and even sly old bitches:
Nothing too large, too small, too late, too soon
(Shakespeare at night, Shaw in the afternoon):
No matter age or race or size, you've played it;
What could be made by zest and art, you've made it.
Signing all protests, lending each good cause a tongue,
You've swept into old age still champion of the young.
And while the scripts may sleep upon the shelf,
You play the last big role of all – YOURSELF.
The calls, the lights, may go but not, my dear, *this part*:
The glowing spirit – the great generous heart.'

Chronology

Theatre

Mrs Rawlings in *When the Devil Was Ill* by Charles McEvoy

Artemis in *Hippolytus* by Euripides

Caroline Blizzard in *Gentlemen of the Road* by Charles McEvoy

Lady Denison in *The Charity That Began at Home* by St John Hankin

Mrs Barthwick in *The Silver Box* by John Galsworthy

Nurse Price in *Cupid and the Styx* by J Sackville Martin

Bettina in *The Vale of Content* by Hermann Sudermann

Thora in *The Feud* by Edward Garnett

Gertrude Eckersley in *Tresspassers Will Be Prosecuted* by M A Arabian

1910	
January	Sal Fortescue in *Peg Woffington's Pearls* by C Duncan Jones and Dennis Cleugh, Court (Play Actors)
February	Columbine in *The Marriage of Columbine* by Harold Chapin, Court (Play Actors)
March–June	Duke of York's repertory season.
	Winifred in *The Sentimentalists* by George Meredith
	Emma Huxtable in *The Madras House* by Granville Barker
	Romp in *Prunella* by Granville Barker and Laurence Housman
	Maggie Massey in *Chains* by Elizabeth Baker
September	Emily Chapman in *Smith* by Somerset Maugham, Empire, New York
1911	
Spring and Summer	Tour of *Smith* in USA
1912	
June	Beatrice Farrer in *Hindle Wakes* by Stanley Houghton, Gaiety company at Aldwych (Stage Society); then Playhouse.
August 1912–	Gaiety, Manchester repertory season.
May 1913	Jennie Rollins in *The Question* by John J Wickham
	Mrs Eversleigh in *The Charity That Began at Home*
	Romp (later Privacy) in *Prunella*

Renie Dalrymple in *Revolt* by George Calderón
Ann Wallwyn in *The Pigeon* by John Galsworthy
Judith Anderson in *The Devil's Disciple* by Bernard Shaw
Julia in *The Rivals* by Richard Brinsley Sheridan
Malkin in *The Whispering Well* by Frank H Rose
Jane Clegg in *Jane Clegg* by St John Ervine

1913
May | Gaiety company at the Court.
Lady Philox in *Elaine* by Harold Chapin
Malkin in *The Whispering Well*
Jane Clegg in *Jane Clegg*
Ann Wellwyn in *The Pigeon*

September–
December | Gaiety, Manchester repertory season.
Annie Scott in *The Price of Thomas Scott* by Elizabeth Baker
Miss Stormit in *Nothing Like Leather* by Allan Monkhouse
Hester Dunnybrig in *The Shadow* by Eden Phillpotts
Portia in *Julius Caesar*
Mrs Cleland in *What the Public Wants* by Arnold Bennett
Jane Clegg in *Jane Clegg*
Mrs Barthwick in *The Silver Box*

October | Hester in *The Shadow*, Court

November 1914 | Four seasons of Shakespeare at the Old Vic. Played most of
–May 1918 | the main female characters, plus:
Prince Hal in *Henry IV Part 1*
The Fool in *King Lear*
Ferdinand in *The Tempest*
Launcelot Gobbo in *The Merchant of Venice*
Rugby in *The Merry Wives of Windsor*
Puck in *A Midsummer Night's Dream*
Other parts:
Lady Teazle in *The School for Scandal* by Richard Brinsley
Sheridan
Peg Woffington in *Masks and Faces* by Charles Reade and
Tom Taylor
Kate Hardcastle in *She Stoops to Conquer* by Oliver
Goldsmith
Angel Gabriel in *The Star of Bethlehem* (mystery play)

Nancy in *Oliver Twist* by Charles Dickens, adapted by
Russell Thorndike and E A Ross

Two revues: *The Sausage String's Romance, or a New Cut
Harlequinade* and *Seaman's Pie, a Naval Review of Revues
and Other Things*. Also appeared in the summer of 1916 in 12
Old Vic productions at the Shakespeare Memorial Theatre,
Stratford-upon-Avon.

1918	
May	Foible in *The Way of the World* by William Congreve (Stage Society)
June	Mrs Lopez in *The Profiteers*, in a variety bill, London Pavilion
	Françoise Regnard in 'The Kiddies in the Ruins', in *The Better 'Ole*, New Oxford, London
1919	
February	Princess Savitri in *Savitri* by Kedar Nath das Gupta, Comedy
	Cherry in *The Beaux' Stratagem* by George Farquhar, Haymarket
March	Sygne de Coûfontaine in *The Hostage* by Paul Claudel, Scala (Pioneer Players)
April	Naomi Melsham in *The Chinese Puzzle* by Marion Bower and Leon M Lion, New
July	James Barry in *Dr James Barry* by Olga Racster and Jessica Grove, St James'
September	Clara Borstwick in *The Great Day* by Louis N Parker and George R Sims, Drury Lane
October	Anna Wickham in *Napoleon* by Herbert Trench, Queen's (Stage Society)
	Hecuba in *The Trojan Women* by Euripides, Old Vic
November	Sakuntala in *Sakuntala* by Kalidasa, Winter Garden
December	Hecuba in *The Trojan Women*, Holborn Empire
1920	
February–March	Season at Holborn Empire.
	Hecuba in *The Trojan Women*
	Candida in *Candida*
	Medea in *Medea* by Euripides

	Mary Hey in *Tom Trouble* by John Burley
	Beryl Napier in *The Showroom* by Florence Bell
May	Mathilde Stangerson in *The Mystery of the Yellow Room* by Gaston Leroux, St James'
June	Céline in *The Children's Carnival* by Saint-Georges de Bouhélier, Kingsway (Pioneer Players)
September 1920 –June 1922	Two seasons of Grand Guignol at the Little. 24 parts played.

1921

February	Wife of Scrooge's Nephew in *A Christmas Carol* by Charles Dickens, Lyric
April	Mother Sawyer in *The Witch of Edmonton* by Thomas Dekker, John Ford and William Rowley, Lyric Hammersmith (Stage Society)
May	Lady Wraithe in *Shall We Join the Ladies?* by J M Barrie, Palace
June	Lady Macbeth in *Macbeth*, Odéon, Paris
November	Evadne in *The Maid's Tragedy* by Francis Beaumont and John Fletcher, Lyric Hammersmith (Phoenix Society)

1922

April	Old Lady in *Thirty Minutes in the Street* by Beatrice Mayor, Kingsway (Playwrights' Theatre)
May	Hecuba in *The Trojan Women*, Palace and Drury Lane
July	Jane in *Jane Clegg*, New
	His Betrothed in *Rounding the Triangle* by Eliot Crawshay-Williams, New
	Tosca in *La Tosca* (excerpts) by Victorien Sardou, Coliseum
September	Charlotte Fériol in *Scandal* by Henri Bataille, New
October	Medea in *Medea*, New
November	Beatrice in *The Cenci* by Percy Bysshe Shelley, New

1923

January	April Mawne in *Advertising April* by Herbert Farjeon and Horace Horsnell, Criterion
June	Provincial tour with *Jane Clegg*, *Medea*, *Scandal*, *Advertising April*
September	Imogen in *Cymbeline*, New
October	Elinor Shale in *The Lie* by Henry Arthur Jones, New

1924

January	Gruach in *Gruach* by Gordon Bottomley, St Martin's
March	Joan in *Saint Joan* by Bernard Shaw, New
May	Sonia in *Man and the Masses* by Ernst Toller, New (Stage Society)
	Madge Ashley in *Two Women and a Telephone* by Rice Bromley-Taylor, Aldwych (Play Actors)
July	Rosalind in *As You Like It*, Regent (Fellowship of Players)
October	Hecuba in *The Trojan Women*, New

1925

January	Joan in *Saint Joan*, Regent
February	Phaedra and Artemis in *Hippolytus*, Regent
March	Claire in *The Verge* by Susan Glaspell, Regent (Pioneer Players)
May	Daisy Drennan in *The Round Table* by Lennox Robinson, Wyndham's
	Elinor Shale in *The Lie*, Wyndham's
June	Medea in *Medea*, Christ Church College, Oxford
December	Queen Katharine in *Henry VIII*, Empire

1926

March	Beatrice in *The Cenci*, Empire
	Joan in *Saint Joan*, Lyceum
April	Duchesse de Croucy in *Israel* by Henry Bernstein, Strand
	Gertrude in *Hamlet*, Lyceum
June	Judith in *Granite* by Clemence Dane, Ambassador's
July	Helen Stanley in *The Debit Account* by Eliot Crawshay-Williams, New (Interlude Players)
December	Lady Macbeth in *Macbeth*, Prince's

1927

February	Nadejda Ivanovna Pestoff in *The Greater Love* by J B Fagan, Prince's
March	Angela Guiseley in *Angela* by Florence Bell, Prince's
April	Medea in *Medea*, Prince's
June	*Saint Joan* and *Medea*, Théâtre des Champs-Elysées, Paris
September 1927	Old Vic company at Lyric Hammersmith.
–February 1928	Katharina in *The Taming of the Shrew*
	Portia in *The Merchant of Venice*

Beatrice in *Much Ado About Nothing*
Chorus and Katherine in *Henry V*

1928

February   Judith in *Judith of Israel* by E de Marnay Baruch, Strand
April   Queen Elizabeth in *The Making of an Immortal* by George
                Moore, Arts
                Rosamund Withers in *The Stranger in the House* by Michael
                Morton and Peter Traill, Wyndham's
April 1928–   Tour of South Africa, appearing in *Saint Joan*, *Macbeth*, *The*
February 1929   *Lie*, *Jane Clegg*, *Henry V*, *Much Ado About Nothing*, plus:
                Mrs Phelps in *The Silver Chord* by Sidney Howard

1929

March   Barbara Undershaft in *Major Barbara* by Bernard Shaw,
                Wyndham's
April   Lily Cobb in *Mariners* by Clemence Dane, Wyndham's
                Lady Wraithe in *Shall We Join the Ladies?*, Palace
                Princess Halm Eberstein in *Daniel Deronda*, Palace
May   Jane Clegg in *Jane Clegg* and Medea in *Medea* (double-bill)
June   Lady Lassiter in *The Donkey's Nose* by Eliot Crawshay-
                Williams, Prince of Wales (Sunday Play Society)
December   Madame de Beauvais in *Madame Plays Nap* by Brenda
                Girvin and Monica Cozens, New

1930

January   Dorothy Lister in *The Devil* by Benn Levy, Arts
February   Ronnie's Mother in *To Meet the King* by H C G Stevens,
                Coliseum
March   Phèdre in *Phèdre* by Jean Racine, Arts
                Sylvette in *The Fire in the Opera House* by Georg Kaiser,
                Everyman Hampstead
April   Mrs Alving in *Ghosts* by Henrik Ibsen, Everyman
                Hampstead
May   Emilia in *Othello*, Savoy
August   Provincial tour, appearing in *Granite*, *Ghosts*, plus:
                Dolores Mendez in *The Squall* by Jean Bart
                Jess Fortune in *The Matchmaker* by Ashley Dukes

1931

March	Marcelle in *The Medium* by Pierre Mille and C de Vylar, Palladium
April	Joan in *Saint Joan*, His Majesty's, then Haymarket
	Monica Wilmot in *Dark Hester* by Walter Ferris, New
May	Eloise Fontaine in *Marriage by Purchase* by Steve Passeur, Embassy
December	Mrs Page in *Rosalind* by J M Barrie, Brighton Hippodrome

1932

January	The Citizen's Wife in *The Knight of the Burning Pestle* by Francis Beaumont and John Fletcher, Old Vic
February	Julie Renaudin in *The Dark Saint* by François de Curel, Fortune
April 1932– April 1933	Tour of Egypt, Palestine, Australia and New Zealand, appearing in *Saint Joan, Macbeth, Madame Plays Nap, Granite, Advertising April, Ghosts, The Silver Chord*, plus: Lady Cicely Waynflete in *Captain Brassbound's Conversion* by Bernard Shaw Kitty Fane in *The Painted Veil* by Somerset Maugham Gertrude Rhead in *Milestones* by Arnold Bennett and Edward Knoblock

1933

September	Evie Millward in *The Distaff Side* by John van Druten, Apollo
November	Mrs Siddons in *Mrs Siddons* by Naomi Royde Smith, Apollo

1934

March	Victoria Van Brett in *Double Door* by Elizabeth McFadden, Globe
April	Gertrude in *Hamlet*, Sadler's Wells
May	Nourmahal in *Aureng-Zebe* by John Dryden, Westminster
June	Passenger Z in *Village Wooing* by Bernard Shaw, Little
September	Evie Millward in *The Distaff Side*, Booth, New York

1935

June	Blanche Oldham in *Grief Goes Over* by Merton Hodge, Globe
November	Lady Bucktrout in *Short Story* by Robert Morley, Queen's

December	Lisha Gerart in *The Farm of Three Echoes* by Noel Langley, Wyndham's (1930 Players)
1936	
June	Mary Herries in *Kind Lady* by Edward Chodorov, Lyric
August–November	Provincial tour, appearing as:
	Passenger Z in *Village Wooing*
	Doris Gow in *Fumed Oak* by Noël Coward
	Lady Maureen Gilpin in *Hands Across the Sea* by Noël Coward
	Mrs Gascoigne in *My Son's My Son* by D H Lawrence
	Aphrodite and the Nurse in *Hippolytus*
1937	
February–May	Provincial tour, appearing as Betty Loveless in *Six Men of Dorset* by H Brooks and Miles Malleson
June	Ann Murray in *Yes, My Darling Daughter* by Mark Reed, St James'
December	Hecuba in *The Trojan Women*, Adelphi
1938	
January	Mrs Conway in *Time and the Conways* by J B Priestley, Ritz, New York
April	Volumnia in *Coriolanus*, Old Vic
September	Miss Moffat in *The Corn is Green* by Emlyn Williams, Duchess
1939	
December	Miss Moffat in *The Corn is Green*, Piccadilly
1940–1942	Toured towns and villages in Wales and the north, appearing as Lady Macbeth, Candida and Medea, plus: Rebekah and Chorus in *Jacob's Ladder* by Laurence Housman
1941	
March	Joan in *Saint Joan*, Palace
July	Constance in *King John*, New
1942	
September	Woman of Peace in *Cathedral Steps*, compiled by Clemence Dane, St Paul's Cathedral
December	Georgina Jeffreys in *The House of Jeffreys* by Russell Thorndike, Playhouse

1943
February   Spokeswoman in *Salute to the Red Army*, Royal Albert Hall
March   Mrs Alving in *Ghosts*, Gaiety Dublin
                    Lady Cicely Waynflete in *Captain Brassbound's Conversion*,
                    Gaiety Dublin
May   Mrs Hardcastle in *She Stoops to Conquer*, Theatre Royal,
                    Bristol
                    Lady Beatrice Cuffe in *Queen B* by Judith Guthrie, Theatre
                    Royal, Bristol
July   Mrs Dundass in *Lottie Dundass* by Enid Bagnold,
                    Vaudeville
November   The Goddess of Ignorance in *The Rape of the Locks* by
                    Menander, Queen Mary Hall, London
December   Queen of Hearts and White Queen in *Alice in Wonderland*
                    and *Alice Through the Looking-Glass* by Lewis Carroll, Scala

1944
August 1944–   Old Vic company at the New. Appeared as:
April 1945   Aase in *Peer Gynt* by Henrik Ibsen
                    Catherine Petkoff in *Arms and the Man* by Bernard Shaw
                    Queen Margaret in *Richard III*
                    Marina the Nurse in *Uncle Vanya* by Anton Chekhov
December   Queen of Hearts and White Queen in *Alice in Wonderland*
                    and *Alice Through the Looking-Glass*, Palace

1945
May-July   Toured with Old Vic company in Belgium, Germany and
                    France, with *Peer Gynt*, *Arms and the Man* and *Richard III*
September 1945   Old Vic company at the New.
–April 1946   Mistress Quickly in *Henry IV, Parts 1 and 2*
                    Jocasta in *Oedipus Rex* by Sophocles
                    The Justice's Lady in *The Critic* by Richard Brinsley
                    Sheridan
                    Marina the Nurse in *Uncle Vanya*
                    Catherine Petkoff in *Arms and the Man*

1946
May   Edith Bolling Wilson in *In Time to Come* by Howard Koch
                    and John Huston, King's Hammersmith
June   Clytemnestra in *Electra* by Euripides, King's Hammersmith

1947
April   Mrs Fraser in *Call Home the Heart* by Clemence Dane, St
               James'
August   Isobel Linden in *The Linden Tree* by J B Priestley, Duchess
1948
October   Isobel Linden in *The Linden Tree*, Glasgow Citizens'
November   Mrs Jackson in *The Return of the Prodigal* by St John
               Hankin, Globe
1949
February   Isabel Brocken in *The Foolish Gentlewoman* by Margery
               Sharp, Duchess
September   Aunt Anna Rose in *Treasure Hunt* by M J Farrell and John
               Perry, Apollo
1950
August   Lady Randolph in *Douglas* by John Home, Lyceum
               Edinburgh
1951
April   Mrs Whyte in *Waters of the Moon*, Haymarket
1953
November   Laura Anson in *A Day by the Sea*, Haymarket
1955
March–July   Tour of Australia and New Zealand, appearing as:
               The Grand Duchess in *The Sleeping Prince* by Terence
               Rattigan
               Mrs Railton-Bell in *Separate Tables* by Terence Rattigan
1956
June   Amy, Lady Monchensey in *The Family Reunion* by T S
               Eliot, Phoenix
1957
January   Mrs Callifer in *The Potting Shed* by Graham Greene, Bijou,
               New York
July 1957–   Tour of Australia and New Zealand, appearing as:
June 1958   Mrs St Maugham in *The Chalk Garden* by Enid Bagnold
1959
January   Dame Sophia Carrell in *Eighty in the Shade* by Clemence
               Dane, Globe
Autumn   Toured as Mrs Kittridge in *The Sea Shell* by Jess Gregg

1960
September   Lotta Bainbridge in *Waiting in the Wings* by Noël Coward,
                 Duke of York's

1961
October   Teresa in *Teresa of Avila* by Hugh Ross Williamson,
                 Vaudeville

1962
July   Marina the Nurse in *Uncle Vanya*, Chichester Festival
                 Theatre

November   Miss Crawley in musical of *Vanity Fair* by William
                 Thackeray, Queen's

1963
July   Marina the Nurse in *Uncle Vanya*, Chichester Festival
                 Theatre

September   Toured as Lady Beatrice Cuffe in *Queen B*

1964
January   Dowager Countess of Lister in *The Reluctant Peer* by
                 William Douglas-Home, Duchess

September   Mrs Storch in *Season of Goodwill* by Arthur Marshall,
                 Queen's

1965
March   Doris Tate in *Return Ticket* by William Corlett, Duchess

1966
February   Abby Brewster in *The Viaduct* by Marguerite Duras, Yvonne
                 Arnaud, Guildford

1968
February   Mrs Basil in *Call Me Jacky* by Enid Bagnold, Yvonne
                 Arnaud, Guildford

April   Toured as Mrs Bramson in *Night Must Fall* by Emlyn
                 Williams

1969
September   The Woman in *There Was an Old Woman* by John Graham,
                 Thorndike Leatherhead

Film

1921

Mrs Brand in *Moth and Rust*

1922

Various parts in *Tense Moments from Great Plays*

1928

Edith Cavell in *Dawn*

1929

The Mother in *To What Red Hell*

1931

Madame Duval in *A Gentleman of Paris*

Mrs Hawthorn in *Hindle Wakes*

1936

Ellen in *Tudor Rose*

1941

General Baines in *Major Barbara*

1947

Mrs Squeers in *Nicholas Nickleby*

1948

Mrs Mouncey in *Britannia Mews*

1950

Mrs Gill in *Stage Fright*

Mrs Marston in *Gone to Earth*

1951

Miss Bosanquet in *The Lady with the Lamp*

The Aristocratic Client in *The Magic Box*

1953

Queen Victoria in *Melba*

Mabel in *The Weak and the Wicked*

1957

The Queen Dowager in *The Prince and the Showgirl*

1958

Dora in *Alive and Kicking*

Granny McKinley in *Smiley Gets a Gun*

1959

Lady Fitzhugh in *Shake Hands with the Devil*

Emma Morgan in *Jet Storm*

1960
Lady Caroline in *Hand in Hand*
1961
Aunt Cathleen in *The Big Gamble*
1963
Marina the Nurse in *Uncle Vanya*

Television

1939
Widow Cagle in *Sun Up*
1954
Miss Cicely in *The Heirloom*
Catherine in *Mr Sampson*
1959
Dame Sophia Carroll in *Eighty in the Shade*
Mrs Whyte in *Waters of the Moon*
1960
Mauyra in *Riders to the Sea*
Sara Champline in *A Matter of Age*
1964
The Dowager Countess of Lister in *The Reluctant Peer*
1965
Mrs Moore in *A Passage to India*
Isobel in *Man and Mirror*
1966
A Forger in *Don't Utter a Note*
1968
Nurse in *The Father*
1970
Mother in *The Great Inimitable Mr Dickens*

Radio

1924
The Tragedy of Mr Punch
Columbine
Medea

1929
Saint Joan

1933
Coriolanus

1938
The Winter's Tale

1939
The Persians

1942
Abraham and Isaac

1944
Jane Clegg
Peer Gynt
Matrimonial News

1945
Henry IV, Parts 1 and 2

1946
The Trojan Women

1947
The Cenci
The Blue Bird

1948
The White Devil
Coriolanus
The Corn is Green

1949
Brand

1951
Comédienne

1952
The Women of Troy

1953
Saviours

1954
Henry VIII

1959
The Linden Tree
Henry VIII
Riders to the Sea
1961
The Sunday Market
A Picture of Autumn
1962
Spooner
1963
Waiting in the Wings
1965
God and Kate Murphy
The Sacred Flame
1966
The Loves of Cass McGuire
The Foolish Gentlewoman
Jane Clegg
1967
The Distaff Side
The Potting Shed
Saint Joan (scenes)
A Passage to India
Captain Brassbound's Conversion
1968
Peace
The Father
Your Loving Sybil
1969
Night Must Fall
The Son
The Captain's Log
1971
The Viceroy's Wife
Arsenic and Old Lace
1975
The Evening is Calm

Bibliography

Brooks Atkinson, *Broadway*, Cassell 1970

Michael Billington, *State of the Nation: British Theatre since 1945*, Faber 2007

Colin Chambers, *The Story of Unity Theatre*, Lawrence & Wishart, 1989

Katherine Cockin, *Women and Theatre in the Age of Suffrage*, Palgrave 2001

Gordon Crosse, *Shakespearean Playgoing 1890–1952*, Mowbray 1953

Basil Dean, *The Theatre at War*, Harrap 1956

Bernard F Dukore (ed), *The Collected Screenplays of Bernard Shaw*, George Pryor 1980

Tyrone Guthrie, *On Acting*, Studio Vista 1971

Richard J Hand and Michael Wilson, *London's Grand Guignol and the Theatre of Horror*, University of Exeter Press 2007

Holly Hill (ed), *Playing Joan*, Theater Communications Group 1987

Julie Holledge, *Innocent Flowers: Women in the Edwardian Theatre*, Virago 1981

Michael Sanderson, *From Irving to Olivier: A Social History of the Acting Profession 1880–1983*, Athlone Press 1984

J Thompson and A Toynbee (eds), *Essays in Honour of Gilbert Murray*, Allen & Unwin 1936

John Vickers, *The Old Vic in Photographs*, Saturn Press 1947

Harcourt Williams, *Old Vic Saga*, Winchester 1949

Audrey Williamson, *Old Vic Drama*, Rockliff 1948

Biographies

(Listed in alphabetical order according to their subject.)

Michael Billington, *Peggy Ashcroft*, Mandarin 1991

Eric Salmon, *Granville Barker: A Secret Life*, Heinemann 1983

Richard Findlater, *Lilian Baylis: The Lady of the Old Vic*, Allen Lane 1975

Elizabeth Shafer, *Lilian Baylis: A Biography*, University of Hertfordshire Press, 2006

Winifred Bannister, *James Bridie and His Theatre*, Rockliff 1955

James Harding, *Cochran*, Methuen, 1988

Philip Hoare, *Noël Coward*, Sinclair-Stevenson 1995

Eleanor Adland (ed), *Edy: Recollections of Edith Craig*, Muller 1949

Katherine Cockin (ed), *Edith Craig: Dramatic Lives*, Cassell 1998

Bryan Forbes, *Ned's Girl: The Life of Edith Evans*, Elm Tree Books 1977

Marion Cole, *Fogie: The Life of Elsie Fogerty*, Peter Davies 1967

Martial Rose, *Forever Juliet: The Life and Letters of Gwen Ffrangcon-Davies*, Larks Press 2003

Jonathan Croall, *Gielgud: A Theatrical Life*, Methuen 2000

Linda Ben-Zvi, *Susan Glaspell: Her Life and Times*, OUP New York 2005

Winifred Isaac, *Ben Greet and the Old Vic*, Greenbank Press 1964

Sheila Goodie, *Annie Horniman: A Pioneer in the Theatre*, Methuen 1990

Rex Pogson, *Miss Horniman and the Gaiety Theatre*, Rockliff 1952

Christopher Fitz-Simon, *The Boys: A Biography of Micheál Maclíammóir and Hilton Edwards*, Nick Hern 1994

Terry Coleman, *Olivier*, Bloomsbury 2005

Anthony Holden, *Olivier*, Weidenfeld & Nicolson, 1988

John Heilpern, *John Osborne: A Patriot for Us*, Chatto & Windus 2006

Judith Cook, *Priestley*, Bloomsbury 1997

Alan Strachan, *Secret Dreams: A Biography of Michael Redgrave*, Weidenfeld & Nicolson 2004

John Miller, *Ralph Richardson*, Sidgwick & Jackson 1995

Michael Darlow, *Terence Rattigan: The Man and His Work*, Quartet 2000

Martin Duberman, *Paul Robeson*, Bodley Head, 1989

Angela V John, *Elizabeth Robins: Staging a Life 1862–1952*, Routledge 1995.

Kenneth Barrow, *Flora: The Life of Dame Flora Robson*, Heinemann 1981

Allan Chappelow, *Shaw the Villager and Human Being*, Charles Skilton 1961

Archibald Henderson, *Shaw, Playwright and Prophet*, D Appleton 1932

Michael Holroyd, *Bernard Shaw: Vol 3 The Lure of Fantasy*, Chatto & Windus 1991

Lawrence Langner, *GBS and the Lunatic*, Hutchinson 1964

Margot Peters, *Bernard Shaw and the Actresses*, Doubleday, 1980

Joy Melville, *Ellen and Edy*, Pandora Press 1987

Milly Barranger, *Margaret Webster*, University of Michigan Press, 2004

James Harding, *Emlyn Williams: A Life*, Weidenfeld & Nicolson 1993

Wendy Trewin, *All on Stage: Charles Wyndham and the Alberys*, Harrap 1980

Memoirs

Gary Powell (ed), *Robert Atkins: An Unfinished Autobiography*, Society for Theatre Research 1994

George Baker, *The Way to Wexford*, Headline 2002

E Martin Browne, *Two Into One*, Cambridge University Press 1981

C B Cochran, *Secrets of a Showman*, Heinemann 1935

Basil Dean, *Seven Ages: An Autobiography 1888–1927*, Hutchinson 1970

Alec Guinness, *Blessings in Disguise*, Hamish Hamilton 1985

Tyrone Guthrie, *A Life in the Theatre*, Hamish Hamilton 1960

Charles Hickman, *Directed by – *, New Horizon 1981

Leon M Lion, *The Surprise of My Life: The Lesser Half of an Autobiography*, Hutchinson, 1945

Micheál Maclíammóir, *All for Hecuba: An Irish Theatrical Autobiography*, Methuen 1946

Constance Malleson, *After Ten Years*, Jonathan Cape 1931

Arthur Marshall, *Life's Rich Pageant*, Hamish Hamilton 1984

Claude Marks, *Theatre Sketchbook*, Amber Lane Press 1982

Raymond Massey, *A Hundred Different Lives*, Robson Books 1979

Nora Nicholson, *Chameleon's Dish*, Paul Elek 1973

Laurence Olivier, *Confessions of an Actor*, Weidenfeld & Nicolson 1982

Joan Plowright, *And That's Not All: The Memoirs of Joan Plowright*, Orion 2001

Michael Powell, *Million Dollar Movie*, Heinemann 1992

Graham Robertson, *Time Was*, Hamish Hamilton 1931

J B Priestley, *Particular Pleasures*, Heinemann, 1975

Ned Sherrin, *The Autobiography*, Little, Brown 2005

Ernest Thesiger, *Practically True*, Heinemann 1927

Ben Travers, *A-Sitting on a Gate*, W H Allen 1978

Margaret Webster, *The Same Only Different: Five Generations of a Great Theatre Family*, Gollancz 1969

Margaret Webster, *Don't Put Your Daughter on the Stage*, Alfred Knopf 1972

Arnold Wesker, *As Much as I Dare*, Century 1994

Herbert Wilcox, *Twenty-Five Thousand Sunsets*, Bodley Head 1967

Critics

James Agate, *Contemporary Theatre*, 1923, 1924, 1925, 1926

James Agate, *At Half Past Eight*, Cape 1923

James Agate, *The Amazing Theatre*, Harrap 1939

James Agate, *A Short View of the English Stage 1900–1926*, Herbert Jenkins 1926

Beverley Baxter, *First Nights and Footlights*, Hutchinson 1955

George W Bishop, *My Betters*, Heinemann 1957

Caryl Brahms, *The Rest of the Evening's My Own*, W H Allen 1964

W A Darlington, *Six Thousand and One Nights: Forty Years a Critic*, Harrap 1960

Alan Dent, *Preludes and Studies*, Macmillan 1942

Archibald Haddon, *Green Room Gossip*, Stanley Paul 1922

Harold Hobson, *Theatre*, Longman 1948

Desmond MacCarthy, *Drama*, Putnam 1940

Hannen Swaffer, *Who's Who*, Hutchinson 1929

J C Trewin, *The Gay Twenties*, Macdonald 1958

J C Trewin, *The Turbulent Thirties*, Macdonald 1960

J C Trewin, *The Theatre since 1900*, Dakers 1951

Audrey Williamson, *Theatre of Two Decades*, Rockcliff 1951

A E Wilson, *Playgoer's Pilgrimage*, Stanley Paul 1938

T C Worsley, *The Fugitive Art: Dramatic Commentaries 1947–1951*, John Lehmann 1952

Diaries, Letters

James Agate, *Ego* 1: Hamish Hamilton 1935, 2: Gollancz 1936, 3–9: Harrap 1938–1948

Colin Clark, *The Prince, the Showgirl and Me*, HarperCollins 1995

L W Connolly (ed), *Bernard Shaw and Barry Jackson*, University of Toronto Press 2002

Alan Dent (ed), *Bernard Shaw and Mrs Patrick Campbell: Their Correspondence*, Gollancz 1952

Dan Laurence (ed), *The Collected Letters of Shaw*, vols 1–4, Max Reinhardt 1965–88

Sources and Notes

My principal sources have been the interviews I conducted with nearly two hundred people who knew or worked with Sybil Thorndike, who are listed in the Acknowledgements. I have also drawn throughout on the books written by or about the Thorndike and Casson families, listed below; on Sybil's letters to her family, friends, and colleagues in the theatre; and on the scores of articles and reviews by or about her in newspapers, books and periodicals.

John Casson, *Lewis and Sybil: A Memoir*, Collins, 1972

Patricia Casson (ed), *'My Dear One': A Victorian Courtship*, Julia MacRae 1984 (PC)

Diana Devlin, *A Speaking Part: Lewis Casson and the Theatre of His Time*, Hodder & Stoughton, 1982 (DD)

Sheridan Morley, *Sybil Thorndike: A Life in the Theatre*, Weidenfeld & Nicolson 1977

Elizabeth Sprigge, *Sybil Thorndike Casson*, Gollancz 1971 (ES)

Russell Thorndike, *Sybil Thorndike*, Thornton Butterworth, 1930; Eyre & Spottiswoode, 1950 (RT)

Sybil Thorndike and Russell Thorndike, *Lilian Baylis*, Chapman & Hall, 1938

J C Trewin, *Sybil Thorndike*, Rockcliff, 1955

1 When Arthur Met Agnes

Much of the family history is described by Sybil in a fragment of autobiography, included in the account of her parents' Victorian courtship (PC).

2 A Kentish Lass

The principal source is Russell Thorndike's lively and detailed biography (RT), a delightful if not always reliable account of their Rochester childhood. The letters between their parents appear in PC.

3 The Young Musician

Sybil's short musical career is described in RT.

4 Drama School and Ben Greet

Her drama student year is also covered in RT. Information about Greet and his company is in Winifred Isaac's book on Ben Greet.

5 An Innocent Abroad

Most of Sybil's letters from America appear in RT.

6 Fallen Among Highbrows

Lewis' history is drawn from Diana Devlin's informative biography of her grandfather (DD). Julie Holledge's book on women in the Edwardian theatre contains useful material on the Women's Social and Political Union and the Actress' Franchise League.

7 Annie Horniman and the Gaiety

Valuable sources for Sybil's time at the Gaiety are the two biographies of Annie Horniman by Sheila Goodie and Rex Pogson, and Basil Dean's memoir *Seven Ages*.

8 Granville Barker and America

The 1910 repertory season at the Duke of York's is dealt with in detail in Eric Salmon's biography of Granville Barker.

9 The Gaiety Revisited

The two Horniman biographies are again useful sources for the 1912–13 Gaiety years.

10 The Old Vic and Lilian Baylis

The early history and wartime years of the theatre are covered in the biographies of Lilian Baylis by Richard Findlater, Elizabeth Shafer, and Sybil and Russell Thorndike, and the books on the Old Vic by Harcourt Williams and Audrey Williamson.

11 The Pity of War

As for Chapter 10.

12 The New Tragedienne

Sybil's memories of Edy Craig can be found in Eleanor Adland's volume of recollections, in her essay 'The Festival in the Barn Theatre – 1947'.

13 Grand Guignol

Further valuable detail appears in Richard J Hand and Michael Wilson's book on London's Grand Guignol, which includes the text of ten of the plays performed at the Little.

14 The Albery Partnership

Wendy Trewin's book on Wyndham and the Alberys covers the managerial partnership with Bronson Albery.

15 Saint Joan

The books on Shaw listed in the Bibliography have all proved useful.

16 Top of the Tree

Linda Ben-Zvi's book on Susan Glaspell covers *The Verge*.

17 Lady Macbeth and Nurse Cavell

The kind of voice exercises Elsie Fogerty gave to Sybil and many others to work on is spelt out in Marion Cole's biography of the founder of the Central School.

18 Into Africa

The main source here is Sybil's own account of the trip to Africa, as told to Elizabeth Sprigge (ES).

19 Shaw to Ibsen

A detailed account of the founding of Equity appears in Michael Sanderson's social history of the acting profession.

20 Robeson, Guinness and a Dame

The background to the production of *Othello* is covered in Martin Duberman's biography of Paul Robeson. Alec Guinness' account of his meeting with Sybil and Lewis is in his memoir *Blessings in Disguise*.

21 Australia and Beyond

The main source is Sybil's own account of the Australia and New Zealand trip, as told to Elizabeth Sprigge (ES).

22 Back in the USA

Brooks Atkinson's comprehensive history *Broadway* is useful for this and Sybil's later trips to America.

23 On the Road

Among other sources, I have based the description of the tour of *Six Men of Dorset* on Sybil's own account (ES), and on Nora Nicholson's memoir.

24 J B Priestley to Emlyn Williams

James Harding's biography of Emlyn Williams has been a key source for the account of *The Corn is Green*.

25 A Pacifist at War

The difficulties of filming *Major Barbara* in wartime are spelt out in Bernard Dukore's book on Shaw's screenplays.

26 Shakespeare for the Miners

Background information and correspondence about the CEMA tours can be found in the Theatre Museum collection within the Victoria and Albert Museum.

27 Red Army to White Queen

Basil Dean's *The Theatre at War* provides more detailed descriptions of *Salute to the Red Army* and *Cathedral Steps*.

28 Triumph at the New

Sources for the celebrated 1944–45 season include the biographies of Olivier and Richardson by Anthony Holden and John Miller, and John Burrell's introduction to John Vickers' photographic volume of the Old Vic productions.

29 Among the Ruins

The main source for the tour of Europe is the private correspondence between Sybil and Lewis.

30 A New Age

The Olivier and Richardson biographies are again essential sources.

31 Cavalcanti, Hitchcock and Powell

Winifred Bannister's biography of James Bridie is useful background for John Casson's time at the Glasgow Citizens'. Michael Powell's memoir is valuable for *Gone to Earth*.

32 Sybil and Edith at the Haymarket

Their relationship, both here and earlier, is well covered by Bryan Forbes' biography of Edith Evans.

33 Gielgud and a Jubilee

Details of the Gielgud affair are mainly drawn from my own biography of the actor.

34 Far Horizons

Sybil and Lewis' travels to Australia and elsewhere are drawn mainly from her own account (ES).

35 Waiting for Marilyn

There are detailed accounts of the troubled filming of *The Prince of the Showgirl* in Terry Coleman's biography of Olivier, and in Colin Clark's diary.

36 Fifty in the Sun

Brooks Atkinson's *Broadway* is again a valuable background source for Sybil's final American visit. For the trip to Australia and New Zealand, I have mainly used her own account, as told to Elizabeth Sprigge (ES).

37 Noël Coward and Saint Teresa

Margaret Webster provides a blow-by-blow account of *Waiting in the Wings* in her memoir *Don't Put Your Daughter on the Stage*.

38 Olivier and Chekhov at Chichester

The memoirs of Olivier and Joan Plowright, and Alan Strachan's biography of Redgrave, provide detailed descriptions of this memorable production of *Uncle Vanya*.

39 Vanity Fair to TW3

George Baker's memoir *The Road to Wexford* includes an inside account of the accident-prone production of *Vanity Fair*, while Ned Sherrin in his autobiography describes Sybil's involvement in *That Was the Week That Was*.

40 Later Stages

A detailed description of *Season of Goodwill* is to be found in Arthur Marshall's memoir *Life's Rich Pageant*.

Chapters 41–44 are based principally on my interviews.

My thanks go to the publishers listed in the Bibliography from whose books I have quoted material.

Acknowledgements

I owe a huge debt to the many people who gave me their time, their memories and, in many cases, their hospitality. I must thank first members of Sybil Thorndike's family, for talking to me and giving me invaluable access to her letters and other material. My particular thanks go to her daughter Mary Casson, for patiently in several sessions providing me with recollections of her mother and their family life. I'm also most grateful to Ben Campbell, Dirk Campbell, Douglas Campbell, Teresa Campbell, Tom Campbell, Anthony Casson, Bronwen Casson, Glynis Casson, Jane Casson, Diana Devlin, Ian Haines, Sybil Mitchell, Penny Pocock, Tom Pocock, Janet Ritchie, Daniel Thorndike, Dickon Thorndike and Phyllis Mary Walshaw.

I am greatly indebted to the following for kindly allowing me to plunder their memories in interviews: David Andrews, Renée Asherson, Richard Attenborough, George Baker, Jill Balcon, Peggy Batchelor, Timothy Bateson, Stanley Baxter, Sam Beazley, Richard Bebb, Derek Bond, Bette Bourne, Peter Bowles, Rosalind Boxall, Margot Boyd, Richard Briers, Ian Burford, David Burke, Sheila Burrell, Anna Calder-Marshall, Judy Campbell, Heather Chasen, Peter Copley, Helen Cotterill, John Crocker, Frances Cuka, Peggy Cummins, Ann Davies, Alan Dobie, Clive Francis, John Gordon, Dulcie Gray, Kenneth Griffith, Walter Hall, Rosemary Harris, Thelma Holt, David Horovitch, Peter Howell, William Hutt, Saeed Jaffrey, Pauline Jameson, Barbara Jefford, Nicholas Jones, Miriam Karlin, Rachel Kempson, Jean Kent, Rosalind Knight, Robert Lang, Barbara Leigh-Hunt, Helen Lindsay, Terence Longdon, William Lucas, Violet Luckham, John McCallum, Ian McKellen,

Virginia McKenna, Carol MacReady, Hugh Manning, Jehane Markham, Kika Markham, Petra Markham, John Mills, Barry Morse, John Moffatt, Perlita Neilson, Milo O'Shea, Richard Pasco, Siân Phillips, Joan Plowright, Ann Queensberry, Corin Redgrave, Joyce Redman, Terence Rigby, Paul Rogers, Prunella Scales, Margaretta Scott, Gerald Sim, Donald Sinden, Heather Stoney, John Stride, Virginia Stride, Janet Suzman, Richard Todd, Margaret Tyzack, Jane Wenham, Bay White, Sonia Williams, Margaret Wolfit, Susan Wooldridge, Peter Woodthorpe, Edgar Wreford.

Roy Ward Baker, Michael Bakewell, Frith Banbury, Doris Barry, Richard Digby-Day, Patrick Dromgoole, Frank Dunlop, Graham Gauld, Philip Grout, Peter Hall, Waris Husein, Martin Jenkins, John Powell, James Roose-Evans, Ned Sherrin, Wendy Toye, Hallam Tennyson, John Tydeman, Hugh Wooldridge, William Corlett, Christopher Fry, John Graham, Robin Miller, Johnny Dankworth, Antony Hopkins, Cleo Laine, Charles Mackerras, Blanche Mundlak, Julian Slade, Tanya Moisiewitch.

Patsy Ainley, Jessica Andrews, Catherine Ashmore, Philippa Astor, John Bickersteth, Kitty Black, James Crathorne, Sylvia Crathorne, Ronald Hayman, Julia Jarrett, Jane-Ann Jones, Megan Jones, Bruce Lewisohn, Neville Lewisohn, Barbara Niemskaya, Duncan Noel-Paton, Tarquin Olivier, Sheila Ronald, Adam Rowntree, Bruce Sharman, George Speaight, Mary Speaight, Natasha Spender, Ion Trewin, Hazel Vincent Wallace, Adrian Walmsley and Shirley Williams.

I am grateful to the following for corresponding with me about Sybil: Michael Anderson, Tony Barlow, Elizabeth Bird, Kevin Brownlow, John Butler, George Cole, Marie Dakin, Richard Fleischer, Bryan Forbes, Brian Glanvill, Pauline Jameson, Philip Jones, Patricia Kennedy, Barbara Laurenson, Frank Long, Kathleen McCreery, Vi Marriott, Vivian Matalon, Alexander Murray, John Neville, Graham Payn, Judith Payne, Evelyn Pugh, Amanda Saunders, Paul Scofield, Judith Searle, Muriel Spark, David Spenser, John Sumner, Guy Thomas, Norman Tozer, Phyllis Urch, Mary Walker, Stanley Wells and David William.

Other biographers have in different ways been generous with help and information: Milly Barringer, John Butler, Katherine Cockin, Terry Coleman, Angela John, Martial Rose, Eric Salmon, Alan Strachan and Irving Wardle. I am also grateful for help from Fran Abrams, Don Chapman, Suzanne Farrington, Helen Grime, Marie Hartley, Peter Hiley, Jinx Nolan, David Paramor, Michaela Schwarz-Santos G Henriques, Ben Thompson, Harriet Ward, Colin Ward and Siân Williams.

I owe a special word of thanks to Megan Jones, who kindly made available to me her substantial collection of material relating to Sybil's career; to Richard Mangan at the Mander and Mitchenson Theatre Collection, for his sustained help and expertise in theatre history; to Brian McFarlane, who provided me with invaluable newspaper coverage of Sybil's trips to Australia; to Rebekah Maggor and Lydia Budianto, for helping me to find letters and other material in libraries in America; to Ian Godfrey, who allowed me to listen to his many recordings of Sybil; and to the Society of Authors, for an Authors' Foundation research grant.

I would also like to thank the staff at the following libraries and other institutions: Fales Library, New York University; Leeds University Library; King's College, Cambridge Library; the National Library of Wales; the John Rylands Library, Manchester University; the Royal College of Music; the Theatre Museum; the Modern Records Centre, Warwick University; Glasgow University Library; the Shakespeare Institute Library, Stratford-upon-Avon; the National Library of Australia; the Ellen Terry Museum, Smallhythe; the Library of Congress, Washington DC; McMaster University Library, Ontario; Pennyslvania State University Libraries; The New Bodleian Library, Oxford University; Northwestern University Library, Illinois; the Templeman Library, Kent University; the BBC Written Archives Centre at Reading University; the Harry Ransom Humanities Research Center, University of Texas at Austin; King Alfred's College Library, Winchester; Medway Archives and Local Studies Centre; the British Library Sound Archive; the Theatre Collection, Bristol University; the Shakespeare Centre Library, Stratford-upon-Avon; Houghton Library, Harvard University; St John's College Library, Cambridge University; the New York Library of Performing Arts; the British Film Institute Library. I must also thank my editors at Haus Publishing – Barbara Schwepcke, Robert Pritchard and Stephen Chumbley – for their friendly and very helpful assistance.

I am grateful to the following for permission to quote from copyright material: Tom Priestley for 'Epilogue for Sybil' by J B Priestley; the Society of Authors on behalf of the Estate of Bernard Shaw, for the letters of Shaw; Joan Plowright for letters from Laurence Olivier; Alexander Murray for letters from Gilbert Murray.

Index